HARCOURT BRACE & COMPANY

Orlando Atlanta Austin Boston San Francisco Chicago Dallas New York
Toronto London

Printed in the United States of America
ISBN 0-15-301867-4
2 3 4 5 6 7 8 9 10   048   97   96   95   94   93

■ ACKNOWLEDGMENTS ■

Some computer lessons in this book are based on AppleWorks® by Claris Corporation. © 1989
by Claris Corporation. All rights reserved. Claris is a registered trademark of Claris Corporation.
AppleWorks is a registered trademark of Apple Computer, Inc. licensed to Claris Corporation.
Apple is a registered trademark of Apple Computer, Inc.

Logo lessons in this book present the Terrapin Logo version. Terrapin is a registered trademark of
Terrapin Software, Inc.

See page H107 for photo and art credits.

AUTHORS

Grace M. Burton
Professor, Department of Curricular Studies
University of North Carolina at Wilmington
Wilmington, North Carolina

Jerome D. Kaplan
Professor of Education
Seton Hall University
South Orange, New Jersey

Martha H. Hopkins
Associate Professor
University of Central Florida
Orlando, Florida

Leonard Kennedy
Professor Emeritus
California State University at Sacramento
Sacramento, California

Howard C. Johnson
Chair, Mathematics Education
Professor of Mathematics and Mathematics Education
Syracuse University
Syracuse, New York

Karen A. Schultz
Professor, Mathematics Education
Georgia State University
Atlanta, Georgia

SENIOR EDITORIAL ADVISORS

Francis (Skip) Fennell
Professor of Education
Western Maryland College
Westminster, Maryland

Evan M. Maletsky
Professor of Mathematics
Montclair State College
Upper Montclair, New Jersey

ADVISORS

Janet S. Abbott
Curriculum Coordinator
Chula Vista Elementary School District
Chula Vista, California

Michael C. Hynes
Professor
University of Central Florida
Orlando, Florida

Sid Rachlin
Mathematics Education Coordinator
East Carolina University
Greenville, North Carolina

Don S. Balka
Professor
Saint Mary's College
Notre Dame, Indiana

Marsha W. Lilly
Mathematics Coordinator, K–12
Alief Independent School District
Alief, Texas

Kay Sammons
Supervisor of Mathematics - Elementary
Howard County School District
Ellicott City, Maryland

George W. Bright
Professor of Mathematics Education
The University of North Carolina at
  Greensboro
Greensboro, North Carolina

Douglas McLeod
Professor of Mathematics
San Diego State University
San Diego, California

Dorothy S. Strong
Manager, Mathematics Support
Chicago Public Schools
Chicago, Illinois

MULTICULTURAL ADVISORS

Pat A. Browne
Director, African Centered Multicultural
  Education
Indianapolis Public Schools
Indianapolis, Indiana

Asa G. Hilliard III
Fuller E. Callaway Professor of Urban
  Education
Georgia State University
Atlanta, Georgia

Young Pai
Chairman, Div. of Social-Philosophical
  Foundations of Education
University of Missouri
Kansas City, Missouri

Gilbert Cuevas
Professor of Education
University of Miami
Coral Gables, Florida

Genevieve M. Knight
Professor of Mathematics
Coppin State College
Baltimore, Maryland

Susan Cashman Paterniti
School Board Member
Port Charlotte, Florida

CONTENTS

2 Adding and Subtracting Whole Numbers and Decimals

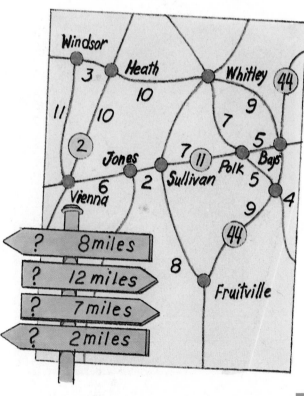

3 Multiplying Whole Numbers and Decimals

4 Dividing Whole Numbers and Decimals

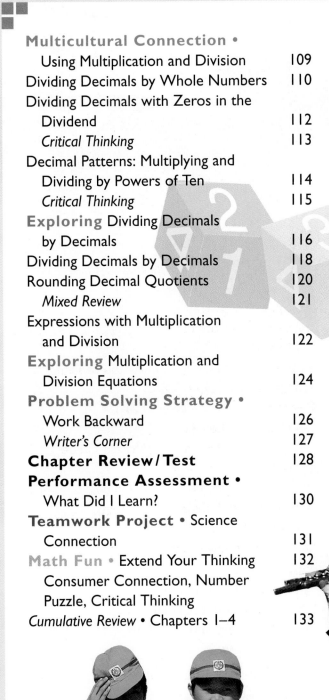

5 Graphing, Statistics, and Probability

6   Number Theory

9 Measurement

12 Perimeter, Area, and Volume

THEME: Arts and Crafts 378

13 Integers

THEME: Geography   412

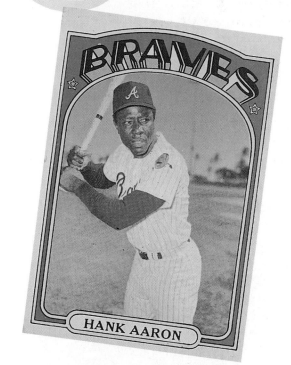

HANK AARON

14 Getting Ready for Algebra

THEME: The Future   444

Joe Carter

Bo Jackson

JOSE CANSECO OF

TOM
LAWLESS

Welcome to

MATHEMATICS PLUS

Mathematics is an important part of your daily life. You use it at school, at home, and everywhere you go. As you study math this year, think about how the ideas you are learning help you with other school subjects and with your everyday activities.

This year you are going to use ideas you have already learned in interesting, new ways. You will learn more about how to solve problems. You will also learn how to use the calculator and the computer as problem-solving tools. You will use whole numbers, fractions, and decimals to solve problems. You will explore ideas about the perimeter and area of plane figures and about the volume of solid figures. You will learn more about collecting, organizing, and analyzing data. You will explore ideas that will help you understand algebra. You will learn more about how to estimate and how to use an estimate to check that an answer is reasonable.

Math is fun! You will work in groups to share what you are learning. You will have fun solving the puzzles and problems in the **Math Fun Magazine** at the back of this book.

This year
you can make mathematics
a learning adventure!

The Authors

▶ ▶ ▶ ▶ ▶ ▶ ▶ ▶

How Do You Use Math Every Day?

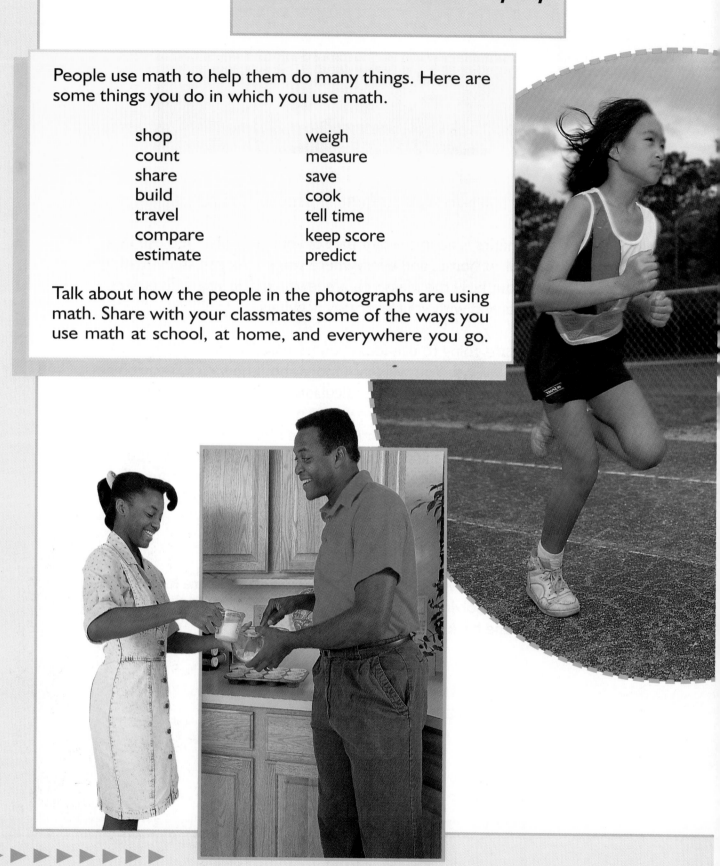

People use math to help them do many things. Here are some things you do in which you use math.

shop	weigh
count	measure
share	save
build	cook
travel	tell time
compare	keep score
estimate	predict

Talk about how the people in the photographs are using math. Share with your classmates some of the ways you use math at school, at home, and everywhere you go.

How Will You Solve Problems?

You use math every day to solve problems. In this book you will learn how to solve problems by asking yourself questions. These questions will help you

- UNDERSTAND the problem.
- PLAN a solution.
- SOLVE the problem.
- LOOK BACK and check your solution.

Kevin has a problem to solve. Read his problem slowly and carefully.

Kevin won first prize in a photography contest. The prize is a $100.00 gift certificate from Shutterbug Camera Shop. He plans to buy a tripod that costs $57.98 and a camera bag that costs $27.29. How much of the prize money will he have left to spend on film?

How can Kevin find out? Think along with Kevin as he solves the problem.

Understand the Problem

First, Kevin must UNDERSTAND the problem.

He restates the problem to himself. He wants to be sure he knows what the problem is about. Then he asks himself these questions.

What must I find?
I must find how much I will have left to spend on film after I buy the tripod and camera bag I want.

What facts do I have?
The gift certificate is worth $100.00. The tripod costs $57.98. The camera bag costs $27.29.

How would you restate Kevin's problem in your own words?

Plan a Solution

Then, Kevin must PLAN how to solve his problem.

He thinks about the ways he solves problems. He chooses one of these strategies.

- Draw a picture
- Make a model
- Work backward
- Guess and check
- Write a number sentence
- Make a table or graph

Then he makes a plan by asking himself these questions.

How can I solve the problem?
Since I must find how much money I will have left after purchasing two items, I can write a number sentence to solve the problem.

What number sentence should I write?

$$\text{price of tripod} + \text{price of camera bag} = \text{total spent}$$

I can then subtract the total from the $100.00 to find how much I will have left for film.

What other plan could Kevin have made?

Solve the Problem

Next, Kevin must SOLVE the problem.

He must decide how to solve the problem. He must choose the method of computation he will use to find the answer.

PAPER AND PENCIL   **MENTAL MATH**   **CALCULATOR**   **MANIPULATIVES**

$57.98
$27.29

I can use a calculator to find the answer.

price of tripod	+	price of camera bag	=	total spent
$57.98	(+)	$27.29	(=)	(85.27)

value of gift certificate		total spent		amount left for film
$100.00	(−)	$85.27	(=)	(14.73)

Why do you think Kevin chose a calculator to solve the problem? What method would you choose?

Last, Kevin can LOOK BACK and check whether his answer is correct.

He thinks about a way to check his answer. He thinks about whether his solution answers the question.

He asks himself these questions.

How can I check my answer?
I can add the prices of the tripod and the camera bag and the amount I have left for film. If the total is $100, then my answer is correct.

Does my solution answer the question?
Since I found the amount left after buying the tripod and camera bag with the $100 gift certificate, my solution answers the question.

How else could Kevin check his answer?

Kevin solved his problem. He used math to help him find how much money he will have left from his $100 gift certificate.

In Mathematics Plus you will learn to be a problem solver!

How Will You Learn Math?

In Mathematics Plus you will learn math in different ways. All of the ways to learn involve *thinking*.

WORKING TOGETHER

- Listen carefully to other people's ideas.
- Encourage others to share their ideas.
- Discuss ideas in a friendly way.
- Plan how your group is going to share the work.

You will learn math by

- working with a group.
- modeling problems, using objects and diagrams.
- listening to your teacher and your classmates.
- talking about math ideas.
- writing about math ideas.
- recording the meanings of new words.
- choosing problem-solving strategies.
- making decisions about how to solve problems.
- using math in school, at home, and everywhere.

PLACE VALUE
WHOLE NUMBERS
AND
DECIMALS

Did you know...

... that people who work in highly technical fields use both very large and very small numbers?

TALK ABOUT IT

NASA's budget in the year 2000 is predicted to exceed $23 billion. While accountants work with such large amounts, engineers may be working with intervals of time that are smaller than 0.0001 second. Explain what the numbers 23 billion and 0.0001 mean to you.

Numeration systems are ways of counting and naming numbers. Here are three different ways to represent the number in a dozen.

- Which way of representing the number in a dozen is most familiar to you?

Ancient Egyptians used everyday objects as symbols to name numbers.

	Lotus Flower	Coiled Rope	Arch	Stroke
Egyptian →				
Decimal →	1,000	100	10	1

The Egyptian system was based on groups of 10. Numbers were formed by writing a series of symbols.

 → 1,428

- Tell the decimal value of each Egyptian number.

A.

B.

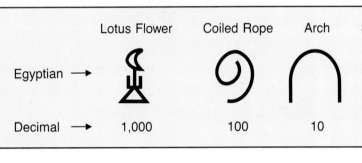

- How would you write the day of the month on which you were born, using the Egyptian system?

- How would you write the year you were born, using the Egyptian system?

MULTICULTURAL NOTE: The bottom photo shows an ancient Egyptian calendar. Our 365-day calendar is probably based on the Egyptian system of dividing the year into 12 months of 30 days each. This system left five extra days, which were used for holidays.

Comparing Numeration Systems

The people of ancient Rome used letters as symbols to name numbers.

Roman →	M	D	C	L	X	V	I
Decimal →	1,000	500	100	50	10	5	1

Roman numerals are read from left to right. You add or subtract the value of each symbol to find the value of the number. A symbol can be repeated only three times.

If the value of the symbols from left to right decreases or stays the same, you add.

CLVI → 156   MCXXIII → 1,123

If the value of the symbols from left to right increases, you subtract.

XC → 90   CMIV → 904

• Tell whether to add or to subtract to find the value of the number.

a. LXV   **b.** CD   **c.** MCMXC

• How would you write the year you were born using Roman numerals?

Talk About It

▶ How is the Roman system like the Egyptian system?

▶ How is the Roman system different from the Egyptian system?

Comparing Numeration Systems

The numeration system you use is called a **decimal system** because it is based on ten numerals: 0, 1, 2, 3, 4, 5, 6, 7, 8, and 9. You use place value and these numerals to name numbers.

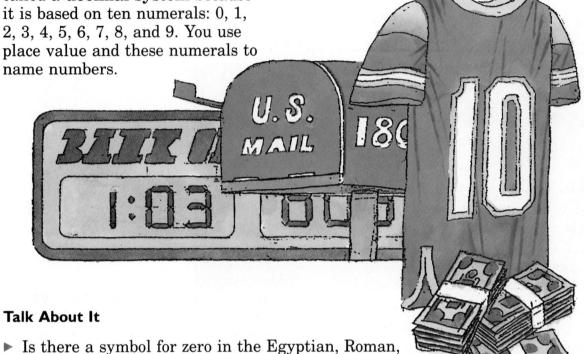

Talk About It

▶ Is there a symbol for zero in the Egyptian, Roman, and decimal systems? Explain.

▶ Which systems repeat symbols to show greater values?

▶ Which system uses place value?

▶ In which systems is the order of the symbols important?

▶ How many symbols are needed in each system to write the current year?

Check for Understanding

Write the Roman numeral and the Egyptian numeral.

1. 8   **2.** 24   **3.** 35   **4.** 101   **5.** 1,000

Write the decimal numeral.

6. XXXIV   **7.** 𓏤𓏤𓏤𓎆𓈐𓏭   **8.** MCMXXV   **9.** 𓏤𓏤𓎆𓈐𓏭

10. 𓐍𓈐𓏭   **11.** DCCXLV   **12.** 𓏤𓂋𓂋𓏭   **13.** MXII

Practice

Copy and complete the table.

14. Decimal	38	■	■	1,432	■	■
15. Roman	■	CXLVII	■	■	MDCCCXLV	■
16. Egyptian	■	■	𓆼𓆼∩∩	■	■	𓏤𓈖𓈖///

Mixed Applications

17. When will you be sixteen years old? Write the year in the decimal system, the Roman system, and the Egyptian system.

18. The decimal number 215 means 200 + 10 + 5. Do the values of the 2 and the 1 change if you change the order of the digits? Explain your answer.

19. By pressing ⌨ 1 + = and then = repeatedly on a calculator, Liz can count the beats to music while she listens. Use a calculator. How quickly can you count to 500?

20. **Number Sense** Create your own number system. Make a table to explain your symbols. Then use your number system to write your age and the year you were born.

COMPUTER CONNECTION

You can use any number as a base to make up a numeration system. Sometimes computer programmers use a base-8 system in which only the digits 0, 1, 2, 3, 4, 5, 6, and 7 are used to name numbers.

Base 10:	1	2	3	4	5	6	7	8	9	10 ... 16 24 32 ...
Base 8:	1	2	3	4	5	6	7	10	11	12 ... 20 30 40 ...

21. Use the table to explain each example.

A. $9_{10} \rightarrow 11_8$

base 10 — base 8

B. $21_8 \rightarrow 17_{10}$

22. Write the base-8 equivalent.
$13_{10} \rightarrow$ ■

23. Write the base-10 equivalent.
$32_8 \rightarrow$ ■

24. Write your age in base 8.

25. Write the number of days in September in base 8.

Name an advantage of the decimal system.

WRAP UP...

More Practice, Lesson 1.1, page H34

UNDERSTANDING LARGE NUMBERS

Joe estimates that it will take about 800 truckloads of sand to repair a ten-mile stretch of beach.

Eight hundred truckloads will contain about 122,039,680,000 grains of sand.

The chart can help you read and write large numbers. Notice that commas separate each three-digit period.

A tablespoon contains about 2,400 grains of sand.

A cubic foot contains about 353,100 grains of sand.

Place Value											
Billions			**Millions**			**Thousands**			**Ones**		
H undreds	T ens	O nes	H undreds	T ens	O nes	H undreds	T ens	O nes	H undreds	T ens	O nes
1	2	2,	0	3	9,	6	8	0,	0	0	0

A dump truck contains about 152,549,600 grains of sand.

Read:

Short Word Form → 122 billion, 39 million, 680 thousand
Word Form → one hundred twenty-two billion, thirty-nine million, six hundred eighty thousand

Write:

Standard Form → 122,039,680,000
Expanded Form → 100,000,000,000 + 20,000,000,000 + 2,000,000,000 + 30,000,000 + 9,000,000 + 600,000 + 80,000

Talk About It

▶ What is the value of the underlined digit in the number 42,736?

▶ What are some careers in which people use large numbers?

Check for Understanding

Write the value of the underlined digit.

1. 45,301,276,489   **2.** 174,057   **3.** 18,426   **4.** 77,100,264,993   **5.** 694,132

Practice

Write the value of the underlined digit.

6. 43,8<u>7</u>5,000

7. 5<u>2</u>1,976,000

8. 881,7<u>6</u>4

9. 43,0<u>4</u>1,000,000

10. 5,432,0<u>1</u>4

11. 3<u>9</u>8,004,213

12. 2,6<u>6</u>4,902,000

13. <u>4</u>2,908,000,000

14. 9,087,6<u>5</u>4,321

Write the number in short word form.

15. 3,603,542

16. 36,542,000

17. 507,090,000

18. 103,058,200,753

19. 45,034,126

20. 3,043,987,000

21. 356,080

22. 6,780,200,000

Write the number in standard form.

23. twenty-six billion, three hundred fourteen million, one hundred ten thousand, nine hundred ninety-six

24. eight million, twenty-four thousand, two hundred one

25. 500 billion, 24 thousand, 12

26. 1,000,000,000 + 2,000,000 + 800,000 + 70,000 + 4,000 + 300 + 50 + 8

27. 6,000,000 + 400,000 + 60,000 + 8,000

Mixed Applications

28. The circulation of a magazine is eight million, ninety-one thousand, seven hundred fifty-one. Write the number in standard form.

29. A movie studio reports that rentals of a video are 2,000,000 + 600,000 + 50,000 + 7,000 + 800. Write the number in word form.

30. **Number Sense** How is the value of each place in a decimal number related to the value of the place at its right?

31. **Critical Thinking** Three box labels read as follows: (a) Pen is here, (b) Pen is not here, and (c) Pen is in Box **a.** Only one label is correct. In which box is the pen?

How do you know that the values of 160,000 and 100,600 are not the same?

UNDERSTANDING SMALL NUMBERS

In Kenya, Africa, a thickened cornmeal porridge called *ugali* is hardened, cut into cubes, and then served with broth, vegetables, and meat. The cornmeal is made by grinding whole corn kernels into fine, sandlike particles. A speck of this cornmeal may be as small as 0.0025 inch in diameter.

The place-value chart for whole numbers can be expanded to help you read and write decimal numbers.

Place Value				
Ones	Tenths	Hundredths	Thousandths	Ten-Thousandths
0	0	0	2	5

Read:

Word Form → twenty-five ten-thousandths
Short Word Form → 25 ten-thousandths

Sometimes people read a number by saying the digits. → zero point zero zero two five

Write:

Standard Form → 0.0025

Talk About It

▶ Why do people say the number by reading the digits?

▶ What are some careers in which people use small numbers?

MULTICULTURAL NOTE: Corn is a major part of the Kenyan diet. Ugali has a taste similar to Italian polenta or American corn mush.

Check for Understanding

Write the number in short word form.

1. 0.3421   2. 0.87   3. 0.8905

4. 0.739   5. 0.73   6. 1.034

Write the value of the underlined digit.

7. <u>4</u>.5   8. 0.21<u>4</u>   9. 0.0<u>3</u>   10. 0.00<u>5</u>   11. 0.000<u>1</u>

Practice

Write the number in standard form.

12. 45 hundredths

13. eight hundredths

14. two hundred one and two thousandths

15. seven ten-thousandths

Copy and complete the table.

	Standard Form	Short Word Form	Word Form
16.	0.4	■	■
17.	■	■	thirty-two and eight tenths
18.	■	35 thousandths	■
19.	43.0834	■	■
20.	■	80 and 9 hundredths	■
21.	■	■	one hundred twenty-one ten-thousandths

Mixed Applications

22. A grain of coarse sand may be as large as eighty-three thousandths inch. Write the number in standard form.

23. The world's smallest cut diamond is 0.0009 inch in diameter and weighs 0.0012 carat. Write both numbers in short word form.

VISUAL THINKING

About how much of each geometric figure is shaded? Write **a, b,** or **c**.

24.

a. 0.3   **b.** 0.6   **c.** 0.9

25.

a. 0.3   **b.** 0.6   **c.** 0.9

26.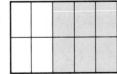

a. 0.3   **b.** 0.6   **c.** 0.9

How do you know that 2.3 and 2.003 are not the same?

COMPARING AND ORDERING NUMBERS

Sue is a buyer for a men's clothing chain. Her inventory shows the numbers of shirts still in the store. The smaller the number in the Total column of the inventory, the more popular the shirt.

Inventory			
Item: <u>Men's Shirts</u>		Date: <u>Nov. 2, 1993</u>	
Identification	Color	Size	Total
# 0723001	red	sm.	12,010
# 0723002	red	med.	12,583
# 0723003	red	lg.	12,924
# 0723004	blue	sm.	11,403
# 0723005	blue	med.	10,010
# 0723006	blue	lg.	12,031
# 0723007	green	sm.	13,040
# 0723008	green	med.	13,001
# 0723009	green	lg.	13,945

- Which size red shirt is the most popular?

- Which color shirt is the least popular?

- Which shirt is the most popular of all?

You can use these symbols when you compare and order numbers.

< means "is less than."
> means "is greater than."

Example List the numbers of large shirts in the inventory in order from least to greatest.

12,031 < 12,924 < 13,945

Talk About It

▶ Would you solve the problem differently if you were asked to order the numbers of large shirts from greatest to least? Explain your answer.

▶ How do you use comparison to order numbers?

Check for Understanding

Compare the numbers. Write <, >, or =.

1. 8,234 ● 8,324   2. 42,697 ● 42,079   3. 23,431 ● 23,431   4. 9.550 ● 9.55

Write the numbers in order from least to greatest. Use <.

5. 42,697; 42,079; 42,597   6. 45.7; 45.57; 45.07   7. 2.05; 2.07; 2.01

Practice

Compare the numbers. Write <, >, or =.

8. 23.001 ● 23.010   **9.** 5,788 ● 5,787   **10.** 41.030 ● 41.03   **11.** 13,945.2 ● 13,954.6

12. 17.099 ● 17.090   **13.** 4.707 ● 4.770   **14.** 0.21 ● 0.22   **15.** 5.401 ● 5.4010

Write the numbers in order from greatest to least. Use >.

16. 23,511; 23,611; 23,116   **17.** 0.0009; 9; 0.009; 0.09   **18.** 423,173; 423,317; 423,137

19. 0.001; 0.101; 0.011   **20.** 6,552; 6,525; 6,255   **21.** 5.004; 5.040; 5.005

Mixed Applications

Use the inventory on page 10 for Exercises 22–23.

22. Write in order from greatest to least the numbers of medium-sized shirts. Use >.

23. Write in order from least to greatest the numbers of all the shirts in the inventory. Use <.

CRITICAL THINKING

Use the table for Exercise 24 a–c.

24. Sue is saving shares of Regal stock. She keeps a list of the average yearly values so that she knows whether the value of her stock is increasing or decreasing.

Average Yearly Values of Regal Stock	
Year	Value
1989	$12.075
1990	$13.106
1991	$12.100
1992	$12.195
1993	$12.989

a. Which year would have been the best year to buy some stock? Why?

b. Which year would have been the best year to sell some stock? Why?

c. Explain how Sue's stock has changed in value from 1989 to 1993.

Name a career in which people must compare and order numbers.

WRAP UP...

PROBLEM SOLVING

Strategy • Make and Use a Table

Dr. Lee's list shows the average daily calorie consumption of nine clients. Suppose that the most active clients consume the greatest number of calories. How can you show the data in a way that Dr. Lee can easily see which clients are most active?

If you have access to a database program, you can use a computer to organize the data.

Client	Calories Consumed
Ellen	2,641
Frank	3,089
Juan	2,915
Karen	3,140
Lani	2,689
Louis	2,908
Maria	2,402
Ron	2,654
Wayne	3,273

► UNDERSTAND

What are you asked to do?

What information are you given?

► PLAN

How will you solve the problem?

You can make a table in which you list the clients in order by the number of calories they consumed.

► SOLVE

How can you make a table?

List the clients in order from greatest to least number of calories consumed. Label the columns and title the table.

Use the data in the table to see which clients are most active.

Daily Calorie Consumption	
Client	Calories Consumed
Wayne	3,273
Karen	3,140
Frank	3,089
Juan	2,915
Louis	2,908
Lani	2,689
Ron	2,654
Ellen	2,641
Maria	2,402

► LOOK BACK

How can you check your solution?

WHAT IF... ...you were asked who consumed the least number of calories? What would be your answer?

 Connection, pages 488–489

Apply

1 Make a table to organize the meteorologist's report of average January temperatures and amounts of precipitation in four cities.

> **Report:** In Chicago the average temperature is 21°F, and the average precipitation is 1.6 inches. In Los Angeles the temperature is 57°F, and the precipitation is 3.7 inches. In Atlanta the temperature is 42°F, and the precipitation is 4.9 inches. In Dallas the temperature is 44°F, and the precipitation is 1.7 inches.

Use your table for Exercises 2–5.

2 Which of the four cities have average temperatures between 40°F and 50°F?

3 Which two cities have about the same average amount of precipitation?

4 List the average temperatures in order from coldest to warmest. Use <.

5 Compare the average amount of precipitation in Chicago with that in Atlanta. Use < or >.

Mixed Applications ➔ **STRATEGIES** Make and Use a Table • Act It Out • Guess and Check • Draw a Diagram

Choose a strategy and solve.

6 Every day Carrie drives 7 miles to work and 5 miles to a health club. Then she takes the same route home. How many miles does she drive each day?

7 W, X, and Y each stand for different whole numbers. If W + X + Y < Z, can Z equal 2? Can Z equal 7? Can Z equal 10? Justify your answers.

8 Al is a commercial artist who uses colored pencils to sketch. How many pencils does Al have if all of them are blue except 2, all of them are yellow except 2, and all of them are red except 2?

9 Leonard wants to buy a pen and a pencil that together cost $15. The pen costs $10 more than the pencil. How much does the pencil cost?

WRITER'S CORNER

10 Using the information in your table from Exercise 1, write and solve as many word problems as you can.

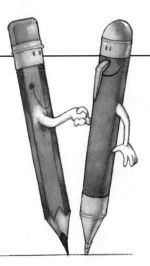

Sara estimates her company's average annual sales by rounding to the nearest ten-thousand dollars to make a pictograph for a presentation.

Look at the 1978 sales. The estimated amount is $80,000. What could the actual sales for 1978 be?

Think: What is the least whole number amount that rounds to $80,000?
What is the greatest whole number amount that rounds to $80,000?

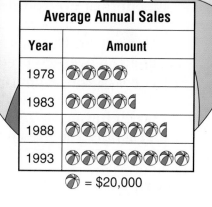

Average Annual Sales	
Year	**Amount**
1978	🏐🏐🏐🏐
1983	🏐🏐🏐🏐🏐
1988	🏐🏐🏐🏐🏐🏐🏐
1993	🏐🏐🏐🏐🏐🏐🏐🏐

🏐 = $20,000

Least amount: $75,000   Greatest amount: $84,999

So, the actual sales for 1978 could be any amount from $75,000 to $84,999.

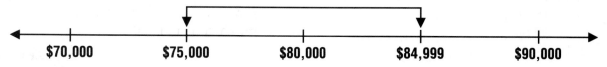

More Examples

A. For 1993 the sales could be any amount from $155,000 to $164,999.

B. For 1983 the sales could be any amount from $85,000 to $94,999.

Talk About It

▶ Why do you think Sara used estimated amounts in the pictograph?

▶ Why do you think Sara decided to round to ten thousands rather than to hundreds?

▶ In the examples above, what pattern do you see in the least amounts and the greatest amounts?

Check for Understanding

The number has been rounded to the place indicated. Write the least and greatest whole number that round to the given number.

1. 500
   hundreds

2. 750
   tens

3. 1,000,000
   millions

4. 3,600
   hundreds

5. 6,000,000,000
   billions

6. 60¢
   ten cents

7. 12,000
   thousands

8. 1,530,000
   ten thousands

Practice

Estimate by rounding to the place indicated.

9. 92
tens

10. $12.58
10 cents

11. 229
hundreds

12. $43.25
10 cents

13. $15.75
dollar

The number has been rounded to the place indicated. Write the
least and greatest whole number that round to the given number.

14. 76,000
thousand

15. 80,000
ten thousand

16. 900,000
hundred thousand

17. 23,000,000
million

18. 500,000,000
hundred million

19. $3.50
ten cents

20. Use the digits 3, 4, 5, 6, 6, and 6.
Write two numbers that each round
to 500 when you round them to the
nearest hundred.

21. Use the digits 2, 3, 4, 5, 9, 9, 9, and
9. Write two numbers that each
round to 3,000 when you round
them to the nearest thousand.

Mixed Applications

Use the pictograph on page 14 for Exercise 22.

22. Compare the sales for 1978 with
those for 1993. Which statement is
true? **(a)** Sales are about the same.
(b) Sales have doubled.

23. Find Data Ask ten classmates what
size shoes they wear. Make a list of
the data you collect.

24. Organize Data List the shoe sizes
from Exercise 23 in order from
largest to smallest. Make a
pictograph to display your data.

MIXED REVIEW

Write the number in short word form.

1. 5,066

2. 0.02

3. 0.5432

4. 0.087

5. 600,002

6. 2.011

Write the numbers in order from greatest to least. Use >.

7. 43,231; 43,132; 43,223

8. 5.02; 5.0202; 5.022

9. 0.049; 0.005; 0.0489

What is meant by "a range"
of estimates?

WRAP
UP...

1. Suppose you will give a report about the Egyptian, Roman, and decimal numeration systems. Make a table to show the symbols and their values.

Use scrap paper to plan your table.

2. Write the Roman numeral MCM in decimal form.

3. Write the decimal number 34 using Roman numerals.

4. A pattern of numbers begins with 0. If each number in the pattern is 5 more than the number before, what are the fourth and the fifth numbers in the pattern?

Write the value of the underlined digit.

5. 26,0<u>9</u>8,751,084

6. 2<u>6</u>,098,751,084

7. 956.071<u>3</u>4

Write the number in short word form.

8. 7,011,011

9. 6,005,000,031

10. 3.0028

Write the number in word form.

11. 15,010,003

12. 14,012,000,005

13. 9.0017

Write the number in standard form.

14. 102 million and twelve hundredths

15. 57 billion and ten thousandths

16. twenty and two ten-thousandths

Write the numbers from least to greatest. Use <.

17. 5.2, 5.13, 5.123

18. 6.07, 6.7, 6.007

19. 7.06, 7.1, 7.024

Estimate by rounding to the place indicated.

20. 29,683,425,000 millions

21. 29,683,425,000 billions

22. 523.098647 ten-thousandths

Write the range of numbers that round to the given number.

23. 25,000 thousands

24. 500 hundreds

25. 45,000,000 millions

26. 50 tens

27. 6,000,000 millions

28. 640,000 ten-thousands

Data Given as Estimates

NORTH AMERICA

Costa Rica

Costa Rica is one of the seven countries of Central America. It has an area of 19,575 square miles and a population of approximately 3,000,000.

Much of the land in Costa Rica is covered with rich, volcanic soil, and agriculture is an important industry. The table shows four of the country's major agricultural products and the number of metric tons of each produced in a recent year.

Agricultural Production in Costa Rica	
Product	Amount Produced (metric tons)
Coffee	145,000
Bananas	1,150,000
Sugar	230,000
Cocoa	4,000

Use the table to solve the problems.

1. For which agricultural product was the number of metric tons produced the greatest? the least?

2. Suppose the number showing the amount of cocoa produced had been rounded to the nearest thousand. What is the least amount of cocoa that could have been produced?

3. Suppose the number showing the amount of bananas produced had been rounded to the nearest ten thousand. What is the greatest amount of bananas that could have been produced?

4. The Central American country of Nicaragua produced 250,000 metric tons of sugar in a recent year. Is this more or less than the amount produced by Costa Rica? How much more or less?

ORDER OF OPERATIONS
Using Algebra

When Melvin leaves for work, he must choose to put his car in forward gear or reverse gear.

• In which gear should Melvin put his car first?

• Why is it important which gear Melvin chooses first?

In many areas of life, the order in which you perform tasks has a dramatic impact on the results. The same is true in math. To avoid confusion, mathematicians agree on this order of operations.

1. Perform all operations inside the parentheses first.

2. Multiply and divide from left to right.

3. Add and subtract from left to right.

Example

$$2 + (12 \div 3)$$ ← Perform operation inside parentheses.

$$2 + \quad 4$$

$$2 + \quad 4 \quad = 6$$ ← Then add.

More Examples

A. $50 - 10 \times 3$ ← Multiply.
$50 - 30 = 20$ ← Subtract.

B. $4 + 3 \times 5 - 6$ ← Multiply.
$4 + 15 - 6$ ← Add.
$19 - 6 = 13$ ← Subtract.

• How can you rewrite Example **A** so that the correct answer is 120?

Check for Understanding

Tell which operation to perform first.

1. $(3 - 2) \times 5$ **2.** $25 \div 5 - 3$ **3.** $3 + 3 \times 5$ **4.** $7 \times 9 + 3$

Solve.

5. $30 - 15 \div 3$ **6.** $12 + (5 \times 6)$ **7.** $(7 \times 8) \div 2$ **8.** $(5 \times 4 + 13) \div 11$

Practice

Tell which operation to perform first.

9. $7 \times 9 + 8$ **10.** $4 \times (3 + 8)$ **11.** $25 - 3 \times 5$ **12.** $25 - 15 \div 5$

13. $6 + 9 - 5$ **14.** $12 \div 3 - 4$ **15.** $5 \times 4 \div 2$ **16.** $9 + 49 \div 7$

Solve.

17. $(4 + 3) \times 8$ **18.** $8 \times 9 + 7$ **19.** $36 - 7 \times 2$

20. $54 - 81 \div 9$ **21.** $12 + 11 \div 11$ **22.** $63 \div 7 - 2$

23. $144 \div (12 - 8)$ **24.** $(5 + 4) \times (10 - 3)$ **25.** $300 \div (23 - 8)$

26. Rewrite Exercise 10 so that the answer is 20.

27. Rewrite Exercise 12 so that the answer is 2.

28. Rewrite Exercise 23 so that the answer is 4.

29. Rewrite Exercise 24 so that the answer is 42.

Use the digit 7 four times and the order of operations to write problems that have the following answers.

30. 126   **31.** 4   **32.** 10   **33.** 490

Mixed Applications

34. Sam can score 15 points in 5 minutes. May can score twice as many in 5 minutes. How many total points can they score in 5 minutes?

35. May scores 15 fewer points than Ray, who scores 45 points. Fay scores half as many points as May. How many points does Fay score?

36. **Make Up a Problem** Write a word problem that can only be solved by using two operations.

37. **Number Sense • Mental Math** Mr. Jones teaches 5 classes of 25 students each. In his classes 100 students are sixth graders. How many students are not sixth graders?

Why do you think it is important to agree on an order of operations?

WRAP UP...

EXPLORING

Powers and Exponents

Numbers can be written in many forms. For example, you can rename 81 by using nines and threes as factors.

$$81 = 9 \times 9 \qquad 81 = 9 \times 3 \times 3 \qquad 81 = 3 \times 3 \times 3 \times 3$$

Work Together

Building Understanding

Use base-ten blocks to explore writing numbers using powers and exponents.

Ten

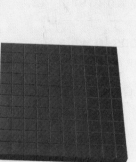

One thousand

One hundred

Another way to write 1,000, or $10 \times 10 \times 10$, is to use an exponent. An **exponent** shows how many times a number called the **base** is used as a factor.

TALK ABOUT IT

- How can you rename 100 using tens as factors?

- How can you rename 1,000 using tens and hundreds as factors?

- How can you rename 1,000 using only tens as factors?

- How many times is 10 used as a factor of 1,000?

exponent
↓

Example $10^3 = 10 \times 10 \times 10 = 1,000$

↑   ⎵   ↑

base   factors   number in standard form

Write: 10^3. **Read:** "ten to the third power," or "ten cubed."

Making the Connection

Compare a multiple of 10 written in exponent form with the same multiple of 10 written in standard form. You will find an interesting pattern.

Copy and complete the place-value chart.

Place Value

Power of Ten	Millions			Thousands			Ones		
	H	T	O	H	T	O	H	T	O
1. 10^1								■	■
2. ■							1	0	0
3. ■						1	0	0	0
4. 10^4					■	■	■	■	■
5. 10^5				■	■	■	■	■	■
6. ■			1	0	0	0	0	0	0

Look at the pattern of zeros in the numbers written in standard form.

7. In the table, what power of 10 results in the least number of zeros when the number is written in standard form?

8. In the table, what power of 10 results in the greatest number of zeros when the number is written in standard form?

9. How does the exponent of a power of 10 compare with the number of zeros in the number written in standard form?

10. A googol is the term used for 10^{100}. How many zeros are in a googol?

Checking Understanding

Tell how many zeros will be in the number when written in standard form.

11. 10^7

12. 10^{11}

13. ten cubed

14. ten to the tenth power

Write the number in standard form.

15. ten to the ninth power

16. 10^8

17. $10 \times 10 \times 10 \times 10 \times 10$

EXPLORING

Squares and Square Roots

Suppose you have a square that is made up of 225 unit squares. How can you find the length of one side of the square?

Work Together

Building Understanding

Choose a manipulative that can be used to make squares. Make a square

- with 9 square units.
- with 36 square units.

Copy and complete this table.

Total square units	9	36
Length of each side	◼	◼

Now look at the square at the right. Extend your table to include this square.

Using your table, discuss any relationships you see between the total number of square units and the length of each side. Share with your classmates any relationships that you discover.

Explain how you can use your discoveries to find the length of each side of a square that is made up of 225 unit squares.

Making the Connection

A **square** is the product of a number and itself. The numbers 9, 36, and 49, which you used on page 22, are perfect squares. A number is a **perfect square** if it is the square of a whole number.

$$3^2 = 3 \times 3 = 9$$

Read: 3 squared

When you find the two equal factors of a number, you are finding the **square root,** $\sqrt{\ }$, of the number.

Example What is $\sqrt{16}$?

Arrange 16 blocks to model the square. Find the two equal factors of 16.

$4 \times 4 = 16$

So, $\sqrt{16} = 4$.

TALK ABOUT IT

• How does a square differ from a square root?

You can use a calculator to find squares and square roots.

Examples

What is 13^2?

 13 $\boxed{\times}$ $\boxed{=}$ 169

So, 13^2 is 169.

What is $\sqrt{625}$?

625 $\boxed{\sqrt{\ }}$ 25.

So, $\sqrt{625}$ is 25.

Checking Understanding

Use the method of your choice to find the square or square root.

1. 8^2

2. 12^2

3. 50^2

4. 35^2

5. $\sqrt{121}$

6. $\sqrt{400}$

7. $\sqrt{1,024}$

8. $\sqrt{0.49}$

9. You know that $\sqrt{4} = 2$ and $\sqrt{9} = 3$. What do you think $\sqrt{5}$ equals? Explain your reasoning.

MIXED REVIEW

Round to the place indicated.

1. $1.87
   ten cents

2. 6,561
   thousands

3. 25,789
   ten thousands

4. 622.411
   hundredths

Tell which operation to perform first. Then solve.

5. $144 \div 12 - 8$

6. $(25 + 15) \div 5$

7. $30 \times 4 - 12$

8. $7 + 45 \div 15 - 2$

PROBLEM SOLVING

STRATEGY • Find a Pattern

Luisa writes training manuals for new employees. The notepad shows the total number of pages she has written by the end of each week. If she continues this pattern, how many pages will she have written by the end of the seventh week?

week 1 = 10 pages
week 2 = 16 pages
week 3 = 23 pages
week 4 = 31 pages

▶ **UNDERSTAND**

What are you asked to find?

What information are you given?

▶ **PLAN**

How can you solve the problem?

Make a table to show the number of pages written by the end of each week.

Week	1	2	3	4	5	6	7
Pages Written	10	16	23	31	▪	▪	▪

+ 6   + 7   + 8   + ?   + ?   + ?

Look for a pattern.

Week 1 = 10 pages
Week 2 = 10 pages + 6 pages
Week 3 = 16 pages + 7 pages
Week 4 = 23 pages + 8 pages

The pattern shows the number of pages increasing by 6, 7, 8. . . .

▶ **SOLVE**

How can you carry out your plan?

Extend the table to Week 7.

Week	1	2	3	4	5	6	7
Pages Written	10	16	23	31	40	50	61

So, Luisa will have written 61 pages by the end of the seventh week.

▶ **LOOK BACK**

How can you check your answer?

WHAT IF... . . . Luisa has written 15 pages by the end of the first week, 26 the second, 36 the third, and 45 the fourth week? If she continues this pattern, how many pages will she write by the end of Week 8?

 Connection, pages 478–479

Apply

Find the pattern. Then solve.

1 Jason has used 15 blocks to build the first 5 steps of a staircase. How many blocks will he need to build a staircase with 10 steps?

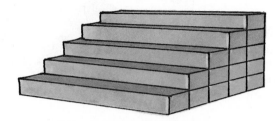

2 A landscaper plants 10 rosebushes the first year. He adds 2 every year after that. How many in all does he plant during 6 years?

3 How many puzzles will you solve on the tenth day if you solve 1 the first day and then solve 2 more puzzles each day than you did the day before?

Mixed Applications ➔ **STRATEGIES** Find a Pattern • Draw a Diagram • Use a Table • Act It Out

Choose a strategy and solve.

4 **Making Choices** Monte will work for his aunt this summer. She has given him the option of being paid (**a**) a total of $20 or (**b**) $1 the first day, $2 the second, $3 the third, and so on for 8 days. For which option will Monte be paid more?

5 Vic works in a pet store. His job is to feed the animals. He feeds the fish first and the reptiles last. He feeds the cats before the dogs and the dogs after the birds. Which animals does Vic feed just before he feeds the reptiles?

6 Ria has a fifty-cent coin. She asks a clerk to give her 6 coins as change. What combination of coins could the clerk give Ria?

7 Suppose Ria had asked the clerk to give her 8 coins as change for a fifty-cent coin. What coins could the clerk give Ria?

Use the table for Exercises 8–11.

8 If the quality of each car is the same, which is the best buy?

9 If the quality of each car is the same, which is the worst buy?

10 Is the price of the Vigro greater than or less than the price of the Tiger?

11 List in order from greatest to least the prices of the Hawk, Tiger, and Vigro.

Car	Price
Hawk	$12,430
Tiger	$14,489
Vigro	$13,999

Vocabulary Check

Choose a word or words from the box to complete each sentence.

Using new words in sentences helps you learn them.

base
exponent
perfect square
square root
standard

1. The number 2,136 is written in __?__ form. *(page 6)*

2. The __?__ shows how many times the __?__ is used as a factor. *(page 20)*

3. A number is a __?__ if it is the square of a whole number. *(page 22)*

4. When you find the two equal factors of a number, you are finding the __?__ of the number. *(page 22)*

Concept Check

5. In which numeration systems is the order of the symbols important—the decimal, the Roman, or the Egyptian system? *(pages 2, 3, 4)*

6. If you were rounding the amount of your $4.75 weekly allowance in order to estimate the total for the year, would you round to the nearest dollar or ten dollars? *(page 14)*

7. Which numeration system uses place value—the decimal, the Roman, or the Egyptian system? *(page 4)*

8. Explain the order of operations. *(page 18)*

9. What does 10^4 mean? *(page 20)*

10. How does a square differ from a square root? *(page 22)*

The number has been rounded to the place indicated.
Write the range of numbers that round to the given number. *(page 14)*

11. 35,000,000
    millions

12. $0.80
    ten cents

13. 100
    hundreds

Tell which operation to perform first. *(page 18)*

14. $5 \times (45 - 25)$

15. $12 + 6 \times 8$

16. $(26 + 12) \div 7$

Tell how many zeros will be in the number when written in standard form. *(page 20)*

17. ten cubed

18. ten squared

19. ten to the ninth power

Skill Check

Write the value of the underlined digit. *(pages 6, 8)*

20. 5,0<u>3</u>0,000,000

21. <u>5</u>,030,000,000

22. 12.008<u>6</u>

Write the number in short word form. *(pages 6, 8)*

23. 6,300,000

24. 6,300,000,000

25. 2.0014

Write the numbers from least to greatest. Use <. *(page 10)*

26. 1.10, 1.01, 1.001

27. 2.04, 2.4, 2.014

28. 3.5, 3.25, 3.185

Estimate by rounding to the place indicated. *(page 14)*

29. 9,705,128,004
billions

30. 9,705,128,004
millions

31. 59,238.60057
ten-thousandths

Use the order of operations. Solve. *(page 18)*

32. $5 \times 3 + 4 \div 2$

33. $35 - 3 \times 6 \div 2$

34. $4 + (6 - 10 \div 5) \times 4$

35. $12 \div 4 + (20 - 11)$

36. $4 \times 5 \div (6 - 2)$

37. $(7 + 6) + (9 \times 5)$

Write the number in standard form. *(pages 20, 22)*

38. 10^7

39. 10^3

40. $\sqrt{100}$

41. 4^2

Problem-Solving Check

Use the table for Exercises 42–43. *(pages 12, 24)*

42. Liz uses the table to make plant food at a nursery. If the pattern continues, how many teaspoons of concentrate will she use with 8 quarts of water?

43. How many teaspoons of concentrate will Liz use with $4\frac{1}{2}$ quarts of water?

44. Make a table that shows the formula so that 4 teaspoons are used with 1 quart of water.

Plant-Food Formula					
Teaspoons of Concentrate	2	4	6	8	10
Quarts of Water	1	2	3	4	5

WHAT DID I LEARN?

1. Explain how to identify the value of each 6 in 20,638,061.0967, and then state each value.

2. Order these numbers from greatest to least: 3,567.1; 3,652.1; 3,526.1. Explain your thinking.

3. Explain how to determine the least whole number and the greatest whole number that, to the nearest thousand, round to 4,000. Identify the numbers.

4. Show where you would place the parentheses in this problem so that the answer is 12: 3 × 2 + 2.

5. Use 16 unit cubes to make a square. Use your square to explain the meaning of a square root.

6. Read Exercise 3 on page 25. Follow the steps on the Problem-Solving Think Along worksheet to show how to solve this problem.

Write About It

7. Describe a personal experience you have had related to one of the concepts in this chapter on place value.

8. Write all you can about the meaning of $\sqrt{25}$. Explain what it means. Draw a picture or model to show your answer.

TEAMWORK Project

Start a Business

Suppose you are going to open a business that sells school supplies. You will need to fill these positions:

Decide Determine which team member or members will fill each position. If there are other jobs that need to be done, decide which members of your team will fill those positions.

Do Each team member should make a list of five or six responsibilities that his or her position might require.

Share Compare the responsibilities of the positions. If more than one person feels responsible for a task, decide as a group which person should accept the responsibility.

Directors
(those who decide which supplies to sell)

Purchasers
(those who order the supplies)

Accountants
(those who keep track of expenses and profits)

Salespeople
(those who sell the supplies)

Work with your teammates to plan your business.

Talk About It

☐ **How would the person filling each position use numbers in the course of his or her work?**

☐ **Why is it important that all the group members work together in the business?**

Decimal High

To play this game, you will need an opponent, a deck of 20 cards labeled with the numbers 0 through 9 twice, and a game board similar to the one shown. The object of the game is to make the greater decimal number. Shuffle the cards and place them facedown in a stack.

The players take turns drawing a card from the stack and placing it faceup in one of the spaces on the game board. A player who draws a zero has three choices: place the zero on the board, switch any two digits already on the board to create a larger number, or move any one card from its space to an empty space. If the zero is not placed on the board, it is set aside. Play continues until the players fill all the spaces on the game board. The player with the greater decimal number wins the round, and the player who wins two out of three rounds wins the game.

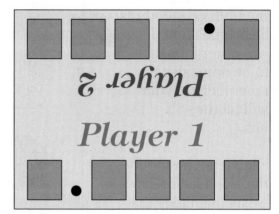

Challenge

Number Sense

Which numbers in the chart have equal value? Find one set of "twins" and one set of "triplets" by determining the value of the numbers.

2^2	2^4	6^2
2^3	1^4	4^2
4^3	10^2	8^2
1^3	3^1	3^4
5^2	3^2	5^3
3^3	2^5	2^6

Critical Thinking

This five-digit number is 20,000 when rounded to the nearest ten thousand. The number contains consecutive digits whose sum is 10. The digit in the hundreds place is the least. The tens digit is less than the thousands digit and the ones digit. What is the number?

Write the letter of the correct answer.

1. Which is the value of the underlined digit? 2̲0,000,000,000

  A. 20 thousand   **B.** 20 million
  C. 20 billion   **D.** 20 trillion

2. Which is the short word form for 0.0005?

  A. 5 tenths   **B.** 5/1,000ths
  C. 5 ten-thousandths   **D.** 5/100,000

3. Which is one million two in standard form?

  A. 1,000,000.2   **B.** 1,000,002
  C. 1,200,000   **D.** not here

4. Which is four and fourteen ten-thousandths in standard form?

  A. 4.00014   **B.** 4.0014
  C. 414,000   **D.** not here

5. Which is two hundred and two thousandths in standard form?

  A. 0.202   **B.** 200.002
  C. 200.2   **D.** 202,000

6. Which is listed in order from least to greatest?

  A. 0.8, 0.9, 0.08   **B.** 0.8, 0.08, 0.9
  C. 0.08, 0.8, 0.9   **D.** not here

7. Which is 4.089765 rounded to the ten-thousandths place?

  A. 4.08977   **B.** 4.089
  C. 4.0898   **D.** 4.09

8. $4 \times 5 + 6 \div 2$

  A. 13   **B.** 22
  C. 23   **D.** 36

9. $25 + (12 - 6 \div 3) \times 2$

  A. 29   **B.** 54
  C. 70   **D.** not here

10. Which is the value of 10^3?

  A. 30   **B.** 100
  C. 1,000   **D.** 3,000

11. When does bus fare cost most?

Bus Schedule	
Time	Cost
9 A.M.–6 P.M.	$12.50
6 P.M.–10 P.M.	$12.05
10 P.M.–12 P.M.	$12.55

  A. 6 P.M.–10 P.M.   **B.** 9 A.M.–6 P.M.
  C. 10 P.M.–12 P.M.   **D.** $12.55

12. Rob is trying to figure out a number series. The first three numbers are 3, 7, and 11. If the pattern continues, which will be the fourth and the fifth numbers in the series?

  A. 11 and 15   **B.** 13 and 17
  C. 15 and 19   **D.** 19 and 23

ADDING AND SUBTRACTING WHOLE NUMBERS AND DECIMALS

Did you know...

...that in college basketball Pearl Moore holds the women's record for most career points?

TALK ABOUT IT

Pearl Moore holds this record with 4,061 points. Philip Hutcheson, with 4,106 points, holds the men's record. Using the information given, write as many problems as you can.

MENTAL-MATH STRATEGIES
for Addition and Subtraction

In the first four basketball games of the season, Wes scored 16, 9, 11, and 24 points. How many points did he score in all?

$$16 + 9 + 11 + 24$$

The properties of addition can help you find pairs of addends that are easy to add using mental math.

$$16 + 9 + 11 + 24$$
$$16 + 24 + 9 + 11 \leftarrow \text{Commutative}$$
$$(16 + 24) + (9 + 11) \leftarrow \text{Associative}$$
$$40 + 20 = 60 \leftarrow \text{Use mental math.}$$

So, Wes scored 60 points in four games.

Properties of Addition

Commutative Property
Numbers can be added in any order.
$$7 + 16 = 16 + 7$$

Zero Property
The sum of any number and zero is that number.
$$36 + 0 = 36$$

Associative Property
Addends can be grouped differently. The sum is always the same.
$$(23 + 20) + 36 = 23 + (20 + 36)$$
$$43 + 36 = 23 + 56$$
$$79 = 79$$

Another Strategy

When you use **compensation**, you make adding and subtracting simple and quick by changing one addend to a multiple of ten and adjusting the other addend to keep the balance.

Addition Example
How many points did Wes score in the first two games?

$$16 + 9$$
$$(16 - 1) + (9 + 1)$$
$$15 + 10 = 25$$

So, Wes scored 25 points in the first two games.

Subtraction Example
How many more points did Wes score in the fourth game than in the first game?

$$24 - 16 \quad \leftarrow 16 + 4 = 20$$
$$(24 + 4) - (16 + 4) \quad \leftarrow \text{Compensate.}$$
$$28 - 20 = 8$$

So, Wes scored 8 more points in the fourth game.

Recall that addition and subtraction are **inverse**, or opposite, operations.

Talk About It

▶ How can you use compensation when you add?

▶ How can you use compensation when you subtract?

▶ Explain how you can use the Commutative and Associative Properties to find the sum $18 + 24 + 76 + 12$.

Check for Understanding

Use mental math and the properties of addition to find the missing addend. Name the property you use.

1. $6 + \blacksquare = 6$

2. $(17 + 3) + \blacksquare = 5 + (17 + 3)$

3. $3 + (4 + \blacksquare) = (3 + 4) + 6$

Use compensation to solve. Show your work.

4. $19 + 8$

5. $8 + 24$

6. $67 + 15$

7. $67 - 38$

8. $21 - 17 - 4$

9. $41 - 29$

10. $127 + 115$

11. $82 - 36$

Practice

Find the sum or difference. Use mental math when possible.

12. $46 - 46$

13. $17 + (3 + 20)$

14. $4 + 23 + 76$

15. $34 + (6 + 23)$

16. $(14 + 22) + 8$

17. $35 + 33 + 5$

18. $92 + 66 + 8$

19. $49 - 21 - 0$

20. $(6 + 22) + 8$

21. $75 + 46 + 25$

22. $42 - 36$

23. $92 - 14$

24. $43 + (17 + 8)$

25. $81 - 25$

26. $11 + 20 + 49$

27. $33 - 28$

Mixed Applications

Use mental-math strategies to solve Exercises 28–29. Explain your strategies.

28. Chee had 14 team pennants. Then he won 6 at a fair, and friends gave him 3 more. How many pennants does Chee have?

29. Bea sold 4 bowls of chili, 16 hamburgers, and 20 orders of french fries. How many items did she sell altogether?

30. Critical Thinking Use the map.

   a. Name the cities missing on the road sign.

   b. Tell where the sign is located.

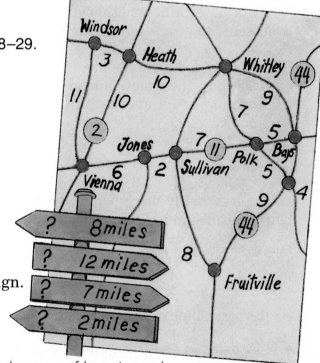

What is one advantage of knowing and using the properties of addition?

WRAP UP...

ESTIMATING
Sums and Differences

You estimate sums or differences when an exact answer is not needed or when you want to check the reasonableness of an answer.

Keena determines that Daley Thompson scored 17,293 total points. Is her answer reasonable?

Olympic Decathlon Champions		
Name	Points	Date
Daley Thompson, U.K.	8,495	1980
Daley Thompson, U.K.	8,798	1984
Christian Schenk, E. Ger.	8,488	1988
Robert Zmelik, TCH	8,611	1992

You can use adjusted front-end estimation.

Add front digits. Then adjust.

$$8,495$$
$$+\ 8,798$$
$$16,000 \leftarrow \text{estimate}$$

$495 + 798 \approx 1,300$

≈ means "is approximately equal to."

$$16,000 + 1,300 = 17,300 \leftarrow \text{adjusted estimate}$$

You can use rounding.

Round.

$$8,495 \rightarrow 8,000$$
$$+8,798 \rightarrow 9,000$$
$$17,000$$

Since 17,293 is close to the estimate, Keena's answer is reasonable.

- How would the example using rounding change if you rounded to the nearest hundred?

You can determine whether an estimated sum is an overestimate or an underestimate.

If both rounded addends are greater than the exact addends, the estimate is an **overestimate**.

$$8,495 \rightarrow 8,500$$
$$+8,798 \rightarrow 8,800$$
$$17,300$$

If both rounded addends are less than the exact addends, the estimate is an **underestimate**.

$$8,445 \rightarrow 8,400$$
$$+8,732 \rightarrow 8,700$$
$$17,100$$

The place to which you round depends on the situation.

About how many more points did Robert Zmelik score than Christian Schenk?

Estimate the difference by rounding.

$$8,611 \rightarrow 8,600$$
$$-8,488 \rightarrow 8,500$$
$$100$$

So, Robert Zmelik scored about 100 more points.

- How can you use front-end digits to estimate the difference?

Check for Understanding

Use adjusted front-end estimation to estimate the sum or difference.

1. $\begin{array}{r} 1,072 \\ +2,550 \\ \hline \end{array}$

2. $\begin{array}{r} 3,244 \\ -2,124 \\ \hline \end{array}$

3. $\begin{array}{r} 8,025 \\ -2,284 \\ \hline \end{array}$

4. $\begin{array}{r} 4,668 \\ +6,432 \\ \hline \end{array}$

5. $\begin{array}{r} 7,312 \\ -4,583 \\ \hline \end{array}$

Round to the nearest thousand. Then estimate the sum or difference.

6. $\begin{array}{r} 1,854 \\ +5,187 \\ \hline \end{array}$

7. $\begin{array}{r} 6,443 \\ +7,248 \\ \hline \end{array}$

8. $\begin{array}{r} 6,153 \\ -5,075 \\ \hline \end{array}$

9. $\begin{array}{r} 5,231 \\ -2,139 \\ \hline \end{array}$

10. $\begin{array}{r} 5,167 \\ +6,860 \\ \hline \end{array}$

Practice

Tell whether the estimate is an overestimate or an underestimate.

11. $6,321 + 8,239 \approx 14,000$

12. $13,772 + 6,559 \approx 21,000$

13. $61,864 + 32,901 \approx 90,000$

14. $82,142 + 23,031 \approx 100,000$

Use adjusted front-end estimation to estimate the sum or difference.

15. $\begin{array}{r} 7,320 \\ +9,989 \\ \hline \end{array}$

16. $\begin{array}{r} 7,381 \\ -3,547 \\ \hline \end{array}$

17. $\begin{array}{r} 5,933 \\ -3,642 \\ \hline \end{array}$

18. $\begin{array}{r} 1,754 \\ +3,748 \\ \hline \end{array}$

19. $\begin{array}{r} 2,329 \\ +7,673 \\ \hline \end{array}$

Round to estimate the sum or difference.

20. $\begin{array}{r} 27,681 \\ -23,216 \\ \hline \end{array}$

21. $\begin{array}{r} 21,050 \\ -12,155 \\ \hline \end{array}$

22. $\begin{array}{r} 61,240 \\ +27,545 \\ \hline \end{array}$

23. $\begin{array}{r} 93,685 \\ +93,216 \\ \hline \end{array}$

24. $\begin{array}{r} 28,803 \\ -17,901 \\ \hline \end{array}$

Mixed Applications

25. Lu says that by driving 14,879 miles and 37,640 miles, she has driven a total of 40,640 miles. Is her calculation reasonable? Explain.

26. **Number Sense** Nancy ran 3 miles farther than Fran. Together they ran 17 miles. How far did Nancy run?

27. Three duffel bags weigh 49, 53, and 77 pounds. About how much is the total weight of the three bags?

28. **Write a Question** Use the facts in the table on page 36. Write a question that can be solved by estimating the sum.

If you reheat a plate of food in a microwave, should you overestimate or underestimate the cooking time?

WRAP UP...

More Practice, Lesson 2.2, page H38

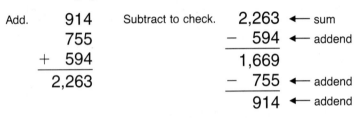

CONNECTING ADDITION AND SUBTRACTION

Since addition and subtraction are inverse, or opposite, operations, you can subtract to check addition and add to check subtraction.

Wayne Gretzky scored 914 points from 1979 to 1984, 755 from 1984 to 1988, and 594 from 1988 to 1992. How many points did he score in all from 1979 to 1992?

Add.
```
    914
    755
 +  594
  2,263
```

Subtract to check.
```
  2,263  ← sum
 −  594  ← addend
  1,669
 −  755  ← addend
    914  ← addend
```

So, Wayne Gretzky scored a total of 2,263 points from 1979 to 1992.

Mark Messier, another hockey player from Canada, scored 1,034 points by 1992. How many more points did Gretzky score than Messier by 1992?

Subtract.
```
  2,263
 −1,034
  1,229
```

Add to check.
```
  1,229
 +1,034
  2,263
```

So, Gretzky scored 1,229 more points than Messier.

Talk About It

▶ Why are two subtraction operations necessary to check the total points Gretzky scored?

▶ Name one other way you could check the answer in each example.

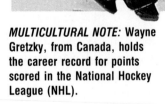

MULTICULTURAL NOTE: Wayne Gretzky, from Canada, holds the career record for points scored in the National Hockey League (NHL).

Check for Understanding

Find the sum or difference. Use the inverse operation to check your answer.

1.
```
   657
 − 549
```

2.
```
   923
 + 578
```

3.
```
  3,342
 −1,849
```

4.
```
  54,321
 −37,768
```

5.
```
  156,123
   82,878
 +717,797
```

Practice

Find the sum or difference. Use the inverse operation to check.

| 6. 768
 +867 | 7. 535
 −396 | 8. 357
 −258 | 9. 6,273
 +3,958 | 10. 7,632
 −5,498 |

| 11. 54,652
 −27,468 | 12. 19,233
 − 6,988 | 13. 25,532
 +33,468 | 14. 113,411
 −109,424 | 15. 636,721
 −365,290 |

| 16. 257
 38
 +766 | 17. 3,431
 1,567
 + 989 | 18. 78,465
 5,821
 +12,473 | 19. 131,522
 2,945
 + 76,798 | 20. 1,454,982
 153,375
 +5,662,866 |

Find the missing digits.

21.
```
   4 8 , 1 ▧ 0
 + ▧ 4 , 2 5 4
 ─────────────
   6 ▧ , 3 7 ▧
```

22.
```
   ▧ , 9 ▧ 2
 − 3 , 5 5 ▧
 ───────────
   3 , ▧ 2 1
```

Mixed Applications

23. The Eagles won 48 games this year. The Bobcats won 77. Jan says the Bobcats won 28 more games. Is she correct? Justify your answer.

24. Lamont and Robert scored a total of 621 points this season. Since Robert scored 276 points, he will win the high-scorer award. Is this true? Justify your answer.

MIXED REVIEW

Use mental math and the properties of addition to find the missing addend.

1. $7 + ▧ = 6 + 7$ 2. $5 + 0 = ▧$ 3. $9 + (1 + ▧) = (9 + 1) + 8$

Use adjusted front-end estimation to estimate the sum or difference.

| 4. 3,240
 +3,685 | 5. 7,673
 −5,113 | 6. 8,203
 +2,451 | 7. 4,186
 −1,157 | 8. 6,223
 −3,779 |

Round to the nearest thousand. Then estimate the sum or difference.

| 9. 7,548
 −3,250 | 10. 1,972
 +9,127 | 11. 19,201
 −12,713 | 12. 15,126
 +14,921 | 13. 26,130
 −21,860 |

Why is it a good idea to estimate an answer before you use a calculator to add or subtract?

WRAP UP...

PROBLEM SOLVING

Choose the Method of Computation

Amy plans to spend $25 for a jogging outfit, $15 for a compact disc, $10 for a birthday present for her brother, and $5 for lunch. How much money should Amy take to the mall?

You can use estimation, paper and pencil, mental math, or a calculator to solve problems. To decide which to use, think about the numbers involved, the questions asked, and the time and tools available to you.

▶ **UNDERSTAND**

What are you asked to find?

What information are you given?

▶ **PLAN**

What will you do to solve the problem? Since you need to find the total cost of the items, you will add.

▶ **SOLVE**

What method of computation can you use? Since the amounts are in multiples of 5 dollars, you can use mental math. Use the Associative Property of Addition to group numbers so that they are easy to add.

($25 + $5) + ($10 + $15)
↓ ↓
$30 + $25 = $55

So, Amy should take $55 to the mall.

▶ **LOOK BACK**

How can you check your answer?

WHAT IF...

... Amy must make sure she has enough money to buy items that cost $8.89, $14.67, and $14.14? What method could she use?

Apply

Solve. Use estimation, paper and pencil, mental math, or a calculator. Justify your choice.

(1) A high school's receipts from three football games are $79.53, $135.53, and $151.79. What are the total receipts?

(2) Daily attendance at a state fair was 176,239; 255,464; 241,950; and 180,715. What was the total four-day attendance?

(3) Li has $5.75. She wants to buy a golf glove for $16.00. How much more money does she need?

(4) Mike gives a clerk $5.00 to pay for a $3.90 pack of golf balls. How much change will he receive?

Mixed Applications ⟩ **STRATEGIES** **Make and Use a Table • Act It Out • Find a Pattern • Draw a Diagram**

Choose a strategy and solve.

(5) Athletes burn 300 calories an hour biking, 600 jogging, 280 playing baseball, 310 playing volleyball, and 720 skating. In which activities do athletes burn about the same number of calories?

(6) Teresa is starting an exercise program. She plans to exercise 5 minutes on the first day, 15 on the second, and 25 on the third. If she continues this pattern, how many minutes will she exercise on the seventh day?

(7) The first number in a pattern is 5. Each number thereafter increases by 3. What is the fifth number in the pattern?

(8) Jan needs a tarpaulin to cover 81 square feet of a cinder track. Should she order the 5-by-5-foot, 7-by-7-foot, or 9-by-9-foot size?

WRITER'S CORNER

(9) Joel rode his bike 10 miles on Monday, 15 on Tuesday, and 12 on Wednesday. Use this information to write a word problem that can be solved using mental math.

(10) Attendance at baseball games was 31,684 on Sunday and 27,241 on Monday. Use this information to write a problem. What method will you use to solve your problem?

ESTIMATING DECIMALS
Sums and Differences

Li and Tong are gymnasts. Both scored well in two gymnastics competitions. Did either gymnast increase his score by more than 12 points from one competition to the other?

You can estimate decimal sums and differences in the same ways you estimate whole-number sums and differences.

Gymnastic Meet Points		
Gymnast	First Meet	Second Meet
Li	106.375	117.675
Tong	100.25	115.275

You can use adjusted front-end estimation.

Li's points:

$$\begin{array}{r} 1\ 1\ 7\ .6\ 7\ 5 \\ -1\ 0\ 6\ .3\ 7\ 5 \\ \hline 1\ \blacksquare\ . \end{array}$$ Subtract the tens.

You can use rounding.

Tong's points:

$$\begin{array}{rcl} 115.275 & \rightarrow & 115 \\ -100.25 & \rightarrow & 100 \\ \hline & & 15 \end{array}$$

Adjust. Since $7.675 - 6.375 \approx 1$,
$117.675 - 106.375 \approx 11$.

So, Tong's score increased by more than 12 points.

Talk About It

▶ Why must you use the ones place and the decimal places to adjust the increase in Li's score?

▶ Suppose Li's score for the first competition was 95.75 points. Would you need to adjust your estimate to answer the question? Explain.

▶ Is the estimate of the increase in Tong's score an overestimate or an underestimate? How do you know?

Check for Understanding

Use adjusted front-end estimation to estimate the sum or difference.

1. $0.352 + 0.859$

2. $\$9.98 - \$5.12$

3. $1.72 + 3.119$

Round to the tenths place. Estimate the sum or difference.

4. $0.975 + 0.325$

5. $0.4488 - 0.2773$

6. $4.091 - 1.58$

MULTICULTURAL NOTE: The photos show Chinese gymnasts during the 1988 Summer Olympics in Seoul, South Korea. The Chinese won 2 medals for gymnastics that year and won 8 medals for gymnastics during the 1992 Summer Olympics in Barcelona, Spain.

Practice

Use adjusted front-end estimation to estimate the sum or difference.

7.	2.9 +7.68	8.	1.84 −0.52	9.	7.22 +0.99	10.	5.96 −1.213	11.	0.5674 +0.0345

Round to estimate the sum or difference.

12.	4.29 +9.4	13.	12.7 − 9.3	14.	16.2 +19.8	15.	5.2 −0.999	16.	5.47 + 1.07

Estimate to compare the sum or difference. Use < or >.

17. $19.23 - 10.7 \bullet 10$

18. $3.65 + 5.99 \bullet 10$

19. $7.72 - 7.70 \bullet 1$

20. $9.2 + 7.001 \bullet 16$

21. $23.99 - 23.19 \bullet 0.5$

22. $0.99 + 0.67 \bullet 1$

Tell whether the estimate is an overestimate or an underestimate.

23. $7.2 + 9.4 \approx 16$

24. $5.28 + 2.17 \approx 7$

25. $11.8 + 5.7 \approx 18$

26. $8.2 + 1.13 \approx 9$

27. $1.29 + 1.11 \approx 2$

28. $2.9 + 1.8 \approx 5$

Mixed Applications

29. In a Summer Olympics, Kristin Otto swam the 100-meter backstroke in 60.89 seconds and the 100-meter freestyle in 54.93 seconds. About how much faster did she swim the freestyle event?

30. In recent Olympic track-and-field events, Florence Griffith-Joyner ran the 100-meter race in 10.54 seconds and the 200-meter race in 21.34 seconds. In theory, about how fast could Griffith-Joyner run a 300-meter race?

31. Number Sense • Mental Math Among the largest freshwater fish ever caught are a 28.5-pound peacock bass and a 22.25-pound largemouth bass. How much more did the peacock bass weigh?

32. Write a Question Among the largest tuna ever caught were a 375.5-pound Atlantic bigeye, a 348.31-pound southern bluefin, a 435-pound Pacific bigeye, and a 388.75-pound yellowfin.

Would you overestimate or underestimate the amount of time it takes to ride a bus to your favorite sporting event?

WRAP UP...

Use the table for Exercises 1–4.

Sometimes I must read a problem more than once.

1. Jersey World's top three salespeople are listed in the table. How many jerseys have the three salespeople sold over the four-month period?

2. If the pattern continues, how many will Bobby sell in September?

3. If the pattern continues, how many will Donna sell in September?

| Number of Jerseys Sold | | | | |
Salesperson	May	June	July	August
Bobby	88	92	95	97
Donna	75	81	88	96
Jim	77	85	92	98

4. If the patterns continue, who will sell the greatest number of jerseys in October?

5. The square of a number is 81. The square root of the same number is 3. What is the number?

Tell which operation to perform first. Then solve.

6. $9 \times 8 - 10$

7. $33 - 10 \times 2$

8. $6 + 9 \div 3$

9. $24 \div (12 - 4)$

10. $60 + 8 \div 2$

11. $(15 \times 2) + 9$

12. $32 - 16 \div 4$

13. $40 \div 8 - 3$

Write the number in standard form.

14. two squared

15. 10^3

16. 3^2

17. ten to the fifth power

Estimate the sum or difference. Tell whether the sum is an overestimate or an underestimate.

18. $6,330 + 8,160$

19. $5,612 - 1,782$

20. $7,321 - 2,405$

21. $8.8 + 1.81$

22. $1.8 - 0.667$

23. $1.013 + 0.247$

Tell whether the estimate is an overestimate or an underestimate.

24. $3.424 + 7.091 \approx 10$

25. $8.920 + 11.675 \approx 21$

26. $1.25 + 12.07 \approx 13$

Find the sum or difference.

27. $\begin{array}{r} 847 \\ -239 \\ \hline \end{array}$

28. $\begin{array}{r} 349 \\ +817 \\ \hline \end{array}$

29. $\begin{array}{r} 20,864 \\ -18,907 \\ \hline \end{array}$

30. $\begin{array}{r} 76,403 \\ 2,091 \\ +10,982 \\ \hline \end{array}$

ASIA

India

Another Way to Add

Bhāskara the Learned was a famous twelfth-century mathematician in India. Most people in India at that time added numbers in the same way that we do. However, in one of Bhāskara's books, he showed a different way to find the sum of these numbers:

2, 5, 32, 193, 18, 10, and 100.

Bhāskara's Method

Sum of the units	2, 5, 2, 3, 8, 0, 0	20
Sum of the tens	3, 9, 1, 1, 0	14
Sum of the hundreds	1, 1	2
Sum of the sums		360

Talk About It

• How is Bhāskara's method similar to the method you use to add? How is it different?

Use Bhāskara's method to find the sum of the numbers. Use a calculator to check your answer.

1. 12, 22, 6, 125, 47

2. 8, 17, 35, 131, 100

3. 5, 10, 30, 120, 255, 186

4. 23, 44, 8, 50, 103, 200

5. 110, 150, 248, 335, 56, 121

6. 77, 84, 92, 134, 255, 400

MULTICULTURAL NOTE: The culture of twelfth-century India included many contributions to literature, painting, and sculpture. The elephant was often represented in the art of the period.

ADDING DECIMALS

The Dodd Middle School relay team won the 400-meter relay at a local meet. Ken ran his leg of the race in 15 seconds, Josh ran his in 14.75 seconds, Bill ran his in 13.125 seconds, and Bobby ran his in 12.8 seconds. What was the team's winning time?

You could round to the nearest whole number to estimate the sum.

15 + 14.75 + 13.125 + 12.8
↓   ↓   ↓   ↓
15 + 15 +   13   + 13 = 56 ← estimate

Find the sum.

Step 1 Align the decimal points.	**Step 2** Place the decimal point. Then add.
15 or 15.000 Placing zeros to the 14.75 14.750 right of the decimal 13.125 13.125 point does not +12.8 +12.800 change the value of the decimal.	15 14.75 13.125 +12.8 ⎯⎯⎯⎯ 55.675

So, the team's winning time was 55.675 seconds.

Talk About It

▶ How do you know it is acceptable to rewrite 15 as 15.000, 14.75 as 14.750, and 12.8 as 12.800?

▶ Why do you align the decimal points?

Check for Understanding

Find the sum.

1. $18 + $2.95 + $13.30   **2.** 14.4 + 231.67 + 24.699   **3.** 63.403 + 2.661

4. 763.114	**5.** $304.42	**6.** 420	**7.** 260	**8.** 25.01
17.58	+ 18.09	76.3	103.403	115.9
+ 0.066		+ 8.5	+254.906	+ 87.99

Practice

Place the decimal point in the sum.

9. $76.551 + 24.59 + 0.054 = 101195$

10. $123.98 + 0.873 + 10.0059 = 1348589$

11. $48.9 + 31.092 + 0.87 = 80862$

12. $0.1209 + 0.236 + 0.279 = 06359$

Find the sum.

13. $6.25 + 4.794$

14. $0.29 + 6.68$

15. $9.3 + 3.708$

16. $30.03 + 40.54$

17. $67.1 + 2.693$

18. $4.6 + 75.188$

19.
```
   76.6
   55.66
 +32.666
```

20.
```
    6.72
   44.5
 +  0.77
```

21.
```
 6,453.5
   960.11
 +  431.7
```

22.
```
 $423.12
   33.42
 + 777.74
```

23.
```
   54.01
    9.3
 +68.776
```

24. $72.44 + 33.93$

25. $4.12 + 832 + 209.7$

26. $0.12 + $53.91 + 43

27. $40.2 + 753.01 + 2,562 + 0.96$

Mixed Applications

Solve. Use the table for Exercises 28–31.

Month	Jan.	Feb.	Mar.	Apr.	May	June	July	Aug.	Sept.	Oct.	Nov.	Dec.
Rainfall (inches)	2.2	3	3.55	4.2	3.45	2.7	0.84	0.4	10.1	2	1.9	2.3

28. How much rain fell during the first three months of the year?

29. How much rain fell during the last three months of the year?

30. How much rain fell during the three wettest months?

31. How much rain fell during the three driest months?

32. Critical Thinking Look at the problems $3.2 + 9.7$ and $32 + 97$. How are they similar? Which problem has the greater sum?

33. Analyze Data Use the table. When do you think outdoor athletic contests were rained out? When could you have left your umbrella at home?

Name an everyday situation in which you add decimals.

SUBTRACTING DECIMALS

Arie Luyendyk drove a record 185.984 miles per hour (mph) to win the Indianapolis 500. The next fastest time was clocked four years earlier when Bobby Rahal drove 170.72 mph. How much faster is Luyendyk's time?

Estimate. You could use the front digits and then adjust if needed.

185.984 − 170.72

Since 0.984 ≈ 1, 0.72 ≈ 1, and 1 − 1 = 0, no adjustment is needed.

185 − 170 = 15

Find the difference.

Step 1	Step 2
Align the decimal points.	Place the decimal point. Then subtract.
$\begin{array}{r} 185.984 \\ -170.72 \\ \hline \end{array}$ or $\begin{array}{r} 185.984 \\ -170.720 \\ \hline \end{array}$	$\begin{array}{r} 185.984 \\ -170.72 \\ \hline 15.264 \end{array}$

So, Luyendyk's time is 15.264 mph faster.

Examples

A. $\begin{array}{r} 24.02 \\ -\ 7.3 \\ \hline 16.72 \end{array}$ B. $\begin{array}{r} 15.007 \\ -12.22 \\ \hline 2.787 \end{array}$ C. $\begin{array}{r} 36.1 \\ -\ 9.73 \\ \hline 26.37 \end{array}$

- How can you check your subtraction?

Check for Understanding

Find the difference.

1. $4.2 - 0.12$

2. $63.039 - 29.84$

3. $739.4 - 56.2$

4. $26.32 - 17.15$

5. $481.201 - 256.893$

6. $261.92 - 89.796$

7. $\begin{array}{r} 42.03 \\ -\ 9.859 \\ \hline \end{array}$ 8. $\begin{array}{r} 78.02 \\ -\ 6.437 \\ \hline \end{array}$ 9. $\begin{array}{r} 34.7 \\ -\ 0.938 \\ \hline \end{array}$ 10. $\begin{array}{r} 12.77 \\ -\ 8.435 \\ \hline \end{array}$ 11. $\begin{array}{r} 77.95 \\ -41.5 \\ \hline \end{array}$

Practice

Place the decimal point in the difference.

12. $98.5 - 6.09 = 9241$ **13.** $4.85 - 0.485 = 4365$ **14.** $680.2 - 92.4 = 5878$

 Find the difference.

15. $5.23 - 0.986$ **16.** $83.12 - 8.6$ **17.** $101.23 - 8.7$

18. $9 - 6.23$ **19.** $0.54 - 0.054$ **20.** $23.5 - 9.6719$

21. $0.67 - 0.2103$ **22.** $41.08 - 8.7$ **23.** $31.02 - 7.8643$

24. $23 - 0.76$ **25.** $6.398 - 4.885$ **26.** $6.5 - 3.92$

27. $8.703 - 4.29$ **28.** $9.7 - 3.872$ **29.** $86.49 - 3.295$

30. $\begin{array}{r} 65.05 \\ -\ 5.2 \\ \hline \end{array}$ **31.** $\begin{array}{r} 0.9 \\ -0.04 \\ \hline \end{array}$ **32.** $\begin{array}{r} 74.7 \\ -\ 0.987 \\ \hline \end{array}$ **33.** $\begin{array}{r} 86.49 \\ -\ 4.32 \\ \hline \end{array}$ **34.** $\begin{array}{r} 9.183 \\ -7.041 \\ \hline \end{array}$

Mixed Applications

35. Last year Maria did an average of 87.5 sit-ups. This year her average is 93.7 sit-ups. How much has her average improved?

36. Juan used 2.6 pounds of a 7-pound block of clay to sculpt a wrestler. He also gave away 1.5 pounds. How much clay was left?

37. **Find Data** Use an encyclopedia, an almanac, or another reference book to find and list five facts about your favorite sport.

38. **Make Up a Problem** Use the facts you found in Exercise 37 to write a problem that can be solved using addition or subtraction.

NUMBER SENSE

39. Copy the puzzle. Fill the yellow boxes with addition or subtraction signs so that the computations both across and down are equal to 18.4.

3.4		8.4		6.6
7.3		14.6		3.5
7.7		4.6		15.3

Name an everyday situation in which you subtract decimals.

USING CALCULATOR MEMORY

Use the memory keys on a calculator when you need to perform more than one operation to solve a problem.

Press [MRC] twice to clear the memory.   ← Always clear the memory first.

[M+] adds a number to the memory.   [MRC] recalls the number.

Example   A checkbook balance shows how much money is in a checking account. Amounts of deposits are added to the balance. Amounts of checks are subtracted. Wade uses a calculator to check his checkbook balance.

Date	Check Number	Checks issued to or Deposit received from	Amount of Deposit	Amount of Check	Balance
4/19		beginning balance			$302.35
4/20		salary	487.24		
4/25	738	Northern Telephone Co.		37.45	
4/26	739	Abe's Oriental grocery		78.43	
4/27		salary	515.31		
4/27	740	Clyde's car loan Co.		256.25	
4/28	741	Lingfat Health Club		178.98	
4/30	742	Hi-Roll Savings Bank		400.00	353.79

sum of beginning balance and deposits − total checks = balance
(302.35 + 487.24 + 515.31) − (37.45 + 78.43 + 256.25 + 178.98 + 400.00)

First, Wade totals the checks. Then, he adds the total to the memory.

37.45 [+] 78.43 [+] 256.25 [+] 178.98 [+] 400 [=] [M+]   [M   951.11]

Next, he finds the sum of the beginning balance and the deposits.

302.35 [+] 487.24 [+] 515.31 [=]   [M   1304.9]

To subtract his checks, he presses [−] [MRC] [=]   [M   353.79].

So, Wade's checkbook balance is $353.79.

• Was the final balance shown in the checkbook correct?

• How can Wade add another check to the memory?

Check for Understanding

 Solve. Use a calculator with memory keys.

1. $(21.75 + 3.45 + 52.57 + 31.49 + 25.75) - (54.31 + 5.43 + 62.98)$

2. $(121,657 + 476,474 + 11,980) - (54,321 + 45,231 + 35,798)$

Practice

Find the balance. Use a calculator with memory keys.

3.

Checks	Deposits
$ 50.25	$851.67
136.29	
525.78	245.25
354.11	
Balance:	■

4.

Checks	Deposits
$475.38	$1,200.00
84.76	
162.04	
260.52	68.52
Balance:	■

5.

Checks	Deposits
$267.54	$750.80
192.48	
12.29	750.80
722.76	
Balance:	■

Mixed Applications

6. In his collection of blocks, Dan has 375 red, 226 blue, 415 yellow, and 387 green blocks. He wants to build a castle that calls for 927 blocks, and a drawbridge with 368 blocks. How many blocks will be left?

7. Kate has $5.00, and Sue gives her $12.00 more for these groceries: cereal, $3.87; bread, $1.29; milk, $2.56; chicken, $5.39; broccoli, $1.78; and juice, $1.98. How much change will Kate receive?

CRITICAL THINKING

You can use a calculator and your knowledge of place value to perform operations with numbers in the hundred-millions place and greater.

Example $354,956,588$ ➞ 354 million + 956,588
            $+ 466,355,244$ ➞ 466 million + 355,244

Use a calculator.

354 + 466 = | 820. | (million)

956,588 + 355,244 = | 1311832. |

Use paper and pencil.

820,000,000 + 1,311,832 = 821,311,832

Use a calculator to solve.

8. $684,923,317 + 722,196,442$

9. $1,234,567,890 - 987,654,321$

Name a way you can use the memory keys on a calculator.

WRAP UP...

VARIABLES AND EXPRESSIONS
Using Algebra

A football team scored 3 more points in the second half than they had scored in the first half of a game. How many points did the team score in the second half?

If the team had scored 7 points in the first half, you could write the **numerical expression** $7 + 3$ to solve the problem. Since you do not know the number of points scored in the first half, you can use a letter, or **variable**, to write an algebraic expression.

Use p for the number of points scored in the first half.

word expression $\longrightarrow$ 3 more than the number of points scored in the first half

algebraic expression $\longrightarrow$ $p + 3$

So, the team scored $p + 3$ points in the second half.

Talk About It

▶ How does the algebraic expression differ from the word expression?

▶ If the team had scored 3 fewer points in the second half, what algebraic expression would you have written?

The table shows examples of word expressions and algebraic expressions.

Word Expression	Algebraic Expression
Four more than a number x	$x + 4$
The sum of 8.6 and a number p	$8.6 + p$
Nine less than a number y	$y - 9$
Seven fewer than a number d	$d - 7$

Check for Understanding

Write an algebraic expression for the word expression.

1. seven more than a number y

2. four less than a number n

3. the sum of a number x and 15

4. nine fewer than a number s

Practice

Write an algebraic expression for the word expression.

5. 30 more than a number b

6. k fewer than 115.75

7. 26 less than a number p

8. w less than 97

9. 12 fewer than a number t

10. the sum of 55 and a number n

11. the sum of 3.2 and a number s

12. d more than 52

Write a word expression for the algebraic expression.

13. $23 + u$

14. $45 - q$

15. $t - 11.075$

16. $b + 452.5$

17. $43.7 + a$

18. $65 - y$

19. $z + 2.5$

20. $b - 67$

21. $w + 12$

22. $x - 5.5$

Mixed Applications

23. James scored 46 more free throws than Nathan. Let n represent the number of free throws Nathan scored. Write an algebraic expression that represents the number of free throws James scored.

24. Which decimal number is greatest, 1.02, 1.20, or 1.022? Which of these numbers is least?

25. June gave Sara $5. Let d represent the amount June had before she gave money to Sara. Write an algebraic expression that represents how much money June had left.

26. Number Sense • Estimation In his best game, a halfback rushed for 9 yards, 21 yards, 17 yards, and 58 yards. About how many total yards did he rush?

Write an algebraic expression that tells how much more time you spend in math class than you spend eating lunch.

WRAP
UP...

EVALUATING EXPRESSIONS
Using Algebra

Each day Juana missed the same number of free throws no matter how many she attempted. She kept this record.

Attempted	10	15	18	24	28	f
Scored	4	9	12	18	22	?

- What pattern does the table show?

- If f represents the number of free throws attempted, what algebraic expression represents the number scored?

Suppose Juana attempts 16 free throws. How many will she score?

Use 16 for f in the expression $f - 6$.   → $f - 6$
$16 - 6 = 10$

So, Juana will score 10 free throws.

When you replace the variable with a number and perform the operation in an algebraic expression, you are **evaluating**, or finding the value of, the expression.

Example   Evaluate $x + 6$, for $x = 7$.

Step 1	**Step 2**
Replace the variable with the number 7.	Perform the operation.
$x + 6 = 7 + 6$	$7 + 6 = 13$

More Examples   Evaluate the expressions for $b = 4.5$ and $c = 12$.

A. $32 - b$
$32 - 4.5 = 27.5$

B. $c + 13$
$12 + 13 = 25$

C. $(c + b) - 2.3$
$(12 + 4.5) - 2.3 = 14.2$

Check for Understanding

Evaluate the expression.

1. $n + 25$, for $n = 7$

2. $w - 13$, for $w = 72$

3. $33 - t$, for $t = 19$

4. $n + 25$, for $n = 2$

5. $w - 13$, for $w = 26$

6. $y - 9.8$, for $y = 21$

Practice

Evaluate the expression $p + 35.57$ for each value of p.

7. $p = 21.42$ **8.** $p = 19.09$ **9.** $p = 43.35$ **10.** $p = 87.09$ **11.** $p = 98.88$

Evaluate the expression $113.25 - p$ for each value of p.

12. $p = 13.89$ **13.** $p = 46.25$ **14.** $p = 51.5$ **15.** $p = 79.93$ **16.** $p = 98.88$

Evaluate the expression.

17. $a - 35$, for $a = 52$ **18.** $a + 7.9$, for $a = 5.2$ **19.** $72 - b$, for $b = 26$

20. $57 + b$, for $b = 64$ **21.** $45.2 - c$, for $c = 36.7$ **22.** $643 + c$, for $c = 597$

23. $65 - k$, for $k = 65$ **24.** $23.8 + k$, for $k = 0$ **25.** $d - 72$, for $d = 72$

26. $(5 + t) + 12$, for $t = 8$ **27.** $(t - 25) + 14$, for $t = 72$

28. $(2.6 + 5.9) + d$, for $d = 11.4$ **29.** $d - (7.8 + 6.5)$, for $d = 15.1$

30. $37 - (41 - f)$, for $f = 13.5$ **31.** $45 - (f + 12.2)$, for $f = 23.7$

32. $m + (2.45 + 5.73)$, for $m = 9.56$ **33.** $(m - 11.3) - 17.8$, for $m = 51.1$

Mixed Applications

Write and evaluate the algebraic expressions for Exercises 34–35.

34. A balcony ticket for a show costs $3.75 less than an orchestra ticket. How much does an orchestra ticket cost if a balcony ticket costs $14.25?

35. Isaac ran 37.6 meters farther than Drew in a contest to raise money for a charity. How far did Drew run if Isaac ran 463.5 meters?

36. Number Sense A number palindrome, such as 545, reads the same when you reverse the digits. You can often make a palindrome by adding a number and its reverse, such as $324 + 423 = 747$. Use 143 and 12,342 to make palindromes.

37. Critical Thinking Tiffany, Deidre, Liza, Bette, and Lori are runners. Bette can outrun Liza and Tiffany, but Deidre can outrun Bette. Liza can outrun Lori, but Deidre can outrun Liza. Which one of the girls is the fastest runner?

If the value of the variable changes, will the value of the expression remain the same? Why?

W R A P
UP...

EXPLORING

Addition and Subtraction Equations

An **equation** is a mathematical sentence that uses an equals sign to show that two quantities are equal. Think of an equation as a balanced scale.

Here are some examples of equations. Notice that some equations contain algebraic expressions.

$$2 + 6 = 8 \qquad 17 - 9 = 8$$
$$n + 5 = 11 \qquad x - 12 = 3$$

Work Together

Building Understanding

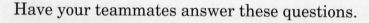

Place yellow cubes on a balance so that it looks like the picture at the right. Have your teammates look away while you place an equal number of blue cubes on each side of the balance. Cover the blue cubes on the left side with a napkin.

Have your teammates answer these questions.

TALK ABOUT IT

- What algebraic expression describes the number of cubes on the left side? Use the variable c. How many cubes are on the right side?

- What equation tells the relationship between one side and the other?

- Remove the 5 yellow cubes from each side. Is the scale still balanced?

- How many cubes are now on the right side? How many cubes must be under the napkin? What is the value of c?

Making the Connection

By using a balance scale, you solved an equation by finding the value of c.

1. What operation did you use to solve the equation and find the value of c?

2. What is the inverse of addition?

Suppose you were asked to solve the equation $c - 5 = 12$.

3. What is the inverse of subtraction?

4. What operation would you use to solve the equation?

5. How would you solve the equation and find the value of c?

Checking Understanding

Tell how to solve the equation.

6. $x + 7 = 21$

7. $y - 6 = 18$

8. $p + 26 = 47$

9. $1.5 + a = 7.75$

10. $t + 19 = 54$

11. $b - 5.25 = 14.75$

12. $c - 9.7 = 4.2$

13. $23.7 + d = 28$

14. $k + 31.8 = 51.8$

Use inverse operations. Solve the equations.

15. $x + 10 = 20$

16. $7 + b = 17$

17. $t - 5 = 20$

MIXED REVIEW

Find the sum or difference.

1. $\begin{array}{r} 8{,}394 \\ + 2{,}493 \\ \hline \end{array}$

2. $\begin{array}{r} 98{,}763 \\ - 97{,}873 \\ \hline \end{array}$

3. $\begin{array}{r} 75.364 \\ + 75.463 \\ \hline \end{array}$

4. $\begin{array}{r} 325{,}433 \\ - 245{,}349 \\ \hline \end{array}$

5. $\begin{array}{r} 75.335 \\ - 33.965 \\ \hline \end{array}$

Write an algebraic expression for the word expression.

6. 11 more than a number b

7. 6 fewer than a number c

8. the sum of t and 3.7

9. y less than 6.2

PROBLEM SOLVING

STRATEGY • Guess and Check

Of the 25 hockey games the Redbirds played, they tied 3 games and won 2 more than they lost. How many games did the Redbirds win?

Guess and check is a good strategy to use when more than one condition must be met to find the solution.

▶ **UNDERSTAND**

What are you asked to find?

What information are you given?

▶ **PLAN**

What strategy will you choose?

Guess an answer that satisfies the first condition. Check to see if your answer satisfies the other conditions. If not, guess again.

▶ **SOLVE**

How will you carry out your plan?

Make a table to keep a record of your guesses and checks. Try to guess in an organized way so that each of your guesses comes closer and closer to the exact answer.

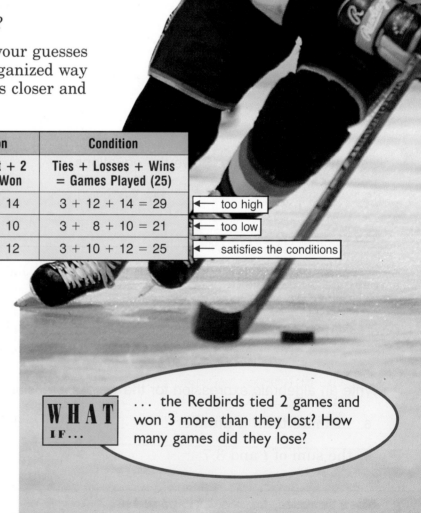

Given	Guess	Condition	Condition	
Games Tied	Games Lost	Games Lost + 2 = Games Won	Ties + Losses + Wins = Games Played (25)	
3	12	12 + 2 = 14	3 + 12 + 14 = 29	← too high
3	8	8 + 2 = 10	3 + 8 + 10 = 21	← too low
3	10	10 + 2 = 12	3 + 10 + 12 = 25	← satisfies the conditions

So, the Redbirds won 12 games.

▶ **LOOK BACK**

How does the table help you find the answer?

WHAT IF... ... the Redbirds tied 2 games and won 3 more than they lost? How many games did they lose?

58

Apply

Solve. Use the strategy *guess and check*. Record your guesses and checks.

(1) Of the 40 photographers and reporters attending a soccer game, there are 16 more photographers than reporters. How many reporters are there?

(2) Mary and Bill collect baseball cards. Mary has 7 more cards than Bill. Together they have a total of 31 cards. How many baseball cards does Bill have?

> **Mixed Applications** **STRATEGIES** Guess and Check • Find a Pattern • Make and Use a Table • Act It Out

Choose a strategy and solve.

(3) Akim exercises 15 minutes in week one, 30 minutes in week two, and 45 minutes in week three. If this pattern continues, how long will Akim exercise in week six?

(4) Of the 95 sixth graders and seventh graders going on a field trip, there are 27 more sixth graders than seventh graders. How many sixth graders are going on the trip?

(5) A park has canoes that carry either 3 or 4 people. There are 5 canoes carrying a total of 17 people. How many four-person canoes are there?

(6) Joyce runs 0.5 kilometer the first day. She adds 0.5 kilometer each day as she trains for a 10-kilometer race. On what day will Joyce run 10 kilometers?

(7) Orange City Little League has 1 coach for every 9 players. If there are 8 coaches, how many players are there?

(8) Chad has 11 coins in his pocket. He has only dimes and quarters. The sum of the coins is $2. How many quarters does Chad have?

(9) A square garden decorates a stadium entrance. If 144 square yards of plastic covers the garden, what is the length of each side?

(10) Janine walks 7 blocks south, 3 blocks east, 5 blocks north, and 8 blocks west. How many blocks has she walked when she crosses her own path?

(11) The difference between two numbers is 37. Their sum is 215. What are the numbers?

(12) The sum of Paco's and José's ages is 14. Paco is 2 years older than José. What are their ages?

More Practice, Lesson 2.12, page H41

CHAPTER REVIEW/TEST

Vocabulary Check

Choose a word from the box to complete each sentence.

algebraic
compensation
equation
evaluating
inverse
variable

1. When you use __?__, you change one addend to a multiple of ten and adjust the other addend by the same amount. *(page 34)*

2. Addition and subtraction are __?__ operations. *(page 34)*

3. A(n) __?__ expression contains a letter of the alphabet. The letter is called a __?__ and is used to represent a number. *(page 52)*

4. When you replace the variable with a number and perform the operation in an algebraic expression, you are __?__ the expression. *(page 54)*

5. In a(n) __?__, or number sentence, the equals sign shows that expressions on both sides represent the same number. *(page 56)*

Concept Check

6. How can you tell whether an estimated sum is an overestimate or an underestimate? *(page 36)*

7. Does the value change or remain the same if you add zeros to the right of a decimal? Explain. *(page 46)*

8. How can you check your answer to a subtraction problem? *(page 38)*

Write an algebraic expression for the word expression. *(page 52)*

9. four more than a number a

10. two fewer than a number c

11. a number n plus 15

12. 25 minus a number z

13. x less than 36

14. b more than 12

Tell what operation you would use to solve the equation. *(page 56)*

15. $h + 15 = 35$

16. $y - 25 = 15$

17. $b - 9 = 45$

18. $25 + b = 43$

Skill Check

Estimate the sum or difference. Then tell whether the sum is an overestimate or an underestimate. *(pages 36, 42)*

How I round determines my estimate.

19. $6.72 - 0.991$

20. $25.342 + 12.25$

21. $1.17 - 0.142$

22. $4.19 + 9.3$

23. $12.6 - 9.714$

24. $28.15 + 17.393$

Find the sum or difference. *(pages 34, 38, 46, 48)*

25. $18 + 12$

26. $12 + 16 + 14$

27. $35 - 17$

28. $56.34 - 38.76$

29. $745 - 259$

30. $811 - 622$

31. $8,140 + 9,205$

32. $8,771 - 2,846$

33. $3.9 + 6.78$

Write an algebraic expression for the word expression. *(page 52)*

34. 14 more than a number n

35. 1.6 less than a number c

Write a word expression for the algebraic expression. *(page 52)*

36. $10 - w$

37. $z + 1.7$

38. $d - 26$

Evaluate the expression. *(page 54)*

39. $n - 8$, for $n = 17$

40. $m + 12$, for $m = 9$

41. $2.1 - k$, for $k = 1.09$

42. $b + 9$, for $b = 7.5$

43. $y - 3.7$, for $y = 9.2$

44. $11.03 + n$, for $n = 9.19$

Problem-Solving Check *(pages 40, 58)*

45. The attendance at the state fair for four days was 168,254; 245,589; 214,520; and 179,065. What was the total attendance? What method of computation did you use?

46. Elsa gave the clerk $10.00 to pay for a package of apples that cost $2.95. How much change did Elsa receive? What method of computation did you use?

47. The sum of Sandy's and Trina's ages is 15. Trina is 3 years older than Sandy. What are Sandy's and Trina's ages?

48. The difference between two numbers is 38. The sum of the two numbers is 212. What are the numbers?

WHAT DID I LEARN?

1. Explain the method you would use, and then estimate 7,321 + 4,929.

2. Explain the method you would use, and then estimate 67.212 − 21.83.

3. Show each step as you find the sum 45.6 + 37.25.

4. Show each step as you find the difference 83.6 − 2.35.

5. Explain how to evaluate $a − 6$ for $a = 10$. Then evaluate the expression.

6. Read Exercise 4 on page 41. Follow the steps on the Problem-Solving Think Along worksheet to show how to solve this problem.

Write About It

7. Which concept in this chapter on adding and subtracting whole numbers and decimals was the easiest for you? Which was the hardest? Explain.

8. Explain what helps you determine the algebraic expression for a given word expression.

TEAMWORK Project

Plan a Bike Trip

A headline in a local newspaper reads, "Couple bikes 1,212 miles in 12 days." Work with your teammates to plan a 1-day bike trip.

Decide ▼ What information will you need for determining the distance you can travel?

Where will you go?
How many hours will you bike?
What supplies will you need to take with you?

Do ▼ As a team, make a map of the route, with the distance between points marked.
Plan your stops and the amount of time you will spend at each stop. Estimate the number of miles per hour you will be able to travel.

Share ▼ Compare your plans with those of other teams. Tell why you chose your particular route. Compare the lists of supplies. How do they differ? Why?

Speed Guidelines	
Type of Terrain	**Miles per Hour**
Up steep hills	6
Downhill with tailwinds	49
Flat stretches	15–20

Talk About It

What are the critical factors that determined where you would bike, how far you would bike, and how long you would bike?

How did you use addition and subtraction of whole numbers and decimals in your planning?

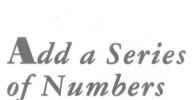

MathFun
Extend Your Thinking

Add a Series of Numbers

Carl Friedrich Gauss (1777–1855) was a famous German mathematician and astronomer. It is believed that he used this shortcut to find the sum of the numbers from 1 to 10.

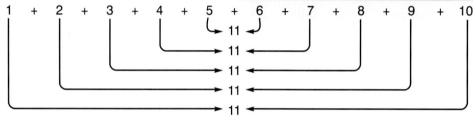

1. What is the sum of each pair of numbers?

2. How many pairs are there?

3. What is the sum of the numbers from 1 to 10?

4. Use this method to find the sum of the numbers from 1 to 100.

Challenge

Critical Thinking

A forester plans to have the same number of trees in Field A as in Field B. Field A contains 752 trees. Workers remove 78 of them. Field B contains 184 trees. Workers plant 265 spruce trees and 229 pine trees in Field B. Do Field A and Field B contain the same number of trees? If not, how many trees should be planted in which field to have the same number of trees in both fields?

Number Puzzles

▶ Place each number in one of the circles so that the sum of every three numbers in a line is the same.

2.1 2.6
2.2 2.7
2.3 2.8
2.4 2.9
2.5

What is the sum? Is there a pattern?

CUMULATIVE REVIEW
CHAPTERS 1–2

Write the letter of the correct answer.

1. Which is the value of 10^2?

   A. 10   B. 100
   C. 1,000 D. 10,000

2. Round 19.514 to the tenths place.

   A. 19   B. 19.5
   C. 19.51 D. 20

3. Use the order of operations to solve $4 + (6 \div 2) - 5$.

   A. 8   B. 10
   C. 12   D. not here

4. What is ten to the fourth power in standard form?

   A. 10,000 B. 40,000
   C. 40   D. not here

5. Choose the best estimate.
   $7.456 - 1.6$

   A. 4   B. 5
   C. 7   D. 8

6. Choose the best estimate.
   $4.16 - 1.9$

   A. 2   B. 3
   C. 3.5   D. 4

7. $5.16 + 3.074$

   A. 8.125   B. 8.234
   C. 8.8174 D. not here

8. $9.2 - 1.305$

   A. 7.1213 B. 7.213
   C. 7.895   D. 8

9. Evaluate $k + 14$, for $k = 7$.

   A. 7   B. 21
   C. 22   D. 98

10. Evaluate $5.1 - m$, for $m = 2.34$.

    A. 2.76   B. 0.183
    C. 18.3   D. 7.44

11. What is an algebraic expression for 3 less than a number x?

    A. $3 - x$ B. $x + 3$
    C. $x - 3$ D. $3x$

12. Which operation would you use to solve the equation $x - 5 = 11$?

    A. addition   B. subtraction
    C. division   D. not here

13. Kevin ran 1 mile (mi) Monday, 5 mi Tuesday, 9 mi Wednesday, and 13 mi Thursday. If the pattern continues, how far will Kevin run on Saturday?

    A. 17 mi   B. 19 mi
    C. 21 mi   D. 35 mi

14. The difference between two numbers is 14. The sum of the two numbers is 56. What are the numbers?

    A. 20 and 36   B. 22 and 34
    C. 21 and 35   D. 14 and 56

MULTIPLYING
WHOLE NUMBERS
AND
DECIMALS

Did you know . . .

. . . that the city of Stockholm, Sweden, is built on 14 islands that are connected by about 50 bridges?

TALK ABOUT IT

Each year Swedish families celebrate Midsummer Day by erecting maypoles. The Bergland family crosses bridges 8 times going to and from a Midsummer Day celebration. Draw a diagram showing 6 islands and 10 bridges. Show one way that you could cross bridges 8 times on a round trip from one place to another.

Lou used 13 packages of light bulbs to replace burned-out lights around a civic center. If each package contained 4 bulbs, how many bulbs did Lou use?

You can use mental math and the Distributive Property to make a simpler problem.

$$
\begin{aligned}
4 \times 13 &= 4 \times (10 + 3) \\
&= (4 \times 10) + (4 \times 3) \\
&= 40 + 12 \\
&= 52 \leftarrow \text{So, Lou used 52 bulbs.}
\end{aligned}
$$

You can also use mental math to solve multiplication problems by changing the order of factors or by grouping factors.

$$
\begin{aligned}
(2 \times 8) \times 5 &= (8 \times 2) \times 5 \leftarrow \text{Commutative} \\
&= 8 \times (2 \times 5) \leftarrow \text{Associative} \\
&= 8 \times 10 \\
&= 80
\end{aligned}
$$

Talk About It

▶ How can you use the Property of One and mental math to solve problems?

▶ How can you use the Zero Property and mental math to solve problems?

▶ Suppose Lou had used 28 packages of light bulbs. How could you find the total number of bulbs he used?

Check for Understanding

Use the properties of multiplication and mental math to find the product.

1. 3×42

2. $9 \times (8 - 8)$

3. $1 \times (6 \times 7)$

4. $(2 \times 9) \times 5$

Properties of Multiplication

Distributive Property
A factor can be thought of as the sum of addends. Each addend can be multiplied by the other factor without changing the product.

$$
\begin{aligned}
2 \times 37 &= 2 \times (30 + 7) \\
&= (2 \times 30) + (2 \times 7) \\
&= 60 + 14 \\
&= 74
\end{aligned}
$$

Commutative Property
Factors can be multiplied in any order without changing the product.

$$3 \times 4 = 4 \times 3$$
$$12 = 12$$

Associative Property
Factors can be grouped in any way without changing the product.

$$(6 \times 5) \times 3 = 6 \times (5 \times 3)$$
$$30 \times 3 = 6 \times 15$$
$$90 = 90$$

Property of One
The product of any factor and 1 is the factor.

$$17 \times 1 = 17$$

Zero Property
The product of any factor and zero is zero.

$$99 \times 0 = 0$$

Practice

Write a number sentence that illustrates each property of multiplication.

5. Zero **6.** Commutative **7.** One **8.** Associative **9.** Distributive

Find the missing factor. Name the property used.

10. $26 \times 37 = \blacksquare \times 26$

11. $42 \times \blacksquare = 0$

12. $24 \times 31 = \blacksquare \times 24$

13. $16 \times 1 = \blacksquare$

14. $67 \times \blacksquare = 67$

15. $\blacksquare \times 6 = (4 \times 6) + (3 \times 6)$

16. $(3 \times 5) \times \blacksquare = 3 \times (5 \times 2)$

17. $1 \times 32 = \blacksquare$

18. $6 \times (4 \times 9) = (4 \times \blacksquare) \times 6$

19. $\blacksquare \times 13 = (6 \times 4) + (6 \times 9)$

20. $0 \times 25 = \blacksquare$

21. $48 \times 7 = 6 \times (\blacksquare \times 7)$

Use mental math and the properties of multiplication to find the product.

22. $7 \times 2 \times 5$

23. $23 \times 3 \times 0$

24. 48×5

25. 35×4

26. $4 \times 25 \times 1$

27. 4×21

28. $3 \times 8 \times 5$

29. 13×9

30. $5 \times 4 \times 9$

31. 5×16

32. $22 \times 2 \times 0$

33. 28×8

34. 4×130

35. $3 \times 9 \times 10$

36. $11 \times 4 \times 2$

37. $12 \times 1 \times 12$

Mixed Applications

38. A flower shop has 5 vases on each of 3 shelves. Each vase holds 24 roses. What is the total number of roses on the shelves? Write a number sentence using one of the properties of multiplication. Then solve.

39. **Critical Thinking** Dea will multiply several different numbers by 12. Next, she will divide each product by 2 twice and then by 3. What will the results be?

40. **Number Sense ● Estimation** Kyle made 3 trips to recycling centers. He took 383 cans, 521 cans, and 415 cans. About how many cans did Kyle take to the recycling centers?

How can you use the properties to multiply 9×510?

WRAP
UP...

ESTIMATING PRODUCTS

There will be a special show at the Sydney Opera House. Tickets have been sold for 48 rows of 28 seats each. About how many programs should be printed for the show?

- Are you asked to find an exact answer or an estimate? How do you know?

One way to estimate a product is to round each factor.

Round and multiply.

$$
\begin{array}{r}
48 \rightarrow 50 \\
\times 28 \rightarrow \times 30 \\
\hline
1{,}500
\end{array}
$$

Sometimes you may need to know whether your estimate is an overestimate or an underestimate.

Both rounded factors are greater than the exact factors. So, 1,500 is an overestimate.

- Why might you want to overestimate the number of programs to print?

So, about 1,500 programs should be printed.

More Examples

Estimate.

$$
\begin{array}{r}
104 \rightarrow 100 \\
\times 34 \rightarrow \times 30 \\
\hline
3{,}000
\end{array}
$$

Both rounded factors are less than the exact factors. So, 3,000 is an underestimate.

$$
\begin{array}{r}
1{,}975 \rightarrow 2{,}000 \\
\times 423 \rightarrow \times 400 \\
\hline
800{,}000
\end{array}
$$

One rounded factor is greater than the exact factor, and one is less. You cannot tell whether 800,000 is an overestimate or an underestimate.

MULTICULTURAL NOTE: The gigantic shell roof of the Sydney Opera House in Sydney, Australia, covers five separate concert and exhibition halls. The opera house can hold 5,500 people.

- Name a situation in which you might want to overestimate a product.

Check for Understanding

Estimate the product. Tell whether your estimate is an overestimate or an underestimate.

1. 345×6 **2.** 68×49 **3.** 495×275 **4.** $5{,}396 \times 422$ **5.** $9{,}164 \times 523$

Practice

Choose the best estimate. Write a, b, or c.

6. 375×185 **a.** 40,000   **b.** 100,000   **c.** 80,000

7. 536×54 **a.** 40,000   **b.** 20,000   **c.** 25,000

8. $2,654 \times 7$ **a.** 30,000   **b.** 14,000   **c.** 21,000

9. $5,560 \times 239$ **a.** 1,200,000   **b.** 1,000,000   **c.** 1,800,000

10. $1,850 \times 46$ **a.** 50,000   **b.** 100,000   **c.** 800,000

Estimate the product.

11. $\begin{array}{r} 53 \\ \times\ 7 \\ \hline \end{array}$	12. $\begin{array}{r} 78 \\ \times\ 5 \\ \hline \end{array}$	13. $\begin{array}{r} \$21 \\ \times\ 9 \\ \hline \end{array}$	14. $\begin{array}{r} 189 \\ \times\ 6 \\ \hline \end{array}$	15. $\begin{array}{r} 232 \\ \times\ 4 \\ \hline \end{array}$
16. $\begin{array}{r} 459 \\ \times\ 9 \\ \hline \end{array}$	17. $\begin{array}{r} 7,951 \\ \times\ 3 \\ \hline \end{array}$	18. $\begin{array}{r} 78 \\ \times 87 \\ \hline \end{array}$	19. $\begin{array}{r} 542 \\ \times\ 41 \\ \hline \end{array}$	20. $\begin{array}{r} 873 \\ \times 429 \\ \hline \end{array}$

Estimate to compare. Use < or >.

21. $32 \times 21 \bullet 600$ 22. $47 \times 39 \bullet 2,000$ 23. $9 \times 17 \bullet 200$

24. $123 \times 62 \bullet 6,000$ 25. $50 \times 38 \bullet 2,000$ 26. $246 \times 41 \bullet 8,000$

Mixed Applications

27. A group of 22 students has tickets to 7 performances by an ethnic dance company. About how many tickets do the students have in all?

28. A theater was filled to capacity for 627 shows. The theater holds 2,398 people. About how many people attended the shows?

29. A total of 7 buses will be driven to a football game. Each bus holds 42 students. About how many students can ride the buses to the game?

30. Each of 8 vendors has an umbrella. Each umbrella has 9 spokes. Attached to each spoke are 4 dolls. About how many dolls are there?

31. **Making Decisions** Tonisha has a list of groceries to buy within her budget. Should she overestimate or underestimate the cost? Explain.

32. **Write a Question** A small-town college has an enrollment of 1,342 students. A city college has an enrollment of 12,078 students.

Why would you want to know whether an estimate is an underestimate or an overestimate?

MULTIPLYING
by Two- and Three-Digit Numbers

Suppose that for each of 23 performances last year, the Odeon in Athens, Greece, sold 5,250 tickets. What was the total number of tickets sold?

Estimate. $5{,}250 \times 23 \longrightarrow 5{,}000 \times 20 = 100{,}000$

$5{,}250 \times 23 \approx 100{,}000$

Multiply.

Step 1 Multiply by the ones.	**Step 2** Multiply by the tens.	**Step 3** Add the partial products.
$\begin{array}{r} 1 \\ 5{,}250 \\ \times\quad 23 \\ \hline 15\,750 \end{array}$ ← $3 \times 5{,}250$	$\begin{array}{r} 1 \\ 5{,}250 \\ \times\quad 23 \\ \hline 15\,750 \\ 105\,000 \end{array}$ ← $20 \times 5{,}250$ You may omit the zero placeholder.	$\begin{array}{r} 5{,}250 \\ \times\quad 23 \\ \hline 15\,750 \\ 105\,00 \\ \hline 120{,}750 \end{array}$

Since 120,750 is close to the estimate of 100,000, the answer is reasonable.

So, the total number of tickets sold was 120,750.

Another Example $3{,}823 \times 408$

Estimate. $4{,}000 \times 400 = 1{,}600{,}000$

Multiply.
$$\begin{array}{r} 3{,}823 \\ \times\qquad 408 \\ \hline 30\,584 \\ 1\,529\,2 \\ \hline 1{,}559{,}784 \end{array}$$

$30\,584 \leftarrow 8 \times 3{,}823$

$1\,529\,2 \leftarrow 400 \times 3{,}823$

• Why are there two partial products for 408?

MULTICULTURAL NOTE: The Odeon is a restored Greek theater in Athens, Greece. The original Odeon was built in about A.D. 160. The word *theater* comes from the Greek word *theatron*, which means "a place for seeing."

Check for Understanding

Find the product.

| 1. $\begin{array}{r} 42 \\ \times 17 \end{array}$ | 2. $\begin{array}{r} 96 \\ \times 24 \end{array}$ | 3. $\begin{array}{r} 1{,}637 \\ \times\quad 34 \end{array}$ | 4. $\begin{array}{r} 2{,}586 \\ \times\quad 41 \end{array}$ | 5. $\begin{array}{r} 23{,}556 \\ \times\quad 270 \end{array}$ | 6. $\begin{array}{r} 15{,}025 \\ \times\quad 136 \end{array}$ |

Practice

Estimate the product. If your estimate is greater than 200,000, use a calculator to find the exact answer.

7. 859
    × 34

8. 3,813
    × 508

9. 511
    × 16

10. 4,763
    × 20

11. 4,887
    × 75

12. 6,502 × 507   13. 683 × 75   14. 3,873 × 48   15. 178 × 498

Find the product.

16. 67
    × 23

17. 67
    × 85

18. 1,723
    × 44

19. 2,246
    × 906

20. 35,631
    × 74

21. 432
    × 336

22. 4,375
    × 697

23. 3,421
    × 56

24. 65,322
    × 635

25. 153,543
    × 732

Mixed Applications

26. Mary likes to exercise at a health club. She does 35 sit-ups in each workout. How many sit-ups will Mary do in 135 workouts?

27. Inez manages 112 apartments. Each rents for $485 a month. If they were all leased in May, how much rent did Inez collect?

28. **Number Sense • Mental Math** There are 24 hours in a day. How many hours are in a 7-day week?

29. **Make Up a Problem** Write a problem about city life that must be solved by adding 4 three-digit numbers.

SCIENCE CONNECTION

At the science museum, Elise learned that light travels about 299,793 kilometers per second through space and about 225,408 kilometers per second through water.

30. About how far does light travel through space in 100 seconds? through water in 10 seconds?

31. About how much faster does light travel through space than it travels through water?

Are the number of partial products always the same as the number of digits being multiplied? Explain.

PROBLEM SOLVING

Making Decisions

Don wants a bicycle to ride to and from school. The bicycle costs $290. Don has saved $225. He earns $40 a week working at a supermarket. He has three options.

Option 1: Don can save until he has $290 to buy the bicycle.
Option 2: Don can pay $90 down and $19 a month for a year.
Option 3: Don can pay nothing down and $28 a month for a year.
Which option should Don choose?

Sometimes solving a problem involves making a decision based on the situation.

▶ UNDERSTAND

What are you asked to find?

What information are you given?

▶ PLAN

How will you solve the problem?

You need to find the total amount Don would pay with each option and to compare the advantages and disadvantages.

▶ SOLVE

How will you carry out your plan?

Find the total amount Don would pay with each option. Consider the following:

A. With which option would Don spend the least?

B. With which options would Don get the bicycle right away?

C. Does Don make enough money to afford each option?

D. Would Don's monthly payment be smaller with Option 2 or with Option 3?

- If you were Don, which option would you choose? Why?

▶ LOOK BACK

Do your reasons make sense considering Don's situation? Explain.

WHAT IF... ... you wanted to buy a bicycle? What options would you consider?

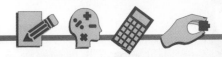

Apply

Yoko wants to buy a home video system that costs $250. She has $225 in a savings account. She earns $35 a week. Yoko considers these options.

Option 1: Continue to save until she can pay for the system in full

Option 2: Pay $65 down and $20 per month for 12 months

Option 3: Pay nothing down and $26 per month for 12 months

(1) How much will the video system cost using Option 3?

(2) What is a disadvantage of Option 1?

(3) Which option will Yoko choose if she wants to keep all the money in her savings account?

(4) Which option will Yoko choose if she wants to pay the lesser amount of money each month?

(5) What is a reason for Yoko to choose Option 2?

(6) What is a reason for Yoko to choose Option 1?

Mixed Applications → **STRATEGIES**

Guess and Check • Find a Pattern • Write a Number Sentence • Draw a Diagram

Choose a strategy and solve.

(7) Joel withdrew $13 the first week, $16 the second, $20 the third, $25 the fourth, and $31 the fifth. If this pattern continues, how much will he withdraw the seventh week?

(8) Sol and Sergio own a total of 59 books. Sergio owns 11 more books than Sol. How many books does Sergio own?

(9) Jean has 3 times as many pens as Joan. If Joan has 5 blue pens and 2 red pens, how many pens does Jean have?

(10) April is making a number puzzle. The first five numbers are 2, 6, 18, 54, and 162. If the pattern continues, what is the next number?

(11) Rae has 72 inches of ribbon to wrap around a package that is 11 inches around. If she wraps the package 4 times, how much ribbon will she have left?

(12) It takes Rich 5 minutes to take out the garbage, 2 times that long to vacuum, and 3 times as long to dust as to vacuum. How long does it take Rich to do all three chores?

WRITER'S CORNER

(13) Write a problem that involves options. Exchange with a classmate, and explain which option you would choose.

ESTIMATING DECIMAL PRODUCTS

You can estimate decimal products in the same way you estimate whole-number products. Estimate decimal products when an exact answer is not needed or to determine the reasonableness of an answer.

Una earns $4.52 an hour at a local radio station. About how much does she earn for working 37.5 hours?

Estimate. $4.52 × 37.5

> Round $4.52 to the nearest dollar. Round 37.5 to the nearest ten.

$5 × 40 = $200

So, Una earns about $200.00.

Una estimates she earns about $100 for working 19.5 hours. Using a calculator, she finds that her exact earnings are $881.40.

- Is Una's estimate reasonable?
- Is Una's calculation reasonable?
- What mistake did Una make?

You can also use estimation to place the decimal point in a product.

A hit song is 3.42 minutes long. If a radio station plays the song 8 times in one day, how many total minutes is the song on the air?

Estimate to place the decimal in the product.

$$\begin{array}{r} 3.42 \\ \times\ 8 \\ \hline 2736 \end{array} \longrightarrow \begin{array}{r} 3 \\ \times\ 8 \\ \hline 24 \end{array}$$

Since the estimate is 24, place the decimal point after the 7.

So, the song is on the air for 27.36 minutes.

Check for Understanding

Choose the best estimate. Write **a, b,** or **c.**

1. $12.6 × 45$ a. 690   b. 500   c. 400

2. $\$119.56 × 38$ a. $4,000   b. $8,000   c. $3,000

3. $91.06 × 7.3$ a. 9,000   b. 450   c. 630

Use estimation to place the decimal point in the product.

4. $6.19 × 75 = 46425$ 5. $435.7 × 8.9 = 387773$ 6. $14 × 2.713 = 37982$

Practice

Estimate. Choose the correct product. Write **a**, **b**, or **c**.

7. 178×4.89
  a. 870.42
  b. 87.042
  c. 8.7042

8. 7.925×234
  a. 18,544.500
  b. 1,854.450
  c. 185.445

9. 83.7×19
  a. 159.03
  b. 15.903
  c. 1,590.3

10. 2.273×3.6
  a. 0.8182
  b. 8.1828
  c. 81.828

Estimate the product.

11. 5.23×9

12. 72.9×8.5

13. 1.3×6.4

14. 2.3×98.4

15. 38.7×1.7

16. 7.05×6.8

17. 51.2×0.9

18. 27.2×12.1

Mixed Applications

Solve. Use the table for Exercises 19–20.

19. Leroy bought 2.5 yards of cotton and 5.75 yards of corduroy. About how much did he spend?

20. If Karen bought 6 yards of acetate and Barbara bought 3.5 yards of cotton, who spent more money?

Fabrics on Sale	
Fabric	Price per Yard
Corduroy	$3.29
Cotton	$1.97
Polyester	$3.98
Acetate	$4.98

21. Number Sense • Mental Math The pep club sells balloons for $2.00 each. If members have sold a total of 150 balloons, what is the total amount of their sales?

22. Number Sense • Estimation Frank calculates that if nails cost $1.09 a pound, 4.25 pounds will cost $4.63. Is Frank's calculation reasonable? Explain.

PATTERNS AND RELATIONSHIPS

Look at the patterns of zeros.

4×6	$= 24$	
40×6	$= 240$	
40×60	$= 2,400$	
400×60	$= 24,000$	
400×600	$= 240,000$	

3.51×10	$= 35.1$
3.51×100	$= 351$
$3.51 \times 1,000$	$= 3,510$
$3.51 \times 10,000$	$= 35,100$
$3.51 \times 100,000$	$= 351,000$

23. How does the number of zeros in the whole-number factors compare with the number of zeros in the product?

24. State a rule for multiplying by multiples of 10.

25. State a rule for multiplying decimals by powers of 10.

How does estimating help you place the decimal point in the product?

WRAP UP...

1. John and Sue run a total of 21 miles every morning. Sue runs 3 more miles than John. How many miles does each run?

2. Sara is 6 years younger than Richard. Sara and Richard have a combined age of 18. Bob and Sara have a combined age of 14. How old are Sara, Bob, and Richard?

Use the situation in the box for Exercises 3–4.

3. Which option would cost Lee the least amount of money?

4. How much more money would Lee pay for the microwave if he chose Option C instead of Option B?

> When you *guess and check*, record your guesses.

> Lee earns $5 a week. He has saved $155. He wants to buy a microwave that costs $180. He can (a) save until he has $180, (b) pay $75 down and $15 a month for 12 months, or (c) pay $25 a month for 12 months.

Find the sum or difference.

5. $9.201 + 76.8$

6. $42.93 - 0.861$

7. $24.9 + 89.075$

8. $91.37 - 6.798$

9.
$$\begin{array}{r} \$21.25 \\ 52.86 \\ +\quad 0.04 \\ \hline \end{array}$$

10.
$$\begin{array}{r} 9.768 \\ -5.332 \\ \hline \end{array}$$

11.
$$\begin{array}{r} 2.32 \\ 69.1 \\ +\quad 0.33 \\ \hline \end{array}$$

12.
$$\begin{array}{r} 2{,}541.6 \\ 913.81 \\ +\quad 692.34 \\ \hline \end{array}$$

Write an algebraic expression for the word expression.

13. 2 more than a number b

14. 30 less than an amount p

15. k fewer than 210

Tell what operation to use to solve the equation.

16. $x + 2 = 25$

17. $y - 8 = 10$

18. $b - 4.5 = 12.8$

19. $68.4 + c = 93$

Estimate the product. Tell whether the estimate is an overestimate or an underestimate.

20. 63×112

21. $1{,}937 \times 791$

22. 42.1×2.4

23. 99.7×17.82

Find the product.

24.
$$\begin{array}{r} 61 \\ \times 18 \\ \hline \end{array}$$

25.
$$\begin{array}{r} 1{,}563 \\ \times\quad 67 \\ \hline \end{array}$$

26.
$$\begin{array}{r} 852 \\ \times 353 \\ \hline \end{array}$$

27.
$$\begin{array}{r} 46{,}924 \\ \times\quad 812 \\ \hline \end{array}$$

Russia

EUROPE

Another Way to Multiply

For hundreds of years, many cultures have used doubling as a way to do multiplication. The doubling method shown below is known as the Russian Peasant Method.

Example Multiply 26 by 35.

Write the numbers at the top of two columns. Halve the number in the left column. Continue to halve the numbers in this column until you reach 1. Ignore all remainders.

Double the number in the right column. Continue doubling until you have a doubled number for each number in the left column.

Cross out any numbers in the right column that are opposite an even number in the left column.

Find the sum of the numbers remaining in the right column. This is the product.

So, 26 × 35 = 910.

26	35
13	70
6	140
3	280
1	560

26 →	3̶5̶
13	70
6 →	1̶4̶0̶
3	280
1	560
	910

Talk About It

- Suppose you halved 35 and doubled 26. Do you think you would still get 910? Explain.

- Could you use this method to find the product 6 × 8? Would you use this method? Explain.

Use the Russian Peasant Method to find the products. Use a calculator to check your answer.

1. 19 × 24   **2.** 32 × 53   **3.** 21 × 105   **4.** 42 × 112

Multicultural Connection • 79

USING MULTIPLICATION
to Estimate Sums

Di is a meteorologist. She will buy sandwiches for $2.95, $3.00, $2.75, and $3.25 from a vending machine at the television station where she works. About how much money does she need?

Step 1 Round to the nearest dollar.	**Step 2** The addends cluster around the same rounded dollar amount. Multiply it by the number of addends.
$2.95 → $3.00 $3.00 → $3.00 $2.75 → $3.00 $3.25 → $3.00	4 × $3.00 = $12.00 $2.95 + $3.00 + $2.75 + $3.25 ≈ $12.00

So, Di needs about $12.00 to pay for the sandwiches.

- Why is multiplying more useful than adding to estimate the sum of a large number of addends that cluster around the same rounded number?

Another Example

Di made this table to show the average monthly rainfall in Albany, New York. About how much is the total rainfall in Albany in a year?

Jan. 2.4	Feb. 2.3	Mar. 3.0	Apr. 2.9	May 3.3	June 3.3	July 3.0	Aug. 3.3	Sept. 3.2	Oct. 2.9	Nov. 3.0	Dec. 3.0

2.4 + 2.3 + 3.0 + 2.9 + 3.3 + 3.3 + 3.0 + 3.3 + 3.2 + 2.9 + 3.0 + 3.0

2 × 2 = 4   10 × 3 = 30

4 + 30 = 34

So, the rainfall in Albany is about 34 inches a year.

Check for Understanding

Use mental math and multiplication to estimate the sum.

1.	2.	3.	4.	5.
0.66 0.79 +1.15	5.21 4.95 +5.45	29.51 27.48 +28.00	9.54 9.78 +9.98	2,450 1,544 2,333 +1,872

Practice

Use mental math and multiplication to estimate the sum.

6.	7.	8.	9.	10.
200	775	5,923	27,032	43,002
185	798	6,221	26,898	42,756
213	802	6,313	24,772	43,135
+221	+787	+6,400	+27,125	+42,999

11.	12.	13.	14.	15.
$2.35	9.07	0.9	87.333	62.005
2.15	9.2	1.02	87.002	61.9
1.98	8.7	0.8	86.701	62.1
1.75	8.821	0.76	87.114	62.355
+ 2.00	+8.88	+1.17	+87.101	+61.8882

16.	17.	18.	19.	20.
0.009	7.2	492	21,823	700,234
0.01	6.3	405	19,934	697,782
0.011	6.2	395	21,009	175
+0.008	+6.1	+501	+19,073	+709,145

Mixed Applications

21. Tyrone is a courier. The list below shows his earnings for six months. About how much did Tyrone earn in this time period?

Jan. $1,895.45	Apr. $1,901.67
Feb. $1,793.33	May $2,113.75
Mar. $2,045.45	June $1,754.91

22. Leslee gives dance lessons at a studio. Her daily schedule is listed below. About how many hours does Leslee teach in one week?

Mon. 3:30 to 7	Thurs. 4 to 8
Tues. 4 to 8:15	Fri. 2 to 6
Wed. 3:30 to 7:30	Sat. 1 to 5

MIXED REVIEW

Find the product. Round money amounts to the nearest cent.

1. 7×192

2. $9,125 \times 611$

3. $\$3.77 \times 8$

4. 76.3×3.67

5.	6.	7.	8.	9.
1,009	56,521	$462.55	22.5	3.72
× 599	× 0.9	× 12.15	× 0.033	×1.005

Evaluate the expression.

10. $95 + b$, for $b = 39$

11. $k - 13.3$, for $k = 24.1$

12. $2 + (x - 8)$, for $x = 32$

How is clustering similar to rounding?

WRAP UP...

MULTIPLYING DECIMALS

Mac adds 16.3 ounces of tint to a gallon of paint. How much tint will Mac need for 132.5 gallons of paint?

Step 1 Choose compatible numbers. Estimate the product.	**Step 2** Multiply.	**Step 3** Use the estimate to place the decimal point.
132.5 × 16.3 ↓ ↓ 100 × 20 = 2,000	132.5 × 16.3 ――― 397 5 7950 1325 ――― 21597 5	132.5 × 16.3 ≈ 2,000 The estimate is in the thousands, so place the decimal after the 9. 132.5 × 16.3 = 2,159.75

So, Mac will need 2,159.75 ounces of tint.

 More Examples

A. 81 × 7.23

Estimate. 80 × 7 = 560
Multiply.
Use paper and pencil.

```
    7.23
  ×   81
  ―――――
    7 23
  578 4
  ―――――
  585 63  →  585.63
```

B. 7.9 × $2.35

Estimate. 8 × $2 = $16
Multiply.
Use a calculator.

7.9 ⊠ 2.35 ⊟ [.18.565]

= $18.57 ↑

Round money amounts to the nearest cent.

- Look at the decimal places in the factors and the product in Example **A** and in the example at the top of the page. State a rule for placing the decimal point in the product when multiplying decimals.

Check for Understanding

Tell how many decimal places will be in the product. Find the product.

1. 24.82 × 5.6	2. 288.7 × 0.52	3. 1.42 × 0.74	4. 64.32 × 20.5	5. 18.88 × 1.75

Practice

Estimate to place the decimal point in the product.

6. $5.7 \times 2.4 = 1368$

7. $1.57 \times 5.5 = 8635$

8. $5.656 \times 8.8 = 497728$

9. $0.44 \times 2.6 = 1144$

10. $0.58 \times 0.89 = 05162$

11. $2.981 \times 0.2 = 05962$

12.
$$\begin{array}{r} 20.74 \\ \times\ \ 4.4 \\ \hline 91256 \end{array}$$

13.
$$\begin{array}{r} 78 \\ \times 4.6 \\ \hline 3588 \end{array}$$

14.
$$\begin{array}{r} 1.564 \\ \times\ \ 0.9 \\ \hline 14076 \end{array}$$

15.
$$\begin{array}{r} 9.67 \\ \times 54.2 \\ \hline 524114 \end{array}$$

16.
$$\begin{array}{r} 45.2 \\ \times 165 \\ \hline 74580 \end{array}$$

Find the product. Round money amounts to the nearest cent.

17.
$$\begin{array}{r} 5.8 \\ \times 2.5 \\ \hline \end{array}$$

18.
$$\begin{array}{r} 3.456 \\ \times\ \ 4.1 \\ \hline \end{array}$$

19.
$$\begin{array}{r} 345.6 \\ \times\ \ 4.1 \\ \hline \end{array}$$

20.
$$\begin{array}{r} \$14.85 \\ \times\ \ 8.5 \\ \hline \end{array}$$

21.
$$\begin{array}{r} 43.6 \\ \times 0.09 \\ \hline \end{array}$$

22.
$$\begin{array}{r} 58.87 \\ \times\ \ 38 \\ \hline \end{array}$$

23.
$$\begin{array}{r} \$13.87 \\ \times\ \ 0.7 \\ \hline \end{array}$$

24.
$$\begin{array}{r} \$763.08 \\ \times\ \ 6.06 \\ \hline \end{array}$$

25.
$$\begin{array}{r} \$543.99 \\ \times\ \ 0.5 \\ \hline \end{array}$$

26.
$$\begin{array}{r} 0.98 \\ \times 0.4 \\ \hline \end{array}$$

27. 14.8×64

28. $\$127.10 \times 4.9$

29. 842.7×1.82

30. 6.49×73

31. 52.33×6.7

32. 0.75×0.25

33. $8{,}392 \times 5.005$

34. 1.5×0.005

Mixed Applications

35. Joe buys ground beef for $1.78 a pound. To the nearest cent, how much will he pay for 3.8 pounds of ground beef?

36. Sam uses 1.5 pounds of cold cuts to make a 6-foot sub. If he makes 2.5, or $2\frac{1}{2}$, subs, how many pounds of cold cuts will he use?

37. **Analyze Data** The deli charges $1.32 for a sandwich and $0.85 for a salad. If Mel spent $5.66, how many sandwiches and salads did he buy?

38. **Number Sense ● Estimation** Rachael bought 3.2 pounds of pears at $1.89 a pound, 1.9 pounds of plums at $0.99 a pound, and 2.7 pounds of apples at $1.76 a pound. About how much did Rachael spend for fruit?

What two methods can you use to place the decimal point in the product?

WRAP UP...

ZEROS IN THE PRODUCT

Students touring a power plant learned that operating a television costs $0.037 an hour. How much does operating a television for 0.75, or $\frac{3}{4}$ hour cost?

- Will your answer be more than or less than $0.037? Explain.

Remember: The number of decimal places in the product equals the sum of the decimal places in the factors.

Step 1	Step 2
Multiply as with whole numbers.	Place the decimal point. Write a zero to hold the correct number of places. Place the dollar sign.
$0.037 × 0.75 ——— 185 259 ——— 2775	$0.037 ← 3 decimal places × 0.75 ← 2 decimal places ——— 185 259 ——— $0.02775 ← 5 decimal places

So, the cost of operating a television for 0.75 hour is $0.02775. To the nearest cent, the cost is $0.03.

Another Example

0.0025 ← 4 decimal places
× 8 ← 0 decimal places
———
0.0200 ← 4 decimal places

- Which zeros are holding places in the product?

Check for Understanding

Choose the correct product. Write **a, b,** or **c.**

1. 4.8 × 0.06   **a.** 0.0288   **b.** 0.288   **c.** 0.00288

2. 0.08 × 453   **a.** 0.03624   **b.** 0.3624   **c.** 36.24

Find the product.

3. $2.40 × 0.2	4. 0.03 × 0.8	5. 0.0056 × 4.2	6. 0.056 × 100	7. $5.04 × 305

Practice

Place the decimal point in the product.
Write zeros where necessary.

8. $\begin{array}{r} 0.03 \\ \times\ 5.8 \\ \hline 174 \end{array}$

9. $\begin{array}{r} 0.002 \\ \times\ 43.6 \\ \hline 872 \end{array}$

10. $\begin{array}{r} 0.037 \\ \times\ 4.8 \\ \hline 1776 \end{array}$

11. $\begin{array}{r} 1.84 \\ \times\ 0.5 \\ \hline 92 \end{array}$

12. $\begin{array}{r} 0.0007 \\ \times\ 36 \\ \hline 252 \end{array}$

Find the product.

13. $\begin{array}{r} 0.038 \\ \times\ 8 \\ \hline \end{array}$

14. $\begin{array}{r} 54.88 \\ \times\ 30.7 \\ \hline \end{array}$

15. $\begin{array}{r} 0.08 \\ \times\ 9 \\ \hline \end{array}$

16. $\begin{array}{r} 25.68 \\ \times\ 0.04 \\ \hline \end{array}$

17. $\begin{array}{r} 0.98 \\ \times\ 702 \\ \hline \end{array}$

18. $\begin{array}{r} 0.032 \\ \times\ 0.4 \\ \hline \end{array}$

19. $\begin{array}{r} 0.0036 \\ \times\ 587 \\ \hline \end{array}$

20. $\begin{array}{r} 7.5 \\ \times\ 0.6 \\ \hline \end{array}$

21. $\begin{array}{r} 0.43 \\ \times\ 2.08 \\ \hline \end{array}$

22. $\begin{array}{r} 0.003 \\ \times\ 59.8 \\ \hline \end{array}$

23. 4.6×100

24. 0.031×10

25. $0.0097 \times 1,000$

26. 0.654×100

27. $16.9 \times 1,000$

28. 276.4×10

Mixed Applications

29. Perfume comes in sample packages of 0.025 ounce. What is the total amount of perfume in a box of 24 sample packages?

30. **Number Sense** Nutritionists say we need 0.0017 gram of riboflavin every day. How much do we need in a week?

MIXED REVIEW

Estimate the sum or difference.

1. $12.76 - 8.25$

2. $49.01 - 14.67$

3. $9.18 - 0.97$

4. $10.341 + 0.882$

Estimate. If your estimate is greater than 100,000, find the exact answer.

5. 17×14

6. 21×52

7. 3.7×209

8. $\$5.25 \times 476$

9. 236×722

When do you place zeros in the product?

WRAP UP...

PROBLEM SOLVING

Multistep Problems

Thirty students at Brook Middle School held a car wash to raise money for a trip to Los Angeles. They charged $1.95 for each car. They washed 93 cars on Saturday and 65 cars on Sunday. How much money did they earn for the trip?

When there is a main question and a hidden question, you may need two or more operations to solve the problem.

▶ UNDERSTAND

What are you asked to find?

What information are you given?

▶ PLAN

How will you solve the problem?
You need to multiply the total number of cars washed by $1.95.

To do this, you must first answer the hidden question: What was the total number of cars washed?

▶ SOLVE

How will you carry out your plan?
First, add to find the total number of cars washed.

93 [+] 65 [=] [158.] [M+]

The students washed 158 cars.

Then, multiply to find the amount of money earned.

1.95 [×] [MRC] [=] [ᴹ   308.1]

So, the students earned $308.10.

▶ LOOK BACK

How can you check your solution by solving the problem in a different way?

WHAT IF... ... each student needs $15.00 for the trip? How much more must the students earn?

86

Apply

Melissa plans to hang a shelf in her room. She finds a kit with all the parts for $15.25. The prices of the separate parts are $7.50 for the wood, $4.80 for the brackets, and $1.75 for the screws.

(1) Which is less expensive, the kit or the separate shelf parts?

(2) What is the difference in price between the kit and the separate shelf parts?

Mixed Applications ⟶ STRATEGIES

Write a Number Sentence
• **Find a Pattern** • **Make a Table**
• **Draw a Diagram**

Choose a strategy and solve.

(3) Francine is making a cabinet for a shop project. She buys 3 boards at $1.75 each and 4 hinges at $0.99 each. What is the total cost of the supplies?

(4) Leon runs 2 miles the first week, 3 miles the second, 5 miles the third, and 8 miles the fourth. If he continues this pattern, when will he run 23 miles?

(5) Teo scored 98 on a math test. On the next test, he scored 16 fewer points. On a third test, he scored 92. What is the difference between Teo's highest and lowest scores?

(6) Carol bought 2.3 pounds of bananas at $0.47 a pound and 3.4 pounds of grapes at $0.89 a pound. How much more money did Carol spend for grapes than she spent for bananas?

(7) Mr. Soni and his family consume 3 pounds of potatoes each day. If Mr. Soni buys a 50-pound sack of potatoes, how many days will it take the family to consume 24 pounds of the potatoes?

(8) A taxicab travels 5 miles west, 2 miles south, 1 mile west, 4 miles north, 8 miles east, 1 mile south, and then 10 miles west. How far has the taxicab traveled when it crosses its own path?

(9) Lin sold 43 pairs of shoes. Frances sold twice as many as Lin. How many pairs of shoes did they sell?

(10) Mrs. Schultz bought bread for $0.98, eggs for $1.17, ground turkey for $3.18, and carrots for $0.55. She gave the clerk $10.03. How much change should Mrs. Shultz receive?

Vocabulary Check

Choose a word from the box to complete each sentence.

Associative
Distributive
overestimate
underestimate
zero

1. If you rewrite the multiplication problem 24×7 as $(20 \times 7) + (4 \times 7)$, you are using the _?_ Property of Multiplication. *(page 68)*

2. An answer will be an _?_ if both rounded factors are less than the exact factors. *(page 70)*

3. The product of any number and zero is _?_. *(page 68)*

4. The _?_ Property of Multiplication states that factors can be grouped in any way without changing the product. *(page 68)*

5. An answer will be an _?_ if both rounded factors are greater than the exact factors. *(page 70)*

Concept Check

6. Will you always be able to determine whether an estimate is an overestimate or an underestimate? Explain. *(page 70)*

> To answer Exercise 6, think about the rounded factor in relation to the exact factor.

7. How can you use estimation to place the decimal point in a product? *(page 76)*

8. Why is it sometimes necessary to add zeros to decimal products? *(page 84)*

9. How can you estimate the sum of several addends that cluster around the same number? *(page 80)*

10. State a rule for multiplying by multiples of 10. *(page 77)*

11. State a rule for multiplying decimals by powers of 10. *(page 77)*

Place the decimal point in the product. Write zeros where necessary. *(pages 82, 84)*

12. $2.11 \times \$62.53 = \$13194$

13. $16.079 \times 0.53 = 852187$

14. $0.23 \times 0.06 = 138$

15. $4.25 \times 0.003 = 1275$

Skill Check

Estimate the product. *(pages 70, 76)*

16. 62
$\times 18$

17. 6,324
$\times\ \ 430$

18. 60.09
$\times\ \ 1.18$

19. 273.65
$\times\ \ 46.89$

Use mental math and multiplication to estimate the sum. *(page 80)*

20. 795
812
834
783
$+779$

21. 26,091
26,234
25,957
$+25,684$

22. 0.008
0.013
0.01
$+0.007$

23. 42.32
41.98
41.18
$+41.86$

Find the product. *(pages 72, 82, 84)*

24. 26
$\times 54$

25. 2,913
$\times\ \ \ 62$

26. 864
$\times 795$

27. 169,846
$\times\ \ \ \ \ \ 392$

28. 6.7
$\times 2.8$

29. $41.80
$\times\ \ \ 7.1$

30. 914.03
$\times\ \ \ 5.06$

31. 1.82
$\times 0.006$

32. 824
$\times 309$

33. 3,089
$\times\ \ \ 725$

34. 4.06
$\times 7.33$

35. 61.8
$\times 0.09$

Problem-Solving Check

Use the information in the box for Exercises 36–37. *(pages 74, 86)*

36. Which option is the least expensive if Ramon must have the garage-door opener installed?

37. Which option should Ramon choose if he wants to install the garage-door opener himself?

> Ramon wants to buy a garage-door opener. He has these options.
> Option A: $149.99 for the opener
> $78.50 for installation
> Option B: $170.99 for the opener
> no installation service
> Option C: $199.99 for the opener
> $25.00 for installation

38. A taxi charged Rachel $7.75 to take her to school and $8.45 to take her to the arena. How much did she spend if she made round trips to both places?

39. Every week, Elsa drives 45 miles on Monday, 17 miles on Tuesday, 88 miles on Wednesday, and 12 miles on Friday. How many miles does she drive in 4 weeks?

1. Estimate the product 2.3 × 56.8. Explain your method.

2. Find the product 72 × 128. Show your work.

3. Find the product 15 × 25.7. Show your work.

4. Read Exercise 10 on page 87. Follow the steps on the Problem-Solving Think Along worksheet to show how to solve this problem.

Using estimation is a good way to check the reasonableness of your answer.

Write About It

5. What was the most challenging activity or lesson for you in this chapter on multiplying whole numbers and decimals? Explain why it was challenging.

6. Explain why the product of a number multiplied by the decimal 0.96 will almost be equal to the number.

TEAMWORK *Project*

Write a Guidebook

 When new people move to your community, how do they locate restaurants, theaters, museums, sporting events, and community activities? Work with your teammates to plan a guidebook about places to go to and things to do in your community.

▲ *Decide*

As a team, brainstorm ideas for your guidebook. List categories of places and events you will include.

▲ Do

As a team, divide the list of categories among your team members. Have each team member research a category and select places and appropriate events.

Conduct interviews or use other sources of information to write a brief description of each place or event. Include

- important data, such as prices, dates and times of operation, and telephone numbers.
- Work together to design, write, and assemble your guidebook.

▲ *Share*

Exchange guidebooks. Tell what new things you have discovered about your community.

Talk About It

Could you combine pages from each team's guidebook to assemble one book for new students at your school?

Would your school newspaper or newsletter be interested in publishing some of your guidebook information?

Your Move!
A Game of Strategy

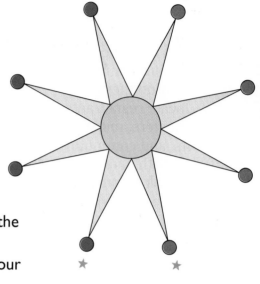

A group of Polynesian people known as Maori discovered and settled New Zealand in the fourteenth century. The Maori played a board game called Mu Torere, which means "your move."

To play the game, you will need a gameboard like the one shown, four game pieces of one color for yourself, and four game pieces of another color for your opponent.

Place the game pieces on the points of the large star as shown.

Players take turns. On each player's first two turns, only the pieces that are next to the small stars may be used. A piece may be moved to any empty adjacent point, to the center if it is empty, or from the center to any empty point.

The game is over when a player can no longer make a move. The other player is the winner.

Challenge

Critical Thinking

Use the clues to find the number.

1. The product of the digits is 0.
2. It is $< (7 \times 9) + 2$.
3. It is $> 8 \times 5$.
4. It is a multiple of 5.
5. It is a multiple of 6.

What is the number?

Patterns

This is a multiples triangle. Complete the fifth row in the triangle.

$$1$$
$$2 \quad 4$$
$$3 \quad 6 \quad 9$$
$$4 \quad 8 \quad 12 \quad 16$$

What patterns can you find in the triangle? What would be the last number in row one hundred?

Write the letter of the correct answer.

1. What is twelve ten-thousandths written in standard form?

   A. 0.0012   **B.** 0.012
   C. 12.0000   **D.** not here

2. Which shows 86.4278 rounded to the nearest thousandth?

   A. 8.6427   **B.** 8.64278
   C. 86.42   **D.** 86.428

3. $2 + 7 \times 5$

   A. 35   **B.** 37
   C. 45   **D.** not here

4. What is the value of 10^6?

   A. 0.6   **B.** 60
   C. 100,000   **D.** 1,000,000

5. Which is the best estimate?
$12.94 + 7.18$

   A. 19   **B.** 20
   C. 21   **D.** 70

6. $6.924 - 4.58$

   A. 1.344   **B.** 2.34
   C. 2.344   **D.** 2.434

7. Choose an algebraic expression for 32 less than x.

   A. $32 - x$ **B.** 32
   C. $x - 32$ **D.** $32 + x$

8. Evaluate the expression $24 - (8 + t)$, for $t = 11$.

   A. 4   **B.** 5
   C. 6   **D.** 27

9. Choose the best estimate.
$5,378 \times 621$

   A. 5,000   **B.** 30,000
   C. 300,000   **D.** 3,000,000

10. Place the decimal point in the product. 5.963×2.34

   A. 1.395342   **B.** 139.5342
   C. 1,395.342   **D.** not here

11. 2.7×0.0099

   A. 0.002672   **B.** 0.02672
   C. 0.02673   **D.** 0.2673

12. $120 \div 12 - 8$

   A. 2   **B.** 4
   C. 20   **D.** 30

13. Wanda works for $4.80 an hour for 3 hours each day of the week. About how many days must she work to earn $105.00?

   A. 4 days   **B.** 7 days
   C. 9 days   **D.** 10 days

14. Dave and Mark have a total of 35 bus tokens. If Dave has 7 more than Mark, how many bus tokens does Mark have?

   A. 14 bus tokens   **B.** 17 bus tokens
   C. 18 bus tokens   **D.** 21 bus tokens

CHAPTER 4

DIVIDING WHOLE NUMBERS AND DECIMALS

Did you know...

... that in India the average number of children in each elementary-school class is much larger than in the United States?

TALK ABOUT IT

India is a huge country, with a population of about 850 million people. What information would you need to know if you wanted to calculate the average number of children in each elementary classroom in India? How could you solve the problem?

EXPLORING

Divisibility

A number is **divisible** by another number if the quotient is a whole number and the remainder is zero.

Remember that a number is divisible by 3 if the sum of the digits of the number is divisible by 3. Use what you know about divisibility by 3 to explore divisibility by 9.

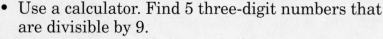

Work Together

Building Understanding

- Divide these numbers by 9. Record the quotients. Which numbers are divisible by 9?

  152   540   438   999   1,989   189   300

- Use a calculator. Find 5 three-digit numbers that are divisible by 9.

TALK ABOUT IT

- Look at the numbers above that are divisible by 9. Find the sum of the digits for each number.

- What patterns did you observe in the sums of the digits?

- Are numbers that are divisible by 9 also divisible by 3? Explain.

- What is the greatest three-digit number that is divisible by 9? What is the least three-digit number that is divisible by 9?

Making the Connection

Learning divisibility rules can help you develop number sense.

Divisibility Rules
A whole number is divisible by
2   if it ends in 0, 2, 4, 6, or 8.
3   if the sum of its digits is divisible by 3.
5   if it ends in 0 or 5.
9   if the sum of its digits is divisible by 9.
10   if it ends in 0.

Examples

A new school cafeteria will hold 396 students. Designers plan to use tables that seat 9 students each. Will there be exactly enough tables for 396 students?

Think: Is 396 divisible by 9?

        Sum of the digits: 3 + 9 + 6 = 18 ← 18 is divisible by 9.

So, there will be exactly enough tables for 396 students.

1. Suppose the designers plan to use tables that seat 5 students each. Will there be exactly enough tables for 396 students? Explain.

Checking Understanding

Tell whether each number is divisible by 2, 3, 5, 9, or 10.

2. 3,750   **3.** 9,882   **4.** 4,516

5. 18,270   **6.** 2,604   **7.** 63,405

Mrs. Fuller's math class is setting up work stations for an Exploring lesson. This particular class has 36 students.

8. Can every student sit in a group of 9 at a work station? Explain.

9. Can every student sit in a group of 3 at a work station? Explain.

10. Are numbers that are divisible by 3 also divisible by 9? Explain.

When you estimate a quotient, you can use rounding or compatible numbers. **Compatible numbers** divide without a remainder, are close to the actual numbers, and are easy to compute mentally.

Estimate. $6{,}134 \div 35$

Use compatible numbers.   Round.

$6{,}134 \div 35$ $6{,}134 \div 35$
$6{,}000 \div 30 = 200$ ← estimate $6{,}000 \div 40 = 150$ ← estimate

Talk About It

► Which estimate would be easier to compute by using mental math?

► When choosing numbers to estimate, why choose compatible numbers?

Remember to estimate when an exact answer is not needed or to determine the reasonableness of an answer.

Example Ann knows that 34 sixth graders can attend the computer lab each hour. She determines that 1,654 students can attend the lab once in 69 hours. Is this reasonable?

Estimate by using compatible numbers.

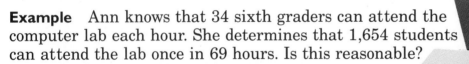

$$34\overline{)1{,}654} \longrightarrow \overset{40 \;\leftarrow\; \text{estimate}}{40\overline{)1{,}600}}$$

So, Ann's answer of 69 hours is not reasonable.

Talk About It

► Why would you not use rounding to estimate the quotient of 1,654 divided by 34?

Check for Understanding

Tell whether you would use compatible numbers or rounding to estimate. Justify your choice. Then estimate the quotient.

1. $7{,}344 \div 8$ 2. $9\overline{)2{,}945}$ 3. $12{,}353 \div 17$ 4. $22\overline{)23{,}650}$ 5. $53{,}350 \div 23$

Practice

Choose the best estimate. Write **a**, **b**, or **c**.

6. 5)‾345‾
   a. 55
   b. 70
   c. 30

7. 18)‾46,170‾
   a. 2,500
   b. 3,000
   c. 5,000

8. 5,474 ÷ 23
   a. 300
   b. 200
   c. 2,000

9. 7)‾749‾
   a. 10
   b. 170
   c. 100

10. 861 ÷ 41
   a. 20
   b. 30
   c. 40

Estimate the quotient.

11. 647 ÷ 7
12. 569 ÷ 3
13. 3,532 ÷ 8
14. 2,435 ÷ 7
15. 1,406 ÷ 6

16. 482 ÷ 7
17. 6,321 ÷ 9
18. 968 ÷ 47
19. 3,456 ÷ 432
20. 5,765 ÷ 26

21. 12)‾23,143‾
22. 30)‾2,552‾
23. 26)‾573‾
24. 57)‾4,339‾
25. 46)‾5,199‾

26. 8)‾4,396‾
27. 7)‾5,276‾
28. 72)‾647‾
29. 46)‾3,321‾
30. 12)‾3,786‾

31. 8)‾639‾
32. 5)‾885‾
33. 3)‾943‾
34. 8)‾752‾
35. 6)‾431‾

36. 9)‾889‾
37. 64)‾25,012‾
38. 37)‾3,663‾
39. 17)‾1,432‾
40. 58)‾32,557‾

Mixed Applications

41. A social studies book has 414 pages. If each chapter is about 35 pages, about how many chapters are in the social studies book?

42. A cafeteria prepares 145 celery sticks to serve 42 students. About how many celery sticks are served to each student?

43. **Number Sense • Mental Math** Sally sold 9 boxes of pencils at the school bookstore. If each box contained 200 pencils, how many pencils did Sally sell?

44. **Making Decisions** Frank can buy a package of 8 ballpoint pens for $14.96, or he can buy the same ballpoint pens for $1.75 each. If Frank needs 8 ballpoint pens, which choice is the better buy?

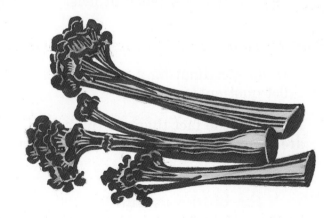

Is 273 ÷ 7 easier to estimate using rounding or compatible numbers?

DIVIDING
with One-Digit Divisors

Dortmund, a college-preparatory school in Germany, has 586 students. There are 7 science teachers. What is the least number of students each teacher will teach?

Estimate.

You can use your estimate to determine about how many digits will be in the exact quotient.

$$7)\overline{586} \rightarrow 7)\overline{560}$$

80 ← estimate

Since the estimate is 80, or 8 tens, you know the first digit will probably be in the tens place, and there will probably be two digits in the quotient.

Divide.

Step 1	Step 2	Step 3
Since the first digit will be in the tens place, divide the 58 tens. Think: $7 \times 8 = 56$.	Bring down the ones. Divide the 26 ones. Think: $7 \times 3 = 21$. Record the remainder.	Use the inverse operation, multiplication, to check. Remember to add the remainder.

Step 1

$$\begin{array}{r} 8 \\ 7)\overline{586} \\ -56 \\ \hline 2 \end{array}$$

Multiply.

Subtract. Compare. $2 < 7$

Step 2

$$\begin{array}{r} 83 \text{ r5} \\ 7)\overline{586} \\ -56\downarrow \\ \hline 26 \\ -21 \\ \hline 5 \end{array}$$

← More than 83 are needed.

Multiply.

Subtract. Compare. $5 < 7$

Step 3

$$\begin{array}{r} 83 \\ \times\ 7 \\ \hline 581 \\ +\ 5 \\ \hline 586 \end{array}$$

← quotient
← divisor

← remainder
← dividend

So, each teacher will teach at least 83 students.

Talk About It

► How does estimating a quotient help you find the exact quotient?

► How does the fact that multiplication and division are inverse operations help you find quotients?

MULTICULTURAL NOTE: In Germany there are different types of high schools. One type, called a Gymnasium, prepares students for college. Another, called a Hauptschule, provides specialized job training. A school that provides a general education is called a Realschule.

Check for Understanding

Estimate. Tell about how many digits will be in the exact quotient.

1. $8)\overline{427}$ 2. $2)\overline{874}$ 3. $4)\overline{3,324}$ 4. $7)\overline{232}$ 5. $9)\overline{843}$

Practice

Estimate the quotient.

6. 5)$\overline{39}$ **7.** 4)$\overline{125}$ **8.** 7)$\overline{506}$ **9.** 8)$\overline{816}$ **10.** $7,123 \div 4$

11. $311 \div 4$ **12.** $1,600 \div 5$ **13.** $16,543 \div 9$ **14.** $1,158 \div 6$ **15.** $587 \div 2$

16. $624 \div 8$ **17.** $51,222 \div 5$ **18.** $13,721 \div 7$ **19.** $5,500 \div 7$ **20.** $24,135 \div 6$

Find the quotient.

21. 4)$\overline{552}$ **22.** 8)$\overline{1,989}$ **23.** 8)$\overline{568}$ **24.** 3)$\overline{6,612}$ **25.** 9)$\overline{6,234}$

26. $5,440 \div 8$ **27.** $699 \div 3$ **28.** $67,663 \div 6$ **29.** $1,845 \div 9$ **30.** $1,242 \div 3$

31. 8)$\overline{3,376}$ **32.** 3)$\overline{3,912}$ **33.** 6)$\overline{49,307}$ **34.** 2)$\overline{6,323}$ **35.** 6)$\overline{548}$

Mixed Applications

36. A bus made 6 trips of 242 miles each. What is the total number of miles the bus traveled?

37. A teacher has 273 milligrams of a chemical to divide equally into 3 solutions. How much will the teacher add to each solution?

  MENTAL MATH

When you multiply and divide each part of the dividend mentally, you are using a method called short division.

Divide the first digit. Write the remainder next to the second digit. The remainder and the second digit become the next number to divide. Repeat until you have completed the division.

Example

$$\begin{array}{c} 1 \\ 8)\overline{9\,^19\ 5} \end{array} \longrightarrow \begin{array}{c} 1\ 2 \\ 8)\overline{9\,^19\,^35} \end{array} \longrightarrow \begin{array}{c} 1\ 2\ 4\ r3 \\ 8)\overline{9\,^19\,^35} \end{array}$$

Divide. Use short division.

38. 5)$\overline{240}$ **39.** 7)$\overline{1,680}$ **40.** 9)$\overline{28,125}$ **41.** 4)$\overline{4,933}$ **42.** 8)$\overline{3,655}$

Why do you estimate a quotient?

 WRAP UP...

DIVIDING
with Two-Digit Divisors

Fans of a hurling team want to place a decorative banner all along a 2,748-foot fence that surrounds the hurling field. If the paper for the banner comes only in 13-foot rolls, how many rolls will they need?

Estimate to place the first digit in the quotient.
$2,748 \div 13 \longrightarrow 2,600 \div 13 = 200$

Divide.

Step 1	**Step 2**	**Step 3**
Since the first digit will be in the hundreds place, divide the 27 hundreds. Think: $13 \times 2 = 26$.	Bring down the tens. Divide the 14 tens. Think: $13 \times 1 = 13$.	Bring down the ones. Divide the 18 ones. Record the remainder.
$\begin{array}{r} 2 \\ 13\overline{)2,748} \\ -26 \\ \hline 1 \end{array}$	$\begin{array}{r} 21 \\ 13\overline{)2,748} \\ -26\downarrow \\ \hline 14 \\ -13 \\ \hline 1 \end{array}$	$\begin{array}{r} 211 \text{ r}5 \\ 13\overline{)2,748} \\ -26\downarrow \\ \hline 14 \\ -13\downarrow \\ \hline 18 \\ -13 \\ \hline 5 \end{array}$

- Why will the fans need more than 211 rolls of paper?

Since the fans cannot buy part of a roll, they will need 212 rolls of paper.

MULTICULTURAL NOTE: Hurling, the national game of Ireland, is similar to American field hockey.

Examples   Sometimes you need to correct the quotient.

A.
$\begin{array}{r} 9 \\ 23\overline{)200} \\ -207 \end{array}$ Since 207 > 200, the digit in the quotient is too large.

B.
$\begin{array}{r} 5 \\ 38\overline{)232} \\ -190 \\ \hline 42 \end{array}$ Since 42 > 38, the digit in the quotient is too small.

Check for Understanding

Tell whether you need to correct the first digit in the quotient. Write *yes* or *no*.

1. $\begin{array}{r} 2 \\ 13\overline{)241} \end{array}$
2. $\begin{array}{r} 4 \\ 91\overline{)420} \end{array}$
3. $\begin{array}{r} 1 \\ 56\overline{)5,765} \end{array}$
4. $\begin{array}{r} 6 \\ 62\overline{)36,743} \end{array}$
5. $\begin{array}{r} 4 \\ 67\overline{)32,264} \end{array}$

Practice

Estimate the quotient.

6. $13 \overline{)254}$ **7.** $52 \overline{)123}$ **8.** $56 \overline{)5,834}$ **9.** $13 \overline{)4,145}$

10. $91 \overline{)440}$ **11.** $36,043 \div 62$ **12.** $12 \overline{)2,564}$ **13.** $91,654 \div 32$

Find the quotient.

14. $35 \overline{)140}$ **15.** $13 \overline{)117}$ **16.** $42 \overline{)892}$ **17.** $29 \overline{)261}$

18. $74 \overline{)4,736}$ **19.** $38 \overline{)8,174}$ **20.** $41 \overline{)11,316}$ **21.** $6,552 \div 91$

22. $1,579 \div 81$ **23.** $42,032 \div 71$ **24.** $22,120 \div 35$ **25.** $2,744 \div 49$

26. $54 \overline{)1,512}$ **27.** $66 \overline{)15,972}$ **28.** $97 \overline{)96,708}$ **29.** $28 \overline{)67,815}$

 Complete the table. You may want to use a calculator.

	Divisor	Dividend	Quotient		Divisor	Dividend	Quotient
30.	36	4,752	▧	**31.**	46	460	▧
32.	42	▧	56	**33.**	97	87,979	▧
34.	▧	456	38	**35.**	▧	3,858	6

Mixed Applications

36. A total of 288 students will play intramural basketball. Into how many teams of 12 can the students be grouped?

37. The principal at Division Middle School has ordered 1,170 desks to divide equally among 45 classrooms. How many desks will be in each classroom?

38. Find Data Use a recent almanac to find information about the number of students and the number of school districts in your state.

39. Make Up a Problem Use the data you found in Exercise 38 to write a word problem that can be solved using division.

How do you know that a digit in the quotient is too large? too small?

WRAP UP...

PROBLEM SOLVING

STRATEGY • Write a Number Sentence

A teacher will distribute 288 new books among several classes of 24 students each. If every student in each class is given a new book, how many classes will have new books?

▶ **UNDERSTAND**

What are you asked to find?

What information are you given?

▶ **PLAN**

What strategy will you use?

Since you know that 288 books will be distributed among groups of 24, you can write a division number sentence.

▶ **SOLVE**

How can you carry out your plan?

Write a division number sentence.
$288 \div 24 = n$

Estimate.

$$288 \div 24$$
$$\downarrow \qquad \downarrow$$
$$300 \div 20 = 15$$

Use a calculator to solve.

288 ÷ 24 =   12.

So, 12 classes will receive new books.

▶ **LOOK BACK**

How do you know your solution is reasonable?

WHAT IF... . . . you were asked to find the total number of students in 3 of the classes? What number sentence would you write to solve the problem?

Apply

Write a number sentence. Then solve.

1. Elizabeth and Mary's school bus averages 328 miles on 41 gallons of gasoline. How many miles does the school bus average on 1 gallon of gasoline?

2. A band teacher is buying 341 sets of sheet music for members of the middle school band. If the sheet music costs $1.79 a set, what is the total cost?

Mixed Applications → **STRATEGIES**

Find a Pattern • Use a Table
• Guess and Check
• Write a Number Sentence

Choose a strategy and solve.

3. Tran is sorting pencils. There are 7 more red pencils than blue pencils in a total of 39 pencils. How many are blue?

4. Julio makes $5.25 an hour working as an assistant to the school librarian. How much will Julio make if he works 36 hours?

5. Of the 2,048 students who competed in a spelling bee, 1,024 were eliminated the first day, 512 the second, and 256 the third. If this pattern continued, on what day did the last two students in the spelling bee compete?

6. Use the table below. If the pattern continues, how far will 6 runners run on the fifth day?

Each Runner's Training Schedule				
Day	1	2	3	4	5
Miles	2	6	10	14	■

7. Janet ran 0.5 mile on Monday, 0.6 mile on Tuesday, and 0.7 mile on Wednesday. If she continues this pattern, how far will Janet run on Friday?

8. Alonzo scored 12 three-point shots and 14 two-point shots in three basketball games. How many total points did Alonzo score?

9. Marissa has 19 coins to spend at a soccer game. She has only dimes and quarters. The value of the coins is $4. How many dimes does Marissa have?

10. Jill has worked 4 more than 3 times as many problems as Dave. Wayne has worked 2 times as many as Dave. If Wayne has worked 28 problems, how many problems has Jill worked?

DIVIDING
Zeros in the Quotient

A total of 27 members of a band-booster club sold 8,235 bumper stickers. What is the average number sold by each member?

Estimate. $8,235 \div 27 \rightarrow 9,000 \div 30 = 300$

Divide.

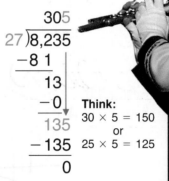

Step 1	Step 2	Step 3
Since the first digit will be in the hundreds place, divide the 82 hundreds.	Bring down the tens. Divide the 13 tens. Think: 27 > 13. Write 0 in the quotient.	Bring down the ones. Divide the 135 ones. Use compatible numbers.

Step 1:
$$\begin{array}{r} 3 \\ 27\overline{)8,235} \\ -81 \\ \hline 1 \end{array}$$

Think:
$30 \times 3 = 90$
or
$25 \times 3 = 75$

Step 2:
$$\begin{array}{r} 30 \\ 27\overline{)8,235} \\ -81\downarrow \\ \hline 13 \\ -0 \\ \hline 13 \end{array}$$

Step 3:
$$\begin{array}{r} 305 \\ 27\overline{)8,235} \\ -81 \\ \hline 13 \\ -0\downarrow \\ \hline 135 \\ -135 \\ \hline 0 \end{array}$$

Think:
$30 \times 5 = 150$
or
$25 \times 5 = 125$

So, each member sold an average of 305 bumper stickers. Since 305 is close to 300, the answer is reasonable.

- When do you write zero in the quotient?

- How can you use your estimate to determine whether a zero has been omitted?

Check for Understanding

Choose the correct quotient. Write **a**, **b**, or **c**.

1. $8\overline{)5,624}$
   - **a.** 703
   - **b.** 730
   - **c.** 73

2. $41\overline{)8,614}$
   - **a.** 21 r4
   - **b.** 201 r4
   - **c.** 210 r4

3. $16\overline{)992}$
   - **a.** 602
   - **b.** 62
   - **c.** 620

4. $24\overline{)14,172}$
   - **a.** 50 r12
   - **b.** 590 r12
   - **c.** 509 r12

5. $63\overline{)25,666}$
   - **a.** 740 r25
   - **b.** 470 r25
   - **c.** 407 r25

Find the quotient.

6. $72\overline{)2,884}$

7. $7\overline{)8,421}$

8. $8\overline{)8,724}$

9. $12\overline{)2,439}$

Practice

Find the quotient.

10. $7\overline{)2,821}$ **11.** $6\overline{)12,014}$ **12.** $9\overline{)7,020}$ **13.** $4\overline{)3,603}$

14. $43\overline{)8,772}$ **15.** $8\overline{)4,803}$ **16.** $32\overline{)22,432}$ **17.** $63\overline{)5,100}$

18. $6\overline{)7,204}$ **19.** $21\overline{)5,260}$ **20.** $5\overline{)4,304}$ **21.** $9\overline{)8,197}$

22. $47\overline{)14,326}$ **23.** $17\overline{)17,599}$ **24.** $70\overline{)4,925}$ **25.** $41\overline{)8,561}$

Use inverse operations to complete the table.

	Divisor	Dividend	Quotient
26.	24	14,544	■
27.	■	16,012	4,003
28.	9	■	60 r7
29.	45	4,815	■

Mixed Applications

30. Davis Middle School library has 62,525 cards in its card catalog. If there are 5 cards for each book, how many books are in the library?

31. **Number Sense • Estimation** A school library must put 35,099 books on 130 shelves. Which numbers would you use to estimate the quotient: $35,000 \div 130$, $36,000 \div 120$, or $35,000 \div 150$? Why?

MIXED REVIEW

Determine whether the number is divisible by 2, 3, 5, 9, or 10. Write all that apply.

1. 650 **2.** 315 **3.** 2,048 **4.** 6,561

Use multiplication to estimate the sum.

5. $3.1 + 2.8 + 3.3 + 2.75$ **6.** $99.11 + 100.32 + 97.954 + 102.004$

Find the quotient.

7. $7\overline{)392}$ **8.** $2,835 \div 9$ **9.** $57\overline{)684}$ **10.** $1,470 \div 98$

Why do you write a zero in the quotient?

1. Tasha sold 234 school newspapers for $0.05 each. If each newspaper cost $0.03 to print, what was the profit from Tasha's sales?

2. Barbara baked 10 dozen muffins for the 36 newspaper club members. If each member has 3 muffins, how many muffins will be left?

When computing with money, I must place the decimal point correctly.

3. Students use a hand-run press to print the school newspaper. The press can print 24 pages every 30 minutes. If the press runs 210 minutes a day, how long will it take to print 504 pages?

4. The school newspaper staff pays $0.03 for every page printed. If the staff decides to print 945 copies of a 4-page newspaper next month, how much will the printing cost?

Estimate the product or the quotient.

5. 9.8×41

6. 279.63×12.2

7. $5,432 \times 61.89$

8. $5,958.24 \times 3.9$

9. $642 \div 27$

10. $946 \div 34$

11. $5,391 \div 94$

12. $7,986 \div 11$

Place the decimal point in the product.

13. $6.8 \times 3.4 = 2312$

14. $5.3 \times 0.07 = 0371$

15. $800 \times 1.8 = 14400$

Find the product.

16. 9.7×5.2

17. $4,562 \times 7.5$

18. 0.066×100

19. $1,321.95 \times 0.38$

20. $3.029 \times 1,000$

21. 754.2×0.98

22. 33.2×21.5

23. 624×9.7

Determine whether the number is divisible by 2, 3, 5, 9, or 10. Write all that apply.

24. 270

25. 16,833

26. 62,390

27. 53,865

Find the quotient.

28. $984 \div 4$

29. $826 \div 6$

30. $3,691 \div 5$

31. $4,251 \div 6$

32. $68,242 \div 2$

33. $276 \div 45$

34. $1,207 \div 90$

35. $7,928 \div 12$

36. $18,496 \div 4$

37. $16,905 \div 42$

38. $62,863 \div 99$

39. $75,342 \div 60$

NORTH
AMERICA

United
States

Using Multiplication and Division

Games are part of every culture. Many children's games involve running, jumping, throwing, and swinging. The game of jump rope is played by children all over the world. There are many types of jumps, such as single, double, backward, crossed feet, and double Dutch.

Double Dutch jump rope is popular in many cities in the United States. In double Dutch, two ropes are turned at the same time in opposite directions.

Use multiplication or division to solve.

1. Shannel is a member of a double Dutch jump rope team. She counted and determined that she takes 250 steps in 1 minute. About how many steps does she take in 1 second?

2. Shannel's routine lasts 6 minutes. How many steps does she take during this time if she jumps at the same rate as described in Exercise 1?

3. At a recent competition, a double Dutch jump rope team used 1 minute 20 seconds of its performance time for a total of 16 moves, including flips, turns, and handsprings. What was the average time for each move? (HINT: Change 1 minute 20 seconds to seconds.)

4. Shannel's team practices for 7.5 hours each week. How many hours does the team practice in one year?

DIVIDING DECIMALS
by Whole Numbers

Gabriel drives 103.6 kilometers every 4 days to take children to and from school. What is the average number of kilometers Gabriel drives each day?

Estimate to place the first digit in the quotient.

$$103.6 \div 4 \quad \longrightarrow \quad 100 \div 4 = 25$$

Divide.

Step 1	**Step 2**
Place a decimal point above the decimal point in the dividend.	Divide as with whole numbers.

$$4\overline{)103.6}$$

$$\begin{array}{r} 25.9 \\ 4\overline{)103.6} \\ -8 \\ \hline 23 \\ -20 \\ \hline 3\,6 \\ -3\,6 \\ \hline 0 \end{array}$$

So, Gabriel drives about 25.9 kilometers each day.

You can also use short division.

Example $6.797 \div 7$

Round to estimate.

$$\begin{array}{r} 1 \\ 7\overline{)7} \end{array}$$
6.797 rounded to the nearest whole number is 7.

Use short division.

$$7\overline{)6.7^4 9 7} \quad 0.9\ 71$$
Since the quotient is less than 1, place 0 in the ones place.

MULTICULTURAL NOTE: In some schools in Ecuador, the school day is divided into sessions. There is one session in the morning for elementary-school-age students, an afternoon session for middle-school-age students, and an evening session for high-school-age students.

Check for Understanding

Choose the correct quotient without computing. Write **a, b,** or **c.**

1. $23\overline{)181.47}$
   a. 0.789
   b. 78.9
   c. 7.89

2. $59\overline{)164.02}$
   a. 27.8
   b. 2.78
   c. 0.278

3. $87\overline{)4.785}$
   a. 0.055
   b. 0.0055
   c. 0.55

4. $36\overline{)2.7972}$
   a. 0.0777
   b. 0.777
   c. 7.77

Practice

Place the decimal point in the quotient.

5. $270.585 \div 63 = 4295$ **6.** $11.919 \div 87 = 137$ **7.** $1591.2 \div 39 = 408$

Find the quotient.

8. $5\overline{)21.5}$ **9.** $2\overline{)\$30.72}$ **10.** $8\overline{)\$31.20}$ **11.** $11\overline{)3.96}$

12. $9\overline{)38.601}$ **13.** $12\overline{)7.2}$ **14.** $7\overline{)33.6}$ **15.** $11\overline{)394.46}$

16. $24\overline{)7.44}$ **17.** $82\overline{)59.86}$ **18.** $17\overline{)85.51}$ **19.** $31\overline{)111.6}$

20. $41\overline{)70.643}$ **21.** $37\overline{)99.9}$ **22.** $47\overline{)86.48}$ **23.** $53\overline{)79.5}$

24. $173.6 \div 8$ **25.** $7.1139 \div 69$ **26.** $70.95 \div 15$ **27.** $474.75 \div 75$

Mixed Applications

28. A total of 31 students signed up for a weekend computer course. They paid a total of $1,418.25. How much did each student pay?

29. A 6-story school building is 19.2 meters high. If each story of the school building is the same height, how high is each story?

30. **Critical Thinking** Fluorine is one of the gaseous elements. Nine molecules of fluorine weigh 638.154 atomic mass units. How much do 2 molecules of fluorine weigh?

31. **Making Decisions** A computer store sells two brands of diskettes of equal quality. Brand A costs $9.23 for 12. Brand B sells for $0.98 each. Which brand is the better buy?

When dividing a decimal by a whole number, why do you need a decimal point in the quotient?

More Practice, Lesson 4.7, page H47

DIVIDING DECIMALS
with Zeros in the Dividend

In science class Jan learns that it takes 4 hours to move a space shuttle 3.4 miles from the assembly building to the launch pad. How far is the shuttle moved in 1 hour?

Estimate. Use compatible numbers.

$$4\overline{)3.4} \rightarrow 4\overset{0.8}{\overline{)3.2}}$$

Sometimes you must place zeros to the right of the decimal in a dividend to complete a division problem. Since 3.4 and 3.40 are equivalent, you can place a zero to the right of the decimal.

Divide.

Step 1	Step 2
Place the decimal point and divide.	Place a zero in the hundredths place. Continue to divide until the remainder is 0.
$$\begin{array}{r} 0.8 \\ 4\overline{)3.4} \\ -3\,2 \\ \hline 2 \end{array}$$	$$\begin{array}{r} 0.85 \\ 4\overline{)3.40} \\ -3\,2\downarrow \\ \hline 20 \\ -20 \\ \hline 0 \end{array}$$

So, the shuttle is moved 0.85 mile in 1 hour.

- Why do you place zeros to the right of the decimal in a dividend?

_____

Zeros are sometimes needed to hold places in decimal quotients just as zeros are sometimes needed in whole-number quotients.

Example

$$\begin{array}{r} 0.026 \\ 5\overline{)0.130} \\ -10 \\ \hline 30 \\ -30 \\ \hline 0 \end{array}$$

Zeros show that there are no whole numbers and no tenths in the quotient.

Check for Understanding

Place the decimal point in the quotient. Add zeros to divide until the remainder is zero.

1. $4.50 \div 2 = 225$

2. $1.610 \div 5 = 322$

3. $0.1040 \div 65 = 16$

4. $0.924 \div 6 = 154$

5. $0.060 \div 4 = 15$

6. $2.135 \div 7 = 305$

Divide until the remainder is zero.

7. $5\overline{)1.61}$

8. $2\overline{)9.87}$

9. $8\overline{)7.9}$

10. $42\overline{)50.19}$

11. $16\overline{)119}$

Practice

Divide until the remainder is zero.

12. $8\overline{)0.7}$

13. $16\overline{)11}$

14. $18\overline{)40.5}$

15. $32\overline{)5.6}$

16. $4\overline{)21.5}$

17. $65\overline{)1.04}$

18. $4\overline{)3.4}$

19. $16\overline{)27}$

20. $98\overline{)121.03}$

21. $4\overline{)0.85}$

22. $342 \div 48$

23. $0.93 \div 6$

24. $0.47 \div 5$

25. $31.5 \div 84$

Mixed Applications

26. In home economics class, Ian made 8 hamburgers for lunch, using 2.8 pounds of ground beef. How much ground beef was in each hamburger?

27. When she set the table for lunch, Jean poured 0.5 liter of milk into each of 4 glasses. What is the total amount of milk she poured?

CRITICAL THINKING

Tell whether each item was bought at Joe's or at Bob's.

28. Sara bought 1 apple for $0.30.

29. Mont bought 1 orange for $0.37.

30. Ira bought 1 pear for $0.43.

31. Ward bought 2 apples for $0.80.

	Apples 3 for	Oranges 3 for	Pears 4 for
Joe's	$0.89	$1.29	$1.69
Bob's	$1.19	$1.09	$1.45

Why do you place zeros to the right of the decimal in some division problems?

WRAP UP...

DECIMAL PATTERNS
Multiplying and Dividing by Powers of Ten

Tonya can walk 0.05 of a mile around the school track in 1 minute (min). If she maintains this pace, how far can she walk in 10 min? in 100 min? in 1,000 min?

Notice the pattern that occurs when you multiply decimals by powers of 10.

10^0, or 1 $\times \ 0.05 = 0.05$ ← 1 min
10^1, or 10 $\times \ 0.05 = 0.0\,5$, or 0.5   ← 10 min
10^2, or 100 $\times \ 0.05 = 0.05\,0$, or 5.0   ← 100 min
10^3, or 1,000 $\times \ 0.05 = 0.050\,0$, or 50.0   ← 1,000 min

So, if Tonya maintains her pace, she can walk 0.5 mile in 10 minutes, 5 miles in 100 minutes, and 50 miles in 1,000 minutes.

- What happens to the product as the power of 10 increases?

- What rule can you state for multiplying decimals by powers of 10?

By standing, Mr. McKinney burns 666.6 calories in the 1,000 hours (hr) he teaches each year. How many calories does he burn in 100 hr? in 10 hr? in 1 hr?

Think: $1,000 \div 10 = 100;\ 100 \div 10 = 10;\ 10 \div 10 = 1.$

Notice the pattern that occurs when you divide decimals by powers of 10.

$666.6 \div 10^0$, or 1 $= 666.6$ ← 1,000 hr
$666.6 \div 10^1$, or 10 $= 66\,6.6$, or 66.66   ← 100 hr
$666.6 \div 10^2$, or 100 $= 6\,66.6$, or 6.666   ← 10 hr
$666.6 \div 10^3$, or 1,000 $= 0\,666.6$, or 0.6666   ← 1 hr

So, Mr. McKinney burns 66.66 calories in 100 hours, 6.666 in 10 hours, and 0.6666 in 1 hour.

- Does the quotient get larger or smaller as the power of 10 increases?

- What rule can you state for dividing decimals by powers of 10?

Check for Understanding

Complete the pattern.

1. $0.15 \times 10 = 1.5$
   $0.15 \times 100 = $
   $0.15 \times 1,000 = $ ▣

2. $235 \div 10 = 23.5$
   $235 \div 100 = $ ▣
   $235 \div 1,000 = $ ▣

3. $1.045 \times 1,000 = 1,045$
   $1.045 \times 100 = $ ▣
   $1.045 \times 10 = $ ▣

Practice

Copy and complete each table.

	×	10^1	10^2	10^3
4.	37.89	▣	▣	▣
5.	0.0643	▣	▣	▣
6.	0.53	▣	▣	▣
7.	0.024	▣	▣	▣

	÷	10^1	10^2	10^3
8.	14.5	▣	▣	▣
9.	8.9	▣	▣	▣
10.	0.06	▣	▣	▣
11.	740	▣	▣	▣

Mixed Applications

12. Troy, Alan, and 8 other members of the school's hiking club will share equally the cost of a cabin rental. If the cost is $455.50, how much will each person pay?

13. Fran tried to lift a bag of mail containing 1,000 letters from students concerned about water pollution. If each letter weighed 0.064 pound, how much did all the letters weigh?

CRITICAL THINKING

Use the table for Exercises 14–17.

10 millimeters	= 1 centimeter
100 centimeters	= 1 meter
1,000 meters	= 1 kilometer

14. How many meters are in 4.6 kilometers?

15. How many meters are in 567 centimeters?

16. How many millimeters are in 1 meter?

17. How many millimeters are in 6.4 meters?

How is multiplying a decimal by a power of 10 different from dividing a decimal by a power of 10?

WRAP UP...

More Practice, Lesson 4.9, page H48

EXPLORING

Dividing Decimals by Decimals

Robbie has $1.65. Into how many groups of $0.05 can he divide his money?

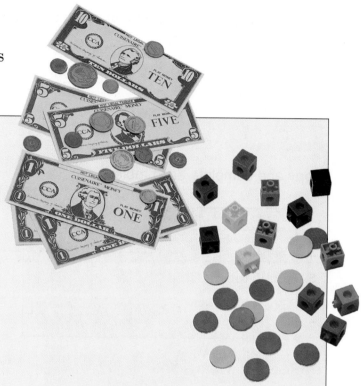

Building Understanding

Use the manipulatives or tool of your choice to model the problem and find a solution.

Explain why you chose the manipulatives or tool that you used.

Write a description of the steps in your model.

Now model these two problems.

• Suppose Robbie has $16.50. Into how many groups of $0.50 can he divide his money?

• Suppose Robbie has $165. Into how many groups of $5 can he divide his money?

TALK ABOUT IT

• Explain what your three models have in common.

• Describe any patterns that you see in the problems and in the solutions.

Be prepared to share your models and explanations with the class.

Making the Connection

One way to show division of decimals by decimals is to use a number line.

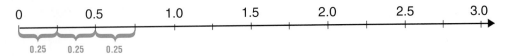

If you continue showing 0.25 on the number line, you find that $2.75 \div 0.25 = 11$.

1. What division problem is shown on this number line? What is the quotient?

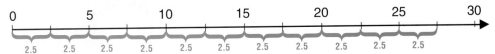

2. Show $275 \div 25$ on a number line.

TALK ABOUT IT

- How are $2.75 \div 0.25$, $27.5 \div 2.5$, and $275 \div 25$ related?

- Multiply both 2.75 and 0.25 by 10. What are the results? Multiply both 2.75 and 0.25 by 100. What are the results?

- How does multiplying the divisor and the dividend by the same power of 10 affect the quotient?

Another Example

$1.92 \div 0.16 = 12$
$19.2 \div 1.6 = 12$ ⟵ $1.92 \times 10 = 19.2$; $0.16 \times 10 = 1.6$
$192 \div 16 = 12$ ⟵ $1.92 \times 100 = 192$; $0.16 \times 100 = 16$

Checking Understanding

Use the method of your choice to find the quotient.

3. $9.9 \div 0.3$
4. $1.44 \div 0.04$
5. $0.63 \div 0.09$
6. $1.35 \div 0.15$

7. What conclusion can you draw about the quotient when the divisor and the dividend have been multiplied by the same power of 10?

More Practice, Lesson 4.10, page H48

DIVIDING DECIMALS
by Decimals

An art teacher gives Bill several containers holding a total of 28.5 liters of paint for a mural and asks him to pour 1.5 liters into each smaller container. How many smaller containers will Bill need?

You have seen that multiplying the divisor and the dividend by the same power of 10 has no effect on the quotient. Think about this relationship when you divide decimals by decimals.

Divide. $1.5\overline{)28.5}$

Step 1	**Step 2**
Make the divisor a whole number. Multiply both the divisor and the dividend by 10.	Place the decimal point in the quotient. Divide as with whole numbers.

Step 1

$1.5 \times 10 = 15\ (1.5)$

$28.5 \times 10 = 285\ (28.5)$

Step 2

```
        19.
   15.)285.
      -15↓
       135
      -135
         0
```

Since the remainder is 0, the answer is a whole number, and you do not need to show the decimal point.

So, Bill will need 19 smaller containers.

More Examples

A.
```
         8  ← whole
  4.3)34.4      number
    -34 4
        0
```

B.
```
          6.6
  0.75)4.95 0
       -4 50↓
         45 0
        -45 0
            0
```
Place a zero to continue to divide.

C.
```
           25
  2.38)59.50
       -47 6↓
         11 90
        -11 90
             0
```
Place a zero in the dividend to make the divisor a whole number.

Check for Understanding

Write the power of 10 needed to make the divisor a whole number.

1. $1.1\overline{)3.67}$

2. $52 \div 3.45$

3. $4.075\overline{)77.88}$

4. $5.2234 \div 0.06$

5. $17.5 \div 2.5$

6. $5.55\overline{)49.95}$

7. $28.16 \div 7.04$

8. $7.8\overline{)11.7}$

Practice

Place the decimal point in the quotient. Add zeros if necessary.

9. $241.5 \div 4.6 = 525$

10. $1{,}449 \div 1.38 = 1050$

11. $258.5 \div 2.5 = 1034$

12. $0.984 \div 2.4 = 41$

13. $4{,}062.5 \div 0.26 = 15625$

14. $1.25 \div 0.5 = 25$

15. $20.25 \div 1.2 = 16875$

16. $138.75 \div 8.88 = 15625$

17. $56.2152 \div 3.54 = 1588$

Find the quotient.

18. $8.1 \div 0.09$

19. $3.9 \div 0.15$

20. $49.3 \div 0.29$

21. $219.3 \div 5.1$

22. $0.28\overline{)0.42}$

23. $0.063\overline{)15.12}$

24. $11.7\overline{)26.208}$

25. $0.133\overline{)5.32}$

26. $20.7\overline{)107.64}$

27. $0.95\overline{)35.055}$

28. $7.7\overline{)480.48}$

29. $33\overline{)488.4}$

30. $105.6 \div 24$

31. $5.382 \div 9$

32. $0.2835 \div 2.7$

33. $4.563 \div 1.2$

Mixed Applications

34. A school parking lot is 71.3 meters long. If each parking space is 2.3 meters wide, how many cars can be parked side by side?

35. Sori made flags for a school fair out of a strip of material 12.6 meters long. Each flag was 0.7 meter long. How many flags did she make?

36. **Number Sense • Estimation** Trina's family owns a sailboat that can travel 6.5 kilometers per hour. About how far can the sailboat travel in 4 hours?

37. **Find Data** Use an almanac to find high school graduation rates in your state and in three neighboring states. Organize and display your data in a table.

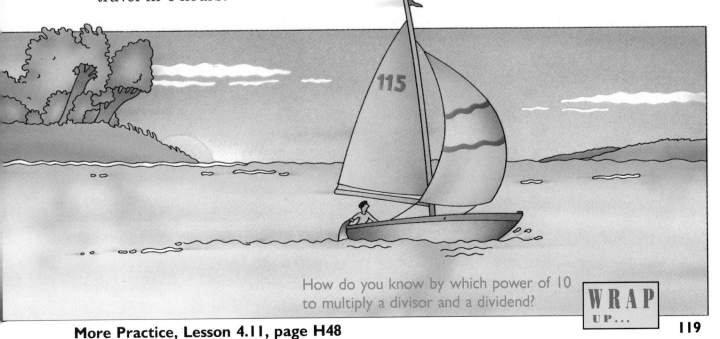

How do you know by which power of 10 to multiply a divisor and a dividend?

WRAP UP...

ROUNDING
Decimal Quotients

A school district is buying 77,250 cases of chalk at a discounted price of $717,867. How much does one case of chalk cost?

 Use a calculator to divide large numbers.

717,867 ÷ 77,250 = `9.2927766`

Since money is commonly expressed in cents, or hundredths, round the answer to the nearest cent.

So, one case of chalk costs $9.29.

Some division problems will continue to have a remainder no matter the number of places to which you divide. When this happens, round your answer to an appropriate place.

To round a decimal quotient to a given place, divide to the next place-value position. Then round to the given place.

Examples

A. Round to the nearest tenth.

$$
\begin{array}{r}
9.44 \rightarrow 9.4 \\
4.3\overline{)40.6\,00} \\
-38\,7 \\
\hline
1\,9\,0 \\
-1\,7\,2 \\
\hline
1\,8\,0 \\
-1\,7\,2 \\
\hline
8
\end{array}
$$

Divide to the hundredths place.

B. Round to the nearest thousandth.

$$
\begin{array}{r}
0.8065 \rightarrow 0.807 \\
8\overline{)6.4520} \\
-6\,4 \\
\hline
0\,5\,2 \\
-4\,8 \\
\hline
4\,0 \\
-4\,0 \\
\hline
0
\end{array}
$$

Divide to the ten-thousandths place.

Check for Understanding

Find the quotient. Round to the place given.

1. $3.447 \div 1.8$
(tenths)

2. $14.5 \div 5$
(ones)

3. $\$14.07 \div 8.4$
(cents)

4. $56.77 \div 9$
(hundredths)

5. $109.5 \div 73$
(ones)

6. $1.4508 \div 6.2$
(hundredths)

7. $4.1049 \div 9$
(thousandths)

8. $13.2154 \div 6$
(thousandths)

Practice

Find the quotient. Round to the nearest whole number or dollar.

9. $8.00 ÷ 3   **10.** 22.1 ÷ 5.6   **11.** 19.5 ÷ 9   **12.** 152 ÷ 5   **13.** 121 ÷ 13

14. 168.7 ÷ 3.5   **15.** 426 ÷ 8   **16.** 87 ÷ 6   **17.** $943 ÷ 7   **18.** $576 ÷ 6.1

Find the quotient. Round to the place given.

19. 113.88 ÷ 73
(tenths)

20. $5)\overline{14.8}$
(ones)

21. $52)\overline{\$87.35}$
(cents)

22. 31.932 ÷ 6
(tenths)

23. 1.29 ÷ 5.5
(hundredths)

24. $1.8)\overline{3.446}$
(thousandths)

25. 7.263 ÷ 9
(hundredths)

26. $7)\overline{4.104}$
(ten-thousandths)

Mixed Applications

Choose the place to which you will round for Exercises 27–28.
Be prepared to defend your choice. Then solve.

27. The cafeteria staff served 82 liters of salad to 335 students. If the salad was divided equally, about how much did each student receive?

28. The 4 students on a middle school relay team ran the 400-meter dash in 45.19 seconds. What was the average time of each runner?

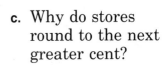

29. Critical Thinking At the school store, pens sell at 3 for $1.53. What is the cost of 1 pen?

a. To the nearest thousandth, what does 1 pen cost if 3 sell for $1.54?

b. What does a store charge for 1 pen if 3 pens sell for $1.54?

c. Why do stores round to the next greater cent?

MIXED REVIEW

Tell how to move the decimal point to find the answer.

1. 10×1.5 **2.** $3.4 ÷ 100$ **3.** 52.55×10^3 **4.** $5,433 ÷ 10^4$

Estimate the quotient.

5. 448 ÷ 9   **6.** 110 ÷ 58   **7.** 3,496 ÷ 18   **8.** 93,245 ÷ 86

Name an everyday situation in which you round decimals to the hundredths place.

WRAP
UP...

EXPRESSIONS
with Multiplication and Division

You can use what you know about algebraic expressions with addition and subtraction to write algebraic expressions with multiplication and division. Recall that an algebraic expression contains a variable.

Word Expression	Algebraic Expression
Twice a number, *y* 5.6 times a number, *c* A number, *d*, multiplied by 3	2*y* 5.6*c* 3*d*
A number, *b*, divided by 12 The quotient of a number, *x*, and 5	$b \div 12$, or $\dfrac{b}{12}$ $x \div 5$, or $\dfrac{x}{5}$

When you write an algebraic expression with multiplication, omit the sign. For example, $4 \times n$ is 4*n*.

Rich spent $9.00 for lunches at school this week. He paid the same price each day. What was the daily cost of his lunch?

Since you do not know how many days Rich bought lunch, you can write an algebraic expression for the daily cost of his lunch. Let *n* equal the number of days he bought lunch.

The daily cost of Rich's lunch was $\dfrac{9}{n}$.

You can evaluate the expression $\dfrac{9}{n}$ if you know how many days Rich bought his lunch.

Example

Find the daily cost when *n* = 5 days and when *n* = 3 days.

Evaluate $\dfrac{9}{n}$, for *n* = 5.   Evaluate $\dfrac{9}{n}$, for *n* = 3.

$\dfrac{9}{5} = 1.8$ $\dfrac{9}{3} = 3$

So, the daily cost was $1.80 if Rich bought lunch 5 days and $3.00 if he bought lunch 3 days.

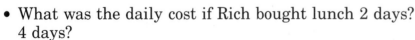

- What was the daily cost if Rich bought lunch 2 days? 4 days?

- Suppose Rich spent $24.00 for lunches for 10 days. What was the daily cost of his lunches?

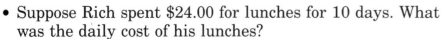

Check for Understanding

Write an algebraic expression for the word expression.

1. 14 times a number, z

2. the quotient of a number, p, and 7

3. a number, h, divided by 12

4. a number, k, multiplied by 54

Evaluate the expression.

5. $x \div 12$, for $x = 60$ **6.** $8t$, for $t = 7$ **7.** $4.5m$, for $m = 4$ **8.** $s \div 10$, for $s = 56.7$

Practice

Evaluate the expression $2.5b$ for each value of b.

9. $b = 21$ **10.** $b = 33$ **11.** $b = 153$ **12.** $b = 722$ **13.** $b = 17.8$

Evaluate the expression $\frac{b}{6}$ for each value of b.

14. $b = 42$ **15.** $b = 252$ **16.** $b = 1{,}503$ **17.** $b = 48.3$ **18.** $b = 72.6$

Evaluate the expression.

19. $35a$, for $a = 7$

20. $\frac{a}{4}$, for $a = 144$

21. $72b$, for $b = 3$

22. $\frac{m}{11}$, for $m = 968$

23. $6.5k$, for $k = 2.5$

24. $\frac{c}{3.6}$, for $c = 19.8$

Mixed Applications

For Exercises 25–26, write an algebraic expression.
Then evaluate the expression.

25. Tina traveled m miles to attend 5 track meets at the same place. How far did she travel to attend 1 meet? Evaluate the expression for $m = 378$ miles.

26. Brett has saved b dollars a week from his allowance for 8 weeks. How much has Brett saved? Evaluate the expression for $b = \$4.45$.

27. Number Sense Copy the puzzle. Write the missing factors so that the products of the factors both across and down are 144.

4		2	
3	12		2
	3	6	
3			2

If Bill drives m miles to work in 1 day, how far will he drive in 5 days?

WRAP UP...

EXPLORING

Multiplication and Division Equations

Remember that the equals sign in an equation shows that expressions on both sides represent the same value.

An equation is like a balanced scale. You can multiply or divide both sides by the same number to maintain the balance and solve the equation.

$$5 + m = 13$$
$$45 - f = 12$$
$$5n = 30$$
$$\frac{x}{7} = 9$$
$$20 = 2t$$
$$6 = \frac{k}{8}$$

Work Together

Building Understanding

Use a balance scale and cubes to explore equations.

Each bag on the left side of the scale has the same number of cubes.

TALK ABOUT IT

- What expression shows the number of cubes on the left side of the scale above? Use the variable c to represent 1 bag.

- How many cubes are on the right side of the scale?

  - What is an equation that shows the relationship between the left side of the scale and the right side?

- Look at the scale on the left. There were 3 bags on the left side. Now there is 1 bag. By what number must you divide $3c$ in order to have only c remaining?

- How many cubes are now on the right side of the scale? Since the scale must have the same number of cubes on each side, how many cubes must be in the bag, or what is the value of c?

Making the Connection

By using a balance scale, you solved the equation $3c = 12$ and found that $c = 4$.

1. What operation did you use to solve the equation and find the value of c?

2. What is the inverse of multiplication?

Suppose you were asked to solve the equation $\frac{c}{3} = 4$.

3. What is the inverse of division?

4. What operation would you use to solve the equation?

5. How would you find the value of c?

Checking Understanding

Tell how to find the value of the variable.

6. $5x = 25$

7. $\frac{x}{4} = 16$

8. $25w = 15$

9. $\frac{w}{9} = 13$

10. $7d = 133$

11. $\frac{a}{12} = 144$

12. $12a = 144$

13. $\frac{t}{9} = 81$

14. $9t = 81$

15. $\frac{k}{2} = 155$

16. $25y = 625$

17. $\frac{z}{25} = 5$

18. $17s = 153$

19. $\frac{p}{155} = 1$

20. $54n = 432$

Use inverse operations to solve the equation.

21. $2t = 20$

22. $5n = 25$

23. $\frac{c}{3} = 11$

PROBLEM SOLVING

STRATEGY • Work Backward

Mrs. Fox, a school cook, has $49.90 left from her paycheck. She paid a 4-week newspaper bill, spent $46.28 for food, and deposited $99.50 in her savings account. If her paycheck is $213.40, what is the weekly cost of the newspaper?

▶ **UNDERSTAND**

What are you asked to find?

What information are you given?

▶ **PLAN**

What strategy will you choose?

Since you know how much Mrs. Fox was paid and how much she spent on other items, *work backward* to find the weekly cost of the newspaper.

▶ **SOLVE**

How can you carry out your plan?

You can make a flowchart to organize the information. Then *work backward* using inverse operations and a calculator to find the weekly cost of the newspaper.

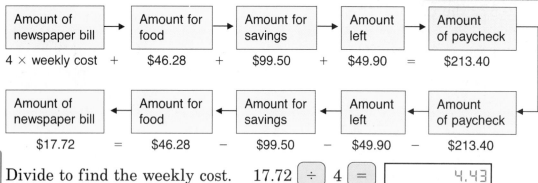

Amount of newspaper bill		Amount for food		Amount for savings		Amount left		Amount of paycheck
4 × weekly cost	+	$46.28	+	$99.50	+	$49.90	=	$213.40

Amount of newspaper bill		Amount for food		Amount for savings		Amount left		Amount of paycheck
$17.72	=	$46.28	−	$99.50	−	$49.90	−	$213.40

Divide to find the weekly cost. 17.72 ÷ 4 = ⌐ 4.43 ⌐

So, the weekly cost of the newspaper is $4.43.

▶ **LOOK BACK**

What other strategy could you use?

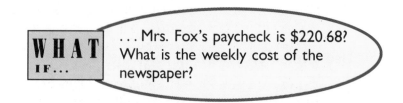

WHAT IF... ... Mrs. Fox's paycheck is $220.68? What is the weekly cost of the newspaper?

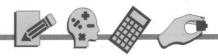
Apply

Make a flowchart and *work backward.* Solve.

(1) Ben spent $6.00 for school supplies. He spent $3.00 for a notebook and $1.75 for a pen. How much did he spend for other supplies?

(2) Carol spent a total of $20.00. She spent $9.45 for tickets, $5.95 for food, and the rest for 2 rings that were on sale at 2 for the price of 1. How much did each ring cost?

Mixed Applications ⟹	STRATEGIES

Guess and Check • Find a Pattern • Write a Number Sentence • Work Backward

Choose a strategy and solve.

(3) If the change from a gift purchase was $3.90 and each of 6 students had donated an equal amount, how much change should each student receive?

(4) A school has computer lab networks for 4 students and networks for 3 students. If 3 networks hold a total of 10 students, how many 3-student networks are there?

(5) Everett has a total of 30 problems for homework. If there are 6 more addition problems than subtraction problems, how many addition problems are there?

(6) While working at the school store, Julie sold a jacket for $39.95 and notebooks for $1.39 each. If she collected $109.45, how many notebooks did she sell?

(7) A school cafeteria sold 1,280 slices of pizza the first week, 640 the second, and 320 the third. If this pattern continues, in what week will the cafeteria sell 40 slices?

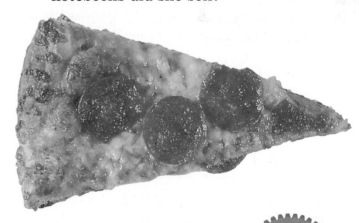

(8) At the school store, Yolanda collected $0.85, $1.25, $2.10, and $1.10. She gave $0.25, $0.05, and $0.15 in change. She has $19.85 in the cash box. How much cash was in the box when Yolanda started?

WRITER'S CORNER

(9) Students in a science class will expose 35 plants to different environments. Some plants will be kept in natural light, some will be exposed to artificial light, and others will be kept in the dark. Use this situation to write a word problem. Solve the problem and explain the strategy you used.

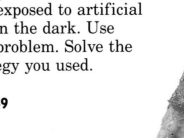

More Practice, Lesson 4.15, page H49

Vocabulary Check

Choose a word from the box to complete each sentence.

> compatible
> divisible
> divisor
> expression
> quotient
> remainder

I read the words in the box before I read the vocabulary sentences.

1. The number of times a _?_ divides the dividend is called the _?_. *(page 96)*

2. Numbers used to estimate that divide without a remainder and are close to the actual numbers are called _?_ numbers. *(page 98)*

3. The _?_ must be less than the divisor. *(page 102)*

4. $\frac{n}{4}$ is an example of an algebraic _?_. *(page 122)*

5. A number is _?_ by another number if the quotient is a whole number and the remainder is zero. *(page 96)*

Concept Check

6. You can use the inverse operation, _?_, to check your answer to a division problem. *(page 100)*

7. Since 4.1 and 4.10 are _?_, you can place zeros to the right of the decimal without changing the value of the number. *(page 112)*

8. When you write an algebraic expression, you can write _?_ for 4 times *n*. *(page 122)*

9. To solve a multiplication equation, you _?_ each side of the equation by the _?_ number. *(page 124)*

Estimate. Choose the correct number of digits in the quotient. *(page 100)*

10. $12\overline{)1,945}$
    a. 1 digit
    b. 2 digits
    c. 3 digits

11. $3\overline{)12,540}$
    a. 3 digits
    b. 4 digits
    c. 5 digits

12. $25\overline{)53,760}$
    a. 4 digits
    b. 3 digits
    c. 2 digits

13. $173\overline{)945}$
    a. 3 digits
    b. 2 digits
    c. 1 digit

14. $965\overline{)492,906}$
    a. 4 digits
    b. 3 digits
    c. 2 digits

Complete the pattern. *(page 114)*

15. $4.707 \times 1,000 = 4,707$
    $4.707 \times 100 = \blacksquare$
    $4.707 \times 10 = \blacksquare$

16. $543 \div 1,000 = 0.543$
    $543 \div 100 = \blacksquare$
    $543 \div 10 = \blacksquare$

17. $8,505 \div 10 = 850.5$
    $8,505 \div 100 = \blacksquare$
    $8,505 \div 1,000 = \blacksquare$

Skill Check

Determine whether the number is divisible by 2, 3, 5, 9, or 10. Write all that apply. *(page 96)*

18. 790   **19.** 1,845   **20.** 2,499   **21.** 4,986

Estimate the quotient. *(page 98)*

22. $547 \div 9$ **23.** $267 \div 91$ **24.** $3,303 \div 16$ **25.** $48,139 \div 71$

Find the quotient. *(pages 100, 102, 106, 110, 116, 118)*

26. $12,611 \div 4$ **27.** $52,836 \div 34$ **28.** $965.25 \div 5$ **29.** $649.2 \div 0.03$

Find the quotient. Round to the place given. *(page 120)*

30. $215.09 \div 89$ (tenths)   **31.** $\$27.15 \div 4.9$ (cents)   **32.** $4,561 \div 6.7$ (hundredths)   **33.** $3.819 \div 6.2$ (thousandths)

Evaluate the expression. *(page 122)*

34. $\dfrac{d}{6}$, for $d = 90$ **35.** $9x$, for $x = 12$ **36.** $\dfrac{n}{5.3}$, for $n = 42.4$

Tell how to solve the equation. *(page 124)*

37. $2x = 10$ **38.** $\dfrac{w}{4} = 36$ **39.** $6d = 844$ **40.** $\dfrac{y}{24} = 35$

Problem-Solving Check *(pages 104, 126)*

41. Jim needs to pick up 213 band uniforms and 27 band capes from the dry cleaner. If each item costs $5.20 to clean, what will be Jim's total bill?

42. Tanya has misplaced 62 of a total of 437 booster club notices. How many classrooms of 25 students can receive copies of the notice?

43. Band boosters collected $187.50 by selling T-shirts for $6.00 each and hats for $4.50 each. If 15 students picked up their shirts and 15 students picked up their hats, how many students must still pick up items?

44. Nina spent $25.00 at the school bookstore. She has $3.54 left after buying 5 pencils for $0.20 each, 2 pens for $1.98 each, 2 notebooks for $3.50 each, and a novel. How much did the novel cost?

1. Explain how to determine whether 420 is divisible by 2, 3, 5, 9, and 10. Then determine the divisibility.

2. Estimate $7,178 \div 8$. Explain your method.

3. Find the quotient $892 \div 41$. Show your work.

4. Find the quotient $3.9 \div 0.15$. Show your work.

5. Explain how to evaluate $6a$ for $a = 4$. Then evaluate the expression.

6. Read Exercise 2 on page 127. Follow the steps on the Problem-Solving Think Along worksheet to show how to solve this problem.

Write About It

7. Describe a situation, other than in school, when dividing whole numbers and decimals could be useful to you.

8. Explain why the solution for b in the following equation is or is not correct:
$$4b = 20$$
$$b = 80$$

TEAMWORK Project

Science Connection

There are nine planets in the solar system. Each planet takes a different length of time to go around the sun once. The table shows how many of the earth's days it takes each planet to go around the sun one time.

Your team's goal is to find how many Earth years it takes each planet to go around the sun once. For this activity, let one Earth year equal exactly 365 days.

Planet	Days to Go Around the Sun once	Earth Years to Go Around the Sun Once
Mercury	87.6 days	■
Venus	222.7 days	■
Earth	365.0 days	■
Mars	693.5 days	■
Jupiter	4,343.5 days	■
Saturn	10,767.5 days	■
Uranus	30,660.0 days	■
Neptune	60,152.0 days	■
Pluto	90,702.5 days	■

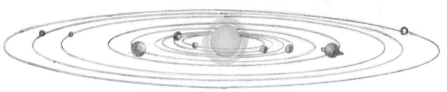

Decide

Discuss how you should go about solving the problem. Divide the calculations among yourselves. Each team member should do at least one calculation.

Do

Use your calculations to complete the table. Check your work carefully.

Share

Compare your team's calculations with those of another team.

Talk About It

What conclusions can you draw about the relationship between the distance of a planet from the sun and the amount of time it takes the planet to go around the sun once?

Consumer Connection

Many organizations, including some schools, allow people to buy season tickets to sporting events at a discounted rate. For example, a professional basketball organization might sell tickets to individual games for $8.00 but offer season tickets to 81 games for $599.40. If you bought a season ticket, how much would a single game cost?

How much would you save per ticket compared with the single-ticket price?

How much would you save by buying season tickets if you went to every game?

Find an organization in your community or school that offers season tickets. Find out how much the season tickets cost and how much tickets to single events cost. How much does each event cost at season-ticket prices? How much can you save by buying season tickets?

Challenge

Number Puzzle

Find a number that is divisible by all of these numbers:

4, 7, 5, 8, 2, and 10.

Critical Thinking

In a New England harbor, the water level at high tide is 36.8 feet. At low tide, the water level is 24.3 feet. It takes the tide 6 hours to go out. The water level drops steadily, going down the same amount each hour. To the nearest tenth, how far does the water drop in 2 hours?

Write the letter of the correct answer.

1. $112 - 70 \div 5$

   A. 37   **B.** 98
   C. 99   **D.** not here

2. What is the value of 10^5?

   A. 1,000   **B.** 10,000
   C. 100,000   **D.** 1,000,000

3. Choose the best estimate.
   $9.257 - 2.81$

   A. 5   **B.** 6
   C. 7.6   **D.** 8

4. $2,463.88 + 712.49$

   A. 3,175.37   **B.** 3,176.37
   C. 3,276.37   **D.** not here

5. Evaluate $b + 21$, for $b = 5.4$.

   A. 15.6   **B.** 25.4
   C. 26.4   **D.** 113.4

6. Choose the best estimate.
   $4,263 \times 18.81$

   A. 75,600   **B.** 76,000
   C. 76,600   **D.** 80,000

7. 35.4×0.086

   A. 2.9444   **B.** 3.0444
   C. 3.1444   **D.** 30.144

8. Choose the best estimate.
   $67.84 \div 8.29$

   A. 7   **B.** 8
   C. 9.5   **D.** 80

9. $9.54 \div 11.25$

   A. 0.0085   **B.** 0.795
   C. 0.848   **D.** 1.179

10. Evaluate $c \div 32$, for $c = 5.1$.

   A. 0.016   **B.** 1.59
   C. 159   **D.** not here

11. Jackie took $6.35 to buy a $1.20 sandwich, a $0.79 muffin, and an $0.80 apple juice. She also bought 2 pencils. If Jackie had $3.06 left, how much did each pencil cost?

   A. $0.25   **B.** $0.50
   C. $1.00   **D.** $1.50

12. Jeremy practices band 4 times a week for 90 minutes each time and for 75 minutes on Friday. If he missed 60 minutes on Wednesday, how many minutes did he practice that week?

   A. 300 minutes   **B.** 375 minutes
   C. 405 minutes   **D.** 435 minutes

GRAPHING, STATISTICS, AND PROBABILITY

Did you know...

... that an opinion poll is a popular way to find out how people feel about important issues?

TALK ABOUT IT

Take an opinion poll in your class. Ask a question of your choice. Record and display your poll results, and share your results with your classmates.

COLLECTING AND ORGANIZING DATA

Statistics is a branch of mathematics dealing with the collection, organization, display, and analysis of data.

Mike and Ann are counting election votes. Mike reads the ballots and Ann writes the names, but Ann cannot keep up. What can Ann do to record the data quickly and easily?

The type of facts you want affects how you collect data.

- To collect data to record for an interview, which often requires long answers, use a questionnaire.

- To collect data to record for an opinion poll, which usually requires short answers, use a tally sheet.

Since Ann is recording votes, which are short answers, she can use a tally sheet.

Ann lists the names in alphabetical order on a **tally sheet.** She tallies the votes. Then Mike organizes the information in a frequency table, listing the candidates in order by the number of votes they received.

Tally Sheet

James	Juan	Kris	Teri
⊮ ⊮	⊮ ⊮ ⊮ ⊮	⊮ ⊮ ⊮ ⊮ ⊮ ⊮ ///	⊮ ///

Frequency Table

Name	Frequency of Votes
Kris	33
Juan	20
James	10
Teri	8

- In which display are the election results easier to read?

Check for Understanding

1. Why did Ann use alphabetical order on the tally sheet?

2. Why did Mike use numerical order in the frequency table?

3. List three situations in which you would use a tally sheet to collect data for a table.

4. List three situations in which you would use a questionnaire to collect data for an interview.

  Idea Bank, pages 490–491, Exercises 7, 9–12, 14

Practice

Tell how to collect or organize the data.

5. Julio will interview a rock star about her career. Should he use a questionnaire or a tally sheet to gather information about the star? Explain your answer.

6. There are columns labeled *yes* and *no* on a tally sheet. Down the left side are names of several brands of cereal. For what might this tally sheet be used?

Suppose you are making a tally sheet and a frequency table. Use the data in the box for Exercises 7–13.

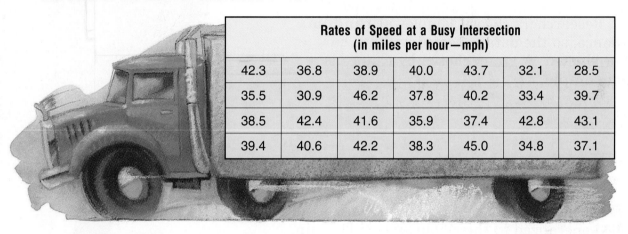

Rates of Speed at a Busy Intersection (in miles per hour—mph)						
42.3	36.8	38.9	40.0	43.7	32.1	28.5
35.5	30.9	46.2	37.8	40.2	33.4	39.7
38.5	42.4	41.6	35.9	37.4	42.8	43.1
39.4	40.6	42.2	38.3	45.0	34.8	37.1

7. Will you write each rate of speed or group the speeds, such as 25 to 30 mph, on your tally sheet? Justify your choice.

8. Will you use decimals or whole numbers to record the rates of speed on your tally sheet? Explain.

9. What will be the lowest rate of speed on your tally sheet?

10. What will be the highest rate of speed on your tally sheet?

11. How will you organize the rates of speed in your frequency table? Explain your answer.

12. Will the number of cars traveling from 40 to 45 mph be easier to find on the tally sheet or in the table?

13. Make a tally sheet for the data in the box. Record the data. Then make a frequency table to organize the data.

Mixed Applications

14. **Find Data** Think of several ways your classmates spend their allowance. Write three questions about spending an allowance. Use a questionnaire to interview at least five classmates.

15. **Organize Data** Use an almanac to find the populations of your state and your surrounding states. Make a table to display the data.

What is a frequency table?

CHOOSING SAMPLES

About 1,000 students attend Blair School. Jon surveyed 100 students by polling 1 out of every 10 as they entered school. He asked whether the student preferred the eagle or the bobcat as the school mascot. Thirty students chose the eagle, and seventy chose the bobcat.

WHICH DO YOU PREFER?

Although the number may vary, people chosen to represent a population or group are called a **sample.** Researchers choose samples at **random,** or by chance, so the data collected will not be biased or slanted. A group chosen by chance is a **random sample.**

Talk About It

▶ What is another method Jon could use to choose a random sample of students?

▶ Do you think the data collected from Jon's sample can be generalized to the whole school? Explain.

▶ If Jon asked the same question of teachers, would his results represent the students? Explain.

▶ If Jon chose to survey only sixth graders, would his results represent the whole school population? Why or why not?

▶ Suppose Jon wanted the eagle to be chosen. If he surveyed only students he knew would vote for the eagle, would his survey represent the whole school population? Explain.

Check for Understanding

Suppose you will survey 1 person out of every 10 for a sample. Tell about how many of each group you will survey.

1. 83 shoppers   2. 521 students   3. 2,987 drivers   4. 326 teachers

Name the people to survey for opinions about each product.

5. diapers   6. dog food   7. chalkboards   8. cereal

Practice

Answer the questions. Give reasons for your answers.

19 out of 20 Voters
SUPPORT
MAYOR ALLEN

Moms!
4 out of 5 kids
prefer

Oatem Cereal

9. Volunteers called 200 voters (1 out of every 10 from a voters' list) to get the data about Mayor Allen's supporters. Is this a random sample? Is the sample large enough for the claim?

10. This billboard advertisement for Oatem cereal is based on a random sample of ten children living in the same block in Dallas, Texas. Is the sample large enough to represent all children?

11. Fay surveys 100 people in a town of 500 and determines that 0.85 of them like to shop at Gee's Grocery. Can Fay claim that 85 out of 100 townspeople like to shop at Gee's?

12. A local radio station polls its audience on issues in the local news. Listeners call in to vote *yes* or *no*. Are the results of these polls representative of all radio listeners?

CONSUMER CONNECTION

Advertisers hope that a consumer will buy what others are buying. A common advertising strategy is to say, "Everyone is buying this soap."

With a team of classmates, discuss the following advertising claims. Are you convinced the product is popular? How specific are the words that tell how many people use the product? Is its popularity a good reason to buy the product? Share your results with other teams.

13. Two out of three people surveyed chose Plastotech toothpaste. Shouldn't you?

14. More and more people are turning to Painfree for headache relief. Shouldn't you get some today?

15. The best athletes and those champions who know quality buy XYZ running shoes.

16. Comfy jeans are the choice of everyone, young and old, who wants to look and feel good.

If you ask twelve boys their opinion, will your results be representative of your class? Explain.

WRAP
UP...

MAKING PICTOGRAPHS AND BAR GRAPHS

Ann and Mike will make graphs of the election results to display on two bulletin boards. What kinds of graphs are appropriate?

The kind of graph you make depends on the type of data you want to show.

To display	You can use	Advantages and Disadvantages
a comparison of data	a bar graph or a pictograph	← can show specific data ← makes an attractive display; difficult to show specific data

Since Ann and Mike will show a comparison of votes, either a bar graph or a pictograph is appropriate.

To make their graphs, both Mike and Ann will follow these guidelines.

• Title the graph.

• Label the vertical axis (from base to top).

• Label the horizontal axis (from left to right).

• In a pictograph, use a key to show the symbol and its value.

• In a bar graph, use bars of equal width.

• In a bar graph, use equal space between bars.

• Use an appropriate numerical scale with equal intervals.

Mike and Ann know that the numerical scale of a graph begins with 0, but they are puzzled by the guideline "Use an appropriate numerical scale with equal intervals." How can Mike and Ann choose an appropriate numerical scale?

A scale that uses the numbers 0, 10, 20, and 30 is a scale with equal intervals. The intervals 0 to 9, 10 to 19, and 20 to 29 contain the same range of numbers. An appropriate scale is one that fits on the page without being too small. An appropriate scale is also one that shows the data without distorting it.

Talk About It

▶ What is the greatest number in Ann and Mike's frequency table?

▶ What is the least number in Ann and Mike's data?

▶ If Ann and Mike use a scale that counts by 2's, how many intervals will they have on their graphs?

▶ If Ann and Mike use a scale that counts by 10's, how many intervals will they have on their graphs?

▶ Which numerical scale will be easier to read, one with intervals of 2 or one with intervals of 10?

▶ Name a numerical scale with equal intervals that you think is appropriate to use to graph this data.

Frequency Table	
Name	*Frequency of Votes*
Kris	33
Juan	20
James	10
Teri	8

Mike and Ann decide to use a scale that counts by 5's: 0, 5, 10, 15, 20, 25, 30, and 35.

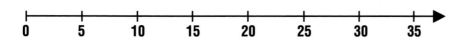

▶ Why did Mike and Ann not stop their scale at 30?

▶ Suppose the greatest number in the data is 30. Should the greatest number of the scale be 30 or 35? Justify your answer.

▶ Suppose the smallest number in the data is 5. How will this affect the scale?

Mike decides to make a pictograph, and Ann decides to make a bar graph.

Mike's Pictograph Guidelines

a. Title the graph.
b. Label the axes.
c. Use a key to show the symbol and its value.
d. Round the numbers in the data as needed.

Ann's Bar-Graph Guidelines

a. Title the graph.
b. Label the axes.
c. Use an appropriate numerical scale with equal intervals.
d. Use equal-width bars.
e. Use equal space between bars.

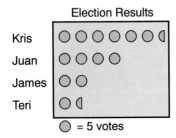

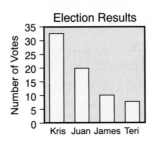

- In which graph is it easier to tell the exact number of votes?

- Which graph do you think is more attractive?

Check for Understanding

Tell how to label the axes to make each graph.

1. favorite television shows

2. rainfall in four cities

3. school enrollment by grade level

4. speeds of 5 fastest cars

Tell what is wrong with each graph.

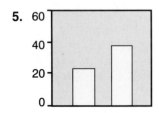

5.

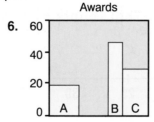

6. Awards

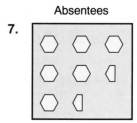

7. Absentees

Write an appropriate numerical scale with equal intervals for each collection of data.

8. 22, 15, 7, 12, 27

9. 86, 15, 25, 45, 30

10. 290, 100, 350, 500, 760

11. 50, 300, 100, 250, 450

Practice

For Exercises 12–13, tell which type of graph is appropriate for displaying the data.

12. Sam is collecting data about the populations of four major United States cities.

13. Rachel is collecting data about the number of large cars bought in a ten-year period.

14. Make a list of guidelines to use when making a bar graph.

15. Choose the data in *A, B,* or *C.* Make a bar graph.

A. Students' Heights

Name	Height (inches)
Kim	32
Joe	37
Mary	41
Lee	47
Carol	55
Babs	63

B. Value of Common Stocks

Name of Company	Current Value
BF&F	$100.00
ABT	$121.00
XYZ Co.	$146.41
Nu-Lite	$177.16
Hi-Si	$214.36
I-Qu	$159.37

C. U.S. Population

Year	Population (millions)
1820	9.6
1850	23.2
1880	50.2
1910	92.2
1940	132.2
1970	203.3

16. Choose the data in *A, B,* or *C.* Make a pictograph.

A. Punt Contest

Name	Distance (feet)
John	32
Jaime	37
Mac	43
Frank	46
Quan	47

B. Public Libraries

City	Volumes (millions)
Queens, NY	5.5
Portland, OR	4.0
Miami, FL	2.4
Dallas, TX	1.8

C. Currency in Circulation

Denomination	Value (billions)
$1	$ 4.8
$5	$ 5.9
$10	$11.7
$20	$65.9
$50	$33.6

17. Choose one of the two collections of data that you did not use to make a pictograph in Exercise 16. Choose the symbol you would use to make a pictograph of the data.

Mixed Applications

18. Organize Data Make a bar graph to display the scores you made on your last three math quizzes or math tests.

19. Make Up a Problem Write a problem that can be solved using one collection of data from Exercise 15 or 16.

Which graph can show more exact information, or a pictograph?

W R A P
U P . . .

RELATING BAR GRAPHS AND HISTOGRAMS

A **bar graph** is used to compare data. A **histogram** is a bar graph that shows the number of times data occurs within a certain range or interval.

Bar Graph

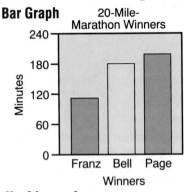

Histogram

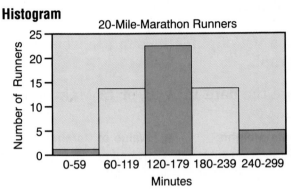

Talk About It

▶ How does what is shown in the bar graph differ from what is shown in the histogram?

▶ How do the bars in the bar graph compare with the bars in the histogram?

▶ In which graph do you find information about individual runners?

▶ Which graph gives more information about the marathon in general?

▶ During which range of time did the most runners finish?

▶ From which graph can you determine the number of runners who finished in 120–179 minutes?

▶ How does the winning time shown in the bar graph compare with that shown in the histogram?

Check for Understanding

Discuss how to display the data. Decide on a bar graph or a histogram.

1. favorite foods

2. shoe sizes

3. birthdays

4. class enrollments

5. favorite sports

6. daily activities

Practice

Tell whether a bar graph or a histogram is more appropriate for Exercises 7–8. Explain your answer.

7. Charmaine is collecting data about the number of people who vote at a polling place from 7:00 A.M. to 7:00 P.M.

8. Todd is collecting data about the number of boys and girls enrolled in five programs at a summer camp.

9. Choose the data in *A, B,* or *C.* Make a bar graph.

A. NBA's Most Valuable Players

Name	Number of Years
Abdul-Jabbar	6
Bird	3
Johnson	3
Jordan	2
Malone	3

B. Tall Buildings in the United States

Name	Height (feet)
Sears Tower	1,454
World Trade Center	1,350
Amoco	1,136
J. Hancock Center	1,127
Chrysler	1,046

C. Largest Freshwater Bass in the World

Type of Bass	Weight (ounces)
Peacock	424
Whiterock	358
Largemouth	356
Smallmouth	191
Redeye	131

10. Choose the data in *A, B,* or *C.* Make a histogram.

A. Speeds of Animals

Animal	Speed (mph)
Cheetah	70
Lion	50
Coyote	43
Greyhound	39.35
Human	27.89

B. Number of Voters

Time of Day	Number
7–8:59 A.M.	321
9–10:59 A.M.	97
11:00 A.M.–12:59 P.M.	298
1–2:59 P.M.	84
3–4:59 P.M.	315
5–6:59 P.M.	534

C. Television Reception

Number of Stations	Percent of Homes
1–4	3
5–8	23
9–12	35
13–16	24
17 or more	11

Mixed Applications

11. Write a Question Make up a question that can be answered by using the information in the double-bar graph.

12. Number Sense • Mental Math How many sixth graders attend Shoreline Middle School?

13. What is the mean of the sixth-grade class?

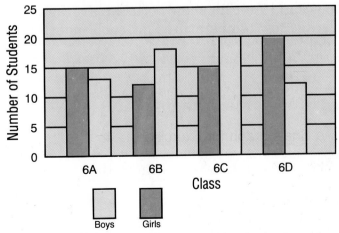

Sixth Graders at Shoreline Middle School

How do the bars in a histogram differ from those in a bar graph?

W R A P
U P...

More Practice, Lesson 5.4, page H51

145

MAKING LINE GRAPHS

Ae-Cha is making a graph to show the average temperature where her grandparents live, in Seoul, South Korea.

Since Ae-Cha wants to show changes over time, she chooses a **line graph.**

Ae-Cha uses the same guidelines for making her line graph that Ann used for making a bar graph, except Ae-Cha will draw lines. Ae-Cha marks a point on the graph to indicate the average temperature for each month. Then she connects the points with straight lines.

MULTICULTURAL NOTE: Most of Korea has a humid climate. The subtropical climate of South Korea allows farmers to plant rice in the summer and other grains in the winter.

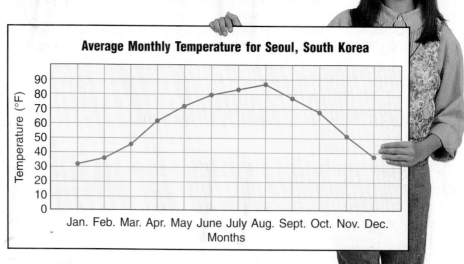

Average Monthly Temperature for Seoul, South Korea

Talk About It

▶ Predict the months in which Seoul might have some snow.

▶ How could Ae-Cha show both the average high and the average low temperatures for each month on the same graph?

Check for Understanding

Use Ae-Cha's graph for Exercises 1–4.

1. What information is shown on the horizontal axis?

2. What information is shown on the vertical axis?

3. How could you find the average temperature for the year?

4. Which two months have approximately the same average temperature?

Practice

Tell whether a line graph or a bar graph is more appropriate.

5. George is collecting data about high tides at the Bay of Fundy during the month of April.

6. Lily is collecting data about the number of people who attend local rock concerts.

7. Choose the data in *A*, *B*, or *C*. Make a line graph. Round the numbers to a convenient place.

A. Humidity in Chicago

Month	Relative Humidity (%)
August	57
September	58
October	56
November	64
December	70

B. Matt's Bank Balance

Month	Amount in Bank
March	$ 578.98
May	$1,245.65
July	$2,077.25
September	$ 895.37
November	$1,003.67

C. Population of St. Louis

Year	Population
1950	856,796
1960	750,026
1970	622,236
1980	453,085
1990	396,685

8. Make a double-line graph. Choose the data in *A*, *B*, or *C* that corresponds to the data you chose in Exercise 7. Use a different color to display this data in the graph you made. Revise the title of your graph.

A. Humidity in Miami

Month	Relative Humidity (%)
August	65
September	67
October	64
November	62
December	60

B. Jan's Bank Balance

Month	Amount in Bank
March	$1,954.35
May	$ 552.24
July	$ 857.85
September	$ 654.99
November	$1,201.44

C. Population of Phoenix

Year	Population
1950	106,818
1960	439,170
1970	584,303
1980	789,704
1990	983,403

CHALLENGE • VISUAL THINKING

9. Use the graph you made in Exercise 7. Write a question that can be answered by using subtraction to compare the data in your graph.

10. Use the graph you made in Exercise 8. Write three questions that can be answered by comparing the data in your graph.

How can you decide whether to use a bar graph or a line graph?

WRAP UP...

USING AND MAKING CIRCLE GRAPHS

A **circle graph** shows the parts of a whole and the relationships among the parts.

The table shows Greg's weekday activities. How can he make a circle graph to display the data for his home economics class?

The circle with dashed lines can be used as a pattern for a circle graph in which the whole has 24 equal parts. Each section represents one hour.

Greg traces the pattern. He marks and labels sections to represent the activities. Then he titles the graph.

Greg's Weekday Activities	
Activity	**Number of Hours**
Sleep	8
School	7
Recreation	5
Meals	2
Homework	1
Other	1

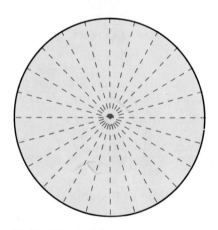

Greg's Weekday Activities

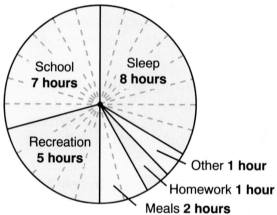

Talk About It

▶ How many more hours does Greg spend attending school and doing homework than sleeping?

▶ How might the graph differ if it showed only Greg's Saturday activities?

▶ If you were asked to make a graph showing Greg's activities during school, would you use this same circle pattern? Why or why not?

Check for Understanding

Tell into how many sections to divide a circle to graph these parts.

1. months in a year **2.** primary colors **3.** $1.00 **4.** a dozen

Practice

Use the graph for Exercises 5–7.

5. Does the graph show that more teenagers prefer to watch informational programs or general drama?

6. Does the graph show that more teenagers prefer to watch situation comedies or feature films?

7. What two types of programs appear to be equally liked by teenagers?

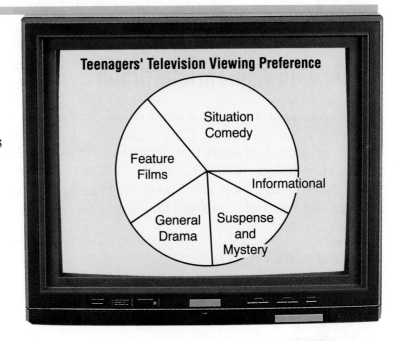

8. Make a table like the one on page 148 to show how you spend your time during a weekday.

9. Use the table you made in Exercise 8. Trace the pattern for a circle graph on page 148. Make a circle graph to display the data about your activities.

10. Choose the data in *A, B,* or *C.* Trace the pattern for a circle graph on page 148. Make a circle graph to display the data.

A. Favorite Colors	
Color	Number of Students
Red	6
Blue	7
Yellow	4
Green	2
Purple	3
Orange	2

B. Favorite Flavors	
Flavor	Number of Students
Vanilla	5
Chocolate	6
Strawberry	5
Peach	2
Pecan	4
Banana	2

C. Sue's Budgeted Expenses	
Item	Amount Spent
Food	$400
Clothing	$100
Rent	$800
Utilities	$200
Car	$400
Savings	$500

Mixed Applications

11. **Write a Question**   Write a question that can be answered by using the *guess and check* or the *work backward* strategy. You may want to use the information in the circle graph you made in Exercise 10.

12. **Making Decisions**   Look at the graph at the top of the page. Suppose you want to advertise to attract teenage buyers. Which type of program would you want to sponsor? Explain your choice.

How can you decide whether to use a line graph or a circle graph?

PROBLEM SOLVING

Choose an Appropriate Graph

Zimbabwe exports great quantities of gold, nickel, and cotton. For a social studies project, Chuma gathered this information about the growth of exports in Zimbabwe: 1984, $1.45 billion; 1985, $1.54 billion; 1986, $2.2 billion; 1987, $1.89 billion; 1988, $2.86 billion. How can Chuma organize and display the data so that other students will find it easy to read and will see the changes?

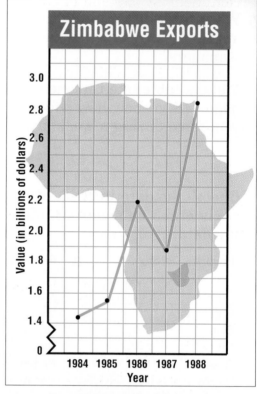

▶ **UNDERSTAND**

What are you asked to do?

What information is given?

▶ **PLAN**

How can you solve the problem? You can organize the data by year and use a graph to display the data.

▶ **SOLVE**

How can you carry out your plan? Choose an appropriate type of graph. Since you will be showing changes in the values of exports over time, you can make a line graph. Organize the data by year.

1. Label the axes, with years on one axis and billions of dollars on the other.

2. Plot the points.

3. Draw lines connecting the points.

4. Title the graph.

▶ **LOOK BACK**

Is the solution reasonable? Explain.

MULTICULTURAL NOTE: Zimbabwe (zihm · BAH · bway) is a country in southern Africa. Gold has been an important part of its economy since the eighth century, when the people of the area traded gold for porcelain and other luxuries with China and India.

WHAT IF... ... you want to display the changes in the values of the exports, in order from the highest to the lowest? What type of graph would you use?

Apply

Make a table or a graph to organize each set of data so that it is easy to read and compare.

1 A newspaper reported this data about businesses that have complied with a new law: By the end of June, 45 businesses had complied. By the end of July, 70 had complied. By the end of August, 120 had complied. By the end of September, 150 had complied. By the end of October, 170 had complied.

2 A group of scientists published a report about bird migration. They caught birds in a net, counted the number of different species, and then released them. They counted birds once a day beginning on March 24. They counted 16, 20, 22, 24, 28, 26, 24, 22, 18, 12, 10, and 10 different species.

Mixed Applications ⟹ **STRATEGIES** Make a Table • Work Backward • Write a Number Sentence • Find a Pattern

Choose a strategy and solve.

3 Nick buys two different nature magazines. The total cost for both is $18.00. The difference in the costs of the magazines is $2.50. How much does each of the magazines cost?

4 Lisa collects postcards. In May she bought 3. Her aunt gave her 5. Lisa traded 2 of hers for 3 of Betty's. If Lisa has 45 postcards now, how many did she have at the beginning of May?

5 Julie began her newspaper route with 12 customers. After 2 months she gained 5 more. After 2 more months, Julie had 22 customers. At this rate, how many customers can Julie expect to have on her route after 6 more months?

6 A newspaper reported the capture of a pet boa constrictor that had been lost in an apartment building. If the pet boa is 0.75 as long as a 24-foot boa (the largest boa ever captured), how long is the pet boa?

WRITER'S CORNER

7 Take a survey of students entering the cafeteria. Ask each to name his or her favorite beverage, salad, entree, or dessert. Use the results of your survey to write an advertisement for the cafeteria.

More Practice, Lesson 5.7, page H51

1. A newspaper reported that 34 people were running for four local offices. A total of 7 were running for manager, 3 for secretary, and 6 for treasurer. If 2 candidates for commissioner dropped out of the race, how many people were running for commissioner?

2. A town council printed 1,045 ballots for three precincts. In the first precinct, 282 people voted. In the second precinct, 309 people voted. A total of 148 ballots were returned blank. How many votes should a news broadcaster report for the third precinct?

To answer Exercises 1 and 2, I must answer the hidden question.

3. If you were going to record data from an interview, would you use a questionnaire or a tally sheet? Defend your answer.

Tell whether a bar graph or a line graph is more appropriate.

4. most-popular household pets

5. change in car prices over 5 years

Find the quotient. Round your answer to the nearest hundredth.

6. $95.71 \div 5$

7. $52 \div 3.4$

8. $533.24 \div 7.1$

9. $1.9527 \div 40.8$

Evaluate the expression.

10. $\dfrac{k}{11}$, for $k = 55$

11. $5.2x$, for $x = 8.1$

12. $12.5y$, for $y = 7$

13. $\dfrac{c}{2.5}$, for $c = 15.9$

14. $30.3a$, for $a = 2.7$

15. $\dfrac{b}{15}$, for $b = 63$

Use the histogram for Exercises 16–19.

16. How many flights does Midstate have between 6:00 A.M. and noon?

17. How many more flights are there from 8:00–8:59 A.M. than from 6:00–6:59 A.M.?

18. For which flight times are the most tickets available for purchase?

19. For which flight times are the fewest tickets available for purchase?

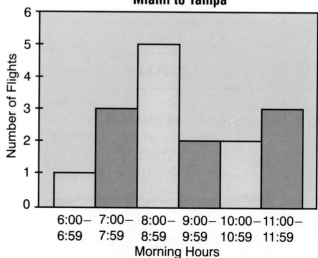

**Midstate Flight Schedule
Miami to Tampa**

Number of Flights vs *Morning Hours* (6:00–6:59, 7:00–7:59, 8:00–8:59, 9:00–9:59, 10:00–10:59, 11:00–11:59)

Different Styles of Graphs

England — EUROPE

People all over the world use graphs to display data. Sometimes a graph from a different country may not look like the graphs you are used to seeing.

Stan lives in England. He plays rugby, a sport similar to football, for the Sheffield team. He wants to show the scores for this season's first ten games and the scores for last season's first ten games. He uses a double-line graph to show these two seasons. Stan sets up his graph like a graph he found in his hometown newspaper.

MULTICULTURAL NOTE: Rugby originated at a school called Rugby in Rugby, England. The idea for this game came from students playing intramural soccer.

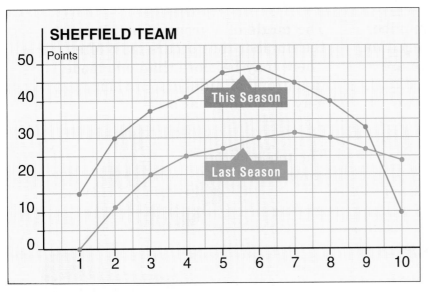

SHEFFIELD TEAM

Points

This Season

Last Season

Use Stan's graph to answer the questions.

1. Why do you think Stan used a double-line graph?

2. How is this graph different from the graph on page 150?

3. What do the numbers on the horizontal axis represent? How do you know?

4. In which season did Stan's team score more points? Explain.

RANGE, MEAN, MEDIAN, AND MODE

Suppose judges gave a figure skater these scores.

7.9   8.0   8.2   7.9

- If you were the skater's parent, which score might you want to report?

- If you were the skater's opponent, which score might you want to report?

- Describe a fair way of reporting these scores.

Here are four ways to analyze and present data fairly.

The **range** of a group of numbers is the difference between the greatest and least numbers. It measures the distance between extremes.

The range of the scores is
8.2 − 7.9 = 0.3

The **mean** is the average of a group of numbers, or the sum of the group divided by the number of addends in the group.

The mean of the scores is
(8.2 + 8.0 + 7.9 + 7.9) ÷ 4 = 8

The **median** is the middle number in a group of numbers arranged in numerical order. When there are two middle numbers, the median is the mean or average of the two middle numbers.

7.9   7.9   8.0   8.2
The median of the scores is
(8.0 + 7.9) ÷ 2 = 7.95.

The **mode** of a group of numbers is the number that occurs most often. There may be more than one mode in a group of numbers, or there may be no mode at all.

The mode of the scores is 7.9.

Check for Understanding

Use the table for Exercises 1–4.

1. Name the gymnast with the median score.

2. Find the mean. Round to the nearest hundredth.

3. What is the range of the scores?

4. What is the mode of the scores?

5. To the nearest hundredth, what is the mean of the three highest scores?

Team "A" Results	
Gymnast	**Score**
Jones	9.1
Dean	8.9
Moss	8.5
Ames	8.1
Keown	7.9
Hilton	6.8
Kent	6.2

Practice

Copy and complete the table.

	Collections of Data	Range	Mean	Median	Mode
6.	27, 27, 30, 85, 46	▦	▦	▦	▦
7.	78, 97, 93, 84, 98	▦	▦	▦	▦
8.	79, 95, 80, 66, 77, 77	▦	▦	▦	▦
9.	86, 95, 59, 74, 58, 83, 70	▦	▦	▦	▦
10.	80, 84, 76, 80, 94, 84, 97	▦	▦	▦	▦
11.	72, 65, 36, 57, 87, 97, 65, 57	▦	▦	▦	▦

Mixed Applications

12. At the *Daily Star,* 2 reporters earn $18,000 a year, 5 earn $22,000, and 3 earn $29,000. What is the mode of the salaries? What is the range?

13. A used-car company advertises 5 cars for sale at $6,212; $5,659; $6,365; $5,719; and $7,140. What is the average price of the used cars? What is the median price?

14. **Critical Thinking** The LCM of three numbers greater than 1 is 12. What are the numbers?

15. **Number Sense** The range of three numbers is 45. Both the mode and the median are 52. Name each of the three numbers.

MIXED REVIEW

Write whether you would use a tally sheet or a questionnaire to record the information.

1. a day in the life of an airline pilot

2. the number of customers who prefer Brand X to Brand Y

Write whether a bar graph, a line graph, a histogram, or a circle graph is most appropriate to display the data.

3. average monthly value of a corporate stock

4. number sold of the three most popular foreign cars

5. votes counted during 1:00–2:59 P.M., 3:00–4:59 P.M., and 5:00–6:59 P.M.

6. a budget showing how you spend your allowance

How do you find the mean of a set of data?

WRAP UP...

EXPLORING

Stem-and-Leaf Plot

Henry (Hank) L. Aaron played for 23 seasons, hitting the following number of home runs:

10	12	20	32	13	27	24	34
26	29	30	40	40	38	39	34
39	44	44	45	44	44	47	

A **stem-and-leaf plot** can be used to organize this set of data and show the distribution.

Hank's Home Runs in 23 Seasons

Stem	Leaves
1	0 2 3
2	0 4 6 7 9
3	0 2 4 4 8 9 9
4	0 0 4 4 4 4 5 7

Work Together

Building Understanding

Work with your teammates to order the data at the top of the page from least to greatest. Separate the data into groups that each have the same digit in the tens place.

TALK ABOUT IT

- Look at your first group of data and the first row of the stem-and-leaf plot. How are the two similar?

- What does the stem represent?

- What do the leaves represent?

- How many home runs are shown by the second stem and its first leaf?

- How many home runs are shown by the fourth stem and its seventh leaf?

Idea Bank, page 491, Exercise 13

Making the Connection

You can use the stem-and-leaf plot to find the range, median, and mode of the data on page 156.

Examples

A. What is the range of the data?

$$\boxed{\begin{array}{c}\text{last stem} \\ \text{and} \\ \text{last leaf}\end{array}} - \boxed{\begin{array}{c}\text{first stem} \\ \text{and} \\ \text{first leaf}\end{array}} = \text{range}$$

$$47 \quad - \quad 10 \quad = \quad 37$$

So, the range of the data is 37.

B. What is the median of the data?

Since there are 23 leaves, the twelfth leaf shows the median ($11 + 1 + 11 = 23$).

Count to the twelfth leaf. The twelfth leaf is 4. The stem is 3.

So, the median of the data is 34.

C. What is the mode of the data?

Find the leaf that is repeated most often for one stem. For the first and second stems, no leaves are repeated. For the third stem, both 4 and 9 appear twice. For the fourth stem, 0 appears twice and 4 appears four times.

So, the mode of the data is 44.

Checking Understanding

Rella's Scores for 20 Rounds of Golf

Stem	Leaves
7	6 7 8 9 9 9
8	0 2 3 5 5 6 8 9
9	0 0 1 2 3 8

1. What is the score shown by the second stem and its third leaf?

2. What are the scores shown by the third stem and its leaves?

3. Which number occurs more often, 80 or 90?

4. What is the mode of Rella's golf scores?

5. What is the median of Rella's golf scores?

6. What is the range of Rella's golf scores?

COUNTING PRINCIPLE

At the grand opening of McKool's Frozen Health Food Shoppe, Marcie can buy a large yogurt parfait for $1. She can choose from the selection of flavors and sauces in the table. How many choices does Marcie have?

One way to find the number of choices is to make a tree diagram that shows the total outcomes.

McKool's Yogurt and Sauce	
Yogurt Flavor	**Sauce**
Vanilla	Apple
Chocolate	Peach
	Blueberry

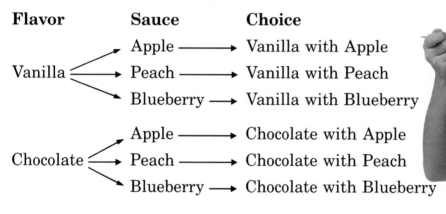

Flavor	Sauce	Choice
Vanilla	Apple	Vanilla with Apple
	Peach	Vanilla with Peach
	Blueberry	Vanilla with Blueberry
Chocolate	Apple	Chocolate with Apple
	Peach	Chocolate with Peach
	Blueberry	Chocolate with Blueberry

So, Marcie has 6 choices.

Another Method

You can also use the counting principle to find the total number of choices. When you use the **counting principle,** you multiply the total outcomes of one set of choices by the total outcomes of the other set of choices.

number of flavors × number of sauces = total choices

$$2 \times 3 = 6$$

Check for Understanding

Find the number of choices by making a tree diagram.

1.

Meat	Gravy
Ham	Redeye
	Mushroom

2.

Crust	Topping
Regular	Pepperoni
Deep-dish	Sausage
	Anchovies

3.

Entree	Beverage
Pizza	Milk
Noodles	Apple juice
Beans	Grape juice

Practice

Make a tree diagram to find the number of choices.

4.

Shoes	Socks
Brown	Argyle
	Black
	White

5.

Entree	Spice
Chicken	Curry
Beef	Mustard
	Garlic

6.

Ink	Paper
Green	Gray
Red	White
Black	

7.

Plate	Napkins
Flowered	Mauve
Checked	Taupe
Polka-dotted	Rust

8.

Shirt	Slacks
Blue	Striped
Red	Checked
Yellow	Plaid

9.

Buttons	Bows
Purple	Striped
Pink	
Chartreuse	

Write the number of choices.

10. 2 vegetables, 3 salads

11. 3 wigs, 5 hats

12. 4 soaps, 7 towels

13. 5 birthdays, 10 cards

14. 5 ink cartridges, 6 pens

15. 150 students, 5 teachers

16. 7 cards, 12 colors

17. 11 pencils, 25 erasers

Mixed Applications

18. Each of 5 airlines offers 3 flights each day from St. Louis to Indianapolis. June wants to take one flight. From how many can June choose?

19. Zed is registering for school. He can choose either English or science at 9:00 A.M. and either art, health, or math at 10:00 A.M. How many pairs of classes can Zed choose from?

20. Critical Thinking In a recent contest, Gary scored fewer points than Barb, who scored more points than Tina. Tim scored more points than Tina but fewer than Gary. Who won?

21. Make Up a Problem Think of a situation that involves choosing from several alternatives. Make up a problem about the total number of choices.

How can you find the number of choices without drawing a diagram?

More Practice, Lesson 5.10, page H52

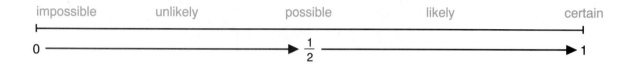

PROBABILITY

Probability (P) is a comparison between the number of favorable events or outcomes and the number of possible events or outcomes. The number line shows that the probability of an event ranges from 0, or impossible, to 1, or certain.

| impossible | unlikely | possible | likely | certain |

$0 \longrightarrow \frac{1}{2} \longrightarrow 1$

A spinner like this one is used on a television show. What is the probability that the spinner will stop on orange?

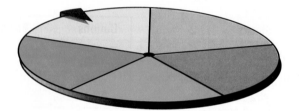

$$P(\text{orange}) = \frac{\text{number of favorable outcomes}}{\text{number of possible outcomes}} = \frac{1}{5}, \text{ or 1 out of 5}$$

The probability of spinning orange is $\frac{1}{5}$.

Since the outcomes are equally likely, the probability of stopping on any one color is $\frac{1}{5}$, or 1 out of 5.

- Are you more likely to stop on orange if 3 of 5 sections of a spinner are orange or if 1 of 5 sections are orange?

What is the probability of spinning either red or blue?

$$P(\text{red or blue}) = \frac{\text{number of favorable outcomes}}{\text{number of possible outcomes}} = \frac{2}{5}, \text{ or 2 out of 5}$$

So, the probability, P(red or blue), is $\frac{2}{5}$.

Check for Understanding

Use the spinner. Find the probability of each event.

1. stopping on red, blue, or yellow

2. not stopping on green

3. P(red or blue or green or yellow or orange)

4. P(purple, pink, or aqua)

Practice

For Exercises 5–10, think of a number cube labeled 2, 4, 6, 8, 10, and 12.

5. What is the probability of tossing an even number?

6. What is the probability of tossing an odd number?

7. What is the probability of tossing a number less than 8?

8. What is the probability of tossing a number greater than 2?

9. What is the probability of tossing a number greater than 4?

10. What is the probability of tossing 2?

Copy and complete the table.

	Experiment	Possible Outcome	Probabilities
11.	Toss a coin once.	heads or tails	P(heads) = ■ P(tails) = ■
12.	Toss a number cube with faces 1 to 6. 	■	P(odd number) = ■ P(even number) = ■ P(3 or 5) = ■
13.	Draw a marble from 3 green, 2 red, and 4 yellow marbles without looking.	■	P(yellow) = ■ P(red or yellow) = ■

Mixed Applications

14. Look at Exercise 13. Which color marble has the greatest probability of being drawn?

15. A coin shows heads five times in a row. What is the probability of heads on the next toss?

16. **Critical Thinking** The mean of five whole numbers is 16.8. What is the sum of the numbers?

17. **Analyze Data** Toss a coin ten times. Compare your results with the results in Exercise 11.

If you are given a choice of three answers to a problem, what is the probability of choosing the correct answer by chance?

WRAP UP...

INDEPENDENT EVENTS

Rosa cannot decide among program choices of comedy, drama, and mystery, so she writes the choices on slips of paper and puts them in a bag. Each time she draws a slip of paper, she returns it to the bag. If she has chosen *comedy* in 2 out of 4 draws, what is the probability she will draw *drama* next time?

Events that have no influence on one another are called **independent events.** Because Rosa always returns the slip of paper to the bag, she creates independent events. Since Rosa always has the same number of possible outcomes, drawing *comedy* does not affect the probability of drawing *drama*.

So, the probability of drawing *drama* is still $\frac{1}{3}$.

Rosa will choose from car and cereal commercials. She puts slips of paper in bags marked *programs* and *commercials*. What is the probability she will draw *car* for the commercial and *drama* for the program?

Commercial	Program	Possible Combination
	Comedy →	Car commercial, Comedy
Car	Drama →	Car commercial, Drama
	Mystery →	Car commercial, Mystery
	Comedy →	Cereal commercial, Comedy
Cereal	Drama →	Cereal commercial, Drama
	Mystery →	Cereal commercial, Mystery

So, the probability of choosing *car* and *drama* is $\frac{1}{6}$.

Check for Understanding

Use Rosa's choices of programs and commercials. Find the probability of each event.

1. drawing mystery program after drawing drama 2 times

2. drawing car commercial after drawing cereal 5 times

3. P(car commercial, comedy program)

4. P(car or cereal, comedy)

Practice

Use the situation described for Exercises 5–8.

Arthur will go to a theater to see a movie and have a snack. *Here With the Wind*, *The Tin Man*, and *Old Blue* are playing at the theater. Arthur's favorite snacks are popcorn, pizza, and burritos.

5. Make a tree diagram to show all of Arthur's possible choices.

6. What is the probability that Arthur will choose *Old Blue* and a burrito?

7. If Claire has the same choices as Arthur, what is the probability she will choose *Here With the Wind* and popcorn?

8. Suppose Claire can choose a fourth movie, *Field Trip*. What is the probability she will choose pizza and *The Tin Man*?

Mixed Applications

9. The weather reporter said the chance of rain is 1 out of 5 this morning. If it rains at 6:00 A.M., what is the probability of rain at 10:30 A.M. and 11:00 A.M.?

10. **Number Sense • Mental Math** Jeffrey must choose a three-piece outfit from 3 pairs of slacks, 4 shirts, and 2 jackets. How many choices does Jeffrey have?

MIXED REVIEW

Evaluate the algebraic expression.

1. $\frac{m}{12}$, for $m = 108$

2. $6.8b$, for $b = 3.5$

3. $35x$, for $x = 10$

Tell which operation you use to solve the equation.

4. $37y = 333$

5. $\frac{n}{62} = 186$

6. $5.9n = 82.6$

Draw a tree diagram to show the number of choices.

7. 1 problem, 4 answers

8. 3 shirts, 3 slacks

9. 4 cats, 5 dogs

If the probability of red is 1 out of 5, what will be the probability of red at the twelfth event?

WRAP UP...

PROBLEM SOLVING

STRATEGY • Find a Pattern

A television station will predict the winner in a close election when 17,200 votes are counted. At 7:00 P.M. 8,700 votes had been counted. By 8:00 P.M. 10,200 votes had been counted. By 9:00 P.M. 11,800 votes had been counted, and by 10:00 P.M. 13,500 votes had been counted. If the pattern continues, when will the station predict the winner?

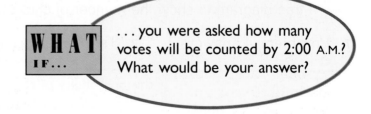

ELECTION UPDATE

Making a table is often a good strategy for solving a problem when you must find a pattern.

▶ **UNDERSTAND**

What are you asked to find?

What information are you given?

▶ **PLAN**

How will you solve the problem?

You can make a table showing the times and the number of votes counted. Then extend the pattern.

▶ **SOLVE**

How will you find the pattern?

Find the number of votes counted during each interval.

Time	7:00 P.M.	8:00 P.M.	9:00 P.M.	10:00 P.M.
Votes Counted	8,700	10,200	11,800	13,500

+1,500   +1,600   +1,700

An additional 100 votes are counted each hour.

 Extend the pattern.

11:00 P.M.   12:00 midnight

13,500 [+] 1,800 [=] ⌗5300.   15,300 [+] 1,900 [=] ⌗7200.

The television station will predict the winner at 12:00 midnight.

▶ **LOOK BACK**

How can you check your answer?

WHAT IF... ... you were asked how many votes will be counted by 2:00 A.M.? What would be your answer?

Apply

Find a pattern and solve.

(1) A print shop's presses must be cleaned regularly to keep them working. A service company cleaned them in October 1984, March 1985, August 1985, and January 1986. During which months in 1988 were the print shop's presses cleaned?

(2) A city has a total of 7 news offices. There are 6 computer terminals in one office, 8 terminals in the second office, and 11 terminals in the third office. If the pattern continues, what is the total number of computer terminals in all 7 offices?

Mixed Applications ⇒	STRATEGIES

Find a Pattern • Guess and Check • Write a Number Sentence • Work Backward

Choose a strategy and solve.

(3) Michael spent a total of $22.70 at a local newsstand. He bought a newspaper for $1.25, a magazine for $3.95, and 2 books that each cost the same. How much did each book cost?

(4) Lydia studies twice as long as James. James and Cathy study a total of 7 hours, but Cathy studies 3 hours longer than James. How long does Lydia study?

(5) Each NBA team has 5 minutes to choose a player in the draft. If the draft begins at 8:00 P.M. and the Nets get the sixth draft choice, at what time will the Nets choose?

(6) Use the information in Exercise 5. Suppose you were the twentieth player chosen in the NBA draft. What is the greatest number of minutes you would have had to wait to be chosen by one of the teams?

(7) One UN delegate will travel 3 hours to get to a session this year. The second will travel 1 hour more than twice the time traveled by the first, and the third will travel 2 times longer than the second. What is the total travel time for the UN delegates?

(8) The UN session will last 4 days. A 6-hour meeting and a 2-hour luncheon are scheduled each day. There will be a 3-hour reception on the opening day and a 4-hour banquet on the closing day. What is the total amount of time scheduled during the session?

MULTICULTURAL NOTE: When the United Nations was organized in 1945, 50 nations joined. One of the original 50 was the African nation of Liberia. Today the United Nations has over 160 member nations.

More Practice, Lesson 5.13, page H53

CHAPTER REVIEW/TEST

Vocabulary Check

Choose a word or words from the box to complete each sentence.

| circle graph |
| histogram |
| line graph |
| median |
| mode |
| probability |
| range |

1. Changes over time can be shown in a __?__. *(page 146)*

2. The number that occurs most often in a set of data is the __?__. *(page 154)*

3. A bar graph that shows how often numbers occur within a certain range is a __?__. *(page 144)*

4. The middle number in a group of numbers arranged in numerical order is the __?__. *(page 154)*

5. The type of graph used to display parts of a whole and relationships among the parts is a __?__. *(page 148)*

6. A comparison between the number of favorable events and the number of possible events is called __?__. *(page 160)*

7. The difference between the greatest and least numbers of a group of numbers is called the __?__. *(page 154)*

Concept Check

8. If you were graphing changes in amount of light over a 24-hour period, would you use a bar graph, a histogram, or a line graph? *(pages 140, 144, 146)*

Tell whether a bar graph, histogram, line graph, or circle graph is most appropriate to display the data. *(pages 140, 144, 146, 148)*

The type of graph I choose will depend on the kind of data to be graphed.

9. number of babies born during a 24-hour period

10. amount of electricity used from month to month for a year

11. heights of tallest mountains

12. speeds of fastest animals

13. number to finish a race in 5-minute intervals

14. daily relative humidity in Puerto Rico for the month of May

Skill Check

Use the information in the stem-and-leaf plot for Exercises 15–19.

Scholastic Bowl Team "B" Tournament Points Scored

Stem	Leaves
3	3 4 4
4	5 6 7 8
5	2 2 2 8

15. How many points are shown by the second stem and its leaves? *(page 156)*

16. What is the range of the scores? *(pages 154, 156)*

17. What is the median of the scores? *(pages 154, 156)*

18. What is the mode of the scores? *(pages 154, 156)*

19. To the nearest hundredth, what is the mean of the scores in the plot? *(page 154, 156)*

Draw a tree diagram. Tell the number of possible choices. *(page 158)*

20.

Jacket	Hat
blazer	beret
	sock hat
	cap

21.

Ink	Card
blue	postcard
red	birthday
	thank you

22.

Course	Day
science	Monday
English	Tuesday
health	Friday

23. A number cube has faces 1 through 6. What is the probability of tossing a 3 or a 5? *(page 160)*

24. A number cube has faces 1 through 6. What is the probability of tossing a 6 if you have already tossed the cube 4 times? *(page 162)*

Problem-Solving Check *(pages 150, 164)*

25. Wendy will replace a radio newscaster every other Friday night, beginning the second Friday in September. If there are 4 Fridays in each month, will Wendy work the last Friday in October?

26. Ms. Malone is a beekeeper. On Monday she tends 2 hives, on Tuesday 4 hives, on Wednesday 8 hives, and on Thursday 16 hives. If she works five days a week and the pattern continues, how many hives will she tend next Tuesday?

27. Ron asked 24 students to name their favorite type of music. Twelve like rock, 2 like jazz, 4 like country, 5 like rap, and 1 likes classical. Make a bar graph, a histogram, or a circle graph for the data.

28. Dan will survey 1 out of every 10 mail carriers. If there are 450 carriers, how many will he survey?

WHAT DID I LEARN?

1. Explain how to collect and organize data to show the number of pets owned by the students in your math class.

2. Identify the type of graph you would use to display the scores of your class on a math test. Explain your choice.

3. Explain how to find, and then find, the range, mean, median, and mode for this set of data.

   63   68   79   81   89   89   91

4. Make a tree diagram to show all the choices that are possible for sandwiches if you have 3 kinds of bread and 4 kinds of filling. Give the total number of choices.

5. There are 2 red marbles and 2 green marbles in a bag. Explain how the probability of drawing a red marble changes if 1 red marble is added to the bag.

6. Read Exercise 2 on page 165. Follow the steps on the Problem-Solving Think Along worksheet to show how to solve this problem.

As you add marbles to the bag, the probability changes.

Write About It

7. Which lesson or activity in this chapter on graphing, statistics, and probability was the most interesting to you? Explain.

8. Suppose the mean score on a math test given to your class is 82. Explain what this tells you about the scores.

Graph the Results

Sometimes you can demonstrate a general rule by testing the rule and making a graph of your results. For example, when you toss a coin, the probability of heads is 1 out of 2.

Work with teammates. Experiment by tossing a coin. Then graph your results.

 Decide

Discuss how to record the data, allowing each member of the team to record his or her own results. Also decide how you will construct your graph.

 Do

Each team member should toss a coin 20 times and record the number of heads and the number of tails. Then the team should make a bar

- graph to show the results.
- Use two bars for each group
- member, shading one bar for
- heads and one for tails.
- Shade or color the bars
- differently.

Share

- Compare your results with
- those of another team.

| *T*alk About It | Are the results easier to understand from each team member's record or from the graph? Explain.

How is your graph similar to the other team's graph?

Is the probability of heads 1 out of 2 in most cases? Why or why not?

Predict Events

If you roll a number cube one time, you will roll 1, 2, 3, 4, 5, or 6.

The probability of rolling a 2 is $\frac{1}{6}$. If you roll the cube 60 times, the best prediction for the number of 2's is 10, because $\frac{1}{6}$ of 60 is 10.

Make a prediction for each situation described below. Then use number cubes to see how close your prediction is to your outcome.

1. How many times will you roll an odd number if you roll one number cube 50 times?

2. How many times will you roll a sum of 7 if you roll two number cubes 180 times?

Challenge

Critical Thinking

1. A player spins each spinner once. How many possible outcomes are there?

2. A player spins each spinner twice. How many possible outcomes are there?

Problem Solving

1. The mean of Evan's scores on three math tests is 72. His last two scores were 76 and 72. What was his first score?

2. Dale's math teacher counts tests twice as heavily as quizzes. Dale scored 80 and 60 on quizzes, but he has an overall average of 82. What was his score on the test?

Write the letter of the correct answer.

1. 9,061.8 − 234.76

    A. 8,827.04   **B.** 8,827.42
    C. 8,837.12   **D.** 9,827.42

2. Evaluate $21.4 - b$, for $b = 5.9$.

    A. 14.5   **B.** 15.5
    C. 16.5   **D.** not here

3. $215 \div 5 - 3$

    A. 33   **B.** 40
    C. 107.5   **D.** not here

4. Evaluate $\dfrac{x}{2.4}$, for $x = 7.92$.

    A. 2.3   **B.** 3.0
    C. 3.3   **D.** 3.4

5. What is the mode of the data?
    2   5   7   9   12   12

    A. 7.8   **B.** 9
    C. 10   **D.** 12

6. $0.0153 \times 6,729$

    A. 102.9537   **B.** 103.9537
    C. 109.5327   **D.** 1,029.537

7. Estimate to place the decimal point.
    $453.8337 \div 9.01$

    A. 5.037   **B.** 50.37
    C. 503.7   **D.** 5,037

8. $2.748 \div 45.8$

    A. 0.6   **B.** 0.62
    C. 6.02   **D.** not here

9. Which type of graph would you use to show the lengths of the 5 longest rivers?

    A. circle   **B.** histogram
    C. bar   **D.** line

10. What is the probability of choosing a 5 from a bag containing cards with the numbers 1–6?

    A. 6 out of 6   **B.** 2 out of 6
    C. 3 out of 6   **D.** 1 out of 6

11. Sara is twice as old as her brother Sean. Sean is 4 years older than Tracey. If Sara will be 13 years old next year, how old is Tracey?

    A. 2   **B.** 3
    C. 4   **D.** 5

12. Lily scored 4 more points on a quiz than Dora scored. If the sum of their scores is 180, how many points did Lily score on the quiz?

    A. 84   **B.** 88
    C. 90   **D.** 92

NUMBER THEORY

Did you know...

... that using number theory when you play games can make you a more competitive player?

TALK ABOUT IT

Suppose the altitude gauge on a flight simulator game shows an increase in altitude of 10 feet for every second you pull back on a joystick. The gauge shows a decrease in altitude while you push forward on the joystick. Using this and any other information you need, write and solve as many problems as you can.

MULTIPLES AND LEAST COMMON MULTIPLE

Nan takes 3 minutes to drive the course of a car-rally video game and return to the starting point. Cladio takes 4 minutes. If they start at the same time, how many minutes will pass before they cross the starting point at the same time?

Multiples of 3 tell when Nan crosses the starting line. To find multiples of 3, multiply 3 by 1, 2, 3, 4, and so on. Multiples of 3 are shaded.

Multiples of 4 tell when Cladio crosses the starting point. To find multiples of 4, multiply 4 by 1, 2, 3, 4, and so on. An *X* is put through each multiple of 4.

Numbers that are both shaded and crossed out are **common multiples.** The smallest common multiple of two or more numbers is called the **least common multiple (LCM).**

1	2	3	4	5	6	7	8	9	10
11	12	13	14	15	16	17	18	19	20
21	22	23	24	25	26	27	28	29	30

- Which numbers in the list are common multiples of 3 and 4?

- Which number is the LCM of 3 and 4?

So, 12 minutes will pass before Nan and Cladio cross the starting point at the same time.

Another Method You can also list multiples of each number to find the LCM of two or more numbers.

What is the LCM of 2 and 5?

Step 1	**Step 2**
List multiples of 2 and 5.	Find the LCM.
2: 2 4 6 8 10 12 14	2: 2 4 6 8 ⑩ 12 14
5: 5 10 15 20 25 30 35	5: 5 ⑩ 15 20 25 30 35

So, the LCM of 2 and 5 is 10.

Talk About It

▶ Is there an LCM of every pair of numbers? How do you know?

Check for Understanding

Use a list of numbers to find the LCM of the numbers.

1. 3, 5   **2.** 4, 12   **3.** 3, 4   **4.** 2, 3, 7   **5.** 3, 5, 6

List multiples to find the LCM of the numbers.

6. 4, 5   **7.** 3, 7   **8.** 4, 6   **9.** 2, 3, 4   **10.** 2, 8, 12

Practice

Write the first three multiples, excluding the number itself.

11. 3   **12.** 5   **13.** 6   **14.** 7   **15.** 9

16. 10   **17.** 11   **18.** 12   **19.** 15   **20.** 20

Find the LCM of the numbers.

21. 6, 7   **22.** 2, 13   **23.** 8, 12   **24.** 20, 3   **25.** 9, 15

26. 5, 35   **27.** 3, 5   **28.** 4, 20   **29.** 6, 12   **30.** 8, 9

31. 9, 6   **32.** 10, 15   **33.** 15, 45   **34.** 12, 24   **35.** 16, 32

36. 18, 54   **37.** 11, 132   **38.** 16, 64   **39.** 15, 40   **40.** 1, 110

41. 50, 100   **42.** 2, 4, 6   **43.** 3, 6, 9   **44.** 12, 15, 18   **45.** 12, 24, 30

Mixed Applications

46. Bob plays tennis every other day, and Caroline plays every fourth day. Some days they compete with each other. If they both play on Monday, on what day will Bob and Caroline both play again?

47. Justine has 12 card games and 14 board games. Rachel has twice as many board games and half as many card games. How many games does Rachel have?

48. **Number Sense** If the LCM of a pair of numbers is 4 and the sum of the pair is 6, what are the numbers?

49. **Critical Thinking** The LCM of three different numbers is 4. What are the numbers?

How can you find the LCM of three numbers?

EQUIVALENT FRACTIONS

Jody and Lyle follow these steps to make a spinner for a board game.

Fold a circle in half. Shade one part.

Fold the circle in half again.

Fold the circle in half a third time.

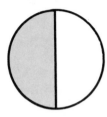

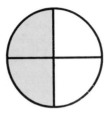

$\frac{1}{2}$ is shaded.

$\frac{2}{4}$ is shaded.

$\frac{4}{8}$ is shaded.

- How can you tell from the circles above that $\frac{1}{2} = \frac{2}{4}$, $\frac{2}{4} = \frac{4}{8}$, and $\frac{1}{2} = \frac{4}{8}$?

- If Jody and Lyle fold the circle in half a fourth time, will the shaded amount remain the same?

- What fraction names the amount shaded if they fold the circle in half a fourth time?

Equivalent fractions are fractions that name the same part. $\frac{1}{2}$, $\frac{2}{4}$, $\frac{4}{8}$, and $\frac{8}{16}$ are equivalent fractions.

Another Method You can also multiply or divide both the numerator and the denominator by the same number to find equivalent fractions.

A. $\frac{1}{2} = \frac{1 \times 2}{2 \times 2} = \frac{2}{4}$
$\frac{2}{2} = 1$

B. $\frac{8}{16} = \frac{8 \div 8}{16 \div 8} = \frac{1}{2}$
$\frac{8}{8} = 1$

C. $\frac{4}{8} \;\; = \;\; \frac{8}{16}$
$\times 2$
$\times 2$

Check for Understanding

Fold a sheet of paper with the given amount shaded to find two equivalent fractions.

1. $\frac{1}{4}$

2. $\frac{2}{3}$

3. $\frac{3}{4}$

Multiply or divide to find two equivalent fractions.

4. $\frac{2}{5}$

5. $\frac{5}{10}$

6. $\frac{5}{6}$

Practice

Write a fraction that tells what part is colored. Identify the
equivalent fractions by comparing Exercises 7–10.

7.

8.

9.

10.

Complete the number sentence.

11. $\dfrac{2}{3} = \dfrac{\blacksquare}{6}$

12. $\dfrac{1}{2} = \dfrac{4}{\blacksquare}$

13. $\dfrac{5}{8} = \dfrac{\blacksquare}{64}$

14. $\dfrac{30}{35} = \dfrac{\blacksquare}{7}$

15. $\dfrac{4}{5} = \dfrac{\blacksquare}{25}$

16. $\dfrac{1}{2} = \dfrac{38}{\blacksquare}$

17. $\dfrac{13}{8} = \dfrac{\blacksquare}{32}$

18. $\dfrac{2}{3} = \dfrac{16}{\blacksquare}$

19. $\dfrac{30}{36} = \dfrac{5}{\blacksquare}$

20. $\dfrac{3}{24} = \dfrac{\blacksquare}{8}$

21. $\dfrac{17}{34} = \dfrac{1}{\blacksquare}$

22. $\dfrac{39}{52} = \dfrac{\blacksquare}{4}$

Write *yes* or *no* to tell whether the fractions are equivalent.
If they are not, write an equivalent fraction for each fraction.

23. $\dfrac{15}{30}, \dfrac{1}{2}$

24. $\dfrac{3}{18}, \dfrac{1}{3}$

25. $\dfrac{2}{3}, \dfrac{12}{18}$

26. $\dfrac{3}{4}, \dfrac{9}{12}$

27. $\dfrac{4}{16}, \dfrac{12}{18}$

28. $\dfrac{10}{12}, \dfrac{13}{24}$

29. $\dfrac{10}{16}, \dfrac{4}{4}$

30. $\dfrac{12}{21}, \dfrac{4}{7}$

Mixed Applications

31. Janis can solve 5 mazes in one day.
If she has 45 new mazes to work,
how many days will Janis need to
solve them?

32. A pizza is cut into fourths. Gwen
will cut it into smaller pieces to
share equally with 5 friends. Into
how many total pieces will Gwen
cut the pizza?

33. **Critical Thinking** Warren played $\frac{1}{2}$
of 18 holes of golf. Robin assembled
$\frac{1}{2}$ of a 500-piece jigsaw puzzle. Are
their efforts equal? Explain.

34. **Making Decisions** You must take
the shorter of two routes to a
friend's house. One route is $\frac{5}{6}$ mile,
and the other is $\frac{1}{3}$ mile. Which
route will you take?

How do you know that $\frac{2}{2}$ and $\frac{8}{8}$
are equal to 1?

WRAP
UP...

EXPLORING

Least Common Denominator

Name some multiples of 2 and 3. What is the LCM of 2 and 3? In this lesson you will look at multiples of 2 and 3 to explore least common denominator.

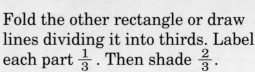

Building Understanding

Use paper, a ruler, and scissors. Draw and cut out two rectangles that are 6 cm by 24 cm each.

Fold one rectangle, or draw a line dividing it into halves. Label each part $\frac{1}{2}$. Then shade $\frac{1}{2}$.

Fold the other rectangle or draw lines dividing it into thirds. Label each part $\frac{1}{3}$. Then shade $\frac{2}{3}$.

Rectangle A

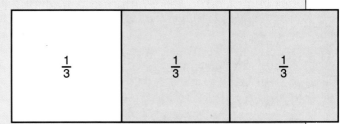

Rectangle B

TALK ABOUT IT

Now divide each rectangle so that both rectangles have the same number of sections.

- Into how many equal sections has each rectangle been folded?

- After the fold, what fraction names the shaded part of Rectangle A?

- After the fold, what fraction names the shaded part of Rectangle B?

- Is $\frac{3}{6}$ the same as $\frac{1}{2}$ of Rectangle A?

- Is $\frac{4}{6}$ the same as $\frac{2}{3}$ of Rectangle B?

- Look at the denominators of the fractions. How is 6 related to 2 and 3?

Making the Connection

A common multiple of the denominators of two or more fractions is called a **common denominator**. You can find a common denominator the same way you find a common multiple.

How can you write $\frac{5}{6}$ and $\frac{1}{9}$ using common denominators?

Find common multiples of 6 and 9.

6: 6 12 ⓲ 24 30 ㊱ 42 48
9: 9 ⓲ 27 ㊱ 45 54 63 72

Write equivalent fractions using denominators that are common multiples.

$\frac{5}{6} = \frac{15}{18}$ $\frac{5}{6} = \frac{30}{36}$ $\frac{1}{9} = \frac{2}{18}$ $\frac{1}{9} = \frac{4}{36}$

So, using common denominators, $\frac{5}{6}$ can be written as $\frac{15}{18}$ and $\frac{30}{36}$, and $\frac{1}{9}$ can be written as $\frac{2}{18}$ and $\frac{4}{36}$.

The **least common denominator (LCD)** for two or more fractions is the least common multiple (LCM) of the denominators.

You can find the LCD the same way you find the LCM.

How can you write $\frac{1}{3}$ and $\frac{4}{5}$ using the LCD?

Step 1 Find the LCD.	**Step 2** Write equivalent fractions.
3: 3 6 9 12 ⑮ 18 21 5: 5 10 ⑮ 20 25 30 35	$\frac{1}{3} = \frac{1 \times 5}{3 \times 5} = \frac{5}{15}$ $\frac{4}{5} = \frac{4 \times 3}{5 \times 3} = \frac{12}{15}$

So, with the LCD, $\frac{1}{3}$ is written $\frac{5}{15}$ and $\frac{4}{5}$ is written $\frac{12}{15}$.

1. What is the LCD for $\frac{1}{5}$ and $\frac{9}{15}$?

2. What is the LCD for $\frac{5}{6}$ and $\frac{1}{9}$? Rewrite $\frac{5}{6}$ and $\frac{1}{9}$ using the LCD.

Checking Understanding

Write each pair of fractions by using the LCD.

3. $\frac{1}{2}, \frac{3}{4}$ 4. $\frac{5}{6}, \frac{1}{9}$ 5. $\frac{1}{5}, \frac{3}{10}$ 6. $\frac{1}{3}, \frac{3}{4}$ 7. $\frac{1}{6}, \frac{5}{8}$

8. Name two fractions in which one of the denominators is the LCD for the fractions.

COMPARE AND ORDER

Amber, Ben, and Chad are playing a game with fraction cards. They each draw a card from the stack and turn it faceup. The person with the greatest fraction takes all the cards. Amber draws $\frac{4}{5}$, Ben draws $\frac{1}{5}$, and Chad draws $\frac{3}{5}$. Who takes all the cards?

$\frac{1}{5}$, $\frac{4}{5}$, and $\frac{3}{5}$ are **like fractions.** They have the same denominator. To compare and order like fractions, compare the numerators.

Since $4 > 3 > 1$, then $\frac{4}{5} > \frac{3}{5} > \frac{1}{5}$.

So, Amber takes all the cards.

Suppose Amber draws $\frac{1}{6}$, Ben draws $\frac{1}{4}$, and Chad draws $\frac{1}{3}$. Who takes all the cards?

$\frac{1}{6}$, $\frac{1}{4}$, and $\frac{1}{3}$ are **unlike fractions.** They have different denominators. To compare and order unlike fractions, you can use fraction bars or write equivalent fractions with like denominators.

Fraction Bars

| $\frac{1}{3}$ | $\frac{1}{3}$ | $\frac{1}{3}$ |

| $\frac{1}{4}$ | $\frac{1}{4}$ | $\frac{1}{4}$ | $\frac{1}{4}$ |

| $\frac{1}{6}$ | $\frac{1}{6}$ | $\frac{1}{6}$ | $\frac{1}{6}$ | $\frac{1}{6}$ | $\frac{1}{6}$ |

$\frac{1}{3} > \frac{1}{4} > \frac{1}{6}$

So, Chad takes all the cards.

Equivalent Fractions

Use the LCD to write equivalent fractions. The LCD is 12.

$$\overset{\times 2}{\frac{1}{6} = \frac{2}{12}}\underset{\times 2}{} \qquad \overset{\times 3}{\frac{1}{4} = \frac{3}{12}}\underset{\times 3}{} \qquad \overset{\times 4}{\frac{1}{3} = \frac{4}{12}}\underset{\times 4}{}$$

$$\frac{1}{3} > \frac{1}{4} > \frac{1}{6}$$

Talk About It

▶ When you compare and order two fractions with a numerator of 1, how can the denominators help you determine which fraction is greater?

▶ How would you order $1\frac{1}{2}$, $2\frac{1}{4}$, and $1\frac{1}{4}$ from least to greatest?

Check for Understanding

Use the LCD to write like fractions. Tell which one is greater.

1. $\frac{3}{5}, \frac{9}{10}$

2. $\frac{4}{9}, \frac{16}{27}$

3. $\frac{6}{7}, \frac{30}{49}$

4. $\frac{2}{3}, \frac{6}{21}$

5. $\frac{5}{6}, \frac{35}{36}$

6. $\frac{4}{7}, \frac{1}{2}$

7. $\frac{3}{5}, \frac{7}{8}$

8. $\frac{4}{15}, \frac{7}{10}$

Practice

Compare. Use < or >.

9. $\frac{2}{3} \bullet \frac{1}{3}$

10. $\frac{5}{8} \bullet \frac{3}{4}$

11. $\frac{4}{7} \bullet \frac{6}{7}$

12. $\frac{39}{40} \bullet \frac{7}{8}$

13. $3\frac{6}{15} \bullet 3\frac{9}{30}$

Use <, >, or = to compare the fractions.

14. $\frac{5}{20} \bullet \frac{6}{20}$

15. $\frac{4}{5} \bullet \frac{2}{3}$

16. $\frac{7}{14} \bullet \frac{4}{6}$

17. $\frac{9}{27} \bullet \frac{11}{33}$

18. $\frac{16}{32} \bullet \frac{9}{12}$

19. $\frac{24}{48} \bullet \frac{27}{36}$

20. $\frac{12}{15} \bullet \frac{10}{12}$

21. $\frac{49}{50} \bullet \frac{56}{100}$

Write in order from least to greatest. Use <.

22. $\frac{4}{5}, \frac{7}{10}, \frac{3}{5}$

23. $\frac{7}{8}, \frac{1}{2}, \frac{2}{3}$

24. $\frac{1}{2}, \frac{1}{3}, \frac{3}{4}$

25. $\frac{4}{6}, \frac{7}{14}, \frac{5}{7}, \frac{1}{3}$

Tell whether the fractions are in order from greatest to least.
Write *yes* or *no*.

26. $\frac{5}{8} > \frac{3}{8} > \frac{5}{6}$

27. $\frac{5}{6} > \frac{3}{4} > \frac{1}{2}$

28. $\frac{2}{3} > \frac{4}{9} > \frac{3}{4}$

29. $\frac{7}{10} > \frac{3}{5} > \frac{4}{15}$

Mixed Applications

30. Of all the markers in Trey's new game, $\frac{1}{6}$ are red, $\frac{1}{2}$ are blue, and $\frac{1}{3}$ are green. Does Trey have more blue markers or green markers?

31. **Making Decisions** A board-game card reads, "You must pay the player to your left 0.3 of your earnings or pay the bank 0.42 of your earnings." Which choice will you make?

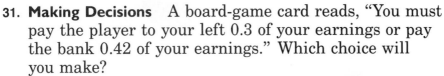

Why is it easier to order like fractions than unlike fractions?

WRAP

UP...

PROBLEM SOLVING

Choose a Strategy

Teresa, Lea, Bart, and Doug are getting ready for a chess tournament. Before play begins, each player shakes hands with each of the other players once. How many handshakes are there in all?

What strategies can you choose?

This problem, like many others, can be solved with more than one strategy. You can *make an organized list* or *act it out*.

Understand
Plan
Solve
Look Back

Strategy: Make an Organized List

You can make a tree diagram, one type of organized list, by showing the names of the players who shake hands.

Players   Handshakes

Teresa and ⎸ Lea
             ⎸ Bart   Teresa shakes hands with
             ⎸ Doug   all the other players.

Lea and ⎸ Bart   Lea's handshake with Teresa
          ⎸ Doug   is shown above.

Bart and —— Doug   Bart's handshakes with Teresa
                            and Lea are shown above.

Doug   All of Doug's handshakes are
                            shown above.

Strategy: Act It Out

You can solve this problem by acting it out. Have four students represent the four chess players.

Have each student shake hands with each of the other students once. Record the handshakes.

So, there are 6 handshakes in all.

WHAT IF... . . . there are 5 players in the chess tournament? How many handshakes will there be?

182

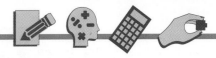

Mixed Applications ▷ **STRATEGIES** Make a Table • Work Backward
• Write a Number Sentence
• Act It Out

Choose a strategy and solve.

(1) There are five reporters for a television show. Before the first show, each of the reporters had one telephone conversation with every other reporter. How many telephone conversations were there in all?

(2) Six girls sat at a round table. Opal sat at Suzanna's right. Suzanna sat across from Pearl. Barb did not sit next to Pearl, but she did sit next to April. Maria sat between Opal and Pearl. Which of the girls sat at Pearl's right?

(3) Tari and Rita have different editions of the same game. Each has 56 markers. Half of Tari's markers are purple, but Rita has 5 fewer purple markers than Tari. How many of Rita's markers are not purple?

(4) Edward and Doris worked crossword puzzles on Monday, Thursday, Sunday, Wednesday, and Saturday. If this pattern continues, when will Edward and Doris work their next crossword puzzle?

(5) Perry had 42 sheets of colored construction paper that he divided among 7 classmates and himself. Could Perry divide the sheets of paper evenly, or did he have some left over? Explain.

(6) When a game was called because of rain, Tom was $\frac{3}{5}$ finished, Mack was $\frac{3}{9}$ finished, Bob was $\frac{1}{3}$ finished, and Dewayne was $\frac{7}{10}$ finished. Which players were tied?

(7) Fran, Harold, Sandy, and Ted enjoy fishing, hunting, skiing, or tennis. No person's name begins with the first letter of the activity he or she enjoys. Fran likes tennis. Sandy does not like hunting. Which activity does each person enjoy?

(8) Colette gave 12 marbles to Jim, got 15 from Lenny, got twice that number from Dee, and gave 16 more to Sally than she had given to Jim. Now she has 62 marbles. How many marbles did Colette have before she gave 12 marbles to Jim?

FACTORS, PRIMES, AND COMPOSITES

Sid and Corey are playing "Factor." They draw from a bag containing the numbers 2 to 100 to determine the number of squares with which to play. The object is to use the squares to make as many rectangles as possible. Players get a point for each rectangle they make.

Corey draws the number 5 and uses 5 squares. How many rectangles can Corey make?

Corey can make two rectangles, one that is 5 squares by 1 square and another that is 1 square by 5 squares. The numbers 1 and 5 are factors of 5.

Factors are numbers that are multiplied to find a product.

Since 5 has only two factors, it is a prime number. A **prime number** has exactly two factors, itself and 1.

Another Example

Sid draws the number 12 and uses 12 squares. How many rectangles can Sid make?

Sid can make 6 rectangles: 1 by 12, 12 by 1, 2 by 6, 6 by 2, 3 by 4, and 4 by 3. The numbers 1, 2, 3, 4, 6, and 12 are factors of 12.

A whole number such as 12 is called a **composite number** because it has more than two factors.

NOTE: The numbers 0 and 1 are neither prime nor composite.

Talk About It

Use unit squares to help you model the questions.

▶ When Sid draws a number, will he score more points if he draws a prime number or a composite number?

▶ Will Corey score more points if he draws 6 or 9?

▶ Will Sid score more points if he draws 28 or 30?

Idea Bank, page 490, Exercises 5–6

Check for Understanding

List the factors. Then tell whether the number is prime or composite.

1. 5   **2.** 14   **3.** 18   **4.** 2   **5.** 16

Practice

Tell whether the number is prime or composite.

6. 12   **7.** 11   **8.** 36   **9.** 37   **10.** 49   **11.** 71   **12.** 83

Write the factors of each number.

13. 9   **14.** 16   **15.** 12   **16.** 21   **17.** 18   **18.** 25   **19.** 121

Mixed Applications

20. Make a list of the prime numbers between 1 and 10.

21. Make a list of the composite numbers between 1 and 10.

22. Alice and Mary have 36 games. Mary has 12 more games than Alice. How many games does Alice have? How many does Mary have?

23. Number Sense Challenge another student to a game of Factor. Draw numbers 2 to 50 from a bag to determine the number of cubes for each player's turn. Keep score.

SOCIAL STUDIES CONNECTION

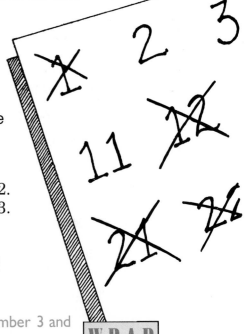

Eratosthenes was a Greek mathematician who lived about 200 B.C. He devised this system of finding the prime numbers between 1 and 100.

List the numbers 1 to 100 on a sheet of paper. Then follow the instructions in *A–D* and complete Exercise 24.

A. Cross out 1.
B. Cross out all the multiples of 2 that are greater than 2.
C. Cross out all the multiples of 3 that are greater than 3.
D. Do the same for multiples of 5 and 7.

24. The remaining numbers are prime. List all the prime numbers from 1 to 100.

Name two factors that the prime number 3 and the composite number 12 have in common.

WRAP UP...

PRIME FACTORIZATION

A composite number can be expressed as a product of prime numbers. This is the **prime factorization** of the number. You can use a factor tree to find the prime factors of a composite number.

What is the prime factorization of 100?

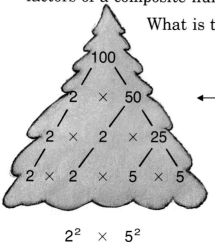

← Choose any two factors of 100. →
Continue until only prime numbers are left.

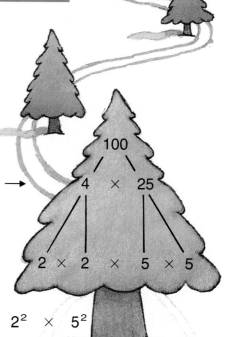

← prime factorization →

prime factorization written
← with exponents →

$2^2 \times 5^2$

$2^2 \times 5^2$

So, the prime factorization of 100 is $2 \times 2 \times 5 \times 5$, or $2^2 \times 5^2$.

Another Method You can also divide until the quotient is 1 to find the prime factors of a number.

What is the prime factorization of 36?

 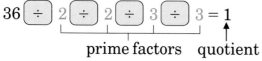
prime factors   quotient

The prime factorization of 36 is $2 \times 2 \times 3 \times 3$, or $2^2 \times 3^2$.

Talk About It

▶ How can you use divisibility rules to help you find the prime factorization of a number?

▶ How do you know that you have finished a prime factorization?

Check for Understanding

Complete the prime factorization.

1. $12 = 2 \times \blacksquare \times 3$

2. $2 \times 5 \times \blacksquare = 70$

3. $81 = 3 \times 3 \times 3 \times \blacksquare$

4. $2^{\blacksquare} = 16$

5. $3 \times \blacksquare \times 7 = 105$

6. $2 \times 7^{\blacksquare} = 98$

Practice

Write the prime factorization. Use a factor tree.

7. 25 **8.** 16 **9.** 21 **10.** 24 **11.** 49 **12.** 56

13. 36 **14.** 44 **15.** 66 **16.** 42 **17.** 98 **18.** 84

Write the prime factorization in exponent form.

19. 9 **20.** 18 **21.** 12 **22.** 32 **23.** 50 **24.** 49

25. 48 **26.** 98 **27.** 64 **28.** 27 **29.** 56 **30.** 72

Mixed Applications

31. Number Sense If a number x is a prime factor of 12, will x be a prime factor of 36? How do you know?

32. Critical Thinking A number f is the least common multiple of 3, 5, and 6. What is f?

MATH CONNECTION

You can use prime factorization to find the LCM.

 Example Find the LCM of 4, 9, and 50.

Step 1 Write the prime factorizations.	**Step 2** Write an expression using each factor once.	**Step 3** Write the greatest exponent of each factor. Then multiply. $2^2 \cdot 3^2 \cdot 5^2$
$4 = 2^2$ $9 = 3^2$ $50 = 2 \times 5^2$	$2 \cdot 3 \cdot 5$ ↑ ↑ Dots mean multiply.	You can use a calculator with an x^2 key. 

So, the LCM of 4, 9, and 50 is 900.

Use prime factorization to find the LCM.

33. 9, 30 **34.** 12, 16 **35.** 10, 15 **36.** 20, 90 **37.** 4, 25, 100

Do the prime factors of a number differ depending on which factors you choose first? Explain.

GREATEST COMMON FACTOR

The Whitmore School Chess Club wants to build a giant chessboard on a playground area. The area measures 40 feet by 50 feet. The chessboard must contain 64 squares, with 8 squares on each side. What is the largest square that can be used?

You must find the largest number that divides into both 40 and 50 without a remainder.

Factors shared by two or more numbers are called **common factors.** The largest common factor is called the **greatest common factor (GCF).**

To find the GCF, list the factors of 40 and 50, identify the common factors, and then find the greatest factor.

Factors of 40: 1, 2, 4, 5, 8, 10, 20, 40
Factors of 50: 1, 2, 5, 10, 25, 50

MULTICULTURAL NOTE: Outdoor chess is a popular game played in many countries.

Work Together

- Would the playground area be big enough to hold 64 squares if they were each 10 feet square?

- What is the largest square that can be used?

So, the largest square that can be used is a 5-foot square.

Another Method   Use prime factorization to find the GCF of 18 and 24.

Prime factorization of 18: 2 × 3 × 3
Prime factorization of 24: 2 × 2 × 2 × 3   ← Find the product of the common factors: 2 × 3 = 6

So, the GCF of 18 and 24 is 6.

Check for Understanding

Find the GCF by listing the factors.

1. 9 and 15   **2.** 24 and 32   **3.** 52 and 78   **4.** 25 and 75

Find the GCF by using prime factorization.

5. 18 and 30   **6.** 12 and 16   **7.** 54 and 72   **8.** 30 and 96

Practice

Write the common factors of each pair of numbers.

9. 9, 12   **10.** 18, 36   **11.** 12, 16   **12.** 32, 60   **13.** 27, 54

14. 9, 64   **15.** 40, 12   **16.** 56, 49   **17.** 25, 50   **18.** 12, 72

Write the GCF of each pair of numbers.

19. 8, 52   **20.** 21, 9   **21.** 18, 99   **22.** 36, 16   **23.** 34, 60

24. 56, 64   **25.** 30, 12   **26.** 33, 99   **27.** 25, 40   **28.** 12, 72

29. 4, 72   **30.** 21, 63   **31.** 24, 72   **32.** 45, 81   **33.** 24, 56

Mixed Applications

34. Rico has 72 red roses and 54 white roses to make bouquets. How many roses can he put in each bouquet if he uses an equal number of each color and makes the largest bouquets possible?

35. Mental Math Sean has six 12-inch pieces of toy train track. Ruth has eight 9-inch pieces of train track. When assembled, will both tracks be the same length? Explain.

MIXED REVIEW

Complete the number sentence.

1. $\frac{1}{3} = \frac{\blacksquare}{6}$ **2.** $\frac{3}{4} = \frac{\blacksquare}{12}$ **3.** $\frac{9}{18} = \frac{1}{\blacksquare}$ **4.** $\frac{4}{5} = \frac{16}{\blacksquare}$ **5.** $\frac{3}{7} = \frac{15}{\blacksquare}$

Write in order from greatest to least. Use $>$.

6. $\frac{1}{5}, \frac{4}{5}, \frac{3}{5}$ **7.** $\frac{2}{7}, \frac{6}{7}, \frac{5}{7}, \frac{4}{7}$ **8.** $\frac{1}{2}, \frac{3}{5}, \frac{2}{3}$ **9.** $\frac{2}{9}, \frac{3}{4}, \frac{2}{3}$ **10.** $\frac{3}{8}, \frac{1}{4}, \frac{1}{3}, \frac{1}{6}$

Write the factors of each number.

11. 4   **12.** 17   **13.** 27   **14.** 39   **15.** 47

How can you use prime factorization to find the GCF of two numbers?

WRAP UP...

REVIEW AND MAINTENANCE

1. At a closeout sale, you can buy 1 game at the regular price of $7.50, 2 for $13.00, 3 for $18.50, and 4 for $24.00. If the pattern continues, how much can you save over the regular price if you buy 6 games?

2. Quiltz is a game of patterns. Denise drew a card with 32, 31, 29, 26, and 22 written on it. She must find the next three numbers in the pattern to score. What are they?

3. Mary, Emily, and Sue drove to a chess match in their own cars. One car was blue, one gray, and one white. Mary met the white car at a traffic light. The blue car passed Mary. Sue does not drive a white car. Which color car does each person drive?

4. After a contest, five winners lined up in order from the fifth- to the first-prize winner. Will was ahead of Dean but behind Pete. Harold was behind Will but ahead of Dean. Dan was ahead of Pete. Who received each prize?

Use the stem-and-leaf plot for Exercises 5–9.

5. What are the ages shown by the first stem and its leaves?

6. What is the range of the ages?

7. What is the mode of the data?

Ages of Baseball Players

Stem	Leaves
2	0 1 2 3 7 8
3	1 2 4 4 6

8. What is the median of the data?

> I read the direction lines very carefully.

9. What is the average age of the baseball players?

Write the number of choices.

10. 2 cars, 4 colors

11. 4 dresses, 6 belts

Write the LCM for each pair of numbers.

12. $20, 40$

13. $12, 18$

14. $15, 35$

15. $9, 10$

16. $3, 75$

Use the LCD to write like fractions.

17. $\frac{2}{3}, \frac{1}{2}$

18. $\frac{1}{8}, \frac{3}{10}$

19. $\frac{4}{21}, \frac{2}{9}$

20. $\frac{7}{15}, \frac{5}{9}$

21. $\frac{11}{12}, \frac{7}{8}$

Write the GCF for each pair of numbers.

22. $9, 63$

23. $12, 16$

24. $25, 60$

25. $35, 75$

26. $18, 42$

Visualize the Solution

Black beans, plantains (a type of banana), and rice are traditional foods in Venezuela. Arepas are a traditional form of corn bread. They are crisp on the outside and doughy on the inside.

Margarita is making arepas for herself and 6 of her friends. Her recipe serves 9 people. She would like to have enough to serve 2 arepas to each person. How many batches will Margarita need to make?

Sometimes visualizing can help you solve a problem. When you visualize a problem, you form a mental picture of the solution.

Work Together

- How many arepas are needed for Margarita and her friends? Visualize the solution.

- How many batches of arepas will Margarita need to make?

- Make a drawing to show what you visualized.

- Do you think it is easier to visualize a solution or to compute a solution?

MULTICULTURAL NOTE: Arepas are made from corn flour, salt, and water. Corn is an important crop in Venezuela.

Visualize a solution to each problem. Then draw a picture of the solution.

1. Eduardo is setting up tables for a local fiesta. The tables seat 8 people on each side and 1 person at each end. Eduardo will use 4 of the tables. How many chairs will he need for the tables?

2. Fredrico bought 12 plantains. He and his two brothers ate $\frac{1}{3}$ of the plantains. His mother used $\frac{1}{2}$ of the remaining plantains to make a dessert. How many plantains are left?

FRACTIONS
in Simplest Form

Jim and Alex were playing Simplest-Form Fraction Match. Jim drew these two cards and called them a match. He said $\frac{16}{24}$ is not in simplest form, but $\frac{2}{3}$ is. Alex challenged the play. Who was correct?

A fraction is in **simplest form,** or lowest terms, when the numerator and the denominator have no common factor greater than 1.

- Is $\frac{2}{3}$ in simplest form? How do you know?

- Is $\frac{16}{24}$ in simplest form? How do you know?

To find who was correct, you must write $\frac{16}{24}$ in simplest form. Use repeated division until no common factors other than 1 remain.

$$\frac{16}{24} = \frac{8}{12} = \frac{4}{6} = \frac{2}{3} \leftarrow \text{simplest form}$$

So, Jim was correct.

Another Method

You can also use the GCF to write a fraction in simplest form.

Write $\frac{6}{8}$ in simplest form.

Divide the numerator and the denominator by the GCF.

$$\frac{6 \div 2}{8 \div 2} = \frac{3}{4} \leftarrow \text{simplest form}$$

- Which method of writing a fraction in simplest form is more efficient? Why?

- What is $\frac{12}{8}$ written in simplest form?

- What is $\frac{10}{10}$ written in simplest form? $\frac{a}{a}$?

- Does the value of the fraction remain the same when you divide both the numerator and the denominator by the GCF? How do you know?

Check for Understanding

Find the GCF of each pair of numbers.

1. 12, 24   **2.** 36, 42   **3.** 16, 48   **4.** 18, 72   **5.** 40, 45

Tell which fraction is written in simplest form.

6. $\frac{21}{23}, \frac{5}{25}$ **7.** $\frac{54}{54}, \frac{4}{9}$ **8.** $\frac{4}{16}, \frac{7}{9}$ **9.** $\frac{2}{4}, \frac{2}{5}, \frac{2}{8}$ **10.** $\frac{3}{7}, \frac{4}{12}, \frac{7}{14}$

Practice

Write the GCF of the numerator and denominator.

11. $\frac{40}{65}$ **12.** $\frac{15}{60}$ **13.** $\frac{28}{63}$ **14.** $\frac{42}{56}$ **15.** $\frac{4}{32}$

16. $\frac{9}{54}$ **17.** $\frac{16}{80}$ **18.** $\frac{20}{70}$ **19.** $\frac{8}{32}$ **20.** $\frac{48}{54}$

Write the fraction in simplest form.

21. $\frac{18}{60}$ **22.** $\frac{10}{16}$ **23.** $\frac{50}{60}$ **24.** $\frac{36}{54}$ **25.** $\frac{14}{21}$

26. $\frac{64}{72}$ **27.** $\frac{16}{32}$ **28.** $\frac{40}{32}$ **29.** $\frac{15}{24}$ **30.** $\frac{25}{30}$

31. $\frac{45}{72}$ **32.** $\frac{75}{55}$ **33.** $\frac{63}{72}$ **34.** $\frac{12}{12}$ **35.** $\frac{48}{42}$

Write the fraction that is in simplest form.

36. $\frac{3}{6}, \frac{1}{2}, \frac{4}{8}, \frac{5}{10}$ **37.** $\frac{6}{9}, \frac{18}{27}, \frac{12}{18}, \frac{2}{3}$ **38.** $\frac{3}{5}, \frac{15}{25}, \frac{30}{50}, \frac{21}{35}$

39. $\frac{4}{24}, \frac{2}{12}, \frac{1}{6}, \frac{3}{18}$ **40.** $\frac{15}{20}, \frac{3}{4}, \frac{9}{12}, \frac{6}{8}$ **41.** $\frac{12}{27}, \frac{8}{18}, \frac{16}{36}, \frac{4}{9}$

Mixed Applications

42. Beth made 24 blueberry, 12 banana, and 12 chocolate muffins. What part of the muffins are blueberry?

43. Critical Thinking How do you know that $\frac{4}{8}$ written in simplest form is not $\frac{1}{3}$?

44. Is $\frac{2}{3}$ greater than $\frac{4}{6}$? Defend your answer.

How do you know that a fraction is in simplest form?

WRAP UP...

After a table-tennis tournament, Patty and two friends will share some pizza. How can they share 1 pizza?

Any whole number can be written as a fraction.

$$1 = \frac{3}{3}$$

So, they can share by dividing the pizza into $\frac{3}{3}$.

- If you buy 11 slices of pizza from a restaurant that cuts pizzas into thirds, how many pizzas will have to be cut?

$$\frac{11}{3}$$

$$3\frac{2}{3}$$

A fraction is greater than 1 if the numerator is greater than the denominator.

A **mixed number** is a whole number and a fraction.

A fraction greater than 1 can be written as a mixed number.	A mixed number can be written as a fraction greater than 1.

A fraction greater than 1 can be written as a mixed number.

Write $\frac{15}{4}$ as a mixed number.

Divide the numerator by the denominator.

$$4\overline{)15} \quad \begin{array}{r} 3 \\ -12 \\ \hline 3 \end{array}$$

Write the remainder as a fraction in simplest form.

$$3\frac{3}{4} \atop 4\overline{)15}$$

A mixed number can be written as a fraction greater than 1.

Write $7\frac{3}{4}$ as a fraction.

Multiply the whole number by the denominator. $7 \times 4 = 28$

Add the numerator to the product. Write the sum as the new numerator. Use the same denominator.

$$3 + 28 = 31$$
$$7\frac{3}{4} = \frac{31}{4}$$

Talk About It

▶ How can you tell whether a fraction can be rewritten as a mixed number?

▶ How can you write $\frac{6}{3}$ as a whole number?

Check for Understanding

Write as a mixed number.

1. $\dfrac{13}{4}$　　　2. $\dfrac{15}{11}$　　　3. $\dfrac{37}{2}$

Write as a fraction.

4. $2\dfrac{2}{3}$　　　5. $3\dfrac{5}{8}$　　　6. $1\dfrac{4}{5}$

Practice

Find the missing digit.

7. $\dfrac{27}{5} = 5\dfrac{2}{\blacksquare}$　　　8. $\dfrac{28}{3} = \blacksquare\dfrac{1}{3}$　　　9. $\dfrac{35}{6} = \blacksquare\dfrac{5}{6}$　　　10. $7\dfrac{31}{4} = \dfrac{\blacksquare}{4}$

11. $\dfrac{39}{11} = \blacksquare\dfrac{6}{11}$　　　12. $\dfrac{29}{10} = 2\dfrac{\blacksquare}{10}$　　　13. $13 = \dfrac{\blacksquare}{3}$　　　14. $7 = \dfrac{\blacksquare}{1}$

Write the fraction as a mixed number or as a whole number.

15. $\dfrac{31}{9}$　　　16. $\dfrac{59}{6}$　　　17. $\dfrac{57}{10}$　　　18. $\dfrac{56}{7}$　　　19. $\dfrac{44}{8}$

Write the mixed number as a fraction.

20. $10\dfrac{4}{5}$　　　21. $9\dfrac{1}{3}$　　　22. $6\dfrac{5}{6}$　　　23. $4\dfrac{2}{7}$　　　24. $6\dfrac{8}{9}$

Mixed Applications

25. **Number Sense** Dave has more games than Jill but fewer than Toni. If Toni has $\dfrac{2}{3}$ of the games, can Dave have $\dfrac{3}{4}$ of the games? Defend your answer.

26. **Make Up a Problem** Kim has played checkers after school for 35 days. Make up a problem that can be solved by writing a fraction.

MIXED REVIEW

Write the GCF of each pair of numbers.

1. $3, 9$　　　2. $8, 16$　　　3. $5, 25$　　　4. $45, 54$　　　5. $7, 11$

Write the fraction in simplest form.

6. $\dfrac{50}{60}$　　　7. $\dfrac{7}{14}$　　　8. $\dfrac{15}{45}$　　　9. $\dfrac{21}{21}$　　　10. $\dfrac{35}{63}$

How can you order $1\dfrac{1}{5}$, $\dfrac{8}{5}$, and $\dfrac{4}{5}$ from least to greatest?

WRAP UP...

PROBLEM SOLVING

Choose a Strategy

To paint the bleachers in a gym, Joanne stood on a step 2.4 meters (m) from the floor. The steps of the bleachers are 0.25 m apart. She went up 6 more steps to paint the top of the bleachers. How many meters from the floor is the top of the bleachers?

Understand
Plan
Solve
Look Back

Sometimes you can use one of several strategies to solve a problem.

What strategies can you use? You can write a *number sentence* or *draw a diagram.*

Strategy: Draw a Diagram

Draw a diagram.

Show the distances between the steps of the bleachers.

Find the sum of the distances.

0.25 m
0.25 m
0.25 m
0.25 m
0.25 m
0.25 m
2.4 m

Strategy: Write a Number Sentence

Write a number sentence.

distance between steps	number of steps climbed	distance of first step from floor	height of bleachers from floor
↓	↓	↓	↓
(0.25 ×	6) +	2.4 =	▨

0.25 ⊠ 6 ⊞ 2.4 ⊜ [3.9   ]

So, the top of the bleachers is 3.9 meters from the floor.

WHAT IF... ... the steps are 0.3 meters apart? How many meters from the floor is the top of the bleachers?

196

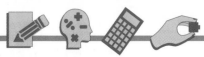
Mixed Applications → **STRATEGIES**

Write a Number Sentence
• Draw a Diagram • Act It Out
• Find a Pattern

Choose a strategy and solve.

(1) Dylan, Croaker, Legs, and Amos competed in a frog-jumping contest. Dylan finished after Legs but before Croaker. Amos finished just before Croaker. Legs finished first. In what order did the frogs finish?

(2) Tammy and Peter are working 45 mazes each. Tammy has completed 7 more than Peter, who has completed 15. How many mazes does Tammy still need to complete?

(3) There are 65 games of pachisi and backgammon on a toy-store shelf. If there are 15 more backgammon games than pachisi games, how many boxes of each game are on the shelf?

(4) Tim spent $\frac{1}{6}$ of his money on a tic-tac-toe game, $\frac{1}{3}$ on mazes, $\frac{5}{12}$ on puzzles, and $\frac{1}{12}$ on marbles. On which item did Tim spend the most?

(5) Guillermo made a spinner with triangles, squares, a circle, and a star. What is the probability he will land on a square if he spins 18 times?

(6) Joyce is decorating the border of a game board. She starts with 3 triangles, 4 squares, and 5 circles. Then she repeats the 3 triangles and 4 squares. What will be the next three designs in the pattern?

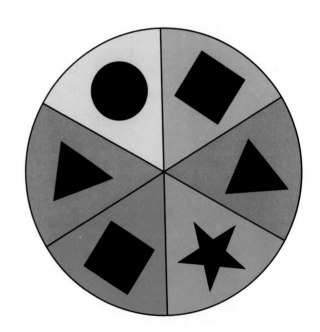

(7) Art invents mazes. He made 2 during the first week, 4 the second week, 6 the third week, and 8 the fourth week. If Art continues this pattern of making mazes, how many mazes will he make during the eighth week?

WRITER'S CORNER

(8) Think about a game you like to play. Write a problem about the game that can be solved using two different strategies. Be sure to name the strategies.

CHAPTER REVIEW/TEST

Vocabulary Check

Choose a word or words from the box to complete each sentence.

composite
greatest common
   factor (GCF)
least common
   denominator (LCD)
least common
   multiple (LCM)
like
mixed
prime
prime factorization

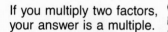

If you multiply two factors,
your answer is a multiple.

1. The smallest number that is a multiple of two or more whole numbers is the __?__ . *(page 174)*

2. A number that has only two factors, itself and 1, is a __?__ number. *(page 184)*

3. A whole number that has more than two factors is a __?__ number. *(page 184)*

4. The __?__ is the LCM of the denominators. *(page 179)*

5. The largest common factor of two or more numbers is called the __?__ . *(page 188)*

6. Fractions that have the same denominator are called __?__ fractions. *(page 180)*

7. When you express a composite number as the product of prime factors, you are using __?__ . *(page 186)*

8. A whole number and a fraction form a(n) __?__ number. *(page 194)*

Concept Check

9. What is the difference between the LCM and the LCD? *(page 179)*

10. What are equivalent fractions? *(page 176)*

11. How can you order fractions with unlike denominators? *(page 180)*

12. What is the difference between prime and composite numbers? *(page 184)*

13. How do you know when a fraction is in simplest form? *(page 192)*

14. When is a fraction greater than 1? *(page 194)*

15. How can you write a fraction as a mixed number? *(page 194)*

Skill Check

Find the LCM for each pair of numbers. *(page 174)*

16. $8, 40$ **17.** $12, 30$ **18.** $10, 16$ **19.** $11, 20$

Complete the number sentence. *(page 176)*

20. $\dfrac{3}{4} = \dfrac{\blacksquare}{12}$ **21.** $\dfrac{2}{3} = \dfrac{\blacksquare}{9}$ **22.** $\dfrac{4}{5} = \dfrac{\blacksquare}{20}$ **23.** $\dfrac{3}{8} = \dfrac{\blacksquare}{24}$

Use $<$, $>$, or $=$ to compare the fractions. *(page 180)*

24. $\dfrac{2}{4} \bullet \dfrac{15}{16}$ **25.** $\dfrac{9}{12} \bullet \dfrac{5}{8}$ **26.** $\dfrac{4}{9} \bullet \dfrac{20}{45}$

27. $\dfrac{3}{5} \bullet \dfrac{2}{15}$ **28.** $\dfrac{1}{9} \bullet \dfrac{7}{12}$ **29.** $\dfrac{3}{8} \bullet \dfrac{5}{12}$

Tell whether the number is prime or composite. Then list the factors. *(page 184)*

30. 18 **31.** 61 **32.** 26 **33.** 97

Write the prime factorization in exponent form. *(page 186)*

34. 63 **35.** 88 **36.** 50 **37.** 120

Write the GCF of each pair of numbers. *(page 188)*

38. $10, 35$ **39.** $15, 90$ **40.** $16, 120$ **41.** $45, 75$

Write the fraction as a mixed number or as a whole number. *(page 194)*

42. $\dfrac{40}{7}$ **43.** $\dfrac{18}{3}$ **44.** $\dfrac{62}{8}$ **45.** $\dfrac{93}{12}$

Problem-Solving Check *(pages 182, 196)*

46. Denny, Greg, and Gene went to a game. One drove, one took a bus, and the other took a train. Greg did not go by bus. Denny did not drive. Gene took a train. Who took a bus?

47. Four girls are running in a marathon. Tora is 10 minutes ahead of Tisha. Tisha is 25 minutes ahead of Lara, and Kim is 15 minutes behind Tora. How far behind Kim is Lara?

48. Maria is working a jigsaw puzzle. If it takes her an average of 7 minutes to assemble 20 pieces, how long will it take her to assemble 160 pieces?

49. Cindy runs 10 miles one day and 4 miles the next. How many days will it take her to run a total of 52 miles if she runs every two days and rests every third day?

WHAT DID I LEARN?

1. Use connecting cubes to determine whether 12 is a prime number or a composite number. Explain your method.

2. Explain how to determine the prime factorization of 24. Then find the prime factorization.

3. Write $\frac{24}{36}$ in simplest form. Show your work and explain.

4. Compare $\frac{3}{4}$ to $\frac{2}{3}$ to find which is greater. Show your work and explain.

5. Write the mixed number $2\frac{3}{4}$ as a fraction. Show your work and explain.

6. Read Exercise 2 on page 183. Follow the steps on the Problem-Solving Think Along worksheet to show how to solve this problem.

Write About It

7. What is something you discovered about fractions that you didn't know before studying this chapter on number theory?

8. Explain how to determine whether $\frac{23}{43}$ is in simplest form.

TEAMWORK *Project*

Make a Math Game

Creating your own game can be both challenging and fun.

Work with your teammates to create a math game and challenge another team in your classroom.

Decide

As a team, decide on a math concept to structure the game.

Will players compete as individuals or teams? How will a player or a team win?

Decide on the format for the game. Will it contain cards, a board, game pieces?

Decide on a method of scoring.

Discuss and limit the length of the game.

Do

- As a team, design and build the game.
- Make the necessary parts.
- Write a set of rules. State how to score and how to win.
- Play the game. Adjust any features that do not work.

Share

- Exchange games with another team. After everyone has had a chance to play, discuss the challenges of both games.

Talk About It

What math skills are required to play each game?

How can you improve your game?

Which game seems to be more popular? Why?

Pico, Centro, Nada

Many people in Venezuela play the game *Pico, Centro, Nada*. Play the game with a partner.

Players take turns. One player thinks of a two-digit number. The other player tries to guess the number. When each guess is made, the first player gives one clue: *pico, centro,* or *nada.*

★ *Pico* means one digit is correct but in the wrong place.

★ *Centro* means one digit is correct and in the correct place.

★ *Nada* means neither digit is correct.

MULTICULTURAL NOTE: The Spanish brought the game *Pico, Centro, Nada* with them when they first came to Venezuela, around 1500.

Players need to keep a record of the number of guesses they make. The player who makes fewer guesses is the winner.

Challenge

Number Sense

Mirror primes are pairs of prime numbers whose digits are reversed. Find the mirror primes in the table.

Prime Numbers Less Than 150
2   3   5   7   11 13 17 19
23 29 31 37 41 43 47 53
59 61 67 71 73 79 83 89
97 101 103 107 109 113 127 131
137 139 149

Twin primes are pairs of prime numbers with a difference of 2. Name the twin primes that are less than 150.

Critical Thinking

The numbers below can be written as the sum of two prime numbers. For example, $71 + 11 = 82$. Find two prime-number addends for each number.

12	94
24	126
38	176
60	222
82	

Find a second pair of prime numbers whose sum is 222.

CUMULATIVE REVIEW
CHAPTERS 1–6

Write the letter of the correct answer.

1. $24.2 - (8.1 \times 2) + 8$

   A. 15   **B.** 16
   C. 40.2   **D.** 161

2. Evaluate $b - 6$, for $b = 18.9$.

   A. 12   **B.** 12.9
   C. 18.3   **D.** not here

3. Estimate $6{,}235 \times 240$.

   A. 120,000   **B.** 1,200,000
   C. 1,800,000   **D.** not here

4. 8.8×0.622

   A. 4.4736   **B.** 5.4636
   C. 5.4736   **D.** 54.736

5. What type of graph is appropriate to show favorite car colors?

   A. bar   **B.** double-line
   C. line   **D.** histogram

6. Choose the number of choices.
2 pairs of shoes, 3 pairs of socks

   A. 2 choices   **B.** 3 choices
   C. 5 choices   **D.** 6 choices

7. $9.66 \div 2.1$

   A. 0.46   **B.** 4.5
   C. 46.   **D.** not here

8. Find the LCM of 10 and 12.

   A. 1   **B.** 2
   C. 60   **D.** 120

9. Find the GCF of 8 and 32.

   A. 2   **B.** 4
   C. 8   **D.** 16

10. What is $7\frac{2}{5}$ written as a fraction?

   A. $\frac{14}{5}$ **B.** $\frac{37}{5}$

   C. $\frac{72}{5}$ **D.** $35\frac{2}{5}$

11. Sandy has the greatest number of hits. Jon has fewer than Kirk, who has fewer than Sandy. Mona is ahead of Jon but behind Kirk. Who has the least number of hits?

   A. Jon   **B.** Kirk
   C. Mona   **D.** Sandy

12. A cat was tangled in 36 inches of yarn. With every attempt to get free, he got rid of 15 inches and then re-entangled himself in 8 inches. How many tries did it take the cat to get free?

   A. 3 tries   **B.** 6 tries
   C. 9 tries   **D.** not here

CHAPTER 7

ADDING AND SUBTRACTING FRACTIONS

Did you know...

... that fractions are commonly used around the home?

TALK ABOUT IT

Suppose a recipe for muffins requires $1\frac{1}{3}$ cups of raisins. A recipe for fruit salad requires $\frac{3}{4}$ cup of raisins. Each recipe serves 2 people. Decide the number of servings of muffins and fruit salad you would need for your family and the amount of raisins you would buy.

ESTIMATING
Fraction Sums and Differences

You can round to estimate fraction sums or differences. Some fractions that can be rounded to 0, $\frac{1}{2}$, or 1 are given.

$\boxed{\frac{1}{9}}\boxed{\frac{1}{8}}\boxed{\frac{1}{6}}\boxed{\frac{2}{9}}\boxed{\frac{1}{4}}$ $\boxed{\frac{1}{3}}\boxed{\frac{3}{8}}\boxed{\frac{4}{9}}\boxed{\frac{1}{2}}\boxed{\frac{5}{9}}\boxed{\frac{5}{8}}\boxed{\frac{2}{3}}$ $\boxed{\frac{3}{4}}\boxed{\frac{7}{9}}\boxed{\frac{5}{6}}\boxed{\frac{7}{8}}\boxed{\frac{8}{9}}$

The numerator is much less than the denominator. So, round to 0.

The numerator is about one half the denominator. So, round to $\frac{1}{2}$.

The numerator is about the same as the denominator. So, round to 1.

Normee and his father are Inuit who live in northern Canada. They are building bookends from wood scrap. One piece of wood is $\frac{1}{4}$ yard, one is $\frac{3}{8}$ yard, and one is $\frac{5}{6}$ yard long. Normee determines that he has $1\frac{11}{24}$ yards of wood scrap. Is his answer reasonable?

$$\frac{1}{4} \ + \ \frac{3}{8} \ + \ \frac{5}{6} \ = \ \blacksquare$$
$$\downarrow \qquad \downarrow \qquad \downarrow$$

Estimate. $0 \ + \ \frac{1}{2} \ + \ 1 \ = \ 1\frac{1}{2}$

So, Normee's answer is reasonable.

You can also round to estimate mixed-number sums and differences.

Example   About how much is $9\frac{9}{10} - 5\frac{7}{8}$?

Step 1 Round to the nearest whole number.	**Step 2** Subtract.
$9\frac{9}{10}$ is a little less than 10. $-\ 5\frac{7}{8}$ is a little less than 6.	$\begin{array}{r} 10 \\ -\ \ 6 \\ \hline 4 \end{array}$ ← estimate

MULTICULTURAL NOTE: Some of the Inuit people still live as their ancestors did hundreds of years ago. Most Inuit, however, have adopted more modern ways.

Check for Understanding

Write *about 0*, *about* $\frac{1}{2}$, or *about 1*.

1. $\frac{14}{27}$

2. $\frac{10}{11}$

3. $\frac{1}{9}$

4. $\frac{11}{24}$

5. $\frac{1}{16}$

6. $\frac{9}{10}$

Practice

Round the fractions to 0, $\frac{1}{2}$, or 1. Then rewrite the problem.

7. $\frac{13}{14} + \frac{10}{17}$

8. $8\frac{1}{3} - 3\frac{1}{15}$

9. $\frac{8}{9} + \frac{1}{2}$

10. $11\frac{4}{5} - 2\frac{7}{9}$

11. $6\frac{1}{4} + 3\frac{2}{9}$

12. $4\frac{1}{20} - 1\frac{4}{5}$

Estimate the sum or difference.

13. $\frac{1}{15} + \frac{9}{20}$

14. $\frac{1}{8} + \frac{5}{6}$

15. $\frac{7}{8} - \frac{4}{9}$

16. $\frac{29}{30} - \frac{9}{10}$

17. $3\frac{3}{7} + 1\frac{1}{14}$

18. $1\frac{5}{26} - \frac{1}{6}$

19. $12\frac{2}{3} - 5\frac{6}{11}$

20. $\frac{4}{5} + \frac{7}{10} + \frac{1}{6}$

21. $4\frac{3}{4} - 1\frac{1}{8}$

22. $\frac{13}{15} + \frac{1}{5}$

23. $3\frac{1}{4} + 4\frac{6}{7}$

24. $5\frac{6}{7} - 2\frac{1}{3}$

25. $\frac{7}{8} - \frac{1}{16}$

26. $4\frac{1}{2} + 2\frac{3}{4}$

27. $9\frac{1}{9} - 7\frac{7}{8}$

28. $\frac{4}{9} - \frac{1}{15}$

Mixed Applications

Estimate to solve.

29. Elsa had $27\frac{7}{8}$ yards of jute. She used $13\frac{1}{4}$ yards to make a plant hanger. Does Elsa have enough jute to make another plant hanger the same size? Defend your answer.

30. Leon has three fabric remnants measuring $2\frac{5}{6}$ yards, $1\frac{1}{4}$ yards, and $1\frac{2}{3}$ yards. He determines that he has a total of about 4 yards. Is his estimate reasonable? Explain.

31. **Number Sense** Prime numbers that differ by two, such as 3 and 5 or 59 and 61, are called **twin primes.** Write 2 other pairs of twin primes between 1 and 50.

32. **Make Up a Problem** Write a problem about everyday life at home that can be solved by estimating fractions. Exchange with a classmate and solve.

Explain how to round fractions.

W R A P U P . . .

ADDING AND SUBTRACTING
Like Fractions

Cher's muffin recipe calls for $\frac{5}{8}$ teaspoon (t) of cinnamon and $\frac{1}{8}$ t of nutmeg. How much spice does she need?

You can use mental math when you add like fractions.

Step 1	Step 2
When the denominators are the same, add the numerators. $\frac{5}{8} + \frac{1}{8} = \frac{6}{8}$	Write the answer in simplest form. $\frac{6 \div 2}{8 \div 2} = \frac{3}{4}$

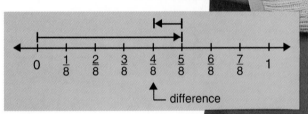

So, the recipe calls for a total of $\frac{3}{4}$ t of spice.

How much more cinnamon than nutmeg is needed for the recipe?

You can also use mental math when you subtract like fractions.

Step 1	Step 2
When the denominators are the same, subtract the numerators. $\frac{5}{8} - \frac{1}{8} = \frac{4}{8}$	Write the answer in simplest form. $\frac{4 \div 4}{8 \div 4} = \frac{1}{2}$

So, $\frac{1}{2}$ t more cinnamon than nutmeg is needed.

More Examples

A. $\frac{5}{7} + \frac{4}{7} = \frac{9}{7}$, or $1\frac{2}{7}$ **B.** $\frac{10}{12} - \frac{5}{12} = \frac{5}{12}$ **C.** $\frac{5}{6} + \frac{5}{6} + \frac{4}{6} = \frac{14}{6} = \frac{7}{3}$, or $2\frac{1}{3}$

Check for Understanding

Find the sum or difference. Write your answer in simplest form.

1. $\frac{1}{4} + \frac{1}{4}$

2. $\frac{2}{6} + \frac{3}{6}$

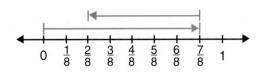

3. $\frac{7}{8} - \frac{5}{8}$

Practice

Tell whether the sum or difference is correct. Write *true* or *false.*
If you write *false,* give the correct answer.

4. $\dfrac{2}{5} + \dfrac{1}{5} = \dfrac{3}{10}$

5. $\dfrac{6}{9} - \dfrac{2}{9} = \dfrac{1}{3}$

6. $\dfrac{7}{16} + \dfrac{9}{16} = 1$

7. $\dfrac{11}{12} - \dfrac{8}{12} = \dfrac{1}{4}$

8. $\dfrac{2}{10} + \dfrac{4}{10} = \dfrac{2}{5}$

9. $\dfrac{19}{20} - \dfrac{3}{20} = \dfrac{4}{5}$

Find the sum or difference. Write your answer in simplest form.

10. $\dfrac{2}{5} + \dfrac{3}{5}$

11. $\dfrac{9}{10} - \dfrac{8}{10}$

12. $\dfrac{6}{12} + \dfrac{11}{12}$

13. $\dfrac{5}{20} - \dfrac{1}{20}$

14. $\dfrac{1}{12} + \dfrac{7}{12}$

15. $\dfrac{4}{9} - \dfrac{2}{9}$

16. $\dfrac{9}{10} + \dfrac{3}{10}$

17. $\dfrac{7}{8} - \dfrac{3}{8}$

18. $\dfrac{1}{15} + \dfrac{8}{15}$

19. $\dfrac{5}{6} - \dfrac{1}{6}$

20. $\dfrac{5}{8} + \dfrac{7}{8}$

21. $\dfrac{13}{16} - \dfrac{5}{16}$

22. $\dfrac{7}{16} - \dfrac{5}{16}$

23. $\dfrac{4}{5} + \dfrac{4}{5}$

24. $\dfrac{13}{14} - \dfrac{3}{14}$

25. $\dfrac{6}{7} + \dfrac{5}{7}$

Mixed Applications

26. A blueberry-pecan muffin recipe calls for $\frac{3}{4}$ cup of whole-wheat flour. If Doug has $\frac{1}{4}$ cup, how much more whole-wheat flour does he need?

27. **Number Sense ● Mental Math** How can you use mental math to add $\frac{2}{5} + \frac{1}{3} + \frac{3}{5} + \frac{2}{3}$?

MIXED REVIEW

Choose the better estimate. Write **a** or **b.**

1. $798 + 521$
   a. 1,100
   b. 1,300

2. $6,245 - 2,198$
   a. 4,000
   b. 5,000

3. 735×57
   a. 3,500
   b. 42,000

4. $5,435 \div 89$
   a. 90
   b. 60

Find the sum or difference.

5. $\begin{array}{r} 473 \\ +698 \\ \hline \end{array}$

6. $\begin{array}{r} 39,100 \\ -\ \ \ \ 678 \\ \hline \end{array}$

7. $\begin{array}{r} \$35.98 \\ +\ 10.52 \\ \hline \end{array}$

8. $\begin{array}{r} 6,519 \\ +2,103 \\ \hline \end{array}$

9. $\begin{array}{r} 870,000 \\ -\ 87,937 \\ \hline \end{array}$

Write as a mixed number or as a fraction greater than 1.

10. $\dfrac{35}{6}$

11. $4\dfrac{5}{8}$

12. $\dfrac{29}{3}$

13. $6\dfrac{1}{4}$

14. $\dfrac{98}{12}$

15. $8\dfrac{3}{7}$

How do you add or subtract like fractions?

WRAP UP...

ADDING AND SUBTRACTING
Unlike Fractions

John has $\frac{3}{4}$ yd of red ribbon and $\frac{1}{12}$ yd of purple ribbon. How much more red than purple ribbon does he have?

- How can you use fraction bars to find the difference $\frac{3}{4} - \frac{1}{12}$?

To add or subtract fractions with unlike denominators, rename the fractions by using the least common denominator.

Step 1
Write equivalent fractions using the LCD.

$$\frac{3}{4} = \frac{3 \times 3}{4 \times 3} = \frac{9}{12} \quad \text{The LCD is 12.}$$
$$-\frac{1}{12} = \qquad \frac{1}{12}$$

Step 2
Subtract. Write the answer in simplest form.

$$\frac{3}{4} = \frac{9}{12}$$
$$-\frac{1}{12} = \frac{1}{12}$$
$$\overline{\qquad \frac{8}{12} = \frac{2}{3}}$$

So, John has $\frac{2}{3}$ yd more red ribbon.

If John uses all the purple ribbon and $\frac{3}{8}$ yd of green ribbon, how much ribbon will he use?

Step 1
Write equivalent fractions using the LCD.

$$\frac{1}{12} = \frac{1 \times 2}{12 \times 2} = \frac{2}{24} \quad \text{The LCD is 24.}$$
$$+\frac{3}{8} = \frac{3 \times 3}{8 \times 3} = \frac{9}{24}$$

Step 2
Add. If necessary, write the answer in simplest form.

$$\frac{1}{12} = \frac{2}{24}$$
$$+\frac{3}{8} = \frac{9}{24}$$
$$\overline{\qquad \frac{11}{24}}$$

So, John will use $\frac{11}{24}$ yd of ribbon.

Check for Understanding

Write equivalent fractions using the LCD.

1. $\frac{9}{14} - \frac{1}{7}$ 2. $\frac{3}{4} + \frac{9}{16}$ 3. $\frac{6}{8} - \frac{2}{5}$ 4. $\frac{1}{2} + \frac{5}{6} + \frac{4}{5}$

Practice

Write equivalent fractions by finding the missing digits.

5. $\dfrac{1}{2} = \dfrac{\blacksquare}{8}$
$+\dfrac{3}{8} = \dfrac{3}{8}$
____
$\dfrac{\blacksquare}{8}$

6. $\dfrac{1}{5} = \dfrac{\blacksquare}{10}$
$+\dfrac{7}{10} = \dfrac{\blacksquare}{10}$
____
$\dfrac{9}{10}$

7. $\dfrac{2}{3} = \dfrac{10}{\blacksquare}$
$-\dfrac{1}{5} = \dfrac{3}{\blacksquare}$
____
$\dfrac{7}{\blacksquare}$

8. $\dfrac{5}{6} = \dfrac{\blacksquare}{\blacksquare}$
$+\dfrac{3}{4} = \dfrac{\blacksquare}{\blacksquare}$
____
$\dfrac{\blacksquare}{\blacksquare}$, or $1\dfrac{7}{12}$

Find the sum or difference. Write your answer in simplest form.

9. $\dfrac{5}{6}$
$+\dfrac{2}{3}$

10. $\dfrac{7}{9}$
$-\dfrac{1}{3}$

11. $\dfrac{3}{4}$
$+\dfrac{1}{6}$

12. $\dfrac{5}{8}$
$-\dfrac{1}{4}$

13. $\dfrac{1}{6}$
$+\dfrac{3}{4}$

14. $\dfrac{2}{3}$
$-\dfrac{1}{2}$

15. $\dfrac{9}{10}$
$-\dfrac{3}{5}$

16. $\dfrac{1}{3}$
$+\dfrac{5}{6}$

17. $\dfrac{7}{12}$
$-\dfrac{1}{3}$

18. $\dfrac{2}{3}$
$+\dfrac{3}{4}$

19. $\dfrac{2}{3}$
$-\dfrac{2}{5}$

20. $\dfrac{1}{2}$
$+\dfrac{1}{3}$

Mixed Applications

21. Brandon is making a pennant. He needs $\dfrac{1}{3}$ yd of red fabric, $\dfrac{1}{2}$ yd of blue fabric, and $\dfrac{3}{4}$ yd of white fabric. How much fabric does Brandon need?

22. **Making Decisions** Beth uses $\dfrac{1}{8}$ of her total daily water consumption to wash dishes by hand, but $\dfrac{1}{80}$ to use a dishwasher. Which method conserves more water?

NUMBER SENSE • ESTIMATION

When you adjust an estimate, you are finding an estimate that is closer to the exact answer.

Estimate. $4\dfrac{3}{5} + 5\dfrac{5}{8} \approx 11$

Acceptable adjustments include:

about 10   more than $9\dfrac{1}{2}$ less than 11   a little more than 10

Adjust the estimate.

23. $2\dfrac{1}{8} + 4\dfrac{2}{5} \approx 6$

24. $8\dfrac{6}{7} + 5\dfrac{3}{4} \approx 15$

25. $7\dfrac{5}{6} + 3\dfrac{8}{9} \approx 11$

How do you know that 24 is the LCD for $\dfrac{1}{12} + \dfrac{3}{8}$?

ADDING MIXED NUMBERS

Connie has $3\frac{3}{4}$ cups of orange juice and $2\frac{3}{4}$ cups of cranberry juice. If she combines the juices, how many cups of juice will Connie have?

Estimate. $3\frac{3}{4} + 2\frac{3}{4} \longrightarrow 4 + 3 = 7$

Add.

Step 1 Add the like fractions.	**Step 2** Add the whole numbers.	**Step 3** Write the fraction in simplest form. Rewrite the sum.
$\begin{array}{r} 3\frac{3}{4} \\ +2\frac{3}{4} \\ \hline \frac{6}{4} \end{array}$	$\begin{array}{r} 3\frac{3}{4} \\ +2\frac{3}{4} \\ \hline 5\frac{6}{4} \end{array}$	$5\frac{6}{4} = 5\frac{3}{2} = 5 + \frac{2}{2} + \frac{1}{2} = 6\frac{1}{2}$

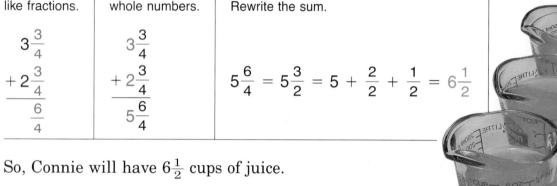

So, Connie will have $6\frac{1}{2}$ cups of juice.

To add mixed numbers with unlike denominators, you must first find the LCD of the fractions.

Example $\quad 3\frac{3}{4} + 1\frac{1}{2}$

Step 1 Write equivalent fractions using the LCD.	**Step 2** Add. Rewrite the sum.
$\begin{array}{r} 3\frac{3}{4} = 3\frac{3}{4} \\ +1\frac{1}{2} = 1\frac{2}{4} \\ \hline \end{array}$ The LCD is 4.	$\begin{array}{r} 3\frac{3}{4} = 3\frac{3}{4} \\ +1\frac{1}{2} = 1\frac{2}{4} \\ \hline 4\frac{5}{4} = 4 + \frac{4}{4} + \frac{1}{4} = 5\frac{1}{4} \end{array}$

Check for Understanding

Write *true* or *false.* If you write *false,* give the correct answer.

1. $5\frac{1}{6} + 3\frac{2}{6} = 8\frac{1}{2}$ **2.** $3\frac{2}{5} + 4\frac{3}{5} = 8$ **3.** $1\frac{2}{5} + 2\frac{3}{10} = 3\frac{3}{5}$

Practice

Estimate the sum.

4. $2\frac{1}{12} + 3\frac{1}{12}$ **5.** $3\frac{1}{5} + 4\frac{2}{3}$ **6.** $5\frac{2}{7} + 6\frac{3}{4}$ **7.** $7\frac{2}{3} + 5\frac{1}{9}$

Find the sum.

8. $\begin{array}{r} 3\frac{1}{10} \\ + 2\frac{3}{10} \\ \hline \end{array}$ **9.** $\begin{array}{r} 6\frac{1}{4} \\ + 2\frac{1}{4} \\ \hline \end{array}$ **10.** $\begin{array}{r} 1\frac{3}{8} \\ + 5\frac{1}{8} \\ \hline \end{array}$ **11.** $\begin{array}{r} 2\frac{2}{7} \\ + 3\frac{3}{7} \\ \hline \end{array}$ **12.** $\begin{array}{r} 4\frac{5}{6} \\ + 7\frac{1}{6} \\ \hline \end{array}$

13. $\begin{array}{r} 1\frac{1}{2} \\ + 2\frac{3}{5} \\ \hline \end{array}$ **14.** $\begin{array}{r} 3\frac{3}{8} \\ + 5\frac{3}{4} \\ \hline \end{array}$ **15.** $\begin{array}{r} 2\frac{2}{3} \\ + 1\frac{1}{2} \\ \hline \end{array}$ **16.** $\begin{array}{r} 1\frac{3}{5} \\ + 4\frac{5}{8} \\ \hline \end{array}$ **17.** $\begin{array}{r} 5\frac{1}{4} \\ + 7\frac{3}{16} \\ \hline \end{array}$

18. $\begin{array}{r} 5\frac{1}{8} \\ + 3\frac{3}{4} \\ \hline \end{array}$ **19.** $\begin{array}{r} 11\frac{7}{12} \\ + 5\frac{1}{4} \\ \hline \end{array}$ **20.** $\begin{array}{r} 9\frac{2}{3} \\ + 8\frac{4}{7} \\ \hline \end{array}$ **21.** $\begin{array}{r} 8\frac{3}{7} \\ + 6\frac{2}{3} \\ \hline \end{array}$ **22.** $\begin{array}{r} 4\frac{5}{8} \\ + 7\frac{3}{5} \\ \hline \end{array}$

Mixed Applications

23. Carlos bought $1\frac{2}{3}$ pounds (lb) of potato salad, $2\frac{3}{5}$ lb of coleslaw, and $4\frac{5}{6}$ lb of chicken at a deli. What is the total weight of his purchases?

24. **Make Up a Problem** Use a newspaper to find the prices of three stocks listed on a stock exchange. Then use the information to write a problem.

CALCULATOR CONNECTION

 You can use a calculator designed to operate with fractions.

Example $4\frac{1}{5} + 6\frac{7}{8}$ 4 [+] 1 [/] 5 [+] 6 [+] 7 [/] 8 [=] | 10   43/40 |

[Ab/c] | 11   3/40 |

25. What does pressing [Ab/c] do?

26. What keystrokes would you use to add two fractions?

How does adding mixed numbers differ from adding fractions?

WRAP UP...

PROBLEM SOLVING

STRATEGY • Draw a Diagram

The steps of a building extend south $20\frac{1}{3}$ yd from the entrance. The south edge of a statue is $15\frac{2}{3}$ yd west of the bottom step. An east-west path begins $24\frac{2}{3}$ yd south of the statue. How far is it from the entrance of the building straight south to the path?

Sometimes drawing a diagram can help you solve a problem. The diagram may help you visualize the solution.

▶ **UNDERSTAND**

What are you asked to find?

What information are you given?

▶ **PLAN**

What strategy can you use?

You can *draw a diagram* that shows the building entrance, the statue, and the path.

▶ **SOLVE**

How will you carry out your plan?

Draw a diagram and label the structures and the distances. Since the direction from the steps to the statue is west, you can ignore it and add the remaining distances.

$$20\frac{1}{3} + 24\frac{2}{3} = 44\frac{3}{3} = 45$$

So, the path is 45 yd from the building entrance.

▶ **LOOK BACK**

What other strategy can you use to solve the problem?

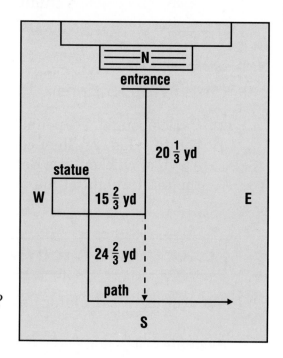

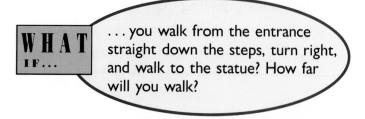

WHAT IF... ...you walk from the entrance straight down the steps, turn right, and walk to the statue? How far will you walk?

Apply

1. Kirk walked $\frac{9}{10}$ mile north, $1\frac{1}{10}$ miles east, $\frac{3}{10}$ mile south, and $1\frac{6}{10}$ miles west in order to visit friends. How far had he walked when he crossed his own path?

2. Carrie's room is 12 feet square. A chair that is $2\frac{1}{4}$ feet deep is against one wall. A 2-foot-wide table is $2\frac{3}{4}$ feet from the chair. How far is the table from the opposite wall?

Mixed Applications → **STRATEGIES**

Draw a Diagram • Make a Table
• Write a Number Sentence
• Find a Pattern

Choose a strategy and solve. Use the table for Exercises 3–4.

Violin Lesson Fees		
1 Lesson	**Cost**	**Book Rental**
at home:	$10.00	no charge
at studio:	$ 7.00	$0.50/week

3. If Jasmine takes one violin lesson a week, how much will it cost her to take four lessons at the studio?

4. How much more will it cost Jasmine to take four lessons at her home than at the studio?

5. Ed wants to put a 1.4-meter chest against a 3.6-meter wall. If he centers the chest, how far will it be from each end of the wall?

6. Wade's baby brother chewed $\frac{1}{4}$ of Wade's baseball cards. What part of the cards were not chewed?

7. Dan's record collection includes $\frac{3}{5}$ rock, $\frac{1}{5}$ country, and $\frac{1}{5}$ classical. How much of his collection is not rock music?

8. Suppose you have 6 blue pens, 5 green pens, and some red pens in your desk. If there is a $\frac{4}{15}$ probability of choosing a red pen from your desk, how many pens are in your desk?

9. Five pads of paper cost $4.50, 10 pads cost $8.05, 20 pads cost $15.15, and 30 pads cost $22.25. If this pattern continues, how much do 50 pads cost?

WRITER'S CORNER

10. Write a word problem that can be solved by drawing a diagram. Draw the diagram on a separate sheet of paper and solve. Then ask a classmate to solve the problem. Is his or her diagram similar to yours?

REVIEW AND MAINTENANCE

1. Lamar is standing on a ladder to paint windows. He is 2.9 meters from the ground. The ladder rungs are 0.2 meter apart. If he moves up 3 rungs, how many meters will he be from the ground?

After I read a problem, I choose a strategy to solve it.

2. Mrs. Smith used $1\frac{1}{2}$ cups (c) of flour to make muffins, $4\frac{1}{3}$ c to make bread, and $\frac{3}{4}$ c to make gravy for a meal. If she has $3\frac{1}{4}$ c left, how much flour did Mrs. Smith have before she started the meal?

3. Mr. Evans is painting squares on a wall. The first is 5 inches (in.) square, the second 8 in., the third 13 in., and the fourth 20 in. If the pattern continues, what will be the size of the sixth square?

Write the GCF of the numerator and denominator.

4. $\frac{10}{15}$
5. $\frac{21}{63}$
6. $\frac{32}{96}$
7. $\frac{12}{36}$
8. $\frac{44}{80}$

Write the fraction as a mixed number.

9. $\frac{62}{10}$
10. $\frac{81}{6}$
11. $\frac{79}{9}$
12. $\frac{24}{5}$
13. $\frac{54}{7}$

Write the mixed number as a fraction.

14. $4\frac{1}{3}$
15. $7\frac{1}{4}$
16. $6\frac{2}{5}$
17. $11\frac{1}{2}$
18. $8\frac{4}{9}$

Estimate the sum or difference.

19. $6\frac{2}{3} + 8\frac{9}{11}$
20. $4\frac{9}{10} - 2\frac{1}{8}$
21. $8\frac{7}{8} + 2\frac{3}{4}$

Find the sum or difference.

22. $\frac{1}{6} + \frac{2}{6} = $ ▨
23. $4\frac{2}{5} + 3\frac{4}{5} = $ ▨
24. $\frac{9}{10} - \frac{3}{10} = $ ▨
25. $\frac{7}{9} + \frac{2}{5} = $ ▨

26. $\frac{6}{15} + \frac{1}{10} = $ ▨
27. $\frac{5}{12} + \frac{1}{4} = $ ▨
28. $\frac{3}{4} - \frac{1}{6} = $ ▨
29. $\frac{2}{3} - \frac{1}{4} = $ ▨

30. $\begin{array}{r} \frac{5}{7} \\ - \frac{1}{14} \\ \hline \end{array}$
31. $\begin{array}{r} 9\frac{2}{3} \\ + 7\frac{1}{4} \\ \hline \end{array}$
32. $\begin{array}{r} 5\frac{1}{9} \\ + 3\frac{2}{3} \\ \hline \end{array}$
33. $\begin{array}{r} 2\frac{3}{4} \\ + 4\frac{3}{5} \\ \hline \end{array}$
34. $\begin{array}{r} 11\frac{3}{8} \\ + 5\frac{2}{16} \\ \hline \end{array}$

ASIA

China

Chinese Fractions

More than 1,000 years ago in China, people used a different method to add fractions. This method did not require the denominators of the addends to be the same. The method was described in a book called *Nine Chapters,* one of the first Chinese mathematics books.

Example $\frac{2}{5} + \frac{3}{8}$

Step 1 Multiply opposite numerators and denominators.

$$\frac{2}{5} \times \frac{3}{8} \qquad \begin{array}{c} 2 \times 8 = 16 \\ 5 \times 3 = 15 \end{array}$$

Step 2 Find the sum of the products.

$$16 + 15 = 31$$

This number becomes the numerator for your answer.

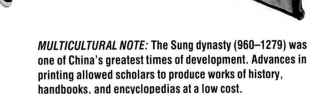

Step 3 Multiply the denominators.

$$\frac{2}{5} + \frac{3}{8} \qquad 5 \times 8 = 40$$

This number becomes the denominator for your answer.

Step 4 $\frac{2}{5} + \frac{3}{8} = \frac{31}{40}$

MULTICULTURAL NOTE: The Sung dynasty (960–1279) was one of China's greatest times of development. Advances in printing allowed scholars to produce works of history, handbooks, and encyclopedias at a low cost.

Work with a partner. See how long it takes to solve the problems by using the ancient Chinese method. Then see how long it takes to solve the problems by using the method you learned earlier in the chapter.

1. $\frac{6}{7} + \frac{1}{8}$

2. $\frac{1}{3} + \frac{1}{4}$

3. $\frac{4}{9} + \frac{1}{2}$

4. $\frac{1}{6} + \frac{5}{9}$

5. $\frac{5}{7} + \frac{1}{3}$

6. $\frac{3}{4} + \frac{1}{8}$

EXPLORING

Subtraction of Mixed Numbers

Mrs. France has $3\frac{1}{4}$ yards of fabric to make placemats and napkins. If she uses $1\frac{3}{4}$ yards to make placemats, how much fabric will be left to make napkins?

Building Understanding

Use fraction squares to subtract mixed numbers with like denominators.

Example $3\frac{1}{4} - 1\frac{3}{4}$

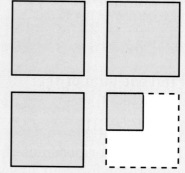

Figure A

TALK ABOUT IT

- What amount in Figure **A** is blue?

- What must you do to change Figure **A** so that you can subtract $1\frac{3}{4}$ from it?

- How does Figure **B** differ from Figure **A**?

- What amount is left in Figure **B** if you remove $1\frac{3}{4}$?

- How much fabric will be left to make napkins?

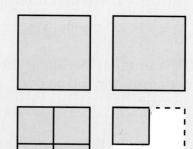

Figure B

Use fraction squares to find the difference.

a. $3 - 1\frac{1}{2}$ **b.** $3 - \frac{3}{4}$ **c.** $1\frac{1}{3} - \frac{2}{3}$ **d.** $3\frac{1}{6} - 2\frac{5}{6}$

Making the Connection

Another way to see subtraction of mixed numbers is to use a number line.

Example $3\frac{1}{3} - 1\frac{2}{3}$

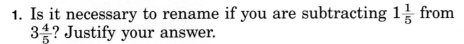

- Look at the number line. What is $3\frac{1}{3} - 1\frac{2}{3}$?

Sometimes you must rename mixed numbers before you can subtract. Renaming mixed numbers is similar to regrouping whole numbers.

Examples

Whole number: $234 = 2$ hundreds, 3 tens, 4 ones
$\qquad\qquad\quad = 1$ hundred, 13 tens, 4 ones

Mixed number: $5\frac{3}{5} = 4 + 1 + \frac{3}{5} = 4 + \frac{5}{5} + \frac{3}{5} = 4\frac{8}{5}$

1. Is it necessary to rename if you are subtracting $1\frac{1}{5}$ from $3\frac{4}{5}$? Justify your answer.

2. When must you rename a mixed number before you can subtract?

3. How do you rename a mixed number?

Checking Understanding

Tell whether or not you must rename the greater number. Write *yes* or *no*. Then rename if necessary.

4. $2\frac{1}{8} - \frac{7}{8}$

5. $1\frac{11}{12} - \frac{7}{12}$

6. $1\frac{1}{5} - \frac{3}{5}$

Find the difference.

7. $6\frac{1}{5} - 4\frac{3}{5}$

8. $4\frac{1}{4} - 2\frac{3}{4}$

9. $5\frac{5}{8} - 3\frac{7}{8}$

10. $8\frac{1}{8} - 2\frac{7}{8}$

11. $8 - 5\frac{3}{4}$

12. $19 - 15\frac{2}{3}$

SUBTRACTING MIXED NUMBERS
with Like Denominators

Isabel's aunt sent her $7\frac{2}{3}$ yards of handwoven wool fabric from South America. Isabel used $3\frac{1}{3}$ yards to make a poncho. How much fabric was left?

Estimate.

$$7\frac{2}{3} - 3\frac{1}{3} = \blacksquare$$

$$8 - 3 = 5 \leftarrow \text{estimate}$$

Step 1 Subtract the fractions.	**Step 2** Subtract the whole numbers. Write the fraction in simplest form.
$7\frac{2}{3}$ $-3\frac{1}{3}$ ___ $\frac{1}{3}$	$7\frac{2}{3}$ $-3\frac{1}{3}$ ___ $4\frac{1}{3}$

So, $4\frac{1}{3}$ yards of fabric were left.

Sometimes you must rename the greater mixed number.

Isabel made a poncho for her sister. If she used $2\frac{2}{3}$ yards of the fabric that remained, how much fabric was left?

Step 1 Decide whether to rename the greater mixed number. Think: $\frac{2}{3} > \frac{1}{3}$. So, rename.	**Step 2** Subtract. If necessary, write the fraction in simplest form.
$4\frac{1}{3} = 3\frac{4}{3}$ $-2\frac{2}{3}$ ___	$4\frac{1}{3} = 3\frac{4}{3}$ $-2\frac{2}{3} = 2\frac{2}{3}$ ___ $1\frac{2}{3}$

MULTICULTURAL NOTE: Ponchos are worn by both men and women in South America. The fabric, made by native South Americans, is known for its bright colors and creative designs.

So, $1\frac{2}{3}$ yards of fabric were left.

Check for Understanding

Find the difference.

1. $7\frac{4}{5} - 3\frac{1}{5}$
2. $5\frac{1}{3} - 3\frac{2}{3}$
3. $10\frac{5}{8} - 8\frac{3}{8}$
4. $19\frac{1}{5} - 12\frac{4}{5}$

Practice

Find the difference.

5. $16\frac{6}{7}$
$-\ \ 3\frac{1}{7}$

6. $5\frac{1}{3}$
$-\ 1\frac{2}{3}$

7. $7\frac{4}{20}$
$-\ 5\frac{3}{20}$

8. 9
$-\ 3\frac{11}{12}$

9. $10\frac{7}{11}$
$-\ \ 4\frac{9}{11}$

10. $9\frac{19}{20}$
$-\ 2\frac{7}{20}$

11. $3\frac{1}{8}$
$-\ 2\frac{5}{8}$

12. $5\frac{3}{8}$
$-\ 2\frac{7}{8}$

13. $8\frac{6}{12}$
$-\ 3\frac{5}{12}$

14. $18\frac{9}{10}$
$-\ \ 9\frac{3}{10}$

15. $4\frac{1}{9}$
$-\ 1\frac{7}{9}$

16. $12\frac{7}{8}$
$-\ \ 4\frac{3}{8}$

17. $15\frac{9}{16}$
$-\ \ 2\frac{13}{16}$

18. $76\frac{19}{20}$
$-\ 31\frac{17}{20}$

19. $49\frac{11}{36}$
$-\ 22\frac{17}{36}$

Mixed Applications

20. Shelby practices the piano $7\frac{3}{4}$ hours a week. He has already practiced $5\frac{1}{3}$ hours. How many more hours will Shelby practice this week?

21. **Number Sense** Look at the fractions. Find the pattern. What are the next three numbers in the pattern?

$\frac{1}{2}, \frac{2}{3}, \frac{5}{6}, \blacksquare, \blacksquare, \blacksquare$

22. **Critical Thinking** Two 2-digit numbers have the same digits, only reversed. The sum of the digits is 6. The difference between the 2-digit numbers is 18. What are the two numbers?

NUMBER SENSE

23. Copy the puzzle. Find the missing numbers so that the sum of the first and second numbers across or down equals the third number. Write your answers in simplest form.

24. Use the puzzle as a model. Make a puzzle that can be solved by subtracting across and down.

$1\frac{1}{10}$	$+$	$\blacksquare$	$=$	$\blacksquare$
$+$		$+$		$+$
$\blacksquare$	$+$	$6\frac{7}{10}$	$=$	10
$=$		$=$		$=$
$\blacksquare$	$+$	$10\frac{9}{10}$	$=$	$15\frac{3}{10}$

How do you know that $6\frac{1}{2} - 4\frac{1}{4}$ is more than 2?

WRAP
UP...

EXPLORING

More Subtraction of Mixed Numbers

Building Understanding

Use fraction bars to explore renaming mixed numbers with unlike denominators in order to subtract.

Example $2\frac{1}{3} - 1\frac{1}{2}$

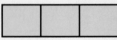

Figure A

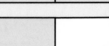

Figure B

TALK ABOUT IT

- What amount is shown in Figure **A**?

- What amount is shown in Figure **B**?

- If you put the blue amount over the pink amount, how can you find the amount of pink still showing?

- What size pieces will fit exactly over both $\frac{1}{2}$ and $\frac{1}{3}$?

- How many pieces the size of $\frac{1}{6}$ will fit over the amount of pink still showing?

- If you remove $1\frac{1}{2}$ from $2\frac{1}{3}$, what amount is left?

Use fraction bars to find the difference.

a. $3 - 1\frac{1}{2}$ **b.** $2\frac{1}{2} - 1\frac{3}{4}$ **c.** $3\frac{1}{3} - 1\frac{3}{4}$

Making the Connection

To model the difference of mixed numbers, you can use two number lines.

Example $2\frac{1}{6} - 1\frac{3}{12}$

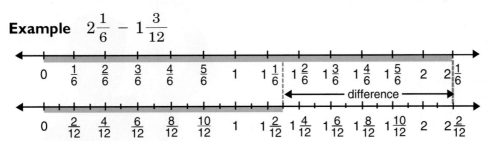

- Look at the two number lines. What is $2\frac{1}{6} - 1\frac{3}{12}$?

Sometimes you must write equivalent fractions and rename before you can subtract mixed numbers.

Example $3\frac{1}{6} - 1\frac{2}{3}$

Step 1 Write equivalent fractions using the LCD.	**Step 2** Rename the greater number.	**Step 3** Subtract. Write the fraction in simplest form.
$\begin{array}{r}3\frac{1}{6} = 3\frac{1}{6}\\ -1\frac{2}{3} = 1\frac{4}{6}\end{array}$	$\begin{aligned}3\frac{1}{6} &= 2 + \frac{6}{6} + \frac{1}{6}\\ &= 2\frac{7}{6}\end{aligned}$	$\begin{array}{r}3\frac{1}{6} = 2\frac{7}{6}\\ -1\frac{4}{6} = 1\frac{4}{6}\\ \hline 1\frac{3}{6} = 1\frac{1}{2}\end{array}$

1. Is it necessary to write equivalent fractions using the LCD if you are subtracting $1\frac{1}{2}$ from $2\frac{1}{3}$? Explain.

Checking Understanding

Change to the LCD if necessary. Then tell whether you must rename to subtract. Write *yes* or *no*.

2. $2\frac{1}{3} - \frac{2}{3}$

3. $2\frac{3}{5} - 1\frac{1}{4}$

4. $3\frac{3}{4} - 1\frac{1}{10}$

Find the difference.

5. $8\frac{5}{6} - 4\frac{8}{9}$

6. $16\frac{3}{8} - 7\frac{1}{2}$

7. $6\frac{1}{3} - 1\frac{5}{9}$

SUBTRACTING MIXED NUMBERS
with Unlike Denominators

Kele has $1\frac{5}{12}$ yards of colonial molding and $3\frac{2}{3}$ yards of quarter-round molding. How much more quarter-round molding does he have?

Estimate. $3\frac{2}{3} - 1\frac{5}{12} = $ ▪

$$4 - 1\frac{1}{2} = 2\frac{1}{2} \leftarrow \text{estimate}$$

Step 1	**Step 2**
Write equivalent fractions using the LCD.	Subtract. Write the fraction in simplest form.
$3\frac{2}{3} = 3\frac{8}{12}$ The LCD is 12. $-1\frac{5}{12} = 1\frac{5}{12}$	$3\frac{2}{3} = 3\frac{8}{12}$ $-1\frac{5}{12} = 1\frac{5}{12}$ $\overline{\quad\quad\quad 2\frac{3}{12} = 2\frac{1}{4}}$

So, Kele has $2\frac{1}{4}$ yards more quarter-round molding.

Another Example $3\frac{2}{3} - 2\frac{8}{9}$

Step 1	**Step 2**
Write equivalent fractions using the LCD.	Rename. Subtract. Write the fraction in simplest form.
$3\frac{2}{3} = 3\frac{12}{18}$ The LCD is 18. $-2\frac{8}{9} = 2\frac{16}{18}$	$3\frac{2}{3} = 3\frac{12}{18} = 2\frac{30}{18}$ $-2\frac{8}{9} = 2\frac{16}{18} = 2\frac{16}{18}$ $\overline{\quad\quad\quad\quad\quad \frac{14}{18} = \frac{7}{9}}$

Check for Understanding

Write equivalent fractions using the LCD.

1. $1\frac{4}{6}$
    $-1\frac{1}{5}$

2. $4\frac{3}{4}$
    $-2\frac{1}{2}$

3. $5\frac{1}{8}$
    $-3\frac{3}{4}$

4. $7\frac{2}{3}$
    $-3\frac{4}{5}$

Practice

Estimate the difference.

5. $5\frac{1}{6}$
$-2\frac{2}{3}$

6. $7\frac{1}{4}$
$-4\frac{2}{5}$

7. $3\frac{9}{10}$
$-1\frac{6}{7}$

8. $5\frac{7}{10}$
$-3\frac{1}{2}$

9. $8\frac{1}{3}$
$-\frac{3}{4}$

Find the difference.

10. $7\frac{4}{9}$
$-3\frac{1}{2}$

11. $8\frac{2}{5}$
$-4\frac{1}{4}$

12. $5\frac{7}{12}$
$-1\frac{1}{6}$

13. $6\frac{2}{3}$
$-2\frac{1}{8}$

14. $9\frac{5}{9}$
$-5\frac{1}{6}$

15. $18\frac{1}{6}$
$-15\frac{3}{4}$

16. $20\frac{4}{5}$
$-16\frac{5}{6}$

17. $26\frac{1}{2}$
$-11\frac{3}{8}$

18. $32\frac{1}{2}$
$-21\frac{7}{8}$

19. $43\frac{1}{2}$
$-32\frac{7}{10}$

20. $15\frac{1}{6} - 3\frac{1}{2}$

21. $19\frac{3}{8} - 12\frac{3}{4}$

22. $28\frac{1}{2} - 21\frac{4}{5}$

23. $37\frac{2}{3} - 4\frac{7}{9}$

24. $36\frac{1}{4} - 14\frac{3}{4}$

25. $21\frac{1}{4} - 13\frac{7}{10}$

Mixed Applications

26. Peter lives $1\frac{3}{4}$ miles from school. Tony lives $1\frac{2}{3}$ miles from school in the same direction. How much farther is Peter's round-trip than Tony's round-trip?

27. Critical Thinking Tim raises chickens and cows. His animals have a total of 25 heads and 70 feet. How many chickens and how many cows does Tim have?

MIXED REVIEW

Estimate the product or quotient.

1. $999 \div 99$

2. 279×19

3. $386 \div 6$

Write the common factors.

4. $6, 12$

5. $9, 15$

6. $9, 18, 27$

7. $12, 16, 24$

8. $36, 54, 72$

How does subtracting mixed numbers with unlike denominators differ from subtracting mixed numbers with like denominators?

PROBLEM SOLVING

Choose a Strategy

A minibus leaves the garage to pick up Louis at the first stop. Then it travels $3\frac{1}{6}$ miles (mi) to pick up Tanya, $4\frac{1}{4}$ mi more to pick up Renee, and $4\frac{5}{12}$ mi more to the school. If the bus travels a total of $21\frac{2}{3}$ mi, what is the distance from the garage to Louis's house?

Understand
Plan
Solve
Look Back

Sometimes you can use different strategies to solve the same problem.

What strategies can you use?

You can *draw a diagram* or *work backward*. First make the problem easier by writing equivalent fractions using the LCD 12.

$$3\frac{1}{6} = 3\frac{2}{12} \qquad 4\frac{1}{4} = 4\frac{3}{12} \qquad 4\frac{5}{12} = 4\frac{5}{12} \qquad 21\frac{2}{3} = 21\frac{8}{12}$$

Strategy: Draw a Diagram

Garage $\longrightarrow$	Louis $\longrightarrow$	Tanya $\longrightarrow$	Renee $\longrightarrow$	School
0	? mi	$3\frac{2}{12}$ mi	$4\frac{3}{12}$ mi	$4\frac{5}{12}$ mi

$\longleftarrow$ $21\frac{8}{12}$ mi $\longrightarrow$

Add the miles to each stop.

$$3\frac{2}{12} + 4\frac{3}{12} + 4\frac{5}{12} = 11\frac{10}{12}$$

Subtract from the total miles.

$$21\frac{8}{12} - 11\frac{10}{12} = 20\frac{20}{12} - 11\frac{10}{12} = 9\frac{10}{12} = 9\frac{5}{6}$$

$\longmapsto$ rename $\longrightarrow$

Strategy: Work Backward

Miles to Louis	$\rightarrow$	Miles to Tanya	$\rightarrow$	Miles to Renee	$\rightarrow$	Miles to school	$\rightarrow$	Total miles
?	+	$3\frac{2}{12}$	+	$4\frac{3}{12}$	+	$4\frac{5}{12}$	=	$21\frac{8}{12}$

Miles to Louis	$\leftarrow$	Miles to Tanya	$\leftarrow$	Miles to Renee	$\leftarrow$	Miles to school	$\leftarrow$	Total miles
$9\frac{5}{6} = 9\frac{10}{12}$	=	$3\frac{2}{12}$	$-$	$4\frac{3}{12}$	$-$	$4\frac{5}{12}$	$-$	$21\frac{8}{12}$

So, the distance from the garage to Louis's house is $9\frac{5}{6}$ mi.

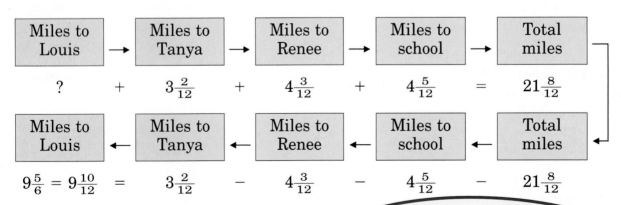

WHAT IF... ...you were asked to find the distance from Tanya's house to the school? What strategy would you use?

Mixed Applications → **STRATEGIES**   Draw a Diagram • Find a Pattern
• Work Backward • Make a Graph

Choose a strategy and solve.

1 Teresa runs a backyard lemonade stand. She sold $\frac{1}{2}$ of the cups of lemonade before lunch. Then she sold 4 cups after lunch. By evening she had 12 cups left. How many cups of lemonade did Teresa have at the beginning of the day?

2 Melanie swam 1 lap in the pool the first week, 4 laps the second week, 9 laps the third week, and 16 laps the fourth week. If she continues this pattern, how many laps will Melanie swim in weeks five, six, and seven?

3 Esther left her backyard and walked $1\frac{1}{3}$ kilometers (km) north. Then she walked $\frac{3}{4}$ km west, $\frac{1}{3}$ km north, $1\frac{1}{4}$ km east, and $1\frac{2}{3}$ km south. How far from her backyard was she?

4 Mrs. Wilson returned home after $1\frac{1}{2}$ hours. During that time she drove $\frac{1}{4}$ hour to take Jeff to scouts and $\frac{1}{3}$ hour to take Karen to ballet, and she then went shopping. How much time did it take her to shop and return home?

Monty drew a bar graph of the time he spent in a week making one model airplane. Use the bar graph for Exercises 5–7.

5 What is the total amount of time Monty spent making the model from Monday to Friday?

6 What is the median length of time Monty spent making the model during the week?

7 On the average, did Monty spend more time making the model during the five weekdays or during the weekend? How much more or less time did he spend per day?

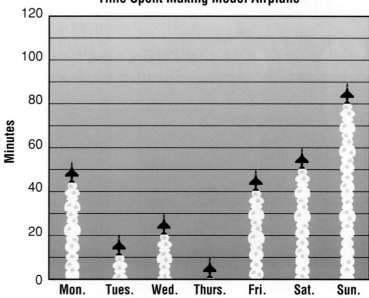

Time Spent Making Model Airplane

Vocabulary Check

Choose a word or words from the box to complete each sentence.

| denominator |
| estimate |
| renaming |
| simplest form |
| unlike |

1. You can round fractions to 0, $\frac{1}{2}$, or 1 to _?_ sums and differences. *(page 206)*

2. When fractions have the same _?_, you can add or subtract the numerators. *(page 208)*

3. To add mixed numbers with _?_ denominators, find the LCD for the fractions. *(page 212)*

4. You divide the numerator and the denominator by the same number to write a fraction in _?_. *(page 208)*

5. Regrouping whole numbers is similar to _?_ mixed numbers. *(page 219)*

Think: When do you need to rename the greater number?

Concept Check

6. If the numerator is much less than the denominator, you round to _?_ when estimating fraction sums and differences. *(page 206)*

7. If the numerator is about the same as the denominator, you round to _?_ when estimating fraction sums and differences. *(page 206)*

8. How does adding or subtracting like fractions differ from adding or subtracting unlike fractions? *(pages 208, 210)*

9. How do you write equivalent fractions? *(page 210)*

10. Do you need to find the LCD to answer $2\frac{1}{4} - 1\frac{1}{6}$? What is the LCD for $\frac{1}{4}$ and $\frac{1}{6}$? *(page 223)*

11. What must you do to subtract $2\frac{1}{4}$ from 4? *(page 223)*

Tell whether you must rename to subtract. Write *yes* or *no*.
(page 223)

12. $5\frac{1}{3} - 3\frac{2}{3}$

13. $6\frac{1}{2} - 2\frac{1}{4}$

14. $7 - \frac{3}{5}$

15. $3\frac{4}{9} - 2\frac{1}{9}$

16. $9\frac{7}{10} - 3\frac{11}{15}$

17. $8\frac{2}{3} - 2\frac{1}{2}$

Skill Check

Estimate the sum or difference. *(page 206)*

18. $\dfrac{1}{8} + \dfrac{3}{4}$

19. $\dfrac{9}{10} - \dfrac{1}{9}$

20. $9\dfrac{5}{7} + 1\dfrac{8}{9}$

21. $6\dfrac{1}{6} - 2\dfrac{7}{8}$

22. $5\dfrac{1}{15} + 5\dfrac{4}{5}$

23. $21\dfrac{1}{4} - 9\dfrac{5}{6}$

Find the sum or difference. *(pages 208, 210, 212, 214, 218, 220)*

24. $\dfrac{8}{11} + \dfrac{2}{11}$

25. $\dfrac{8}{15} - \dfrac{2}{15}$

26. $\dfrac{3}{10} + \dfrac{7}{10}$

27. $\dfrac{7}{9} + \dfrac{4}{5}$

28. $\dfrac{4}{5} - \dfrac{1}{2}$

29. $\dfrac{1}{6} + \dfrac{7}{8}$

30. $10\dfrac{1}{8} + 2\dfrac{5}{8}$

31. $3\dfrac{1}{12} + 7\dfrac{5}{12}$

32. $4\dfrac{1}{6} + 8\dfrac{1}{6}$

33. $12\dfrac{2}{3} - 3\dfrac{1}{3}$

34. $12\dfrac{2}{7} - 9\dfrac{5}{7}$

35. $4\dfrac{1}{8} - 2\dfrac{5}{8}$

Tell whether the sum or difference is correct. Write *true* or *false*. If you write *false*, give the correct answer. *(pages 212, 214, 222, 224)*

36. $4\dfrac{3}{4} + 2\dfrac{2}{5} = 7\dfrac{3}{20}$

37. $8\dfrac{1}{6} + 6\dfrac{1}{8} = 14\dfrac{1}{3}$

38. $9\dfrac{3}{5} + 9\dfrac{2}{3} = 19\dfrac{4}{15}$

39. $7\dfrac{2}{3} - 1\dfrac{2}{9} = 6\dfrac{4}{9}$

40. $8\dfrac{1}{6} - 2\dfrac{1}{15} = 6\dfrac{1}{15}$

41. $15\dfrac{1}{2} - 11\dfrac{5}{8} = 4\dfrac{7}{8}$

42. $3\dfrac{1}{8} - 1\dfrac{3}{4} = 1\dfrac{1}{2}$

43. $9\dfrac{1}{7} + 3\dfrac{11}{14} = 12\dfrac{13}{14}$

44. $7\dfrac{1}{3} - 5\dfrac{3}{8} = 1\dfrac{23}{24}$

Problem-Solving Check *(pages 214, 226)*

45. Kim watched as a cat played for $1\dfrac{1}{4}$ hours, ate for $\dfrac{1}{4}$ hour, played again for $\dfrac{1}{4}$ hour, and then slept. If Kim watched the cat for $2\dfrac{1}{2}$ hours, how long did the cat sleep?

46. Sue walked $1\dfrac{2}{3}$ miles (mi) from school to a store. Continuing in the same direction, she walked 1 mi to Rosa's home and then to her own home. Sue walked a total of $3\dfrac{1}{3}$ mi. How far is her home from Rosa's?

47. Bill has 5 shirts and 4 pairs of jeans. All of the shirts go with all of the jeans. How many different shirt-and-jeans outfits can Bill make with this wardrobe?

48. Paul drives from his home $2\dfrac{1}{2}$ mi south. Next, he drives west $\dfrac{1}{3}$ mi. Then, he drives north 3 mi. In which directions must Paul turn to return home?

WHAT DID I LEARN?

1. Estimate $\frac{1}{6} + \frac{7}{8} + \frac{3}{7}$. Explain your method.

2. Estimate $7\frac{1}{5} - 2\frac{5}{6}$. Explain your method.

3. Show each step as you find the sum $\frac{3}{4} + \frac{2}{3}$.

4. Show each step as you find the difference $5\frac{1}{4} - 1\frac{7}{8}$.

5. Read Exercise 2 on page 227. Follow the steps on the Problem-Solving Think Along worksheet to show how to solve this problem.

Write About It

6. What do you think is the most important thing to understand about adding and subtracting fractions? Explain.

7. Explain how fifths are related to tenths. Draw a picture to go with your explanation.

TEAMWORK *Project*

Create an Invention

Have you ever thought, "If there were only some gadget that would . . . to make my life easier"?

Work with your teammates to create an invention, such as a gadget, a piece of furniture, or an appliance, that could make your lives easier.

Decide Begin by making a list of common tasks or activities with which you could use some help. What kinds of inventions would help?

Choose one invention to work on.

Describe the purpose of the invention.

Do As a team, make a model or draw a sketch of your invention.

Write a description of how the invention would be manufactured and used.

Share Show your model or sketch to another team. If you made a model, demonstrate it. If you drew a sketch, describe how your invention works. Then let the other team do the same with its model or sketch.

Talk About It

How useful is each invention?

What fraction of the students in your class would find your invention helpful?

Suppose you wanted to manufacture your invention. What do you think would be the cost of manufacturing it?

Create a MAZE

MULTICULTURAL NOTE: The photo shows a hedge maze in England. People today still try to find their way through this maze.

In Europe, mazes were sometimes formed out of live, pruned hedges. During the 1600's, in the reign of William III of England, a hedge maze was built at Hampton Court Palace.

WORK WITH A PARTNER to design your own maze. Start by drawing a square, rectangle, or circle on a piece of paper. Then draw passageways inside. Be sure to include dead ends and alternative passageways in your maze. When you have finished designing your maze, exchange with another pair of students and try to find your way through their maze.

Challenge

Magic Square

Complete the square so that the sum of the numbers in every row, column, and diagonal is $3\frac{15}{16}$.

■	■	■
$1\frac{1}{16}$	■	■
■	$1\frac{7}{16}$	$1\frac{1}{8}$

Write a Question

Use the picture to write a question. Tell whether to add or subtract to solve.

$\frac{15}{16}$ inch

A

$\frac{11}{16}$ inch

B

Write the letter of the correct answer.

1. Evaluate $3.45 - c$, for $c = 0.5$.

   A. 2.95   B. 3.4
   C. 3.95   D. not here

2. $3 \times 60.4 - 0.4 + 10$

   A. 150   B. 190
   C. 190.8   D. 210

3. 2.3×5.04

   A. 1.602   B. 11.592
   C. 11.692   D. 115.92

4. $39.8 \div 0.4$

   A. 9.95   B. 99.5
   C. 995   D. not here

5. What is the number of combinations for 3 hats and 4 pairs of shoes?

   A. 3   B. 4
   C. 7   D. 12

6. Which is the appropriate graph for June temperature readings in Miami?

   A. bar   B. line
   C. circle   D. histogram

7. What is the LCM of 8 and 12?

   A. 2   B. 4
   C. 24   D. 96

8. What is the GCF of 15 and 60?

   A. 3   B. 5
   C. 15   D. not here

9. $12\frac{1}{5} + 3\frac{3}{4}$

   A. $15\frac{4}{9}$ B. $15\frac{9}{20}$
   C. 16   D. not here

10. $9\frac{1}{3} - 7\frac{7}{8}$

    A. $\frac{11}{24}$ B. $1\frac{5}{12}$
    C. $1\frac{11}{24}$ D. $2\frac{11}{24}$

11. Jim is in a maze. He goes north 5 ft, west 2 ft, north 2 ft, east 4 ft, and south 3 ft. In what direction should he turn to cross his own path?

    A. east   B. west
    C. north   D. south

12. Ken drove $25\frac{1}{3}$ mi from his house to the store. He stopped at Lisa's, which is $5\frac{1}{2}$ mi from his house. How far is Lisa's from the store?

    A. $19\frac{1}{6}$ mi   B. $19\frac{5}{6}$ mi
    C. $20\frac{5}{6}$ mi   D. $30\frac{5}{6}$ mi

CHAPTER 8

MULTIPLYING AND DIVIDING FRACTIONS

Did you know...

... that hundreds of marching bands participate in holiday parades in the United States every year?

TALK ABOUT IT

Suppose $\frac{1}{4}$ of the 144 members of a marching band play percussion instruments. Describe several different ways to find the number of band members who play percussion instruments.

EXPLORING

Multiplying Fractions by Fractions

To find $\frac{1}{2}$ of 6, you multiply. How would you find $\frac{1}{2}$ of $\frac{3}{4}$? In this lesson you will explore multiplying a fraction by a fraction.

Think: What is $\frac{1}{2}$ of $\frac{3}{4}$?

Figure A

Figure B

Building Understanding

You can use a model to help you find the product $\frac{1}{2} \times \frac{3}{4}$.

TALK ABOUT IT
- What part of Figure **A** is represented by diagonal lines?

- What part of Figure **B** is represented by dots?

- What part of Figure **B** is represented by the area that has both dots and diagonal lines?

- What is $\frac{1}{2}$ of $\frac{3}{4}$?

- Is your answer less than or greater than each factor?

Draw a model to represent each problem. Solve.

A. $\frac{1}{2} \times \frac{1}{3}$

B. $\frac{1}{3} \times \frac{2}{3}$

C. $\frac{1}{3} \times \frac{3}{5}$

TALK ABOUT IT
- How does each product compare with the factors?

- Will the product of two fractions that are each less than 1 always be less than either factor? How do you know?

236

Making the Connection

Multiplying fractions that are less than 1 is similar to
multiplying decimals that are less than 1.

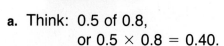

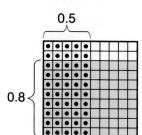

Figure A

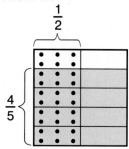

Figure B

a. Think: 0.5 of 0.8,
or $0.5 \times 0.8 = 0.40$.

b. Think: $\frac{1}{2}$ of $\frac{4}{5}$,
or $\frac{1}{2} \times \frac{4}{5} = \frac{4}{10}$, or $\frac{2}{5}$.

1. How do the numbers in the problem for Figure **A**
compare with the numbers for Figure **B**?

2. How does the part that has both shading and dots in
Figure **A** compare with the part that has both shading
and dots in Figure **B**?

3. Is the product 0.5×0.8 the same as the product
$\frac{1}{2} \times \frac{4}{5}$? How can you tell?

Checking Understanding

Use the model to help you find the product. Write the product in
simplest form.

4. $\frac{2}{5} \times \frac{1}{4}$ $\frac{2}{5}$

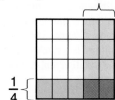

$\frac{1}{4}$

5. $\frac{1}{6} \times \frac{2}{3}$ $\frac{1}{6}$

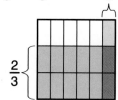

$\frac{2}{3}$

6. $\frac{1}{2} \times \frac{4}{7}$ $\frac{1}{2}$

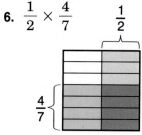

$\frac{4}{7}$

Draw a model for each problem. Tell whether the product in **a** is
the same as the product in **b**.

7. a. $0.5 \times 0.4 = 0.2$

   b. $\frac{1}{2} \times \frac{2}{5} = \frac{1}{5}$

9. a. $\frac{1}{8} \times \frac{4}{5} = \frac{1}{10}$

   b. $0.9 \times 0.8 = 0.72$

8. a. $\frac{3}{4} \times \frac{1}{3} = \frac{1}{4}$

   b. $0.7 \times 0.7 = 0.49$

10. a. $0.1 \times 0.5 = 0.05$

   b. $\frac{1}{10} \times \frac{1}{2} = \frac{1}{20}$

More Practice, Lesson 8.1, page H62

MORE MULTIPLYING
Fractions by Fractions

Susan buys $\frac{2}{3}$ yard of black fabric to trim a scarlet tunic, a type of jacket, for Canada Day. She uses $\frac{5}{6}$ of the fabric. What part of a yard does she use?

Think: What is $\frac{5}{6}$ of $\frac{2}{3}$?

You can use a model to help you solve the problem.

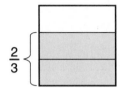

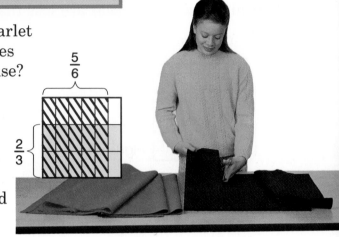

- What part of the model has both shading and diagonal lines?

Another Method   You can also multiply to find $\frac{5}{6}$ of $\frac{2}{3}$.

Step 1 Multiply the numerators.	**Step 2** Multiply the denominators.	**Step 3** Write the answer in simplest form.
$\frac{5}{6} \times \frac{2}{3} = \frac{10}{}$	$\frac{5}{6} \times \frac{2}{3} = \frac{10}{18}$	$\frac{10 \div 2}{18 \div 2} = \frac{5}{9}$

So, Susan uses $\frac{5}{9}$ yard of fabric.

- How is $\frac{2}{3}$ represented in the model?

- How is $\frac{5}{6}$ represented in the model?

- How is $\frac{10}{18}$ represented in the model?

- Why do you divide the numerator and denominator by 2 to simplify?

MULTICULTURAL NOTE: Canada Day is celebrated with colorful costumes, such as the uniform of the Royal Canadian Mounted Police. The scarlet tunic of the uniform is a symbol of justice and is a tradition that is more than 120 years old.

Check for Understanding

Use the model to help you find the product.

1. $\frac{1}{3} \times \frac{1}{2}$

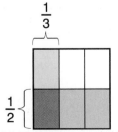

2. $\frac{1}{5} \times \frac{1}{2}$

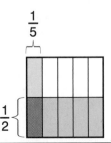

3. $\frac{2}{3} \times \frac{3}{4}$

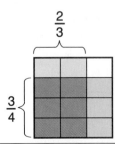

4. $\frac{1}{4} \times \frac{4}{5}$

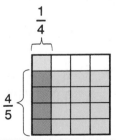

238

Practice

Complete the multiplication sentence.
Write the product in simplest form.

5. $\frac{3}{4} \times \blacksquare = \blacksquare$

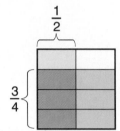

$\frac{1}{2}$

$\frac{3}{4}$

6. $\frac{3}{5} \times \blacksquare = \blacksquare$

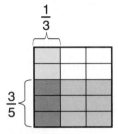

$\frac{1}{3}$

$\frac{3}{5}$

7. $\blacksquare \times \frac{5}{6} = \blacksquare$

$\frac{5}{6}$

$\frac{3}{4}$

Solve. Write the product in simplest form.

8. $\frac{1}{3} \times \frac{2}{3}$

9. $\frac{1}{2} \times \frac{1}{2}$

10. $\frac{3}{4} \times \frac{1}{4}$

11. $\frac{1}{5} \times \frac{2}{3}$

12. $\frac{1}{4} \times \frac{2}{7}$

13. $\frac{7}{8} \times \frac{2}{5}$

14. $\frac{3}{8} \times \frac{4}{7}$

15. $\frac{2}{9} \times \frac{3}{4}$

16. $\frac{4}{5} \times \frac{5}{6}$

17. $\frac{6}{7} \times \frac{7}{8}$

18. $\frac{2}{5} \times \frac{5}{7}$

19. $\frac{1}{9} \times \frac{3}{5}$

20. $\frac{5}{9} \times \frac{3}{10}$

21. $\frac{4}{9} \times \frac{3}{5}$

22. $\frac{5}{7} \times \frac{7}{15}$

Mixed Applications

23. Seth had $\frac{1}{2}$ of a display from the festival. He gave $\frac{2}{3}$ of what he had to Tim. What part did Seth give to Tim?

24. Beth's dad had $\frac{3}{4}$ of a box of sparklers. He used $\frac{1}{2}$ of the sparklers last night. What part of the box did he use?

25. Critical Thinking Write a multiplication problem that has the same answer as $\frac{1}{2} + \frac{1}{2} + \frac{1}{2} + \frac{1}{2}$.

26. Number Sense Use the rules for the order of operations to solve $\frac{1}{5} + \frac{2}{3} \times \frac{3}{5} - \frac{2}{5}$. Write the answer in simplest form.

VISUAL THINKING

Think of the multiplication of a whole number by a fraction as repeated addition. Use a number line to visualize the answer.

Example $6 \times \frac{3}{5}$

$6 \times \frac{3}{5} = \frac{18}{5} = 3\frac{3}{5}$

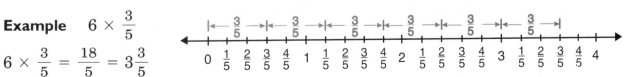

27. Draw a number line to find the product $\frac{1}{4} \times 5$.

How do you multiply fractions?

WRAP
UP...

MULTIPLYING FRACTIONS
Another Method

The first United States flag was adopted in 1777. Many people remember the occasion on June 14 every year by celebrating Flag Day. Yoshi lives $\frac{4}{5}$ mile from the park where the town celebrates Flag Day. On Flag Day he was $\frac{1}{8}$ of the way to the park on his bike when he had a flat tire. How far did he ride before he had the flat tire?

You can often simplify before you multiply.

Step 1	**Step 2**	**Step 3**
Find a common factor of any one numerator and any one denominator.	Divide the numerator and the denominator by the common factor.	Repeat until 1 is the only common factor left. Then multiply.
$\frac{1}{8} \times \frac{4}{5}$ A common factor of 8 and 4 is 2.	$\frac{1}{\overset{}{8}_{4}} \times \frac{\overset{2}{4}}{5}$	$\frac{1}{\underset{2}{8}} \times \frac{\overset{1}{4}}{5} = \frac{1 \times 1}{2 \times 5} = \frac{1}{10}$

So, Yoshi rode $\frac{1}{10}$ mile before he had the flat tire.

Talk About It

▶ What is the product of $\frac{1}{8}$ and $\frac{4}{5}$ if you multiply without simplifying?

▶ What is the greatest common factor (GCF) of 4 and 8?

▶ What fractions would you multiply in Step 2 if you had simplified using the GCF instead of any other common factor?

▶ When you use the GCF, do you need to continue to simplify the fractions? Explain.

More Examples

A. $\frac{5}{8} \times \frac{8}{16} = \frac{5}{\underset{1}{8}} \times \frac{\overset{1}{8}}{16} = \frac{5}{16}$ GCF is 8.

B. $\frac{2}{3} \times \frac{3}{10} = \frac{\overset{1}{2}}{\underset{1}{3}} \times \frac{\overset{1}{3}}{\underset{5}{10}} = \frac{1}{5}$ GCF of 3 and 3 is 3.   GCF of 2 and 10 is 2.

Check for Understanding

Tell what common factors you can use to simplify the fractions.

1. $\frac{1}{2} \times \frac{2}{3}$ **2.** $\frac{1}{5} \times \frac{15}{16}$ **3.** $\frac{14}{27} \times \frac{6}{7}$ **4.** $\frac{4}{9} \times \frac{6}{14}$ **5.** $\frac{6}{4} \times \frac{8}{9}$

Practice

Simplify the factors.

6. $\dfrac{1}{4} \times \dfrac{4}{5}$ 7. $\dfrac{1}{2} \times \dfrac{6}{7}$ 8. $\dfrac{2}{5} \times \dfrac{3}{4}$ 9. $\dfrac{3}{5} \times \dfrac{5}{6}$

10. $\dfrac{2}{3} \times \dfrac{3}{4}$ 11. $\dfrac{4}{20} \times \dfrac{5}{8}$ 12. $\dfrac{2}{3} \times \dfrac{6}{9}$ 13. $\dfrac{4}{9} \times \dfrac{15}{22}$

14. $\dfrac{9}{12} \times \dfrac{6}{18}$ 15. $\dfrac{3}{5} \times \dfrac{1}{6}$ 16. $\dfrac{4}{5} \times \dfrac{5}{16}$ 17. $\dfrac{4}{7} \times \dfrac{21}{28}$

18. $\dfrac{2}{15} \times \dfrac{5}{6}$ 19. $\dfrac{5}{12} \times \dfrac{18}{25}$ 20. $\dfrac{2}{9} \times \dfrac{27}{28}$ 21. $\dfrac{7}{10} \times \dfrac{5}{14}$

22. $\dfrac{3}{4} \times \dfrac{16}{21}$ 23. $\dfrac{1}{2} \times \dfrac{12}{13}$ 24. $\dfrac{5}{8} \times \dfrac{12}{25}$ 25. $\dfrac{6}{8} \times \dfrac{2}{3}$

Choose a method to find the product.
Write the product in simplest form.

26. $\dfrac{2}{3} \times \dfrac{1}{6}$ 27. $\dfrac{5}{6} \times \dfrac{3}{8}$ 28. $\dfrac{7}{10} \times \dfrac{5}{7}$ 29. $\dfrac{4}{5} \times \dfrac{5}{8}$

30. $\dfrac{8}{9} \times \dfrac{3}{4}$ 31. $\dfrac{5}{6} \times \dfrac{3}{10}$ 32. $\dfrac{2}{3} \times \dfrac{9}{10}$ 33. $\dfrac{6}{7} \times \dfrac{5}{8}$

34. $\dfrac{5}{8} \times \dfrac{4}{15}$ 35. $\dfrac{5}{14} \times \dfrac{7}{10}$ 36. $\dfrac{8}{9} \times \dfrac{3}{4}$ 37. $\dfrac{18}{25} \times \dfrac{5}{9}$

38. $\dfrac{4}{5} \times \dfrac{15}{16}$ 39. $\dfrac{21}{22} \times \dfrac{2}{7}$ 40. $\dfrac{3}{16} \times \dfrac{8}{15}$ 41. $\dfrac{5}{24} \times \dfrac{9}{10}$

42. $\dfrac{7}{26} \times \dfrac{13}{35}$ 43. $\dfrac{9}{10} \times \dfrac{5}{27}$ 44. $\dfrac{9}{30} \times \dfrac{5}{18}$ 45. $\dfrac{11}{28} \times \dfrac{7}{22}$

Mixed Applications

46. Mark had $\frac{2}{3}$ of his cake left after his birthday party. If he gave $\frac{3}{4}$ of the remaining cake to Rita, what part of the entire cake did Mark give Rita?

47. Mrs. Chen has used all the red candles from a box of candles and still has $\frac{2}{3}$ left. If $\frac{1}{4}$ of the remaining candles are blue, what part of the entire box was blue?

48. **Visual Thinking** Look at the number line. If C and B are less than 1, does A or D correspond to C × B?

0   A   B   C   D   1

49. **Critical Thinking** Find the values for a and b if a and b are consecutive even numbers and $\frac{a}{b} = \frac{8}{9}$.

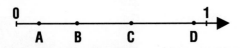

What is the advantage of simplifying before multiplying?

W R A P
UP...

ESTIMATING PRODUCTS OF FRACTIONS

Americans set aside the third Monday of February for Presidents' Day. This is a day to remember all U.S. Presidents throughout history. The park manager has marked off $\frac{7}{8}$ of the park for the Presidents' Day celebration. Of this area, $\frac{3}{5}$ will be used for games and sports. About how much of the park will be used for games and sports?

You can estimate the product of $\frac{7}{8}$ and $\frac{3}{5}$ to answer the question.

Step 1	Step 2	Step 3
Compare the numerator to the denominator.	Round each factor.	Multiply the rounded factors.
$$\frac{7}{8} \times \frac{3}{5}$$ about the same as the denominator / about one half the denominator	$$\frac{7}{8} \times \frac{3}{5}$$ $$\downarrow \qquad \downarrow$$ $$1 \times \frac{1}{2}$$	$$1 \times \frac{1}{2} = \frac{1}{2}$$

So, about $\frac{1}{2}$ of the park will be used for games and sports.

You can also use compatible numbers to estimate. When you estimate using two methods, you can find a range.

Judy had a total of 179 tickets. If she sold about $\frac{4}{9}$ of them, about how many tickets did she sell?

Use rounding.

$$\frac{4}{9} \times 179$$
$$\downarrow \qquad \downarrow$$
$$\frac{1}{2} \times 200 = 100$$

Use compatible numbers.

$$\frac{4}{9} \times 179$$
$$\downarrow \qquad \downarrow$$
$$\frac{4}{9} \times 180 = 80$$

So, Judy sold about 80 to 100 tickets.

Talk About It

▶ What other pairs of compatible numbers can you use?

▶ What method would you use to estimate the product of $\frac{2}{3}$ and 627? Explain your choice.

Check for Understanding

Choose the best range of estimates. Write **a**, **b**, or **c**.

1. $\frac{5}{6} \times 376$
   a. 350 to 900
   b. 300 to 376
   c. 100 to 300

2. $\frac{2}{3} \times 264$
   a. 150 to 200
   b. 50 to 300
   c. 75 to 100

3. $\frac{3}{8} \times 176$
   a. 30 to 50
   b. 40 to 80
   c. 70 to 100

4. $\frac{3}{5} \times 443$
   a. 100 to 400
   b. 300 to 370
   c. 200 to 270

Practice

Use rounding to estimate the product.

5. $\frac{4}{9} \times \frac{7}{8}$

6. $\frac{2}{3} \times \frac{9}{11}$

7. $\frac{2}{5} \times \frac{7}{16}$

8. $\frac{11}{12} \times \frac{6}{7}$

9. $\frac{5}{12} \times \frac{11}{13}$

Use compatible numbers to estimate the product.

10. $\frac{1}{4} \times 79$

11. $\frac{1}{5} \times 451$

12. $910 \times \frac{3}{4}$

13. $\frac{2}{5} \times 299$

14. $\frac{5}{6} \times 538$

Tell whether the estimate is reasonable. Write *yes* or *no*.

15. $\frac{9}{10} \times 30 \approx 20$

16. $\frac{2}{5} \times 20 \approx 10$

17. $\frac{7}{12} \times 314 \approx 300$

18. $\frac{1}{3} \times 300 \approx 100$

19. $\frac{13}{14} \times \frac{7}{15} \approx 1$

20. $\frac{7}{15} \times 210 \approx 75$

21. $\frac{9}{20} \times 425 \approx 100$

22. $\frac{1}{4} \times 600 \approx 150$

Mixed Applications

23. At a dance contest, $\frac{1}{2}$ of the winners received the third prize, fancy socks. If there were 395 winners, about how many received fancy socks?

24. **Visual Thinking** Write the multiplication sentence that the model represents.

MIXED REVIEW

Find the difference.

1. $3\frac{1}{2} - \frac{3}{4}$

2. $5\frac{1}{3} - 1\frac{4}{5}$

3. $6\frac{1}{5} - 4\frac{5}{7}$

4. $1\frac{3}{4} - \frac{7}{8}$

Find the sum. Write your answer in simplest form.

5. $\frac{7}{8} + \frac{1}{2}$

6. $\frac{1}{6} + \frac{5}{18}$

7. $\frac{3}{4} + \frac{2}{3}$

8. $\frac{11}{12} + \frac{3}{4}$

How do you decide which strategy to use when you estimate?

MULTIPLYING
with Mixed Numbers

Gina brought $1\frac{1}{3}$ pans of lasagna to a Kwanzaa festival. If she gave away $\frac{1}{2}$ of the lasagna, how much did Gina give away?

Think: What is $\frac{1}{2}$ of $1\frac{1}{3}$?

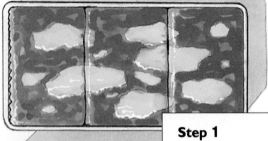

You can make a model like this one to determine the answer, or you can multiply $\frac{1}{2}$ and $1\frac{1}{3}$.

* How many parts are in each pan?

* How many parts are shaded red?

* What part of the pans would the entire shaded area be?

Step 1 Write the mixed number as a fraction.	**Step 2** Simplify.	**Step 3** Multiply.
$\frac{1}{2} \times 1\frac{1}{3}$ $\frac{1}{2} \times \frac{4}{3}$	$\frac{1}{2} \times \frac{4}{3} = \frac{1}{\underset{1}{\cancel{2}}} \times \frac{\overset{2}{\cancel{4}}}{3}$	$\frac{1}{\underset{1}{\cancel{2}}} \times \frac{\overset{2}{\cancel{4}}}{3} = \frac{1}{1} \times \frac{2}{3} = \frac{2}{3}$

So, Gina gave away $\frac{2}{3}$ of a pan of the lasagna.

* Why is the product, $\frac{2}{3}$, greater than one of the factors?

Another Example $3\frac{1}{3} \times 2\frac{1}{4}$

Estimate. Round to the nearest whole number. $3 \times 2 = 6$ ◄— estimate

Multiply.

Step 1 Write the mixed numbers as fractions.	**Step 2** Simplify.	**Step 3** Multiply.
$3\frac{1}{3} \times 2\frac{1}{4} = \frac{10}{3} \times \frac{9}{4}$	$\frac{10}{3} \times \frac{9}{4} = \frac{\overset{5}{\cancel{10}}}{\underset{1}{\cancel{3}}} \times \frac{\overset{3}{\cancel{9}}}{\underset{2}{\cancel{4}}}$	$\frac{\overset{5}{\cancel{10}}}{\underset{1}{\cancel{3}}} \times \frac{\overset{3}{\cancel{9}}}{\underset{2}{\cancel{4}}} = \frac{5}{1} \times \frac{3}{2} = \frac{15}{2}, \text{or } 7\frac{1}{2}$

* Why is the product greater than each factor?

Check for Understanding

Rewrite the problem by changing each mixed number to a fraction.

1. $4\frac{3}{4} \times \frac{1}{8}$ 2. $\frac{2}{7} \times 6\frac{3}{5}$ 3. $1\frac{1}{3} \times 3\frac{3}{4}$ 4. $2\frac{1}{3} \times 1\frac{6}{7}$

Practice

Write each mixed number as a fraction. Then simplify the factors.

5. $1\frac{2}{3} \times \frac{3}{4}$ 6. $\frac{4}{15} \times 4\frac{3}{8}$ 7. $2\frac{2}{3} \times 1\frac{3}{8}$ 8. $4\frac{1}{6} \times 2\frac{14}{25}$

Tell whether the product will be less than both factors, between the factors, or greater than both factors.

9. $\frac{1}{8} \times \frac{3}{5}$ 10. $\frac{1}{9} \times 2\frac{1}{4}$ 11. $\frac{2}{3} \times 1\frac{1}{8}$ 12. $2\frac{4}{5} \times 2\frac{1}{2}$

13. $2\frac{1}{3} \times 1\frac{2}{7}$ 14. $1\frac{5}{6} \times \frac{1}{11}$ 15. $\frac{5}{6} \times 1\frac{1}{3}$ 16. $5\frac{1}{4} \times 4\frac{2}{3}$

Solve. Write the product in simplest form.

17. $3\frac{1}{2} \times \frac{4}{5}$ 18. $6\frac{1}{4} \times 5\frac{3}{5}$ 19. $3\frac{1}{3} \times 2\frac{5}{8}$ 20. $\frac{1}{5} \times 3\frac{1}{3}$

21. $4\frac{2}{3} \times 1\frac{3}{4}$ 22. $1\frac{7}{8} \times 4\frac{2}{3}$ 23. $5\frac{1}{2} \times \frac{1}{6}$ 24. $\frac{1}{2} \times 3\frac{1}{7}$

25. $4\frac{1}{6} \times 3\frac{3}{5}$ 26. $1\frac{3}{4} \times \frac{1}{3}$ 27. $10\frac{1}{5} \times 8\frac{1}{3}$ 28. $5\frac{5}{6} \times \frac{1}{5}$

29. $3\frac{1}{3} \times 2\frac{1}{7}$ 30. $3\frac{1}{4} \times \frac{2}{5}$ 31. $\frac{7}{8} \times 7\frac{3}{7}$ 32. $9\frac{3}{8} \times 4\frac{4}{5}$

Mixed Applications

33. Karen and Cami rode bicycles to the picnic. Karen rode $6\frac{1}{2}$ minutes. Cami rode $1\frac{1}{4}$ times as long. How long did it take Cami to ride her bicycle to the picnic?

34. Richard and Hector walked to a picnic. Richard walked $1\frac{3}{5}$ miles. Hector walked $2\frac{1}{2}$ times as far as Richard. How far did Hector walk?

35. **Number Sense • Mental Math** Julie has completed $\frac{2}{3}$ of an 18-week enrichment course. How many weeks has she completed?

36. **Critical Thinking** Sara has 20 nickels and dimes. The value of the coins is $1.35. How many of each coin does Sara have?

When you multiply two mixed numbers, is the product less than or greater than the factors?

W R A P
UP...

PROBLEM SOLVING

STRATEGY • Write an Equation

Markie and Bill are on a committee to make favors for a New Year's Eve party. If they use $8\frac{2}{3}$ cups of confetti for every dozen favors, how many cups of confetti will they use for $12\frac{3}{4}$ dozen favors?

▶ UNDERSTAND

What are you asked to find?

What information are you given?

▶ PLAN

What strategy will you use?

You can write and solve an equation.

▶ SOLVE

How will you carry out your plan?

Write an equation. Let c represent the number of cups of confetti that will be used.

$$c = 8\frac{2}{3} \times 12\frac{3}{4} \quad c = \frac{26}{3} \times \frac{51}{4}$$

Use a standard calculator.
Multiply the denominators.

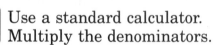 12 M+

 1326 ←Multiply the numerators.

1326 ÷ MRC = ⎡ 110.5 ⎤

Use a calculator designed to operate with fractions.

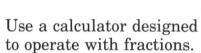 1326/12

Ab/c ⎡ 110 u 6/12 ⎤

Simp 6 = ⎡ 110 u 1/2 ⎤

$110.5 = 110\frac{1}{2}$ 0.5 and $\frac{1}{2}$ name the same amount.

So, Markie and Bill will use $110\frac{1}{2}$ cups of confetti.

▶ LOOK BACK

How can you check your solution?

 WHAT IF... ...Markie and Bill need to make 15 dozen favors? How many cups of confetti will they use?

Apply

Write an equation. Then solve.

(1) The employees of a novelty company worked $\frac{1}{2}$ as many hours this week as they worked last week. If they worked 60 hours last week, how many hours did the employees work this week?

(2) Mr. Gonzalez, the manager of a novelty company, will earn $1\frac{1}{2}$ times as much this year as he earned last year. If he earned $15,000 last year, how much will he earn this year?

(3) For Arbor Day, Nora gave one tiny tree each to $\frac{1}{2}$ of her 36 classmates and $\frac{1}{3}$ of the 33 students on her bus. How many trees did Nora give away?

| Mixed Applications | STRATEGIES | Write an Equation • Guess and Check • Work Backward • Find a Pattern |

Choose a strategy and solve. Use the table for Exercises 6–7.

(4) Nim's Novelty Company employs 16 clerks. Noe's company employs $\frac{3}{4}$ as many clerks as Nim's. How many clerks does Noe's Novelty Company employ?

(5) Amy spent $\frac{1}{3}$ of her allowance for confetti, $\frac{1}{2}$ of what was left for balloons, and the remaining $3.00 for red streamers. How much did Amy spend?

(6) Andy has a package delivery service. If the pattern of delivery charges continues, how much will Andy charge to deliver a package $2\frac{5}{8}$ miles?

Andy's Delivery Service	
Distance	**Fee**
Up to $1\frac{1}{2}$ miles	$1.25
From $1\frac{1}{2}$ to $1\frac{3}{4}$ miles	$1.70
From $1\frac{3}{4}$ to 2 miles	$2.15

(7) Andy delivered a package $2\frac{5}{8}$ miles to one client, returned to the office, and delivered another package 2 miles in the opposite direction. How much money did Andy collect?

(8) Leon placed 2 boxes of party favors on a delivery truck. The boxes weighed a total of 12 pounds. One box was 2 pounds heavier than the other. How much did each of the boxes weigh?

(9) Kevin earns $40 for working an 8-hour day. If he is paid twice his regular rate for overtime, what will Kevin be paid for working a regular 40-hour week and 5 hours of overtime?

More Practice, Lesson 8.6, page H63

REVIEW AND MAINTENANCE

1. A bus leaves a fair to pick up riders at Stop 1. It then goes $2\frac{1}{2}$ miles (mi) to Stop 2, 4 mi to Stop 3, and $3\frac{1}{3}$ mi to Stop 4. If the whole trip is $12\frac{1}{6}$ mi, how far is the fair from Stop 1?

2. Mike sold $\frac{1}{2}$ of his flags on Monday and Tuesday. On Wednesday he sold 3 and had 5 left. How many flags did Mike have before he sold some on Monday?

3. Last year, Tom and Jan ran $1\frac{3}{4}$ mi per hour to come in third in a three-legged race at a Veterans Day picnic. After practicing, they now run $1\frac{3}{5}$ times faster. How fast do they run now?

4. Carla often works 35 hours a week. Since she is taking some of her vacation this week, she will work only 2 hours more than $\frac{1}{5}$ of her usual schedule. How many hours will Carla work this week?

Estimate the difference.

5. $3\frac{1}{3} - 1\frac{2}{3}$

6. $8\frac{1}{6} - 6\frac{1}{8}$

7. $5\frac{3}{5} - 2\frac{1}{4}$

8. $10\frac{1}{5} - 8\frac{7}{8}$

Rename the greater mixed number.

9. $8\frac{1}{4} - 6\frac{3}{4}$

10. $7\frac{1}{3} - 4\frac{2}{3}$

11. $6\frac{1}{6} - 2\frac{5}{6}$

12. $23\frac{1}{8} - 17\frac{5}{8}$

Find the difference. Write your answer in simplest form.

13. $5 - 2\frac{1}{2}$

14. $11\frac{1}{9} - 4\frac{4}{9}$

15. $8\frac{1}{5} - 3\frac{4}{5}$

16. $7\frac{1}{5} - 5\frac{1}{4}$

17. $4\frac{4}{9} - 3\frac{1}{3}$

18. $18\frac{1}{2} - 1\frac{2}{3}$

19. $8\frac{1}{6} - 1\frac{7}{8}$

20. $12\frac{1}{4} - 8\frac{5}{6}$

Tell whether the estimate is reasonable. Write *yes* or *no*.

21. $\frac{3}{4} \times \frac{1}{5} \approx 2$

22. $62 \times \frac{1}{3} \approx 20$

23. $\frac{1}{2} \times 253 \approx 200$

24. $\frac{9}{10} \times \frac{11}{12} \approx 1$

Simplify the factors.

25. $\frac{1}{3} \times \frac{3}{20}$

26. $\frac{2}{5} \times \frac{1}{8}$

27. $\frac{4}{9} \times \frac{3}{10}$

Remember to multiply both the numerators and the denominators.

Find the product. Write the product in simplest form.

28. $\frac{1}{3} \times \frac{3}{4}$

29. $\frac{3}{5} \times \frac{7}{12}$

30. $\frac{1}{2} \times \frac{7}{8}$

31. $1\frac{2}{3} \times 5$

32. $4\frac{1}{2} \times 3$

33. $6\frac{5}{8} \times \frac{4}{5}$

34. $8\frac{1}{3} \times \frac{1}{5}$

35. $3\frac{5}{6} \times \frac{1}{4}$

36. $2\frac{1}{7} \times 2\frac{2}{5}$

Connecting Fractions and Time

The Babylonian civilization developed in an area that is now part of Iraq. The Babylonians used a number system based on 60 and wrote their fractions using a denominator of 60 or 360.

Our division of a circle into 360 degrees and an hour into 60 minutes comes from the ideas developed by the Babylonians.

Since 1 hour = 60 minutes, 1 minute = $\frac{1}{60}$ of an hour. You can use this fact to write measures of time as clock fractions.

ASIA

Iraq
Babylonia

MULTICULTURAL NOTE: The Babylonians were probably the first people to use a sundial, the oldest known device for telling time.

Examples   **A.** Express 40 minutes as a clock fraction.
40 minutes = $\frac{40}{60}$

B. Express 1 hour 15 minutes as a mixed clock fraction.
1 hour 15 minutes = $1\frac{15}{60}$

Express each amount of time as a clock fraction.

1. $\frac{1}{2}$ hour

2. 35 minutes

3. 55 minutes

4. 12 minutes

Express each amount of time as a mixed clock fraction.

5. 2 hours 10 minutes

6. 145 minutes

7. 200 minutes

8. 95 minutes

Tell how much time is expressed by each clock fraction.

9. $\frac{5}{60}$

10. $\frac{23}{60}$

11. $\frac{59}{60}$

12. $\frac{42}{60}$

EXPLORING

Division of Fractions

An artist is painting a mural in the city park. He has 3 quarts of paint that he wants to put in $\frac{1}{2}$-quart containers. How many $\frac{1}{2}$-quart containers will he need?

- Since you must find out how many $\frac{1}{2}$'s are in 3, what operation will you use to solve the problem?

You can use fraction circles to explore dividing whole numbers by fractions.

Work Together

Building Understanding

Use fraction circles. Trace complete circles on your paper to represent the whole numbers. Use circle parts to represent fractions.

Figure A

Think: $3 \div \frac{1}{2}$.

TALK ABOUT IT

- What amount is represented by the white circles in Figure **A**?

- What amount is represented by one part of the blue fraction circle in Figure **A**?

Figure B

- Look at Figure **B**. Into how many parts the size of $\frac{1}{2}$ can 3 be divided? In other words, how many $\frac{1}{2}$-quart containers will the artist need?

Use fraction circles to model each problem.

a. $2 \div \frac{1}{3}$

How many $\frac{1}{3}$'s are in 2?

b. $4 \div \frac{1}{5}$

How many $\frac{1}{5}$'s are in 4?

c. $3 \div \frac{2}{6}$

How many $\frac{2}{6}$'s are in 3?

d. $5 \div \frac{1}{3}$

How many $\frac{1}{3}$'s are in 5?

You can also use fraction circles to explore dividing fractions by fractions.

Work Together

Building Understanding

Use fraction circles to represent the divisor and the dividend.

Example $\frac{1}{2} \div \frac{1}{6}$

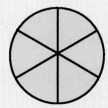

Figure A

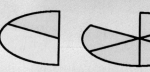

Figure B

TALK ABOUT IT

• What part of a whole is represented in blue in Figure **A**?

• Into how many parts is the yellow circle divided in Figure **A**? What part of a whole is represented by 1 yellow part?

• Look at Figure **B**. How many parts the size of $\frac{1}{6}$ can you fit over $\frac{1}{2}$? In other words, into how many parts the size of $\frac{1}{6}$ can $\frac{1}{2}$ be divided?

• What is the quotient of $\frac{1}{2} \div \frac{1}{6}$?

Use fraction circles to model each problem.

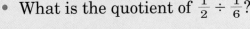

a. $\frac{3}{4} \div \frac{1}{4}$

How many $\frac{1}{4}$'s are in $\frac{3}{4}$?

b. $\frac{1}{3} \div \frac{1}{6}$

How many $\frac{1}{6}$'s are in $\frac{1}{3}$?

c. $\frac{1}{2} \div \frac{1}{8}$

How many $\frac{1}{8}$'s are in $\frac{1}{2}$?

d. $\frac{3}{4} \div \frac{1}{8}$

How many $\frac{1}{8}$'s are in $\frac{3}{4}$?

Making the Connection

Look for a pattern in the division and multiplication number sentences. Use fraction circles to model the problems.

1. $6 \div 2 = \blacksquare$ $6 \times \dfrac{1}{2} = \blacksquare$

2. $1 \div \dfrac{1}{2} = \blacksquare$ $1 \times \dfrac{2}{1} = \blacksquare$

3. $3 \div \dfrac{3}{4} = \blacksquare$ $3 \times \dfrac{4}{3} = \blacksquare$

4. $\dfrac{1}{4} \div \dfrac{1}{2} = \blacksquare$ $\dfrac{1}{4} \times \dfrac{2}{1} = \blacksquare$

$\dfrac{2}{1} = 2$

TALK ABOUT IT

- What is the relationship between the dividend and the first factor? between the quotient and the product?

- Look at the divisor and the second factor. Remember that multiplication and division are inverse operations. What is the product of the divisor and the second factor of each pair of number sentences?

  $2 \times \dfrac{1}{2} = \blacksquare$ $\dfrac{1}{2} \times 2 = \blacksquare$ $\dfrac{3}{4} \times \dfrac{4}{3} = \blacksquare$ $\dfrac{1}{2} \times \dfrac{2}{1} = \blacksquare$

Such number relationships are called **reciprocals.** Two numbers are reciprocals if their product is 1.

- How can you use multiplication to solve a division problem?

Checking Understanding

Write the reciprocal of the divisor.

5. $7 \div \dfrac{1}{3}$

6. $5 \div \dfrac{2}{3}$

7. $\dfrac{4}{5} \div 5$

8. $\dfrac{5}{6} \div 6$

9. $\dfrac{2}{3} \div \dfrac{3}{4}$

10. $\dfrac{1}{2} \div \dfrac{1}{10}$

11. $\dfrac{7}{8} \div \dfrac{1}{8}$

12. $25 \div \dfrac{1}{5}$

13. $36 \div \dfrac{6}{7}$

14. $\dfrac{9}{10} \div \dfrac{1}{2}$

Complete the multiplication sentence. Then find the quotient of the division sentence.

15. $\dfrac{3}{4} \div \dfrac{1}{4} = \blacksquare$ $\dfrac{3}{4} \times \blacksquare = \blacksquare$

16. $12 \div \dfrac{3}{4} = \blacksquare$ $12 \times \blacksquare = \blacksquare$

17. $\dfrac{1}{3} \div \dfrac{1}{6} = \blacksquare$ $\dfrac{1}{3} \times \blacksquare = \blacksquare$

18. $15 \div \dfrac{1}{3} = \blacksquare$ $15 \times \blacksquare = \blacksquare$

19. $\dfrac{2}{3} \div \dfrac{1}{9} = \blacksquare$ $\dfrac{2}{3} \times \blacksquare = \blacksquare$

20. $\dfrac{3}{4} \div \dfrac{1}{10} = \blacksquare$ $\dfrac{3}{4} \times \blacksquare = \blacksquare$

PROBLEM-SOLVING PRACTICE

In the United States, people celebrate their independence on July 4. In Mexico, people celebrate their independence in September.

Social Studies Connection

Every September 15 and 16, Julio and his family go to Guaymas to celebrate Mexican independence. They participate in festivities that include fireworks, parades, and street dances. Julio enjoys the activities, arts and crafts, and ethnic foods that are found in the crowded marketplaces.

1. Julio sees 8 girls who are waiting for a parade to begin. There are 5 carrying castanets, 3 carrying maracas, and 2 carrying both castanets and maracas. How many of the girls are not carrying either castanets or maracas?

2. Aneta likes to watch the street dancers who wear traditional costumes and dance in groups of 4 or 6. She counted a total of 36 dancers. There were more groups of 6 than of 4. How many groups of 4 and how many groups of 6 did Aneta watch?

3. Julio was among 6 contestants in a men's competition. He finished second, and his friend Luis finished next to last. José finished just before Luis, and Benito finished after Luis. If Carlos did not finish first, in what place did Alejandro finish in the competition?

4. Maria is making tissue-paper flowers. She tears a sheet of tissue paper in half. Then she puts 1 piece on top of the other and tears them in half again. If she continues the same process, how many pieces of tissue paper will Maria have after she makes 5 tears?

5. Octavio and Susana found a cafe that accepts U.S. dollars. They had $20.00 to spend for dinner. They each bought 3 tamales for $1.50, a serving of frijoles for $1.75, 2 tostadas for $1.25 each, and 2 enchiladas for $1.50 each. How much change did they receive?

6. In the final $1\frac{1}{2}$ hours of the celebration, Julio watched a shower of rockets for $\frac{1}{4}$ hour, a brilliant fireworks display for $\frac{1}{2}$ hour, and a pinata party in which his little sister participated. For how long did Julio watch the party?

DIVIDING FRACTIONS

Christina's family has gathered to spend Greek National Independence Day together. Christina serves a cold drink called *vissinatch* to her family. She has 4 liters of vissinatch. Each glass holds $\frac{2}{10}$ liter. How many glasses of vissinatch can Christina serve?

Step 1 Use the reciprocal of the divisor to write a multiplication problem.	**Step 2** Simplify.	**Step 3** Multiply.
$4 \div \dfrac{2}{10} = 4 \times \dfrac{10}{2}$	$\dfrac{\overset{2}{\cancel{4}}}{1} \times \dfrac{10}{\underset{1}{\cancel{2}}}$	$\dfrac{2}{1} \times \dfrac{10}{1} = \dfrac{20}{1}$, or 20

So, Christina has enough vissinatch for 20 glasses.

More Examples

A. $\dfrac{3}{8} \div \dfrac{3}{4} = \dfrac{\overset{1}{\cancel{3}}}{\underset{2}{\cancel{8}}} \times \dfrac{\overset{1}{\cancel{4}}}{\underset{1}{\cancel{3}}} = \dfrac{1}{2}$

B. $\dfrac{7}{10} \div \dfrac{2}{5} = \dfrac{7}{\underset{2}{\cancel{10}}} \times \dfrac{\overset{1}{\cancel{5}}}{2} = \dfrac{7}{4}$, or $1\dfrac{3}{4}$

Talk About It

▶ In Examples A and B, how do the divisors compare with the dividends?

▶ In Example A, is the quotient less than or greater than 1?

▶ In Example B, is the quotient less than or greater than 1?

▶ What rule can you write to compare the value of the quotient with the values of the divisor and the dividend?

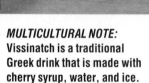

MULTICULTURAL NOTE: Vissinatch is a traditional Greek drink that is made with cherry syrup, water, and ice.

Check for Understanding

Tell whether the quotient will be less than or greater than 1.

1. $7 \div \dfrac{3}{5}$ 2. $\dfrac{7}{9} \div \dfrac{3}{5}$ 3. $\dfrac{1}{2} \div \dfrac{2}{3}$ 4. $\dfrac{2}{3} \div \dfrac{1}{2}$ 5. $\dfrac{1}{2} \div 5$

Practice

Complete.

6. $\dfrac{1}{4} \div \dfrac{1}{2} = \dfrac{1}{4} \times \dfrac{2}{1} = \dfrac{\blacksquare}{\blacksquare}$

7. $6 \div \dfrac{1}{4} = 6 \times \dfrac{\blacksquare}{\blacksquare} = \dfrac{\blacksquare}{\blacksquare}$

8. $3 \div \dfrac{3}{5} = \blacksquare \times \dfrac{5}{3} = \dfrac{\blacksquare}{\blacksquare}$

9. $\dfrac{1}{2} \div \dfrac{3}{5} = \dfrac{1}{2} \times \dfrac{\blacksquare}{\blacksquare} = \dfrac{\blacksquare}{\blacksquare}$

Tell whether the quotient will be greater than or less than 1.

10. $15 \div \dfrac{5}{6}$

11. $10 \div \dfrac{3}{5}$

12. $\dfrac{3}{5} \div \dfrac{1}{8}$

13. $\dfrac{3}{4} \div \dfrac{1}{6}$

14. $\dfrac{5}{6} \div \dfrac{2}{9}$

15. $\dfrac{5}{6} \div \dfrac{7}{3}$

16. $1 \div \dfrac{4}{3}$

17. $9 \div \dfrac{3}{8}$

Find the quotient.

18. $10 \div \dfrac{5}{6}$

19. $4 \div \dfrac{4}{5}$

20. $\dfrac{3}{4} \div \dfrac{1}{3}$

21. $\dfrac{5}{8} \div \dfrac{2}{3}$

22. $8 \div \dfrac{6}{7}$

23. $12 \div \dfrac{3}{5}$

24. $\dfrac{3}{4} \div \dfrac{3}{16}$

25. $\dfrac{2}{3} \div \dfrac{4}{5}$

26. $6 \div \dfrac{3}{4}$

27. $\dfrac{9}{10} \div \dfrac{3}{5}$

28. $2 \div \dfrac{1}{6}$

29. $\dfrac{1}{10} \div \dfrac{5}{6}$

Mixed Applications

30. Brian is grilling hamburgers for a block party. How many $\frac{1}{4}$-pound hamburgers can he grill with 12 pounds of ground beef?

31. **Number Sense** The number 4 is 16 times greater than its reciprocal. If a number is 9 times greater than its reciprocal, what is the number?

NUMBER SENSE

You can use common denominators or the LCD to divide.

A. $\dfrac{9}{8} \div \dfrac{3}{8}$ 8 is a common denominator.

B. $\dfrac{3}{4} \div \dfrac{1}{8}$ LCD is 8.

$\dfrac{9}{8} \div \dfrac{3}{8} = \dfrac{9 \div 3}{8 \div 8} = \dfrac{3}{1} = 3$

$\dfrac{3}{4} \div \dfrac{1}{8} = \dfrac{6}{8} \div \dfrac{1}{8} = \dfrac{6 \div 1}{8 \div 8} = \dfrac{6}{1} = 6$

Use the LCD to divide. Show your work.

32. $\dfrac{3}{4} \div \dfrac{1}{4}$

33. $\dfrac{2}{5} \div \dfrac{1}{5}$

34. $\dfrac{3}{4} \div \dfrac{3}{8}$

35. $\dfrac{14}{15} \div \dfrac{3}{5}$

Describe how you divide fractions by using reciprocals.

WRAP UP...

DIVIDING MIXED NUMBERS

Jian is making greeting cards to celebrate the Chinese New Year. The base of each card is $3\frac{3}{4}$ inches long. A $1\frac{1}{4}$-inch repeating pattern forms a border across the base of the card. How many times does the pattern occur?

You can use a ruler to visualize the answer.

- Into how many parts the size of $1\frac{1}{4}$ inches can $3\frac{3}{4}$ inches be divided?

Or, you can divide $3\frac{3}{4}$ by $1\frac{1}{4}$ to find the answer.

Step 1 Write the mixed numbers as fractions.	**Step 2** Use the reciprocal to write a multiplication problem. Simplify.
$3\frac{3}{4} \div 1\frac{1}{4} = \frac{15}{4} \div \frac{5}{4}$	$\frac{15}{4} \div \frac{5}{4} = \frac{15}{4} \times \frac{4}{5} = \frac{\overset{3}{\cancel{15}}}{\underset{1}{\cancel{4}}} \times \frac{\overset{1}{\cancel{4}}}{\underset{1}{\cancel{5}}}$

MULTICULTURAL NOTE: The Chinese New Year is a celebration that lasts for three days. Many people spend the celebration visiting relatives.

Step 3
Multiply.

$$\frac{\overset{3}{\cancel{15}}}{\underset{1}{\cancel{4}}} \times \frac{\overset{1}{\cancel{4}}}{\underset{1}{\cancel{5}}} = \frac{3}{1} \times \frac{1}{1} = 3$$

So, the pattern occurs 3 times.

More Examples

A. $4\frac{1}{2} \div 3 = \frac{9}{2} \div \frac{3}{1} = \frac{9}{2} \times \frac{1}{3} = \frac{\overset{3}{\cancel{9}}}{2} \times \frac{1}{\underset{1}{\cancel{3}}} = \frac{3}{2}$, or $1\frac{1}{2}$

B. $\frac{4}{5} \div 3\frac{1}{2} = \frac{4}{5} \div \frac{7}{2} = \frac{4}{5} \times \frac{2}{7} = \frac{8}{35}$

- What other method can you use to divide?

- What is the LCD of $\frac{4}{5}$ and $3\frac{1}{2}$?

- How do you use the LCD to divide mixed numbers?

Check for Understanding

Tell whether the multiplication sentence is correct. Write *yes* or *no.*

1. $4\frac{1}{4} \div 2 = \frac{17}{4} \times \frac{1}{2}$

2. $5\frac{1}{4} \div 1\frac{3}{4} = \frac{4}{21} \times \frac{7}{4}$

3. $10\frac{1}{3} \div 5\frac{2}{3} = \frac{31}{3} \times \frac{3}{17}$

Practice

Write the multiplication sentence.

4. $1\frac{1}{4} \div \frac{5}{8}$

5. $\frac{7}{8} \div 1\frac{3}{4}$

6. $2\frac{2}{3} \div 6$

7. $1\frac{1}{8} \div 6\frac{3}{4}$

Find the quotient.

8. $1\frac{1}{2} \div \frac{3}{8}$

9. $3\frac{2}{3} \div \frac{5}{6}$

10. $3\frac{1}{4} \div 1\frac{3}{8}$

11. $\frac{7}{8} \div 3\frac{1}{2}$

12. $1\frac{1}{2} \div 6\frac{1}{2}$

13. $5 \div 1\frac{7}{8}$

14. $2\frac{1}{2} \div 1\frac{1}{4}$

15. $\frac{5}{8} \div 1\frac{1}{2}$

16. $8 \div 2\frac{2}{5}$

17. $4\frac{5}{7} \div 3$

18. $3\frac{1}{4} \div 2\frac{1}{6}$

19. $3\frac{3}{7} \div 8$

20. $1\frac{1}{6} \div 5\frac{1}{4}$

21. $9 \div 3\frac{3}{4}$

22. $4\frac{2}{7} \div 2\frac{1}{2}$

23. $1\frac{3}{8} \div 5\frac{1}{2}$

Mixed Applications

24. A board 12 feet long will be cut into sections for bookshelves. Each shelf will be $1\frac{1}{2}$ feet long. How many shelves can be made from the 12-foot board?

25. Bill has $\frac{3}{4}$ of a pizza left. He wants to give $\frac{1}{2}$ of it to Julie. How can you find the amount Bill wants to give Julie?

MIXED REVIEW

Tell whether the product will be greater than or less than 1.

1. $\frac{2}{5} \times \frac{1}{2}$

2. $\frac{1}{3} \times 97$

3. $45 \times \frac{1}{8}$

4. $\frac{9}{10} \times \frac{2}{3}$

Estimate the sum or difference.

5. $\frac{4}{5} + \frac{9}{18}$

6. $\frac{7}{8} - \frac{9}{10}$

7. $6\frac{2}{3} + 5\frac{3}{4}$

8. $10\frac{3}{8} - 2\frac{2}{5}$

Find the sum or difference. Write your answer in simplest form.

9. $\frac{9}{10} - \frac{2}{10}$

10. $\frac{4}{9} + \frac{2}{9}$

11. $9\frac{7}{8} - 4\frac{3}{8}$

12. $5\frac{1}{2} + 1\frac{1}{2}$

When you divide two mixed numbers, will the quotient be less than or greater than the dividend?

More Practice, Lesson 8.9, page H64

Jim wants to represent $\frac{3}{4}$ on a standard calculator to determine the cost of each serving of juice.

Use the models to visualize $\frac{3}{4}$ as a decimal.

• What part of Figure **A** is green?

• What part of Figure **B** is blue?

• How does the amount in Figure **A** compare with the amount in Figure **B**?

So, Jim can use 0.75 to represent $\frac{3}{4}$ on a calculator.

Figure A   Figure B

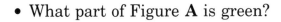

You can change a fraction to an equivalent decimal by dividing the numerator by the denominator.

You can use paper and pencil, or you can use a calculator.

A. $\frac{1}{4}$

$$\begin{array}{r} 0.25 \\ 4\overline{)1.00} \\ -8 \\ \hline 20 \\ -20 \\ \hline 0 \end{array}$$

$\frac{1}{4} = 0.25$

B. $\frac{1}{3}$

$$\begin{array}{r} 0.33 \\ 3\overline{)1.00} \\ -9 \\ \hline 10 \\ -9 \\ \hline 1 \end{array}$$

← The remainder is always 1. The decimal repeats.

$\frac{1}{3} = 0.\overline{3}$ ← The bar shows that the digit 3 repeats.

C. $\frac{2}{9}$

$2 \boxed{\div} 9 \boxed{=}$ $\boxed{0.2222222}$

$\frac{2}{9} = 0.\overline{2}$

Another Method

If the denominator of a fraction is a factor of 10 or 100, write an equivalent fraction using 10 or 100 as the denominator. Then use place value to write the decimal.

A. $\frac{3}{50} = \frac{6}{100} = 0.06$ **B.** $\frac{11}{25} = \frac{44}{100} = 0.44$ **C.** $\frac{1}{5} = \frac{2}{10} = 0.2$

You can change a decimal to an equivalent fraction by using what you know about place value.

A. $0.8 = \frac{8}{10} = \frac{4}{5}$ **B.** $0.25 = \frac{25}{100} = \frac{1}{4}$ **C.** $0.125 = \frac{125}{1,000} = \frac{1}{8}$

Check for Understanding

Tell how you would change to a decimal or a fraction. Write *division* or *place value.*

1. $\dfrac{1}{2}$

2. $\dfrac{13}{20}$

3. $\dfrac{2}{3}$

4. 0.4

5. 0.64

6. 0.45

Practice

Write as a decimal.

7. $\dfrac{1}{2}$

8. $\dfrac{43}{100}$

9. $\dfrac{4}{5}$

10. $\dfrac{3}{10}$

11. $\dfrac{3}{4}$

12. $\dfrac{7}{8}$

13. $\dfrac{13}{20}$

14. $\dfrac{2}{9}$

15. $\dfrac{12}{25}$

16. $\dfrac{17}{50}$

17. $\dfrac{2}{25}$

18. $\dfrac{1}{12}$

 Use a calculator. Find an equivalent decimal.

19. $\dfrac{3}{5}$

20. $\dfrac{2}{3}$

21. $\dfrac{7}{20}$

22. $\dfrac{5}{6}$

23. $\dfrac{7}{8}$

24. $\dfrac{6}{11}$

Write as a fraction in simplest form.

25. 0.5

26. 0.09

27. 0.10

28. 0.15

29. 0.25

30. 0.025

31. 0.8

32. $0.04\dfrac{1}{25}$

33. 0.01

34. 0.75

35. 0.38

36. 1.99

Mixed Applications

37. Marsha needs to know the decimal equivalent of $\dfrac{1}{4}$ in order to determine the cost of each serving of yogurt. Write the decimal equivalent of $\dfrac{1}{4}$.

38. **Critical Thinking** If the repeating decimal that is equivalent to $\dfrac{1}{3}$ is $0.\overline{3}$, what is the repeating decimal that is equivalent to $\dfrac{2}{3}$?

39. **Number Sense** A number is between 24 and 25. There is a 6 in the hundredths place, and the sum of the 4 digits is 13. Write the number as a mixed number.

Name some ways you can change a decimal to a fraction or a fraction to a decimal.

WRAP UP...

PROBLEM SOLVING

STRATEGY • Solve a Simpler Problem

Charity volunteers are holding a Spring Fair raffle on Flag Day. They sold $\frac{1}{2}$ of the raffle tickets and gave away $\frac{1}{4}$ of the remaining tickets. If the volunteers gave away 2,400 raffle tickets, how many tickets did they have in the beginning?

▶ **UNDERSTAND**

What are you asked to find?

What information are you given?

▶ **PLAN**

What strategy will you use?

You can *solve a simpler problem.* Since 24 × 100 is 2,400, use 24 for the number of tickets given away.

▶ **SOLVE**

How can you carry out your plan?

Let 24 equal the number of tickets given away.

Think:

$\frac{1}{4}$ of the number of tickets = 24.
If $\frac{1}{4}$ = 24, then $\frac{4}{4}$ = 96.

Think:

$\frac{1}{2}$ of the number of tickets = 96.
If $\frac{1}{2}$ = 96, then $\frac{2}{2}$ = 192.

If 24 had been given away, there would have been 192 in the beginning. Since 24 × 100 = 2,400 given away, there were 192 × 100 = 19,200 tickets in the beginning.

So, the volunteers had 19,200 raffle tickets in the beginning.

▶ **LOOK BACK**

What other strategy could you use?

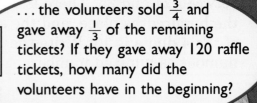

WHAT IF... . . . the volunteers sold $\frac{3}{4}$ and gave away $\frac{1}{3}$ of the remaining tickets? If they gave away 120 raffle tickets, how many did the volunteers have in the beginning?

Apply

Solve by using a simpler problem.

1 Dennis has 500 plastic name tags. He had used $\frac{1}{2}$ of the total for a convention and $\frac{1}{3}$ of the total for a carnival. How many name tags did Dennis have in the beginning?

2 Meg gave away $\frac{1}{2}$ of the pamphlets, and a friend gave away $\frac{1}{3}$ of what was left. If Meg's friend gave away 550 pamphlets, how many did Meg have at first?

Mixed Applications ⟩ **STRATEGIES**

Solve a Simpler Problem
• **Guess and Check** • **Find a Pattern**
• **Write an Equation**

Choose a strategy and solve.

3 A group of 10 girls and 10 boys will play tennis. If each girl plays one match with each boy, how many tennis matches will there be?

4 There are $\frac{1}{3}$ as many rides at the carnival as there are games. The total number of games is 51. How many rides are at the carnival?

5 At the carnival 20 students enter a checkers tournament. If each student plays every other student only once, what is the total number of games the students will play?

6 Together two rides hold 64 people. One ride holds 3 times as many as the other. How many people can each ride hold?

7 Keisha is making tea for the carnival. She can make 2 quarts of tea with 1 tea bag, 5 with 2 tea bags, and 9 with 3 tea bags. At this rate, how many quarts of tea can Keisha make with 6 tea bags?

8 A group of adults and students went to a concert. They spent a total of $51 for tickets. Adult tickets cost $12.75 each, and student tickets cost $8.50 each. How many of each kind of ticket did the group buy?

WRITER'S CORNER

9 You and your family have just been to a Thanksgiving celebration. Write a problem that can be solved by multiplying or dividing fractions. Exchange papers with a classmate and solve.

CHAPTER REVIEW/TEST

Vocabulary Check

Choose a word or words from the box to complete each sentence.

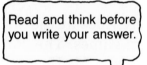

decimal
divisor
fraction
less than
reciprocals
simplify

Read and think before you write your answer.

1. When the product of two numbers is one, the numbers are ___?___. *(page 252)*

2. The product of two fractions that are less than 1 will be ___?___ either factor. *(page 236)*

3. To divide by a fraction, you can use the reciprocal of the ___?___ and then multiply. *(page 252)*

4. You can change a decimal to an equivalent ___?___ by using place value. *(page 258)*

5. You can change a fraction to an equivalent ___?___ by dividing the numerator by the denominator. *(page 258)*

6. You can divide the numerator and the denominator by the GCF to ___?___ a fraction. *(page 238)*

Concept Check

7. To estimate the product of fractions, you can use ___?___ or ___?___ numbers. *(page 242)*

8. To avoid having to change the product to simplest form, you can simplify the ___?___. *(page 240)*

9. Will the product of two mixed numbers be less than the factors, greater than the factors, or between the factors? Why? *(page 244)*

10. If you must find how many $\frac{1}{3}$'s are in 5, what operation will you use? *(page 250)*

Draw a model to help you find the product. Then solve. *(page 238)*

11. $\frac{1}{2} \times \frac{1}{5} = $ ■   12. $\frac{3}{4} \times \frac{2}{3} = $ ■   13. $\frac{1}{4} \times \frac{3}{4} = $ ■   14. $\frac{1}{2} \times \frac{2}{3} = $ ■

Write the reciprocal of the divisor. *(page 252)*

15. $10\frac{1}{2} \div 2$ 16. $6 \div \frac{3}{16}$ 17. $\frac{1}{2} \div \frac{1}{12}$ 18. $3 \div \frac{1}{4}$

Skill Check

Tell whether the estimate is reasonable. Write *yes* or *no*. *(page 242)*

19. $\dfrac{2}{5} \times \dfrac{7}{11} \approx \dfrac{1}{4}$ **20.** $62 \times \dfrac{7}{8} > 8$ **21.** $\dfrac{5}{12} \times \dfrac{13}{15} < 2$ **22.** $\dfrac{1}{6} \times 125 \approx 20$

Simplify the factors. *(page 240)*

23. $\dfrac{2}{7} \times \dfrac{5}{12}$ **24.** $\dfrac{8}{20} \times \dfrac{5}{16}$ **25.** $\dfrac{4}{9} \times \dfrac{3}{10}$ **26.** $\dfrac{1}{6} \times \dfrac{3}{11}$

Find the product. Write your answer in simplest form.
(pages 238, 240, 244)

27. $\dfrac{3}{10} \times \dfrac{1}{3}$ **28.** $\dfrac{5}{9} \times 6$ **29.** $\dfrac{9}{10} \times \dfrac{1}{18}$ **30.** $\dfrac{2}{9} \times \dfrac{3}{5}$

31. $\dfrac{1}{3} \times 3\dfrac{1}{2}$ **32.** $2\dfrac{3}{4} \times \dfrac{2}{3}$ **33.** $4\dfrac{2}{5} \times 1\dfrac{3}{7}$ **34.** $1\dfrac{1}{6} \times 6\dfrac{3}{4}$

Write the reciprocal of the divisor. *(page 252)*

35. $\dfrac{7}{8} \div \dfrac{1}{2}$ **36.** $\dfrac{5}{16} \div 3$ **37.** $1\dfrac{1}{3} \div \dfrac{3}{5}$ **38.** $1\dfrac{1}{2} \div 4\dfrac{1}{4}$

Find the quotient. *(pages 250, 251, 252, 254, 256)*

39. $32 \div \dfrac{4}{5}$ **40.** $16 \div \dfrac{1}{2}$ **41.** $\dfrac{1}{8} \div \dfrac{3}{10}$ **42.** $45 \div \dfrac{1}{5}$

43. $2\dfrac{1}{3} \div \dfrac{3}{4}$ **44.** $9\dfrac{3}{7} \div 4\dfrac{1}{2}$ **45.** $5\dfrac{1}{10} \div \dfrac{2}{5}$ **46.** $12\dfrac{7}{8} \div \dfrac{1}{3}$

Write as a fraction in simplest form. *(page 258)*

47. 0.9 **48.** 0.2 **49.** 0.45 **50.** 0.65 **51.** 0.8

Write as a decimal. *(page 258)*

52. $\dfrac{2}{5}$ **53.** $\dfrac{1}{8}$ **54.** $\dfrac{1}{3}$ **55.** $\dfrac{18}{100}$ **56.** $\dfrac{1}{9}$

Problem-Solving Check *(pages 246, 260)*

57. Burt uses $9\dfrac{1}{2}$ boxes of party streamers to decorate 5 rooms. How many boxes of streamers does he use in each room?

58. Lara received a holiday bonus that was $\dfrac{1}{6}$ of her monthly pay. If she is paid $420 four times a month, how much was her bonus?

59. Tia gave away 50 cups of juice, which was $\dfrac{1}{10}$ what she sold at the fair. How many cups of juice did she sell at the fair?

60. There are 15 students planning a party by telephone. Each student talks to every other student once. How many calls are made?

WHAT DID I LEARN?

1. Show each step as you find the product $2\frac{2}{5} \times \frac{15}{16}$.

2. Estimate $\frac{2}{5} \times \frac{7}{8}$. Explain your method.

3. Show each step as you find the quotient $5\frac{1}{4} \div 1\frac{3}{4}$.

4. Change $\frac{7}{8}$ to a decimal. Show your work.

5. Read Exercise 8 on page 261. Follow the steps on the Problem-Solving Think Along worksheet to show how to solve this problem.

I can use fraction models to show division of fractions.

Write About It

6. Describe an everyday situation in which you would need to multiply fractions.

7. Draw a picture or model to show the solution to $\frac{1}{2} \div \frac{1}{10}$.

Plan Recreational Facilities

Suppose that on Earth Day your community announced plans to build a dome the size of four football fields over your school. Your school building and grounds will be modernized, pollution-free, and environmentally controlled.

You and your teammates have been chosen to plan new recreational activities for your school.

Decide

As a team, discuss the possible choices. Make a list of arts, crafts, and sports you would like to include.

Discuss whether each recreational activity will be in the building or "outdoors," under the dome.

Discuss how to utilize existing facilities and add new ones.

Do

Prepare a plan defining the types of recreation, space, buildings, storage, and equipment needed.

Make a sketch to illustrate your plan.

Share

Compare your team's plan and sketch with those of other teams. Tell why you chose each activity and how each facility will be used.

Talk About It

○ Which type of facility will get the most use?

○ What fraction of the recreational facilities will be used for arts and crafts? for sports?

MATH FUN
Extend Your Thinking

Repeating Decimals

On Earth Day, a power plant revealed that it sends $\frac{5}{11}$ of its electricity to one city. Use a calculator to write a decimal for $\frac{5}{11}$.

 5 $\div$ 11 $=$ | 0.4545454 |

The digits 4 and 5 repeat. Put a bar over the digits that repeat, such as $0.\overline{45}$, instead of writing them several times.

Find patterns in repeating decimals.

Use a calculator. Write the fraction as a repeating decimal.

1. $\frac{1}{11}$ 2. $\frac{2}{11}$

3. $\frac{3}{11}$ 4. $\frac{4}{11}$

5. What pattern do you notice among the numerators and the repeating decimals?

Do not divide. Use the pattern to write the repeating decimal.

6. $\frac{6}{11}$ 7. $\frac{7}{11}$

8. $\frac{8}{11}$ 9. $\frac{9}{11}$

10. What pattern do you see in the repeating decimal equivalents of $\frac{1}{9}$, $\frac{2}{9}$, $\frac{3}{9}$, and so on?

As people are influenced by Earth Day, they are becoming more conscious of the need to preserve natural resources.

Challenge

Critical Thinking

In northern California, steam from the earth heats 99 homes, 3 more than last year. Last year 6 times as many homes were heated by the steam than 10 years ago. How many homes were heated by the steam 10 years ago?

Consumer Connection

It takes an average of $2\frac{1}{2}$ T of coal yearly to make enough electricity for a water heater. It takes $\frac{1}{3}$ T for a range, and $\frac{1}{2}$ T each for a dishwasher, a television, and a clothes dryer. Which requires more coal yearly, a water heater alone or a range, dishwasher, television, and clothes dryer combined?

Write the letter of the correct answer.

1. 7.5×9.24

    A. 68.3   **B.** 69.3

    C. 683   **D.** 693

2. $20.4 \div 1.6$

    A. 0.1275   **B.** 1.275

    C. 12.75   **D.** 127.5

3. $6\frac{1}{8} + 2\frac{1}{3}$

    A. $8\frac{2}{11}$ **B.** $8\frac{11}{24}$

    C. $8\frac{1}{2}$ **D.** $8\frac{11}{12}$

4. What is the median of 0, 2, 3, 3, 4?

    A. 0   **B.** 2

    C. 3   **D.** 4

5. What are combinations for 3 hats and 5 scarves?

    A. 3   **B.** 5

    C. 8   **D.** 15

6. $8\frac{1}{6} - 6\frac{1}{8}$

    A. $1\frac{1}{24}$ **B.** 2

    C. $2\frac{1}{24}$ **D.** $2\frac{1}{2}$

7. Which is the estimate for $\frac{7}{15} \times \frac{9}{10}$?

    A. $\frac{1}{2}$ **B.** 1

    C. $1\frac{1}{2}$ **D.** not here

8. $2\frac{2}{3} \times 1\frac{1}{8}$

    A. $2\frac{1}{12}$ **B.** $2\frac{2}{24}$

    C. $\frac{71}{24}$ **D.** 3

9. $\frac{1}{8} \div 2$

    A. $\frac{1}{4}$ **B.** 4

    C. 16   **D.** not here

10. What is the decimal for $\frac{8}{25}$?

    A. 0.032   **B.** 0.32

    C. 0.33   **D.** 3.2

11. Loretta drives $3\frac{3}{4}$ mi to work. How far does Loretta drive to pick up a friend if the friend lives at the halfway point?

    A. $1\frac{1}{4}$ mi   **B.** $1\frac{7}{8}$ mi

    C. $1\frac{9}{10}$ mi   **D.** $2\frac{1}{4}$ mi

12. Dan sold $\frac{2}{5}$ of the flowers and Rita sold $\frac{1}{3}$ of what remained. If 600 flowers were left, how many did Dan and Rita have at first?

    A. 80 flowers   **B.** 900 flowers

    C. 1,800 flowers   **D.** 1,500 flowers

MEASUREMENT

Did you know . . .

. . . the pull of the moon on the earth causes tides in the ocean?

TALK ABOUT IT

Describe a way to find the difference in water level between the high and low tides at the ocean shore.

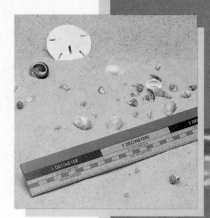

RELATING METRIC UNITS

Metric measurement is based on the decimal system. The relationships among the units are the same as the relationships among place-value positions.

The base unit of length is the **meter.**
The base unit of capacity is the **liter.**
The base unit of mass is the **gram.**

Metric Units of Length		
1 kilometer (km)	=	1,000 meters (m)
	meter (m)	
1 decimeter (dm)	=	0.1 meter
1 centimeter (cm)	=	0.01 meter
1 millimeter (mm)	=	0.001 meter

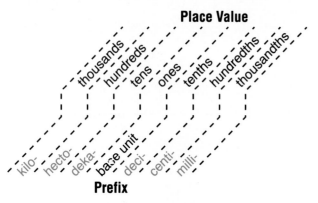

Place Value

thousands, hundreds, tens, ones, tenths, hundredths, thousandths

kilo-, hecto-, deka-, base unit, deci-, centi-, milli-

Prefix

The most commonly used prefixes are *kilo-, deci-, centi-,* and *milli-*. The same prefixes are used for length, capacity, and mass.

Talk About It

▶ How many times lighter or heavier than a gram is a kilogram?

▶ How many times greater or less than a liter is a milliliter?

▶ How many times longer or shorter than a centimeter is a meter?

Use Your Number Sense

a. Name objects in your classroom that are about a meter in length.

b. Name objects in your classroom that are about a centimeter in length.

c. How many of your steps equal about a meter in length?

d. Do you think you could walk a kilometer?

Lea counts her strides as she walks. The distance between her footprints in the sand is 0.75 m. How many centimeters is Lea's stride?

Use place value to change from one unit to another.

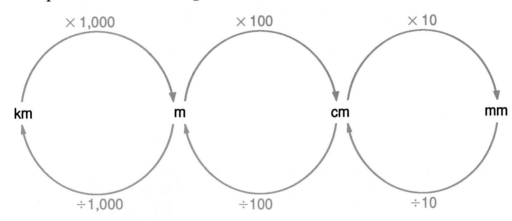

To change from larger units to smaller units, multiply.

To change from smaller units to larger units, divide.

Talk About It

▶ When you change from meters to centimeters, will there be more units or fewer units?

▶ Should you divide or multiply to change from meters to centimeters?

▶ How do you know by what number to multiply or divide?

▶ By what number will you multiply to change from meters to centimeters?

▶ How many centimeters is Lea's stride?

▶ How can you change any metric unit to a smaller unit?

Lea walked 2,800 m. How many kilometers is that?

▶ When you change from meters to kilometers, will there be more units or fewer units?

▶ Should you divide or multiply to change from meters to kilometers?

1,000 m = 1 km
2,800 ÷ 1,000 = 2.8   So, Lea walked 2.8 km.

▶ How can you change any metric unit to a larger unit?

Check for Understanding

Tell which unit is greater.

1. centimeter or decimeter
2. liter or milliliter
3. milligram or kilogram

4. liter or deciliter
5. gram or kilogram
6. meter or millimeter

Tell by what number you must multiply or divide to change the unit.

7. $25\,km = \blacksquare\,m$
8. $2\,L = \blacksquare\,mL$
9. $18\,mg = \blacksquare\,g$

Practice

Complete the pattern.

10. $1\,mL = 0.001\,L$
$10\,mL = \blacksquare\,L$
$100\,mL = \blacksquare\,L$
$1,000\,mL = \blacksquare\,L$

11. $0.001\,m = 0.1\,cm$
$0.01\,m = \blacksquare\,cm$
$0.1\,m = \blacksquare\,cm$
$1\,m = \blacksquare\,cm$

12. $1,000\,g = 1\,kg$
$100\,g = \blacksquare\,kg$
$10\,g = \blacksquare\,kg$
$1\,g = \blacksquare\,kg$

Find the missing number.

13. $0.34\,m = \blacksquare\,km$
14. $480\,cm = \blacksquare\,m$
15. $15\,mL = \blacksquare\,L$

16. $425\,g = \blacksquare\,mg$
17. $37\,cm = \blacksquare\,mm$
18. $16\,L = \blacksquare\,mL$

19. $320\,mm = \blacksquare\,cm$
20. $6\,L = \blacksquare\,mL$
21. $1,000\,g = \blacksquare\,kg$

22. $0.44\,kL = \blacksquare\,L$
23. $1\,km = \blacksquare\,m$
24. $0.086\,kg = \blacksquare\,g$

Mixed Applications

25. If Rosa fills her sand pail with 1.5 L of water, how many milliliters is she using?

26. Jim's beach bag weighs 3,000 g when filled. How many kilograms does it weigh?

27. **Critical Thinking** To get to a beach resort, Don will travel 4 hours, including a $\frac{1}{4}$-hour stop. If he travels at a rate of 88 km per hour, how far will he travel?

28. **Number Sense • Estimation** Will Donna travel a distance of 250 km if she drives an average of 71 km per hour for $2\frac{1}{4}$ hours?

WRAP UP... Why is the metric system easy to use?

More Practice, Lesson 9.1, page H66

Joan and her family went to the beach for the weekend. While she was sleeping one night, Joan had a math-filled dream about three unusual players in a strange game.

Eight-Arms Octopus wanted to play toss-a-plate on the beach. When he wandered onto the sand, looking for company, he met Two-Hands Mermaid. "How about a game of toss-a-plate?" he asked. "The first to score 20 points gets the Catch of the Day." Two-Hands knew the odds were in Eight-Arms' favor. But she was tempted to try for the Catch of the Day, which she knew was her favorite, Seaweed Surprise. Then Stretch-Neck Seal appeared and wanted to help Two-Hands. He made the odds better, 8 to 3.

1. Two-Hands has two options. Which is the better choice, (a) play alone against Eight-Arms, making the odds 8 to 2 in favor of Eight-Arms, or (b) play with Stretch-Neck, making the odds 8 to 3 in favor of Eight-Arms?

2. Two-Hands has to take a dip in the water every few minutes to keep her scales from drying out. She goes into the water after throws 1, 3, 6, 10, 15, and 21. If this pattern continues, after which throw will she return to the water next?

3. Two-Hands is 150 cm tall. Her reach extends upward 55 cm. If the toss-a-plate is thrown in the air to a height of 268 cm, how far must she jump to catch it?

4. The toss-a-plate playing field is 100 m long. Stretch-Neck ran 20 m less than $\frac{1}{2}$ its length to catch the toss-a-plate. How many meters did Stretch-Neck run?

5. Each team is allowed 30 throws in a half. In the first half, Eight-Arms missed 5 throws. Stretch-Neck missed 15, and Two-Hands missed 5 fewer than Stretch-Neck. In the second half, Eight-Arms missed 1, Stretch-Neck 5, and Two-Hands 2. Make and use a table. Who missed 1 out of 10 throws?

6. Eight-Arms can catch equally well with each of his eight arms, and you can never predict with which arm he will catch the toss-a-plate. What are the chances of his catching one throw of the toss-a-plate with any one of three particular arms?

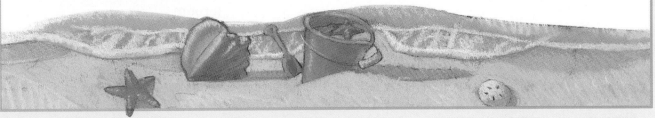

METRIC UNITS OF LENGTH

HAWAII

Joji and his family live on the island of Hawaii. They are planning to drive along the highway from Kalapana to Hilo. Joji determines the distance to be about 45 km. His father says it is closer to 80 km. Whose answer is more reasonable?

Talk About It

▶ How can you use the map to find how many kilometers it is from Kalapana to Hilo?

▶ Whose answer is more reasonable?

Some people visualize the width of a door frame to estimate a meter.

• What items can you use to visualize a millimeter, a centimeter, a meter, and a kilometer?

Examples

A.

B.

C.

about 1 mm thick   about 1 cm thick   about 1 m wide

• What metric unit would you use to measure the length of your classroom? Why?

• What metric unit would you use to measure the distance from your home to school?

Check for Understanding

Choose the appropriate unit. Write *cm, m,* or *km.*

1. distance from Earth to the moon

2. width of your desk

3. length of a room

Choose the more reasonable estimate. Write **a** or **b.**

4. length of a car
   a. 4 m   **b.** 40 m

5. length of your shoe
   a. 250 cm   **b.** 25 cm

6. length of a pin
   a. 2 mm   **b.** 20 mm

Practice

Choose the most reasonable estimate. Write **a** or **b**.

7. width of a mall hallway
   a. 8 m
   b. 8 km

8. length of a pencil
   a. 14 m
   b. 14 cm

9. a walk around a park
   a. 2.4 km
   b. 240 km

10. thickness of a paper clip
    a. 1 mm
    b. 10 mm

11. distance between two towns
    a. 10 mm
    b. 10 km

12. diameter of a baseball
    a. 10 mm
    b. 10 cm

Choose the appropriate unit. Write *mm, cm, m,* or *km.*

13. length of a house

14. length of a skirt

15. diameter of a penny

16. length of an ant

17. height of a flagpole

18. height of a mountain

Estimate the length.

19.

   ___?___ mm

20.

   ___?___ cm

21.

   ___?___ cm

Mixed Applications

22. Sue needs 3 m of paper to wrap a gift. If she has 195 cm, how much more paper does she need?

23. **Analyze Data**   Measure your classroom. Use a meter stick. Ask a classmate to measure the room. Did you get the same measurement? Why or why not?

CALCULATOR CONNECTION

You can use a calculator to change units.

How many centimeters are in 450 mm?   How many meters are in 0.9 km?

450 ÷ 10 = [45.] ← 45 cm   0.9 × 1000 = [900.] ← 900 m

Use a calculator to change units.

24. 7.9 m = ▇ mm

25. 288 m = ▇ km

26. 402 cm = ▇ m

What are the four most commonly used metric units of length?

WRAP UP...

PROBLEM SOLVING

STRATEGY • Use Estimation

Mr. Ray is figuring the cost to build a lattice screen for a client. He made a list of costs for materials, and he noted a labor charge of $12.00 an hour for 6 hours. Mr. Ray will add $15.00 to allow for errors. About how much will his estimate be?

Amount	Materials	Cost	Total Cost
2	lattice panels, $\frac{1}{4}$ in. × $1\frac{1}{2}$ in.	$42.10 each	$84.20
6	boards, 1 in. × 4 in.	2.30 each	13.80
4	boards, 1 in. × 6 in.	3.72 each	14.88
$\frac{1}{2}$	drywall screws, $1\frac{5}{8}$ in., 8 oz	2.08 a lb	1.04
3	concrete mix, 2-lb sack	1.96 a sack	5.88

If weather or changing prices must be considered when determining a total cost, an exact answer is impossible.

▶ **UNDERSTAND**

What are you asked to find?

What information are you given?

▶ **PLAN**

What strategy will you use?

Since you cannot determine an exact answer, you can estimate the cost of the screen.

▶ **SOLVE**

How will you carry out your plan?

Round the total costs to the nearest dollar, write a number sentence, and then use a calculator.

labor + panels + ⌐ boards ⌐ + screws + concrete + errors = estimate

12 × 6 + 84 + 14 + 15 + 1 + 6 + 15 = 207.

So, Mr. Ray's estimate will be about $207.

▶ **LOOK BACK**

How will the actual cost relate to the estimate? Why?

WHAT
IF...

. . . Mr. Ray built 2 lattice screens and allowed a total of $10 for errors? How much might his estimate be?

Apply

Use estimation to solve.

1 A mechanic tells John that the parts needed to repair his car cost $27.90 and that labor is $37.00 an hour. If it takes the mechanic about $1\frac{1}{2}$ hours, about how much will the repairs cost?

2 Sixth graders will paint sets for the school play, *Sandstorm*. If 1 quart of paint covers 50 square feet and 448 square feet must be painted, is 25 quarts a reasonable estimate of the amount of paint needed? If not, what is?

| Mixed Applications → | STRATEGIES | **Use Estimation • Guess and Check • Find a Pattern • Draw a Diagram** |

Choose a strategy and solve.

3 The distance from Edna's house to Cape Cod is 120 miles. If her car gets 27 miles to a gallon of gasoline, about how many gallons of gasoline will she need to make the round trip?

4 The Jones family always takes 10 towels with them when they go to the beach. If they take 2 more beach towels than bath towels, how many of each do they take?

5 On a scavenger hunt, Lydia found a scarf 3 blocks east of her home. Then, she ran north $1\frac{1}{2}$ blocks for a key ring. Next, she ran east $2\frac{1}{4}$ blocks for a glove, and north $\frac{3}{4}$ block for a left shoe. Finally, she ran $5\frac{1}{4}$ blocks west to the park. How far north of Lydia's home is the park?

6 Together, Ruta's banner and Bill's banner are as long as Gene's banner, which is 60 m long. The length of Bill's banner minus the length of Ruta's banner is equal to the length of Lu's banner. Gene's banner is twice as long as Lu's. How long is Ruta's banner? How long is Bill's banner?

7 A clerk at Cozy Snack Bar sold 92 burritos for $1.90 each and 124 fruit drinks for $1.10 each. The clerk must tell his boss about how much money he collected. What is a reasonable estimate?

8 A civic club is selling tickets to a beach concert. In four days the club has sold 110 tickets, 70 tickets, 40 tickets, and 20 tickets. If the pattern continues, how many tickets will be sold on the fifth day?

METRIC UNITS OF CAPACITY AND MASS

Janet plans to mix a little more than 3 L of orange juice, a little more than 4 L of pineapple juice, and 1,200 mL of papaya juice in an 8-L thermos jug to take to the beach. Will she have enough juice to fill the jug?

Change mL to L. 1,200 mL = 1.2 L

Estimate.

a little more than 3	3^+
a little more than 4	4^+
1.2 is a little more than 1.	$\underline{+1^+}$
	8^+ ← more than 8

Capacity

1 L

Janet will have more than enough juice to fill the jug.

- What metric unit would you choose for the capacity of a glass of water?

_____

1 mL

A sign says, "Win a free fish dinner! Guess the mass of 262 flounder in today's catch." Eric thinks that one flounder has about the same mass as his radio, 0.7 kg. He guesses 175 kg. Is Eric's guess reasonable?

Estimate.

Try an overestimate. $300 \times 1.0 = 300$.

Try an underestimate. Think: $0.7 \approx \frac{1}{2}$.
$$250 \times \frac{1}{2} = 125.$$

The flounder probably weigh between 125 and 300 kg.

So, Eric's guess is reasonable.

Mass

1 g

Talk About It

▶ Would Eric's best guess be closer to 125 kg or 300 kg? How do you know?

▶ How can you change 125 kg to grams?

▶ What metric unit would you choose for the mass of the sand in an egg timer?

▶ How can you change grams to kilograms?

1 kg

Check for Understanding

Choose the better estimate. Write **a** or **b**.

1. cup of tea
   a. 240 mL   **b.** 240 L

2. slice of bread
   a. 300 g   **b.** 30 g

3. gold nugget
   a. 25 g   **b.** 25 kg

Practice

Change to the given unit.

4. $2\,mL = \blacksquare\,L$

5. $0.35\,L = \blacksquare\,mL$

6. $1{,}205\,mL = \blacksquare\,L$

7. $10\,kg = \blacksquare\,g$

8. $0.2\,g = \blacksquare\,kg$

9. $210\,g = \blacksquare\,kg$

10. $24\,L = \blacksquare\,mL$

11. $5.5\,L = \blacksquare\,mL$

12. $10{,}000\,mL = \blacksquare\,L$

13. $44{,}000\,g = \blacksquare\,kg$

14. $1.5\,kg = \blacksquare\,g$

15. $620\,g = \blacksquare\,kg$

Mixed Applications

16. Vanna has coins whose total mass of gold is 33 g. If each coin has a mass of gold of about 5.5 g, how many coins does she have?

17. **Critical Thinking** Amy is without any tools. She must estimate the length and width of a room. How can she determine the dimensions?

SCIENCE CONNECTION

Water has a unique property. The number of units of its capacity is equal to the number of units of its mass. You can verify this. Find the mass of an empty container. Then find the mass of the container filled with water. Determine the mass of the water. To determine the capacity of the water, pour the water into a graduated beaker that measures milliliters. Repeat with containers of different sizes.

1 L = 1 kg

Tell the mass of the water.

18. 1 mL

19. 500 mL

20. 1,000 mL

Tell the capacity of a container filled with each mass of water.

21. 25 g

22. 500 g

23. 2,000 g

Is the capacity of a liter of oil the same as a liter of water? How do you know?

WRAP UP...

EXPLORING

Precision

Jason has to replace a wall on a model of a house. He measures the old wall to the nearest centimeter and records a width of 28 cm and a height of 20 cm. The wall is actually a little wider than 28 cm and a little shorter than 20 cm. How can Jason get more precise measurements?

Work Together

Building Understanding

Work in your group to measure the length of each item in centimeters. Record your results.

- a paper clip

- a pencil

Now measure the same items to the nearest millimeter. Record the results.

TALK ABOUT IT

- For each length that you measured, which measurement do you think is more precise? Explain.

- For each length that you measured, which unit of measure is smaller?

- Why is it sometimes important to have the most precise measurement you can get?

- How can Jason get more precise measurements for his wall?

- What relationship do you see between the size of the unit of measure and the precision of a measurement?

Check for Understanding

Use a centimeter ruler. Write the measurement to the nearest centimeter and to the nearest millimeter.

1. ____

2. _____

3. _____

4. _____

5. ____

6. _____

7. _____

8. _____

Practice

Tell which measurement is more precise.

9. 7 cm or 71 mm

10. 979 m or 1 km

11. 7 km or 7,120 m

12. 53 mm or 5 cm

13. 9 km or 8,903 m

14. 9.1 cm or 90 mm

15. 6.27 cm or 6.2 cm

16. 4 cm or 44 mm

17. 1 km or 1.3 km

18. 2 L or 1.7 L

19. 1 kg or 1.4 kg

20. 3.05 mm or 3.1 mm

Mixed Applications

21. Marty has 60 mL of water in his 1-L thermos. How much water must he add to fill the thermos?

22. Why is 1.8 L more precise than 2 L?

23. Lisa fills a container with 2 L of milk. How many 250-mL glasses can she pour?

24. Jed's 4 books have a mass of 1.5 kg, 2 kg, 2.5 kg, and 1.8 kg. What is their average mass?

25. **Number Sense • Mental Math** Tate wants to stack 4 books that are each 20 mm thick and a lunch box that is 70 mm thick in a beach bag that is 20 cm deep. Will everything fit in the beach bag?

26. **Making Choices** For his pet store, Theo wants to buy a fish tank that is small enough to fit on a stand 2 m long. Should he buy a tank that is 160 cm long or 205 cm long?

Name situations in which you are careful to make precise measurements.

More Practice, Lesson 9.5, page H67

281

CHOOSING TO ESTIMATE OR MEASURE

Choosing to estimate or to use a measuring tool is an everyday decision based on the situation. If you decide to use a tool, you must also decide which tool to use.

Talk About It

▶ For each situation, tell whether an estimate is acceptable or if you should use a tool to measure. If you would use a tool, tell which tool.

A. Ian is marking an area 9 m by 18 m so he and some friends can play a game of volleyball.

B. Amy works at a beach boutique that sells gold chains at $35.00 a decimeter.

C. Nicole wonders if the water is too cold for swimming at a Maine beach.

D. Robert checks the time so he will not miss a flight from Los Angeles to New York.

Sometimes you must compute after you have measured.

Hanna has shells that measure 1.5 cm, 3.2 cm, 4.6 cm, and 2.2 cm. If she mounts them edge-to-edge in a row on a large flat shell, how long will the row of small shells be?

1.5 + 3.2 + 4.6 + 2.2 = 11.5

So, the row will be 11.5 cm long.

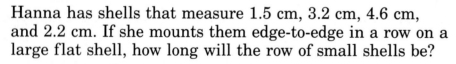

Check for Understanding

Tell whether to estimate or use a tool to measure. If you would use a tool, tell which tool.

1. amount of water to add to a swimming pool

2. time it takes to run a 100-meter dash

3. lengths of boards to make a railing

Practice

Give one example for each type of measurement.

4. mass that must be measured with a tool

5. length that can be estimated

6. capacity that must be measured with a tool

Estimate the sum.

7. $10.3\,g + 8.0\,g + 4.8\,g + 2.3\,g$

8. $7.2\,L + 12.3\,L + 0.32\,L + 0.92\,L$

Find the sum or difference.

9. $60\,m + 201.9\,m + 95.4\,m + 0.31\,m$

10. $0.8\,L + 42\,L + 16.1\,L + 45.9\,L$

11. $10.01\,g - 6.4\,g - 2.03\,g - 0.05\,g$

12. $244.06\,L - 99.2\,L - 2.95\,L - 0.88\,L$

Mixed Applications

13. Jane uses 25 mL of an expensive liquid soap per 1 L of water. Should she estimate or use a tool to measure?

14. Cindy had 305 g of blue sand, 790 g of green sand, and 120 g of white sand. She gave $\frac{1}{3}$ of the sand to Dwight. How much sand did she give Dwight?

15. In second grade, Elliot wore jeans with a 42-cm waist. He has grown taller, and his waist measurement has grown by 5.25 cm each year. If Elliot is in sixth grade, what waist size are his jeans?

MIXED REVIEW

Find the quotient.

1. $2\frac{1}{2} \div 1\frac{2}{3}$

2. $1\frac{2}{7} \div 2\frac{1}{4}$

3. $2\frac{1}{10} \div 1\frac{1}{5}$

4. $1\frac{1}{4} \div 2\frac{1}{2}$

Write as a fraction in simplest form or as a decimal.

5. 0.2

6. 0.8

7. $\frac{3}{5}$

8. $\frac{9}{25}$

9. 0.05

Change to the given unit.

10. $35\,L = \blacksquare\,mL$

11. $2.7\,g = \blacksquare\,kg$

12. $0.4\,cm = \blacksquare\,mm$

What influences your decision to estimate or to choose a tool to measure?

REVIEW AND MAINTENANCE

1. Peter rented $\frac{1}{3}$ of his beach chairs. He disposed of $\frac{1}{6}$ of the remaining chairs, which were damaged. If he disposed of 40 chairs, how many did he have before any were rented?

2. Rona mailed $\frac{1}{3}$ of 8,400 letters, and a co-worker mailed $\frac{1}{4}$ of the remainder. There are 4,200 left. How many letters did Rona mail?

3. A carpenter is estimating the cost of building a ramp. The materials cost $52.29. Labor will be $13.50 an hour for about 7 hr. About how much will she charge?

The word "about" tells me to find an estimate.

Write the multiplication problem.

4. $\frac{1}{6} \div \frac{2}{5}$

5. $1\frac{1}{3} \div \frac{4}{9}$

6. $\frac{1}{2} \div 2$

7. $3\frac{1}{6} \div \frac{11}{12}$

Find the quotient.

8. $6 \div \frac{2}{3}$

9. $\frac{1}{4} \div \frac{3}{5}$

10. $\frac{2}{7} \div \frac{1}{10}$

11. $6\frac{1}{8} \div 8\frac{10}{11}$

Write as a fraction in simplest form or as a decimal.

12. $\frac{2}{5}$

13. $\frac{7}{10}$

14. 0.62

15. $\frac{7}{8}$

16. 0.25

17. 0.8

Choose the better estimate. Write **a** or **b**.

18. length of a magazine
    a. 30 cm **b.** 300 cm

19. capacity of a glass of milk
    a. 200 mL **b.** 20 L

20. mass of a can of beans
    a. 30 kg **b.** 0.3 kg

Change to the given unit.

21. $16 \text{ cm} = \blacksquare \text{ m}$

22. $1.5 \text{ g} = \blacksquare \text{ mg}$

23. $6 \text{ L} = \blacksquare \text{ kL}$

24. $90 \text{ mm} = \blacksquare \text{ cm}$

25. $1.2 \text{ kg} = \blacksquare \text{ dg}$

26. $81 \text{ cL} = \blacksquare \text{ mL}$

Tell whether to estimate or to use a tool to measure. If you would use a tool, tell which tool.

27. a picture frame

28. legs for a table

29. milk for cereal

Tell which measurement is more precise.

30. 0.04 g or 50 mg

31. 6 cm or 62 mm

32. 8 kL or 7,920 L

Using Measurement

Jamaica is an island country known for its beautiful beaches. Many Jamaicans work in agriculture, growing and selling bananas, pineapples, and other tropical fruits. Some Jamaicans work as artists, creating arts and crafts that are very popular with both native Jamaicans and tourists.

NORTH
AMERICA

Jamaica

Solve.

1. Batik is a form of art that uses wax and dye to create patterns on fabric. Dawn is using a piece of fabric 2 m long for a batik design. Her design is 18 cm long. How many times can she put her design on this fabric?

2. Bouvier bought 750 g of bananas from a sidewalk vendor. The price was $1.00 per kilogram. How much did he pay for the bananas?

3. Dennis wants to buy 3 kg of sugar. Each kilogram of sugar costs $0.85. How much does Dennis pay for 3 kg of sugar?

4. Suppose it takes a batik vendor 3 hours to make a design on a shirt. How many shirts can she complete in 8 hours?

5. David buys 2 tropical fruit baskets. Each fruit basket costs $12.50. He also buys 2 coconuts that cost $0.75 each. How much does David pay for 2 fruit baskets and 2 coconuts?

6. Leila has a container with 2 L of coconut milk. How many 250-mL glasses of coconut milk can she fill?

MULTICULTURAL NOTE: Jamaican arts and crafts are sold in commercial galleries and by sidewalk vendors.

CUSTOMARY UNITS OF LENGTH

Joe's father is a tuna fisherman in American Samoa. To determine the amount of fishnet on a bolt, Joe uses the length of a $2\frac{1}{4}$-yd-long table. The fishnet covers the length of the table $8\frac{1}{2}$ times. About how much fishnet is on the bolt?

Estimate when an exact answer is not needed.

$$2\frac{1}{4} \times 8\frac{1}{2} \longrightarrow 2 \times 9 = 18$$

So, about 18 yd of fishnet is on the bolt.

You can use this table to help you change from one customary unit of length to another.

Customary Units of Length	
1 foot (ft)	= 12 inches (in.)
1 yard (yd)	= 3 ft, or 36 in.
1 mile (mi)	= 1,760 yd, or 5,280 ft

Elena wants to carpet her family room, which is 26 ft long. How many yards long should the carpet be?

- When you change from feet to yards, will there be more units or fewer units?

- To the nearest yard, how long should the carpet be?

MULTICULTURAL NOTE: Samoan fishermen use nets to catch fish. The largest industry in American Samoa is tuna canning.

You can write a remainder as the smaller unit or as a fraction of the larger unit.

Examples

A. 8 ft = ▦ in.
   8 × 12 = 96
   8 ft = 96 in.

B. 45 in. = ▦ ft ▦ in.
   45 ÷ 12 = 3 r9
   45 in. = 3 ft 9 in.

C. 19 ft = ▦ yd
   $19 \div 3 = 6\frac{1}{3}$
   $19 \text{ ft} = 6\frac{1}{3} \text{ yd}$

- In Example B, 45 in. = ▦ ft.

- In Example C, 19 ft = 6 yd. ▦ ft.

Check for Understanding

Tell by how much you must multiply or divide to change the units.

1. feet to inches

2. yards to miles

3. inches to yards

4. miles to feet

5. feet to miles

6. yards to inches

Practice

Estimate the product or the quotient.

7. $49\frac{1}{2}$ ft $\times$ $12\frac{1}{4}$

8. $3{,}921$ ft $\div$ 2

9. 712 yd $\times$ $2\frac{1}{2}$

10. $74{,}256$ in. $\div$ 36

11. $4{,}823 \times 31$ mi

12. $26{,}487$ ft $\div$ $5{,}280$

Tell by what number to multiply or divide. Then change the units.

13. 24 feet to inches

14. 3,520 yards to miles

15. 144 inches to yards

16. 31,680 feet to miles

17. 12 yards to feet

18. 3 miles to feet

19. 5 yards to inches

20. 144 inches to feet

21. 54 feet to yards

Change to the given units.

22. 371 ft $=$ ▨ yd ▨ ft

23. 408 in. $=$ ▨ yd ▨ ft

24. $6{,}000$ ft $=$ ▨ mi ▨ yd

25. 215 ft $=$ ▨ yd ▨ ft

26. 2 mi $=$ ▨ yd

27. 124 in. $=$ ▨ ft ▨ in.

Change to the given unit. Write the remainder in fraction form.

28. 80 in. $=$ ▨ ft

29. 204 in. $=$ ▨ yd

30. $6\frac{1}{2}$ ft $=$ ▨ yd

31. 18 in. $=$ ▨ yd

32. $2{,}640$ ft $=$ ▨ mi

33. 97 in. $=$ ▨ ft

Mixed Applications

34. Bruce can walk 240 in. along a straight line from his patio to a gazebo, and then to the shore, which is 60 ft from the gazebo. How many feet is it from the patio to the shore?

35. Melba's shoe is 9 in. long. She wants to measure the room but has no ruler. The room is 11 shoe lengths long. About how many feet long is the room?

36. Organize Data The distance from the lighthouse to the shore is 880 yd; from the cabin to the Seaweed Cafe, 1,800 ft; and from the cabin to Stu's Surf Shop, $\frac{1}{3}$ mi. Make a table that shows the distances listed in order from shortest to longest.

37. Make Up a Problem Dolores likes to play volleyball. Her team won game 1, game 5, and game 9. They are playing game 12 today.

Without stopping, can you run 50 ft? 50 mi?

WRAP
UP...

CUSTOMARY UNITS OF CAPACITY AND WEIGHT

You can use your measurement sense to determine whether an estimate is reasonable. Which is the more reasonable estimate? Why?

1 fl oz or 1 gal?

Since 1 fl oz is about 2 tablespoons, 1 gal is the more reasonable estimate.

200 lb or 1 T?

Since 1 T is more than a person can lift, 200 lb is the more reasonable estimate.

You can use these tables to help you change from one customary unit of capacity or weight to another.

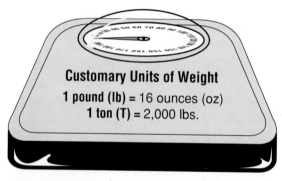

Customary Units of Weight
1 pound (lb) = 16 ounces (oz)
1 ton (T) = 2,000 lbs.

Customary Units of Capacity
1 cup (c) = 8 fluid ounces (fl oz)
1 pint (pt) = 2 c, or 16 fl oz
1 quart (qt) = 2 pt, or 4 c
1 gallon (gal) = 4 qt, or 8 pt

Talk About It

▶ When you change from tons to pounds, will there be more or fewer units?

▶ By how much must you multiply or divide to change pounds to ounces?

▶ When you change from pints to quarts, will there be more or fewer units?

Examples

A. 7 qt = ■ gal

$7 \div 4 = 1\frac{3}{4}$

7 qt = $1\frac{3}{4}$ gal

B. 27 c = ■ qt ■ c

$27 \div 4 = 6$ r3

27 c = 6 qt 3 c

C. $\frac{3}{4}$ gal = ■ pt

$\frac{3}{4} \times 8 = 6$

$\frac{3}{4}$ gal = 6 pt

Check for Understanding

Tell whether to multiply or divide to change units.

1. pounds to ounces
2. gallons to pints
3. pints to quarts

Choose the better estimate. Write **a** or **b**.

4. loaf of bread
   a. 1 oz   **b.** 1 lb
5. bowl of soup
   a. 1 c   **b.** 1 gal
6. box of detergent
   a. 5 lb   **b.** 5 T

Practice

Change to the given unit.

7. $10 \text{ c} = \blacksquare \text{ fl oz}$
8. $9 \text{ qt} = \blacksquare \text{ pt}$
9. $4{,}500 \text{ lb} = \blacksquare \text{ T}$
10. $96 \text{ fl oz} = \blacksquare \text{ pt}$

11. $10 \text{ lb } 2 \text{ oz} = \blacksquare \text{ oz}$
12. $3\frac{1}{2} \text{ pt} = \blacksquare \text{ c}$
13. $\frac{3}{5} \text{ T} = \blacksquare \text{ lb}$
14. $5\frac{1}{2} \text{ gal} = \blacksquare \text{ qt}$

15. $2\frac{3}{4} \text{ lb} = \blacksquare \text{ oz}$
16. $25 \text{ pt} = \blacksquare \text{ qt}$
17. $15 \text{ qt} = \blacksquare \text{ gal}$
18. $8 \text{ oz} = \blacksquare \text{ lb}$

Mixed Applications

19. Gerald had 20 guests, who each drank 4 cups of orange punch. Gerald's punch bowl holds $2\frac{1}{2}$ gal. Did Gerald need to refill the punch bowl?

20. **Write a Question** Don wants to go to a movie and to a party. The movie starts at 7:30 P.M. and lasts 105 minutes. The party starts at 8:00 P.M. and lasts 120 minutes.

SCIENCE CONNECTION

Mass is the amount of matter in an object. Mass does not change.

Weight, however, is determined by gravity. The less gravity, the less the object weighs.

A person whose mass is 45.5 kg weighs 100 lb on the earth, 16 lb on the moon, 38 lb on Mars, 89 lb on Venus, and $264\frac{1}{2}$ lb on Jupiter.

Tell how much a 4.55-kg object would weigh on each.

21. the moon
22. Jupiter
23. Mars

Is it easier to change customary units or metric units? Why?

W R A P
U P . . .

USING CUSTOMARY UNITS

Jay built a sand castle 4 ft 10 in. long. Cathy built one next to Jay's that was 3 times as long.

What is the length of Cathy's sand castle?	What is the total length of the two sand castles?
Multiply to find the answer.	Add to find the answer.

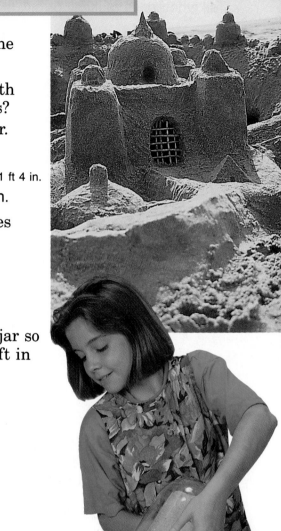

4 ft 10 in.		4 ft 10 in.	
× 3	30 in. = 2 ft 6 in.	+14 ft 6 in.	16 in. = 1 ft 4 in.
12 ft 30 in. = 14 ft 6 in.		18 ft 16 in. = 19 ft 4 in.	

So, Cathy's sand castle is 14 ft 6 in. long.	So, the two sand castles are 19 ft 4 in. long.

Sometimes, you must rename when you subtract.

Robin wants to remove 4 lb 12 oz of sand from a 5-lb jar so she can tint the sand blue. How much sand will be left in the jar?

$$\begin{array}{r} \overset{4\ lb\quad 16\ oz}{\cancel{5}\ lb} \\ -\ 4\ lb\ 12\ oz \\ \hline 0\ lb\ 4\ oz \end{array}$$ ← Rename 1 lb as 16 oz.

So, 4 oz of sand will be left in the jar.

Another Example

$$\begin{array}{r} \overset{5\quad 5}{\cancel{6}\ gal\ \cancel{1}\ qt} \\ -\ 2\ gal\ 3\ qt \\ \hline 3\ gal\ 2\ qt \end{array}$$ Rename 1 gal as 4 qt.
1 qt + 4 qt = 5 qt

Check for Understanding

Find the sum.

1. 3 lb 12 oz + 2 lb 9 oz   **2.** 1 gal 3 qt + 3 gal 2 qt   **3.** 4 ft 11 in. + 5 ft 10 in.

Tell how to rename before subtracting. Then find the difference.

4.	**5.**	**6.**	**7.**
2 c 4 fl oz	3 ft 1 in.	10 lb 2 oz	9 gal 1 qt
−1 c 9 fl oz	−1 ft 2 in.	− 7 lb 9 oz	−5 gal 2 qt

Practice

Rename using the unit given.

8. 1 qt 1 pt = ▨ pt

9. 4 lb 6 oz = 3 lb ▨ oz

10. 5 c 3 fl oz = 4 c ▨ fl oz

11. 2 T 400 lb = 1 T ▨ lb

Find the sum or difference.

12.
   10 ft 6 in.
+ 1 ft 3 in.

13.
   3 ft 2 in.
+ 1 ft 9 in.

14.
   5 ft 4 in.
+ 2 ft 8 in.

15.
   1 yd 2 ft
+ 7 yd 1 ft

16.
   4 yd 2 ft
+ 5 yd 2 ft

17.
   3 ft 9 in.
+ 7 ft 5 in.

18.
   9 ft 2 in.
− 4 ft 1 in.

19.
   8 ft 1 in.
− 6 ft 2 in.

20.
   2 yd
− 1 yd 1 ft

21.
   6 ft 9 in.
− 4 ft 10 in.

22.
   7 ft 8 in.
− 5 ft 11 in.

23.
   8 yd 1 ft
− 6 yd 2 ft

Mixed Applications

24. Consuela is 5 ft 4 in. tall. Her brother is 6 ft 2 in. tall. How much taller is her brother?

25. A young oak tree is 180 in. tall. How many feet tall is the oak tree?

26. Hugh can run 8 mi in 2 hours. How many feet can he run in 1 hour?

27. Arlene bought 16 yd of fabric. She used 33 ft. How many yards did she have left?

28. **Organize Data** Organize the data so the lengths of the lakes are in order from the longest to the shortest.

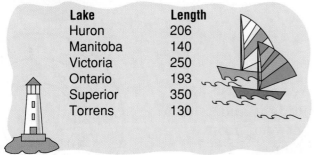

Lake	Length
Huron	206
Manitoba	140
Victoria	250
Ontario	193
Superior	350
Torrens	130

29. **Analyze Data** Use the table. What is the range in population of the six cities? What is the median of the populations?

City	Population
Los Angeles	3,485,398
Atlanta	394,017
Miami	358,548
San Diego	1,110,549
Las Vegas	258,295
Phoenix	983,403

How is renaming customary units of measure different from renaming metric units?

WRAP UP...

COMPUTING WITH INTERVALS OF TIME

Peter's flight to Palm Beach departs at 10:50 A.M. He must be at the airport 30 minutes (min) before departure time, and the trip to the airport takes 45 min. At what time should Peter leave for the airport?

Step 1 Add to find the total time before departure.	**Step 2** Subtract the total from the departure time.
30 min +45 min ‾‾‾‾‾‾‾‾‾ 75 min = 1 hour (hr) 15 min	10:50 − 1:15 ← 1 hr 15 min ‾‾‾‾‾‾‾‾‾ 9:35

So, Peter should leave for the airport at 9:35 A.M.

A.M. hours are those between midnight and noon, and P.M. hours are those between noon and midnight.

The flight takes 1 hr 45 min. If it takes Peter 30 min to get his luggage and 20 min to ride to the hotel, at what time will he arrive at the hotel? Will it be A.M or P.M.?

Step 1 Add to find the total time after departure.	**Step 2** Add the total to the departure time.

1 hr 45 min
    30 min
+   20 min
‾‾‾‾‾‾‾‾‾
1 hr 95 min = 2 hr 35 min
	10:50
	+ 2:35 ← 2 hr 35 min
	‾‾‾‾‾‾‾‾‾
	12:85 = 1:25 ← 12:85 is 85 minutes after
	                        12:00 noon, or 1:25 P.M.

So, Peter will arrive at the hotel at 1:25 P.M.

On a 24-hour clock, such as the kind used for computers, 24:00 to 12:00 hours are the times between midnight and noon, and 12:00 to 24:00 hours are the times between noon and midnight. The clock shows 03:00 or 15:00 hours.

- What would be Peter's arrival time at the hotel on a 24-hour clock?

Connection, pages 486–487

Check for Understanding

Write the time of day, using A.M. or P.M.

1. 8:30 A.M. + 55 min
2. 11:45 P.M. + 1 hr 5 min
3. 12:30 P.M. − 2 hr 25 min
4. 15:20
5. 06:15
6. 20:06

Practice

Change to the given unit. Use a 24-hour clock for Exercises 13–15.

7. 120 min = ▓ sec
8. 1 hr = ▓ sec
9. 144 hr = ▓ days

10. 540 min = ▓ hr
11. 7 days = ▓ hr
12. 24 hr = ▓ min

13. 9:30 A.M. = ▓ : ▓ hr
14. 10:05 P.M. = ▓ : ▓ hr
15. 1:15 P.M. = ▓ : ▓ hr

Find the sum or difference.

16. 4 hr 40 min
    +1 hr 50 min

17. 3 min 50 sec
    +   30 sec

18. 5 min 35 sec
    −4 min 42 sec

Mixed Applications

19. The bell rings for school at 8:30 A.M. Al must be there 15 min before the bell. If the trip to school takes 35 min, when should Al leave for school?

20. **Number Sense • Mental Math** What is the difference between the number of hours in 7 days and the number of hours in 5 days?

MIXED REVIEW

Choose the more reasonable estimate. Write **a** or **b**.

1. $3\frac{5}{8} + 5\frac{11}{12}$
   a. 10   b. 8

2. $4\frac{3}{4} \times 7\frac{1}{9}$
   a. 24   b. 35

3. $5\frac{2}{3} \div 1\frac{7}{8}$
   a. 5   b. 3

Tell which measurement is more precise.

4. 5 kL or 4,920 L
5. 750 cm or 8 m
6. 100 g or 99,000 mg

Change to the given unit.

7. 108 in. = ▓ yd
8. 32 oz = ▓ lb
9. 8 c = ▓ pt

How can you find the number of hours you spend traveling to school each year?

WRAP UP...

PROBLEM SOLVING

STRATEGY • Use a Schedule

Becky wants to fly from Tampa to Fort Lauderdale. Of the flights listed, which one is the fastest?

Airline Schedule Tampa to Fort Lauderdale		
Flight Number	Departure Time	Arrival Time
435 (nonstop)	9:50 A.M.	11:20 A.M.
563 (nonstop)	12:30 P.M.	1:40 P.M.
768 (1 stop)	1:00 P.M.	2:55 P.M.

▶ **UNDERSTAND**

What are you asked to find?

What information are you given?

▶ **PLAN**

What strategy will you use?

You can use the airline schedule. Subtract each departure time from each arrival time, and compare to determine the fastest flight.

▶ **SOLVE**

How will you carry out your plan?

Since nonstop flights are faster than the flights that stop, you can eliminate Flight 768 from consideration. Subtract the departure times from the arrival times for the other two flights.

Flight 435:

    11:20 → 10:80
  − 9:50 → 9:50
    ───────────────
              1:30
           1 hr 30 min

Flight 563:

     1:40 → 13:40 ← 1:40 is 1 hr 40 min
  − 12:30 → − 12:30   after 12 noon.
   ───────────────   12:00 + 1:40 = 13:40
              1:10
           1 hr 10 min

So, Flight 563 is the fastest flight.

▶ **LOOK BACK**

How can you check your answer?

 WHAT IF... ...you need to know the time difference between the fastest and the slowest flights? What is the difference?

Apply

Use the schedule on page 294 to solve Exercises 1–2.

(1) Chad must fly to Fort Lauderdale on business. It takes $\frac{1}{2}$ hr to reach his office from the airport, and his business will take 2 hr. If he will return to Tampa on a 5:30 P.M. flight, should he take Flight 563 or 768?

(2) It takes 45 minutes to drive from Fort Lauderdale's airport to Fran's favorite restaurant. If it takes Fran 15 minutes to get her luggage, can she meet a friend for lunch at 12:30 P.M. at the restaurant?

Mixed Applications ⟹ **STRATEGIES**

Use a Schedule • Work Backward • Use Estimation • Act It Out

Choose a strategy and solve.

(3) Randy will pick up his brother at a bus station at 2:00 P.M. The bus spends 1 hr 40 min on the road and makes two stops, one for 15 min and one for 20 min. Bus 1 departs at 11:35 A.M., Bus 2 at 12:00 noon, and Bus 3 at 12:20 P.M. Which bus should Randy's brother take?

(4) Jill must take her pets—an alligator, a bird, and a cat—to a pet show. She can carry only one pet at a time on her bike. She cannot leave the alligator with the cat or the cat with the bird. How can Jill get all the pets to the pet show?

(5) Kevin sold 12 beach umbrellas on Monday. He put 4 green umbrellas in the storeroom. Then he divided the remaining umbrellas into 2 equal piles of 24 each. How many umbrellas did Kevin have before he opened the store on Monday?

(6) If an elevator holds more than 1,000 lb, an alarm goes off. Seven adults whose average weight is 132 lb and five children whose average weight is 93 lb enter the elevator. Does the alarm go off?

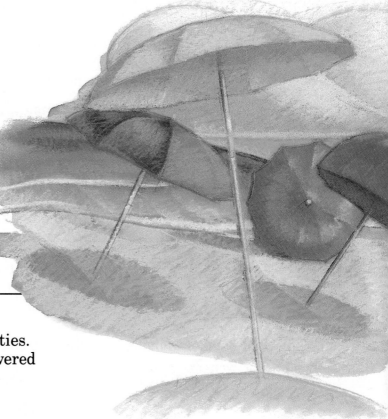

WRITER'S CORNER

(7) Make a schedule of your daily activities. Make up a problem that can be answered by using the schedule.

Vocabulary Check

Choose a word or words from the box to complete each sentence.

| capacity |
| customary |
| gram |
| inches |
| liter |
| meter |
| metric |
| ounces |
| precision |
| weight |

1. The relationships among place-value positions are the same as the relationships among ___?___ units. *(page 270)*

2. The base unit of length in the metric measurement system is the ___?___. *(page 270)*

3. The base unit of capacity in the metric measurement system is the ___?___. *(page 270)*

4. The base unit of mass in the metric measurement system is the ___?___. *(page 270)*

5. The degree of accuracy needed for a particular measurement is called ___?___. *(page 280)*

6. In the ___?___ measurement system, ___?___ and feet are units of length, pints and quarts are units of ___?___, and ___?___ and pounds are units of ___?___. *(pages 286, 288)*

Remember that metric is different from customary measurement, so read the exercises carefully.

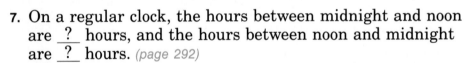

Concept Check

7. On a regular clock, the hours between midnight and noon are ___?___ hours, and the hours between noon and midnight are ___?___ hours. *(page 292)*

8. When you change from centimeters to meters, will there be more or fewer units? *(page 271)*

9. When you change to fewer units, should you multiply or divide? *(page 271)*

10. Within one day's time, would you be able to walk 100 m? 100 km? Explain. *(page 270)*

11. What metric unit would you use to measure the length of a new pencil? What customary unit would you use? *(pages 274, 286)*

Tell by what number to multiply or divide to change the units. *(pages 271, 286, 288)*

12. cm to mm   **13.** mL to L   **14.** in. to ft   **15.** oz to lb   **16.** qt to pt

Skill Check

Tell which unit is greater. *(page 270)*

17. meters or centimeters

18. grams or kilograms

19. millimeters or liters

Choose the better estimate. Write a or b. *(pages 274, 288)*

20. baseball bat
   a. 1 m   **b.** 5 m

21. baseball
   a. 5 oz   **b.** 30 oz

22. cup of milk
   a. $\frac{1}{2}$ pt   **b.** 1 gal

Tell whether to estimate or to use a tool to measure. If you would use a tool, tell which tool. *(page 282)*

23. distance from house to mall

24. amount of expensive perfume

Tell which measurement is more precise. *(page 280)*

25. 12 cm or 120 mm

26. 4 kg or 3,900 g

27. 180 mL or 0.18 L

Change to the given unit. *(pages 271, 274, 278, 286, 288, 292)*

28. 2 L = ■ mL

29. 620 mm = ■ cm

30. 53 g = ■ dg

31. 15 m = ■ km

32. 0.26 kL = ■ dL

33. 10 mg = ■ g

34. 45 in. = ■ ft.

35. 120 ft = ■ yd

36. 288 fl oz = ■ qt

37. 7 lb = ■ oz

38. 10 gal = ■ pt

39. 960 min = ■ hr

Find the sum or difference. *(pages 290, 292)*

40.   2 gal 3 qt
       +1 gal 3 qt

41.   5 ft 9 in.
       −2 ft 11 in.

42.   6 lb 8 oz
       +1 lb 8 oz

43.   9 hr 10 min
       −   50 min

Problem-Solving Check *(pages 276, 294)*

44. Kareem delivered 6 T of sand to a construction site. If workers used 3 T 400 lb on Monday and $\frac{1}{2}$ T on Tuesday, about how much sand was left at the site?

45. A regular flight leaves New York at 4:35 P.M., stops in Atlanta for 45 min, and arrives in Miami at 8:15 P.M. How long does it take to travel on this flight?

46. Mia has 52 yd of canvas to cover beach chairs. If it takes $3\frac{1}{4}$ yd of canvas to cover 1 chair, will Mia have enough canvas to cover the 20 chairs on the hotel veranda?

47. Suppose commuter flights arrive in Jackson from Macon every $3\frac{1}{2}$ hr beginning at 7:00 A.M. If the flight takes 45 min, when will the fourth flight leave Macon?

1. Name the metric units to use for measuring the length of a pencil, the capacity of a drinking glass, and the mass of a pony. Explain each of your choices.

2. Two people measure the length of a pencil. One records 15 cm and the other, 148 mm. Explain how you know which measurement is more precise.

3. Show each step as you find the difference 4 ft 3 in. − 1 ft 6 in.

4. Explain how to change 100 lb to ounces. Then identify the number of ounces.

5. Read Exercise 2 on page 295. Follow the steps on the Problem-Solving Think Along worksheet to show how to solve this problem.

Some measurement tools show both metric and customary measures.

Write About It

6. Which system of measurement, metric or customary, do you feel more comfortable using? Explain.

7. Explain how changing units in the metric system of measurement is different from changing units in the customary system.

TEAMWORK Project

*P*hysical Education Connection

*P*hysical fitness is important for a well-rounded and healthful life-style. There are many ways to exercise and keep physically fit. Work with a team to plan a fitness course around a jogging track in your community.

Decide

Discuss the types of exercises that can be done at different stations of a fitness course. Make a list of the exercises.

Decide how many exercise stations will be on your fitness course.

Decide on the exercises and their order.

Do

As a team, draw a map of the fitness course. Divide the exercise stations among yourselves.

Include a description and a diagram of each exercise.

Use metric units to mark the distances between stations.

Share

Show your map to another team. Tell why you chose each exercise. Let the other team show you their map.

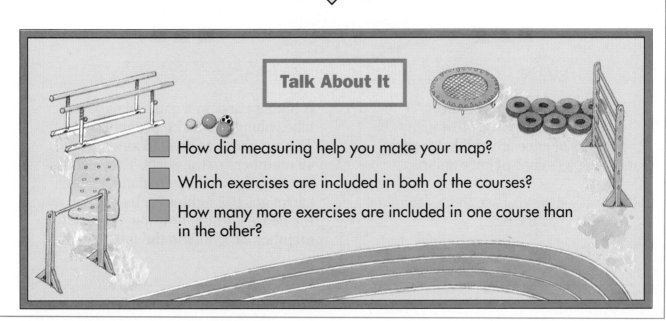

Talk About It

How did measuring help you make your map?

Which exercises are included in both of the courses?

How many more exercises are included in one course than in the other?

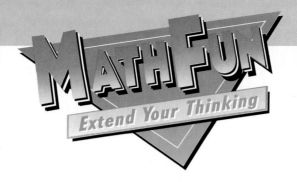

Estimating Distances

Did you ever wonder just how far you walked when you strolled along a beach or hiked through the woods?

Estimate the distance from the front of your classroom to the back by counting the number of steps you take to walk this distance.

▶ How many paces is this?

▶ Assume each pace is 5 ft. Calculate the length of your classroom in feet.

Using a yardstick or tape measure, determine the exact length of the room.

▶ How does your estimate compare with the actual measurement?

The ancient Romans invented the unit called the mile. The mile was equivalent to 1,000 paces. Each pace was equal to 2 steps, or 5 ft. The Roman mile was 5,000 ft long. It was not until the sixteenth century that the mile's length was fixed at 5,280 ft.

1 pace

Challenge

■ ■ ■
Number Sense

A pitcher holds 1.5 L of juice. A cup holds 250 mL of juice. How many pitchers of juice are needed to give 12 people 2 cups of juice apiece?

■ ■ ■
Critical Thinking

A hiking party in a national park takes along 299.25 kg of supplies. The supplies are divided among the 19 members of the party. They use the supplies as they go along, so their packs get 10% lighter each day. To the nearest gram, how much is each member carrying on the fourth day?

Write the letter of the correct answer.

1. Evaluate $5.12 - b$, for $b = 2.3$.

   A. 2.3   **B.** 2.82

   C. 2.92   **D.** 3.09

2. $20 \div 4 + 3 \times 5$

   A. 15.2   **B.** 20

   C. 25.5   **D.** 30.5

3. Find the number of combinations. 7 colors, 5 fabrics

   A. 5   **B.** 7

   C. 35   **D.** 53

4. Which fraction is equal to 0.4?

   A. $\dfrac{1}{5}$ **B.** $\dfrac{2}{10}$

   C. $\dfrac{1}{4}$ **D.** $\dfrac{2}{5}$

5. $3\dfrac{1}{2} + 2\dfrac{2}{5}$

   A. $5\dfrac{3}{10}$ **B.** $5\dfrac{3}{7}$

   C. $5\dfrac{9}{10}$ **D.** not here

6. $9\dfrac{1}{4} - 5\dfrac{1}{3}$

   A. $3\dfrac{2}{3}$ **B.** $3\dfrac{3}{4}$

   C. $3\dfrac{11}{12}$ **D.** $4\dfrac{1}{12}$

7. $\dfrac{1}{5} \times 3\dfrac{1}{4}$

   A. $\dfrac{19}{20}$ **B.** $3\dfrac{1}{20}$

   C. $4\dfrac{1}{20}$ **D.** not here

8. $\dfrac{1}{6} \div \dfrac{11}{12}$

   A. $\dfrac{2}{11}$ **B.** $\dfrac{3}{11}$

   C. $\dfrac{11}{3}$ **D.** $\dfrac{11}{2}$

9. Change to the given unit.
33 mL = ▓ L

   A. 0.033   **B.** 0.33

   C. 3,300   **D.** 33,000

10. Change to the given unit.
9 pt = ▓ qt

   A. $2\dfrac{1}{4}$ **B.** $4\dfrac{1}{2}$

   C. 18   **D.** 36

11. About how much will a custom-made suit cost if fabric is $85, labor is $9 an hour, and 12 hr of labor are needed?

   A. $100   **B.** $185

   C. $285   **D.** $300

12. Maggie's house is 12 min from the station. She is 7 min early for an 11:20 A.M. train. What time did she leave her house?

   A. 10:59 A.M.   **B.** 11:01 A.M.

   C. 11:13 A.M.   **D.** 11:39 A.M.

RATIO, PROPORTION, AND PERCENT

Did you know...

. . . that the relationship between the length and width of the screen is just the same for a large television as for a small television?

TALK ABOUT IT

How could you find the number of small television screens that would equal the size of one of the large television screens?

RATIOS

In a scene from *Play Basketball,* a camera zooms in on 3 players in white uniforms and 2 players in blue uniforms. What is the ratio of white uniforms to blue uniforms?

A **ratio** is a comparison of two numbers. You can write a ratio to compare one amount to another amount, a part to the whole, or the whole to a part.

There are three ways to write a ratio.

Write: 3 to 2, 3:2, or $\frac{3}{2}$
Read: three to two

So, the ratio of white to blue uniforms is $\frac{3}{2}$.

Another Example

What is the ratio of the number of players wearing blue to the total number of players in the scene?

$$\frac{\text{first term} \longrightarrow \quad 2 \longleftarrow \text{ number of players wearing blue}}{\text{second term} \longrightarrow \quad 5 \longleftarrow \text{ total number of players}}$$

So, the ratio of the number of players wearing blue to the total number of players is 2:5.

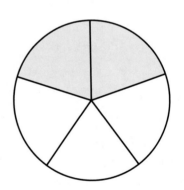

• How would you write the ratio of the number of players jumping to the total number of players?

• What does the ratio $\frac{5}{2}$ compare?

Check for Understanding

Name the items being compared. Then write the ratio by comparing the first amount to the second amount. Use the form ■ : ■.

1. Of the 120 mi Ed drives a week, he drives 80 mi to and from work.

2. A store carries socks that come 3 pairs to a package.

3. The map's scale shows that 2 in. represents 5 mi.

4. Heidi's bicycle travels 42 ft for every 3 pedal revolutions.

5. Of Andrea's 120-card collection of postcards, 45 show pictures of flowers.

6. In Aaron's aquarium, 1 of every 3 fish is a guppy.

Practice

Draw a picture to show the ratio.

7. The ratio of blue boxes to red boxes is 4:6.

8. The ratio of yellow shoes to green shoes is $\frac{7}{2}$.

9. The ratio of stars to crescents is two to five.

10. The ratio of math books to total books is 1:6.

Write the ratio in two other ways.

11. 10:7   **12.** 4:9   **13.** 8:3   **14.** 5:6   **15.** 12:2

16. $\frac{10}{1}$ **17.** $\frac{5}{8}$ **18.** $\frac{9}{5}$ **19.** $\frac{3}{13}$ **20.** $\frac{10}{15}$

21. nine to three   **22.** twelve to fifteen   **23.** twenty-two to fifty

Mixed Applications

24. Lucy buys 4 rolls of color film and 7 rolls of black-and-white film. What is the ratio of color film to the total amount of film?

25. Making Decisions Suppose apples are your favorite fruit. Would you rather buy a sack where the ratio of apples to oranges is $\frac{1}{2}$ or $\frac{3}{1}$?

MATH CONNECTION

When you solve a probability problem, you are using a ratio. Look at the table. If Mandy is a sixth grader, what is the probability she prefers partially animated movies?

$$P \text{ (partial animation)} = \frac{40}{90}$$

So, the probability is $\frac{40}{90}$, or 40:90.

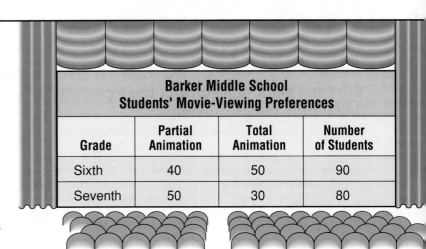

Barker Middle School Students' Movie-Viewing Preferences			
Grade	Partial Animation	Total Animation	Number of Students
Sixth	40	50	90
Seventh	50	30	80

Use the table. Find the probability of the event.

26. sixth graders who prefer total animation

27. seventh graders who do not prefer total animation

28. sixth and seventh graders who prefer partial animation

Use your own words to explain the meaning of *ratio.*

WRAP UP...

RATES

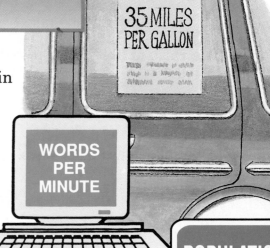

There are 135 students enrolled in 5 photography classes. If the same number of students is enrolled in each class, how many students are in each class?

A **rate** is a ratio that compares one quantity to a different quantity. If the second term of a rate is 1, the rate is called a **unit rate.**

- What are the two different quantities that you must compare to answer this question?

$$\begin{array}{c} \text{students} \rightarrow \\ \text{classes} \rightarrow \end{array} \quad \dfrac{135}{5} \quad \leftarrow \text{rate}$$

- How can you change the rate so that the second term is 1?

$$\frac{135}{5} = \frac{135 \div 5}{5 \div 5} = \frac{27}{1} \quad \leftarrow \text{unit rate}$$

So, there are 27 students per class.

Best Photo Shop sells 12 rolls of film for $28.68. Ace Photo Shop sells 15 rolls of the same film for $32.85. What is the unit price of film in each shop?

You can find a unit price in the same way you find a unit rate, by dividing.

Step 1	**Step 2**
Write ratios that compare the number of rolls of film to the price.	Divide the price by the quantity to find the unit price.
Best: $\dfrac{28.68}{12}$	$\dfrac{28.68}{12} = \dfrac{28.68 \div 12}{12 \div 12} = \dfrac{2.39}{1} = 2.39$
Ace: $\dfrac{32.85}{15}$	$\dfrac{32.85}{15} = \dfrac{32.85 \div 15}{15 \div 15} = \dfrac{2.19}{1} = 2.19$

So, the price at Best Photo is $2.39 per roll, and the price at Ace Photo is $2.19 per roll.

- Which is the better buy?

Check for Understanding

Tell how to find the unit rate or unit price.

1. 4 apples for $1.00

2. 310 words per 7 min

3. 16 stickers for $0.80

4. 140 mi per 7 gal of gasoline

Practice

Write a ratio that describes each rate.

5. 5 tickets for $20

6. a dozen eggs for $0.99

7. 3 for a dime

8. 33 mi to a gal

9. 52 words per min

10. 10 for $2

11. 20 pages per 5 min

12. 12 lb per 6 mo

13. 10 for fifty cents

Find the unit rate or unit price. Remember to express the second term.

14. 5 for $1.00

15. $0.95 for 5

16. $1.44 a dozen

17. 200 mi per 8 gal

18. $10 for 2

19. 14 for $31.50

20. $13.05 for 9

21. 900 people per 10 sq mi

22. 350 per 10 sq mi

23. 324 mi per 12 gal

24. 12 lessons for $155.40

25. 1,600 words per 25 min

Mixed Applications

26. Mr. Kerr buys 16 cassette tapes for $79.84. What is the unit price of each tape?

27. Lana has 9 rolls of film developed for $35.91. How much is the cost per roll of film?

28. A drugstore sells photo album pages at 5 for $4.25. If the rate remains the same, how much will 12 pages cost?

29. Chantel has a camera that produces instant photos. If film is $7.45 a roll, how much will 4 rolls cost?

30. At For-Les, the price of video-cassettes is 3 for $28.35. You can buy the same cassettes at Sav-Mor at 5 for $46.75. Which store has the better buy?

31. **Make Up a Problem** On Tuesdays, Fill-It-Up gasoline station sells high-performance gasoline at the special rate of $20.04 for 12 gal.

What is the difference between a ratio and a rate?

EQUIVALENT RATIOS

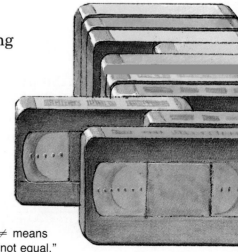

Ralph works at a video store. On Monday he rented 4 drama videos and 6 comedy videos. On Tuesday he rented 8 dramas and 12 comedies. On Wednesday he rented 16 dramas and 24 comedies. Are the ratios of dramas to comedies rented each day equivalent?

Use counters to visualize whether the ratios are equivalent.

There are 4 red for every 6 blue.

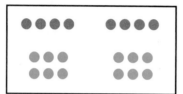

There are 4 red for every 6 blue.

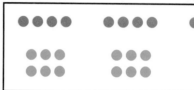

There are 4 red for every 6 blue.

If you can multiply or divide both terms by a common factor, the ratios are equivalent.

$$\frac{\text{dramas}}{\text{comedies}} \rightarrow \quad \frac{4}{6} = \frac{4 \times 2}{6 \times 2} = \frac{8}{12} \qquad \frac{8}{12} = \frac{8 \times 2}{12 \times 2} = \frac{16}{24} \qquad \frac{4}{6} = \frac{8}{12} = \frac{16}{24}$$

So, the ratios of dramas to comedies are equivalent.

Another Example

Ralph rents 3 comedy videos. How many drama videos can he expect to rent if the ratio remains the same?

$$\frac{\text{dramas}}{\text{comedies}} \rightarrow \quad \frac{4}{6} = \frac{\blacksquare}{3} \qquad \frac{4}{6} = \frac{4 \div 2}{6 \div 2} = \frac{2}{3} \quad \leftarrow \text{ratio in simplest form}$$

So, Ralph can expect to rent 2 drama videos.

• How does finding an equivalent ratio compare with finding an equivalent fraction?

• Study the examples. Talk about how you can determine whether two ratios are equivalent.

A. $\dfrac{6}{10} = \dfrac{\blacksquare}{5}$

$\dfrac{6 \div 2}{10 \div 2} = \dfrac{3}{5}$

B. $1:2 = 12:\blacksquare$

$\dfrac{1 \times 12}{2 \times 12} = \dfrac{12}{24}$

C. $\dfrac{4}{32} \overset{?}{=} \dfrac{5}{8}$

$\dfrac{5 \times 4}{8 \times 4} = \dfrac{20}{32}$

$\dfrac{4}{32} \neq \dfrac{5}{8} \quad \leftarrow \neq \text{ means "not equal."}$

Check for Understanding

Complete. Write = or ≠ to tell whether the ratios are equivalent.

1. $\frac{1}{2} \bullet \frac{6}{12}$

2. $1:3 \bullet 5:17$

3. $3 \text{ to } 1 \bullet 9 \text{ to } 3$

4. $7:2 \bullet 21:8$

Write two ratios that are equivalent to the given ratio.

5. $\frac{1}{2}$

6. $3:4$

7. $2 \text{ to } 3$

8. $5:1$

9. $3 \text{ to } 2$

10. $2 \text{ to } 1$

11. $\frac{4}{5}$

12. $\frac{7}{2}$

13. $6:12$

14. $5 \text{ to } 9$

Tell whether the ratios are equivalent. Write *yes* or *no*.

15. $\frac{2}{1}; \frac{8}{4}$

16. $2:5; 6:12$

17. $1:3; 7:21$

18. $\frac{4}{5}; \frac{16}{25}$

19. $\frac{27}{63}; \frac{3}{7}$

20. $20:45; 4:9$

21. $\frac{16}{32}; \frac{2}{4}$

22. $18:48; 3:8$

Find the term that makes the ratios equivalent.

23. $\frac{1}{2}; \frac{\blacksquare}{10}$

24. $\frac{\blacksquare}{7}; \frac{4}{14}$

25. $2 \text{ to } 5; 6 \text{ to } \blacksquare$

26. $9 \text{ to } 3; \blacksquare \text{ to } 27$

27. $\frac{12}{3}; \frac{4}{\blacksquare}$

28. $\frac{\blacksquare}{7}; \frac{3}{1}$

29. $8 \text{ to } 4; \blacksquare \text{ to } 2$

30. $36:15; 12:\blacksquare$

Mixed Applications

31. Karl took 5 photographs of friends for every 3 photographs of scenery. How many pictures of friends does he have if he has 15 photographs of scenery?

32. Dara's contract calls for her to work in 3 films and then 9 commercials. If her contract is renewed, will her fifteenth job be a film or a commercial?

33. **Analyze Data** The table shows the number of trivia games Sean and Sonia won over five days. The ratio of Sean's winning to Sonia's winning the first day is $\frac{2}{1}$. On which other day is the ratio of Sean's winning to Sonia's winning $\frac{2}{1}$?

Number of Trivia Games					
Day	1	2	3	4	5
Sean won	2	1	6	1	4
Sonia won	1	3	3	2	3

Explain in your own words how to find equivalent ratios.

W R A P
U P...

More Practice, Lesson 10.3, page H70

EXPLORING

Proportions

These photographs are in proportion because there is a balance in the relationship of their widths to their lengths. Numbers can help you determine whether items are in proportion.

Work Together

Building Understanding

Use counters to help you.

Is $\frac{3}{5}$ equivalent to $\frac{6}{10}$?

Set A

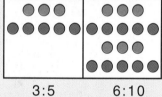

3:5   6:10

Is $\frac{1}{2}$ equivalent to $\frac{2}{3}$?

Set B

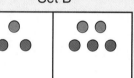

1:2   2:3

TALK ABOUT IT

• In Set A, is the number of red counters in the second box a multiple of the number of red counters in the first box? blue counters?

• How does the ratio of red to blue counters on the left compare with the ratio of red to blue counters on the right?

• In Set B, is the number of red counters in either box a multiple of the number of red counters in the other box? blue counters?

• How does the ratio of red to blue counters on the left compare with the ratio of red to blue counters on the right?

A **proportion** is a number sentence or an equation that states that two ratios are equivalent.

$$\frac{3}{5} = \frac{6}{10} \quad \longleftarrow \text{ a proportion}$$

Use counters. Tell whether the ratios make a proportion. Write = or ≠.

a. $\frac{3}{5} \bullet \frac{5}{1}$ **b.** $\frac{1}{2} \bullet \frac{6}{12}$ **c.** $\frac{2}{3} \bullet \frac{3}{5}$ **d.** $\frac{9}{10} \bullet \frac{18}{36}$

Making the Connection

You can use cross products to determine whether ratios are proportions. The cross products of a proportion are equivalent.

a. $\dfrac{12}{18}$ 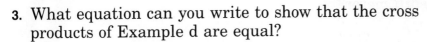 $\dfrac{2}{3}$

   $3 \times 12 = \blacksquare$
   $18 \times 2 = \blacksquare$
   $18 \times 2 \overset{?}{=} 3 \times 12$

b. $\dfrac{2}{3}$ $\dfrac{5}{15}$

   $3 \times 5 = \blacksquare$
   $2 \times 15 = \blacksquare$
   $3 \times 5 \overset{?}{=} 2 \times 15$

1. What are the cross products in Example a? in Example b?

2. Do the ratios in each example form a proportion? Explain your answer.

You can use cross products to find the missing term in a proportion.

c. $\dfrac{y}{4} = \dfrac{12}{16}$ Find the cross products.

   $16y = 4 \times 12 \longleftarrow 4 \times 12 = 48$
   $16y = 48$

d. $\dfrac{18}{6} = \dfrac{n}{2}$ Find the cross products.

3. What equation can you write to show that the cross products of Example d are equal?

4. What would you do to solve the equations?

Checking Understanding

Tell whether the ratios make a proportion. Write *yes* or *no*.

5. $\dfrac{2}{3}; \dfrac{12}{18}$

6. $1:5; 3:15$

7. $\dfrac{4}{5}; \dfrac{32}{8}$

8. $9:2; 15:3$

Write the cross products.

9. $\dfrac{3}{1} = \dfrac{9}{3}$

10. $\dfrac{2}{3} = \dfrac{4}{6}$

11. $\dfrac{1}{8} = \dfrac{t}{40}$

12. $\dfrac{3}{x} = \dfrac{4}{36}$

13. $\dfrac{a}{6} = \dfrac{5}{8}$

14. $\dfrac{4}{b} = \dfrac{7}{9}$

15. $\dfrac{4}{5} = \dfrac{7}{y}$

16. $\dfrac{3}{11} = \dfrac{d}{10}$

RATIO AND PROPORTION
Using Algebra

Animators made 2,880 drawings for 3 minutes of an animated movie. How many drawings would they make for 15 minutes of animation?

Use what you know about equivalent ratios to find the missing term in a proportion.

Step 1 Write a proportion.	**Step 2** Write the cross products.	**Step 3** Solve the equation.
drawings → $\dfrac{2{,}880}{3} = \dfrac{n}{15}$ ← minutes	$\dfrac{2{,}880}{3} \diagdown = \diagdown \dfrac{n}{15}$ $3n = 2{,}880 \times 15$	$3n = 2{,}880 \times 15$ $3n = 43{,}200$ $n = 14{,}400$

So, they would make 14,400 drawings.

Another Example For a movie that is set in Chicago, Henk is making scale models of the Sears Tower, which is 550 m tall, and the John Hancock Center, which is 444 m tall. If Henk's model of the Sears Tower is 10 m tall, what will be the height of his model of the John Hancock Center to the nearest hundredth meter?

$$\frac{\text{model height}}{\text{actual height}} \rightarrow \frac{10}{550} \diagdown = \diagdown \frac{t}{444} \qquad 550t = 444 \times 10 \qquad t = \frac{444 \times 10}{550}$$

 You can use a calculator to find the answer.

444 $\boxed{\times}$ 10 $\boxed{\div}$ 550 $\boxed{=}$ $\boxed{\text{8.0727272}}$

So, to the nearest hundredth meter, the height of Henk's model of the John Hancock Center will be 8.07 m.

Check for Understanding

Write the cross products.

1. $\dfrac{1}{x} = \dfrac{3}{6}$ 2. $\dfrac{3}{8} = \dfrac{t}{24}$ 3. $\dfrac{c}{3} = \dfrac{2}{6}$ 4. $\dfrac{15}{18} = \dfrac{5}{y}$ 5. $\dfrac{a}{16} = \dfrac{1}{4}$

Practice

Tell whether the ratios make a proportion. Write *yes* or *no*.

6. $\frac{2}{5}; \frac{10}{25}$

7. $\frac{9}{3}; \frac{3}{1}$

8. $\frac{18}{25}; \frac{7}{10}$

9. $\frac{3}{8}; \frac{9}{24}$

10. $\frac{7}{8}; \frac{28}{32}$

11. $\frac{5}{6}; \frac{3}{4}$

12. $\frac{20}{32}; \frac{5}{8}$

13. $\frac{2}{9}; \frac{14}{64}$

14. $\frac{3}{14}; \frac{5}{12}$

15. $\frac{2}{7}; \frac{6}{28}$

16. $\frac{4}{9}; \frac{12}{27}$

17. $\frac{3}{5}; \frac{4}{6}$

Write the cross products. Then solve.

18. $\frac{6}{8} = \frac{n}{12}$

19. $\frac{9}{15} = \frac{a}{10}$

20. $\frac{3}{9} = \frac{b}{21}$

21. $\frac{12}{9} = \frac{t}{12}$

22. $\frac{15}{20} = \frac{x}{16}$

23. $\frac{14}{4} = \frac{d}{12}$

24. $\frac{p}{6} = \frac{2.5}{4}$

25. $\frac{4}{m} = \frac{1.6}{2.8}$

Mixed Applications

26. The ratio of rolls of film to exposures is 1 to 12. How many exposures are in 7 rolls of film?

27. There are 5 videotapes to a package. If Leon buys 8 packages of videotapes, how many videotapes will he have?

28. **Critical Thinking** If the ratio of cartoon videos to adventure videos in 2 packages is 6 to 14, how many packages must you buy to have 15 cartoon videos?

MIXED REVIEW

Find the sum or difference.

1. 5 hr 45 min
    −2 hr 30 min

2. 7 min 12 sec
    +6 min 55 sec

3. 12 min 5 sec
    − 8 min 45 sec

4. 2 hr 55 min
    +6 hr 25 min

5. 5 gal − 3 qt

6. 2 T − 1,200 lb

7. 5 km − 3,000 m

Write the ratio in two other ways.

8. four to two

9. five to eight

10. one to nine

11. seven to eleven

How can you tell whether two ratios make a proportion?

W R A P
UP...

More Practice, Lesson 10.5, page H71

313

EXPLORING

Scale Drawings

Martha is making this scale drawing of an auditorium to use as a prop in a mystery movie.

A **scale drawing** is like a photograph. It can be a reduced or an enlarged version of the actual object.

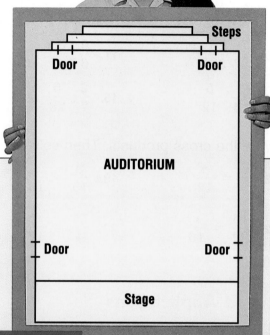

Work Together

Building Understanding

Use centimeter graph paper and a centimeter ruler.

1. Measure the length and the width of the scale drawing.

2. On your graph paper, make a drawing that is twice the size of the scale drawing Martha made.

3. On your graph paper, make a drawing that is half the size of the scale drawing Martha made.

Tell whether you would reduce or enlarge the dimensions to make a scale drawing.

a. a birthstone   b. your bedroom

c. an office   d. an amoeba

TALK ABOUT IT

- What is the ratio of the length to the width in your first drawing? in Martha's drawing? Are the ratios equivalent?

- What is the ratio of the length to the width in your second drawing? in Martha's drawing? Are the ratios equivalent?

- Name some examples of scale drawings that you find in everyday life.

- If you were making a scale drawing of a classroom, would you reduce or enlarge the dimensions?

- If you were making a scale drawing of a thumbtack, would you reduce or enlarge the dimensions?

Making the Connection

The **scale** of a drawing is the ratio of the size of the object in the drawing to the actual size of the object. If you know the scale, you can find a missing dimension.

Use a centimeter ruler and the scale drawing of the office suite.

An interior decorator's drawing of an office suite is 60 mm long. You can write and solve a proportion to find the actual length of the suite.

The scale of the drawing tells you that every distance of 10 mm in the drawing represents an actual distance of 2 m in the office suite.

Office Suite

| Reception Area | Office 1 |
| Office 2 | Hall / Office 3 |

Scale: 10 mm = 2 m

$$\frac{\text{mm}}{\text{m}} \rightarrow \frac{10}{2} = \frac{60}{s} \leftarrow \frac{\text{drawing length}}{\text{actual length}}$$

$$10s = 2 \times 60$$
$$10s = 120$$
$$s = 12$$

So, the actual length of the suite is 12 m.

- What proportion can you write to find the actual length of Office 2?

Checking Understanding

Use the scale drawing of the office suite. Write the proportion you can use to find the actual dimensions.

1. length of the hall

2. width of the suite

3. length of Office 1

4. dimensions of the reception area

Make a scale drawing to enlarge the shape to twice its size.

5.

6.

7.

8.

9.

10.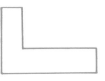

PROBLEM SOLVING

Use a Scale Drawing

Denny wants to be an engineer and help companies make decisions about building large structures. Denny made a presentation to his mechanical drawing class about a theater called Bard Production Hall. He used a scale drawing of the hall. In his drawing, 1 cm represents 6 m. Someone asked Denny, "What is the actual length of the makeup room?"

▶ **UNDERSTAND**

What are you asked to find?

What information are you given?

▶ **PLAN**

How will you solve the problem?

Use the scale drawing. Measure the length of the makeup room. Then write and solve a proportion.

▶ **SOLVE**

How will you carry out your plan?

Use a centimeter ruler. The length of the makeup room in the drawing is 2 cm. Write a proportion.

$$\frac{\text{cm}}{\text{m}} \rightarrow \frac{1}{6} \;=\; \frac{2}{n} \leftarrow \frac{\text{drawing length}}{\text{actual length}}$$

$$1n = 6 \times 2 \quad \leftarrow \; 1 \times n = n$$

$$n = 12$$

So, the actual length of the makeup room is 12 m.

▶ **LOOK BACK**

How can you check your answer?

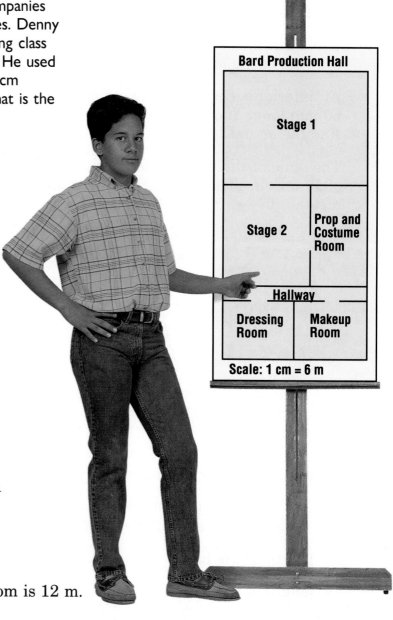

Bard Production Hall

Stage 1

Stage 2

Prop and Costume Room

Hallway

Dressing Room

Makeup Room

Scale: 1 cm = 6 m

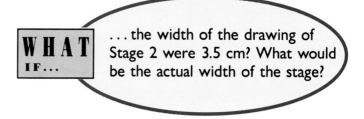

WHAT IF... ...the width of the drawing of Stage 2 were 3.5 cm? What would be the actual width of the stage?

Apply

Use a centimeter ruler and the scale drawing on page 316. Solve.

1 What is the actual width of the prop and costume room?

2 What is the actual width of the dressing room?

3 What are the actual length and width of the hallway?

4 What are the actual length and width of the production hall?

> **Mixed Applications**

STRATEGIES **Write an Equation • Draw a Diagram • Find a Pattern • Work Backward**

Choose a strategy and solve. Use the scale drawing on page 316 for Exercise 6.

5 A costumer uses $\frac{2}{3}$ yd of fabric to make a blouse and $1\frac{4}{5}$ yd to make a skirt for a turn-of-the-century costume. How much fabric will the costumer use to make the 150 blouses and 75 skirts needed for a crowd scene?

6 Leanna and Drew are on the set crew for the next production. They are making a blue curtain that will run the entire length of Stage 1. What will be the actual length of the curtain?

7 To build a long staircase for the filming of *Halt,* the set crew will use 5 blocks for the first step, 10 for the second, 15 for the third, 20 for the fourth, and 25 for the fifth. If the pattern continues, what will be the total number of blocks used for ten steps?

8 Dan took pictures while on vacation. He used $\frac{3}{4}$ roll of film on day 1, $1\frac{1}{2}$ rolls on day 2, $2\frac{1}{4}$ rolls on day 3, and 3 rolls on day 4. If the pattern continued, how much film did Dan use on day 8?

9 In a movie scene, an elevator travels from the fifth floor to the first floor. It then travels to the third floor and back down to the first floor. If the floors are 10 ft apart, how far does the elevator travel?

10 The budget to produce a film is $2,500,000. The producer budgeted $350,000 for costumes; $600,000 for sets; $1,500,000 for actors; and the rest for miscellaneous expenses. How much was budgeted for miscellaneous expenses?

11 The entire cast of an epic film was invited to the premiere. Of those invited, 4 out of 5 planned to attend. If there were 960 people in the cast, how many planned to attend the premiere?

1. George leaves home for work at 7:30 A.M. He rides a train for 35 min and then walks 10 min to his office. If he is 15 min early, at what time is he supposed to begin work?

2. Train A leaves Nokesville at 9:45 A.M., arriving in the city at 10:57 A.M. Train B leaves at 1:35 P.M. and arrives in the city at 2:53 P.M. Which train takes longer?

3. The blueprints for Jan's house use a scale of 1 cm = 4 m. The kitchen is 6 m long. How long is the kitchen in the drawing?

I would write a proportion to solve Exercise 3.

Change to the given unit.

4. $7.9 \text{ m} = \blacksquare \text{ mm}$

5. $6 \text{ lb} = \blacksquare \text{ oz}$

6. $22{,}000 \text{ g} = \blacksquare \text{ kg}$

Find the sum or difference.

7. $\begin{array}{r} 12 \text{ m } 75 \text{ cm} \\ + 9 \text{ m } 45 \text{ cm} \\ \hline \end{array}$

8. $\begin{array}{r} 7 \text{ ft } 7 \text{ in.} \\ -4 \text{ ft } 9 \text{ in.} \\ \hline \end{array}$

9. $\begin{array}{r} 6 \text{ min } 45 \text{ sec} \\ +8 \text{ min } 55 \text{ sec} \\ \hline \end{array}$

10. $\begin{array}{r} 5 \text{ lb } 10 \text{ oz} \\ -3 \text{ lb } 11 \text{ oz} \\ \hline \end{array}$

Write the ratio in two other ways.

11. two to one

12. $5:6$

13. $3:8$

14. three to nine

Find the unit rate.

15. $3.24 a dozen

16. 825 words per 15 min

17. 8 for $12.80

Tell whether the ratios are equivalent. Write *yes* or *no*.

18. $3:2; 9:4$

19. $6:8; 9:12$

20. $4:5; 32:35$

21. $5:15; 20:60$

Find the number that makes the ratios equivalent.

22. $4:3; 32:\blacksquare$

23. $16:8; \blacksquare:2$

24. $5:7; \blacksquare:63$

Tell whether the ratios make a proportion. Write *yes* or *no*.

25. $\frac{6}{9}; \frac{2}{3}$

26. $\frac{1}{9}; \frac{2}{5}$

27. $\frac{3}{5}; \frac{7}{15}$

28. $\frac{3}{8}; \frac{6}{16}$

Write the cross products.

29. $\frac{30}{15} = \frac{x}{5}$

30. $\frac{n}{4} = \frac{9}{1.2}$

31. $\frac{21}{9} = \frac{a}{3}$

32. $\frac{80}{b} = \frac{10}{3}$

Using Data

The Indian movie industry is one of the world's largest, employing about two million people. This industry supplies India with many types of films.

Many of India's movies use only a few popular actors. These actors often work on twenty productions at once! The most popular movies recently have been about the role of women in society and have been love stories.

Use the given data to solve the problems.

1. What is the ratio of the number of people who work in the movie industry in India to the Indian population of 853,000,000?

2. About 800 movies are produced in India each year. In the United States about 330 movies are produced each year. What is the ratio of the number of movies produced in India to the number of movies produced in the United States?

3. About 70,000,000 Indians go to movie theaters each week. At this rate, about how many movie tickets are sold each year?

4. Actually, only a small part of the Indian population attend movies regularly. Use the information given in Exercises 1 and 3 to find the ratio of the number of Indians who go to the movies each week to the population of India.

ASIA

India

MULTICULTURAL NOTE: Music and dance are important parts of Indian culture. Most Indian films contain music, dancing, and singing.

5. The Indian government collects in taxes $6 of every $10 that a movie theater makes in sales. If a theater sells $7,653 worth of tickets in one week, how much is left after the taxes are paid?

EXPLORING

Percent

You can use a 10-by-10 grid to explore percent.

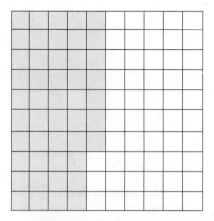

TALK ABOUT IT

- How many squares are in the grid?

- How many squares are shaded?

- What is the ratio of shaded squares to the total number of squares in the grid?

- What percent of the grid is shaded?

Percent is the ratio of a number to 100. **Percent** means "per hundred." The symbol for percent is %.

Work Together

Building Understanding

Use graph paper to make a 10-by-10 grid. Color 20 squares red, 50 squares blue, and 5 squares yellow.

TALK ABOUT IT

- How does your grid show 20%? 50%? 5%?

- What percent of the grid is not colored?

- Does 50% differ from the ratio $\frac{1}{2}$, $\frac{5}{10}$, $\frac{50}{100}$ when shaded on a grid? Why or why not?

- How can you show the ratio $\frac{2}{5}$ on a 10-by-10 grid?

Use graph paper to make three 10-by-10 grids. Color a grid to show the ratio given. Tell what percent is colored.

a. $\frac{75}{100}$ b. $\frac{6}{10}$ c. $\frac{4}{5}$

Making the Connection

The table shows the results of a survey that asked camera users which camera they felt was the most reliable. Use the table for Exercises 1–5.

1. How many people were surveyed?

2. What percent of those surveyed prefer the Minte Maxx?

3. What percent of those surveyed do not prefer the Karron XX?

4. Do more than half of the people surveyed prefer any one type of camera over the others?

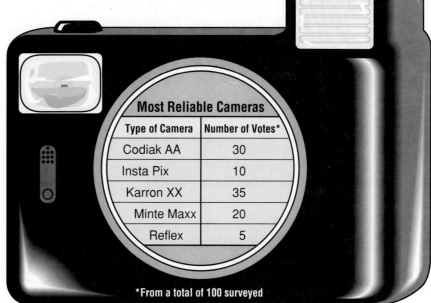

Most Reliable Cameras

Type of Camera	Number of Votes*
Codiak AA	30
Insta Pix	10
Karron XX	35
Minte Maxx	20
Reflex	5

*From a total of 100 surveyed

5. Suppose that the table showed that 15 people preferred the Reflex, but nothing else was changed. Would that mean that 15% of those surveyed preferred the Reflex? Why or why not?

Checking Understanding

Tell what percent each is of one dollar.

6. 1 dime and 1 nickel

7. 1 quarter and 1 dime

8. 1 quarter and 2 dimes

9. 2 quarters and 1 nickel

10. 2 dimes and 3 nickels

11. 1 quarter, 2 dimes, and 1 nickel

12. 1 quarter, 1 dime, and 4 pennies

13. 3 quarters, 1 nickel, and 4 pennies

Solve.

14. If sales tax is 6%, how much tax will you pay if you buy an item that costs $1.00?

15. If sales tax is 5%, how much tax will you pay if you buy an item that costs $10.00?

16. If you surveyed 10 people and 8 said yes to a question, what percent of the people said yes? How do you know?

17. If you surveyed 10 people and 6 said yes to a question, what percent of the people said no?

CONNECTING PERCENTS AND DECIMALS

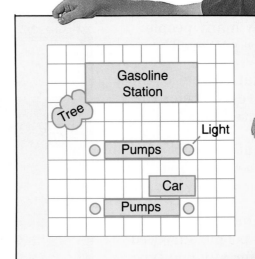

Aliya used a 10-by-10 grid to make a scale drawing of the set of *Tomorrow, Tomorrow, and Tomorrow*. What decimal shows the amount of space taken by the gasoline station?

The gasoline station takes up 12 squares.

12 out of 100 means 12 hundredths or 0.12.

So, 0.12 shows in decimal form the amount of space taken by the gasoline station.

- What percent shows the amount of space taken by the gasoline station?

You can write a decimal as a percent, and you can write a percent as a decimal.

More Examples

A. Write 0.05 as a percent.
0.05 = 5 out of 100

So, 0.05 = 5%.

B. Write 80% as a decimal.
80% = 80 out of 100

So, 80% = $\frac{80}{100}$ = 0.80, or 0.8.

C. Write a decimal and a percent that describe the amount shaded.

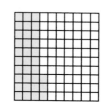

$\frac{33}{100}$ = 0.33 = 33%

Talk About It

Think of place value when you write a decimal as a percent and a percent as a decimal.

▶ Write 6% and 66% as decimals. By what number do you divide to change a percent to a decimal?

▶ Write 0.07 and 0.7 as percents. How many places did you move each decimal point?

▶ What pattern do you see when you write a percent as a decimal?

▶ What pattern do you see when you write a decimal as a percent?

Check for Understanding

Write a decimal and a percent that describe the amount shaded.

1.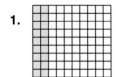
2.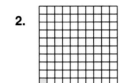
3.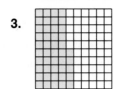
4.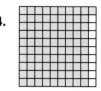

Practice

Use graph paper. Draw a 10-by-10 grid. Then shade the amount.

5. 20%   6. 0.6   7. 45%   8. 75%   9. 51%

Write the decimal as a percent.

10. 0.37   11. 0.44   12. 0.13   13. 0.21   14. 0.16

15. 0.6   16. 0.3   17. 0.03   18. 0.14   19. 1.45

Write the percent as a decimal.

20. 18%   21. 37%   22. 24%   23. 68%   24. 94%

25. 3%   26. 7%   27. 1%   28. 25%   29. 13%

30. 71%   31. 75%   32. 8%   33. 2%   34. 130%

Mixed Applications

35. A local restaurant has 100 autographed photographs of movie stars. Of these, 32 are in color. What percent of the photographs are in color?

36. If you can buy 5 posters for $9, how much does one poster cost?

37. Rich has a poster of a scene from *Dust Busters*. The poster is 150% larger than the original photograph. What decimal expresses the same amount?

38. If you can buy 3 posters for $6, what percent of a dollar does 1 poster cost?

How can you use place value to change a percent to a decimal?

PERCENTS AND FRACTIONS

Ballet companies in cities around the world perform *The Nutcracker*. In one city's version, $\frac{1}{5}$ of the dancers are children. What percent of the dancers are children?

Since percent means per hundred, you can write an equivalent fraction to answer the question.

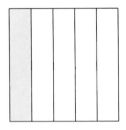

$$\frac{1}{5} = \frac{\blacksquare}{100} \qquad \frac{1 \times 20}{5 \times 20} = \frac{20}{100}$$

So, 20% of the dancers are children.

Another Method In a dance scene that includes the Mouse King and his soldiers, $\frac{2}{3}$ of the dancing mice are children. What percent of the dancing mice are children?

Sometimes you may want to write a fraction as a decimal and then write a percent.

$$0.66\tfrac{2}{3} = 66\tfrac{2}{3}\%$$

Divide to write a two-digit decimal.
Write the remainder as a fraction.

$$3\overline{)2.00}$$
$$\underline{1\ 8}$$
$$20$$
$$\underline{18}$$
$$2$$

So, $66\frac{2}{3}\%$ of the dancing mice are children.

You can change a percent to a fraction by writing the percent as the numerator and 100 as the denominator. Remember to simplify the fraction.

Examples

A. $75\% = \frac{75}{100} = \frac{3}{4}$ **B.** $45\% = \frac{45}{100} = \frac{9}{20}$ **C.** $12\% = \frac{12}{100} = \frac{3}{25}$

- How do you write a decimal as a fraction?

Check for Understanding

Write a fraction in simplest form and a percent that describe the amount shaded.

1. 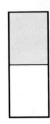 **2.** 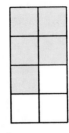 **3.**   **4.**

Practice

Write the fraction as a percent.

5. $\dfrac{1}{10}$ **6.** $\dfrac{1}{5}$ **7.** $\dfrac{1}{4}$ **8.** $\dfrac{9}{10}$ **9.** $\dfrac{4}{5}$

10. $\dfrac{17}{20}$ **11.** $\dfrac{7}{10}$ **12.** $\dfrac{3}{4}$ **13.** $\dfrac{3}{5}$ **14.** $\dfrac{3}{20}$

Write the percent as a fraction in simplest form.

15. 25% **16.** 15% **17.** 45% **18.** 16% **19.** 95%

Mixed Applications

20. A survey of customers at a theater indicates that $\dfrac{2}{5}$ are preteens. What percent of the customers are preteens?

21. Number Sense • Mental Math If $\dfrac{1}{4}$ of 96 students spend 1 hour a night on homework, what percent of students is this? How many students is this?

 NUMBER SENSE

Use a calculator to change a fraction to a percent. Any remainder can be written as a decimal part of the percent.

Write $\dfrac{1}{3}$ as a percent.

1 ÷ 3 = ⟦ 0.3333333 ⟧

$0.3333333 = 0.33\overline{3}$

So, $\dfrac{1}{3}$ can be written as $33.\overline{3}\%$.

The bar shows that the decimal repeats.

Write $\dfrac{2}{3}$ as a percent.

2 ÷ 3 = ⟦ 0.6666666 ⟧

$0.6666666 = 0.66\overline{6}$

So, $\dfrac{2}{3}$ can be written as $66.\overline{6}\%$.

Use a calculator to change the fraction to a percent.

22. $\dfrac{3}{8}$ **23.** $\dfrac{1}{6}$ **24.** $\dfrac{5}{9}$ **25.** $\dfrac{4}{11}$ **26.** $\dfrac{11}{12}$

How is changing a percent to a fraction similar to changing a decimal to a fraction?

WRAP UP...

More Practice, Lesson 10.10, page H72

EXPLORING

Percent of a Number

Kaitlin likes to shop for bargains. She finds a $20 video tape marked "25% off." How can she find the amount she would save, or 25% of $20?

Building Understanding

Use the manipulative of your choice to model the problem.

Write a description of the steps in your model. Explain how you found 25% of $20.

Be prepared to discuss your model.

TALK ABOUT IT

• Suppose Kaitlin could save 50%. Describe how you can change your model to show 50% of $20.

• How would you model the problems if you thought of 25% and 50% as fractions?

Present your model to the class.

Making the Connection

You can use two-color counters to find a percent of a number.

Example What is 30% of 10?

Since 10 counters represent 100%, 1 counter represents 10%.

- How many counters represent 30%?

  So, 30% of 10 = 3.

You can use several other methods to find a percent of a number.

What is 40% of 85?

Method 1	Method 2
Use a ratio in simplest form to name the percent. Then multiply.	Use a decimal to name the percent. Then multiply.
$40\% = \dfrac{40}{100} = \dfrac{2}{5}$	$40\% = 0.40$, or 0.4
$\dfrac{2}{5} \times \dfrac{85}{1} = \dfrac{170}{5} = 34$	$\begin{array}{r} 85 \\ \times\ 0.4 \\ \hline 34.0 \end{array}$

So, 40% of 85 is 34.

Checking Understanding

Use the method of your choice to find the percent of a number.

1. 20% of 55   2. 40% of 40   3. 45% of 90   4. 25% of 140

5. 50% of 150   6. 25% of 80   7. 90% of 60   8. 45% of 40

9. Describe how you can use a calculator to find the percent of a number.

You can use benchmarks and mental math to help you find the percent of many numbers.

In Olivia's school 50% of the 440 students polled said their favorite movie was *Dude*. How many students chose *Dude* as their favorite movie?

Benchmarks for Percent
200% means twice as much.
100% is the same as the number.
50% means $\frac{1}{2}$ as much.
25% means $\frac{1}{4}$ as much.
10% means $\frac{1}{10}$ as much.

Talk About It

▶ How can you write 50% as a fraction?

▶ How can you write 50% as a decimal?

▶ Describe two methods you could use to find the answer to the question.

▶ With which method could you find the answer by using mental math?

$50\% = \frac{1}{2}$ → Multiplying by $\frac{1}{2}$ is the → $440 \div 2 = 220$
same as dividing by 2.

So, 220 students chose *Dude* as their favorite movie.

More Examples

A. What is 20% of 340?

Think:

10% + 10% = 20%
10% of 340 = 34
34 + 34 = 68

So, 20% of 340 = 68.

B. What is 25% of 400?

Think:

$25\% = \frac{1}{4}$
$400 \div 4 = 100$

So, 25% of 400 = 100.

• How can you find 75% of 400?

• What is 150% of 10?

• What is 200% of 10?

• What is 50% of 10?

Check for Understanding

Tell how you can use benchmarks to find the percent of the number.

1. 25% of 400   **2.** 50% of 100   **3.** 200% of 400   **4.** 30% of 300

Practice

Use mental math to find the percent of the number.

5. 30% of 200   **6.** 5% of 500   **7.** 15% of 500   **8.** 20% of 600

9. 50% of 400   **10.** 10% of 12   **11.** 25% of 800   **12.** 100% of 35

13. 10% of 6   **14.** 25% of 440   **15.** 200% of 100   **16.** 50% of $6.50

17. 75% of $12   **18.** 100% of $9.38   **19.** 10% of $75.45   **20.** 65% of $100

Mixed Applications

21. Carolyn scored 100% on a quiz about movie stars. If 45 questions were on the quiz, how many did she get correct?

22. Of 800 people surveyed, 425 prefer rock theme songs to jazz theme songs in movies. How many prefer jazz theme songs?

23. Critical Thinking Use the information in Exercise 22. What percent of the people do not prefer rock theme songs?

MIXED REVIEW

Find the unit rate.

1. 4 rings for $1.00   **2.** 275 words per 5 min   **3.** 285 mi per 15 gal

Tell whether the ratios make a proportion. Write *yes* or *no*.

4. $\frac{1}{5}; \frac{5}{25}$ **5.** $\frac{3}{6}; \frac{2}{5}$ **6.** $\frac{4}{7}; \frac{12}{21}$ **7.** $\frac{35}{45}; \frac{7}{9}$ **8.** $\frac{1}{3}; \frac{3}{16}$

Write as a percent.

9. 0.25   **10.** $\frac{4}{5}$ **11.** $\frac{3}{4}$ **12.** 0.35   **13.** $\frac{3}{10}$

How can you find 110% of a number by using mental math?

WRAP UP...

ESTIMATING PERCENT

Kim reads in the newspaper that the Minte Maxx camera is marked down 9% from the regular price at a local camera shop. If the camera usually sells for $47.99, about how much is the markdown?

Consumers often estimate percents to find a sale price, to compare prices, or to determine how much money to leave as a tip at a restaurant.

9% ≈ 10% $47.99 is about $50.00. ◄— Use rounding.

10% of $50.00 = $5.00

Since 9% is rounded to the next ten percent and $47.99 is rounded to the next ten dollars, the estimate is an overestimate.

So, the markdown is about $5.00.

- Suppose the markdown is 12% and the regular price $53.99. If you round to 10% and $50.00, will your estimate be an overestimate or an underestimate?

- Since the markdown is about $5.00, about how much will the camera cost?

Another Example

Karen wants to leave a 15% tip at a restaurant. The bill is $12.34. How much should she leave?

15% is 10% + 5%. $12.34 is about $12.00.

10% of $12.00 = $1.20 ◄— 0.10 × 12 = 1.2

5% is $\frac{1}{2}$ of 10%, so 5% of $12.00 is $\frac{1}{2} \times$ $1.20 = $0.60.

$1.20 + $0.60 = $1.80

So, Karen should leave about $1.80.

Check for Understanding

Estimate.

1. 12% × 111   2. 29% × 315   3. 42% × 1,050   4. $33\frac{1}{3}$% × 897   5. 50% of 721

Practice

Suppose you know about what 10% of a number is. Tell how you can estimate the given percent.

6. 15%   **7.** 80%   **8.** 20%   **9.** 25%   **10.** 45%

11. 75%   **12.** 40%   **13.** 35%   **14.** 95%   **15.** 12%

Choose the best estimate. Write **a, b,** or **c.**

16. 12% of 115
  a. 10% of 100
  b. 20% of 100
  c. 20% of 200

17. 57% of 198
  a. 60% of 150
  b. 60% of 200
  c. 55% of 200

18. 79% of 1,337
  a. 70% of 2,000
  b. 100% of 1,300
  c. 75% of 1,000

19. 28% of 32
  a. 30% of 40
  b. 20% of 35
  c. 30% of 30

20. 19% of 78
  a. 20% of 50
  b. 20% of 80
  c. 20% of 100

21. 82% of $36.85
  a. 80% of $40
  b. 80% of $30
  c. 90% of $40

Tell whether the estimate is an overestimate or an underestimate.

22. 18% of 36 ≈ 8   **23.** 12% of 124 ≈ 10   **24.** 98% of 599 ≈ 599

25. 16% of 125 ≈ 25   **26.** 55% of 700 ≈ 350   **27.** 25% of 315 ≈ 75

Mixed Applications

28. Reed's advertises 35-mm film for 75% of the regular price of $4.85. About how much is the new price?

29. Fred wants to leave the server at a cafe a 10% tip. If the bill for Fred and his family is $19.85, about how much should he leave?

30. **Making Decisions**   If the price of a poster is 80% of $6 at Store A and 75% of $7 at Store B, where would you get the better buy?

31. **Mental Math**   Sam's Wholesale is having a sale on compact discs. They are marked down 50% below the regular price of $12. What is the sale price of the compact discs?

How can you use the value of 10% of a number to help you estimate other percents of the number?

PROBLEM SOLVING

Choose a Strategy

Understand
Plan
Solve
Look Back

Jason is making a casserole for an after-the-movie dinner. His recipe calls for 3 tomatoes for every 2 onions, but Jason wants to make more than the recipe yields. How many onions should he use with 15 tomatoes?

What strategies can you choose?

You could use one of several strategies. You might *write an equation* in the form of a proportion or *make a table*.

Strategy: Write an equation

$$\text{tomatoes} \longrightarrow \frac{3}{2} = \frac{15}{n} \longleftarrow \text{tomatoes}$$
$$\text{onions} \longrightarrow \qquad\qquad \longleftarrow \text{onions}$$

Use cross products to solve.

$$3n = 15 \times 2$$
$$3n = 30$$
$$n = 10$$

Strategy: Make a table

You can use multiples of 3 and 2 to extend the table.

Casserole Recipe					
Vegetable	Number Needed				
	× 1	× 2	× 3	× 4	× 5
Tomatoes	3	6	9	12	15
Onions	2	4	6	8	10

So, Jason should use 10 onions with 15 tomatoes.

▶ **LOOK BACK**

What other strategy could you use?

WHAT IF... ...Jason uses 18 tomatoes? How many onions should he use?

Mixed Applications ➤ **STRATEGIES** **Write an Equation • Work Backward • Use Estimation • Make a Table**

Choose a strategy and solve.

1 Larry made a scale model of a movie theater, using a scale of 1 in. = 2 ft. The actual length of the theater is 56 ft. What is the length of the model?

2 Use the information in Exercise 1. Larry's model is three-dimensional. The height of the model is 13 in. What is the actual height of the theater?

3 Fewer than 300 people attended a movie one Saturday. The next Saturday, about twice as many people attended the movie. If different people attended each Saturday, about how many people attended the movie?

4 Sue Ann spent the $15 she received on her birthday. Then she bought film for $13 and a flash for $9. She had $3 left. How much money did Sue Ann have before her birthday?

5 Mr. Sanchez had $\frac{1}{2}$ roll of film left in his camera. He divided it evenly among pictures of his 3 sons. How much of the whole roll of film was used for pictures of each son?

6 Rita painted the scenery for a play. She used 1 gallon of paint to cover 18 square yards of wall space. How many gallons did she use to cover 54 square yards of wall space?

7 Mrs. Chen found that a set of camera equipment costs $45.25 at one store and $33.75 at a second store. She needs 12 sets for her class. How much money will she save by buying the equipment at the second store?

8 Ned wants to buy a $20.00 camera. He plans to save $0.01 the first day. Each day after that he will save double the amount he saved the day before. If he keeps to this plan, how long will it take him to save enough money to buy the $20.00 camera?

WRITER'S CORNER

9 Write a word problem that can be solved by using two different strategies. Have several classmates solve your word problem. Which strategy was used more often to solve the problem?

CHAPTER REVIEW / TEST

Vocabulary Check

Choose a word or words from the box to complete each sentence.

percent
proportion
rate
ratio
scale
unit rate

1. A comparison of two numbers is called a ___?___ . *(page 304)*

2. A ratio that compares one quantity to a different quantity is a ___?___ . *(page 306)*

3. A number sentence or an equation that states that two ratios are equivalent is a ___?___ . *(page 310)*

4. In a ___?___ , the second term is 1. *(page 306)*

5. The ratio of the actual size of an object to the size of the object in a drawing is called the ___?___ . *(page 315)*

6. The ratio of a number to 100 is called ___?___ . *(page 320)*

Concept Check

7. How does finding an equivalent ratio compare with finding an equivalent fraction? *(page 308)*

8. How can you find the percent of a number? *(page 327)*

9. How can you estimate 24% of $79.99? *(page 330)*

Name the items being compared. *(page 304)*

10. Martha drove 5 mi in 3 hr.

11. The gasoline tank of Hal's car holds 17 gal.

12. There are 100 tissues in a box.

Tell how to find the unit rate or unit price. *(page 306)*

13. a dozen oranges for $2.40

14. $21.00 for 15 gal of gasoline

Tell whether the ratios make a proportion. Write *yes* or *no*.
(pages 310, 312)

15. $\frac{2}{5} ; \frac{5}{15}$

16. $\frac{3}{4} ; \frac{9}{12}$

17. $\frac{8}{1} ; \frac{16}{4}$

18. $\frac{2}{26} ; \frac{4}{50}$

19. $\frac{0.3}{15} ; \frac{1.2}{60}$

20. $\frac{8}{6} ; \frac{200}{150}$

Skill Check

Write the ratio in two other ways. *(page 304)*

21. ten to nine   **22.** $\dfrac{18}{7}$ **23.** $33:46$ **24.** five to three

Find the unit rate. *(page 306)*

25. $1.08 a dozen   **26.** 195 mi per 3 hr   **27.** 960 words per 12 min

Tell whether the ratios are equivalent. Write *yes* or *no.* *(page 308)*

28. $2:9; 15:45$ **29.** $\dfrac{7}{27}; \dfrac{21}{81}$ **30.** $\dfrac{4}{5}; \dfrac{9}{24}$ **31.** $6:16; 42:112$

Write the cross products. *(page 311)*

32. $\dfrac{10}{c} = \dfrac{5}{10}$ **33.** $\dfrac{b}{6} = \dfrac{2}{12}$ **34.** $\dfrac{6}{d} = \dfrac{3}{4}$ **35.** $\dfrac{1}{7} = \dfrac{x}{5}$

Write the decimal or the fraction as a percent. *(pages 322, 324)*

36. 0.04 **37.** $\dfrac{11}{20}$ **38.** $\dfrac{11}{12}$ **39.** $\dfrac{1}{8}$ **40.** 1.3

Estimate. *(page 330)*

41. 63% of 196 **42.** 21% of 27 **43.** 9% of 81

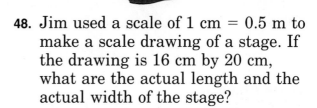

To check a problem, I use my answer and work backward.

Find the percent of the number. *(page 328)*

44. 30% of 30 **45.** 25% of 44 **46.** 20% of 15

Problem-Solving Check *(pages 316, 332)*

47. A movie set covers a 20-m by 25-m area of a soundstage. If a scale drawing of the set is 4 cm by 5 cm, what scale was used?

48. Jim used a scale of 1 cm = 0.5 m to make a scale drawing of a stage. If the drawing is 16 cm by 20 cm, what are the actual length and the actual width of the stage?

49. Sue now has 10 theater tickets that cost $18.95 each. If she sold $227.40 worth of tickets yesterday, how many tickets did she have in the beginning?

50. Jill sold 40 more than 6 times as many rolls of film for $2 each as for $4 each. If she sold a total of $144 worth of film, how many rolls of film did Jill sell at each price?

WHAT DID I LEARN?

1. Explain how to find the ratio of girls to boys in your class. Then find the ratio.

2. The ratio of rainy days to sunny days last month was 2 to 5. Use a proportion to find how many days were rainy if 20 days were sunny. Explain your work.

3. Find a fraction and a decimal equivalent to 60%. Show your work.

4. Use mental math to find 25% of 80. Explain your method.

5. Estimate 48% of 206. Explain your method.

6. Read Exercise 4 on page 333. Follow the steps on the Problem-Solving Think Along worksheet to show how to solve this problem.

Think: A ratio compares two numbers.

Write About It

7. Which lesson or activity in this chapter on ratio, proportion, and percent was the most challenging for you? Explain.

8. Use mental math and benchmark numbers to tell which is greater: 26% of 83 or 51% of 25. Explain your thinking.

TEAMWORK Project

Plan a Commercial

Most television commercials are 30 sec to 1 min long.
Work with your teammates to plan a commercial.

Decide

As a team, discuss different products and decide on a real or make-believe product for your commercial.

Decide on the length of your commercial. Determine the number of frames you will need for filming at 24 frames per second.

Decide on the action in your commercial.

Do

Divide the action into equal parts, and assign each team member a part of the commercial to write.

Describe the action and the roles of the actors. Include in the description the number of frames you will need.

Assemble the parts into one script summary.

Share

Present your summary to other teams. Then watch as other teams present their summaries to you.

Talk About It

What is the difference in the number of frames needed for a 1-min commercial and a 30-sec commercial?

Why do you think commercials are so expensive?

School-Home Connection, page H30

NAVAJO DESIGN

The Navajo are the largest group of Native American people in the United States. Today many Navajo are teachers, engineers, farmers, and technicians.

The Navajo are noted for their use of various geometric patterns on their blankets and rugs.

Look at the Navajo design on the grid. Use a piece of graph paper to enlarge the design.

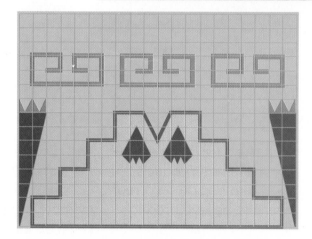

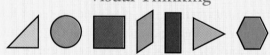

- Describe how you enlarged the design.

- Assume the squares on the graph paper are twice as large as those shown here. What ratio might represent the two drawings?

Write the letter of the correct answer.

1. $7\frac{1}{5} + 2\frac{1}{4}$

   A. $9\frac{1}{9}$ **B.** $9\frac{2}{9}$

   C. $9\frac{9}{20}$ **D.** not here

2. $4\frac{1}{8} - 2\frac{1}{3}$

   A. $1\frac{19}{24}$ **B.** 2

   C. $2\frac{1}{5}$ **D.** $2\frac{19}{24}$

3. Name the appropriate graph for comparing favorite snacks.

   A. bar   **B.** line
   C. circle   **D.** histogram

4. Change to the given unit.
53 cm = ▇ mm

   A. 0.53   **B.** 5.3
   C. 530   **D.** 5,300

5. $5\frac{1}{7} \times \frac{7}{9}$

   A. 4 **B.** $5\frac{1}{9}$

   C. $5\frac{7}{63}$ **D.** 6.6

6. $\frac{7}{8} \div \frac{3}{4}$

   A. $\frac{1}{8}$ **B.** $1\frac{1}{6}$

   C. $1\frac{1}{2}$ **D.** not here

7. Change to the given unit.
240 in. = ▇ ft

   A. 12   **B.** 20
   C. 80   **D.** 2,880

8. Find one cross product of $\frac{6}{8} = \frac{96}{x}$.

   A. 6×96 **B.** $8x$
   C. 6×8 **D.** not here

9. Find the unit rate. $15 for 5

   A. $\frac{3}{1}$ **B.** $\frac{5}{1}$

   C. $\frac{10}{1}$ **D.** $\frac{15}{1}$

10. What is 20% of 80?

   A. 16   **B.** 20

   C. 40   **D.** 160

11. A scale model of a house is 40 cm by 60 cm. The scale used was 4 cm = 1 m. What are the actual dimensions of the house?

   A. 4 m by 6 m   **B.** 10 m by 15 m
   C. 16 m by 24 m   **D.** 40 m by 60 m

12. The ratio of pens to pencils is 9:3. If 1 pencil is added, how many pens must be added to maintain the same ratio?

   A. 1 pen   **B.** 3 pens
   C. 9 pens   **D.** 3:1 pens

CHAPTER 11

GEOMETRY

Did you know...

... that without geometric ideas, you would find it difficult to talk about many concepts in nature that you take for granted?

TALK ABOUT IT

What geometric shapes and relationships can you identify in a daisy?

BASIC IDEAS OF GEOMETRY

The North Star is at the end of the Little Dipper's handle. The stars in the Little Dipper suggest points in planes.

These words and symbols will help you describe geometric figures.

The Little Dipper

C

B

D

A

North Star

Geometric Ideas			
Description	**Example**	**Symbol**	**Read**
A **point** is an exact location.	•P	no symbol	point P
A **line** is a straight path that goes on forever in both directions. It has no endpoints.	A B	$\overleftrightarrow{AB}$ or $\overleftrightarrow{BA}$	line AB or line BA
A **line segment** is part of a line. It has two endpoints.	X Y	$\overline{XY}$ or $\overline{YX}$	line segment XY or line segment YX
A **ray** is part of a line that begins at one endpoint and goes on forever in only one direction.	M N	$\overrightarrow{MN}$	ray MN
An **angle** is formed by two rays that have a common endpoint. The endpoint is the **vertex.**	P M Q	∠PMQ, ∠QMP, or ∠M	angle PMQ, angle QMP, or angle M
A **plane** is a flat surface that goes on forever in all directions.	G F M	no symbol	plane FGM

Talk About It

▶ Look at the picture of the Little Dipper. What geometric figure is suggested by a line from star *A*, through star *B*, continuing forever?

▶ Name objects in nature that suggest a line segment and an angle.

▶ How does knowing these geometric terms help you describe what you see?

Check for Understanding

Name the figure suggested by each in the drawing
of the Little Dipper on page 342.

1. North Star   **2.** *ABC*   **3.** *B* of *ABC*   **4.** *A* to *D*

Practice

Tell what geometric figure is suggested.

5. sunbeam   **6.** straight road   **7.** tabletop   **8.** fork in the road

Use Figure **A** for Exercises 9–10.

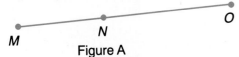

Figure A

9. Name three points.

10. Name three line segments.

Use Figure **B** for Exercises 11–12.

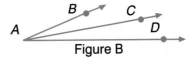

Figure B

11. Name three rays.

12. Name three angles.

Mixed Applications

Use the map for Exercises 13–18. Name the
geometric figure suggested by each example.

13. Brian's house

14. a straight path from Brian's house north

15. path from Brian's house to Betty's house

16. Courtney Street intersected by Elm Drive

17. the baseball field

18. Main Street

19. **Write a Question** Describe Figure **C.** Ask a classmate to draw the figure from your description.

20. To get to school, Tisha must climb steps to walk across an overpass. Is her path in one plane? Explain.

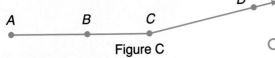

Figure C

Can a line segment be part of a ray?

Sometimes we do not think about the fact that points and lines make up much of what we see around us. Lines are everywhere in nature and everyday life, even in these crystals.

These words and symbols will help you describe the relationships among lines.

Description	Example	Symbol	Read
Parallel lines are lines in a plane that are always the same distance apart. They never intersect and have no common points.		$\overleftrightarrow{AB} \parallel \overleftrightarrow{CD}$	Line *AB* is parallel to line *CD*.
Intersecting lines are lines that cross at exactly one point.		no symbol	Line *RS* intersects line *PQ* at point *X*.
Perpendicular lines are lines that intersect to form 90° angles, or right angles.		$\overleftrightarrow{EF} \perp \overleftrightarrow{GH}$	Line *EF* is perpendicular to line *GH*.
Skew lines are not parallel and do not intersect. Skew lines are in different planes.		no symbol	Line *AB* and line *CE* are skew lines.

Talk About It

▶ In the cerussite crystal, what relationship is suggested by $\overline{AB}$ and $\overline{CD}$?

▶ What relationship is suggested by $\overline{EF}$ and $\overline{GH}$?

▶ What relationship is suggested by $\overline{AB}$ and $\overline{EF}$?

▶ What relationship is suggested by $\overline{JK}$ and $\overline{LM}$?

▶ If two lines are in the same plane, must they be either intersecting or parallel? Explain.

Constructing Congruent Line Segments

All line segments of the same length are **congruent.**

Place the compass point on point A. Open the compass to the length of $\overline{AB}$. Without changing the compass opening, move the compass to an endpoint of $\overline{EF}$. Use the compass to measure the length of $\overline{EF}$.

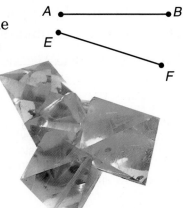

Talk About It

▶ What is the relationship between the length of $\overline{AB}$ and the length of $\overline{EF}$?

_____

You can use a compass and a straightedge to construct congruent line segments. Trace $\overline{AB}$.

Construct a line segment congruent to $\overline{AB}$.

Step 1	**Step 2**	**Step 3**
Draw a ray that is longer than $\overline{AB}$. Label the endpoint C.	Place the compass point on point A. Open the compass to the length of $\overline{AB}$.	Using the same opening, put the compass point on point C. Make a mark where the compass meets the ray. Label it X.
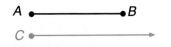	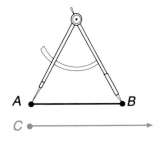	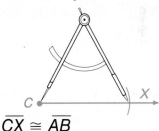 $\overline{CX} \cong \overline{AB}$ $\cong$ means "is congruent to."

Talk About It

▶ In Step 1, why should you draw the ray longer than $\overline{AB}$ instead of shorter than $\overline{AB}$?

▶ Why might you need to know how to construct a pair of congruent line segments?

▶ What are some examples of congruent line segments that you can see in your classroom?

▶ What are some careers in which people must know how to construct geometric figures?

Bisecting a Line Segment

You can also use a compass and a straightedge to bisect a line segment. When you **bisect** a line segment, you divide it into two equal segments. Trace $\overline{RS}$.

Bisect $\overline{RS}$. R •———————• S

Step 1
Place the compass point on point R. Open the compass to a little more than half the distance from R to S on $\overline{RS}$. Draw an arc through $\overline{RS}$ as shown.

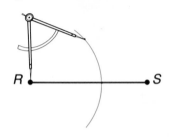

Step 2
Keep the same compass opening. Place the compass point on point S. Draw an arc as shown. Label the points T and U where the arcs intersect.

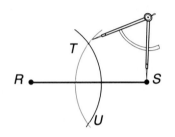

Step 3
Use a straightedge to draw a line from T to U. Label the point P where $\overline{TU}$ intersects $\overline{RS}$.

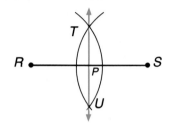

$\overline{TU}$ bisects $\overline{RS}$.

Talk About It

▶ Would you describe $\overline{RS}$ and $\overline{TU}$ as parallel or intersecting?

▶ $\angle TPS$, $\angle SPU$, $\angle UPR$, and $\angle RPT$ are right angles. How many degrees are in each angle?

▶ In addition to intersecting, what other line relationship exists between $\overline{RS}$ and $\overline{TU}$?

Check for Understanding

Look at objects in your classroom. Find examples of these relationships among lines.

1. intersecting   **2.** parallel   **3.** perpendicular   **4.** skew

Tell whether $\overline{XY}$ bisects the line segment. Write *yes* or *no*.

5.

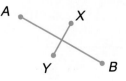

6.

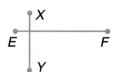

7.

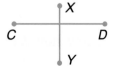

8.

Practice

Tell what the blue symbol means.

9. $\overrightarrow{CD}$ **10.** $\angle ABC$ **11.** $\overline{AB}$ **12.** $\overrightarrow{AB}$ **13.** $\overleftrightarrow{EF}$

14. $\overleftrightarrow{KL} \perp \overleftrightarrow{MN}$ **15.** $\overline{RS} \| \overline{TU}$ **16.** $\angle D$ **17.** $\overline{DE} \perp \overline{FG}$ **18.** $\overleftrightarrow{PQ} \| \overleftrightarrow{RS}$

Use the drawing for Exercises 19–22.
Tell whether the lines are parallel or skew.

19. $\overleftrightarrow{CD}$ and $\overleftrightarrow{GH}$ **20.** $\overleftrightarrow{BC}$ and $\overleftrightarrow{EH}$

21. $\overleftrightarrow{EF}$ and $\overleftrightarrow{CG}$ **22.** $\overleftrightarrow{AE}$ and $\overleftrightarrow{GH}$

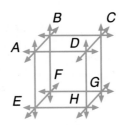

Use a compass and a straightedge.

23. Construct $\overline{AB}$ congruent to $\overline{MN}$.   M •————————• N

24. Use $\overline{AB}$, which you constructed in Exercise 23. Now, bisect $\overline{AB}$. Label point P where the lines intersect.

25. What is the relationship between $\overline{AP}$ and $\overline{PB}$?

Mixed Applications

Use the drawing for Exercises 26–31. Find two examples of each.

26. angle

27. plane

28. parallel lines

29. perpendicular lines

30. intersecting lines

31. skew lines

32. Dan has striped wallpaper in his dining room. There are 125 stripes along one wall. If 60% of the stripes are blue, how many stripes along the wall are blue?

33. $\overline{AB} \perp \overline{CD}$, $\overline{AB} \perp \overline{EF}$, and $\overline{GH} \perp \overline{CD}$. What is the relationship between $\overline{AB}$ and $\overline{GH}$?

What relationship exists between the two line segments of a bisected line segment?

More Practice, Lesson 11.2, page H74

347

EXPLORING

Angles

Look at this clock. What geometric shape is suggested by the hands?

You can use a clock to help you visualize angles.

Angles are measured in degrees.

An acute angle is less than 90°.

A right angle is 90°.

⌐ means 90° angle.

An obtuse angle is more than 90° and less than 180°.

A straight angle is 180°.

Building Understanding

You can use a protractor to measure angles.

A. Trace the angle formed by the hands on the clock and extend the hands.

B. Place the base of the protractor along the hour hand, with the center of the base at the vertex.

C. Read the protractor scale from right to left, starting at 0, to find the measure of the angle.

TALK ABOUT IT
- What is the measure of the angle formed by the clock hands? What type of angle is it?

- How could you use a protractor to measure the angle formed by the unshaded area on the clock? What is the measure of this angle?

- How could you find the total number of degrees around the clock?

- How many degrees are around the clock? Will any circle have the same number of degrees?

Try This

Use a protractor and a straightedge to draw an acute angle, a right angle, and an obtuse angle. Label the rays and write the number of degrees.

Making the Connection

Angles in the same plane sometimes show special relationships with one another, just as lines in the same plane show special relationships.

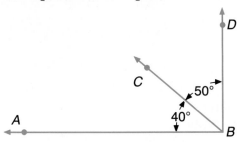

Complementary angles are two angles whose sum is 90°.

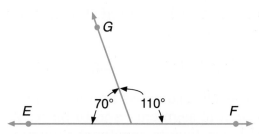

Supplementary angles are two angles whose sum is 180°.

Not all supplementary or complementary angles share the same ray. The sum of the measures of ∠*JKL* and ∠*MNO* is 90°. So, ∠*JKL* and ∠*MNO* are complementary. The sum of the measures of ∠*PQR* and ∠*STU* is 180°. So, ∠*PQR* and ∠*STU* are supplementary.

Trace the angles and extend the rays.
Find the measure of each angle.

1.

2.

3.

4. Which two angles form complementary angles?

5. Which two angles form supplementary angles?

Checking Understanding

Measure the angles. Write *acute*, *right*, or *obtuse*.

6.

7.

8.

9.

10.

11.

12. Use a protractor to draw two complementary angles.

13. Use a protractor to draw two supplementary angles.

CONSTRUCTING
Congruent Angles

The shapes of the two large peaks suggest congruent angles.

● You know what congruent line segments are. What are congruent angles?

● What other objects in nature suggest congruent angles?

You have used a compass and a straightedge to construct congruent line segments and to bisect a line segment. Now you will learn how to construct congruent angles.

Trace ∠XYZ. Construct an angle congruent to ∠XYZ.

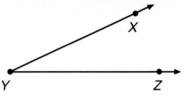

Step 1
Draw $\overrightarrow{MN}$.

Step 2
Draw an arc through ∠XYZ.

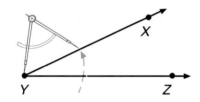

Step 3
Use the same opening to draw an arc through $\overrightarrow{MN}$.

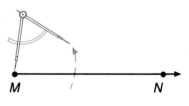

Step 4
Use a compass to measure the arc.

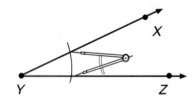

Step 5
Use the same opening to locate point O.

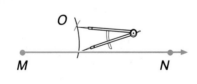

Step 6
Draw $\overrightarrow{MO}$.

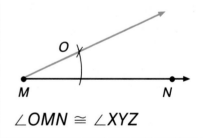

∠OMN ≅ ∠XYZ

Check for Understanding

Use a protractor to measure each pair of angles. Tell whether the two angles are congruent. Write *yes* or *no*.

1.

2.

3.

350

Practice

Use a protractor to measure each pair of angles. Tell whether
the angles are congruent. Write *yes* or *no.*

4. 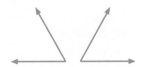 **5.**  **6.**

Use a compass and a straightedge.

7. Construct $\angle ABC \cong \angle XYZ$.

8. Construct $\angle DEF \cong \angle UVW$.

9. Construct $\angle GHI \cong \angle RST$.

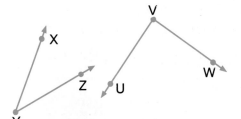

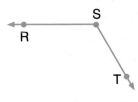

Mixed Applications

Use a protractor and the drawing of the kite for Exercises 10–16.

10. What is the relationship of $\overline{AB}$ to $\overline{CD}$?

11. Name a pair of complementary angles.

12. Name a pair of supplementary angles.

13. Name two acute angles whose vertex is B.

14. Name two obtuse angles.

15. Name one right angle whose vertex is not E.

16. Number Sense How do you know the measure of $\angle CAD$
is the sum of the measures of $\angle CAB$ and $\angle BAD$?

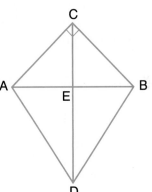

MIXED REVIEW

Tell whether the ratios make a proportion. Write *yes* or *no.*

1. $\dfrac{1}{3}$; $\dfrac{4}{12}$ **2.** $\dfrac{1}{2}$; $\dfrac{14}{24}$ **3.** $\dfrac{5}{3}$; $\dfrac{25}{12}$ **4.** $\dfrac{32}{28}$; $\dfrac{8}{7}$ **5.** $\dfrac{2}{4}$; $\dfrac{25}{50}$

Tell what the blue symbols mean.

6. $\overline{CD}$ **7.** $\angle ABC$ **8.** $\overleftrightarrow{EF} \parallel \overleftrightarrow{GH}$ **9.** $\overline{JK} \perp \overline{LM}$ **10.** $\overrightarrow{DE}$

Explain how to construct
congruent angles.

WRAP UP...

PROBLEM SOLVING

Make a Circle Graph

Mr. Morris's hobby is mineralogy. He hunts for minerals in his spare time. His collection includes 55% nuggets, 35% crystals, and 10% fibers. How can he present this information in a graph?

▶ **UNDERSTAND**

What are you asked to do?

What facts are you given?

▶ **PLAN**

How will you solve the problem?
You can make a circle graph.

▶ **SOLVE**

How can you carry out your plan?

First you must find the number of degrees represented by each percent. Since there are 360° in a circle, multiply each percent by 360° to find the number of degrees for each type of mineral.

Write each percent as a decimal. Then multiply.

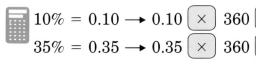

$10\% = 0.10 \rightarrow 0.10 \boxed{\times} 360 \boxed{=}$ | 36. | ← fibers, 36°
$35\% = 0.35 \rightarrow 0.35 \boxed{\times} 360 \boxed{=}$ | 126. | ← crystals, 126°
$55\% = 0.55 \rightarrow 0.55 \boxed{\times} 360 \boxed{=}$ | 198. | ← nuggets, 198°

Make the graph. Use a compass to draw a circle. Draw one radius. Place the center of the base of a protractor on the center of the circle and an edge along the radius.

1. Draw a 36° angle.

2. Place the protractor on the new radius. Draw a 126° angle.

3. Title and label the graph.

• Why did you not have to draw the last angle?

Forms of Minerals

crystals 35%
fibers 10%
nuggets 55%

▶ **LOOK BACK**

What other type of display could you use?

WHAT IF...

... 25% of the minerals are nuggets, 50% are crystals, and 25% are fibers? How many degrees would be needed to represent each in a circle graph?

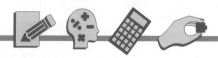

Apply

(1) Dennis determines that when he goes fishing, he catches large fish 5% of the time, medium fish 60%, small fish 25%, and no fish 10% of the time. Make a circle graph showing what happens when Dennis goes fishing.

(2) Suppose that the U.S. gross national product (GNP) for this year indicates that industry accounts for 40%, services for 45%, and agriculture for 15%. Make a circle graph showing this GNP.

Mixed Applications ▷ **STRATEGIES**

Choose a strategy and solve.
Use the graph for Exercises 3–5.

(3) If there are 300 flowers in the garden, how many are zinnias?

(4) If there are 100 flowers in the garden, how many are either marigolds or zinnias?

(5) If there are 60 tulips in the garden, how many daisies are there?

Make a Circle Graph • Work Backward • Write an Equation • Guess and Check

Julie's Flower Garden

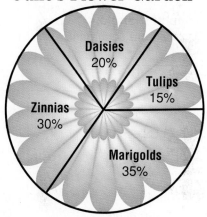

Daisies 20%
Tulips 15%
Zinnias 30%
Marigolds 35%

(6) In all, 70 girls and boys belong to Shell-Finders' Club. The ratio of boys to girls is 3:11. How many boys and how many girls are in the club?

(7) Maria spent $260 on clam-digging equipment. She sold her first catch for $350. If she spends 10% of her profit on more equipment, how many dollars will she spend?

(8) The Simons had $3,000 in savings. They added $460 in June and then spent 25% of the total to buy camping equipment for a family vacation. How much is left in the Simons' savings account?

(9) Pete and Dan went fishing with their father. Pete caught 5 more fish than his father. His father caught 2 fewer fish than Dan, who caught 5 fish. How many fish did Pete and his father each catch?

(10) Lita divides her rock collection according to shape. She has 12 cone-shaped, 44 spherical, 8 triangular, 32 fan-shaped, and 4 oddly shaped rocks. Make a circle graph for the shapes.

(11) Rich is a forester. He planted 25 trees one day and 36 the next day. He gave Tina 62 trees. He gave Sam $\frac{1}{2}$ as many as he planted the second day. If Rich will plant the remaining 46 trees tomorrow, how many trees did he have before he began to plant?

TRIANGLES

The shape of these pines suggests a certain triangle. A **triangle** is a three-sided closed plane figure whose sides are line segments. A triangle can be named by its vertices. The table shows how to classify triangles by sides and by angles.

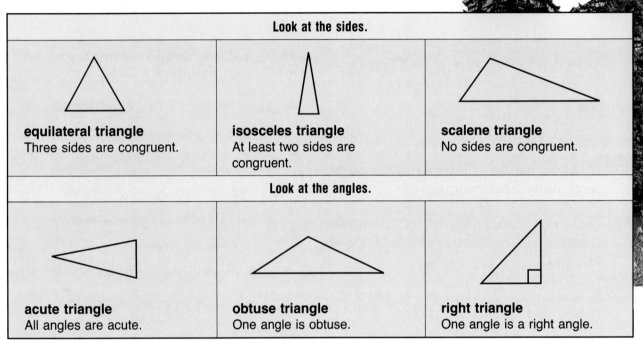

Look at the sides.		
equilateral triangle Three sides are congruent.	**isosceles triangle** At least two sides are congruent.	**scalene triangle** No sides are congruent.

Look at the angles.		
acute triangle All angles are acute.	**obtuse triangle** One angle is obtuse.	**right triangle** One angle is a right angle.

Work Together

Trace three of the triangles in the chart. Extend the sides so that you can use a protractor to measure each angle. Record the measure of each angle. Then label the angles.

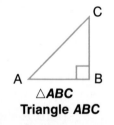

$\triangle ABC$
Triangle *ABC*

Talk About It

▶ What is the sum of the measures of the angles of each of the three triangles you traced and measured?

▶ What conclusion can you draw about the sum of the measures of the angles of a triangle?

▶ The measure of one angle of triangle *ABC* is 90°, and the measure of another angle is 45°. What is the measure of the third angle of $\triangle ABC$?

▶ How can a triangle be both right and isosceles?

▶ Can a triangle be both right and equilateral?

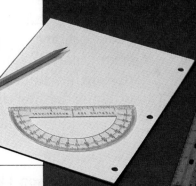

Check for Understanding

Classify the triangle by the sides and then the angles.

1. $9\frac{1}{2}$ 8 2

2. 5 3 5

3. 5 5 5

4. 7 5 5

Practice

Use the drawing for Exercises 5–10. Find and name each type of triangle.

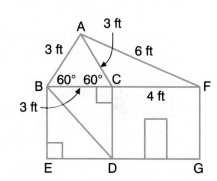

5. equilateral

6. scalene

7. acute

8. right

9. obtuse

10. isosceles

Write the measure of the third angle of the triangle.

11. $100°, 35°, \blacksquare°$

12. $90°, 60°, \blacksquare°$

13. $45°, 45°, \blacksquare°$

14. $25°, 15°, \blacksquare°$

Mixed Applications

15. Don is building a birdhouse of equilateral triangles. The angles of an equilateral triangle are congruent. What is the measure of each angle?

16. **Visual Thinking** Name several examples where triangles are used in the structure and design of homes and other buildings with which you are familiar.

CHALLENGE

In the triangle, ∠1, ∠2, and ∠3 are **exterior** angles. ∠4 is an **interior** angle. ∠1 is supplementary to ∠4.

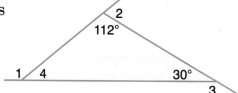

17. What is the sum of the measures of the angles of a triangle?

18. What is the measure of ∠4?

19. What is the sum of the measures of supplementary angles?

20. What is the measure of ∠1?

21. What is the sum of the measures of the exterior angles?

Can one of the interior angles of a right triangle be obtuse?

EXPLORING

Other Polygons

A **polygon** is a closed plane figure whose sides are line segments. Polygons are classified by the number of their sides and angles.

Common Polygons	
Name	**Sides and Angles**
Triangle	3
Quadrilateral	4
Pentagon	5
Hexagon	6
Octagon	8

Work Together

Building Understanding

Use geoboards and rubber bands to model examples of each type of polygon. Copy your polygons on dot paper.

TALK ABOUT IT

- Compare your models with those of other classmates. How are your polygons similar or different?

- How many different types of triangles can you model on the geoboard?

Just as there are many types of triangles, there are many types of quadrilaterals.

Quadrilaterals				
parallelogram	**rectangle**	**rhombus**	**square**	**trapezoid**
Opposite sides parallel and congruent	Parallelogram that has four right angles	Parallelogram that has four congruent sides	Rectangle that has four congruent sides	Only two sides parallel

Use geoboards and rubber bands to model examples of each type of quadrilateral. Copy them on dot paper.

TALK ABOUT IT

- Model a quadrilateral that has no congruent sides, no right angles, and no parallel sides. How is this quadrilateral similar to the quadrilaterals above?

- How can you change your trapezoid model to a parallelogram model?

Making the Connection

A **diagonal** is a line segment that joins two vertices (plural of *vertex*) of a polygon but is not a side. A diagonal can be used to divide a polygon into two new polygons.

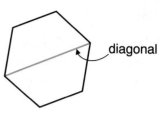
diagonal

1. What new polygons are formed by the diagonal in the hexagon?

A **regular polygon** has all sides congruent and all angles congruent.

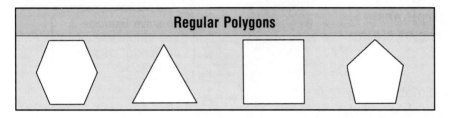

Regular Polygons

2. Which regular polygons can you draw on dot paper?

Checking Understanding

Name the quadrilateral.

3. 4 right angles, 4 congruent sides

4. 2 sides parallel, 2 sides not parallel

5. opposite sides congruent and parallel

6. 4 right angles, 2 congruent sides

7. 4 congruent sides

8. right angles, opposite sides congruent

Name the new figures formed by the diagonal $\overline{AD}$.

9.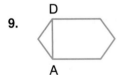

10.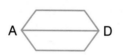

11.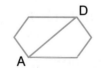

12.

Tell whether the figure is a regular polygon. Write *yes* or *no*.

13.

14.

15.

1. When Tom goes for walks in the desert, he applies 10 mL of sunscreen every 30 min. If he used 35 mL of sunscreen today, how many hours did he walk?

2. Sue mixed 4 oz of strawberries with 8 oz of yogurt. She added 2 oz of banana slices. How much yogurt must she add to keep the ratio of fruit to yogurt 1 to 2?

3. A circle graph shows stamps in a collection. It shows 144° for animal stamps, 108° for flowers, and 54° each for ships and for airplanes. What percent of each type of stamp is in the collection?

To solve Exercise 3, I need to know the number of degrees in a circle.

Write as a percent or as a decimal.

4. 0.81 **5.** 0.2 **6.** 1.52 **7.** 18% **8.** 108%

Write as a percent or as a fraction in simplest form.

9. $\frac{1}{4}$ **10.** $\frac{7}{10}$ **11.** 12% **12.** $\frac{3}{8}$ **13.** 35%

Estimate.

14. 53% of 110 **15.** 29% of 280 **16.** 81% of 27 **17.** 62% of 112

Find the percent of the number.

18. 30% of 30 **19.** 10% of 80 **20.** 6% of 20 **21.** 200% of 50

Write the symbol for each figure.

22. ray *AB* **23.** angle *CDE* **24.** line *FG* **25.** triangle *HIJ*

Name the angle. Write *acute, right, obtuse,* or *straight.*

26. 110° **27.** 90° **28.** 25° **29.** 180° **30.** 91°

Name the figure.

31. 3 congruent sides, 3 congruent angles

32. one of 3 angles obtuse

33. none of 3 sides congruent

34. only 2 of 4 sides parallel

35. parallelogram with 4 right angles

36. rectangle with 4 congruent sides

Making a Part Whole

Sometimes archaeologists find only partial remains of pottery or other decorative objects. They may use a fragment of a geometric design to re-create the design that probably covered the entire piece. Mirror images (reflections) are often used to complete the design.

The use of calabash gourds as decorative objects has a long tradition in Nigeria. The gourds are dried, cut, and decorated for use as food bowls or even as the base for a type of musical instrument. Intricate geometric designs are carved into the bowls.

MULTICULTURAL NOTE: These Nigerian bowls were made from calabash gourds.

Suppose each of the two pieces of calabash bowls below shows only one fourth of the whole design. Copy each partial design on graph paper. Use mirror images to create a drawing of each whole design.

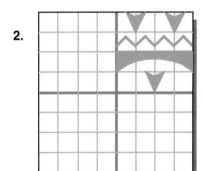

1.

2.

3. Create one fourth of a design on graph paper, and have your partner complete the design, using mirror images.

SIMILAR AND CONGRUENT FIGURES

These photos show different sizes of the same image, Mount Kilimanjaro. Are the images similar or congruent?

Congruent figures have the same size and shape. **Similar** figures have the same shape. Two shapes that are congruent are also similar. However, two similar shapes may not be congruent.

Since the images are the same shape but not the same size, they are similar but not congruent.

- Think of the relationship of any one circle to any other circle. Are the circles similar or congruent?

Work Together

Discover the relationship among the sides and among the angles of similar polygons.

1. Draw any polygon. Label it *A*.

2. Make a transparency of *A*. Show it on a wall by using an overhead projector. Trace the image on a sheet of paper. Label the tracing *B*.

3. Use a ruler to measure the length of the sides and a protractor to measure the angles of polygons *A* and *B*.

Talk About It

▶ Do you think polygons *A* and *B* are similar? Why?

▶ Are the sides of polygon *A* congruent to the sides of polygon *B*? Are the angles of polygon *A* congruent to the angles of polygon *B*?

▶ What conclusion can you draw about similar polygons?

▶ Is a square a regular polygon? How do you know?

▶ Are all squares congruent? similar? How do you know?

▶ Are all regular polygons that have the same number of sides congruent? How do you know?

▶ What conclusions can you draw about regular polygons that have the same number of sides?

MULTICULTURAL NOTE:
Coffee beans, corn, and bananas are grown at elevations of 4,000 to 6,000 feet on the slopes of Mount Kilimanjaro.

Check for Understanding

Tell which pairs of figures are similar and which are congruent.

1.

2.

3.

4.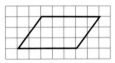

5.

6.

Practice

Using graph paper, draw two figures. Make one similar but not congruent to the one shown. Make the other figure congruent to the one shown.

7.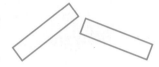

8.

9.

10.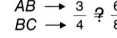

Mixed Applications

11. How many 1-in.-square tiles do you need to cover a square with 20-in. sides? How many 2-in.-square tiles?

12. **Write a Question** Think of objects in your surroundings. Write a question that can be answered with either *similar* or *congruent*.

MATH CONNECTION

If the ratios of the lengths of their matching sides are equivalent, two polygons are similar.

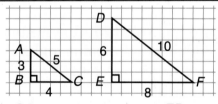

$AB \rightarrow \dfrac{3}{4} \overset{?}{=} \dfrac{6}{8} \leftarrow DE$
$BC \rightarrow$

$\dfrac{3}{4} \overset{?}{=} \dfrac{6}{8}$

$24 = 24$

$BC \rightarrow \dfrac{4}{5} \overset{?}{=} \dfrac{8}{10} \leftarrow EF$
$CA \rightarrow$

$\dfrac{4}{5} \overset{?}{=} \dfrac{8}{10}$

$40 = 40$

$CA \rightarrow \dfrac{5}{3} \overset{?}{=} \dfrac{10}{6} \leftarrow FD$
$AB \rightarrow$

$\dfrac{5}{3} \overset{?}{=} \dfrac{10}{6}$

$30 = 30$

So, the triangles are similar.

Tell whether the polygons are similar. Write *yes* or *no*. If not, tell why.

13.

14.

15.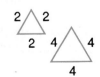

SYMMETRY

The butterfly's wings show how symmetry exists in nature.

A figure has **line symmetry** if it can be folded into congruent parts that match exactly. The fold line is the **line of symmetry.**

Which of these letters have line symmetry?

A B C D E F G

Since *A, B, C, D,* and *E* can be folded into two congruent parts, they have line symmetry.

Some figures have two or more lines of symmetry.

Olivine Crystal

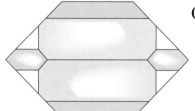

Snowflake

• How many lines of symmetry does the crystal have? the snowflake?

Trace the crystal and the snowflake. Cut out the tracings and place them on top of the original figures.

A figure has **rotational symmetry** if it can be turned less than 360° around a point and still match the original.

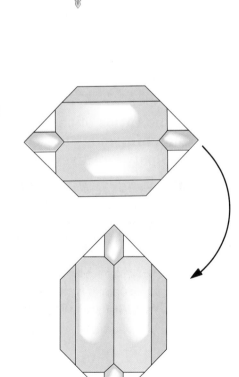

Talk About It

▶ Turn the crystal and the snowflake 90°. Are the images the same as the original images?

▶ Turn the crystal 180°. Is its image the same as the original image?

▶ How do you know that the crystal and the snowflake have rotational symmetry?

▶ Think of a circle. Does a circle have line symmetry? How do you know?

▶ How do you know a circle has rotational symmetry?

Check for Understanding

Tell whether the dotted lines are lines of symmetry. Write *yes* or *no*.

1.   **2.**   **3.**   **4.**

Practice

Trace the figure. Then draw the lines of symmetry.

5.   **6.**  **7.**  **8.**

Trace the figures. Then complete them to make figures that are symmetric. Name the figures you have made.

9.   **10.**   **11.**   **12.**

Tell whether the figure has rotational symmetry. Write *yes* or *no*.

13.  **14.**   **15.**   **16.**

Mixed Applications

17. Name three common items you can find in your classroom that have line symmetry and three items that have rotational symmetry.

18. Sophia has a round of cheese. Her brother challenges her to cut it into 8 congruent pieces with only 3 cuts. How can she do this?

19. Number Sense Write a ratio that compares the number of lines of symmetry with the number of sides of a square.

20. Critical Thinking Use only capital letters that have line symmetry to solve the puzzle.
T▮E ▮EST P▮RT ▮F SC▮O▮L IS ▮AT▮.

Why must the rotation be less than 360° to be an example of rotational symmetry?

WRAP UP...

TRANSLATIONS, ROTATIONS, AND REFLECTIONS

This is what a new sign on a window looked like from inside the store. Alex's boss, Mr. Weeks, was not happy. Do you know why?

Mr. Weeks was unhappy because people approaching the store could not read the sign.

You can move a geometric figure three ways.

You can slide the figure along straight lines. This is called a **translation.**

You can turn the figure around a point. This is called a **rotation.**

You can flip the figure over a line. This is called a **reflection.**

Translation   Rotation   Reflection

Draw a block-letter T on a sheet of paper and cut it out. Use the T and graph paper to show translations, rotations, and reflections. Place the T on the graph paper and trace around it to record a starting position.

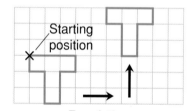

Translation
A. Slide the T five units right and three units up.

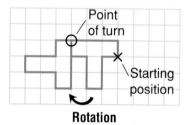

Rotation
B. Hold the corner of the T and turn 90°.

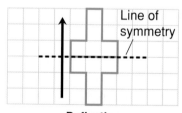

Reflection
C. Flip the T over a line of symmetry.

Talk About It

▶ How does the size of the figure change when you slide, turn, or flip it?

▶ How does the shape of the figure change when you slide, turn, or flip it?

▶ Is the original figure similar or congruent to the final figure? Explain.

▶ What are some practical ways you use translations, rotations, and reflections in everyday life?

Check for Understanding

Tell whether the second figure is a translation, a rotation, or a reflection.

1.

2.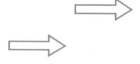

3.

4.

5.

6.

Practice

Read the description of how the figure has been moved. Write *true* or *false*.

7.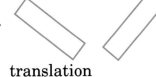

translation

8.

rotation

9.

reflection

10.

translation

11.

rotation

12.

reflection

Trace and label a translation, a rotation, and a reflection of the given figure.

13.

14.

15.

16.

Mixed Application

17. Critical Thinking Hector was fishing at a lake. He saw his reflection when he looked into the water. He moved to the right. Which way did his reflection move?

18. Of Alice's 50 drawings, $\frac{3}{5}$ are reflections. How many of the drawings are reflections?

Can you think of a word that would look the same before and after a flip?

WRAP UP...

SOLID FIGURES

Solid figures exist in more than two planes. These gold crystals display cube-like figures.

A solid figure can be made from polygons, circles, and curved surfaces.

In a solid figure made from polygons, each polygon is a **face**, the faces meet to form **edges**, and the edges meet to form **vertices**. The solid figure rests on a **base** and is named by the shape of the base.

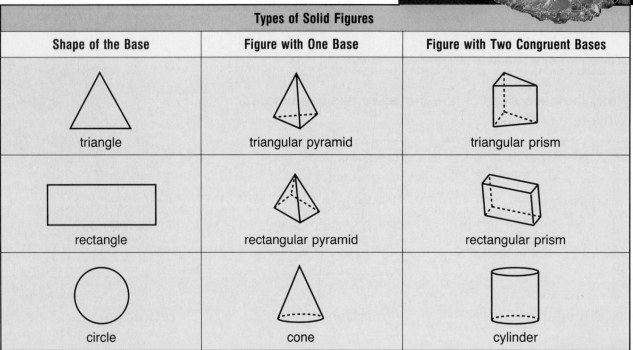

Types of Solid Figures		
Shape of the Base	**Figure with One Base**	**Figure with Two Congruent Bases**
triangle	triangular pyramid	triangular prism
rectangle	rectangular pyramid	rectangular prism
circle	cone	cylinder

Talk About It

▶ A cube has six square faces. What type of prism is a cube?

▶ Is a cylinder more like a prism or a pyramid?

▶ Is a cone more like a prism or a pyramid?

▶ What is the difference between a hexagonal pyramid and a hexagonal prism?

▶ Which has more faces, an octagonal prism or an octagonal pyramid?

▶ A solid figure is made up of four triangles. What is it?

366

Check for Understanding

Name the figure.

1.

2.

3.

4.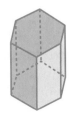

Practice

Complete the table by naming the type of solid figure.

	Type of Solid Figure	Number of Bases and Faces	Number of Edges	Number of Vertices
5.	■	2 square bases 4 square faces	12	8
6.	■	1 base 3 other faces	6	4
7.	■	2 bases	none	none
8.	■	2 bases 5 other faces	15	10
9.	■	2 bases 6 other faces	18	12
10.	■	2 rectangular bases 4 other faces	12	8

Mixed Applications

11. Della has 30 pieces of igneous rock in her collection. If 60% of her collection is igneous rock, how many rocks does she have in her collection?

12. **Critical Thinking** Why do you think contractors choose materials in the shape of prisms rather than pyramids to build walls?

MIXED REVIEW

Write the ratio. Then find the unit rate or unit price.

1. $12 for 3

2. 90 per 2 min

3. $24 a dozen

4. 420 mi per 12 gal

Why is food stored in cans instead of cone-shaped containers?

More Practice, Lesson 11.11, page H77

EXPLORING

Stretching, Shrinking, and Twisting

What would happen if you drew a square on a piece of elastic and then stretched the elastic? What would the square look like?

In this lesson, you will explore what happens when you change the shape of a figure.

Work Together

Building Understanding

Use a geoboard, a ruler, and rubber bands.

A. Place a rubber band on the center peg of the top row of the geoboard. Loop the rubber band around the second and fourth pegs of the fourth row of the geoboard.

B. Measure the length of each side of the triangle.

C. Now stretch the triangle by moving the rubber band from the fourth row to the first and last pegs of the fifth row.

D. Measure the length of each side of the stretched triangle.

E. Now shrink the triangle by moving the rubber band from the last row to the second and fourth pegs of the third row.

F. Measure the length of each side of this reduced triangle.

TALK ABOUT IT

• How is the stretched triangle the same as the original triangle? How is it different?

• How is the reduced triangle the same as the original triangle? How is it different?

• Suppose you drew a square on a balloon and then blew up the balloon. What would happen to the square?

• Suppose you drew a circle on an inflated balloon and then let out the air. What would happen to the circle?

Making the Connection

Twisting is a more complex way to change the shape of a figure than stretching or shrinking. Cut newspaper into three strips that are each 3 in. wide by 18 in. long.

Tape the ends of one strip together, making a loop. Draw a line down the center of the outside surface.

Twist the ends of another strip one time and then tape them together, making a second loop. Draw a line down the center of the outside surface.

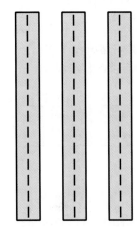

1. How does the line on the second loop differ from the line on the first loop?

Cut along the center line of each loop.

2. What happens to the first loop? the second loop?

Twist the ends of the last strip two times and then tape them together, making a third loop. Draw a line down the center of the outside surface.

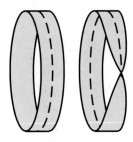

3. Is the line on the third loop like the line on the first loop or the line on the second loop?

Cut along the center line of the third loop.

4. What happens to the third loop?

5. A conveyor belt is one example of twisting rectangles. Where are conveyor belts used? You may want to use an encyclopedia.

Checking Understanding

Use a geoboard and rubber bands. Begin with a 3-by-3 square. Make changes as directed. Then name the new shape.

6. Stretch both bases the same amount.

7. Stretch both ends of one base the same amount.

8. Shrink one base to a point.

9. Move one base to the left or right without stretching or shrinking it.

PROBLEM SOLVING

STRATEGY • Find a Pattern

The Incas of South America are noted for their innovative use of geometric designs. The design below is similar to a design on a piece of Incan tapestry. A pattern has been created by using translations, reflections, and rotations of the design. Eight images in the pattern are shown. What will be the ninth image?

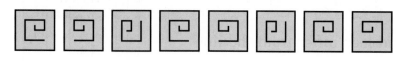

▶ UNDERSTAND

What are you asked to find?

What information are you given?

▶ PLAN

How will you solve the problem?
You must *find the pattern* in the series of images.

▶ SOLVE

How will you carry out your plan?

You can copy and number the images and then compare each image to the one before.

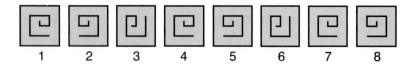

1. original design	3. reflection/rotation	5. reflection	7. rotation
2. reflection	4. rotation	6. reflection/rotation	8. reflection

The pattern is reflection, reflection/rotation, rotation. The eighth image is a reflection.

So, the ninth image in the series will be a reflection/rotation.

▶ LOOK BACK

What other strategy could you use?

MULTICULTURAL NOTE: The Incas were skilled in metalworking, carving, weaving, and pottery. Many beautiful Incan designs have been found by explorers and archaeologists.

 **WHAT IF...** ...you are asked to find the thirteenth image? What will be your answer?

Apply

1 Monty watches birds daily. Monday he saw 2 wrens, Tuesday he saw 5 wrens, Wednesday he saw 3 wrens, Thursday he saw 6 wrens, and Friday he saw 4 wrens. If the pattern continues, how many wrens will he see Sunday?

2 Kay is using black tiles and gray tiles to cover her floor. If the pattern she uses is B, G, B, B, G, B, B, G, B, B, what will be the color of the twentieth tile?

Mixed Applications ➔ **STRATEGIES** | **Write an Equation • Find a Pattern • Work Backward • Draw a Diagram**

Choose a strategy and solve.

3 A triangular prism has 6 vertices. A rectangular prism has 8. How many vertices are there in a 12-sided prism?

4 A certain pyramid has 9 faces, including its base. What is the shape of the pyramid's base?

5 Jane buys 5 gal of gasoline to travel 135 mi. Sally's car uses gasoline at the same rate. How much gasoline must Sally buy to take a 675-mi trip to the mountains?

6 Rangers found that $\frac{3}{4}$ of the giraffes in an African animal preserve stay in one area. What percent of the giraffes do not stay in that area?

7 Paul made a flower bed in the shape of an equilateral triangle. Then he divided the triangle, using all possible lines of symmetry. If he plants 1 rose in each of the newly formed triangles, how many roses will he need?

8 Mrs. Smith went to a nursery, where she spent $5.30 for pansies, $3.98 for daisies, $6.75 for begonias, and $11.50 for geraniums. If she had $22.47 when she returned home, how much money did she take with her when she went to the nursery?

9 Don sends messages to Greg, using a secret code: A=2, B=3, C=6, D=8, E=9, F=12, G=14, H=15, I=18, and J=20. If the pattern continues, how would Don use the code to write the word *school*?

10 Carrie's aunt sent her some samples of moon rocks. Carrie gave half to her brother and divided the rest equally among herself and 2 friends. She has 6 rocks left. How many rocks did her aunt send?

WRITER'S CORNER

11 Create a pattern. Then write a problem that can be solved by finding and extending the pattern.

More Practice, Lesson 11.13, page H77

Vocabulary Check

Choose a word or words from the box to complete each sentence.

> congruent
> diagonal
> isosceles
> obtuse
> perpendicular
> plane
> polygon
> ray
> rotational
> similar
> skew

1. A part of a line that begins at one endpoint and goes on forever in one direction is called a(n) __?__ . *(page 342)*

2. A flat surface that goes on forever in all directions is a(n) __?__ . *(page 342)*

3. An angle that is more than 90° but less than 180° is __?__ . *(page 348)*

4. Two lines that intersect to form right angles are __?__ lines. *(page 344)*

5. A closed plane figure whose sides are line segments is a(n) __?__ . *(page 356)*

6. Figures with the same size and shape are __?__ . Figures with the same shape are __?__ . *(page 360)*

7. A triangle that has two congruent sides is a(n) __?__ triangle. *(page 354)*

8. Lines that are in different planes, are not parallel, and do not intersect are __?__ lines. *(page 344)*

9. A line segment that joins two vertices of a polygon but is not a side is called a(n) __?__ . *(page 356)*

Think: What is the sum of the measures of two supplementary angles?

10. If a figure can be turned less than 360° around a point and still match the original, it has __?__ symmetry. *(page 362)*

Concept Check

11. Can each of two supplementary angles be acute? Why or why not? *(page 349)*

12. Why is a trapezoid not a parallelogram? *(page 356)*

13. If two triangles are similar, are their angles congruent? How do you know? *(page 360)*

14. The sum of the measures of all the angles of a triangle is __?__ °. *(page 354)*

Skill Check

Identify the geometric shape. Use Figure A for Exercises 15–20. *(pages 342, 344)*

15. $\overline{BD}$

16. $\overrightarrow{DC}$

17. $\overline{AB}$ and $\overline{CD}$

18. $\angle ABD$

19. $\triangle ABD$

20. $\angle ADB$

Figure A

Use a compass and a straightedge. Use Figure B for Exercises 21–22. *(pages 345, 350)*

Figure B

21. Construct $\overline{AB} \cong \overline{YZ}$.

22. Construct $\angle CAB \approx \angle XYZ$.

Classify the triangle by the sides and by the angles. *(page 354)*

23.

24.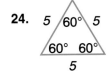

25.

Name the polygon. *(page 356)*

26. 6 sides, 6 angles

27. 4 sides, 4 angles

28. parallelogram with 4 congruent sides

Tell whether the second figure is a translation, rotation, or reflection. *(page 364)*

29.

30.

31.

32. Name the solid figure with one hexagonal base. *(page 366)*

Problem-Solving Check *(pages 352, 370)*

33. A circle graph shows the membership of the Save-the-Whales Club. A 288° section shows members who have paid their dues. What percent have paid their dues?

34. Make a circle graph to show that the membership of a recycling club is 45% men, 30% women, 10% boys, and 15% girls.

35. Four hikers reached camp on Day 1, 6 on Day 2, 10 on Day 3, 12 on Day 4, 16 on Day 5, and 18 on Day 6. If the pattern continues, how many hikers will reach camp on Day 7?

36. Dan drove 2 mi Monday, 4 mi Tuesday, 8 mi Wednesday, 16 mi Thursday, and 32 mi Friday. If the pattern continues, how far will he drive next Tuesday?

1. Name objects in the classroom that remind you of a line segment, an angle, a parallelogram, and a rectangular prism. Explain your choices.

2. Look at page 351. Construct an angle congruent to $\angle ABC$ in the drawing of the kite. Explain your method.

3. Choose and describe two figures that are similar but not congruent. Explain your choices.

4. Explain how the size, shape, and position of a figure are changed in a translation.

5. Read Exercise 2 on page 371. Follow the steps on the Problem-Solving Think Along worksheet to show how to solve this problem.

Write About It

6. Which activity or lesson in this chapter on geometry did you enjoy the most? What did you enjoy about it?

7. Explain why the following statement is or is not reasonable:

   Lines that are skew also intersect each other.

   Draw a picture to go with your explanation.

TEAMWORK Project

Three-Dimensional Figures

*T*he patterns make a prism, a cylinder, a cone, and a pyramid.

Decide

As a team, discuss which pattern makes each figure.

Each team member should choose one figure to make.

Brainstorm ways to build each figure from objects such as toothpicks or straws and connectors such as gumdrops or clay.

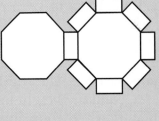

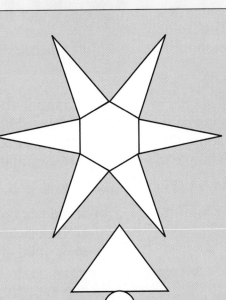

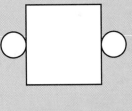

Do

Build the figure. Do not use an object that is already the shape you need.

Make sure the figures that you build have the same properties as the solid shapes you have learned about.

Share

Show the figure and explain its properties to your teammates.

Talk About It

■ **Are some figures easier to build than others? Which ones?**

■ **How did building the figure make you more aware of the shapes of everyday objects?**

MATH**F**UN

Extend Your Thinking

The Golden Ratio

Architects and artists in ancient Greece discovered that some rectangles are more pleasing to the eye than others. The ratio of the sides of the pleasing rectangles is called the Golden Ratio. This Ratio is about $1:1\frac{1}{2}$ or, more precisely, 1:1.6.

1 The ancient Parthenon still stands in Athens, Greece. The width is about 101 feet, and the height is about 60 feet. Is the Parthenon an example of the Golden Ratio?

2 Examine these common rectangular objects. Measure the length and the width of each object. Which items are examples of the Golden Ratio?

a. television   **b.** license plate
c. American flag   **d.** window
e. framed artwork   **f.** sign on building

Challenge

—*Critical Thinking*—

Drawing one straight line across a circle creates two regions, or parts. Drawing two straight lines across a circle creates three or four regions.

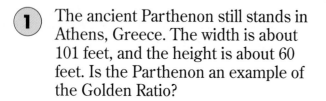

Draw three straight lines across a circle to create the following.

   a. four regions   b. five regions
   c. six regions   d. seven regions

a.   b.   c.   d.

—*Number Puzzles*—

What is this creature? Solve the code to find the answer.

△⬡5   7▭5∠△

▭▱⬡◇ 9 14 24   ⬡6

5↔   7 9 26∠   5 7 25•△

For each geometric symbol or shape, substitute the first letter in its name (*t* for triangle, for example). Each number stands for a letter's place in the alphabet (*a* = 1, *b* = 2, *c* = 3, and so on).

Write the letter of the correct answer.

1. $2\frac{1}{2} \times 1\frac{3}{10}$

   A. $2\frac{3}{20}$ **B.** $3\frac{1}{4}$

   C. 3.3   **D.** not here

2. $2\frac{1}{12} \div 1\frac{1}{4}$

   A. $\frac{3}{5}$ **B.** 0.6

   C. $1\frac{2}{3}$ **D.** $2\frac{1}{3}$

3. Change to the given unit.
2.09 g = ■ mg

   A. 0.00209   **B.** 20.9

   C. 209   **D.** 2,090

4. Change to the given unit.
3,520 yd = ■ mi

   A. 1   **B.** 2

   C. 3   **D.** not here

5. Find the missing number.
$\frac{3}{5} = \frac{18}{■}$

   A. 6   **B.** 11

   C. 30   **D.** 90

6. Name the triangle with angles of 45°, 60°, and 75°.

   A. equilateral   **B.** isosceles

   C. obtuse   **D.** not here

7. What is 12% of 80?

   A. 0.96   **B.** 9.6

   C. 96   **D.** 960

8. Name the figure that connects two endpoints.

   A. angle   **B.** line segment

   C. ray   **D.** plane

9. Describe lines that never meet.

   A. bisect   **B.** parallel

   C. intersect   **D.** perpendicular

10. Which figure has two circular bases?

   A. cone   **B.** cube

   C. pyramid   **D.** cylinder

11. A circle graph shows that a cereal contains 5% fiber, 25% whey, and 70% oat bran. What is the measure of the largest angle in the graph?

   A. 75°   **B.** 126°

   C. 252°   **D.** 324°

12. A design has two trapezoids followed by one circle, three pentagons, and one rhombus. The design is then repeated. What is the twelfth shape in the design?

   A. circle   **B.** pentagon

   C. rhombus   **D.** trapezoid

PERIMETER, AREA, AND VOLUME

Did you know...

... that artists and craftspersons often use their knowledge of perimeter, area, and volume to complete their projects?

Talk about it

Suppose you were going to make a quilt. Draw a picture to explain how you would find the number of inches of ribbon you would need to wrap one time around the outside of the quilt.

ESTIMATING AND MEASURING PERIMETER

Zack paced off two display booths at a craft fair. For a jewelry booth, he walked 9, 12, and 15 paces. For a leather-crafts booth, he walked 16 paces for each of four sides. How many paces did Zack walk for each booth?

Perimeter (P) is the distance around a polygon. To determine the perimeter, find the sum of the lengths of the sides.

You can write a formula to find the perimeter of the jewelry booth. $\qquad P = a + b + c$

* If you use the variable s for the length of each of the four sides, what formula can you write to find the perimeter of the leather-crafts booth?

Jewelry booth
$P = 9 + 12 + 15$
$P = 36$ paces

Leather-crafts booth
$P = 16 + 16 + 16 + 16$
$P = 64$ paces

So, Zack walked 36 paces for the jewelry booth and 64 paces for the leather-crafts booth.

Talk About It

▶ Would the perimeter of the booths be different if someone other than Zack paced the distances? Why?

▶ How can you determine the actual perimeter of the jewelry and the leather-crafts booths?

▶ If you use the variable s for the length of each of the five sides, what formula can you write to find the perimeter of a regular pentagon?

▶ When might you need to find the perimeter of an object?

Check for Understanding

Write a formula for finding the perimeter of the figure.

1.
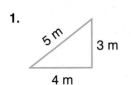
5 m   3 m
4 m

2.
4 in.   4 in.
4 in.   4 in.
4 in.

3.
7 ft
7 ft   7 ft
7 ft   7 ft
7 ft

4.
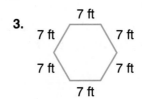
3 cm   3 cm   3 cm
3 cm
5 cm

Practice

Estimate the perimeter of the polygon. Round to the nearest whole number.

5.
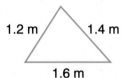

6.
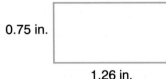

7.
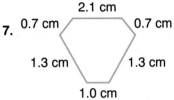

Find the perimeter of the polygon.

8.
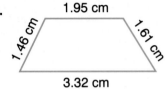

9.
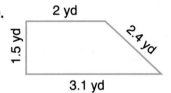

10.
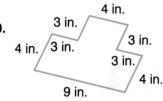

11.
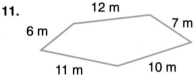

12.
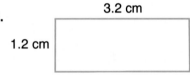

13.
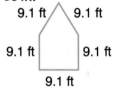

Mixed Applications

14. When Sue leaves home, she drives 6 km, turns right, and drives 8 km more to a crafts fair. Her route home is a straight road that is 4 km shorter than her route to the crafts fair. How long is her round trip?

15. Critical Thinking If a square picture frame measures 1 ft on each side, would the perimeter of the frame be more than a yard?

CHALLENGE • GEOMETRY

16. The perimeter of the regular hexagon in the figure is 42 cm. The star is made from two equilateral triangles whose sides are 21 cm each. What is the perimeter of the star?

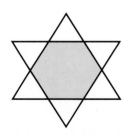

Can you use the formula $P = 5s$ to find the perimeter of an irregular pentagon? Explain.

AREA OF RECTANGLES

Manuel is making a mosaic tile design with square centimeter tiles. Part of his design is in the shape of a rectangle that is 4 cm wide and 6 cm long. What is the area of the rectangle?

Area is the number of square units needed to cover a surface. Square units are shown as m^2, ft^2, and so on.

Look at the rectangle outlined on the graph paper.

- How many square units are needed to cover the rectangle?

So, the area of the rectangle is 24 cm^2.

MULTICULTURAL NOTE: Mosaic is an art form that has been used for many centuries in countries such as India, Italy, Greece, and Mexico. Architects in Mexico have used mosaics on modern buildings.

Talk About It

▶ What is the length of the rectangle? the width?

▶ What is the relationship between the length and the width of the rectangle and its area?

▶ If you use l for length and w for width, what formula can you write to find the area, A, of a rectangle?

▶ A square is a special rectangle. What makes a square special?

▶ If you use s for the length of each side, what formula, other than $A = lw$, can you write to find the area of a square?

▶ When might you or your family need to find the area of an object?

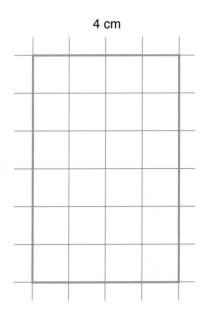

4 cm

6 cm

Use your formulas to find the area of rectangles. You can check your answers by using graph paper to count the square units.

Examples

9 m

12 m

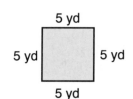

5 yd

5 yd   5 yd

5 yd

A. $A = lw$ ← length × width
   $= 12 \text{ m} \times 9 \text{ m}$
   $= 108 \text{ m}^2$

B. $A = s^2$ ← side squared
   $= 5 \text{ yd} \times 5 \text{ yd}$
   $= 25 \text{ yd}^2$

Checking for Understanding

Write a formula for finding the area of the figure.

1.
5 in.
5 in.

2.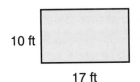
10 ft
17 ft

3.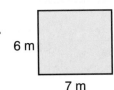
6 m
7 m

4.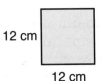
12 cm
12 cm

Practice

 Find the area.

5.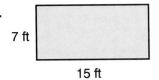
7 ft
15 ft

6.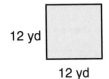
12 yd
12 yd

7.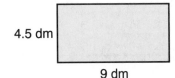
4.5 dm
9 dm

8.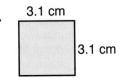
3.1 cm
3.1 cm

9.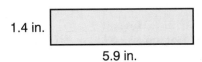
1.4 in.
5.9 in.

10.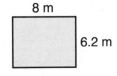
8 m
6.2 m

11. $l = 9\,\text{ft},\ w = 3\,\text{ft}$

12. $l = 18\,\text{cm},\ w = 8\,\text{cm}$

13. $l = 25\,\text{yd},\ w = 40\,\text{yd}$

14. $l = 162\,\text{m},\ w = 95\,\text{m}$

15. $l = 20\,\text{cm},\ w = 20\,\text{cm}$

16. $l = 8\,\text{m},\ w = 0.12\,\text{m}$

Mixed Applications

17. A square box lid has a length and width of 4 cm. What is the area of the box lid?

18. The area of a square table is 25 ft². What is the perimeter?

19. Sally and Todd have 26 art prints. If Sally has 4 more than Todd, how many prints does Todd have?

20. A rectangle has a width of 3 cm. The length is 3 less than 4 times the width. What is the area?

21. The width of a rectangle is x. The length is $x + 5$. If the perimeter is 18 yd, what are the length and the width of the rectangle?

22. Number Sense The area of a rectangle is 20 cm². If the lengths of the sides are whole numbers, what lengths and widths could they be?

If you know the area of a square, how can you find the length of the sides?

Kirsten wants to cover this parallelogram with decorative foil. How much decorative foil does she need?

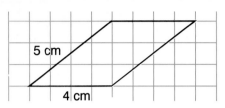

Copy the parallelogram on graph paper and draw a dotted line as shown. Cut along the line.

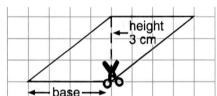

Slide the cutting across the original figure as shown. Label the new figure *ABCD*.

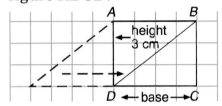

- What new shapes does the dotted line create?

- What new shape does the translation create?

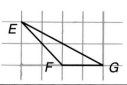

You cut the parallelogram into two congruent triangles.

Talk About It

▶ What is the line relationship between $\overline{AD}$ or $\overline{BC}$ and the base of the parallelogram?

▶ How can you find the area of rectangle *ABCD*?

▶ Is the area of the parallelogram the same as the area of rectangle *ABCD*? How do you know?

▶ If you use *b* for the base and *h* for the height, what formula can you write to find the area of the parallelogram?

$A = bh$ ◄— base times height

$A = 4 \times 3 = 12$ So, Kirsten needs 12 cm² of foil.

What is the area of △ *BCD*?

- How does the area of triangle *BCD* compare with the area of parallelogram *ABCD*? What formula can you write for the area of the triangle?

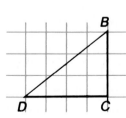

$A = \frac{1}{2}bh$ $\frac{1}{2} \times 4 \times 3 = 6$ The area of △ *BCD* is 6 cm².

The height is measured on a segment perpendicular to the base.

- What is the height of △ *EFG*?

Checking for Understanding

Write a formula for finding the area of the figure.

1.
9 cm
12 cm

2.
3 in.
5 in.
4 in.

3.
6 m
7 m

4.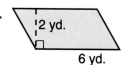
2 yd.
6 yd.

Practice

 Find the area of the parallelogram.

5. $b = 2\,\text{cm}, h = 3\,\text{cm}$

6. $b = 12\,\text{ft}, h = 8\,\text{ft}$

7. $b = 1.5\,\text{m}, h = 2.6\,\text{m}$

8.
2 cm
4 cm

9.
$4\frac{1}{2}$ ft
6 ft

10.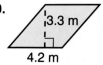
3.3 m
4.2 m

Find the area of the triangle.

11. $b = 10\,\text{yd}, h = 7\,\text{yd}$

12. $b = 82\,\text{m}, h = 4.8\,\text{m}$

13. $b = 6\,\text{in.}, h = 20\,\text{in.}$

14.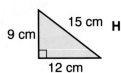
9 cm
15 cm H
12 cm

15.
6 in.
2.4 in.

16.
0.8 m
2.8 m

Mixed Applications

17. A baseball field is divided into two congruent triangles. If the area of one triangle is 50 m², what is the area of the baseball field?

18. **Critical Thinking** You wrote a formula for finding the area of a parallelogram by making a rectangle. Into what 2 familiar figures could you divide a trapezoid to find its area?

MIXED REVIEW

Find the sum or difference.

1. $34.23 - 9.07$

2. $12\frac{5}{9} + 6\frac{2}{3}$

3. $2.073 + 0.909$

4. $8\frac{1}{2} - 6\frac{5}{6}$

5. $45.07 + 12.909$

6. $121 - 12.35$

7. $3.5 + 1.059$

8. $30 - 27.989$

How can you find the area of a rhombus?

WRAP UP...

PROBLEM SOLVING

STRATEGY • Use a Formula

Nancy is tiling a rectangular tabletop and a square bench with imported tile. The tabletop has a width of 18 in. and a length of 22 in. The sides of the bench are each 20 in. long. How many square inches of tile will she need?

Using a formula is a common problem-solving strategy. You can use the formulas you wrote in previous lessons to help you solve problems.

▶ **UNDERSTAND**

What are you asked to find?

What information are you given?

▶ **PLAN**

What strategy can you use?

Since you need to find the area of two figures, you can use the formulas for finding the area of a rectangle and the area of a square. Then add the two areas.

▶ **SOLVE**

How can you carry out your plan?

Use the formulas for finding the area of a rectangle and the area of a square.

rectangle: $A = lw$ square: $A = s^2$
$A = 22 \times 18$ $A = 20^2$
$A = 396$ $A = 400$

$$396 + 400 = 796$$

So, Nancy needs 796 in.^{2} of tile.

▶ **LOOK BACK**

What other strategy can you use?

WHAT IF... . . . the lengths of the sides of the tabletop were increased? What would happen to the area?

Apply

1 Liza has a rectangular toolbox with a base 21 in. long and 9 in. wide. She wants to cover the bottom of the tool box with felt material. How many square inches of felt does she need to cover the bottom of the toolbox?

2 The beads Jose bought to make jewelry came in a container with a lid shaped like a right triangle. If the base of the triangle is 4 cm and its area is 16 cm², what is the height of the lid?

| Mixed Applications ⟶ | STRATEGIES | **Write an Equation • Find a Pattern • Work Backward • Draw a Diagram** |

Choose a strategy and solve.

3 Fencing is on sale at a local lumber yard. Maria wants to fence a square section of her yard that is 42 ft on each side. How many feet of fencing should Maria buy?

4 Dean roped a 215-ft by 170-ft rectangular section of a parking lot to make an unloading zone. What is the area of the unloading zone?

5 Burt found a store where he can purchase a package of 5 carriage bolts for $2.78. If he needs 13 carriage bolts to complete his project, how much will he spend on the carriage bolts?

6 During three days, Lani sold 35 picture frames and gave away 9 as samples. If she sold 12 frames on the third day, how many frames did she sell the first two days?

7 Lindsay's goal was to sell $250 worth of aprons and pot holders. Aprons sell for $5 and pot holders for $3. If she has sold 35 aprons, how many pot holders must she sell to reach her goal?

8 An express bus travels at a speed of 50 mi an hour. If James takes the 9:00 A.M. express bus to travel 45 mi, at what time will he reach his destination?

WRITER'S CORNER

9 Look at the black shape on the graph paper. Write everything you know or can figure out about this shape.

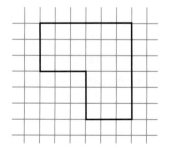

EXPLORING

Area of Irregular Figures

One way to find the area of an irregular figure is to use graph paper and count the number of square units.

Work Together

Building Understanding

Look at the shaded figures that are drawn on graph paper. Each figure covers a certain number of square units.

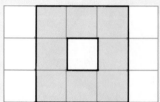

Figure A

Figure B

Figure C

TALK ABOUT IT

- How can you find the area of Figure **A**?

- What is the area of Figure **A**?

- How can you find the area of Figure **B** without counting?

- What is the area of Figure **B**?

- How can you find the area of Figure **C**?

- What is the area of Figure **C**?

- Can two figures with different shapes have the same area? Explain.

Tell how to find the area of the figure.

a. 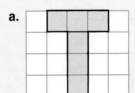   b. 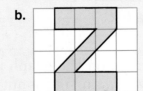   c.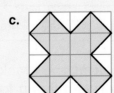

Making the Connection

You can also find the area of an irregular figure that is not drawn on graph paper. Divide the figure into familiar shapes. Measure and then find the area of the familiar shapes. Then add the areas together or subtract the areas from each other.

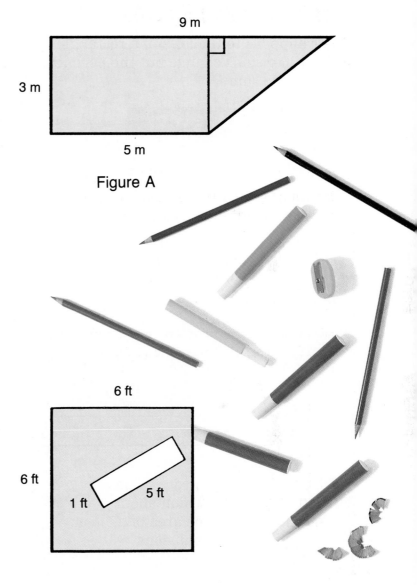

Figure A

1. Into what familiar shapes does the line divide Figure **A**?

2. What is the area of each shape?

3. How do you find the area of Figure **A**?

4. What is the area of Figure **A**?

Look at Figure **B**.

How can you find the area of the shaded part of Figure **B**?

5. What familiar shapes do you see in Figure **B**?

6. What is the area of each shape?

7. How do you find the area of the shaded part of Figure **B**?

8. What is the area of the shaded part of Figure **B**?

Figure B

Checking Understanding

Find the area of the shaded part of the figure.

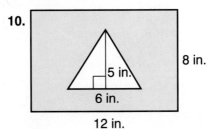

9.

6 mi
8 mi
6 mi
11 mi

10.

6 ft
6 ft
1 ft
5 ft

12 in.
8 in.
5 in.
6 in.

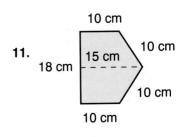

11.

10 cm
10 cm
15 cm
18 cm
10 cm
10 cm

EXPLORING

Relating Perimeter and Area

What happens to the area of a rectangle if the dimensions change but the perimeter remains the same?

Work Together

Building Understanding

Model at least three rectangles that have the same perimeter.

Find the area of each rectangle. Make and complete a table like the one shown. List your rectangles in order from the greatest length to the least length.

Rectangle	Length	Width	Perimeter	Area
1	▪	▪	▪	▪
2	▪	▪	▪	▪
3	▪	▪	▪	▪

Discuss the data in your table. Then write a conclusion about what happens to the area of a rectangle if the dimensions change but the perimeter remains the same.

Share your results and conclusions with your classmates.

390

Making the Connection

One way to model rectangles is to use dot paper.

Example   Three rectangles, each having a perimeter of 24 units, are modeled on dot paper.

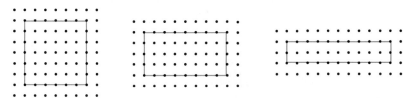

1. Which rectangle has the greatest area?

2. Is it possible to model a rectangle that has the same perimeter but a greater area? Explain.

Suppose you doubled the length and width of each of the rectangles in the example.

TALK ABOUT IT

- What happens to the perimeter of a rectangle when the dimensions are doubled?

- What happens to the area of a rectangle when the dimensions are doubled?

Checking Understanding

Using the perimeter given, model the rectangle with the greatest area. Record the lengths of the sides.

3. $P = 20$ 4. $P = 32$ 5. $P = 60$ 6. $P = 100$

Draw a rectangle that has double the dimensions of the given rectangle. Find the perimeter and area of each.

7. $l = 3 \, \text{cm}; w = 1 \, \text{cm}$ 8. $l = 15 \, \text{mm}; w = 9 \, \text{mm}$ 9. $s = 4 \, \text{cm}$

10. Explain what happens to the perimeter and area of the given rectangle in Exercise 8 when the dimensions are halved.

1. George swims 7 days a week. He swam 6 laps on Sunday. By Saturday he was swimming 24 laps. If George increased the laps by the same number each day, what was that number?

2. Mary uses a design in four ways for a quilt. First she uses the design itself, second a rotation, third a reflection, and fourth another rotation. What is the tenth pattern?

3. A hexagon is divided into 6 equilateral triangles. One triangle has a 5-cm base and a 4-cm height. What is the area of the hexagon?

In Exercise 1, I must find the intervals in the pattern.

4. A rectangle has a length 7 in. less than twice the width. The perimeter is 34 in. What is the length?

Tell which figures are similar and which are congruent.

5.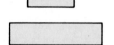

6.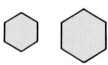

7.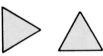

Name the solid figure.

8. 1 base, 5 faces

9. 1 base, 3 faces

10. 2 bases, 6 faces

Find the perimeter of the polygon.

11.
5 m
5 m

12.
3 ft
2 ft   2 ft
3 ft   4 ft

13.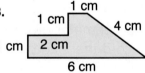
1 cm
1 cm   4 cm
1 cm   2 cm
6 cm

Find the area of the square or the rectangle.

14. $l = 10\,\text{cm}, w = 2\,\text{cm}$

15. $l = 11\,\text{m}, w = 5\,\text{m}$

16. $s = 12\,\text{ft}$

Find the area of the parallelogram.

17. $b = 4\,\text{cm}, h = 7\,\text{cm}$

18. $b = 8\,\text{in.}, h = 6\,\text{in.}$

19. $b = 16\,\text{ft}, h = 10\,\text{ft}$

Find the area of the triangle.

20. $b = 8\,\text{cm}, h = 2\,\text{cm}$

21. $b = 15\,\text{m}, h = 4\,\text{m}$

22. $b = 9\,\text{in.}, h = 6\,\text{in.}$

ASIA

China

Tangrams

The tangram is a geometric puzzle that comes from China. The true tangram consists of seven shapes: two large congruent triangles, one medium-size triangle, two small congruent triangles, one square, and one parallelogram.

Trace the shapes, color them, and cut them out.

Work Together

1. Can the orange square fit inside one of the blue triangles?

2. How can you rearrange the yellow triangles to form a parallelogram congruent to the red parallelogram?

3. How can you rearrange the yellow triangles to cover the orange square?

4. How can the yellow triangles be placed to form a triangle that is similar to the blue triangles?

5. How can the yellow triangles be placed to form an isosceles triangle that is congruent to the green triangle?

6. How can you rearrange all the shapes to form a square? HINT: You may flip any of the figures.

CIRCLES

Needlecrafters use embroidery hoops, which are often in the shape of circles, to hold fabric in place as they embroider.

A **circle** is a special closed figure made up of all the points in a plane that are the same distance from a point called the **center**.

• Where is the center of the circle B?

Parts of a circle have special names.

A **chord** is a line segment with endpoints on a circle.

A **diameter** is a chord that passes through the center of the circle.

A **radius** is a line segment with one endpoint at the center of a circle and the other endpoint on the circle.

Use a compass to construct a circle.

A. Open the compass to the width you desire for the radius.
B. Using the point of the compass as the center of the circle, rotate the pencil.

Talk About It

▶ How is the diameter related to the radius?

▶ Name two chords in Circle *B*. Which is longer?

▶ Name a radius and a diameter in Circle *B*. How is a radius related to a diameter?

▶ Can a radius be a chord? How do you know?

▶ Are all diameters chords? Are all chords diameters? Why?

NOTE: A circle is named by its center.

Check for Understanding

Label the circle you constructed *M*. Using a straightedge, draw and label each part.

1. a diameter, $\overline{JK}$ **2.** two chords, $\overline{RS}$ and $\overline{TU}$ **3.** two radii, $\overline{MN}$ and $\overline{MP}$

Practice

Use Figure *A* for Exercises 4–10. Identify each.

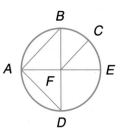

Figure A

4. the center

5. two diameters

6. two radii

7. two chords

8. the circle

9. intersecting line segments

10. If *FE* = 6 cm, what is *AE*? *CF*?

Copy and use Figure **B** for Exercises 11–16.

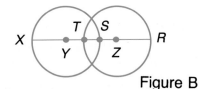

Figure B

11. What is $\overline{XS}$?

12. What is $\overline{RT}$?

13. What is $\overline{XY}$?

14. What is $\overline{TZ}$?

15. Draw one chord that is in each of the two circles.

16. Name a radius in Circle *Y* that intersects Circle *Z*.

Mixed Applications

17. A museum is square shaped. The entry doors cover $\frac{1}{2}$ the length of one side. If the perimeter of the building is 440 ft, what is the length of the entry doors?

18. **Number Sense** Think about a circle. How many diameters would you have to draw through the circle to divide it into 8 parts?

MIXED REVIEW

Write each percent as a decimal.

1. 33%   2. 48%   3. 6%   4. 80%   5. 30%   6. 12%

Write each percent as a fraction in simplest form.

7. 25%   8. 50%   9. 20%   10. 30%   11. 28%   12. 55%

Write = or ≠.

13. $\frac{1}{8}$ ● $\frac{3}{24}$ 14. $\frac{4}{7}$ ● $\frac{2}{3}$ 15. $\frac{5}{9}$ ● $\frac{4}{7}$ 16. $\frac{6}{20}$ ● $\frac{3}{10}$ 17. $\frac{5}{10}$ ● $\frac{3}{6}$

Name some everyday items that would not work if they were not in the shape of a circle.

WRAP UP...

EXPLORING

Circumference of a Circle

Perimeter is found by adding the lengths of the sides of a polygon. Circles do not have sides, so you must find the distance around a circle by using a different method. The distance around a circle is called **circumference.**

Work Together

Building Understanding

Use a compass, string, paper, and a ruler to explore the circumference of a circle.

A. Construct a circle with a $3\frac{1}{2}$-in. radius. Wrap string around the circle. Use a ruler to measure the length of string.

TALK ABOUT IT

- What is the length of the diameter of the circle?

- What is the circumference of the circle?

- Use a calculator. How many times longer than the diameter is the circumference?

B. Construct a circle with a different diameter. Use string to measure the circumference and a ruler to measure the string.

- How many times longer than the diameter is the circumference?

Choose four circular objects in your classroom. You might use a roll of tape, a clockface, a coin, or the rim of a trash can. Copy the table. List and measure the objects. Then use a calculator and complete the table.

Object	Diameter (d)	Circumference (C)	$C \div d$
?	▪	▪	▪
?	▪	▪	▪
?	▪	▪	▪
?	▪	▪	▪

Making the Connection

You know that the circumference of a circle is always a little more than three times the diameter. This means that the ratio of the circumference to the diameter is a little more than 3. This ratio, $\frac{C}{d}$, is called **pi**, π. To find the circumference of a circle, you can use the formula $\frac{C}{d} = \pi$, $C = \pi d$, or $C = 2\pi r$.

Use a calculator with a π key, $\frac{22}{7}$, or 3.14 as an approximation for π, whichever makes a calculation easier. Since π is an approximation, write $\approx$ instead of $=$ in your answer.

Examples

A. Find the circumference of a circle with a diameter of 7 in. Use $\frac{22}{7}$ for π.

$$C = \pi d$$
$$C \approx \frac{22}{7} \times 7$$
$$C \approx 22 \text{ in.}$$

B. To the nearest whole number, what is the circumference of a circle with a diameter of 5 cm? Use a calculator.

Standard calculator

5 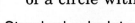 3.14 $=$ | 15.7 |

$C \approx 15.7 \text{ cm}$

Calculator with a π key

5 $\times$ π $=$ | 15.707963 |

L The display shows | 3.1415927 |

$C \approx 15.707963 \text{ cm}$

So, to the nearest whole number, the circumference is 16 cm.

Checking Understanding

Find the circumference. Round your answer to the nearest tenth. You may want to use a calculator.

1.
7 m

2.
15 cm

3.
5 in.

4. diameter = 8 in.

5. diameter = 25 cm

6. radius = 12 ft

7. diameter is 14 m

8. radius is 10 yd

9. radius is 19 in.

AREA OF CIRCLES

Kishi had a circular piece of clay 4 inches in diameter. She cut the clay into 8 equal pieces and pressed the pieces together to form a small tray.

A circle can be rearranged as an approximate parallelogram. You can use the formula for the area of a parallelogram to develop the formula for the area of a circle.

Talk About It

▶ In relation to the circle, what is the length of the base of the approximate parallelogram?

▶ How can you find the circumference of a circle when you know the radius?

▶ In relation to the circle, what is the height of the approximate parallelogram?

MULTICULTURAL NOTE: The Japanese are widely known for their clay figures and ceramics. Other traditional arts include flower arranging and origami.

Now you can develop the formula for the area of a circle. Recall that the area of a parallelogram is $A = bh$.

Think how the base and the height of the approximate parallelogram relate to the parts of the circle.

base (b) = $\frac{1}{2}$ the circumference of a circle ($\frac{1}{2} \times C$)
height (h) = radius (r) of a circle

$A = bh$ ← Replace with terms relating to the circle.

$\quad = (\frac{1}{2} \times C) \times r$ ← $C = 2\pi r$

$\quad = \frac{1}{2} \times 2\pi r \times r$ ← $\frac{1}{2} \times 2\pi r = \pi r$

$\quad = \pi r \times r$, or πr^2 Area of a circle → $A = \pi r^2$

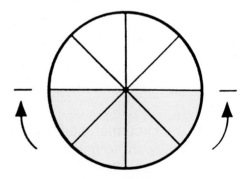

$\frac{1}{2}$ circumference

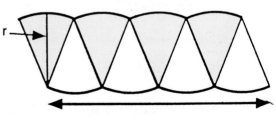

$\frac{1}{2}$ circumference

What was the area of Kishi's circle?
$A = \pi r^2$ ← $r = 2$ and $\pi \approx 3.14$
$\quad \approx 3.14 \times 2^2$
$\quad \approx 3.14 \times 4$
$\quad \approx 12.56$

So, the area of Kishi's circle was about 12.56 in.^{2}

Check for Understanding

Find the area of the circle. Round to the nearest tenth.

1.
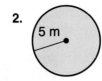
10 in.

2.
5 m

3.
20 cm

Practice

Find the area of the circle. Round to the nearest tenth.

4. $r = 2$ in.

5. $d = 14$ in.

6. $r = 7$ m

7. $d = 8$ ft

8. $r = 3.1$ cm

9. $r = 0.5$ m

10. $r = 12$ cm

11. $r = 12.4$ in.

Mixed Applications

12. Critical Thinking Consuela has two flat, round griddle pans. One has a radius of 8 in., and the other has a diameter of 12 in. Which pan has the greater area?

14. Visual Thinking Look at Figure *A*. If a square represents one square mile, about how many square miles is the area of Lake Walton?

13. Jon has a square coin whose sides measure 2.3 cm. What is the area of the coin? What is the perimeter?

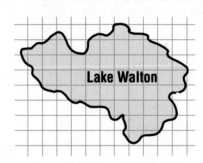

Lake Walton

Figure A

CRITICAL THINKING

You can use what you know about finding the area of polygons and circles to find the number of square meters in the shaded area of this figure. Find the area of each part in this order.

15. the square

16. the circle

17. the triangle

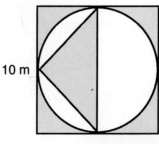

10 m

10 m

Now add and subtract to find the shaded area.

18. How many square meters are in the shaded area?

If you know the area of a circle, what other parts of the circle can you compute?

WRAP
UP...

EXPLORING

Surface Area

You have already learned how to find the area of polygons. In this lesson you will learn how to find the surface area of a rectangular prism.

Surface area is the sum of the areas of the faces of a solid figure.

Building Understanding

Use the drawings and a calculator to help you find the surface area.

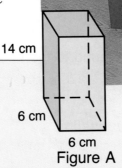
14 cm

6 cm

6 cm
Figure A

Figure B

Top Base — 6 cm

Back Face	Left Face	Front Face	Right Face
6 cm	6 cm	6 cm	6 cm

14 cm

Bottom Base — 6 cm

TALK ABOUT IT

- Counting the bases, how many faces does the rectangular prism in Figure **A** have?

- In Figure **A,** what is the area of the front face of the prism?

Look at Figure **B.** What faces are congruent to the front face?

- What is the combined area of the four faces?

- What is the area of the bottom base of the prism?

Look at Figure **B.** What base is congruent to the bottom base?

- What is the combined area of the two bases?

- How can you find the surface area of the rectangular prism?

- What is the surface area of the rectangular prism?

Find the surface area of the rectangular prism.

a.

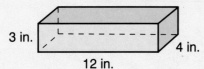

3 in.

4 in.

12 in.

b.

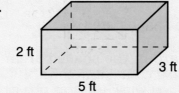

2 ft

3 ft

5 ft

c.

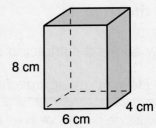

8 cm

4 cm

6 cm

Making the Connection

You can use what you know about finding the area of polygons to find the surface area of other solid figures.

A square-based pyramid has a base that is 6 cm square. The other faces are isosceles triangles with heights of 6 cm. What is the surface area of the pyramid?

1. Including the base, how many faces does the pyramid have?

2. What is the area of the base of the pyramid?

3. What is the area of one of the triangular faces?

4. What is the combined area of the 4 congruent triangular faces?

5. What is the surface area of the rectangular pyramid?

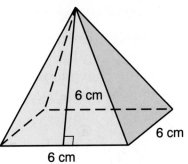

6 cm
6 cm
6 cm

Use the drawing of the cube for Exercises 6–9.

6. Including the base, how many faces does the cube have?

7. What is the area of any face of the cube?

8. How can you find the surface area of the cube?

9. What is the surface area of the cube?

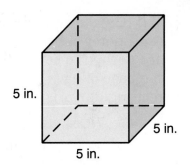

5 in.
5 in.
5 in.

Checking Understanding

Name the solid figure and tell the number of its faces.

10.   11.  12.   13.   14.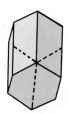

Find the surface area.

15.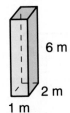
6 m
2 m
1 m

16. 12 cm 8 cm
12 cm
6 cm
15 cm

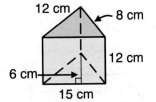

17.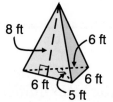
8 ft
6 ft
6 ft
6 ft
6 ft
5 ft

You can use the drawings of the solid figures in the Student Handbook to practice finding surface area.

EXPLORING

Volume

Volume is the number of cubic units needed to fill a container.

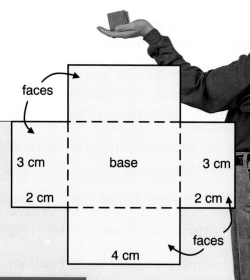

faces

3 cm   base   3 cm

2 cm   2 cm

faces

4 cm

Work Together

Building Understanding

Use centimeter cubes and the pattern for a rectangular prism. Draw the pattern using the given dimensions, transfer it to heavy paper, and cut it out.

Tell how many centimeter cubes are needed to cover the base of each rectangular prism below.

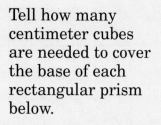

a.

4 cm

4 cm

4 cm

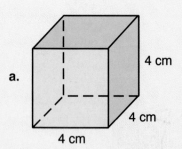

b.

1 cm

3 cm

5 cm

TALK ABOUT IT

- What dimensions does the base of the prism above have?

- Fold and tape the faces to make an open box. What dimension have you added?

- Cover the base with one layer of cubes. How many cubes are there?

- How many cubes will fit in a second layer?

- What is the total number of cubes that will fit in the rectangular prism?

- What is the volume of the rectangular prism in cubic units?

- Why do you express volume in cubic units?

Tell the total number of cubes that will fit in each rectangular prism.

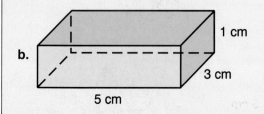

c. $l = 1, w = 1, h = 2$ **d.** $l = 4, w = 4, h = 4$ **e.** $l = 5, w = 3, h = 1$

Making the Connection

You can use multiplication to find the number of cubic units needed to fill a cube or a rectangular prism.

1. What formula do you use to find the area of a rectangle?

2. What dimension does a rectangular prism have that a rectangle does not have?

3. How can you use the length, width, and height of a rectangular prism to find its volume?

4. What formula can you write to find the volume of a rectangular prism?

5. Suppose a rectangular prism is 10 ft long, 9 ft wide, and 8 ft high. How would you find the volume?

Remember that you express the square units that show the area of a plane figure by using cm^2, m^2, ft^2, and so on.

6. Since solid shapes have three dimensions and their volume is expressed in cubic units, would you show cubic units as m^2 and ft^2 or m^3 and ft^3?

7. What is the volume of a rectangular prism that is 10 ft long, 9 ft wide, and 8 ft high?

Checking Understanding

Tell what numbers to multiply to find the volume of the rectangular prism.

8.

9.

10.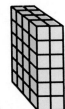

Find the volume.

11.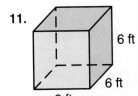
6 ft
6 ft
6 ft

12.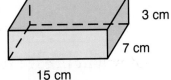
3 cm
7 cm
15 cm

13.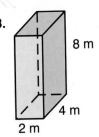
8 m
4 m
2 m

PROBLEM SOLVING

STRATEGY • Make a Model

Mrs. Wise must design a carton to hold 12 cereal boxes. Each box is a prism 11 in. long, 8 in. wide, and 2 in. high. The carton must be a rectangular prism having exactly 1-in. total clearance on the top and sides. The carton must be no taller than 10 in. and no cereal box may lie on its 2-in. side. What is the tallest carton Mrs. Wise can design?

▶ **UNDERSTAND**

What are you asked to find?

What information are you given?

▶ **PLAN**

What strategy can you use?

You can make models of the cereal boxes and arrange the boxes in a rectangular prism shorter than 10 in.

▶ **SOLVE**

How can you carry out your plan?

Use heavy paper and tape to make models of the cereal boxes. Arrange the boxes in rectangular prisms that meet the conditions.

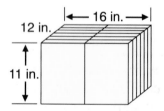

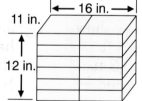

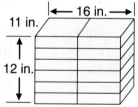

Add clearance.
8 + 1 = 9

So, the tallest carton Mrs. Wise can design is 9 in.

▶ **LOOK BACK**

What other strategy can you use?

 ... the carton must be no taller than 7 in. What is the length of the tallest carton Mrs. Wise can design?

404

Apply

1 Stuart made a basket in the shape of a rectangular prism 10 in. long, 6 in. wide, and 8 in. high. He wants to cover the bottom with plastic cubes that are 2 in. long on each side. Stuart has 12 cubes. Does he have enough to cover the bottom of the basket? Explain.

2 Lesli wants to store a ceramic bowl in a cube-shaped box. The widest part of the bowl has a diameter a little less than 14 in. The height of the bowl is a little less than 14 in. What is the smallest box Lesli can use?

> **Mixed Applications** → **STRATEGIES** Make a Model • Find a Pattern • Act It Out • Write an Equation

Choose a strategy and solve.

3 Fran, Harold, Susan, and Ted each sketched a design for a ceramic building: a fire station, a house, a school, and a theater. No person's first name begins with the same letter as the building. Fran designed the theater. Neither Ted nor Susan designed the fire station. What did Harold design?

4 Tyrone will travel to a crafts exhibit on a high-speed train that travels 158 mi an hour. If the train stops for the first time after traveling 79 mi, how many minutes will it take for the train to reach the first stop?

5 Rose makes dolls. She made 2 dolls the first week, 3 dolls the second week, 5 dolls the third week, and 8 dolls the fourth week. If the pattern continues, how many dolls will she make the seventh week?

6 When Arnold leaves home to attend an art class, he travels 8 mi by bus. He then takes a taxi that travels 6 mi an hour for 12 min. How far is the art class from Arnold's home?

7 A refreshment stand at an art show is a rectangle 10 ft long and 9 ft wide. A counter 7 ft long and 3 ft wide will be put inside the stand. How many square feet of space will be left after the counter is added?

8 Joanne bought a new kiln to fire her pottery. In the first five weeks, she fired 1, 4, 9, 16, and 25 pieces. If the pattern continues, how many pieces of pottery will Joanne fire in the sixth week? the seventh week?

Vocabulary Check

Choose a word from the box to complete each sentence.

> area
> chord
> circumference
> diameter
> perimeter
> pi
> radius
> volume

1. The distance around a polygon is called the __?__. *(page 380)*

2. The distance around a circle is called the __?__. *(page 396)*

3. A line segment in a circle with endpoints on the circle is called a(n) __?__. *(page 394)*

4. A ratio showing that the circumference of a circle is a little more than three times the diameter is __?__. *(page 397)*

5. The number of square units needed to cover a surface is the __?__. *(page 382)*

6. The number of cubic units needed to fill a container is the __?__. *(page 402)*

7. A chord that passes through the center of the circle is called a(n) __?__. *(page 394)*

8. A line segment with one endpoint at the center of a circle and the other endpoint on the circle is a(n) __?__. *(page 394)*

Concept Check

9. How do you find the perimeter of a polygon? *(page 380)*

10. How do you find the area of a rectangle? *(page 382)*

11. How can you find the area of an irregular figure? *(page 388)*

12. Tell how a chord may also be a diameter of a circle. *(page 394)*

13. How do you know that every radius of a circle is congruent to every other radius of the same circle? *(page 394)*

14. How do you find the surface area of a rectangular prism? *(page 400)*

15. What dimension must you consider when finding the volume of a rectangular prism but not when finding the area of a rectangle? *(page 403)*

I try to visualize the figures in the exercises.

Skill Check

Find the perimeter or the circumference. Use $\frac{22}{7}$ for π. *(pages 380, 396)*

16.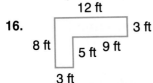
12 ft
3 ft
8 ft
5 ft 9 ft
3 ft

17.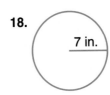
2 m   3 m   2 m
4 m   4 m
4 m   4 m
5 m

18.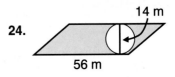
7 in.

Find the area of the parallelogram. *(page 384)*

19. $b = 3\,\text{ft}, h = 4\,\text{ft}$

20. $b = 12\,\text{m}, h = 8.1\,\text{m}$

21. $b = 2.2\,\text{m}, h = 2.1\,\text{m}$

Find the area of the shaded part of the figure. *(page 388)*

22.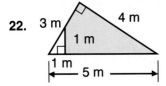
3 m   4 m
1 m
1 m
5 m

23.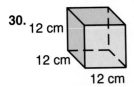
2 in.
4 in.
2 in.

24.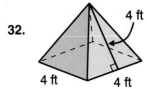
14 m
56 m

Find the area of the circle. Use 3.14 for π, and round your answer to the nearest tenth. *(page 398)*

25. $r = 2\,\text{yd}$ **26.** $d = 12\,\text{cm}$ **27.** $r = 3.2\,\text{ft}$ **28.** $r = 4.4\,\text{cm}$ **29.** $r = 1.5\,\text{m}$

Find the surface area. *(page 400)*

30.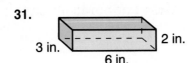
12 cm
12 cm
12 cm

31.
3 in.
2 in.
6 in.

32.
4 ft
4 ft
4 ft

33. Find the volume of the rectangular prism in Exercise 31. *(page 402)*

Problem-Solving Check *(pages 386, 404)*

34. Ray sells bowls with a circumference of 11 in. What size lid is needed to fit the bowls if the lids are sized by the radius? Use $\frac{22}{7}$ for π.

35. Carla added a square room to her house. The room is 100 ft². What is the perimeter of Carla's new room?

36. Lena wants to fill a sandbox that is 4 ft long, 3 ft wide, and $\frac{1}{2}$ ft deep. If sand is sold by the cubic foot, how much sand does she need?

37. Larry left a chair to walk 27 ft west to a bird feeder. He turned south and walked 36 ft to a bush. Then he walked 45 ft back to the chair. How far did he walk?

WHAT DID I LEARN?

1. Explain how to find the perimeter of the classroom.

2. Look at the shapes on page 384. Explain how the area of the rectangle is related to the areas of the parallelogram and the triangle.

3. Explain how to find the circumference and the area of a circle with a radius of 10 cm. Then find the circumference and the area, using 3.14 for π. Show your work.

4. Look at Figure **a** on page 402. Find the surface area and the volume of the figure. Explain your method.

5. Read Exercise 1 on page 405. Follow the steps on the Problem-Solving Think Along worksheet to show how to solve this problem.

> Remember that volume is the number of cubic units that can fill a container.

Write About It

6. Which concept or lesson in this chapter on perimeter, area, and volume was the easiest for you? Which was the hardest? Explain.

7. Draw a 5-cm × 7-cm rectangle. Inside the rectangle, draw a triangle with a base of 4 cm and a height of 5 cm. Shade all of the rectangle except for the triangle inside. Find the area of the shaded part. Explain how you found the area.

TEAMWORK *Project*

Make Tessellations

A **tessellation** is an arrangement of shapes that completely covers a plane, with no gaps and no overlaps. A square tessellates a plane.

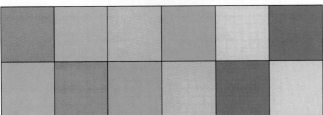

Work as a team to make a tessellation design.

DECIDE Choose a polygon that you will use for your tessellation. NOTE: Not all polygons will tessellate.

Decide how large your design will be and what colors you will use.

Do Design your tessellation. Different assignments should be given to different team members.

Draw your tessellation, making it colorful and appealing.

SHARE Compare your tessellation with those of other teams. Tell why you chose the polygon that you did.

TALK ABOUT IT

Give some examples of tessellations in your classroom or at home. What kinds of polygons are used?

What polygons do you think will not tessellate? Explain.

Use Polygons and Circles

You can use polygons to draw almost any figure. Doing this can help you find the area of a complex figure.

If you know the areas of the individual polygons, you can add them together to find the area of the whole figure. What is the area of the tree?

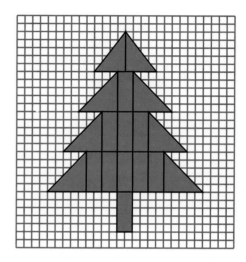

Draw the figure by using polygons. Then find the area of the figure.

1. a dog
2. a shoe
3. a telephone
4. a rabbit

Use circles and polygons to draw these figures.

5. a calculator
6. a school bus
7. an airplane
8. a lamp

Find the area of each figure in Exercises 5–8. Exchange drawings and area calculations with a classmate. Did each of you use the same polygons for the same purposes?

Challenge

Problem Solving

If the mass of an object is less than the mass of an equal volume of water, the object will float; otherwise, the object will sink. For 1 mL of water, mass = 1 g and volume = 1 cm³.

A cube has edges measuring 2 cm. If it has a mass of 5 g, will it sink or float?

Critical Thinking

Sometimes you can place congruent shapes next to each other to make a larger shape that is similar. How can you do this by using the triangle below four times?

Write the letter of the correct answer.

1. $1\frac{1}{2} \div 2\frac{1}{4}$

A. $\frac{2}{3}$ B. $1\frac{1}{2}$

C. $2\frac{1}{8}$ D. $2\frac{1}{4}$

2. 15 lb = ▮ oz

A. $\frac{15}{16}$ B. 1.8

C. 120   D. 240

3. What is 15% of 100?

A. 1.5   B. 15
C. 150   D. not here

4. Which parallelogram has 4 congruent sides?

A. triangle   B. pentagon
C. rhombus   D. trapezoid

5. $5\frac{1}{3} \times 4\frac{1}{4}$

A. $20\frac{2}{3}$ B. $22\frac{2}{3}$

C. $22\frac{11}{12}$ D. $23\frac{1}{6}$

6. 16:12 = ▮:3

A. 4   B. 6

C. 9   D. 12

7. What is the volume of the rectangular prism?
$l = 5$ m, $w = 4$ m, $h = 7$ m

A. 16 m³   B. 32 m³
C. 60 m³   D. not here

8. What is the perimeter of the square?
$s = 6$ cm

A. 6 cm   B. 12 cm
C. 24 cm   D. 36 cm

9. What is the circumference of the circle? $r = 3$ cm

A. 9.42 cm   B. 18 cm
C. 18.84 cm   D. 28.26 cm

10. What is the area of the triangle?
$b = 6$ ft, $h = 18$ ft

A. 6 ft²   B. 12 ft²
C. 27 ft²   D. 54 ft²

11. John has an oriental carpet that is 6 ft long and 10 ft wide. What is the area of the carpet?

A. 16 ft   B. 32 ft²
C. 60 ft²   D. 120 ft²

12. Sue put a small box 12 in. long, 8 in. wide, and 4 in. high inside a box 20 in. long, 15 in. wide, and 9 in. high. How many cubic inches of space are left in the larger box?

A. 1,200 in.³   B. 2,316 in.³
C. 2,341 in.²   D. 1,500 in.²

INTEGERS

Did you know...

...that temperatures vary with altitude?

TALK ABOUT IT

Mount Everest in the Himalayas is the highest mountain in the world. Explain how you could find the difference in temperature between that of snow-topped Mount Everest and the foothills where the family lives.

INTEGERS

The highest point in Israel is Mount Meron, in the Galilee region of the country. It is 3,963 feet above sea level. The lowest point in Israel is the Dead Sea, where the elevation is 1,310 feet below sea level. Sea level equals zero feet. What numbers can you use to represent the highest and lowest points in Israel?

You can use integers to represent the elevations. **Integers** include all whole numbers, their opposites, and zero. For example, the opposite of $^+10$ is $^-10$.

So, the elevation of Mount Meron can be represented as $^+3,963$ and that of the Dead Sea as $^-1,310$.

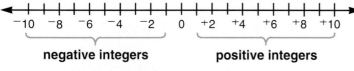

Zero is neither positive nor negative.

Many situations arise in daily life where both positive and negative integers can be used.

MULTICULTURAL NOTE: Israel extracts salt and other minerals from the Dead Sea.

Examples   Name an integer to represent each situation.

A. a loss of 5 yd in a football game

$^-5$

B. a temperature of 3 degrees below zero

$^-3$

C. a bank deposit of $100

$^+100$

Talk About It

▶ Describe the opposite of the situation in Examples A, B, and C.

▶ Name an integer to represent the opposite situation.

▶ Name some situations in everyday life where positive and negative integers are useful.

Check for Understanding

Name an integer to represent the situation.

1. a gain of 7 yd

2. a loss of 10 yd

3. a profit of $100

4. a loss of $50

5. a bank deposit of $75

6. a withdrawal of $25

Practice

Describe the opposite of the situation.

7. 3 steps forward

8. 6 degrees above 0

9. 81 ft above sea level

Name an integer to represent the situation. Then describe the opposite situation and give an integer to represent it.

10. up 2 flights of stairs

11. 19 ft above sea level

12. 68 ft below ground

13. 252 ft above ground

14. an increase of $250

15. a loss of $28

16. a weight loss of 6 lb

17. a 6-yd gain in football

Mixed Applications

18. If you deposit $25 and later withdraw $25, what is the new account balance?

19. If the temperature is 0° and drops 5 degrees, what will be the new temperature?

20. New York's Holland tunnel is 8,557 ft long. Virginia's Midtown Tunnel is 4,194 ft long. How much longer is the Holland Tunnel than the Midtown Tunnel?

21. Find Data Use an almanac to find the elevations for the highest and lowest points in the United States. Then use integers to name each elevation.

MIXED REVIEW

Find the product or the quotient.

1. $\frac{3}{4} \times \frac{8}{15}$

2. $\frac{9}{15} \div \frac{1}{5}$

3. $1\frac{3}{8} \times 4\frac{4}{11}$

4. $10\frac{2}{3} \div 1\frac{5}{6}$

Tell whether whole numbers, decimals, and fractions are integers.

PROBLEM SOLVING

STRATEGY • Act It Out

The Tigers took possession of the football on the Cougars' 45-yd line. On the first play they gained 34 yd. On the second play they lost 12 yd. They gained 9 yd on the third play but lost 5 yd on the fourth play. On what yard line were the Tigers after four plays?

▶ **UNDERSTAND**

What are you asked to find?

What information are you given?

▶ **PLAN**

What strategy will you use?

You can act out the situation to help you visualize how the events are related to each other.

▶ **SOLVE**

How can you carry out your plan?

Draw a diagram of half a football field. Cut a small piece of paper in the shape of a football. Model the play action. Move your football toward the goal line for all the yards the Tigers gained. Move it away from the goal line for all the yards the Tigers lost.

So, after four plays the Tigers were on the Cougars' 19-yd line.

▶ **LOOK BACK**

What other strategy could you use?

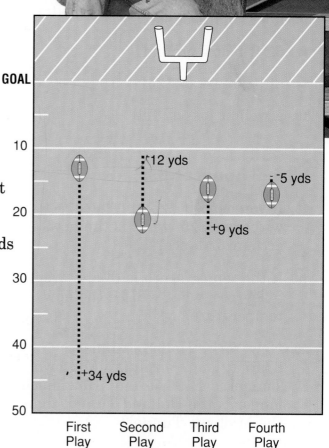

... the Tigers started on the Cougars' 32-yd line, gained 10 yd, 15 yd, and 5 yd, and then lost 2 yd? On what yard line would they be after the four plays?

WHAT IF ...

Apply

Act out the situation to solve each problem.

1 Jan is exploring a mountain cave. One room is a 30-ft wide and 50-ft long rectangle. The long sides face north and south. Jan enters the exact center of the south side and walks 20 ft north. Then she walks 15 ft east. How far is she from the east side of the cave's room?

2 Matt leaves a guest ranch and rides horseback 5 mi west, where he finds a cow's skull, and then 8 mi south, where he finds a cave. Then he rides 1 mi east and 11 mi north and 4 mi east to a large stone mesa. How far north is the mesa from the guest ranch?

Mixed Applications ⟹ STRATEGIES **Draw a Diagram • Guess and Check • Act It Out • Work Backward**

Choose a strategy and solve.

3 The water flow at an electric plant is increased by 2,000 gal per sec at 7 A.M. At 8 A.M. the water flow is doubled to 8,000 gal per sec. What was the water flow per second before 7 A.M.?

4 Ann, Joe, Luis, and Juana won the first four prizes in a design contest. Joe won second prize. Luis did not win third prize. Juana won fourth prize. What prize did Ann win?

5 A cave has 8 columns along one wall. The columns are each 3 ft wide, and they are spaced 7 ft apart. The columns at each end are 12 ft from the cave walls. How wide is the cave?

6 The road from Sun City extends south 20 mi, where it becomes a divided highway, and continues 15 mi to King City. The road extends 4 mi through King City and then another 24 mi south to Jewett. How far is Jewett from Sun City?

WRITER'S CORNER

7 Draw a diagram of a football field. Describe the result of 4 plays. Write a word problem about the plays. Exchange with a classmate. Solve. Then check your classmate's solution.

8 Write a problem similar to Exercise 4. Exchange with a classmate and solve.

More Practice, Lesson 13.2, page H82

COMPARING AND ORDERING INTEGERS

The lowest average temperature in Yakutsk, Siberia, in January is ⁻53 degrees Fahrenheit. The lowest average temperature in February is ⁻40 degrees Fahrenheit. Which temperature is the warmer of the two?

You can use a number line to help you visualize integers. As you move to the right on the number line, the value of the integers becomes greater.

$$\longleftrightarrow \quad {}^{-}53 \quad {}^{-}52 \quad {}^{-}51 \quad {}^{-}50 \quad {}^{-}49 \quad {}^{-}48 \quad {}^{-}47 \quad {}^{-}46 \quad {}^{-}45 \quad {}^{-}44 \quad {}^{-}43 \quad {}^{-}42 \quad {}^{-}41 \quad {}^{-}40$$

Talk About It

▶ Do the numbers become less or greater as you move to the right on the number line?

▶ Is ⁻40 to the left or to the right of ⁻53?

▶ Is ⁻40 greater than or less than ⁻53?

▶ Which temperature is warmer, ⁻40 degrees Fahrenheit or ⁻53 degrees Fahrenheit?

So, ⁻40 degrees Fahrenheit is warmer.

MULTICULTURAL NOTE: Because of the cold and snowy winters, many people in Siberia use a horse and sleigh for transportation.

You can use the symbols <, >, and = to compare and order integers.

Examples

A. Compare. Write <, >, or =.

⁻10 ● ⁻2

⁻10 < ⁻2

> ⁻2 is to the right of ⁻10.

B. Order from least to greatest. Use <.

⁻3, ⁺7, ⁺15, ⁻20

⁻20 < ⁻3 < ⁺7 < ⁺15

Pairs of integers that are the same distance from 0 on the number line are called **opposites**. For example, ⁻5 and ⁺5 are opposites.

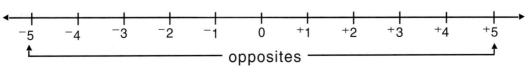

opposites

Check for Understanding

Tell which number is greater.

1. ⁻5 or ⁻3   2. ⁻5 or 0   3. ⁻10 or ⁺10   4. ⁻5 or ⁻8

Name the opposite of the given integer.

5. ⁻10   6. ⁺8   7. ⁺4   8. ⁻7   9. ⁺16   10. ⁻12

Practice

Use the number line. Write an integer for the given point.

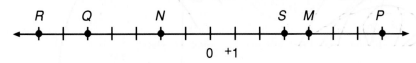

11. M 12. N 13. P 14. Q 15. R 16. S

Compare. Use <, >, or =.

17. ⁻7 ● ⁻9   18. ⁻8 ● ⁺8   19. ⁺2 ● ⁻9   20. ⁺3 ● ⁻4   21. ⁻12 ● ⁺2

22. ⁻10 ● ⁻9   23. 0 ● ⁻6   24. ⁻7 ● ⁺1   25. ⁻5 ● ⁻5   26. ⁻15 ● ⁻10

Order the integers from least to greatest. Use <.

27. 0, ⁻5, ⁺7, ⁻1

28. ⁺9, ⁻7, ⁺5, ⁻3

29. ⁺10, ⁻10, 0, ⁺7, ⁻2

30. ⁻8, ⁻4, ⁻7, ⁻9, 0

31. ⁻3, ⁺4, ⁻1, ⁺7, ⁻12

32. ⁺8, ⁻6, ⁻9, ⁻5, ⁺10, ⁺15

Mixed Applications

Write *sometimes*, *always*, or *never* for Exercises 33–34.

33. A negative integer is less than a positive integer.

34. A negative integer is less than another negative integer.

35. The lowest recorded temperature in Moscow, Russia, is ⁻33° Celsius. The highest recorded temperature is 35° Celsius. Which temperature is the warmer of the two?

36. **Number Sense** Numbers in a pattern are 1, 2, 3, 5, 8, 13, and 21. What are the next two numbers?

Tell why ⁺2 is greater than ⁻3.

EXPLORING

Addition of Integers

Adding positive integers is similar to adding whole numbers.

Building Understanding

Use blue counters. Let each blue counter represent $^+1$. What is $^+5$ and $^+3$?

TALK ABOUT IT

- How many counters do you need to model $^+5$? $^+3$?

- How can you use counters to model $^+5 + ^+3$?

- What is $^+5 + ^+3$?

- How does $^+5 + ^+3$ compare to $^+3 + ^+5$?

- Is addition of positive integers commutative?

You can show addition of positive integers on a number line.

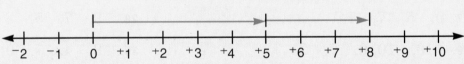

TALK ABOUT IT

- Use the number line. At what point do you begin?

- In what direction do you move to model positive integers?

- How would you show $^+3 + ^+5$ on the number line?

- Think about the number line. Why is the sum of two positive integers always positive?

Use counters or a number line to model adding positive integers. Find the sum.

a. $^+2 + ^+7$

b. $^+1 + ^+5$

c. $^+6 + ^+2$

d. $^+8 + ^+2$

Adding negative integers is similar
to adding positive integers.

ANOTHER ACTIVITY

Use red counters.
Let each red counter
represent $^-1$.
What is $^-3 + {}^-7$?

TALK ABOUT IT

- How many counters
  do you need to model
  $^-3$? $^-7$?

- If you combine the counters, how many do
  you have?

- What is $^-3 + {}^-7$?

- How does $^-3 + {}^-7$ compare to $^-7 + {}^-3$?

- Is addition of negative integers
  commutative?

You can show
addition of negative
integers on a number line.

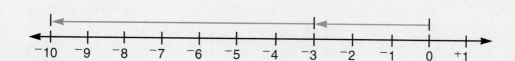

TALK ABOUT IT

- Use the number line. At what
  point do you begin?

- In what direction do you move to
  model negative integers?

- How would you show $^-7 + {}^-3$ on
  the number line?

- Think about the number line.
  Why is the sum of negative
  integers always negative?

Use counters or a number
line to model adding negative
integers. Find the sum.

a. $^-2 + {}^-5$ b. $^-1 + {}^-3$

c. $^-4 + {}^-1$ d. $^-6 + {}^-4$

e. $^-2 + {}^-6$ f. $^-11 + {}^-5$

Adding a positive integer and a negative integer is different from adding whole numbers.

Work Together

Building Understanding

Use red and blue counters. Let each blue counter represent $^+1$ and each red counter represent $^-1$.

Since red and blue counters are opposites, 1 red counter and 1 blue counter equal 0.
What is $^-3 + {}^+5$?

TALK ABOUT IT

- How many counters of each color do you need to model $^-3 + {}^+5$?

- How many pairs of counters can you make if each pair has one red and one blue counter?

- How many counters are left unpaired? Which color?

- What is $^-3 + {}^+5$?

- Which moves on the number line model $^-3 + {}^+5$?

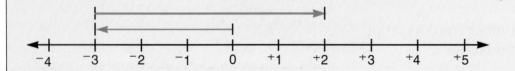

- Which moves on the number line model $^+5 + {}^-8$? What would the sum be?

Write *sometimes, always,* or *never.*

a. The sum of positive integers is __?__ positive.

b. The sum of negative integers is __?__ negative.

c. The sum of a positive integer and a negative integer is __?__ a positive integer.

d. The sum of opposite integers is __?__ zero.

Making the Connection

Think about a thermometer.

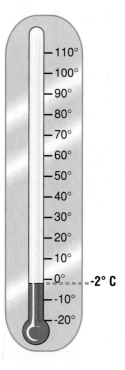

1. If the temperature is 2 degrees below zero and then drops 3 degrees, will the final temperature be higher than or lower than zero?

2. Will the final temperature be positive or negative?

3. What is $^-2 + {}^-3$?

4. If the temperature is 5 degrees above zero and then drops 10 degrees, will the final temperature be positive or negative?

5. What is $^+5 + {}^-10$?

6. Make up a word problem showing how addition of integers applies to temperature changes on a thermometer.

Checking Understanding

Use counters or a number line. Find the sum.

7. $^+6 + {}^+2$	8. $^+12 + {}^+7$	9. $^-10 + {}^-10$	10. $^-12 + {}^-7$
11. $^-9 + {}^+5$	12. $^+12 + {}^-7$	13. $^-12 + {}^+7$	14. $^-1 + {}^+10$
15. $^-7 + {}^-1$	16. $^-8 + {}^+20$	17. $^+18 + {}^+9$	18. $^-11 + {}^+10$
19. $^+13 + {}^-7$	20. $^+8 + {}^+10$	21. $^-6 + {}^-6$	22. $^-18 + {}^+11$
23. $^+12 + {}^+12$	24. $^-19 + {}^-19$	25. $^+17 + {}^-24$	26. $^-13 + {}^+27$

MIXED REVIEW

Find the product or quotient.

1. $3 \times \dfrac{1}{3}$

2. $\dfrac{5}{6} \div \dfrac{1}{12}$

3. $4\dfrac{1}{5} \times 3\dfrac{1}{2}$

4. $9\dfrac{5}{8} \div \dfrac{3}{8}$

Find the area of the figure. Use 3.14 for π.

5. 2 m, 12 m

6. 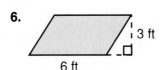 3 ft, 6 ft

7. 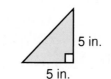 5 in., 5 in.

8. 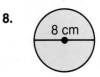 8 cm

EXPLORING

Subtraction of Integers

Use counters to explore subtraction of integers.

Work Together

Building Understanding

Let each blue counter represent $^+1$ and each red counter represent $^-1$.

TALK ABOUT IT

What is $^-7 - {}^-3$?
Put down counters to represent $^-7$.

- How many red counters are left if 3 are removed from the original 7?

- What is $^-7 - {}^-3$?

- What is $^-7 + {}^+3$? How does the answer to $^-7 + {}^+3$ relate to the answer to $^-7 - {}^-3$?

TALK ABOUT IT

What is $^-6 - {}^+2$?

- How many blue counters can you remove from 6 red counters?

- All the boxes represent $^-6$. Why? Show other ways to represent $^-6$.

Recall that the sum of 1 blue counter and 1 red counter is zero. Adding zero does not change the value.

- From which box can you remove 2 blue counters?

- Use Box C to subtract $^+2$. How many red counters are left after you remove 2 blue counters?

- What is $^-6 - {}^+2$?

- What is $^-6 + {}^-2$? How does the answer to $^-6 + {}^-2$ relate to the answer to $^-6 - {}^+2$?

Box A

Box B

Box C

424

Making the Connection

Addition and subtraction of integers are related.

Examples

Study these examples. Think about the relationship between
an integer and its opposite.

A. $^-7 - {^-3} = {^-4}$ and $^-7 + {^+3} = {^-4}$
  So, $^-7 - {^-3} = {^-7} + {^+3}$.

B. $^-6 - {^+2} = {^-8}$ and $^-6 + {^-2} = {^-8}$
  So, $^-6 - {^+2} = {^-6} + {^-2}$.

1. Write a rule telling how to subtract integers.

Checking Understanding

2. Tell which model to use to find $^-5 - {^+3}$.

 a.   **b.**   **c.**

3. The model below shows $^-4$. How can you use counters to
   find $^-4 - {^+2}$?

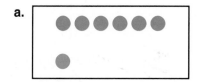   

Use counters to find the difference.

4. $^-7 - {^-5}$ 5. $^-8 - {^-7}$ 6. $^-5 - {^+3}$ 7. $^-2 - {^-5}$

Complete each of the following.

8. $^+7 - {^-4} = {^+7} + {\blacksquare}$ 9. $^-8 - {^-6} = {^-8} + {\blacksquare}$ 10. $^-4 - {^+2} = {^-4} + {\blacksquare}$

11. $^-6 - {^+3} = {^-6} + {\blacksquare}$ 12. $^+6 - {^+3} = {^+6} + {\blacksquare}$ 13. $^-2 - {^-5} = {^-2} + {\blacksquare}$

Rewrite each subtraction expression as an addition expression.
Then solve.

14. $^-7 - {^-10}$ 15. $^-9 - {^+4}$ 16. $^+14 - {^+8}$ 17. $^-14 - {^-12}$

18. $^+17 - {^+9}$ 19. $^-7 - {^+9}$ 20. $^+8 - {^-7}$ 21. $^+9 - {^+25}$

1. Devan has a box 9 in. long, 4 in. wide, and 2 in. high. He has another box 7 in. long, 5 in. wide, and 1 in. high. Will the small box fit inside the large box?

2. Estella has cut a piece of yellow ribbon 25 in. long to wrap around a tree that has an $8\frac{1}{2}$-in. diameter. Will the ends of the ribbon touch when wrapped around the tree?

3. Carole travels 200 mi west of the city. Then she visits an uncle who lives 24 mi off her route. She backtracks and then continues traveling west for another 153 mi to the mountains. What is the direct distance from the city to the mountains?

4. Wade threw a ball 15 ft south to Cal, who caught it and threw it 9 ft east to Jason. Jason threw it 20 ft north to Gene. Gene threw it to Cal. The boys remain in the same positions. How far must Cal throw to reach Wade?

Find the circumference or the area. Round your answer to the nearest tenth.

5. $r = 5\,\text{cm}$
   $A \approx \blacksquare$

6. $r = 16\,\text{in.}$
   $C \approx \blacksquare$

7. $r = 0.2\,\text{m}$
   $C \approx \blacksquare$

8. $r = 1.8\,\text{cm}$
   $A \approx \blacksquare$

9. $r = 22\,\text{in.}$
   $C \approx \blacksquare$

Find the volume of the rectangular prism.

10. $l = 4\,\text{m}, w = 3\,\text{m}, h = 5\,\text{m}$

11. $l = 9\,\text{cm}, w = 6\,\text{cm}, h = 1\,\text{cm}$

> Volume is expressed in cubic units.

Name an integer to represent the situation.

12. temperature of 8 degrees above 0

13. a weight loss of 2 lb

Compare. Use <, >, or =.

14. $^-6 \bullet ^-10$

15. $^+9 \bullet ^-1$

16. $^-12 \bullet ^-12$

17. $^+5 \bullet ^-5$

18. $^+9 \bullet ^+9$

Rewrite each subtraction expression as an addition expression.

19. $^-20 - ^+4$

20. $^-10 - ^+6$

21. $^-12 - ^-2$

22. $^-7 - ^-15$

23. $^+2 - ^-9$

Find the sum or difference.

24. $^+12 + ^+8$

25. $^-10 + ^-6$

26. $^+15 - ^+5$

27. $^-22 - ^+9$

28. $^-15 + ^+27$

29. $^-13 + ^+7$

30. $^+32 - ^-17$

31. $^-5 + ^+2$

32. $^-7 - ^-29$

33. $^+6 - ^-54$

Negative and Positive Integers

Games have been played for thousands of years. Drawings of games in progress have been found on walls in Egyptian tombs. Gameboards have been uncovered in ruins in Egypt, Mesopotamia, Assyria, Crete, and Cyprus. Today, the rules for many of these early games are unknown.

You can use the gameboard from Egypt shown here to practice adding negative and positive integers.

Play the game with one other person. You will need two game pieces, a pair of number cubes, and a copy of the gameboard. Begin by placing both players' game pieces on the space marked with a star.

Roll the cubes. Let even numbers on the cube be positive and odd numbers be negative. Add the two numbers. Move toward the snake's head if the sum is positive and toward the tail if the sum is negative. The first person to reach the snake's head is the winner.

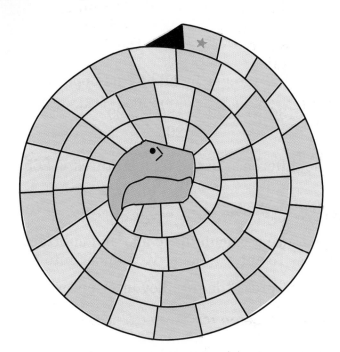

Work Together

1. Is it possible to get a 0 for the total sum of the two number cubes?

2. Write all the possible ways to roll the number cubes and get a sum of $^+1$.

3. Write all the possible ways to roll the number cubes and get a sum of $^-1$.

4. Suppose you are 3 spaces away from landing on the snake's head. On your roll, one cube shows a $^+6$. What do you need on the other cube to get a sum of $^+3$?

The highest recorded temperature occurred in Libya, where the temperature reached 136°F. The lowest recorded temperature occurred in Antarctica, where the temperature reached ⁻129°F. What is the difference between the highest and lowest temperatures?

Since you need to find the difference in temperatures, you must subtract.

136 − ⁻129   When the sign is not written, the integer is always positive.

Subtract the integer by adding its opposite.

$$136 - {}^-129 = 136 + 129$$
$$= 265$$

So, the difference in the temperatures is 265°F.

136° F

Another Method

You can use a calculator to add and subtract integers. To enter a negative number into a calculator, press the [+/-] key after entering the number.

136 − ⁻129
136 [−] 129 [+/-] [=]   265.

A temperature of ⁻4°F was recorded one morning. By noon the temperature had risen 7°F. What was the temperature at noon?

Since the temperature rose, you must add the integers.

$$^-4 + 7 = 3$$

So, the temperature was 3°F at noon.

Talk About It

▶ When would you press [+/-] when entering ⁻4 + 7 on a calculator?

⁻129° F

Check for Understanding

Find the sum.

1. $^-8 + ^-2$

2. $17 + ^-3$

3. $20 + 10$

4. $^-13 + ^-12$

Find the difference.

5. $7 - 3$

6. $^-16 - 3$

7. $^-21 - ^-3$

8. $^-11 - 5$

Practice

 Find the sum or difference.

9. $^-20 + 12$

10. $12 - 19$

11. $3 + ^-12$

12. $^-17 + ^-12$

13. $21 + ^-13$

14. $16 - ^-12$

15. $14 + ^-28$

16. $19 - ^-3$

17. $^-26 - ^-16$

18. $^-12 - 6$

19. $20 + ^-7$

20. $^-14 - ^-7$

21. $^-15 + ^-3$

22. $25 - ^-6$

23. $^-31 - 6$

24. $21 + ^-5$

25. $16 + ^-14$

26. $12 + 9$

27. $12 + ^-9$

28. $^-12 - ^-9$

29. $7 + ^-6 + ^-2$

30. $^-8 + ^-5 + 1$

31. $^-2 + ^-9 + ^-10$

Mixed Applications

Write a number sentence to solve Exercise 32.

32. A mountain climber climbs up 15 yd to a ledge. Then she climbs down 7 yd, 8 yd, and 9 yd to get to another ledge. Which ledge is higher, the first or the second?

33. **Write a Question** The highest recorded temperature in California is 134°F. The lowest recorded temperature is $^-45$°F.

CONSUMER CONNECTION

A bank account is said to be in the black if the balance is positive and in the red if the balance is negative.

34. Heather's account had a balance of $120. Then she made withdrawals of $25, $45, and $30. Use a calculator to find her new balance. Is Heather's final balance in the red or in the black?

How is subtraction of integers related to addition?

WRAP
UP...

EXPLORING

Ordered Pairs

This map shows a city divided into blocks.

Work Together

Building Understanding

Use the map to follow and give directions to different locations in the city.

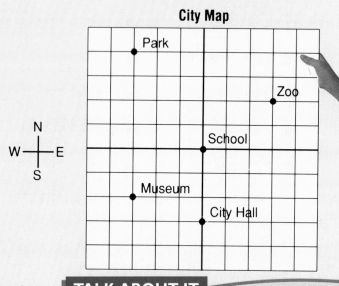

City Map

TALK ABOUT IT

- Start at the school. Go three blocks east. and then 2 blocks north. Where will you be?

- Start at the school. Go 3 blocks west and then 2 blocks south. Where will you be?

- How are the directions for locating the zoo similar to the directions for locating the museum?

- How are the directions for locating the zoo different from those for locating the museum?

- If you tell someone to walk 3 blocks from the school, does he or she have enough information to find City Hall? Explain.

- What directions would guide someone from the school to the park?

Making the Connection

Points on a map can be located by an **ordered pair** of numbers. The first number tells the number of blocks east or west of the starting point. The second number tells the number of blocks north or south of the starting point.

Use the map. How would you tell someone how to get from the starting point to the baseball field?

From start, go 6 blocks east. Then go 2 blocks south.

So, to get from the starting point to the baseball field, you would go 6 blocks east and 2 blocks south.

The ordered pair that names the location of the baseball field is (6, ⁻2).

Checking Understanding

Use the map. Tell the directions needed to get from the starting point to the given location.

1. pool
2. mall
3. fire station
4. post office

Trace the map. Locate each point on the map by following the given directions. Name the ordered pairs.

5. Go 4 blocks west and then 3 blocks south.

6. Go 1 block east and then 4 blocks north.

7. Go 3 blocks east and then 3 blocks south.

8. Go 5 blocks east and then 3 blocks south.

9. Go 3 blocks west and then 0 blocks north.

10. Go 3 blocks east and then 2 blocks north.

The city of Brasília, Brazil, is shown below on a grid. Locations on a map are often given by using a letter and a number as an ordered pair. For example, the Bank of Brazil can be located using the ordered pair D3.

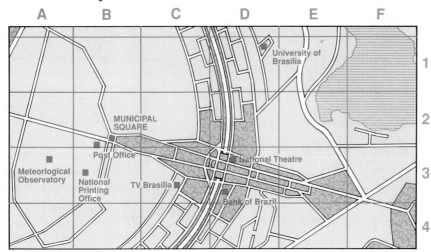

MULTICULTURAL NOTE: Brasília, the capital of Brazil, is one of the newest cities in the world. Construction of the city began in 1956.

Just as points on a map can be located by an ordered pair, points on a **coordinate plane**, or grid, can be located by an ordered pair of numbers.

A coordinate plane is formed with two perpendicular lines, called **axes**. The point where both axes intersect is called the **origin**. The ordered pair describing the origin is (0,0).

The horizontal axis is called the **x-axis.** The vertical axis is called the **y-axis**. Ordered pairs tell you how far and in what direction to move from the origin.

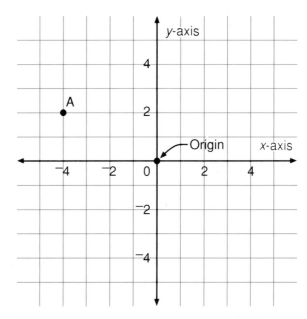

Order is important! The first number in the ordered pair always tells you how far to move horizontally. The second number tells you how far to move vertically.

The ordered pair ($^-4$,2) gives the location of point A in the coordinate plane shown. The first number, the x-coordinate, means you start at the origin and move 4 units to the left, since $^-4$ is negative. The second number, the y-coordinate, tells you to move 2 units up, since 2 is positive.

Connection, pages 476–477

Examples

A. How would you locate the point (3, ⁻4) in the coordinate plane?

Since the first number in the ordered pair is positive, move 3 units to the right (horizontally). Since the second number is negative, move 4 units down (vertically).

B. How would you locate the point (⁻5,7) in the coordinate plane?

Since the first number in the ordered pair is negative, move 5 units to the left. Since the second number is positive, move 7 units up.

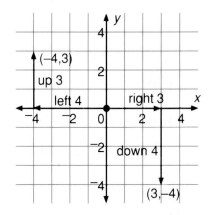

More Examples

C. What ordered pair names each point on the coordinate plane at the right?

1. The ordered pair for point *D* is (1,1).

2. The ordered pair for point *E* is (4,4).

3. The ordered pair for point *F* is (2, ⁻4).

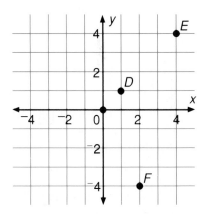

D. What ordered pair names each point on the coordinate plane at the right?

1. The ordered pair for point *R* is (⁻2, ⁻4).

2. The ordered pair for point *S* is (⁻4, ⁻2).

3. The ordered pair for point *T* is (⁻2,4).

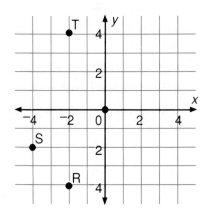

Talk About It

▶ Why is the location of the point (3, ⁻4) different from the location of the point (⁻4,3)?

▶ Look at the ordered pairs for points *R* and *S*. How are the ordered pairs similar?

▶ How are the ordered pairs for points *R* and *S* different?

▶ How are the ordered pairs for points *S* and *T* similar? different?

Check for Understanding

Tell the ordered pair that names each point on the coordinate plane.

1. point D
2. point E

3. point F
4. point G

5. What is the ordered pair for the origin?

6. On what axis is the point (6,0)?

7. On what axis is the point (0,6)?

8. How would you locate the point ($^-2$, $^-5$)?

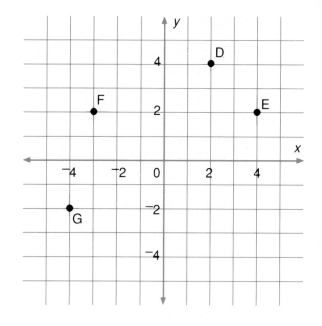

Practice

Write the ordered pair for each point.

9. point M
10. point N

11. point P
12. point Q

13. point W
14. point Z

15. point K
16. point V

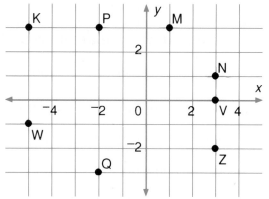

Use graph paper to make a coordinate plane. Locate the point for each ordered pair.

17. A (5,7)
18. B (4,$^-$6)
19. C (3,$^-$5)

20. D ($^-$1,$^-$1)
21. E ($^-$6,6)
22. F (3,7)

23. G (5,0)
24. H (0,5)
25. J ($^-$2, $^-$2)

Remember to move to the left or right first.

26. Locate the points (0,0), (4,0), and (0,4) on the same coordinate plane. Then connect these points in order. What geometric figure is formed?

27. Use the figure you made in Exercise 26. Add a point to make the figure a square. What are the coordinates of the new point?

28. Locate the points (1,1), (5,1), (5,5), and (1,5) on the same coordinate plane. Then connect these points in order. What geometric figure is formed?

Mixed Applications

Copy the figure on a coordinate plane that is at least 8 units square.

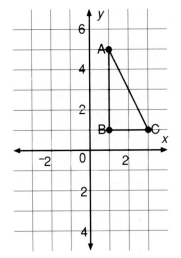

29. Name the coordinates for points *A, B,* and *C.*

30. Add 5 to the *x*-coordinate of points *A, B,* and *C.* Graph the new figure. How does adding 5 to the *x*-coordinates affect the figure?

31. Subtract 5 from the original *x*-coordinates of each point. Graph the figure. How does subtracting 5 from the *x*-coordinates affect the figure?

32. Add 5 to the *y*-coordinates of each point. Graph the figure. How does adding 5 to the *y*-coordinates affect the figure?

33. What do you think would happen to the figure if you subtracted 5 from the original *y*-coordinates?

34. **Visual Thinking** If you reflect the word WOW over a line of symmetry, the word becomes MOM. How else can you move WOW so that it becomes MOM?

GEOMETRY CONNECTION

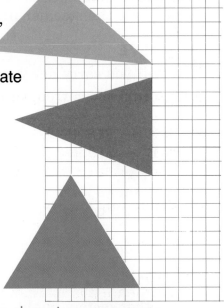

Remember that triangles can be classified as equilateral, isosceles, or scalene.

Use graph paper. Plot each set of ordered pairs on a separate coordinate plane. Then connect each set of points.

a. $(4,0)$, $(^-4,0)$, $(0,7)$
b. $(^-3,^-1)$, $(3,2)$, $(2,^-1)$
c. $(^-6,^-2)$, $(0,3)$, $(6,^-2)$
d. $(^-2,0)$, $(0,3\frac{1}{2})$, $(2,0)$

35. Which triangle is scalene?

36. Which triangles are isosceles?

37. Which triangle is equilateral?

Explain how to locate the point $(3, ^-5)$ on a coordinate plane.

PROBLEM SOLVING

Making Decisions

Lori wants to invest $20 in stock that shows a steady increase in price per share. Her broker listed the original price of two stocks and their gains and losses over a four-year period. Which stock should Lori choose?

Stock A—Price per Share				
Original Price	Yr 1	Yr 2	Yr 3	Yr 4
$15	$^{+}5$	$^{-}6$	$^{+}10$	$^{-}4$

Stock B—Price per Share				
Original Price	Yr 1	Yr 2	Yr 3	Yr 4
$10	$^{+}1$	$^{+}1$	$^{+}1$	$^{+}2$

▶ **UNDERSTAND**

What are you asked to find?

What information are you given?

▶ **PLAN**

How can you solve the problem?
Add to find the present price of each stock. Compare the changes to determine which stock shows the steadier increase per share.

▶ **SOLVE**

How will you carry out your plan?
Add to find the current price of each stock.

Stock A ⟶ $15 + $^{+}5$ + $^{-}6$ + $^{+}10$ + $^{-}4$ = $20
Stock B ⟶ $10 + $^{+}1$ + $^{+}1$ + $^{+}1$ + $^{+}2$ = $15

Stock A shows large gains and losses from year to year while Stock B shows slight gains each year.

So, Lori should choose Stock B.

▶ **LOOK BACK**

What other factors might Lori consider?

WHAT IF... ...Lori wants to buy stock that will give her the highest return on her money in one year? How will this affect her choice?

Apply

Ramon plans to play golf for 8 weeks this summer. He can buy a pass, pay regular fees, or buy a permit. He made a table to analyze the fees.

Choice 1

A season pass costs $290.

Choice 2

The regular fee is $18 per round.

Choice 3

A permit costs $90 in advance. Then the cost is $11 per round.

Copy and complete the table.

Times Played per Week	Cost		
	Choice 1	Choice 2	Choice 3
① 1	▦	▦	▦
② 2	▦	▦	▦
③ 3	▦	▦	▦
④ 4	▦	▦	▦

⑤ What does the table show about the cost of the three choices for the golfer who wants to play more than twice a week?

⑥ Ramon decided he would play twice a week. He selected Choice 1. Give one advantage of this choice.

Mixed Applications **STRATEGIES** **Guess and Check • Draw a Diagram • Make a Table • Write an Equation**

Choose a strategy and solve.

⑦ Use the table. Eve plans to play golf about twice a week for 8 weeks. She selected Choice 3. Give one of the advantages of her choice.

⑧ Mountain climbers lead tours for 6 people and for 4 people. If there are 4 tours with a total of 22 people, how many 4-person tours are there?

⑨ Bill enters a fun house and walks 4.5 m along a ground-level passage. The passage rises vertically 3 m and then is horizontal for 5.5 m. Suddenly, the passage drops 1 m and opens into a room. How far above ground is the room?

⑩ One year a forest ranger planted 10 trees. Every year he plants 3 more trees. How many trees will he plant in 6 years?

More Practice, Lesson 13.9, page H85

Vocabulary Check

Choose a word or words from the box to complete each sentence.

axes
coordinate plane
negative
opposites
origin
positive

1. An integer that has a value greater than zero is called a(n) __?__ integer. *(page 414)*

2. You can locate points on a(n) __?__ by using an ordered pair of numbers. *(page 432)*

3. The point where both axes of a coordinate plane intersect is called the __?__ . *(page 432)*

4. An integer that has a value less than 0 is __?__ . *(page 414)*

5. A coordinate plane is formed with two perpendicular lines called __?__ . *(page 432)*

6. Two integers that are the same distance from 0 on a number line are __?__ . *(page 418)*

Concept Check

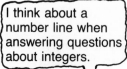

I think about a number line when answering questions about integers.

7. Is zero a positive integer or a negative integer? *(page 414)*

8. The sum of opposite integers is always __?__ . *(page 422)*

9. Is 8 a positive or a negative integer? *(page 428)*

10. Explain how to change subtraction of integers to addition of integers without changing the results. *(page 428)*

11. If you tell someone to turn to the title page of this book, have you given him or her enough information to find the copyright date? *(page 430)*

12. On a coordinate plane, how does the *x*-axis differ from the *y*-axis? *(page 432)*

13. How do you make a coordinate plane from a sheet of plain graph paper? *(page 432)*

14. Why is it important to use an ordered pair to name a point on a coordinate plane? *(page 432)*

15. Explain how to locate the point (⁻2,6) on a coordinate plane. *(page 432)*

Skill Check

Name an integer to represent the situation. *(page 414)*

16. a loss of 3 yards

17. a bank deposit of $6

18. 4 degrees below 0

Order the integers from least to greatest. Use $<$. *(page 418)*

19. $^-1, ^-3, 7, 0, 11$

20. $12, ^-6, 8, ^-7, ^-9$

21. $7, 3, ^-4, ^-9, ^-12$

Use the number line. Write an integer for the given point. *(page 418)*

22. A

23. B

24. C

25. D

26. E

27. F

Find the sum or difference. *(pages 420, 422, 424, 428)*

28. $^-4 + 9$

29. $^-5 + ^-1$

30. $^-5 + 7$

31. $^-7 - 3$

32. $15 - ^-9$

33. $^-10 - ^-2$

34. $8 - ^-10$

35. $^-1 - ^-3$

36. $20 + ^-12$

37. $^-2 + ^-46$

Use graph paper to make a coordinate plane. Locate the point for each ordered pair. *(page 432)*

38. $A\,(2, 6)$

39. $B\,(4, ^-2)$

40. $C\,(^-6, 2)$

41. $D\,(^-1, ^-5)$

Problem-Solving Check *(pages 416, 436)*

42. On Saturday Jayne hiked 4 mi north, 3 mi west, and 2 mi farther north. On Sunday she hiked 2 mi east and 6 mi south. Over the two-day period, how many miles had Jayne hiked when she crossed her own path?

43. Paul's team began on their own 25-yd line. Then they gained 10 yd, lost 26 yd, lost 4 yd, and gained 5 yd. On what yard line are they?

44. Jo must rent a car. Car 1 rents for $139.00 a week, including mileage. Car 2 rents for $109.00 a week plus $0.05 a mile after the first 50 mi. If Jo plans to drive 500 mi, which car option is less expensive?

45. Mr. Kim plans to attend 5 plays. A season ticket costs $175.00 for 7 plays. Individual tickets cost $35.50 each. Which option is less expensive, buying a season ticket or buying an individual ticket to each of 5 plays?

1. Use a number line to help you order these numbers from least to greatest: $^-2$, $^+6$, $^+10$, $^-8$. Explain your method.

2. Use blue counters and red counters to illustrate the sum $^-2 + 6$. Explain your method.

3. Find the difference $8 - {}^-4$. Explain your method.

4. Locate the point $(^-3, 5)$ on a coordinate plane. Explain your method.

5. Read Exercise 2 on page 417. Follow the steps on the Problem-Solving Think Along worksheet to show how to solve this problem.

Remember that the sum of a positive number and its opposite is zero.

Write About It

6. Describe a recent situation in which you or someone in your family used negative integers.

7. Tell whether the following statement is or is not reasonable. Explain.

   If an integer is greater than $^+6$, then its opposite is greater than $^-6$.

TEAMWORK *Project*

Use a Coordinate Plane

Use a coordinate plane to make a scale drawing of your classroom.

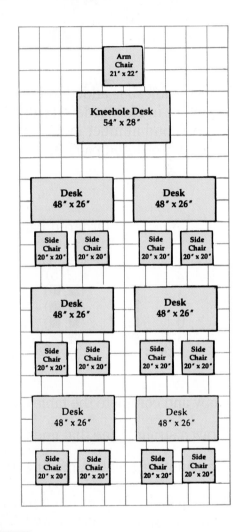

Decide

Decide how to show the exact center of your classroom. This will be (0,0) on your scale drawing.

Decide how your team will work together to complete the scale drawing.

Let one unit on the coordinate plane equal 3 feet in your classroom.

Do

You will need to show chalkboards, tables, bookcases, sinks, and the other large objects in your classroom.

Use ordered pairs to locate the objects on the scale drawing.

Write the ordered pairs for the classroom door, the teacher's desk, and each teammate's desk.

Share

Compare your scale drawing with those of other teams.

TALK ABOUT IT

In what ways is your team's scale drawing similar to those of other teams?

Did you expect most of the drawings to be similar? Why or why not?

Are most of the drawings actually similar?

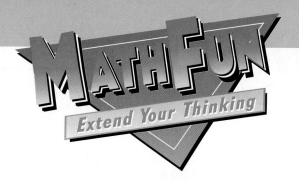

Points on a Straight Line

*I*n this table, 3 is added to the first number in each ordered pair to make the second number in the pair. The first two ordered pairs have been graphed.

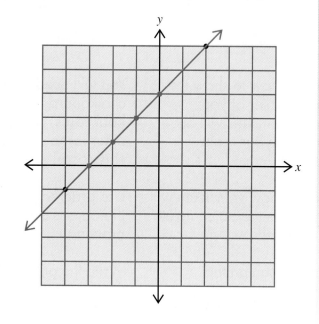

Add 3		Ordered Pair
⁻4	⁻1	(⁻4,⁻1)
2	5	(2, 5)
⁻1	■	(■,■)
⁻2	■	(■,■)
0	■	(■,■)
⁻3	■	(■,■)

1. Copy and complete the table and the graph of ordered pairs.

2. Draw a straight line that goes through all the points on your graph.

3. Find another point on the line. Write the ordered pair for that point.

4. Make a table of six ordered pairs of integers that have a sum of 0. Locate the ordered pairs on a graph. Can you draw a straight line through all the points?

Challenge

Number Puzzle

Arrange integers to complete the magic square so that the sums for the rows, columns, and diagonals are the same.

4	■	■
■	⁻5	8
■	0	⁻14

Problem Solving

A positive integer is twice as many units from 0 on a number line as a negative integer. The two integers are 48 units apart. Find the two integers.

Write the letter of the correct answer.

1. $3\frac{1}{4} \times 2\frac{1}{2}$

  A. $5\frac{1}{8}$ **B.** $5\frac{5}{8}$

  C. $8\frac{1}{8}$ **D.** $8\frac{3}{4}$

2. 93 yd = ▮ ft

  A. 7.75   **B.** 31

  C. 279   **D.** 1,116

3. $\dfrac{▮}{9} = \dfrac{2}{3}$

  A. 3   **B.** 4

  C. 5   **D.** 6

4. What is 20% of 16?

  A. 0.32   **B.** 3.2

  C. 8   **D.** not here

5. Which shows the symbol for parallel lines?

  A. $\overleftrightarrow{AB} \parallel \overleftrightarrow{CD}$ **B.** $\overleftrightarrow{AB} \perp \overleftrightarrow{CD}$

  C. $\overleftrightarrow{AB} \cong \overleftrightarrow{CD}$ **D.** not here

6. What is the third angle in the triangle? 60°, 45°, ▮

  A. 15°   **B.** 105°

  C. 155°   **D.** not here

7. What is the area of the circle?
$r = 5$ cm

  A. 15 cm   **B.** 15.7 cm^2

  C. 78.5 cm   **D.** 78.5 cm^2

8. What is the area of the rectangle?
$l = 12$ ft, $w = 10$ ft

  A. 22 ft   **B.** 44 ft

  C. 60 ft^2 **D.** 120 ft^2

9. On what axis is (7,0)?

  A. x-axis   **B.** y-axis

  C. z-axis   **D.** not here

10. $6 - {}^-2$

  A. $^-2$ **B.** 4

  C. 6   **D.** 8

11. A football team began on their own 20-yd line. First, they gained 10 yd. Next, they lost 5 yd. Then, they gained 15 yd. On what yard line are they?

  A. 20-yd line   **B.** 35-yd line

  C. 40-yd line   **D.** 50-yd line

12. At Ace, Greta can buy 3 brushes for $1.99. At Deuce, she can buy the same kind of brushes at 4 for $2.29. At which store will Greta get the better buy?

  A. Ace   **B.** Deuce

  C. same   **D.** need more facts

GETTING READY
FOR ALGEBRA

Did you know...

... that in the future your homes may be powered completely by solar energy cells that are controlled by a personal computer?

TALK ABOUT IT

Suppose a 1 m² solar panel can collect 1,000 watts of power per day. How can you find the number of panels needed to provide power for your home for a day?

THE LANGUAGE OF ALGEBRA

Cable television did not gain popularity until the late 1960's when the high costs began to decrease. By the year 2020, the cost of cable television may decrease by $12 a month. What expression can you write to show the decrease in cost?

To solve the problem, first choose a variable to represent the present cost of cable television. Then write the expression.

Let the variable c represent the present cost of cable television.

Word expression: c decreased by twelve

Algebraic expression: $c - 12$

So, the algebraic expression $c - 12$ shows the decrease in cost.

More Examples

word expressions

five more than z two times a t divided by twelve

$z + 5$ $2a$ $\dfrac{t}{12}$

algebraic expressions

When you use variables to represent unknown quantities, you are using **algebra**. Solving equations and evaluating expressions are ways to find unknown quantities.

Remember that an equation is a number sentence. It has an equals sign.

$$y + 8 = 20 \qquad 3 + 5 = 8 \qquad 22 - w = 11 \qquad d \div 2 = 12$$

Talk About It

▶ Does the variable in an expression always represent the same number? Explain.

▶ How is an equation different from an expression?

Check for Understanding

Write a word from the box to complete each sentence.

algebra	equation	expression	variable

1. The number sentence $x + 8 = 12$ is a(n) __?__ .

2. In the equation $x + 8 = 12$, x is called a(n) __?__ .

3. In the equation $x + 8 = 42$, $x + 8$ is a(n) __?__ .

4. When you use variables to represent unknown quantities, you are using __?__ .

Practice

Write a word expression for the algebraic expression.

5. $x - 4$

6. $t + 8$

7. $7 + s$

8. $y - 10$

9. $3 - w$

10. $5b$

11. $10a$

12. $\dfrac{x}{5}$

13. $z + 6$

14. $8m$

15. $\dfrac{r}{6}$

16. $10 - y$

Copy and complete the table. Write an algebraic expression, an equation, or a word phrase.

	Word Expression or Sentence	Algebraic Expression or Equation
17.	y plus twelve	■
18.	n and seven equals nine	■
19.	__?__	$^-4 + \dfrac{1}{2}n$
20.	five less than p is 12	■
21.	d divided by four	■
22.	16 is four times h	■

Mixed Applications

23. Jane Tallchief, a Navajo, was 7 years old in 1990. How old will she be in 2020?

24. **Mental Math** Use c for cost. Write an expression to show an increase of $5.

MULTICULTURAL NOTE: Most of the Navajo people live in Arizona, New Mexico, and Utah.

How can you change the expression $a + 6$ to an equation?

WRAP UP...

RATIONAL NUMBERS

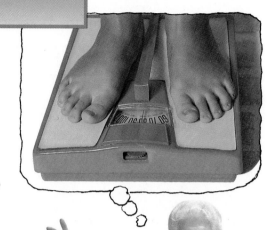

Raphael Perez is an economist who studies future trends. Recently, he predicted that by the year 2000, 90% of all Americans will be overweight. Is 90% a rational number?

A **rational number** can be written as the ratio $\frac{a}{b}$ where a and b are integers and $b \neq 0$. Rational numbers include whole numbers, decimals, fractions, mixed numbers, percents, and integers.

You can write 90% as the ratio $\frac{9}{10}$.

Since you can write 90% as $\frac{90}{100}$, or $\frac{9}{10}$, 90% is a rational number.

Examples

Write the number in the form $\frac{a}{b}$.

$12 = \frac{12}{1}$ $1\frac{3}{5} = \frac{8}{5}$ $2.5 = \frac{25}{10}$, or $\frac{5}{2}$ $75\% = \frac{3}{4}$ $^-3 = \frac{^-3}{1}$

The type of rational number you use depends on the situation.

Examples

A. Money is usually expressed in decimal form, such as $12.35.

Sometimes, you use fractions to express money amounts, such as $\frac{1}{2}$ dollar.

 B. When you use a standard calculator, a fraction is expressed as a decimal. For example, $\frac{3}{5}$ is expressed as 0.6.

$3 \boxed{\div} 5 = \boxed{\quad 0.6}$

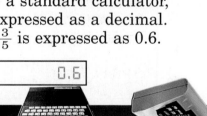

Talk About It

▶ Which rational numbers do you use to count?

▶ Which rational numbers do you use to measure when you cook?

Check for Understanding

Write in the form $\frac{a}{b}$.

1. 0.2 **2.** $1\frac{3}{4}$ **3.** 25% **4.** 1.5 **5.** $3\frac{1}{3}$

Practice

Write the rational number in the form $\frac{a}{b}$.

6. 0.99   **7.** 1.2   **8.** 0.6   **9.** 0.75   **10.** 0.95

11. $\frac{4}{5}$ **12.** $5\frac{11}{12}$ **13.** 90%   **14.** $1\frac{9}{11}$ **15.** 0.11

16. 7%   **17.** $4\frac{1}{2}$ **18.** 16%   **19.** 10.3   **20.** 100%

Tell which rational numbers you would use in the given situation.

21. to express the amount in your bank account

22. to express the amount of spice needed to make muffins

23. to express your shoe size

24. to express a temperature below 0°

25. Is every rational number a whole number? Explain.

26. Is every integer a rational number? Explain.

Mixed Applications

27. Critical Thinking Can you write all the possible fractions equivalent to $\frac{1}{2}$? Explain. Write five fractions equivalent to $\frac{1}{2}$.

28. Critical Thinking The normal body temperature for a human is 98.6°F. Show that 98.6 is a rational number.

29. Only 2% of the apples in a market are bruised. How many apples are bruised if the market has 100 apples?

30. Number Sense How many degrees must the maker of a circle graph use to show 25%?

MIXED REVIEW

Find the least common multiple (LCM) for each pair of numbers.

1. 3, 5   **2.** 15, 45   **3.** 24, 48   **4.** 10, 15   **5.** 2, 18

Find the missing number.

6. 240 mg = ▇ g   **7.** 50 cm = ▇ mm   **8.** 0.2 kL = ▇ L   **9.** 50 cm = ▇ m

Explain why you usually use fractions instead of decimals to express part of a foot.

VARIABLES AND EXPRESSIONS

In the future, jets will travel much faster than today's jets. The Concorde travels at 1,500 mph. How fast will jets travel if they travel 100 mph faster than the Concorde? 500 mph faster? 1,000 mph faster?

You know the speed of the Concorde is 1,500 mph. Since you must find three possible speeds for jets of the future, you can use an expression.

Write an expression. Let c represent the number of miles per hour faster a jet of the future will travel than the Concorde.

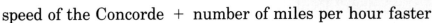

speed of the Concorde + number of miles per hour faster

$$1,500 + c$$

To evaluate an algebraic expression, replace the variable with the given value for the variable. Then perform the operation. Use a calculator with memory keys.

 Enter 1,500 [M+].

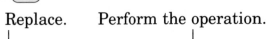

	Replace.	Perform the operation.

1,500 + c

[MRC]	[+]	100	[=]	1600.
[MRC]	[+]	500	[=]	2000.
[MRC]	[+]	1,000	[=]	2500.

So, the jets of the future will travel at 1,600 mph, 2,000 mph, or 2,500 mph.

MULTICULTURAL NOTE: The Concorde, one of the first supersonic transport planes, was built by Britain and France and began carrying passengers in 1976.

Examples

Evaluate the expressions for $d = 10$, $z = \frac{1}{2}$, and $t = ^-12$.

A. $\dfrac{d}{2.5}$

$10 \div 2.5 = 4$

B. $13z$

$13 \times \dfrac{1}{2} = \dfrac{13}{2}$, or $6\dfrac{1}{2}$

C. $t + 10$

$^-12 + 10 = ^-2$

• Why is $y + 12$ the same as $12 + y$?

Check for Understanding

Evaluate the expression.

1. $8 + x$, for $x = 5$

2. $y + 10$, for $y = 12$

3. $z - 3$, for $z = 15$

4. $5w$, for $w = 6$

5. $\dfrac{81}{t}$, for $t = 3$

6. $\dfrac{b}{5}$, for $b = 55$

Practice

Evaluate the expression $y - 12$ for each value of y.

7. $y = 24$

8. $y = 36$

9. $y = 15\dfrac{2}{5}$

10. $y = 33.05$

11. $y = {}^-2$

Evaluate the expression $d \div 3$ for each value of d.

12. $d = 24$

13. $d = \dfrac{1}{3}$

14. $d = 6\dfrac{2}{3}$

15. $d = 27.9$

16. $d = 111$

Evaluate the expression $7s$ for each value of s.

17. $s = 9$

18. $s = 3\dfrac{1}{5}$

19. $s = 5.5$

20. $s = 45\%$

21. $s = 4.02$

Mixed Applications

22. Critical Thinking The dimensions of Bette's rectangular yard are twice the dimensions of Ian's rectangular yard. How does the area of Bette's yard compare with the area of Ian's yard?

23. John has 9 more apples than Rose. Let x equal the number of apples John has. Write an equation, using 9 for the number of apples Rose has.

CHALLENGE • GEOMETRY CONNECTION

Look at the figure. Try to visualize it as a combination of familiar geometric figures.

Let A = area, P = perimeter, r = radius, s = side, and d = diameter.

24. Write a formula for finding the perimeter.

25. Write a formula for finding the area.

26. Use your formulas to find the perimeter and the area.

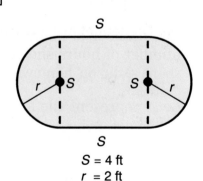

$S = 4$ ft
$r = 2$ ft

If the value of x changes, will the value of $x - 5$ remain the same? Explain.

Marshall thinks a twenty-first century baseball player will reach a lifetime record of 807 home runs, beating Henry Aaron's record of 755. The new record would be a meaningful increase over Aaron's record. What would be the increase in the number of home runs?

You can write and solve an equation to answer this question. Let n represent the increase.

Talk About It

▶ What expression, using n and 755, shows the increase in the number of home runs?

▶ How can you use the expression and 807 to form an equation?

▶ What is the inverse of the operation in the equation?

Use the inverse operation to solve the equation.

$$n + 755 = 807$$
$$n + 755 - 755 = 807 - 755 \quad \longleftarrow \text{ Subtract 755 from each side of the equation.}$$
$$n = 52$$

So, the increase would be 52 home runs.

You can solve equations with fractions in the same way you solve equations with whole numbers.

The number of hours Lily spent reading decreased by the number of hours she spent doing homework is $1\frac{3}{4}$. If she spent $\frac{3}{4}$ hr on homework, how long did she read?

Let r represent the amount of time for reading.

$$r - \frac{3}{4} = 1\frac{3}{4}$$
$$r - \frac{3}{4} + \frac{3}{4} = 1\frac{3}{4} + \frac{3}{4}$$
$$r = 2\frac{2}{4} = 2\frac{1}{2}$$

So, Lily read for $2\frac{1}{2}$ hr.

Check for Understanding

Tell how to solve the equation.

1. $x - 50 = 127$ **2.** $122 + y = 200$ **3.** $x - 1\frac{1}{2} = 4$

4. $m + \frac{3}{4} = 3$ **5.** $w - 10\frac{3}{8} = 10\frac{7}{8}$ **6.** $a + 1\frac{1}{5} = 3\frac{4}{5}$

Practice

Tell the inverse of the operation in the equation.

7. $x - 4 = 1$ **8.** $t + 8 = 17$ **9.** $\frac{3}{7} + s = 9$ **10.** $a - 12 = 62$

11. $y - \frac{1}{10} = 25$ **12.** $w - 3 = 17\frac{1}{3}$ **13.** $18 = x + 6$ **14.** $11 + c = 45$

Solve the equation. Use inverse operations.

15. $x + 321 = 500$ **16.** $y - 212 = 347$ **17.** $a + 347 = 459$ **18.** $b + 13 = 500$

19. $x + \frac{3}{8} = \frac{7}{8}$ **20.** $y - \frac{5}{6} = 1$ **21.** $m + 2\frac{1}{2} = 6$ **22.** $y - \frac{1}{2} = \frac{3}{4}$

23. $a + \frac{1}{5} = \frac{7}{20}$ **24.** $x - \frac{2}{3} = \frac{3}{4}$ **25.** $w + 3\frac{5}{12} = 7\frac{1}{3}$ **26.** $z - 2\frac{1}{5} = 11\frac{6}{10}$

27. $m + 17,345 = 28,000$ **28.** $a - 76,298 = 100,000$ **29.** $n + 7\frac{5}{12} = 23$

Mixed Applications

30. By the year 2000, U.S. exports of wheat, rice, and corn may increase by 15,000,000 tons. If exports now total 45,763,000 tons, how much may be exported by 2000?

31. Write a Problem Write a problem that can be solved by writing an equation involving fractions.

MIXED REVIEW

Write the greatest common factor (GCF) for each pair of numbers.

1. $9, 33$ **2.** $7, 35$ **3.** $24, 60$ **4.** $18, 99$ **5.** $5, 45$

Write the prime factorization in exponent form.

6. 15 **7.** 45 **8.** 60 **9.** 54 **10.** 75

Explain how to use inverse operations to solve equations.

WRAP UP...

PROBLEM SOLVING

STRATEGY • Write an Equation

The fastest trains in the world today can travel at an average speed of 135 mph. In the future, underground vacuum tubes may travel at an average speed of 14,000 mph. How much faster than today's trains could the vacuum tubes travel?

Sometimes you can solve a problem by writing an equation that relates the quantities you know to the quantity you are trying to find.

▶ **UNDERSTAND**

What are you asked to find?

What facts are given?

▶ **PLAN**

What strategy will you use?

You can *write an equation* that shows how the average speed of trains relates to the average speed of vacuum tubes. To do this, choose a variable to represent the amount of increase.

▶ **SOLVE**

How will you solve the problem?

Let n represent the increase in speed. Then *write an equation* relating the given facts to n.

$$n + 135 = 14,000$$

Use the inverse of addition. Subtract 135 from each side.

$$n + 135 - 135 = 14,000 - 135$$
$$n = 13,865$$

So, the vacuum tubes could travel 13,865 mph faster than today's trains.

▶ **LOOK BACK**

How can you check your answer?

WHAT IF... . . . you write the equation $135 + n = 14,000$ instead of $n + 135 = 14,000$? How will this affect your answer?

Apply

Write an equation. Then solve.

1 Suppose that a football player breaks Fran Tarkenton's lifetime record of 47,003 yd gained. If the new record is 50,000 yd gained, what is the increase over Tarkenton's record?

2 Alice is saving money to buy a computer printer that costs $399. She has already saved $150. How much more does she need to save?

Mixed Applications ⟹ **STRATEGIES** Write an Equation • Make a Table • Guess and Check • Draw a Diagram

Choose a strategy and solve.

3 Mike will save $10 this month, $20 next month, $30 the third month, and so on. If the pattern continues, how much will Mike save the sixth month?

4 The temperature was 28°F at 6 A.M. By noon it was 40°F. How much did the temperature increase during the six hours?

5 Thea walks 5 blocks east, 2 blocks north, 4 blocks west, and 5 blocks north. Is she north or south of the point where she began?

6 Aldo has 10 coins in his pocket. He has only dimes and quarters. The total value of the coins is $1.30. How many quarters does he have?

7 The sum of Angelo's age and Mai's age is 29. Angelo is 3 years younger than Mai. How old are Angelo and Mai?

8 A square patio has an area of 121 ft². What is the length of each side of the patio?

WRITER'S CORNER

9 Today's jet planes travel between New York and Los Angeles in 378 min. In the future, underground vacuum tubes may travel the same distance in 54 min. Use this information to write a problem that can be solved by writing an equation.

Use the table for Exercises 1–2.

I need to determine the total cost of each option.

1. Saoni wants to buy a robot. She has $50 and earns $60 a month at a part-time job. Which option could Saoni choose? Why?

2. Which of the options is the most expensive? the least expensive?

Robot Purchase Options

1. Pay $145 cash.
2. Pay $18 a month for 12 months.
3. Pay $45 down and $12 a month for 12 months.

3. Paul starts a salad while he microwaves his dinner for 15 min. The salad is ready in 21 min. How much longer does it take Paul to make the salad than to microwave the dinner?

4. A monorail car at an amusement park holds 45 passengers. The park manager wants to be sure he has enough cars to accommodate 1,255 passengers. How many monorail cars does he need?

Find the sum or difference.

5. $2 + {}^-3$

6. ${}^-10 - 8$

7. $11 - {}^-9$

8. ${}^-12 + {}^-6$

Write the ordered pair for each point on the coordinate plane.

9. point A

10. point B

11. point C

12. point D

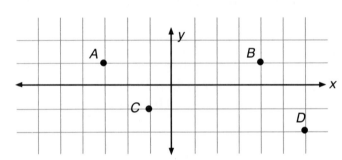

Write an algebraic expression for the word expression.

13. 12 times a

14. 9 more than r

15. 8 less than d

16. c divided by 16

Write the rational number in the form $\frac{a}{b}$.

17. 0.33

18. 5%

19. 2.1

20. 0.35

21. $1\frac{1}{2}$

22. 0.10

Evaluate the expression.

23. $10 - x$, for $x = 9$

24. $y + 4$, for $y = {}^-2$

25. $2z$, for $z = 52$

Solve the equation. Use inverse operations.

26. $a - \frac{3}{4} = \frac{1}{8}$

27. $x + 99 = 220$

28. $y - 9 = {}^-18$

29. $\frac{3}{5} + w = 3\frac{1}{3}$

Expressions for Prime Numbers

Mathematicians have studied prime numbers for over two thousand years. The Greek mathematician Eratosthenes was one of the first to develop a method for finding prime numbers (see page 185).

The French mathematician Pierre de Fermat (1601–1665), who is called the founder of modern number theory, spent much of his time exploring prime numbers. He developed the following expression to find prime numbers.

$$2^{2^n} + 1$$

Using Fermat's expression to find a prime number would involve a lot of calculation. This is a simpler expression that you can use to find some prime numbers:

$$2^n - 1$$

Example Let $n = 3$.
So, $2^n - 1 = 2^3 - 1$
$= 2 \times 2 \times 2 - 1$
$= 8 - 1$
$= 7$

MULTICULTURAL NOTE: Pierre de Fermat was one of many French mathematicians who made contributions to the study of numbers and geometry.

Use the expression $2^n - 1$ to find a prime number for the value of n.

1. $n = 2$ **2.** $n = 5$ **3.** $n = 7$ **4.** $n = 13$

In 1992 David Slowinski and Paul Cage, computer scientists in England, broke the record for the largest known prime number. The prime number they discovered is $2^{756,839} - 1$. This number has 227,832 digits.

5. Write as many digits as you can on one line of a sheet of notebook paper. Count and record the number of digits that you wrote. Then estimate how many lines and how many sheets of notebook paper it would take to write the prime number described above.

EQUATIONS
with Integers

Homes of the future may be built beneath the ocean's surface. Suppose the entrance to an ocean home is 15 m below the surface. The base of the home is 25 m lower than the entrance. How far below the ocean's surface is the base of the home?

You can use integers to write and solve an equation. Let n represent how far the base is from the surface.

Talk About It

▶ What is an expression that shows how far the base is beneath the ocean's surface?

▶ How can you use the expression and n to write an equation?

$$^-15 + {^-25} = n \longleftarrow \text{Add the integers.}$$
$$^-40 = n$$

So, the base of the home of the future is 40 m beneath the ocean's surface.

More Examples

A. $x + {^-8} = {^-2}$

Use the inverse operation. Subtract $^-8$ from each side.

$$x + {^-8} - {^-8} = {^-2} - {^-8}$$

Rewrite as addition. Then add.

$$x + {^-8} + 8 = {^-2} + 8$$
$$x = 6$$

B. $y - {^-45} = 52$

Rewrite as addition.

$$y + 45 = 52$$

Use the inverse operation. Subtract 45 from each side.

$$y + 45 - 45 = 52 - 45$$
$$y = 7$$

Talk About It

▶ In Example **A**, how can you solve the equation by adding the same integer to each side?

▶ In Example **B**, how can you solve the equation by adding the same integer to each side?

Check for Understanding

Tell how to solve the equation.

1. $n = {}^-6 + 8$

2. $^-8 + {}^-6 = y$

3. $n - 2 = {}^-8$

4. $x - {}^-6 = 10$

5. $y + {}^-2 = {}^-9$

6. $m + 4 = 1$

Practice

Tell what integers to add or subtract to solve the equation.

7. $a = 10 + {}^-3$

8. $m = {}^-14 + {}^-5$

9. $x = {}^-12 + 2$

10. $x - 5 = 2$

11. $m - {}^-7 = 8$

12. $c - 3 = {}^-4$

13. $r + {}^-20 = 13$

14. $x + {}^-5 = {}^-9$

15. $n + 29 = 20$

Solve the equation.

16. $a = 17 + {}^-3$

17. $x = 17 - {}^-2$

18. $r = {}^-8 - {}^-1$

19. $b = {}^-11 - {}^+12$

20. $x + {}^-8 = {}^-11$

21. $x - 8 = {}^-6$

22. $m + {}^-70 = 100$

23. $x - {}^-9 = 33$

24. $x - 13 = 2$

25. $a + {}^-7 = {}^-17$

26. $a + 7 = 1$

27. $x + 9 = {}^-33$

28. $x + 14 = 3$

29. $m - 12 = 2$

30. $r - {}^-6 = 10$

31. $s + {}^-12 = 35$

32. If x is 7, what is $x + 12$?

33. If y is 22, what is $56 - y$?

34. If b is $^-5$, what is $b + 9$?

35. If c is $^-6$, what is $15 - c$?

Mixed Applications

36. **Number Sense** Look at these numbers: 2, 3, 5, 8, and 12. What are the next two numbers in the pattern?

37. A diver was 78 ft below the surface of the water. She rose to 50 ft below the surface. How many feet did the diver ascend?

38. **Write a Question** Daytime temperatures on the moon reach 250°F. At night, temperatures on the moon drop to $^-260°$F.

Tell how to solve the equation
$x - {}^-7 = 4.$

INEQUALITIES

A scientist predicts that the United States will begin to explore Mars in less than 12 years. What inequality can you write to represent the statement?

Remember that an equation has an equals sign. An **inequality** has either $<$ or $>$.

Since you do not know the exact number of years, you can use the variable n to represent the number of years. Then write the inequality.

$$n < 12$$

An inequality may have more than one solution. For $n < 12$, there are 11 whole-number solutions.

$1 < 12$	$2 < 12$	$3 < 12$	$4 < 12$	$5 < 12$	$6 < 12$
$7 < 12$	$8 < 12$	$9 < 12$	$10 < 12$	$11 < 12$	

The choices of fraction, mixed-number, decimal, and integer solutions continue forever.

Another Method

You can use a number line to visualize solutions.

$$n > 2$$

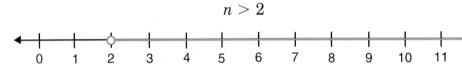

The circle above 2 shows that the number 2 is not included. The line segment to the right of 2 shows that all numbers greater than 2 are included.

- Are $6\frac{1}{2}$, 4.7, and $\frac{14}{5}$ also solutions of $n > 2$?

Example

$$y < 8$$

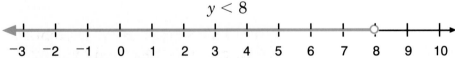

- How will the number line that shows $y > 8$ differ from the number line that shows $y < 8$? Draw the number line.

Check for Understanding

Tell whether the given number is a solution of the inequality in the box. Write *yes* or *no*.

$$x < 5$$

1. 0   **2.** $2\frac{1}{2}$ **3.** 7   **4.** ⁻5   **5.** 5   **6.** 10   **7.** 2

$$x + 4 > {}^-2$$

8. 0   **9.** ⁻4   **10.** ⁻2   **11.** ⁻5   **12.** 20   **13.** ⁻15   **14.** ⁻3

Practice

Tell whether ⁻1 is a solution of the inequality. Write *yes* or *no*.

15. $y > 0$ **16.** $x < {}^-2$ **17.** $x + 3 > 1$ **18.** $y < 12$

Tell whether 3 is a solution of the inequality. Write *yes* or *no*.

19. $x - 2 < 0$ **20.** $y + 5 > {}^-4$ **21.** $m - 3 > 0$ **22.** $n - 4 > {}^-2$

23. Tell which number line shows solutions of $x < 2$.

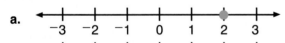

24. Tell which number line shows solutions of $y > {}^-3$.

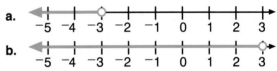

Draw a number line that shows the solutions of the inequality.

25. $m > {}^-4$ **26.** $x < {}^-2$ **27.** $m > 5$ **28.** $b + 2 > 0$

29. $a < 3\frac{1}{2}$ **30.** $t > 1\frac{2}{3}$ **31.** $x < 10$ **32.** $d - 5 < 10$

Mixed Applications

33. Use the variable x to write an inequality. The amount in Sally's savings account is less than $50.

34. **Write a Problem** Write a problem that can only be solved by using negative integers.

Explain why 3.4 and $2\frac{1}{2}$ are solutions of $a < 4$.

WRAP UP...

EXPLORING

Relations

When you use algebra, you are exploring how numbers relate to one another and often create patterns.

Work Together

Building Understanding

Use the rectangular prism to explore relations.

TALK ABOUT IT

- How many cubes are in each layer? How many layers are in the prism?

- If the prism had 6 layers, how many cubes would there be?

- How is the total number of cubes related to the number of layers?

- Let n represent the number of layers. What expression can you write to describe the number of cubes?

Copy and complete the table to find the pattern.

Number of layers	1	2	3	4	5
Total number of cubes	■	■	■	■	■

Another Activity

Brett is 11 years old, and his sister Heather is 9.

Copy and complete the table to show the pattern.

Brett's age	11	12	13	14	15
Heather's age	9	■	■	■	■

TALK ABOUT IT

- How is Brett's age related to Heather's age?

- Let h represent Heather's age. What expression can you write to describe Brett's age?

Making the Connection

When two quantities create a pattern, they are said to form a **relation**. One way to show a relation is to write an expression.

In the rectangular prism, the total number of cubes can be represented by the expression $20n$.

Likewise, Brett's age can be represented by the expression $h + 2$.

Another Example

Suppose the car of the future uses 15 watts of solar power for each mile it travels. What expression can you write to show the number of watts used?

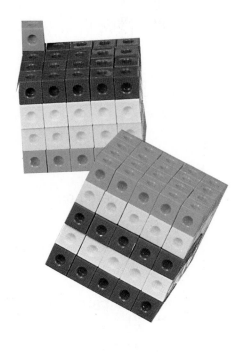

Let x represent the number of miles.

Let y represent the number of watts.

x	1	2	3	4	5
y	15	30	45	60	75

$\longrightarrow 15x$

So, the expression $15x$ shows the number of watts used.

Checking Understanding

Copy and complete the table. Then write an expression using x to show the value of y.

1.

x	3	4	5	6	7	8	9
y	7	8	9	▧	▧	▧	▧

 2.

x	0	1	2	3	4	5	6
y	0	3	6	9	▧	▧	▧

3.

x	2	3	4	5	6	7	8	9
y	0	1	2	3	▧	▧	▧	▧

4.

x	5	10	15	20	25	30
y	1	2	3	▧	▧	▧

5.

x	0	1	2	3	4	5	6	7	8
y	0	$\frac{1}{2}$	1	$\frac{3}{2}$	2	▧	▧	▧	▧

6. In Exercise 3, what expression can you write, using y, to show the value of x?

GRAPHING RELATIONS

Japanese engineers are developing trains that will be able to travel 300 miles per hour. A train traveling 300 miles per hour is going 5 miles per minute. This relationship is shown in the table.

Number of miles	5	10	15	20	25
Number of minutes	1	2	3	4	5

Let m represent the number of miles traveled. Then the expression $\frac{m}{5}$ shows the number of minutes used to travel this distance.

This relation can also be shown by a set of ordered pairs.

(5,1)   (10,2)   (15,3)   (20,4)   (25,5)

You can use the set of ordered pairs to graph a relation.

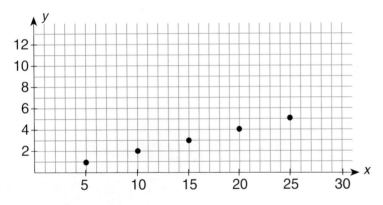

MULTICULTURAL NOTE: The Japanese are developing a high-speed train that is called the magnetically levitated vehicle (MLV).

Example

Name the ordered pairs in the table.

x	⁻3	⁻2	⁻1	0	1	2
y	3	2	1	0	⁻1	⁻2

The ordered pairs are (⁻3,3), (⁻2,2), (⁻1,1), (0,0), (1,⁻1), and (2,⁻2).

Talk About It

▶ What expression, using x, can you write to show the value of y in the example?

  Idea Bank, page 490, Exercises 1–4

Check for Understanding

Name the ordered pairs in the table.

1.

x	8	7	6	5	4
y	5	4	3	2	1

2.

x	4	8	12	16	20
y	1	2	3	4	5

3. What expression, using y, can you write to show the value of x in Exercise 1?

4. What expression, using y, can you write to show the value of x in Exercise 2?

5–6. Use graph paper to make two coordinate planes. Then graph the relation in Exercise 1 and in Exercise 2.

Practice

Use the expression to help you complete the table.

7. $x + 2$

x	0	1	2	3	4
y	2	3	▢	▢	▢

8. $2x$

x	1	2	3	4	5
y	2	4	▢	▢	▢

9. $x - 5$

x	15	14	13	12	11
y	10	9	▢	▢	▢

10. $2x + 1$

x	2	3	4	5	6
y	5	7	▢	▢	▢

11. $2x - 1$

x	1	2	3	4	5
y	1	3	▢	▢	▢

12. $3x - 3$

x	1	2	3	4	5
y	0	3	▢	▢	▢

13–18. Use graph paper. Draw a coordinate plane for each exercise. Graph the ordered pairs for Exercises 7–12.

Mixed Applications

Use the table for Exercises 19–20.

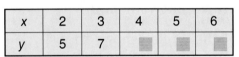

Scientists (s)	1	2	3	4	5
Moons explored (m)	5	8	11	14	17

19. What expression, using s, describes the number of moons explored?

20. Use Data If the pattern continues, how many moons can 10 scientists explore?

What expression can you write to describe the number of students per table in your school cafeteria?

WRAP UP...

PROBLEM SOLVING

Logical Reasoning

The sixth-grade class has 28 students. There are 14 who play in the band, 9 who are on the swim team, and 4 who participate in both activities. Kay drew this diagram to show student participation. How many students do not participate in either activity?

Band Participants   Swim Team Participants

10   4   5

Some problems involving relationships among groups (or sets) of people can be solved by using logical reasoning.

▶ **UNDERSTAND**

What are you asked to find?

What information are you given?

▶ **PLAN**

How can you solve the problem?

Use logical reasoning to determine the number of students not participating in either activity.

▶ **SOLVE**

How can you carry out your plan?

The overlap of the circles shows that 4 students participate in both activities.

There are 10 students in the band who are not on the swim team. There are 5 students on the swim team who are not in the band.

Therefore, there are 4 + 10 + 5, or 19, students in the band or on the swim team or both. This leaves 28 − 19, or 9, students who do not participate in either activity.

So, 9 students in the sixth-grade class do not participate in either activity.

▶ **LOOK BACK**

What other strategy could you use?

WHAT IF... ...you were asked the number of students who participate in only one activity? What would be your answer?

Apply

Solve. Use logical reasoning.

1 A language club has 35 members. Of these members, 15 speak Spanish, 11 speak French, and 5 speak both Spanish and French. How many members do not speak Spanish or French?

2 The results of a survey of 50 people show 11 who ski but do not play tennis, 8 who play tennis but do not ski, and 3 who do both. How many people do not ski or play tennis?

| Mixed Applications ⟹ STRATEGIES | **Draw a Diagram • Guess and Check • Make a Table • Find a Pattern** |

Choose a strategy and solve.

3 The difference between two numbers is 10. Their sum is 90. What are the numbers?

4 The first number in a pattern is 7. Each number thereafter increases by 4. What is the seventh number in the pattern?

5 If the area of a square picture is 81 in.², what is the length of each side of the picture?

6 Anna is 4 years older than Julio. If the sum of their ages is 22, how old is Julio?

7 Adult tickets to a concert cost $5. Student tickets cost $2. A group of 10 people will attend the concert. The total cost is $29. How many students will attend?

8 Wallace plans to practice his trumpet 3 hr in Week 1 and 4 hr in Week 2. He will add 1 hr to his practice time each week for 10 weeks. For how many hours will he practice in Week 7?

9 In a group of 60 students, 16 are in the choir, 25 are in the computer club, and 12 are in both. How many students do not participate in either the choir or the computer club?

10 Jalim walks 3 blocks north, 5 blocks east, 2 blocks south, and 6 blocks west. How many blocks will he have walked when he crosses his own path?

11 Look at the table. How many passengers will fit in 5 personal jets?

Personal jets	1	2	3	4
Passengers	1	4	9	16

CHAPTER REVIEW / TEST

Vocabulary Check

Choose a word from the box to complete each sentence.

algebra
equation
inequality
rational
relation
variable

1. When you use variables to represent unknown quantities, you are using __?__ . *(page 446)*

2. A number that can be written in the form $\frac{a}{b}$ where a and b are integers and $b \neq 0$ is a(n) __?__ number. *(page 448)*

3. When two quantities create a pattern, they form a(n) __?__ . *(pages 462, 463)*

4. A letter that represents an unknown number is a(n) __?__ . *(pages 446, 450)*

5. A mathematical number sentence that uses < or > is a(n) __?__ . *(page 460)*

6. A mathematical number sentence that uses an equals sign is a(n) __?__ . *(page 446)*

7. What is the difference between an expression and an equation? *(page 446)*

8. How do you know whether a number is a rational number? *(page 448)*

9. How do you evaluate algebraic expressions? *(page 450)*

10. How do you solve the equation $t - 5 = 12$? *(page 452)*

Tell whether the given number is a solution to the inequality in the box. Write *yes* or *no*. *(page 460)*

$$x + 2 > 4$$

11. 10   12. 2   13. 18   14. ⁻5   15. 0   16. 3

Write an expression using *x* that shows the value of *y*. *(page 462)*

17.
x	2	4	6	8	10	12	14
y	1	2	3	4	5	6	7

18.
x	2	5	10	15	20	25	30
y	4	10	20	30	40	50	60

Inequalities have more than one correct answer.

Skill Check

Write a word expression for the algebraic expression. *(page 446)*

19. $8 - y$ **20.** $9 + x$ **21.** $\dfrac{z}{7}$ **22.** $(a + 6) - 10$

Write an algebraic expression for the word expression. *(page 446)*

23. six less than b **24.** x plus eleven **25.** twelve divided by a

Write the number in the form $\frac{a}{b}$. *(page 448)*

26. $9\dfrac{1}{5}$ **27.** 9% **28.** $7\dfrac{1}{2}$ **29.** $10\dfrac{1}{2}$ **30.** 0.55 **31.** 25

Evaluate the expression. *(page 450)*

32. $x + 16$, for $x = 5$ **33.** $\dfrac{y}{0.5}$, for $y = 28$ **34.** $z - {}^-3$, for $z = 50$

Solve the equation. Use inverse operations. *(pages 452, 458)*

35. $x + 75 = 205$ **36.** $y - {}^-54 = 55$ **37.** $z - \dfrac{1}{9} = \dfrac{1}{3}$

Tell whether ${}^-7$ is a solution of the inequality.
Write *yes* or *no*. *(page 460)*

38. $x > {}^-1$ **39.** $y < 10$ **40.** $z + 11 > {}^-7$ **41.** $r > 1$

42. $b > {}^-7$ **43.** $c < {}^-8$ **44.** $h - 20 < 45$ **45.** $d < {}^-7$

46. Copy and complete the table. Then
write the expression that shows the
value of y. *(page 462)*

x	1	2	3	4	5	6	7	8
y	2	4	6	8	▨	▨	▨	▨

Problem-Solving Check *(pages 454, 466)*

47. The winning football team was
ahead 35 to 10. Then the losing
team scored 10 points. How many
more points must the losing team
score to tie the game?

48. Mona had 10 yd of material. She
used 4.8 yd to make a suit. How
much material does she have left?

49. A survey of 130 people showed that
55 carried only umbrellas, 50
carried only briefcases, and 15
carried both. How many people did
not carry umbrellas or briefcases?

50. Of the 51 people who ate in a
cafeteria, 32 had salads, 10 had hot
meals, 3 had both, and the rest had
sandwiches. How many people had
sandwiches?

1. Write an expression to describe the number of books in Pete's desk if Pete has 3 more books than John and x equals the number of books in John's desk. Explain.

2. Give examples of situations in which you might express a rational number as a decimal, as a fraction, as a mixed number, and as an integer.

3. Show each step as you solve $x - {}^-3 = 8$. Explain your method.

4. Show the solutions for the inequality $m > {}^-2$ on a number line.

5. Look at the table in Exercise 3 on page 463. Use graph paper to graph the relation shown in this table. Explain your method.

6. Read Exercise 2 on page 455. Follow the steps on the Problem-Solving Think Along worksheet to show how to solve this problem.

Write About It

7. Explain why you think it is important for you to get ready for algebra.

8. Explain how you know whether $^-5$ is a solution of the inequality $a - 15 < 35$.

TEAMWORK
Project

Twenty-First Century Products

*I*n 1975 who could have believed there would be a pocket-size color television set? Let your mind wander into the twenty-first century. What kinds of products will you be using? Work with your teammates to design a future-products catalog.

Decide

Brainstorm products that you might expect to see in the future.

Think about the products' durability, price, and usefulness.

Discuss what products should be in the catalog. Choose ten products.

Decide the products' prices, sizes, and descriptions.

Do

Design and make a catalog that shows or explains these ten products.

Share

Compare your team's catalog with those of other teams. Tell why you chose each product. Did other teams include similar products?

Talk About It

How did you determine the prices of the products?

What new technology will be required to produce the products?

How did you use rational numbers in your catalog?

NUMBERS AND GEOMETRY

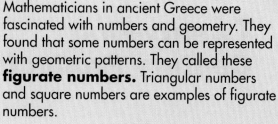

Mathematicians in ancient Greece were fascinated with numbers and geometry. They found that some numbers can be represented with geometric patterns. They called these **figurate numbers.** Triangular numbers and square numbers are examples of figurate numbers.

1. These diagrams show the first four triangular numbers. What is the next triangular number? Draw a diagram to show it.

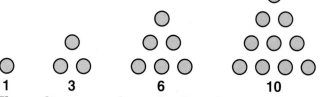

1   3   6   10

2. These diagrams show the first four square numbers. What is the next square number? Draw a diagram to show it.

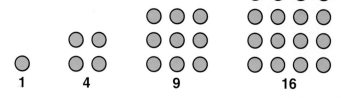

1   4   9   16

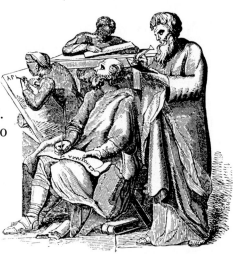

Challenge

Starring Equations

Copy the equations. Use three of the four numbers in the box to replace the stars in each equation, making it correct. You can make the numbers positive or negative. You may want to use a calculator.

2	5	8	11

* + * + * = ⁺15

* + * + * = ⁺2

* + * + * = ⁻8

* + * + * = ⁻11

Algebraic Patterns

Use the expressions to continue each pattern.

$2n$ 2, 4, 6, 8, ■, ■, ■

$2n + 1$ 3, 5, 7, 9, ■, ■, ■

$2n - 1$ 1, 3, 5, 7, ■, ■, ■

Continue this pattern.
1, 4, 9, 16, ■, ■, ■

Write an algebraic expression to show the pattern.

Continue this pattern.
0, 3, 8, 15, ■, ■, ■

Write an algebraic expression to show the pattern.

CUMULATIVE REVIEW
CHAPTERS 1–14

Write the letter of the correct answer.

1. $1\frac{2}{3} + 2\frac{1}{5}$

   A. $3\frac{3}{8}$ B. $3\frac{13}{15}$

   C. $4\frac{13}{15}$ D. not here

2. $3\frac{3}{4} \times \frac{4}{9}$

   A. $1\frac{2}{3}$ B. $2\frac{1}{3}$

   C. 3   D. not here

3. What is the decimal for $\frac{7}{5}$?

   A. 0.14   B. 0.71

   C. 1.4   D. 7.1

4. What is the GCF of 9 and 21?

   A. 3   B. 9

   C. 21   D. 189

5. Solve. $a + 8 = {}^-12$

   A. $a = {}^-20$ B. $a = {}^-12$

   C. $a = 12$ D. $a = 20$

6. What is 12% of 27?

   A. 0.324   B. 3.24

   C. 32.4   D. not here

7. What is the area of a circle with a radius of 11?

   A. 6.908   B. 37.994

   C. 69.08   D. 379.94

8. What is the area of a triangle with $b = 2$ and $h = 6$?

   A. 6   B. 12

   C. 18   D. 36

9. Evaluate $2x$, for $x = 1.6$.

   A. 0.8   B. 0.32

   C. 32   D. not here

10. Which is a solution of $x > {}^-7\frac{1}{2}$?

   A. $^-12$ B. $^-9$

   C. $^-7\frac{1}{2}$ D. $^-7$

11. Apples cost $3.00 a dozen. Oranges cost $0.10 less than $\frac{1}{2}$ the price of apples. How much does a dozen oranges cost?

   A. $1.30   B. $1.40

   C. $1.50   D. $1.75

12. Of the 48 people surveyed, 33 like corn, 11 like tomatoes, and 3 like corn and tomatoes. How many people do not like either?

   A. 4 people   B. 7 people

   C. 10 people   D. 12 people

COMPUTER Connection

Computers are powerful tools for doing many kinds of tasks quickly and accurately. They are used by programmers, graphic artists, word processors, accountants, doctors, and even by students in mathematics.

In this section you will explore LOGO, use a word processing program, make a spreadsheet, and build a data base. You will be using the same types of software that many people use at home and at work.

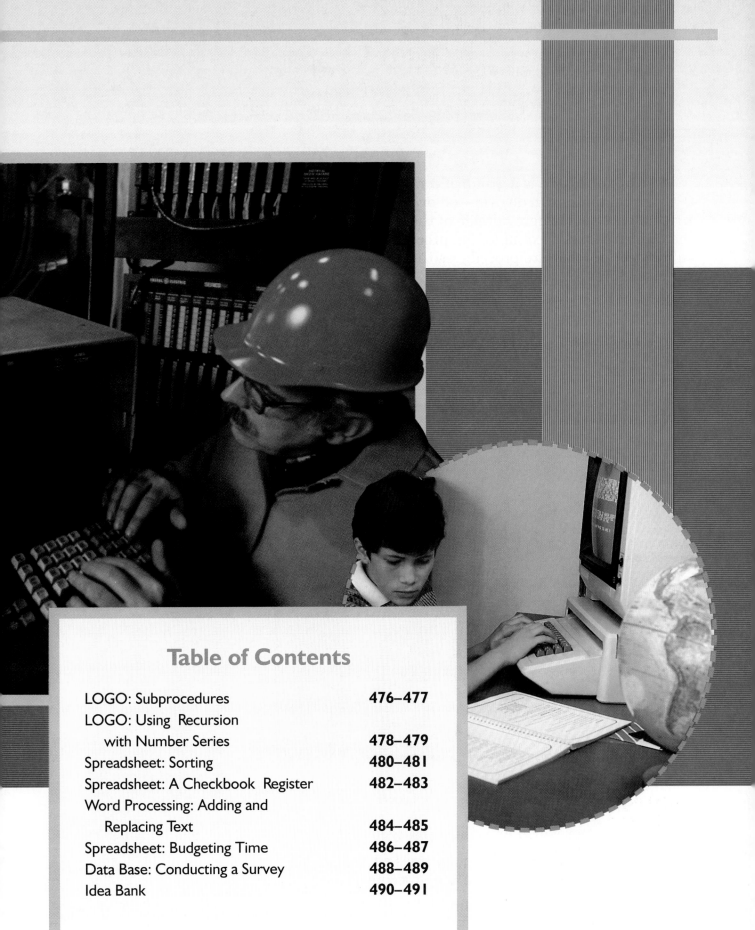

Table of Contents

LOGO Graphics

Subprocedures

A **subprocedure** is a group of commands or a procedure that the computer can do over and over. The subprocedure is written once somewhere outside of the procedure that calls the commands. For example, the procedure STAR calls two subprocedures that are procedures themselves. The subprocedures are called TRIANGLE and MOVE.

At the Computer

Type the procedures TRIANGLE, MOVE, and STAR in that order to draw the picture below.

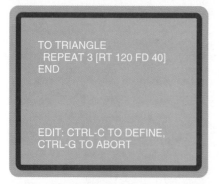

Talk About It

▶ Does it matter which procedure you type first?

▶ What do you think the computer does when it reads the name of the subprocedure in the procedure?

▶ Why are subprocedures useful?

Applying Math

The following computer screens illustrate how to draw a coordinate grid by using LOGO. The procedure GRAPH contains a subprocedure called LINE, which draws the segments on each axis. The lines are 10 turtle steps apart.

The LOGO program has a command called SETXY that directs the turtle to a point on the graph.

At the Computer

1. Type the procedures to make the graph.

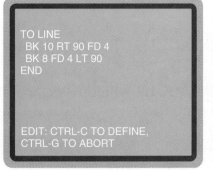

```
TO ARROW
  LT 135 FD 8 BK 8 RT 270
  FD 8 BK 8 LT 135
END




EDIT: CTRL-C TO DEFINE,
CTRL-G TO ABORT
```

```
TO LINE
  BK 10 RT 90 FD 4
  BK 8 FD 4 LT 90
END




EDIT: CTRL-C TO DEFINE,
CTRL-G TO ABORT
```

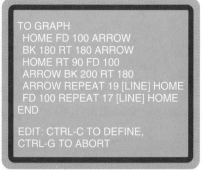

```
TO GRAPH
  HOME FD 100 ARROW
  BK 180 RT 180 ARROW
  HOME RT 90 FD 100
  ARROW BK 200 RT 180
  ARROW REPEAT 19 [LINE] HOME
  FD 100 REPEAT 17 [LINE] HOME
END

EDIT: CTRL-C TO DEFINE,
CTRL-G TO ABORT
```

2. After you have a grid on your computer screen, you can use the SETXY command to direct the turtle to a point on the graph. The command SETXY 20 (–30) tells the turtle to move 20 steps to the right and 30 steps down. (Some LOGO programs require that the second negative number be enclosed by parentheses.) The ordered pair (20,⁻30) describes the point where the turtle stops.

```
PLEASE WAIT...
GRAPH DEFINED
?GRAPH
?
```

Notice that the negative signs in computer commands are not raised as in ordered pairs.

3. Using the SETXY command, write four commands, each sending the turtle to a different section of the graph. Bring the turtle home after each command. For example, SETXY –30 (–10) HOME will draw a line from the center, (0,0), to the stopping point, (⁻30,⁻10), in the left lower section of the grid. HOME brings the turtle back to (0,0) ready for the next command.

4. Write commands for these ordered pairs.

      a. (⁻50,70)   b. (40,60)

      c. (⁻30,⁻50)   d. (10,⁻20)

Recursion is a way of repeating a group of commands over and over. To understand what that means, apply computer recursion to a number sequence discovered by Leonardo Fibonacci in the thirteenth century. The Fibonacci sequence (1, 1, 2, 3, 5, 8, 13, 21, 34, 55, . . .) is recursive because the relationship between the numbers can be expressed in a formula that can be repeated over and over.

At the Computer

1. Type the procedure FIBONACCI1, which prints the sequence.

2. Type the procedure FIBONACCI2, which uses a counter to limit the numbers in the sequence.

```
TO FIBONACCI1 :NUM1 :NUM2
  PRINT :NUM1 + :NUM2
  FIBONACCI1 :NUM2 :NUM1 + :NUM2
END




EDIT: CTRL-C TO DEFINE,
CTRL-G TO ABORT
```

```
TO FIBONACCI2 :NUM1 :NUM2 :COUNTER
  IF :COUNTER = 0 THEN STOP
  PRINT :NUM1 + :NUM2
  FIBONACCI2 :NUM2 :NUM1 + :NUM2 :COUNTER - 1
END




EDIT: CTRL-C TO DEFINE,
CTRL-G TO ABORT
```

FIBONACCI1 1 1
will start the sequence.

FIBONACCI2 1 1 10
will start the sequence.

Talk About It

▶ How are the Fibonacci numbers related?

▶ How can you stop printing the sequence in FIBONACCI1?

▶ Explain what the procedure FIBONACCI1 does.

▶ Why is the procedure FIBONACCI1 recursive?

▶ What are the names of the variables used in FIBONACCI1?

▶ How can you pick out a variable name in a LOGO procedure?

Talk About It

▶ Is the procedure FIBONACCI2 recursive? Why or why not?

▶ Why did the program stop at 144?

▶ What steps in the procedure tell the computer to stop printing the numbers in the sequence?

▶ What can you do to print 20 numbers in the sequence?

▶ What would happen if you start the sequence with two numbers other than 1 and 1?

Many number patterns or sequences are found in architecture, music, or nature. In the nineteenth century, scientists began to discover the Fibonacci sequence in spirals of sunflower heads and snail shells, in pine cones, and even in animal horns. The Fibonacci sequence is found in the chambered nautilus shell. The following procedure uses the sequence to draw the pattern found in the shell.

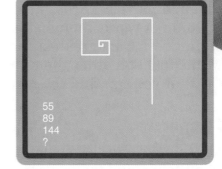

At the Computer

3. Type the procedure FIBONACCI3, which will draw a design of the number sequence found in nature.

```
TO FIBONACCI3 :NUM1 :NUM2 :COUNTER :ANGLE
 IF :COUNTER = 0 THEN STOP
 PRINT :NUM1 + :NUM2
 FD :NUM1 + :NUM2
 RT :ANGLE
 FIBONACCI3 :NUM2 :NUM1 + :NUM2 :COUNTER - 1 :ANGLE
END


EDIT: CTRL-C TO DEFINE,
CTRL-G TO ABORT
```

```
55
89
144
?
```

FIBONACCI3 0 1 11 90
will draw a spiral.

4. Use the procedure FIBONACCI3 to experiment with different number values to make your own designs.

5. Write a procedure to print your own number sequence.

6. Use the number sequence from the procedure written for Exercise 5 to draw a design. Use FIBONACCI3 as a guide.

Spreadsheet

Sorting

Jay organized baseball batting information for some of the players of the Chicago White Sox in the spreadsheet below. He will use the data to find the mean, median, mode, and range for these baseball statistics: Average (AVG), At Bat (AB), Runs (R), Hits (H), Home Runs (HR), Runs Batted In (RBI).

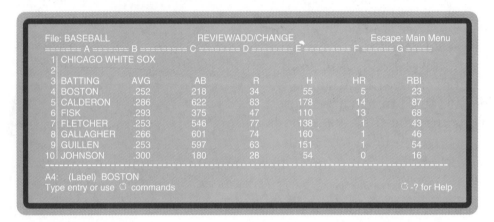

```
File: BASEBALL              REVIEW/ADD/CHANGE              Escape: Main Menu
======= A ======= B ========= C ======== D ======== E ========= F ====== G =====
 1| CHICAGO WHITE SOX
 2|
 3| BATTING      AVG        AB        R        H        HR        RBI
 4| BOSTON       .252       218       34       55        5         23
 5| CALDERON     .286       622       83       178      14         87
 6| FISK         .293       375       47       110      13         68
 7| FLETCHER     .253       546       77       138       1         43
 8| GALLAGHER    .266       601       74       160       1         46
 9| GUILLEN      .253       597       63       151       1         54
10| JOHNSON      .300       180       28       54        0         16
--------------------------------------------------------------------------------
A4:    (Label) BOSTON
Type entry or use ⌂ commands                               ⌂ -? for Help
```

The spreadsheet program has a tool that will sort the information in a particular column. You can tell the computer to sort a column of words alphabetically. It will also sort a column of numbers from greatest to least or from least to greatest. This tool will order the numbers in each of the columns so that you can find the median, mode, and range.

At the Computer

1. Use an almanac or a newspaper to collect information about a baseball team, and make a spreadsheet like the one shown.

2. Type the example spreadsheet (or your own) so that the names of the people are not in alphabetical order. Then use the arrange or sorting tool on *your* computer to alphabetize the list.

3. Using the layout tools, align the numbers and titles on your spreadsheet. Numbers with decimals should have the same number of decimal places, and whole numbers should not have decimals.

4. Use the sorting command on *your* computer to arrange the numbers in column B from greatest to least.

At the Computer

5. Sort the numbers in each of the columns to help you find the mode and range for each baseball statistic. Keep track of your discoveries on a separate sheet of paper or on another section of the same spreadsheet.

6. Finally, copy a formula that will calculate the mean for each column of numbers. For example, the following formula in cell B13 calculates the mean for the numbers in column B.

$$((B4+B5+B6+B7+B8+B9+B10)/7)$$

You can make a relative, or similar, copy of this formula in other columns.

The following baseball spreadsheet shows where the mean, median, mode, and range for the first column of numbers are organized.

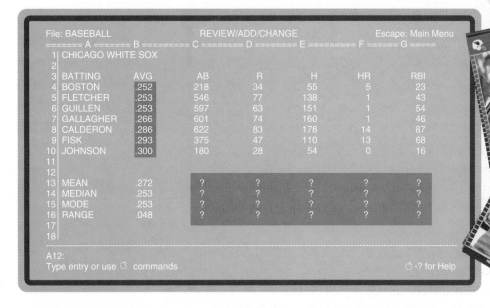

```
File: BASEBALL               REVIEW/ADD/CHANGE              Escape: Main Menu
====== A ====== B ========= C ======= D ======= E ======= F ===== G =====
 1| CHICAGO WHITE SOX
 2|
 3| BATTING     AVG        AB        R         H        HR       RBI
 4| BOSTON      .252       218       34        55        5        23
 5| FLETCHER    .253       546       77       138        1        43
 6| GUILLEN     .253       597       63       151        1        54
 7| GALLAGHER   .266       601       74       160        1        46
 8| CALDERON    .286       622       83       178       14        87
 9| FISK        .293       375       47       110       13        68
10| JOHNSON     .300       180       28        54        0        16
11|
12|
13| MEAN        .272        ?         ?         ?         ?         ?
14| MEDIAN      .253        ?         ?         ?         ?         ?
15| MODE        .253        ?         ?         ?         ?         ?
16| RANGE       .048        ?         ?         ?         ?         ?
17|
18|
-----------------------------------------------------------------------
A12:
Type entry or use ⌃ commands                              ⌃-? for Help
```

Talk About It

▶ How can you be sure a formula is working correctly in a spreadsheet?

▶ When you arrange a column, what happens to the information in the other columns?

▶ How does ordering the numbers help you to find the median, the mode, and the range?

▶ What happens to the formulas when you sort a column?

Spreadsheet

A Checkbook Register

Tammy set up the following spreadsheet to use as a checkbook register. She started with a balance of $514.00 in the bank account. Withdrawals and bank fees are subtracted from the balance. Deposits are added to the balance.

At the Computer

Use the following guidelines to finish Tammy's spreadsheet.

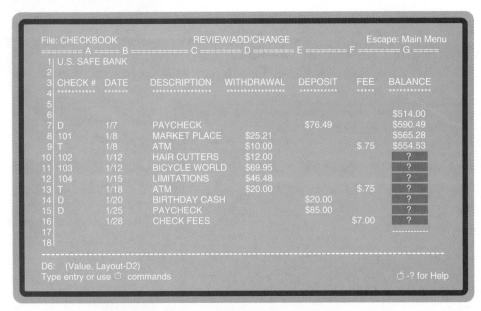

ATM stands for Automated Teller Machine.

1. Type the check numbers and the dates as characters, not number values. Some computer programs interpret 1/7 as 0.14286 instead of the date January 7. In most spreadsheet programs if you type a " symbol before the number, the computer will read the number as a character.

2. Most spreadsheet programs align the number values at the right of a column. Align the number values and titles into a neat format.

3. Add *** or ---- patterns to highlight titles.

4. Use $ and . symbols for dollar values.

5. Type a formula in cell G7 that will subtract or add withdrawals, deposits, and fees, and adjust the balance. HINT: (G6-__+__-__)

6. Copy the formula to cells G7 through G16.

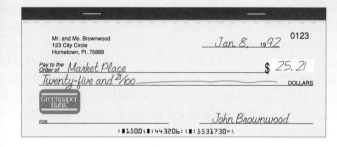

At the Computer

Work in a group of three or four people. Make a checkbook spreadsheet that will record transactions for one month. Follow these steps.

7. Imagine that as a group you will get $200 a month from extra chores, recycling paper and aluminum cans, and allowances.

8. Make a list of six or eight activities to do as a group. Write down how much each activity will cost the group. For example, a trip to a movie might cost $20.00 for four people.

9. Put the transactions to pay for the activities in a spreadsheet. Make up dates and check numbers for your checks. Decide when you can get cash from an Automated Teller Machine (ATM) to pay for an activity.

10. Type a formula that will subtract the costs of the activities from the balance.

11. Include these unexpected transactions.

a. bank fee	$ 0.75	**b.** work bonus	$10.00
c. check fee	$ 8.00	**d.** bank fee	$ 0.75

Talk About It

▶ What happens if the total cost of the activities is greater than the current balance?

▶ What can you do if you forget to type in a transaction?

▶ What happens to the balance if you change the amount of one of the transactions?

Word Processing

Adding and Replacing Text

Word processors have features that allow you to add or replace text (words or characters) in a document. You can also move text to other word processing, spreadsheet, or data base documents. A **clipboard** stores text to be moved from one document to another.

Before you can move information from one document to another, you must create the files. A **desktop index** will let you choose which files you want to work with. To avoid retyping, the workers at U.S. Safe Bank copied the highlighted list of checks from the CHECKBOOK file to the word processing file CHECK SUMMARY.

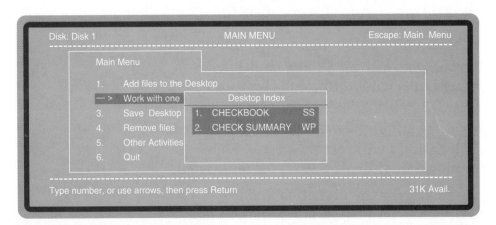

Disk: Disk 1   MAIN MENU   Escape: Main Menu

Main Menu

1. Add files to the Desktop
— > Work with one   Desktop Index
3. Save Desktop   1. CHECKBOOK   SS
4. Remove files   2. CHECK SUMMARY   WP
5. Other Activities
6. Quit

Type number, or use arrows, then press Return   31K Avail.

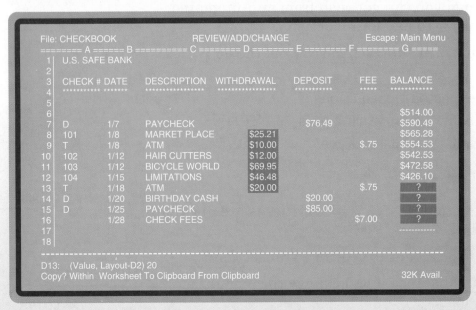

File: CHECKBOOK   REVIEW/ADD/CHANGE   Escape: Main Menu
======== A ===== B ========== C ======== D ======== E ======== F ======== G =====

	CHECK #	DATE	DESCRIPTION	WITHDRAWAL	DEPOSIT	FEE	BALANCE
1	U.S. SAFE BANK						
6							$514.00
7	D	1/7	PAYCHECK		$76.49		$590.49
8	101	1/8	MARKET PLACE	$25.21			$565.28
9	T	1/8	ATM	$10.00		$.75	$554.53
10	102	1/12	HAIR CUTTERS	$12.00			$542.53
11	103	1/12	BICYCLE WORLD	$69.95			$472.58
12	104	1/15	LIMITATIONS	$46.48			$426.10
13	T	1/18	ATM	$20.00		$.75	?
14	D	1/20	BIRTHDAY CASH		$20.00		?
15	D	1/25	PAYCHECK		$85.00		?
16		1/28	CHECK FEES			$7.00	?

D13:   (Value, Layout-D2) 20
Copy? Within Worksheet To Clipboard From Clipboard   32K Avail.

At the Computer

Here is the word processing file that contains information taken directly from the spreadsheet file.

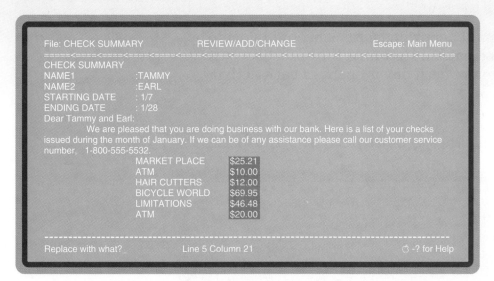

```
File: CHECK SUMMARY          REVIEW/ADD/CHANGE              Escape: Main Menu
=====<====<====<====<====<====<====<====<====<====<====<====<====<====<====<==
CHECK SUMMARY
NAME1            :TAMMY
NAME2            :EARL
STARTING DATE    : 1/7
ENDING DATE      : 1/28
Dear Tammy and Earl:
        We are pleased that you are doing business with our bank. Here is a list of your checks
issued during the month of January. If we can be of any assistance please call our customer service
number,   1-800-555-5532.
                MARKET PLACE     $25.21
                ATM              $10.00
                HAIR CUTTERS     $12.00
                BICYCLE WORLD    $69.95
                LIMITATIONS      $46.48
                ATM              $20.00

---------------------------------------------------------------------------------
Replace with what?_          Line 5 Column 21                        ⌂ -? for Help
```

Suppose that U.S. Safe Bank wants to send Tammy and Earl a summary of their checks every month by changing only certain information. Most word processors have a function that will find and replace characters or numbers.

1. Type the CHECK SUMMARY file on your word processor.

2. Use the **find** and **replace** functions to change January information to February information.

a.	1/7	2/8
b.	1/28	2/22
c.	1-800-555-5532	1-800-555-5528
d.	$25.21	$35.81
e.	$20.00	$30.00

Talk About It

▶ What is the difference between moving information and copying it?

▶ What happens if the word or number you need to find and replace occurs more than once in the file?

▶ If you use a long word like *mathematics* in a document many times, how can the code *mmm* and the find and replace tool help?

Spreadsheet
Budgeting Time

Jerry Kent set up the following spreadsheet to budget the time he spends on recreation. He wants the spreadsheet to calculate what percent of each day is spent in each activity.

At the Computer

Use the following guidelines to finish Jerry's spreadsheet.

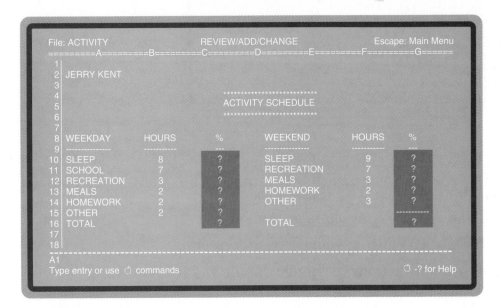

```
File: ACTIVITY              REVIEW/ADD/CHANGE              Escape: Main Menu
========A========B=========C=========D=========E========F=========G=====
 1|
 2| JERRY KENT
 3|
 4|                          ***********************
 5|                          ACTIVITY SCHEDULE
 6|                          ***********************
 7|
 8| WEEKDAY      HOURS      %        WEEKEND      HOURS      %
 9| ---------    -------    ---      ---------    -------    ---
10| SLEEP        8          ?        SLEEP        9          ?
11| SCHOOL       7          ?        RECREATION   7          ?
12| RECREATION   3          ?        MEALS        3          ?
13| MEALS        2          ?        HOMEWORK     2          ?
14| HOMEWORK     2          ?        OTHER        3          ?
15| OTHER        2          ?                          -----------
16| TOTAL                   ?        TOTAL                   ?
17|
18|
--------------------------------------------------------------------
A1
Type entry or use ○ commands                           ○ -? for Help
```

1. Align the number values and titles in a neat format. Most spreadsheet programs will align the number values at the right of a column. Therefore, you can tell the computer to also align the titles of these columns at the right.

2. Add *** or --- patterns to highlight titles.

3. Type a formula in cell B16 that will check that the sum of the hours in each day is 24. Copy a variation of the formula to cell F16.

4. Type a formula in cells C10 through C15 that will calculate the percent of time spent on each activity each weekday. HINT: Try (B10/B16). Tell the computer to translate decimals into percents.

5. Repeat Exercise 4 to calculate the percent of time spent on each activity for weekend days.

Applying Math

Some software programs will translate data from the spreadsheet to a circle graph, or pie chart. Make a circle graph showing Jerry's activities. Use a sheet of paper or a graphing computer program.

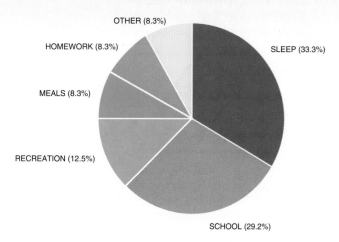

WEEKDAY ACTIVITY SCHEDULE
PERCENT OF TIME

OTHER (8.3%)
HOMEWORK (8.3%)
MEALS (8.3%)
RECREATION (12.5%)
SCHOOL (29.2%)
SLEEP (33.3%)

Use the circle graphs or the spreadsheet on page 486 to answer the following questions about Jerry's schedule.

6. About what percent of time does Jerry spend on recreation and eating during a weekday? a weekend day?

7. What cells contain information about the time Jerry spends on homework?

8. What cells contain 8.3%? Which activities take up this percent of time?

9. About how much more time does Jerry spend sleeping than doing homework and other things during the week?

Talk About It

▶ What happens to the value of the percent on the spreadsheet if you change the number of hours of sleep time from 8 to 7?

▶ How would you add one hour of soccer practice to the weekday schedule?

▶ Why is a spreadsheet an effective way to analyze your daily activities?

Data Base
Conducting a Survey

Jenny and Dave conducted a survey to investigate how different groups of people view optical illusions. They asked a group of middle school students to answer a question about these three pictures. They used a specific code for each result to establish consistency in the answers.

picture 1
What do you see?

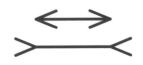

picture 2
Which line is longer?

picture 3
What is wrong?

ANSWER CODES

FA - faces	SA - same	TH - the
VA - vase	TO - top	NO - nothing

They also used codes to collect information about the people they interviewed.

INTERVIEWEE CODES

Age Group		Gender	Eye Color
10	12	MA - male	BL - blue
11	13	FE - female	BR - brown
			GR - green

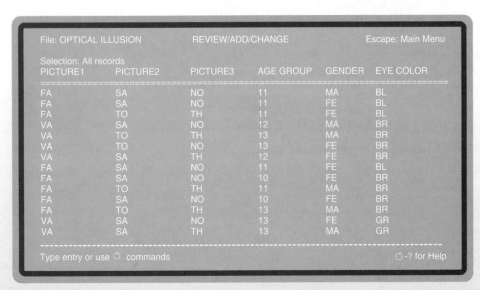

This data base shows how Jenny and Dave organized the results of the optical illusions survey.

File: OPTICAL ILLUSION	REVIEW/ADD/CHANGE			Escape: Main Menu	

Selection: All records

PICTURE1	PICTURE2	PICTURE3	AGE GROUP	GENDER	EYE COLOR
FA	SA	NO	11	MA	BL
FA	SA	NO	11	FE	BL
FA	TO	TH	11	FE	BL
VA	SA	NO	12	MA	BR
VA	TO	TH	13	MA	BR
VA	TO	NO	13	FE	BR
VA	SA	TH	12	FE	BR
FA	SA	NO	11	FE	BL
FA	SA	NO	10	FE	BR
FA	TO	TH	11	MA	BR
FA	SA	NO	10	FE	BR
FA	TO	TH	13	MA	BR
VA	SA	NO	13	FE	GR
VA	SA	TH	13	MA	GR

Type entry or use ⌂ commands   ⌂-? for Help

Investigate

1. Look at the code descriptions and the data base on page 488 to answer these questions.

   a. How many females with blue eyes thought picture 1 was two faces?

   b. How many 13-year-olds thought picture 1 was a vase, or that the lines in picture 2 were the same?

   c. How many people with green eyes thought the lines in picture 2 were the same and that there was nothing wrong with picture 3?

   d. Why is a data base program better for answering the questions?

2. What does the following computer screen show?

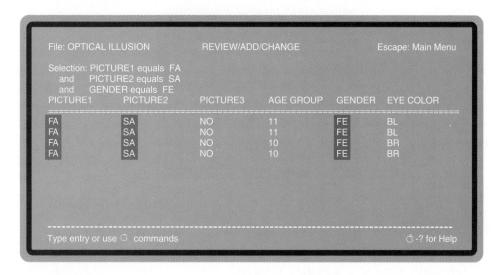

At the Computer

3. Trace the optical illusions on page 488. Conduct a survey like the example, and put your results in a data base.

4. Create your own format and layout. Decide which categories give you valuable information. Determine the widths of the fields.

5. Sort each of the picture fields to see whether there are any interesting results.

6. Print lists of the selections that show patterns or trends.

IDEA BANK

LOGO IDEAS

1. Use a TRIANGLE or SQUARE procedure in a subprocedure for drawing a triangle or a square.
2. Add a variable to the procedure in Exercise 1 to change the size or shape of the figure.
3. Using recursion, write a procedure to draw a figure like this one.

PLEASE WAIT...
CORNERS DEFINED
?CORNERS
?

4. Add a variable to the procedure in Exercise 3 to change the size or shape of the figure.

WORD PROCESSING IDEAS

5. Write directions explaining how to find factors of a large number like 2,464 with a calculator. Type example problems.
6. Use the find and replace functions to change the example problems in Exercise 5.
7. Write a plan for a survey about sports. Make a list of the questions you will ask and the people you will interview. Think about how you can organize the information in a data base program.
8. Write directions on how to copy text from one document to another with your word processor.

SPREADSHEET AND DATA BASE IDEAS

9. Collect statistics from an almanac or a newspaper about your favorite athlete. Put the information in a spreadsheet.

10. Conduct the survey from Exercise 7. Organize the information in a data base.

11. Make a schedule of your day at school. Organize it in a spreadsheet.

12. To the spreadsheet in Exercise 11, add the percent of time each class takes up in the school day.

13. Project. Keep track of your television viewing for one week. Use a spreadsheet to find the total hours you watched television during the week. Calculate the mean, median, range, and mode for the week.

14. Make a data base of the television shows you watch every week. Answer these questions.

    a. How long does each show last?

    b. Who is your favorite performer in the show?

    c. How many years or months have you been watching the show?

    d. How many of your classmates watch the show?

15. Make a data base containing this information about your family and friends.

    a. name

    b. address

    c. phone number

    d. birth date

    e. age

Student Handbook

Bridge Lessons

## CHAPTER 1

Place Value: Whole Numbers and Decimals

Rounding

A newspaper office reports a circulation of 36,475 newspapers. To the nearest ten thousand, how many newspapers are circulated?

You can use a number line to help you.

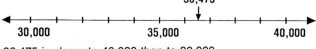

36,475 is closer to 40,000 than to 30,000.

You can also use rounding rules.
Look at the digit to the right of the   36,475
place to which you are rounding.   6 > 5

If that digit is less than 5, the digit being rounded remains the same.

If that digit is 5 or greater, the digit being rounded increases by 1.

So, to the nearest ten thousand, 40,000 newspapers are circulated.

Newspaper ads vary in length. Sally wants to place three ads at the lengths given in the table. Estimate each length to the nearest centimeter.

You can use the rules for rounding whole numbers to round decimals.

Newspaper Ads	
Display Ad	**Length (in cm)**
Car	12.3
Grocery	12.5
Tire	12.7

Examples

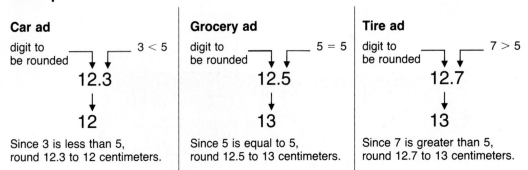

Car ad

digit to be rounded ——— 3 < 5

12.3
↓
12

Since 3 is less than 5, round 12.3 to 12 centimeters.

Grocery ad

digit to be rounded ——— 5 = 5

12.5
↓
13

Since 5 is equal to 5, round 12.5 to 13 centimeters.

Tire ad

digit to be rounded ——— 7 > 5

12.7
↓
13

Since 7 is greater than 5, round 12.7 to 13 centimeters.

• The price of gasoline at a gasoline pump may appear as $1.239. Why is the total amount purchased rounded to the nearest cent?

Practice

Round to the nearest ten thousand.

1. 37,205   **2.** 58,936   **3.** 324,520   **4.** 845,625

Round to the nearest hundred thousand.

5. 483,267   **6.** 678,090   **7.** 449,300   **8.** 12,786,500

Round to the nearest million.

9. 35,458,936   **10.** 20,843,267   **11.** 135,984,600   **12.** 1,452,935,278

Round to the nearest tenth.

13. 84.07   **14.** 89.93   **15.** 0.98   **16.** 0.32

17. 103.506   **18.** 165.094   **19.** 2,045.055   **20.** 1,390.039

Round to the nearest hundredth.

21. 0.934   **22.** 7.783   **23.** 37.839   **24.** 45.005

25. 0.014   **26.** 0.996   **27.** 93.097   **28.** 198.894

Round to the nearest dollar.

29. $2.93   **30.** $11.67   **31.** $0.98

32. $4.02   **33.** $32.39   **34.** $199.49

Round to the nearest whole number.

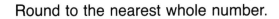

35. 3.75   **36.** 87.42   **37.** 18.9   **38.** 42.09   **39.** 100.54

Use the table for Exercises 40–41.

40. Which kinds of magazines have a circulation of about 5,000,000?

41. Round to the nearest million, and write about how many more news magazines are sold than travel magazines.

42. The number 149 is the greatest three-digit number that can be rounded to 100. What is the greatest four-digit number that can be rounded to 1,000?

Circulation of Magazines	
Kinds of Magazines	**Number Circulated**
News magazines	5,748,324
Sports magazines	4,928,165
Food magazines	1,875,692
Travel magazines	1,379,685

Multiplying Whole Numbers and Decimals

Multiplying Multiples of Ten

Bryan found that the average person uses about 40 gallons of hot water for a shower. If each of 5 family members takes a shower daily, about how much hot water would the family use for showers in one day?

You know about how much hot water 1 person uses. Multiply to find about how much a family of 5 uses.

Find $5 \times 40 = n$.

$$
\begin{array}{r}
4 \text{ tens} \\
\times\ 5 \\
\hline
20
\end{array}
\longrightarrow
\begin{array}{r}
40 \\
\times\ 5 \\
\hline
200
\end{array}
$$

Think:
Since $5 \times 4 = 20$,
$5 \times 40 = 200$.

So, the family of 5 would use about 200 gallons of hot water for showers in one day.

You can use a calculator to find patterns with multiples of 10.

Entry		**Display**	
6 M+ × 7 =		M 42.	The M+ key stores one factor in memory.
MRC × 70 =		M 420.	The MRC key recalls that factor from memory.
MRC × 700 =		M 4200.	
MRC × 7000 =		M 42000.	

Examples

A.
$8 \times 1 = 8$
$8 \times 10 = 80$
$8 \times 100 = 800$
$8 \times 1,000 = 8,000$

B.
$9 \times (3 \times 1) = 9 \times 3 = 27$
$9 \times (3 \times 10) = 9 \times 30 = 270$
$9 \times (3 \times 100) = 9 \times 300 = 2,700$
$9 \times (3 \times 1,000) = 9 \times 3,000 = 27,000$

Talk About It

▶ How is the pattern in Example B different from the pattern in Example A?

▶ How can you use mental math to find 5×7, 5×70, 5×700, and $5 \times 7,000$?

Practice

Use mental math to find the product.

1. 50
    × 5

2. 30
    × 7

3. 800
    ×   2

4. 900
    ×   4

5. 500
    ×   6

6. 400
    ×   8

7. 900
    ×   3

8. 4,000
    ×   6

9. 2,000
    ×   7

10. 7,000
    ×   9

Complete the number sentence.

11. $700 \times 9 = $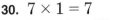

12. $400 \times 5 = $

13. $\blacksquare \times 30 = 240$

14. $3 \times 200 = $

15. $500 \times 5 = $

16. $800 \times \blacksquare = 4,800$

17. $2 \times \blacksquare = 600$

18. $\blacksquare \times 40 = 320$

19. $6 \times \blacksquare = 3,000$

Multiply each number by 10, 100, and 1,000.

20. 2

21. 4

22. 5

23. 7

24. 9

25. 10

26. 15

27. 23

28. 45

29. 123

Use a calculator to complete the pattern.

30. $7 \times 1 = 7$
    $7 \times 10 = $
    $7 \times 100 = $
    $7 \times 1,000 = $

31. $8 \times (6 \times 1) = 48$
    $8 \times (6 \times 10) = $
    $8 \times (6 \times 100) = $
    $8 \times (6 \times 1,000) = $

32. $11 \times (11 \times 1) = 121$
    $11 \times (11 \times 10) = $
    $11 \times (11 \times 100) = $
    $11 \times (11 \times 1,000) = $

Use the table to solve Exercises 33–34.

Cost of Gas and Electricity at Bryan's House	
Month	Amount
January	$150
April	$ 95
July	$200
October	$ 90

33. There are 10 houses on Bryan's block. If each household paid the same amount for gas and electricity in October, how much would all the households on the block have paid?

34. Suppose 1,000 households have the same average gas and electricity bill as Bryan. How much would all the households have paid in January? in July?

CHAPTER 3

Multiplying Whole Numbers and Decimals

Multiplying by One-Digit Numbers

Solar collectors attached to the roof of a house capture energy from sunlight. If the system for one house uses 6 collectors, how many solar collectors are needed to supply 213 houses with the same kind of solar energy system?

Estimate. $6 = 6 \qquad 213 \approx 200$

$\qquad 6 \times 200 = 1,200 \leftarrow$ estimate

You can use four different colors of counters to make a model to solve the problem.

Let ● = 1,000, ● = 100, ● = 10, and ○ = 1.

Step 1
Model the problem.
6 groups of 213

$$\begin{array}{r} 213 \\ \times \quad 6 \end{array}$$

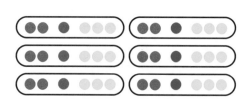

Step 2
Group all counters by color.

Hundreds	Tens	Ones

6 groups of 200, or 12 hundreds   6 groups of 10, or 6 tens   6 groups of 3, or 18 ones

---

Step 3   Thousands   Hundreds   Tens   Ones
Regroup.

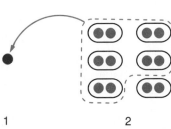

1   2   7   8

$$\begin{array}{r} 213 \\ \times \quad 6 \\ \hline 18 \leftarrow 6 \times 3 \\ 60 \leftarrow 6 \times 10 \\ +1,200 \leftarrow 6 \times 200 \\ \hline 1,278 \end{array}$$

You can also use the standard method of multiplication to find the number of solar collectors needed.

$$\begin{array}{r} {\scriptstyle 1} \\ 213 \\ \times \quad 6 \\ \hline 1,278 \end{array}$$ So, 1,278 solar collectors are needed.

- How is regrouping done in the standard method?

Practice

Solve. Use counters to model each regrouping.

1. $2 \times 346 = $ ▪

2. $3 \times 604 = $ ▪

3. $6 \times 365 = $ ▪

Estimate each product by rounding.

4. $\begin{array}{r} 37 \\ \times\ 4 \\ \hline \end{array}$

5. $\begin{array}{r} 63 \\ \times\ 5 \\ \hline \end{array}$

6. $\begin{array}{r} 367 \\ \times\ \ \ 7 \\ \hline \end{array}$

7. $\begin{array}{r} 276 \\ \times\ \ \ 3 \\ \hline \end{array}$

8. $\begin{array}{r} 129 \\ \times\ \ \ 3 \\ \hline \end{array}$

9. $\begin{array}{r} 649 \\ \times\ \ \ 8 \\ \hline \end{array}$

10. $\begin{array}{r} 592 \\ \times\ \ \ 7 \\ \hline \end{array}$

11. $\begin{array}{r} 2{,}105 \\ \times\ \ \ \ \ 5 \\ \hline \end{array}$

12. $\begin{array}{r} 7{,}952 \\ \times\ \ \ \ \ 6 \\ \hline \end{array}$

Multiply.

13. $\begin{array}{r} 42 \\ \times\ 3 \\ \hline \end{array}$

14. $\begin{array}{r} 28 \\ \times\ 7 \\ \hline \end{array}$

15. $\begin{array}{r} 64 \\ \times\ 6 \\ \hline \end{array}$

16. $\begin{array}{r} 102 \\ \times\ \ \ 5 \\ \hline \end{array}$

17. $\begin{array}{r} 63 \\ \times\ 5 \\ \hline \end{array}$

18. $\begin{array}{r} 77 \\ \times\ 4 \\ \hline \end{array}$

19. $\begin{array}{r} 702 \\ \times\ \ \ 4 \\ \hline \end{array}$

20. $\begin{array}{r} 200 \\ \times\ \ \ 5 \\ \hline \end{array}$

21. $\begin{array}{r} 401 \\ \times\ \ \ 8 \\ \hline \end{array}$

22. $\begin{array}{r} 4{,}623 \\ \times\ \ \ \ \ 9 \\ \hline \end{array}$

23. $\begin{array}{r} 1{,}982 \\ \times\ \ \ \ \ 6 \\ \hline \end{array}$

24. $\begin{array}{r} 3{,}746 \\ \times\ \ \ \ \ 7 \\ \hline \end{array}$

25. $\begin{array}{r} 582 \\ \times\ \ \ 2 \\ \hline \end{array}$

26. $\begin{array}{r} 1{,}045 \\ \times\ \ \ \ \ 5 \\ \hline \end{array}$

27. $\begin{array}{r} 3{,}456 \\ \times\ \ \ \ \ 8 \\ \hline \end{array}$

28. $\begin{array}{r} 8{,}143 \\ \times\ \ \ \ \ 4 \\ \hline \end{array}$

29. $2 \times 453 = $ ▪

30. $7 \times 2{,}450 = $ ▪

31. $3{,}129 \times 7 = $ ▪

32. $9{,}767 \times 8 = $ ▪

33. Sally has a recipe that makes 54 whole-wheat rolls. She will make 6 recipes for a bake sale. How many rolls will she make?

34. Suppose that a row of seats on a jetliner will seat 9 passengers. How many passengers can be seated in 43 rows?

35. Americans recycle 78 million aluminum cans daily. At this rate, how many aluminum cans do Americans recycle in one week?

36. Is 37,000 a reasonable product for the factors 740 and 5? Explain.

## CHAPTER 4

Dividing Whole Numbers and Decimals

Exploring Decimal Division

Work Together

You can use base-ten blocks to explore dividing with decimals.

Divide. $5.36 \div 4 = n$

Work with a classmate. Model 5.36 using base-ten blocks.

If you let the flat represent 1, you can make the following chart.

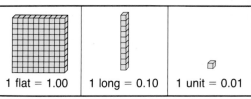

| 1 flat = 1.00 | 1 long = 0.10 | 1 unit = 0.01 |

- What blocks can you use to model 5.36?

- How many flats can be sorted evenly into 4 groups?

- Are there any flats left over?

- What regrouping can be made?

Regroup.
- How many longs are there now?

- How many longs can be sorted evenly into each of the 4 groups?

- Are there any longs left over?

- What regrouping can be made to use the other long?

Regroup.
- How many units are there now?

- How many units can be sorted evenly into each of the 4 groups?

- Did you use all of the blocks?

- What blocks are in each of the 4 groups?

Talk About It

▶ What decimal number represents the amount in each of the 4 equal groups?

▶ How can you compare division to this sorting process?

Practice

Use base-ten blocks to model the problem. Let one flat represent 1, one long represent 0.10, and one unit represent 0.01. Find the quotient.

1. $1.5 \div 5$

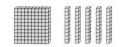

2. $3.2 \div 8$

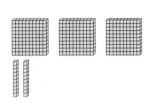

3. $4.4 \div 2$

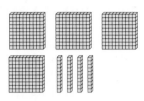

4. $3.74 \div 2$

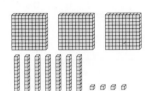

5. $5.28 \div 3$

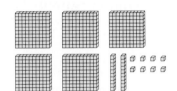

6. $2.10 \div 6$

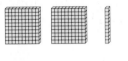

7. $3\overline{)7.5}$

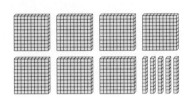

8. $4\overline{)4.8}$

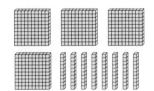

9. $3\overline{)6.3}$

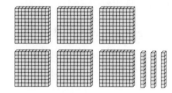

10. $3\overline{)2.79}$

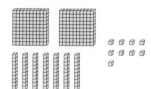

11. $4\overline{)5.36}$

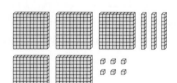

12. $5\overline{)2.95}$

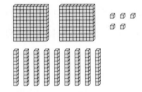

13. Painters at a new school took 9 hours to paint a section of a wall that is 26.1 meters long. How long a section of wall did they paint in 1 hour?

14. A school district administration building is 37.2 meters tall. It was built by attaching 12 identical concrete sections together. How tall is each section?

15. A small van will deliver 2,541.6 kilograms of supplies to the school today. If the van makes 6 trips, what is the average amount of supplies it will carry on each trip?

16. Amy has $1.44. She bought 3 notebooks, a package of pencils for $1.98, and a pen for $3.25. Amy had $16.00 to begin, and each notebook cost the same amount. What did each notebook cost?

CHAPTER 5

Graphing, Statistics, and Probability

Range, Mode, Median, and Mean

Carla surveyed sixth-grade students to find out how many hours a week they watch television. The frequency table shows the results of Carla's survey.

Analyze the data so that you can prepare a report.

Use connecting cubes to model the number of hours each student watches television.

Find the difference between the number of cubes in the tallest and the shortest stacks. This is called the **range.**

Hours of TV Watched Weekly	
Student	Hours
Kyle	8
Leandra	10
Tanya	5
Jody	2
Steven	5

$10 - 2 = 8$ The range is 8.

Look for any stacks that have the same number of cubes. The number that appears most often is called the **mode.** The number 5 appears most often.
So, 5 is the mode.

Place the stacks of cubes in order from greatest to least. The number in the middle stack is called the **median.** The middle stack contains 5 cubes.
So, 5 is the median.

Put the cubes in one stack. Separate the stack into five equal stacks. Count the cubes in each new stack. This number, called the **mean,** is the average number of cubes in the original stacks. To compute the mean, follow these steps.

Step 1	**Step 2**
Find the total number of cubes. $8 + 10 + 5 + 2 + 5 = 30$	Divide the sum of the data by the number of addends. $30 \div 5 = 6$ $\llcorner$ mean

So, the mean is 6.

Talk About It

▶ If you wanted a station to carry more programs of interest to sixth graders, which number would you report? Why?

Practice

Use the data from each table to find the range, mean, median, and mode.

1.

Pet Owners	
Student	Number Of Pets
Peggy	7
Ella	3
Rafael	2
Dennis	3
Kelko	5

Range ▪
Mean ▪
Median ▪
Mode ▪

2.

School Clubs	
Name	Membership
Computer	19
Math	9
Reading	7
Stamp	5
Yearbook	5

Range ▪
Mean ▪
Median ▪
Mode ▪

3.

Fifth-Grade Classes	
Teacher	Number of Students
Mrs. Larson	27
Ms. Stone	31
Mr. Freeman	34
Mrs. Lo	31
Mrs. Ortiz	32

Range ▪ Mean ▪

Median ▪ Mode ▪

4.

Girls' Heights	
Name	Inches
Adela	55
Sandy	59
Melba	60
Luanne	59
Gloria	57

Range ▪ Mean ▪

Median ▪ Mode ▪

Find the range, mean, median, and mode.

5. 24, 37, 42, 37, 15

6. $28, $42, $59, $42, $64

7. $270, $299, $271, $270, $275

8. 575, 630, 720, 575, 525

9. A football team has scored 14 points, 7 points, 10 points, and 17 points in its last four games. Find the mean of the points scored in the four games.

10. Sheila scored 95, 82, 90, and 83 on four tests. After the fifth test, the mode of her scores was 83. What did she score on the fifth test?

11. Use the information in Exercise 9. What is the range of the points that the football team scored?

12. Use the information in Exercise 10. What is the mean of Sheila's five test scores?

13. Use the information in Exercise 10. What is the range of Sheila's five test scores?

14. Use the information in Exercise 10. What is the median of Sheila's five test scores?

CHAPTER 6

Number Theory

Comparing Fractions

Simon and Takenya played a round of Plan-a-Garden. Simon planted watermelon seeds in $\frac{4}{5}$ of the garden. Takenya planted $\frac{2}{5}$ of the garden with cantaloupe seeds. Is more of the garden planted with watermelon or cantaloupe?

To compare fractions with like denominators, compare numerators or use fraction bars.

$\frac{1}{5}$	$\frac{1}{5}$	$\frac{1}{5}$	$\frac{1}{5}$	$\frac{1}{5}$

$\frac{1}{5}$	$\frac{1}{5}$	$\frac{1}{5}$	$\frac{1}{5}$	$\frac{1}{5}$

The fraction bars show that $\frac{4}{5}$ is greater than $\frac{2}{5}$. Also, look at the numerators. $4 > 2$

So, more of the garden is planted with watermelons.

You can also use fraction bars to compare fractions with unlike denominators.

Which is greater, $\frac{2}{3}$ or $\frac{3}{9}$?

$\frac{1}{3}$	$\frac{1}{3}$	$\frac{1}{3}$

$\frac{1}{9}$	$\frac{1}{9}$	$\frac{1}{9}$	$\frac{1}{9}$	$\frac{1}{9}$	$\frac{1}{9}$	$\frac{1}{9}$	$\frac{1}{9}$	$\frac{1}{9}$

The fraction bars show that $\frac{2}{3}$ is greater than $\frac{3}{9}$.

So, $\frac{2}{3} > \frac{3}{9}$.

Another Method

You can also compare $\frac{2}{3}$ and $\frac{3}{9}$ by writing equivalent fractions with like denominators.

Step 1	Step 2	Step 3
Find the least common multiple (LCM) of 3 and 9.	Write an equivalent fraction. Use the LCM as the denominator.	Compare the numerators.
3: 3, 6, 9 9: 9	$\frac{2}{3} = \frac{\blacksquare}{9}$ $\quad$ $\frac{2}{3} = \frac{6}{9}$	$\frac{6}{9} > \frac{3}{9}$ $\quad$ So, $\frac{2}{3} > \frac{3}{9}$

Bridge Lesson

Practice

Use fraction bars to model the problem. Tell which fraction is greater.

1. $\dfrac{3}{4}, \dfrac{1}{4}$

2. $\dfrac{1}{2}, \dfrac{2}{3}$

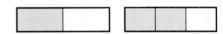

3. $\dfrac{3}{4}, \dfrac{1}{3}$

4. $\dfrac{5}{6}, \dfrac{3}{8}$

Use the least common denominator (LCD) to write equivalent fractions.

5. $\dfrac{1}{8}, \dfrac{5}{6}$
LCD = 24

6. $\dfrac{2}{9}, \dfrac{5}{6}$
LCD = 18

7. $\dfrac{1}{3}, \dfrac{3}{7}$
LCD = 21

8. $\dfrac{5}{8}, \dfrac{3}{16}$
LCD = 16

9. $\dfrac{3}{8}, \dfrac{5}{6}$
LCD = ▦

10. $\dfrac{1}{9}, \dfrac{1}{5}$
LCD = ▦

11. $\dfrac{2}{3}, \dfrac{3}{7}$
LCD = ▦

12. $\dfrac{5}{8}, \dfrac{9}{16}$
LCD = ▦

Compare. Write <, >, or = for ●.

13. $\dfrac{2}{4}$ ● $\dfrac{3}{4}$

14. $\dfrac{1}{4}$ ● $\dfrac{1}{8}$

15. $\dfrac{2}{3}$ ● $\dfrac{5}{6}$

16. $\dfrac{7}{8}$ ● $\dfrac{5}{6}$

17. $\dfrac{5}{6}$ ● $\dfrac{3}{4}$

18. $\dfrac{1}{2}$ ● $\dfrac{3}{6}$

19. $\dfrac{5}{8}$ ● $\dfrac{2}{3}$

20. $\dfrac{6}{8}$ ● $\dfrac{3}{4}$

21. $\dfrac{3}{4}$ ● $\dfrac{5}{8}$

22. $\dfrac{1}{8}$ ● $\dfrac{1}{6}$

23. $\dfrac{1}{2}$ ● $\dfrac{3}{8}$

24. $\dfrac{2}{3}$ ● $\dfrac{4}{6}$

25. Anna used $\dfrac{2}{3}$ bag of fertilizer for her apple trees and $\dfrac{4}{6}$ bag for her pear trees. Did she use more for her apple or her pear trees?

26. Derek made some fruit sauce for his pancakes. He used $\dfrac{3}{4}$ cup of lemons and $\dfrac{7}{8}$ cup of limes. Did he use more lemons or more limes?

27. The members of the buyers' club are purchasing vegetables. One catalog advertises $\dfrac{5}{6}$ pound of chard for \$1, and another catalog offers $\dfrac{7}{8}$ pound of chard for \$1. Which is the better buy?

28. Brent planted $\dfrac{1}{3}$ of his garden with tomato plants, and Jill planted $\dfrac{2}{5}$ of her garden with tomato plants. Who has more tomato plants if they both have the same number of plants in their gardens?

Number Theory

Mixed Numbers

You can use fraction circles and fraction bars to help you understand mixed numbers.

Some fractions greater than 1 can be written as whole numbers.

Method 1

Here is one way to rename $\frac{16}{8}$.

$$\frac{8}{8} = 1 \qquad \frac{8}{8} = 1$$

$$\frac{8}{8} \quad + \quad \frac{8}{8} \quad = \quad \frac{16}{8}$$
$$1 \quad + \quad 1 \quad = \quad 2$$

Method 2

You can also divide to rename a fraction greater than 1 as a whole number.

$$\frac{16}{8} \rightarrow 8\overline{)16} \atop \underline{-16} \atop 0 }$$

$$\begin{array}{r} 2 \\ 8\overline{)16} \\ -16 \\ \hline 0 \end{array}$$

So, another name for $\frac{16}{8}$ is 2.

Some fractions greater than 1 can be written as mixed numbers.

Method 1

A **mixed number** is a whole number with a fraction. Here is one way to rename $\frac{9}{8}$.

$$\frac{8}{8} = 1 \qquad \frac{1}{8}$$

$$1 \quad + \quad \frac{1}{8} \quad = \quad 1\frac{1}{8}$$

Method 2

You can also divide to rename a fraction greater than 1 as a mixed number.

$$\frac{9}{8} \rightarrow \begin{array}{r} 1 \\ 8\overline{)9} \\ -8 \\ \hline 1 \end{array} \quad \frac{1}{8}$$

So, another name for $\frac{9}{8}$ is $1\frac{1}{8}$.

All mixed numbers can be written as fractions greater than 1.

Method 1

$$2\frac{1}{3} \qquad 1 = \frac{3}{3} \qquad 1 = \frac{3}{3} \qquad \frac{1}{3}$$

Add the numerators.

$$\frac{3}{3} + \frac{3}{3} + \frac{1}{3} = \frac{3 + 3 + 1}{3} = \frac{7}{3}$$

The denominator remains 3.

Method 2

You can also use multiplication and addition to change a mixed number to a fraction greater than 1.

$$2\frac{1}{3} = \frac{(3 \times 2) + 1}{3} = \frac{6 + 1}{3} = \frac{7}{3}$$

So, another name for $2\frac{1}{3}$ is $\frac{7}{3}$.

Practice

Use the model. Rewrite as a whole number.

1. $\dfrac{5}{5}$

2. $\dfrac{12}{4}$

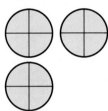

3. $\dfrac{8}{2}$

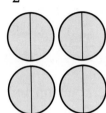

Use the model. Rewrite as a mixed number in simplest form.

4. $\dfrac{3}{2}$

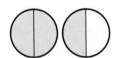

5. $\dfrac{15}{6}$

6. $\dfrac{11}{3}$

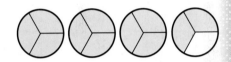

Use the model. Rewrite as a fraction.

7. $3\dfrac{1}{2}$

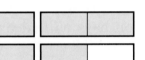

8. $2\dfrac{1}{3}$

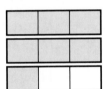

9. $1\dfrac{4}{5}$

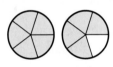

Rewrite as a whole number or a mixed number in simplest form.

10. $\dfrac{6}{6}$ **11.** $\dfrac{12}{3}$ **12.** $\dfrac{24}{4}$ **13.** $\dfrac{36}{6}$ **14.** $\dfrac{81}{9}$

15. $\dfrac{9}{7}$ **16.** $\dfrac{14}{4}$ **17.** $\dfrac{21}{2}$ **18.** $\dfrac{39}{5}$ **19.** $\dfrac{52}{7}$

Rewrite as a fraction.

20. 2 **21.** $1\dfrac{3}{5}$ **22.** $2\dfrac{1}{4}$ **23.** $1\dfrac{2}{3}$ **24.** $3\dfrac{5}{6}$

25. A cook uses $5\dfrac{1}{4}$ loaves of bread to make sandwiches. How many fourths of loaves is this?

26. There are $6\dfrac{2}{3}$ baskets of apples to be divided. How many thirds of baskets will there be?

27. Some students share a pizza. There are $3\dfrac{1}{3}$ pizzas. Each student receives $\dfrac{1}{3}$ of a pizza. How many students can share?

28. There are $2\dfrac{3}{8}$ pounds of spaghetti. One serving takes $\dfrac{1}{8}$ of a pound. How many servings are there?

## CHAPTER 7

Adding and Subtracting Fractions

Adding and Subtracting Unlike Fractions

Work Together

You can use fraction bars to model addition and subtraction of unlike fractions.

<table>
<tr><td>

Addition

$\frac{1}{2} + \frac{2}{5}$

</td><td>

Subtraction

$\frac{1}{2} - \frac{1}{3}$

</td></tr>
</table>

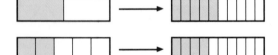

<table>
<tr><td>

Talk About It

▶ What fraction bars will fit exactly over both $\frac{1}{2}$ and $\frac{2}{5}$?

▶ How many tenths does it take to make $\frac{1}{2}$? $\frac{2}{5}$?

▶ What is $\frac{5}{10} + \frac{4}{10}$?

So, $\frac{1}{2} + \frac{2}{5} = \frac{9}{10}$.

</td><td>

Talk About It

▶ What fraction bars will fit exactly over both $\frac{1}{2}$ and $\frac{1}{3}$?

▶ How many sixths does it take to make $\frac{1}{2}$? $\frac{1}{3}$?

▶ What is $\frac{3}{6} - \frac{2}{6}$?

So, $\frac{1}{2} - \frac{1}{3} = \frac{1}{6}$.

</td></tr>
</table>

Another Method   Write equivalent fractions, using the least common multiple (LCM). Then add or subtract.

A. $\frac{1}{5} + \frac{2}{3}$

$\frac{1}{5}$ Multiples of 5: 5, 10, 15

$\frac{2}{3}$ Multiples of 3: 3, 6, 9, 12, 15

$$\frac{1}{5} = \frac{3}{15}$$
$$+\frac{2}{3} = \frac{10}{15}$$
$$\overline{\phantom{+\frac{2}{3} =\;} \frac{13}{15}}$$

B. $\frac{3}{4} - \frac{1}{6}$

$\frac{3}{4}$ Multiples of 4: 4, 8, 12

$\frac{1}{6}$ Multiples of 6: 6, 12

$$\frac{3}{4} = \frac{9}{12}$$
$$-\frac{1}{6} = \frac{2}{12}$$
$$\overline{\phantom{-\frac{1}{6} =\;} \frac{7}{12}}$$

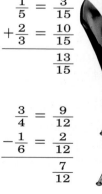

Bridge Lesson

Practice

Use fraction bars to find the sum or difference.

1. $\dfrac{1}{4} + \dfrac{1}{2}$

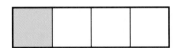

2. $\dfrac{1}{2} - \dfrac{3}{10}$

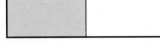

3. $\dfrac{1}{4} + \dfrac{1}{3}$

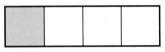

4. $\dfrac{3}{4} - \dfrac{1}{3}$

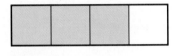

5. $\dfrac{5}{6} - \dfrac{1}{3}$

6. $\dfrac{3}{4} + \dfrac{5}{6}$

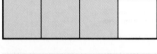

Find the least common denominator (LCD).

7. $\dfrac{1}{5}, \dfrac{2}{3}$

8. $\dfrac{3}{4}, \dfrac{4}{10}$

9. $\dfrac{2}{9}, \dfrac{5}{6}$

10. $\dfrac{1}{2}, \dfrac{4}{5}$

11. $\dfrac{2}{5}, \dfrac{3}{10}$

12. $\dfrac{1}{5}, \dfrac{2}{7}$

13. $\dfrac{1}{6}, \dfrac{2}{5}$

14. $\dfrac{1}{2}, \dfrac{3}{7}$

15. $\dfrac{1}{3}, \dfrac{7}{9}$

Rewrite the problem, using equivalent fractions.
Then find the sum or difference.

16. $\dfrac{1}{5} + \dfrac{2}{3}$

17. $\dfrac{3}{4} - \dfrac{1}{10}$

18. $\dfrac{2}{9} + \dfrac{5}{6}$

19. $\dfrac{4}{5} - \dfrac{1}{2}$

20. $\dfrac{2}{5} + \dfrac{3}{10}$

21. $\dfrac{2}{3} - \dfrac{1}{5}$

22. An explorer in the Arctic needed electricity to power some scientific equipment. He used a windmill to produce the electricity. Suppose the wind blew $10\frac{2}{5}$ hours one day and $8\frac{1}{3}$ hours the next day. How many more hours did the wind blow the first day?

23. A reporter is traveling by nonstop train from Rome to Paris to cover an international summit meeting. The trip to Paris takes $5\frac{1}{4}$ hours, and the return takes $4\frac{3}{8}$ hours. What is the total time for the round trip?

Measurement

The Metric System

Math Club members worked on a project, using only units from the **metric system.** They used metric units of length, capacity, and mass. They discovered that the same prefixes are used with different base units to name all the other units in the system. The prefixes relate to place value.

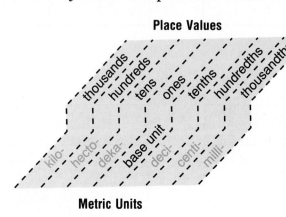

Place Values

Metric Units

Prefix	Base Unit	Measurement
centi-	meter	0.01 meter
milli-	liter	0.001 liter
kilo-	gram	1,000 grams

Metric measurements are given using a prefix and a base unit.

centi*meter*   milli*liter*   kilo*gram*

Decimals show how the prefix relates to the base unit.

centimeter	milliliter	kilogram
0.01 meter	0.001 liter	1,000 grams
(one hundredth of a meter)	(one thousandth of a liter)	

Examples

1 centimeter = 0.01 meter	1 milliliter = 0.001 liter	1 kilogram = 1,000 grams
4 centimeters = ▦ meter	3 milliliters = ▦ liter	7 kilograms = ▦ grams
4 × 0.01 = 0.04 meter	3 × 0.001 = 0.003 liter	7 × 1,000 = 7,000 grams

Talk About It

▶ Which prefixes are used to show units that are smaller than the base units?

▶ Which prefix shows a unit 1,000 times greater than the base units?

▶ Which prefix shows a unit 100 times smaller than the base units?

Practice

Choose the smaller unit of measure. Write **a** or **b**.

1. **a.** milliliter
   b. liter

2. **a.** gram
   b. milligram

3. **a.** kilometer
   b. meter

4. **a.** kilogram
   b. milligram

5. **a.** kilometer
   b. centimeter

6. **a.** liter
   b. kiloliter

Choose the larger unit of measure. Write **a** or **b**.

7. **a.** gram
   b. kilogram

8. **a.** milliliter
   b. liter

9. **a.** decimeter
   b. centimeter

10. **a.** gram
    b. milligram

11. **a.** kilometer
    b. centimeter

12. **a.** liter
    b. kiloliter

Complete the table.

		km	m	dm	cm	mm
13.	3 m	0.003	3	30	300	■
14.	9 m	0.009	9	90	■	9,000
15.	15 m	0.015	15	■	1,500	15,000
16.	25 m	■	25	250	2,500	25,000
17.	30 m	0.03	30	■	3,000	■
18.	45 m	■	45	■	■	■

Use the place-value poster on page H18. Write each as a decimal, using the base unit.

19. 5 dm
20. 3 mL
21. 8 g
22. 2 mm
23. 9 mg

24. 2 mL
25. 13 mL
26. 6 cm
27. 12 mg
28. 25 mg

29. Kristen and Sara need string for their projects. Kristen needs 2.5 m of string, and Sara needs 3.4 m of string. How much string do both girls need?

30. For her science project, Lois needs a board that is 1 m long. Alex needs a board that is 1 dm long. Who needs a longer board?

31. Ricardo is painting his display board. He already has 0.25 L of paint. If the board requires 1.5 L of paint, how much more paint does he need?

32. Cornelius is using an object that weighs 1 kg. Mark is using an object that weighs 1 mg. Who is using the lighter object?

Measurement

Using a Customary Ruler

Lisa did an experiment on plant growth. She measured and recorded the height of a plant in five different ways over four weeks.

Customary Units of Length	
12 inches (in.)	= 1 foot (ft)
3 ft	= 1 yard (yd)
5,280 ft or 1,760 yd	= 1 mile (mi)

Plant Height		
Measurement	**Week 1**	**Week 4**
To the nearest inch.	4 in.	4 in.
To the nearest $\frac{1}{2}$ in.	4 in.	4 in.
To the nearest $\frac{1}{4}$ in.	$3\frac{3}{4}$ in.	$4\frac{1}{4}$ in.
To the nearest $\frac{1}{8}$ in.	$3\frac{7}{8}$ in.	$4\frac{1}{8}$ in.
To the nearest $\frac{1}{16}$ in.	$3\frac{13}{16}$ in.	$4\frac{3}{16}$ in.

1	1 inch
1	$\frac{1}{2}$ inch
1	$\frac{1}{4}$ inch
1	$\frac{1}{8}$ inch
1	$\frac{1}{16}$ inch

- If Lisa measures to the nearest inch or to the nearest $\frac{1}{2}$ in., what would she record?

- Why are some measurements from Week 1 the same as Week 4?

- Using precise measurements, what was the height of the plant in Week 1? Week 4?

- To the nearest $\frac{1}{16}$ in., how much did Lisa's plant grow in four weeks?

Measure the width of your math book to the nearest inch, $\frac{1}{2}$ in., $\frac{1}{4}$ in., $\frac{1}{8}$ in., and $\frac{1}{16}$ in.
Record the measurements.

Talk About It

▶ Which measurement is the most precise?

▶ Why is measuring to the nearest $\frac{1}{16}$ in. more precise than measuring to the nearest $\frac{1}{2}$ in., $\frac{1}{4}$ in., or $\frac{1}{8}$ in.?

▶ When is a precise measurement necessary? When are precise measurements less important?

Practice

Measure each line segment to the part of the inch that gives the most precise measurement.

1. _____

2. _____

3. _____

4. _____

Draw a line to the given length.

5. $5\frac{1}{4}$ in.   6. $2\frac{3}{8}$ in.   7. $6\frac{1}{2}$ in.   8. $7\frac{5}{16}$ in.   9. $\frac{3}{4}$ in.

10. $4\frac{3}{4}$ in.   11. $1\frac{3}{8}$ in.   12. $\frac{5}{16}$ in.   13. $7\frac{1}{2}$ in.   14. $4\frac{5}{8}$ in.

Measure the given part of the figure to the nearest $\frac{1}{16}$ in.

15. the length of the straight yellow bar

16. the long sides of the blue triangle

17. the short side of the blue triangle

18. the red line

19. the green line

20. the purple line

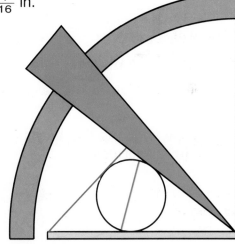

Solve. For Exercises 21–23, complete the riddle.

21. I measure long distances. There are 5,280 ft in me. My name is _?_, and my abbreviation is _?_.

22. I measure small things. There are 12 of me in 1 ft. My name is _?_, and my abbreviation is _?_.

23. I measure large things. There are 3 ft in me. My name is _?_, and my abbreviation is _?_.

24. Caroline measured a butterfly's wing span at $2\frac{3}{8}$ in. What is the measurement to the nearest $\frac{1}{2}$ in.?

25. Mills measured his plant twice a week. If the plant grew $2\frac{1}{3}$ in. each time he measured it, how much did the plant grow in 4 weeks?

26. Dillan measured the height of 5 flowers in his mother's garden. They measured 7 in., 5 in., $8\frac{3}{4}$ in., $7\frac{1}{4}$ in., and 7 in. What is the average height of the flowers?

CHAPTER 10

Ratio, Proportion, and Percent

Ratios

In Mrs. Appleton's class, 3 of the 5 students who ride bicycles to school ride red bicycles.

You can compare the number of students who ride red bicycles to the total number of students who ride bicycles. A **ratio** is a comparison of two numbers.

Work Together

Draw pictures to show comparisons and to explore ratio.

- Draw a rectangle and divide it into five equal parts. Let each part represent one student.

- Shade the number of parts equal to the number of students with red bicycles.

Talk About It

▶ How many students who ride bicycles do *not* ride red bicycles?

The rectangle showing the bicycle riders in Mrs. Appleton's class has three sections.

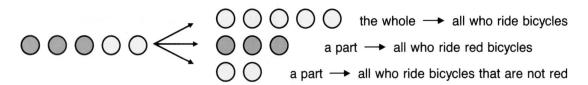

	the whole → all who ride bicycles
	a part → all who ride red bicycles
	a part → all who ride bicycles that are not red

Here are other ratios for Mrs. Appleton's class.

| part:whole
not red:all
2:5 | whole:part
all:red
5:3 | part:part
red:not red
3:2 |

Talk About It

▶ For Mrs. Appleton's class, what does the ratio $\frac{5}{2}$ describe?

▶ Does the ratio $\frac{5}{2}$ describe the same comparison as the ratio $\frac{2}{5}$? Explain.

Practice

Use the shapes in the box. Write the ratio in three ways.

1. stars to circles

2. circles to all shapes

3. all shapes to stars

4. squares to stars

5. squares to all shapes

6. all shapes to squares

7. circles to stars

8. stars to all shapes

9. circles to squares

10. all shapes to circles

11. stars to squares

12. squares to circles

Describe the comparison by using the shapes in the box. Write
part to whole, whole to part, or *part to part.*

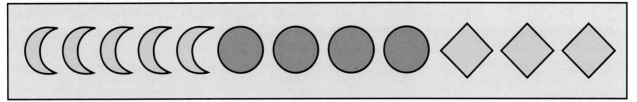

13. crescents to circles

14. circles to crescents

15. circles to diamonds

16. circles to all shapes

17. all shapes to crescents

18. diamonds to all shapes

19. diamonds to circles

20. diamonds to crescents

21. crescents to diamonds

22. all shapes to diamonds

23. crescents to all shapes

24. all shapes to circles

Choose shapes of your own. Draw a picture to show the ratio.

25. The ratio of red to green is $1:2$.

26. The ratio of red to all is $\frac{3}{10}$.

27. The ratio of short to long is $5:2$.

28. The ratio of fat to thin is $\frac{2}{9}$.

29. The ratio of small to all is $\frac{4}{11}$.

30. The ratio of all to thin is $30:25$.

31. Jane and Angela have 2 pairs of yellow shoelaces, 3 pairs of orange shoelaces, and 2 pairs of skates. What is the ratio of pairs of orange shoelaces to pairs of skates? What information is not needed to answer the question?

32. There are 2 wooden bowls, 3 wooden statues, and 4 metal bowls in the garage. What is the ratio of wooden objects to metal objects?

## CHAPTER 11

Geometry

Quadrilaterals

Quadrilaterals are closed plane figures that have four sides and four angles. There are several different kinds of quadrilaterals. Some of them you already know.

Work Together

Building Understanding

Make larger drawings of these figures. Make cardboard strips from your drawings. Punch holes in the cardboard strips and connect them with fasteners. Record the figures on a sheet of paper.

Make a rectangle.   Make a square.   Make a trapezoid.

Talk About It

▶ How many different shapes did you make?

▶ Which figures have four right angles?

▶ Which figure has acute and obtuse angles?

▶ Which figures have two pairs of parallel sides?

▶ Which figure has only one pair of parallel sides?

Adjust the cardboard strips of the square and the rectangle to form a different kind of quadrilateral for each. Trace these new figures on a sheet of paper.

▶ Describe the new figures you made.

▶ Do your new figures have any right angles?

▶ Do any of your figures have parallel sides? If so, how many?

Practice

Describe the relationship among the sides of the quadrilaterals.

Quadrilaterals Classified by Sides		
Name	**Example**	**Description**
1. Rectangle		?
2. Square		?
3. Trapezoid		?
4. Parallelogram		?
5. Rhombus		?

Describe the relationship among the angles of the quadrilaterals.

Quadrilaterals Classified by Angles		
Name	**Example**	**Description**
6. Rectangle		?
7. Square		?
8. Trapezoid		?
9. Parallelogram		?
10. Rhombus		?

11. parallelogram   trapezoid

Compare the sides of a parallelogram with the sides of a trapezoid. How is the trapezoid different?

12. parallelogram   rectangle

Compare the sides of a parallelogram with the sides of a rectangle. How are they the same?

13. rhombus   trapezoid

Compare the sides of a rhombus with the sides of a trapezoid. How is the rhombus different?

14. rectangle   square

Compare the angles of a rectangle with the angles of a square. What are their measures?

School-Home Connection

CHAPTER 1
Place Value: Whole Numbers and Decimals

Application: Comparing Yearly Salaries

The figures in the table are for 1990. These figures, from the Bureau of Labor, show the average yearly salary of workers in five different states.

Write the names of the states in order from the state with the highest average salary to the state with the lowest.

State	Average Yearly Salary
Connecticut	$28,995
Florida	$21,032
Mississippi	$17,718
New York	$28,873
South Dakota	$16,430

Now Try This

What factors do you think affect the salaries of people in a particular state?

Look at employment advertisements in your newspaper. What salaries are listed for jobs you might like to have when you finish school?

CHAPTER 2
Adding and Subtracting Whole Numbers and Decimals

Application: Using a Budget

Budgeting helps you manage your money. A budget shows whether you have enough money to pay for expenses and to save for extras.

If your income is $25 a week and you need money for school lunches, clothes, school supplies, and extras, your budget might be like this.

Budget	
Lunches	$10
Clothes	7
School supplies	3
Extras	+ 5
TOTAL	$25

Now Try This

Suppose your allowance is $7 a week. Make a budget to show how you would spend your allowance during four weeks.

School-Home Connection

CHAPTER 3

Multiplying Whole Numbers and Decimals

Application: Making Change

Knowing how to make change is an everyday life skill. When making change, use as few bills and as few coins as possible. Suppose you must give your parent $6.46 in change. You might use any of these combinations.

a. six $1 bills, 1 quarter, 2 dimes, 1 penny
b. six $1 bills, 4 dimes, 1 nickel, 1 penny
c. one $5 bill, one $1 bill, 1 quarter, 2 dimes, 1 penny

Which combination is the best way to make the change?

Now Try This

Make a table like the one below. Show the best way to make change of $3.22, $2.36, $6.73, and $5.98.

Change Due	Change: Number of					
	$5 bills	$1 bills	Quarters	Dimes	Nickels	Pennies
$3.22						

CHAPTER 4

Dividing Whole Numbers and Decimals

Application: Planning for Transportation

If you are planning a trip for a group of people, you must arrange for transportation. Suppose 35 people in your neighborhood are planning a trip. They will travel in vans that each hold 6 people. How many vans will they need?

$$5.8 \leftarrow \text{They will need 6 vans.}$$
$$6)\overline{35.0}$$

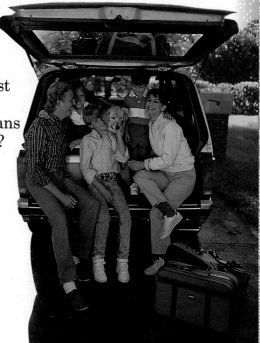

Now Try This

Plan a trip for a group of people in your neighborhood. The people will ride in vans. How many vans will you need to rent? Will all the vans be full? What else will you need to consider if the people ride in vans?

CHAPTER 5

Graphing, Statistics, and Probability

Application: Reading Stock Reports

A stock consists of shares of a company that are bought and sold on a stock market. The prices are listed in the newspaper each day. A line in the stock listings may look like this.

Stock	Div.	PE	Sales hds.	High	Low	Close	Chg.
ABC	1.68	13	63	14	13	14	$+\frac{3}{4}$

The column labeled *Div.* indicates the value of the annual dividend for one share. It is based on the most recent quarterly or semiannual dividend. ABC paid $1.68 per share.

Now Try This

Look in the financial pages of a newspaper for the stock listings. Find the section that tells you how to read the listings. What does each column heading mean?

CHAPTER 6

Number Theory

Application: Adjusting Shutter Speed

On some cameras there is an adjustment for shutter speed. The shutter speed determines how long the shutter remains open to receive light. The larger the number on the dial, the less time the shutter is open.

A setting of 250 means the shutter will be open for $\frac{1}{250}$ of a second. A setting of 15 means the shutter will be open for $\frac{1}{15}$ of a second. Which setting will let more light into the camera? If you take a picture in a dark room, which setting will you use?

Now Try This

Look at a camera your family or a friend owns. Does it have an adjustment for the shutter speed, or is the shutter speed automatic? What do you think are some advantages of an automatic shutter? some disadvantages?

CHAPTER 7

Adding and Subtracting Fractions

Application: Egyptian Fractions

Scientists discovered an ancient document in Egypt that they call the Rhind Papyrus. This document shows how Egyptians wrote fractions. It was written in 1700 B.C., so you know that people have been using fractions for a long time.

Egyptians used 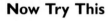 to represent a numerator of 1. They used their whole-number symbols to represent the value of the denominator.

How did the ancient Egyptians write $\frac{1}{14}$?

Now Try This

Make up your own system and symbols for writing fractions. Make a poster that explains your system. What are some advantages of your system?

CHAPTER 8

Multiplying and Dividing Fractions

Application: Adjusting Recipes

Most recipes are written to provide 4 to 6 servings. If you cook for a larger number of people, you must adjust the recipe so you will have enough food to serve everyone.

Suppose a casserole recipe calls for $\frac{3}{4}$ cup of broccoli for each serving. How much broccoli would you need for a casserole large enough to serve 15 people?

$\frac{3}{4} \times 15 = 11\frac{1}{4}$ ← You will need $11\frac{1}{4}$ cups of broccoli.

Now Try This

Find a casserole recipe. Divide the amount of each ingredient by the number of servings the recipe makes. This will give you the amount needed for 1 serving. Then adjust the amounts so that the casserole will serve 15 people.

School-Home Connection

CHAPTER 9

Measurement

Project: Ordering Carpet

Carpet is sold in 9-ft and 12-ft widths. You can buy almost any length. To buy carpet, first measure the length and the width of a room. Next, determine which measurement is less than or equal to 9 ft or 12 ft. Then, use the other measurement to determine the length of carpet needed.

Suppose you want to carpet the floor of a room that is 8 ft wide and 18 ft long. Would you order carpet that has a 9-ft or a 12-ft width? What length would you order if you wanted to have 1 more foot than is actually needed?

Now Try This

Measure one room in your home to determine how much carpet you would need to cover the floor. Suppose that you can order the carpet in 9-ft widths and in 12-ft widths. How much carpet of each width would you need?

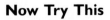

CHAPTER 10

Ratio, Proportion, and Percent

Application: Tipping

When you purchase a meal in a restaurant, you usually tip the server for good service. The amount of the tip is usually between 10% and 20% of the bill.

Suppose a meal costs $18.00 and the service was good. You may decide to leave a 15% tip.

Think:
$$18 \times 0.10 = 1.80 \quad (10\%)$$
$$\tfrac{1}{2} \times 1.80 = \underline{0.90} \quad (5\%)$$
$$2.70$$

You would leave $2.70 for a tip.

Now Try This

The next time your family goes to a restaurant, ask if you can figure the tip. Ask a family member what percent to leave for the tip, and then determine the amount by multiplying the bill by the percent.

CHAPTER 11

Geometry

Application: Making a Scale Drawing

A scale drawing is usually smaller than the actual object. The scale of the drawing relates the size of the drawing to the size of the object.

Suppose the scale of a drawing is 1 in. = 20 ft. This means that a length of 1 in. in the drawing represents 20 ft in the actual object.

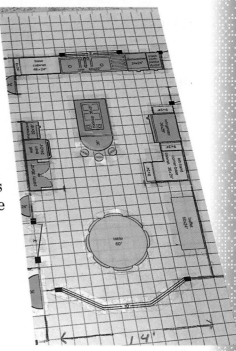

Now Try This

Make a scale drawing of two or three rooms in your home. Use the scale $\frac{1}{2}$ in. = 1 ft. Leave spaces in your drawing where there are doorways.

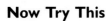

CHAPTER 12

Perimeter, Area, and Volume

Application: Measuring Volume of Containers

Suppose you want to know if several small items will fit in a container. You can find out by comparing the volume of the container to the volume of the items.

Denny has 85 1-in. cubes and a box that is 2 in. wide, 5 in. long, and 10 in. deep. Will all the cubes fit in the box?

Volume of the cubes	Volume of the box
85 × 1 × 1 = 85	2 × 5 × 10 = 100
85 in.³	100 in.³

Since 100 in.³ is greater than 85 in.³, the cubes will fit in the box.

Now Try This

Find several differently shaped boxes that look as if they have the same volume. Then measure to determine the volume of each box. Do the boxes actually have about the same volume?

CHAPTER 13

Integers

Application: Watching Stock Changes

A stock consists of shares of a company that are bought and sold on a stock market. The prices are listed in the newspaper each day. Lines in the stock listings may look like this.

Stock	Div.	PE	Sales hds.	High	Low	Close	Chg.
ABC	1.68	13	63	14	13	14	$+\frac{3}{4}$
XYZ	1.00	58	5557	$49\frac{7}{8}$	$48\frac{7}{8}$	$49\frac{1}{8}$	$-\frac{7}{8}$

Chg. means "change." It is the difference between the closing price shown (Close) and the closing price of the day before.

Now Try This

Choose a stock and follow it for two weeks. Record the change each day. Are the changes, or differences, mostly gains (positive) or mostly losses (negative)?

CHAPTER 14

Getting Ready for Algebra

Application: Computing Commission

In many sales jobs, employees are paid a salary plus a commission. A commission is an amount of money equal to a percent of the employee's sales.

Suppose Josh receives a weekly salary of $250 plus a commission of 5% of his sales. How much would he be paid if he sold $2,500 of merchandise in one week?

salary + (5% × sales) = salary + commission
250 + (0.05 × 2,500) = 250 + 125 = 375

So, Josh would be paid $375 for one week.

Now Try This

In your town, what are some sales jobs in which employees are paid a salary and a commission? Why do you suppose employers want to pay their employees this way? Why do you think people in sales like to be paid this way?

CHAPTER I

Lesson I.I *(pages 2–5)*

Write the Roman numeral.

1. 32	**2.** 568	**3.** 9	**4.** 97
5. 411	**6.** 1979	**7.** 39	**8.** 2010
9. 1546	**10.** 250	**11.** 1887	**12.** 780
13. 19	**14.** 2915	**15.** 44	**16.** 907

Lesson I.2 *(pages 6–7)*

Write the value of the underlined digit.

1. 245,9<u>8</u>6	**2.** 5,7<u>8</u>6,341	**3.** 6,4<u>3</u>5
4. 4,<u>3</u>75,129	**5.** 10,916,<u>4</u>89	**6.** 2<u>9</u>,633,824
7. 11,924,01<u>5</u>	**8.** 6,<u>8</u>12	**9.** 8<u>9</u>,542

Write the number in short word form.

10. 1,908,665	**11.** 761,249	**12.** 396
13. 300,000,268	**14.** 45,836,000	**15.** 1,032
16. 12,801	**17.** 90,100,010	**18.** 6,008

Write the number in standard form.

19. seven thousand, ninety-five

20. six million, four hundred fifty-two thousand, three hundred sixty-nine

21. forty-thousand, six hundred eight

22. two hundred fifteen billion, one million, three thousand two

23. 22,000,000,000 + 55,000,000 + 600 + 20 + 5

24. 4,000,000 + 600,000 + 70,000 + 200 + 40 + 3

Lesson 1.3 *(pages 8–9)*

Write the number in short word form.

1. 0.4 **2.** 0.8925 **3.** 0.468

4. 2.63 **5.** 0.482 **6.** 0.69

7. 11.03 **8.** 0.6253 **9.** 6.812

Write the value of the underlined digit.

10. 0.3$\underline{9}$ **11.** 0.56$\underline{8}$ **12.** $\underline{2}$.03 **13.** 0.234$\underline{5}$

14. 4.$\underline{1}$5 **15.** 0.0$\underline{2}$4 **16.** 10.999$\underline{9}$ **17.** 9.75$\underline{2}$

Write the number in standard form.

18. 96 thousandths **19.** 21 hundredths **20.** 6 tenths

21. 402 ten-thousandths **22.** seventy-two and three tenths

23. 1 and 15 hundredths **24.** 612 thousandths **25.** 5 hundredths

26. 10 and 8 ten-thousandths **27.** six and twelve hundredths

Lesson 1.4 *(pages 10–11)*

Compare the numbers. Write $<$, $>$, or $=$.

1. 10.009 ⬤ 10.090 **2.** 3,232 ⬤ 3,323 **3.** 40.345 ⬤ 40.354

4. 39.0045 ⬤ 39.0450 **5.** 6.120 ⬤ 6.1200 **6.** 0.550 ⬤ 0.549

7. 9.350 ⬤ 9.35 **8.** 4.854 ⬤ 4.844 **9.** 600,910 ⬤ 609,100

List the numbers in order from least to greatest. Use $<$.

10. 33,546; 33,645; 33,564 **11.** 0.020; 0.200; 0.002 **12.** 4,698; 4,869; 4,689

13. 0.301; 0.0301; 0.101 **14.** 2,421; 2,412; 2,422 **15.** 6.009; 6.090; 6.008

16. 4,532; 5,234; 3,254 **17.** 160,329; 180,528; 610,329

18. 2.911; 2.191; 1.921 **19.** 395.005; 295.005; 352.009

20. 0.195; 0.095; 0.189 **21.** 6.918; 6.098; 9.006

22. 0.071; 0.171; 0.0018 **23.** 600,201; 601,002; 600,120

24. 2.3077; 2.0377; 2.3773 **25.** 2,738; 2,728; 2,078

Lesson 1.5 *(pages 12–13)*

1. Sue wants to make a report on the heights and weights of some of her classmates. Later she will gather facts about their parents' and grandparents' heights and weights. Make a table from the information below.

> Report: Linda is 5 feet 4 inches and weighs 120 pounds; Alex is 6 feet 2 inches and weighs 190 pounds; Jason is 5 feet 7 inches and weighs 180 pounds; Herb is 5 feet 8 inches and weighs 200 pounds; Michelle is 5 feet 5 inches and weighs 120 pounds.

Use your table for Exercises 2–5.

2. Which classmates' weights are between 150 pounds and 210 pounds?

3. Compare Michelle's height with that of Alex. Use < or >.

4. List all the heights from tallest to shortest. Use >.

5. Which classmates weigh the same?

Lesson 1.6 *(pages 14–15)*

Estimate by rounding to the place indicated.

1. $4.68
   10 cents

2. 451
   hundreds

3. 84
   tens

4. $3.63
   dollar

5. 890,000,000,000
   hundred billions

The number has been rounded to the place indicated. Write the range of numbers that round to the given number.

6. 600
   hundred

7. 55,000
   thousand

8. 700,000
   hundred thousand

9. 4,000,000
   million

10. 100
    hundred

11. $8.50
    ten cents

12. $2.00
    dollar

13. 8,000,000
    million

Lesson 1.7 *(pages 18–19)*

Solve.

1. $6 \times 5 + 3$

2. $3 \times 4 + 5$

3. $36 \div 3 - 10$

4. $(7 + 4) \times 2$

5. $(5 - 2) \div 3$

6. $12 + 5 \times 3$

7. $66 \div (14 - 3)$

8. $4 \times (3 + 2)$

9. $(6 - 4) \times (4 + 6)$

10. $18 - 2 \times 6$

11. $7 + 10 \div 2$

12. $(8 + 2) \times 10$

Lesson 1.8 (pages 20–21)

Tell how many zeros will be in the number when written in standard form.

1. 10^5
2. 10^6
3. ten squared
4. ten to the sixth power

5. $10 \times 10 \times 10$
6. $10 \times 10 \times 10 \times 10$
7. 10^8

8. ten to the twelfth power
9. $10 \times 10 \times 10 \times 10 \times 10$
10. 10^{10}

Write the number in standard form.

11. $10 \times 10 \times 10 \times 10 \times 10$
12. ten to the eighth power
13. 10^{12}

14. ten to the third power
15. $7 \times 10 \times 10 \times 10$
16. 6×10^2

Lesson 1.9 (pages 22–23)

Use a calculator. Write the square or the square root of the number in standard form.

1. 21^2
2. 1.01^2
3. 40^2
4. 3.2^2

5. $\sqrt{36}$
6. $\sqrt{0.25}$
7. $\sqrt{169}$
8. $\sqrt{0.0025}$

9. $\sqrt{324}$
10. $\sqrt{1.21}$
11. $\sqrt{256}$
12. $\sqrt{4.41}$

13. 60^2
14. 0.7^2
15. 2.8^2
16. 12^2

Lesson 1.10 (pages 24–25)

Find the pattern. Then solve.

1. Pat spent 10 minutes on her rowing machine the first time she used it. If she increases her workout by 4 minutes each time, for how many minutes will she exercise on the sixth time?

2. You plant 2 flowers on the first day and then plant 3 more each day than the day before. If you follow this pattern, how many flowers will you plant on day 8?

3. A stamp collector buys 25 stamps the first month. After that, he buys 15 more stamps every month than the month before. How many stamps does he buy in the sixth month?

4. Tom builds 3 miniature car models the first day and 4 more cars each day than the day before. If he follows this pattern how many cars does he build on the fifth day?

CHAPTER 2

Lesson 2.1 *(pages 34–35)*

Find the sum or difference. Use mental math when possible.

1. $(3 + 10) - 12$
2. $6 + (5 + 9)$
3. $12 + 13 + 5$
4. $42 + (8 + 4)$

5. $(7 + 5) + 10$
6. $22 + 35 + 8$
7. $15 + 35 + 9$
8. $18 - 6 - 2$

9. $(6 + 24) + 7$
10. $43 - 13 - 7$
11. $68 - 9$
12. $46 - 27$

13. $35 + 20 + 65$
14. $54 - 27$
15. $23 + 35 + 17$
16. $50 - 10 - 15$

Lesson 2.2 *(pages 36–37)*

Use adjusted front-end estimation to estimate the sum or difference.

1. $\begin{array}{r} 8,545 \\ -5,328 \\ \hline \end{array}$
2. $\begin{array}{r} 2,989 \\ +4,156 \\ \hline \end{array}$
3. $\begin{array}{r} 3,849 \\ -1,314 \\ \hline \end{array}$
4. $\begin{array}{r} 3,758 \\ +2,455 \\ \hline \end{array}$
5. $\begin{array}{r} 9,243 \\ -6,411 \\ \hline \end{array}$

6. $\begin{array}{r} 3,971 \\ +6,428 \\ \hline \end{array}$
7. $\begin{array}{r} 12,810 \\ -\ 4,202 \\ \hline \end{array}$
8. $\begin{array}{r} 2,178 \\ +8,695 \\ \hline \end{array}$
9. $\begin{array}{r} 20,244 \\ -\ 8,127 \\ \hline \end{array}$
10. $\begin{array}{r} 6,954 \\ +9,821 \\ \hline \end{array}$

Round to estimate the sum or difference.

11. $\begin{array}{r} 32,564 \\ +26,383 \\ \hline \end{array}$
12. $\begin{array}{r} 42,345 \\ -13,859 \\ \hline \end{array}$
13. $\begin{array}{r} 18,941 \\ +17,865 \\ \hline \end{array}$
14. $\begin{array}{r} 29,310 \\ -12,980 \\ \hline \end{array}$
15. $\begin{array}{r} 14,258 \\ +17,637 \\ \hline \end{array}$

16. $\begin{array}{r} 78,432 \\ -10,927 \\ \hline \end{array}$
17. $\begin{array}{r} 3,932 \\ -2,121 \\ \hline \end{array}$
18. $\begin{array}{r} 62,403 \\ +\ 7,380 \\ \hline \end{array}$
19. $\begin{array}{r} 8,526 \\ +1,254 \\ \hline \end{array}$
20. $\begin{array}{r} 9,645 \\ -4,462 \\ \hline \end{array}$

Lesson 2.3 *(pages 38–39)*

Find the sum or difference. Use the inverse operation to check.

1. $\begin{array}{r} 631 \\ +348 \\ \hline \end{array}$
2. $\begin{array}{r} 291 \\ -156 \\ \hline \end{array}$
3. $\begin{array}{r} 547 \\ -396 \\ \hline \end{array}$
4. $\begin{array}{r} 4,546 \\ +5,219 \\ \hline \end{array}$
5. $\begin{array}{r} 9,341 \\ -8,934 \\ \hline \end{array}$

6. $\begin{array}{r} 43,642 \\ -29,835 \\ \hline \end{array}$
7. $\begin{array}{r} 3,101 \\ -1,898 \\ \hline \end{array}$
8. $\begin{array}{r} 32,675 \\ +48,325 \\ \hline \end{array}$
9. $\begin{array}{r} 245,147 \\ -\ 96,639 \\ \hline \end{array}$
10. $\begin{array}{r} 683,473 \\ -197,789 \\ \hline \end{array}$

11. $\begin{array}{r} 541 \\ 63 \\ +371 \\ \hline \end{array}$
12. $\begin{array}{r} 2,539 \\ 1,983 \\ +\ 818 \\ \hline \end{array}$
13. $\begin{array}{r} 3,568 \\ 2,479 \\ +10,238 \\ \hline \end{array}$
14. $\begin{array}{r} 45,109 \\ 31,802 \\ +23,005 \\ \hline \end{array}$
15. $\begin{array}{r} 999,999 \\ 876,543 \\ +\ \ \ \ \ \ 5 \\ \hline \end{array}$

Lesson 2.4 *(pages 40–41)*

Solve. Use estimation, paper and pencil, mental math, or a calculator. Justify your choice.

1. Yolanda's three deposits last month were $239.00, $154.00, and $175.00. How much money did Yolanda deposit last month?

2. Steven gives a clerk $20.00 to pay for a $1.49 pack of pencils. How much change will he receive?

3. Adam gave a clerk $10.00 for frozen yogurt and received $7.01 in change. How much was the frozen yogurt?

4. Marcy bought 3 tapes for $36.97. The first tape cost $12.99 and the second cost $10.99. How much did the third tape cost?

Lesson 2.5 *(pages 42–43)*

Use adjusted front-end estimation to estimate the sum or difference.

1. 0.893 $+0.145$	2. 3.92 -1.25	3. 0.83 -0.192	4. 4.1 $+2.85$	5. 0.435 $+1.569$
6. 62.62 $+31.90$	7. 7.15 -6.05	8. 12.44 $+\ 3.78$	9. 3.75 -2.16	10. 0.0862 $+0.228$

Round to estimate the sum or difference.

11. 2.54 -1.23	12. 4.72 $+3.01$	13. 41.6 -29.8	14. 1.59 $+0.33$	15. 4.15 -3.91
16. 75.9 $+20.6$	17. 54.07 -28.05	18. 32.16 $+61.4$	19. 90.01 -82.15	20. 99.81 $+\ 6.95$

Lesson 2.6 *(pages 46–47)*

Find the sum.

1. $2.05 + 6.453$

2. $6.8 + 5.234$

3. $0.45 + 9.761$

4. $\$12.99 + \$65.36$

5. $3.2 + 1.684$

6. $0.003 + 6.58$

7. 1.024 3.913 $+0.276$	8. 4.5 0.013 $+2.46$	9. 39.126 0.486 $+23.725$	10. 435.1 1.7 $+\ \ \ 0.452$	11. 39.62 1.01 $+456.789$

12. $0.015 + 2.5 + 32.16$

13. $\$3.19 + \$4.28 + \$5.07$

Lesson 2.7 (pages 48–49)

Find the difference.

1. $6.12 - 0.054$

2. $61.39 - 3.4$

3. $215.62 - 9.8$

4. $21 - 0.025$

5. $0.78 - 0.678$

6. $45.4 - 29.489$

7. $0.5 - 0.4982$

8. $7.25 - 5.025$

9. $8.1 - 0.467$

10. $6.315 - 3.125$

11. $4.2 - 3.199$

12. $234.1 - 0.927$

13. $\begin{array}{r} 0.09 \\ -0.008 \\ \hline \end{array}$

14. $\begin{array}{r} 32.12 \\ -29.98 \\ \hline \end{array}$

15. $\begin{array}{r} 89.6 \\ -\ 1.998 \\ \hline \end{array}$

Lesson 2.8 (pages 50–51)

Find the balance. Use a calculator with memory keys.

1.

Checks	Deposits
375.00	510.91
80.00	
69.79	490.91
12.03	
Balance: ■	

2.

Checks	Deposits
35.49	425.00
68.87	
119.13	
387.34	400.00
Balance: ■	

3.

Checks	Deposits
679.85	2,930.14
498.39	
215.67	
3.04	
Balance: ■	

Lesson 2.9 (pages 52–53)

Write an algebraic expression for the word expression.

1. 8 less than a number, t

2. the sum of 39 and a number, x

3. m fewer than 42

4. b more than 85

5. the sum of 0.5 and a number, g

6. 25 fewer than a number, k

7. d less than 145

8. a more than 300

Write a word expression for the algebraic expression.

9. $41 + t$

10. $95 - m$

11. $1.2 + x$

12. $e - 35.2$

13. $n + 4.56$

14. $d - 33$

15. $x - 1$

16. $b + 409$

Lesson 2.10 *(pages 54–55)*

Evaluate the expression.

1. $b + 3.5$, for $b = 0.7$
2. $a + 99$, for $a = 3$
3. $d - 65$, for $d = 65$
4. $g - 19$, for $g = 50$
5. $46 - x$, for $x = 24$
6. $403 - y$, for $y = 108$
7. $29.3 - w$, for $w = 29$
8. $m + 0$, for $m = 16$
9. $n + 5$, for $n = 5$
10. $(10 + x) + 5$, for $x = 3$
11. $(6 - m) + 11$, for $m = 2.5$
12. $43 - (n + 2.1)$, for $n = 0.9$
13. $51 + (t + 25)$, for $t = 7.6$
14. $(a - 6) + 8$, for $a = 12$
15. $b - (21 - 9)$, for $b = 31.6$
16. $b + (8 - 3)$, for $b = 15$
17. $37 - (z - 12)$, for $z = 24$

Lesson 2.11 *(pages 56–57)*

Tell how to solve the equations.

1. $x - 12 = 4$
2. $y + 3 = 5$
3. $m + 9 = 33$
4. $4.3 + b = 9.2$
5. $a + 5.6 = 23.7$
6. $d - 4 = 5$
7. $8.2 + k = 10$
8. $z - 2.5 = 1$
9. $g + 3.2 = 5.3$

Use inverse operations. Solve the equations.

10. $y - 9 = 20$
11. $6 + c = 13$
12. $d + 4 = 25$
13. $a + 35 = 42$
14. $b - 10 = 2$
15. $x + 16 = 26$

Lesson 2.12 *(pages 58–59)*

Solve. Use the strategy *guess and check.* Record your guesses and checks.

1. Pam and Lew collect buttons. Pam has 17 more buttons than Lew. Together they have a total of 267 buttons. How many buttons does Lew have?

2. Of the 90 members of the marching band, there are 20 more female members than males. How many males are there?

3. John bought two banners at the baseball game. The total cost for both was $10. One banner cost $2 more than the other banner. What was the cost of each banner?

4. A hiking club hikes 15 miles in two days. On the second day they hike twice as far as they did on the first day. How far do they hike each day?

CHAPTER 3

Lesson 3.1 *(pages 68–69)*

Find the missing factor. Name the property used.

1. $15 \times 11 = \blacksquare \times 15$
2. $39 \times 1 = \blacksquare$
3. $\blacksquare \times 8 = (4 \times 2) + (4 \times 6)$
4. $9 \times \blacksquare = 0$
5. $16 \times (2 \times 8) = (16 \times \blacksquare) \times 8$
6. $5 \times (6 \times 8) = (8 \times \blacksquare) \times 6$
7. $16 \times \blacksquare = 16$
8. $\blacksquare \times 5 = (8 \times 5) + (7 \times 5)$
9. $36 \times 5 = 5 \times \blacksquare$

Use mental math and the properties of multiplication to find the product.

10. $18 \times 12 \times 0$
11. 15×1
12. 40×3
13. 50×4
14. 10×80
15. 5×12
16. $6 \times 8 \times 1$
17. $11 \times 5 \times 2$
18. $6 \times 3 \times 3$
19. 3×15
20. $40 \times 6 \times 0$
21. 36×3
22. 12×20
23. $2 \times 2 \times 7$
24. $10 \times 9 \times 2$
25. $5 \times 5 \times 2$

Lesson 3.2 *(pages 70–71)*

Estimate the product.

1. $\begin{array}{r} 42 \\ \times\ 3 \\ \hline \end{array}$
2. $\begin{array}{r} 31 \\ \times\ 5 \\ \hline \end{array}$
3. $\begin{array}{r} 49 \\ \times\ 4 \\ \hline \end{array}$
4. $\begin{array}{r} 99 \\ \times\ 8 \\ \hline \end{array}$
5. $\begin{array}{r} 324 \\ \times\ \ 3 \\ \hline \end{array}$

6. $\begin{array}{r} 685 \\ \times\ \ 7 \\ \hline \end{array}$
7. $\begin{array}{r} 6,215 \\ \times\ \ \ \ 4 \\ \hline \end{array}$
8. $\begin{array}{r} 22 \\ \times 56 \\ \hline \end{array}$
9. $\begin{array}{r} 291 \\ \times\ 52 \\ \hline \end{array}$
10. $\begin{array}{r} 615 \\ \times 481 \\ \hline \end{array}$

11. $\begin{array}{r} 45 \\ \times\ 5 \\ \hline \end{array}$
12. $\begin{array}{r} 62 \\ \times\ 8 \\ \hline \end{array}$
13. $\begin{array}{r} 82 \\ \times 15 \\ \hline \end{array}$
14. $\begin{array}{r} 54 \\ \times 59 \\ \hline \end{array}$
15. $\begin{array}{r} 312 \\ \times\ 45 \\ \hline \end{array}$

16. $\begin{array}{r} 42,108 \\ \times\ \ \ \ \ 97 \\ \hline \end{array}$
17. $\begin{array}{r} 3,920 \\ \times\ \ \ \ 35 \\ \hline \end{array}$
18. $\begin{array}{r} 4,086 \\ \times\ \ \ \ 24 \\ \hline \end{array}$
19. $\begin{array}{r} 450 \\ \times\ 82 \\ \hline \end{array}$
20. $\begin{array}{r} 18,420 \\ \times\ \ \ \ \ 62 \\ \hline \end{array}$

Estimate to compare. Use < or >.

21. $8 \times 28 \bullet 240$
22. $50 \times 19 \bullet 800$
23. $63 \times 31 \bullet 1,800$
24. $215 \times 52 \bullet 10,000$
25. $85 \times 9 \bullet 810$
26. $38 \times 68 \bullet 2,800$
27. $45 \times 5 \bullet 250$
28. $9 \times 27 \bullet 300$
29. $11 \times 82 \bullet 800$
30. $190 \times 5 \bullet 1,000$
31. $41 \times 32 \bullet 1,200$
32. $680 \times 97 \bullet 70,000$

Lesson 3.3 *(pages 72–73)*

Find the product.

1. 85 × 41	**2.** 39 × 97	**3.** 247 × 368	**4.** 1,236 × 39	**5.** 3,039 × 165
6. 46,164 × 58	**7.** 6,352 × 24	**8.** 3,815 × 242	**9.** 4,998 × 906	**10.** 136,761 × 525
11. 81 × 32	**12.** 618 × 79	**13.** 9,845 × 68	**14.** 259 × 28	**15.** 8,954 × 71
16. 486 × 351	**17.** 5,876 × 34	**18.** 8,644 × 142	**19.** 9,514 × 529	**20.** 1,012 × 426

Lesson 3.4 *(pages 74–75)*

Frederick wants to buy a television that costs $469. He has $250 in a savings account. He saves $60 from his paycheck each week. He is considering these options.

Option 1: Continue to save until he can pay for the television in full.
Option 2: Pay $30 per month for 18 months.
Option 3: Pay $100 down and $23 per month for 18 months.

1. How much will the television cost using Option 2?

2. With which option will he pay the least amount of money each month?

3. How much will he save by choosing Option 3 instead of Option 2?

4. Which option is the least expensive of all the options?

Lesson 3.5 *(pages 76–77)*

Estimate. Choose the correct product. Write **a, b,** or **c.**

1. 43.6×38
a. 16.568
b. 165.68
c. 1,656.8

2. 8.234×8.25
a. 67.9305
b. 6.79305
c. 679.305

3. 3.24×6.76
a. 219.024
b. 21.9024
c. 2.19024

4. 841×5.13
a. 43.1433
b. 431.433
c. 4,314.33

Estimate the product.

5. 34.2×9.6

6. 2.1×5.9

7. 4.3×12.4

8. 1.6×48.6

9. 6.75×4.93

10. 37.2×9.5

11. 49.6×1.23

12. 3.6×8.7

Lesson 3.6 *(pages 80–81)*

Use mental math and multiplication to estimate the sum.

1. 390 412 420 +375	**2.** 885 902 873 +900	**3.** 1,954 2,431 2,145 +1,837	**4.** 12,342 11,785 12,040 +11,827
5. 8.91 8.82 8.75 +8.69	**6.** $3.75 4.19 3.68 + 4.19	**7.** 0.8 1.4 0.06 +0.9	**8.** 44.001 43.631 43.72 +44.26
9. 34,800 35,020 34,641 +35,293	**10.** 810,462 777,888 763,141 +782,205	**11.** $ 9.97 10.21 9.80 + 10.12	**12.** 721,108 681,926 662,044 +710,802
13. 5.9 5.7 6.3 +6.1	**14.** 3.03 3.09 2.8 +2.7	**15.** 9,105 9,080 8,970 +8,790	**16.** 160.8 158.9 162.1 +159.4

Lesson 3.7 *(pages 82–83)*

Find the product. Round money amounts to the nearest cent.

1. 4.3 ×7.6	**2.** 6.578 × 2.8	**3.** 437.2 × 9.8	**4.** $22.69 × 9.5
5. 67.89 × 45	**6.** $49.95 × 0.4	**7.** $492.45 × 5.12	**8.** 0.38 × 0.6
9. 22.61 × 0.52	**10.** 0.047 × 0.63	**11.** 4.28 ×0.75	**12.** 22.2 ×2.78
13. 29.5 × 38	**14.** 42.91 × 0.03	**15.** 286.5 × 2.91	**16.** 4.76 × 59

17. 38.76×4.6 **18.** 0.125×0.65 **19.** 5.1×0.06 **20.** 33.33×0.003

21. 1.01×99 **22.** 6.008×0.2 **23.** 200.8×3.45 **24.** 106×3.03

25. 4.9×0.01 **26.** 4.02×1.6 **27.** $\$11.20 \times 6.2$ **28.** 1.5×0.002

Lesson 3.8 *(pages 84–85)*

Place the decimal point in the product. Write zeros where necessary.

1.	0.02	2.	0.004	3.	0.054	4.	0.0013
	$\times$ 6.7		$\times$ 25.2		$\times$ 2.3		$\times$ 1.43
	134		1008		1242		1859

5.	0.0006	6.	0.006	7.	0.302	8.	0.012
	$\times$ 35		$\times$ 16		$\times$ 0.03		$\times$ 0.82
	21		96		906		984

9.	120.1	10.	0.8	11.	.011	12.	8.18
	$\times$ 3.3		$\times$1.6		$\times$0.55		$\times$2.07
	39633		128		605		169326

Find the product.

13.	0.015	14.	63.75	15.	0.06	16.	13.68
	$\times$ 10		$\times$ 1.93		$\times$ 8		$\times$ 0.03

17.	0.062	18.	0.0049	19.	6.8	20.	0.64
	$\times$ 0.2		$\times$ 331		$\times$0.5		$\times$3.48

21.	0.031	22.	0.89	23.	0.55	24.	200.75
	$\times$ 60.4		$\times$ 316		$\times$0.93		$\times$ 0.26

25. 1.2×10 26. 0.005×100 27. $1.425 \times 1,000$

28. 0.23×100 29. 0.006×10 30. $3.002 \times 10,000$

31. 33.06×10 32. 0.79×100 33. 0.5132×100

Lesson 3.9 *(pages 86–87)*

1. A hospital held a bake sale to raise money for a new nursery. It sold 240 breadsticks at $0.75 each, 125 muffins at $0.89 each, and 500 rolls at $0.25 each. How much money did the hospital raise?

2. Mirriam bought 12 cucumbers at 4 for $1.00 and 3 pounds of tomatoes at $0.89 a pound. How much more money did Mirriam spend for cucumbers than she spent for tomatoes?

3. Jim drove 132 miles to the city. His father drove twice as many miles to the next big city. How far did they drive in all?

4. Rose bought 10 rolls of film. There are 24 pictures on each roll. If she used all except 2 rolls of film, how many pictures did she take?

More Practice

CHAPTER 4

Lesson 4.1 *(pages 96–97)*

Determine whether the number is divisible by 2, 3, 5, 9, or 10.
Write all that apply.

1. 779   **2.** 302   **3.** 2,515   **4.** 891   **5.** 640

Lesson 4.2 *(pages 98–99)*

Estimate the quotient.

1. $259 \div 9$ **2.** $625 \div 3$ **3.** $4,749 \div 7$ **4.** $321 \div 6$ **5.** $428 \div 5$

6. $1,125 \div 21$ **7.** $353 \div 8$ **8.** $614 \div 7$ **9.** $412 \div 9$ **10.** $514 \div 6$

11. $1,254 \div 22$ **12.** $740 \div 19$ **13.** $430 \div 18$ **14.** $3,119 \div 60$ **15.** $461 \div 15$

16. $19,350 \div 90$ **17.** $16,500 \div 220$ **18.** $185 \div 8$ **19.** $961 \div 9$ **20.** $2,624 \div 24$

21. $13,629 \div 14$ **22.** $822 \div 5$ **23.** $2,618 \div 12$ **24.** $839 \div 7$ **25.** $64,877 \div 29$

Lesson 4.3 *(pages 100–101)*

Find the quotient.

1. $639 \div 2$ **2.** $408 \div 8$ **3.** $414 \div 6$ **4.** $807 \div 3$ **5.** $2,564 \div 4$

6. $777 \div 5$ **7.** $1,920 \div 8$ **8.** $2,532 \div 2$ **9.** $3,402 \div 6$ **10.** $3,000 \div 7$

11. $2,067 \div 3$ **12.** $272 \div 4$ **13.** $5,589 \div 9$ **14.** $2,835 \div 8$ **15.** $2,996 \div 7$

16. $6,242 \div 6$ **17.** $5,326 \div 4$ **18.** $5,476 \div 3$ **19.** $26,547 \div 5$ **20.** $43,852 \div 7$

Lesson 4.4 *(pages 102–103)*

Find the quotient.

1. $162 \div 54$ **2.** $584 \div 40$ **3.** $475 \div 19$ **4.** $154 \div 11$

5. $984 \div 82$ **6.** $3,787 \div 71$ **7.** $182 \div 13$ **8.** $1,854 \div 36$

9. $2,755 \div 19$ **10.** $522 \div 23$ **11.** $9,027 \div 51$ **12.** $918 \div 27$

13. $273 \div 39$ **14.** $1,701 \div 27$ **15.** $18,397 \div 28$ **16.** $13,425 \div 15$

17. $502 \div 31$ **18.** $2,244 \div 18$ **19.** $7,295 \div 51$ **20.** $6,271 \div 11$

21. $2,791 \div 62$ **22.** $20,780 \div 18$ **23.** $8,188 \div 33$ **24.** $42,927 \div 26$

Lesson 4.5 (pages 104–105)

Write a number sentence. Then solve.

1. Christian's car averages 312 miles on 12 gallons of gasoline. How many miles does his car average on 1 gallon?

2. Renee makes $5.35 an hour working as a cashier. How much will Renee make if she works 32 hours?

3. Sallie earned $281.25 working 45 hours as a pharmacy technician. How much does Sallie earn per hour?

4. Zach picked 15 three-leaf clovers and 8 four-leaf clovers. How many clover leaves does he have in all?

Lesson 4.6 (pages 106–107)

Find the quotient.

1. $8 \overline{)5,120}$
2. $9 \overline{)1,082}$
3. $3 \overline{)603}$
4. $7 \overline{)763}$

5. $14 \overline{)2,870}$
6. $21 \overline{)4,368}$
7. $26 \overline{)13,239}$
8. $33 \overline{)2,314}$

9. $5 \overline{)7,500}$
10. $12 \overline{)1,680}$
11. $4 \overline{)3,080}$
12. $8 \overline{)6,448}$

13. $18 \overline{)36,414}$
14. $37 \overline{)15,133}$
15. $50 \overline{)2,502}$
16. $29 \overline{)8,912}$

Lesson 4.7 (pages 110–111)

Find the quotient.

1. $3.2 \div 4$
2. $0.96 \div 8$
3. $43.7 \div 46$
4. $450.8 \div 98$

5. $93.24 \div 18$
6. $3.528 \div 84$
7. $75.02 \div 62$
8. $155.4 \div 42$

9. $0.416 \div 16$
10. $243.46 \div 47$
11. $35.28 \div 84$
12. $146.4 \div 8$

13. $131.2 \div 82$
14. $89.54 \div 74$
15. $0.7 \div 10$
16. $9.45 \div 63$

Lesson 4.8 (pages 112–113)

Divide until the remainder is zero.

1. $1.075 \div 5$
2. $0.336 \div 12$
3. $25.555 \div 19$
4. $5.35 \div 2$
5. $90.662 \div 22$

6. $0.3 \div 4$
7. $2.064 \div 16$
8. $6.015 \div 3$
9. $56.25 \div 18$
10. $35.595 \div 35$

11. $0.448 \div 8$
12. $1.225 \div 7$
13. $0.2208 \div 32$
14. $19.067 \div 46$
15. $150.75 \div 18$

16. $15.025 \div 5$
17. $147.24 \div 6$
18. $0.546 \div 12$
19. $1.7567 \div 11$
20. $6.8835 \div 15$

Lesson 4.9 (pages 114–115)

Copy and complete each table.

×	10^1	10^2	10^3
1. 15.27	■	■	■
2. 0.038	■	■	■
3. 0.004	■	■	■
4. 1.2	■	■	■

÷	10^1	10^2	10^3
5. 2.3	■	■	■
6. 0.6	■	■	■
7. 67.4	■	■	■
8. 480	■	■	■

Lesson 4.10 (pages 116–117)

Use the method of your choice to find the quotient.

1. $8.8 \div 2.2$
2. $2.8 \div 1.4$
3. $3.9 \div 1.3$

Write whether the quotients will be the same or different.

4. $640 \div 320$
   $6.4 \div 3.2$
5. $34.5 \div 1.15$
   $3.45 \div 11.5$
6. $6.6 \div 2.2$
   $0.66 \div 0.022$

Lesson 4.11 (pages 118–119)

Place the decimal point in the quotient. Add zeros if necessary.

1. $134.3 \div 3.4 = 395$
2. $1.475 \div 2.5 = 59$
3. $3.933 \div 1.9 = 207$
4. $9.057 \div 0.3 = 3019$
5. $60.84 \div 0.15 = 4056$
6. $40.12 \div 5.9 = 68$

Find the quotient.

7. $4.8 \div 0.08$
8. $5.922 \div 0.94$
9. $62.712 \div 13.4$

Lesson 4.12 (pages 120–121)

Find the quotient. Round to the nearest whole number or dollar.

1. $135 \div 8$
2. $\$16.00 \div 5$
3. $22.1 \div 6.7$
4. $\$13.00 \div 6$

Find the quotient. Round to the place given.

5. $68.3 \div 9$
   (ones)
6. $4.591 \div 1.41$
   (hundredths)
7. $25.63 \div 15$
   (tenths)

8. $\$93.45 \div 12$
   (cents)
9. $9.965 \div 8$
   (ten-thousandths)
10. $245.82 \div 39$
    (thousandths)

Lesson 4.13 *(pages 122–123)*

Write an algebraic expression for the word expression.

1. a number, m, divided by 9

2. a number, t, multiplied by 3

3. the quotient of a number, y, and 8

4. 35 times a number, w

Evaluate the expression.

5. $23a$, for $a = 14$

6. $2.9d$, for $d = 6.8$

7. $86a$, for $a = 2$

8. $\dfrac{n}{14}$, for $n = 126$

9. $\dfrac{b}{5}$, for $b = 235$

10. $\dfrac{a}{7.2}$, for $a = 48.96$

11. $15.3x$, for $x = 12$

12. $\dfrac{15}{t}$, for $t = 3$

13. $0.5y$, for $y = 35$

Lesson 4.14 *(pages 124–125)*

Tell how to solve the equation.

1. $3x = 99$

2. $\dfrac{x}{5} = 45$

3. $11c = 121$

4. $\dfrac{t}{6} = 144$

5. $9d = 369$

6. $\dfrac{m}{12} = 48$

7. $\dfrac{d}{15} = 225$

8. $29a = 435$

9. $\dfrac{n}{4} = 240$

Use inverse operations. Solve the equation.

10. $4m = 100$

11. $3x = 18$

12. $\dfrac{t}{6} = 9$

13. $91x = 910$

14. $\dfrac{b}{5} = 7$

15. $\dfrac{y}{10} = 55$

Lesson 4.15 *(pages 126–127)*

Make a flowchart and *work backward.* Solve.

1. Bea spent a total of $30.00. She spent $12.95 for a blouse, $9.95 for a T-shirt, $5.95 for a book, and the rest for a birthday card. How much was the birthday card?

2. Jane collected $119.10 for selling 3 jackets at $29.95 each and $29.25 for 15 souvenir pins. How much does one souvenir pin cost?

3. A sandwich shop sells a 6-inch sandwich for $2.95 and a 12-inch for $4.95. On Monday they sold 48 6-inch sandwiches. How many 12-inch sandwiches did they sell if they sold $314.85 worth of sandwiches that day?

4. Emilio bought $15.00 worth of school supplies. He bought 4 book binders at $2.75 each and spent the rest on scratch pads that sell for 3 pads for $1.00. How many pads did Emilio buy?

CHAPTER 5

Lesson 5.1 *(pages 136–137)*

Suppose you are making a tally sheet and a frequency table.
Use the data in the box for Exercises 1–4.

1. Will you write the number of pages in groups of 10 pages, such as 200-210, on your tally sheet? Justify your choice.

2. What will be the highest group of 10 pages on your tally sheet?

Number of Pages in Paperback Books				
245	127	200	395	218
392	195	229	456	376
369	248	345	512	189
412	341	420	259	526

3. How will you organize the number of pages in your frequency table?

4. Will the number of books with 512 pages be easier to find on the tally or the table?

Lesson 5.2 *(pages 138–139)*

Answer the questions. Give reasons for your answers.

1. A local TV station polls its audience on issues in national politics. Viewers call a 900 number to vote *yes* or *no*. Are the results of these polls representative of the whole country?

2. Farrah polled voters in a predominantly Republican neighborhood about the governor who is a Democrat. Will their opinions be biased?

3. Byron surveys 500 people in a town of 20,000 and determines that 0.75 of the group like coffee. Can Byron claim that 75 out of 100 townspeople like coffee?

4. Sarah determines that 10 out of 10 students in the drama club like to read. Can she claim that 100% of the school population likes to read? Why or why not?

Lesson 5.3 *(pages 140–143)*

Choose the data in A and B. Make one bar graph and one pictograph.

A.

Throwing Contest	
Name	Distance (feet)
Kim	98
John	110
Frank	105
Mac	120
Carol	115

B.

Bowling Scores	
Name	Score
Lee	145
Jamie	210
Joe	199
Mary	125
Barb	188

Lesson 5.4 *(pages 144–145)*

Use the data in A to make a bar graph. Use the data in B to make
a histogram.

A.

Amount of Sales	
Store	Sales
Store A	$25,000
Store B	$10,000
Store C	$45,000
Store D	$22,000
Store E	$60,000

B.

Number of Shoppers	
Time	Number
8:00–9:59 A.M.	35
10:00–11:59 A.M.	49
12:00–1:59 P.M.	92
2:00–3:59 P.M.	54

Lesson 5.5 *(pages 146–147)*

Choose the data in A or B. Make a line graph.

A.

Jay's Bank Balance	
Month	Balance
March	$ 659.95
April	$1,635.00
May	$1,392.49
June	$ 848.11
July	$ 900.56

B.

Jane's Weight Loss	
Month	Weight Loss (pounds)
December	7
January	5
February	6
March	4
April	8

Lesson 5.6 *(pages 148–149)*

Choose the data in A or B. Make a circle graph.

A.

Favorite Sports	
Sport	Number of Students
Football	40
Tennis	20
Bowling	10
Baseball	20
Skiing	6

B.

Favorite Vacation	
Vacation	Number of Travelers
Beach	36
Ranch	6
City	15
Cruise	15
Europe	24

Lesson 5.7 *(pages 150–151)*

Make a table or a graph to organize each set of data so that it is
easy to read and compare.

1. An ice-cream store sold 1,500 cones in July, 1,800 in August, 1,200 in September, 900 in October, and 600 in November.

2. The Sooner family rode their exercycle 50 miles on Monday, 60 on Tuesday, 80 on Wednesday, 100 on Thursday, and 150 on Friday.

Lesson 5.8 (pages 154–155)

Copy and complete the table.

	Collection of Data	Range	Mean	Median	Mode
1.	75, 86, 73, 80, 86, 80	■	■	■	■
2.	86, 90, 76, 42, 98, 88	■	■	■	■
3.	48, 52, 75, 47, 83, 49	■	■	■	■
4.	16, 20, 19, 16, 15, 19, 15, 16	■	■	■	■

Lesson 5.9 (pages 156–157)

This stem-and-leaf plot shows 20 students' heights in inches. Use this plot for Exercises 1–6.

Stem	Leaves
5	8 8 9 9
6	0 0 0 1 2 3 4 5 6 6
7	0 0 1 2 2 3

1. How many leaves does the second stem have?

2. What numbers are shown by the third stem and its leaves?

3. Which height occurs more often, 60 in. or 59 in.?

4. What is the range of the students' heights?

5. What is the median of the students' heights?

6. What is the mode of the students' heights?

Lesson 5.10 (pages 158–159)

Make a tree diagram to find the number of choices.

1.

Purses	Shoes
Black	Navy
Beige	White
Blue	Brown

2.

Curtains	Paint
Orange	Green
White	Mauve
	Taupe

3.

Paper	Pen
Blue	Red
Pink	Black

Write the number of choices.

4. 5 brands, 6 sizes

5. 20 scarves, 12 pairs of earrings

6. 9 slacks, 21 shirts

7. 8 pens, 4 colors

Lesson 5.11 *(pages 160–161)*

Use the spinner. Find the probability of each event.

1. stopping on 1

2. stopping on an even number

3. stopping on a number less than 5

4. stopping on a number greater than 8

5. stopping on a number less than or equal to 8

6. stopping on a number greater than 1

7. stopping on 1, 2, or 4

8. stopping on 1, 2, 3, 4, 5, 6, 7, or 8

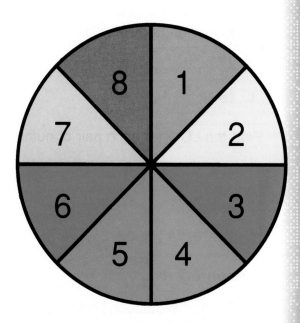

Lesson 5.12 *(pages 162–163)*

Use the situation in the box for Exercises 1–4.

1. Make a tree diagram to show all of Judy's possible choices.

2. How many choices does Judy have for interior and exterior colors?

3. What is the probability that Judy will choose white exterior and red interior?

> Judy bought a new car. The color choices for the interior of the car were blue, red, gray, and white. Her choices for the exterior were light blue, black, and white.

4. What is the probability that Judy will choose white interior and white exterior?

Lesson 5.13 *(pages 164–165)*

Find a pattern and solve.

1. Jean worked 12 hours the first week, 15 hours the second week and 18 hours the third week. How many hours will she work in the sixth week if the pattern continues?

2. Alan saved $100 in March, $125 in April, $160 in May and $205 in June. If the pattern continues, how much money will he save in September?

3. A worker lays 4 design bricks in the first row of a patio, 6 in the third row, and 8 in the fifth row. If the pattern continues, in which row will he lay 12 design bricks?

4. A video store rents one movie for $1.50, 2 movies for $2.00, and 3 for $2.50. If the pattern continues, how much will 6 movies cost?

CHAPTER 6

Lesson 6.1 *(pages 174–175)*

Write the first three multiples, excluding the number itself.

1. 2   2. 4   3. 8   4. 13   5. 14

6. 16   7. 17   8. 18   9. 19   10. 21

Find the LCM for each pair of numbers.

11. 4, 5   12. 3, 17   13. 6, 13   14. 7, 15   15. 8, 10

16. 4, 16   17. 3, 9   18. 7, 9   19. 7, 21   20. 6, 18

21. 12, 16, 24   22. 25, 50   23. 2, 3, 12   24. 1, 4, 32   25. 7, 13, 91

Lesson 6.2 *(pages 176–177)*

Complete the number sentence.

1. $\frac{2}{5} = \frac{\blacksquare}{10}$ 2. $\frac{1}{3} = \frac{\blacksquare}{9}$ 3. $\frac{3}{4} = \frac{\blacksquare}{32}$ 4. $\frac{\blacksquare}{24} = \frac{5}{6}$

5. $\frac{8}{9} = \frac{\blacksquare}{72}$ 6. $\frac{\blacksquare}{33} = \frac{5}{11}$ 7. $\frac{4}{13} = \frac{\blacksquare}{39}$ 8. $\frac{\blacksquare}{45} = \frac{8}{15}$

9. $\frac{21}{23} = \frac{\blacksquare}{92}$ 10. $\frac{5}{12} = \frac{\blacksquare}{144}$ 11. $\frac{19}{38} = \frac{\blacksquare}{2}$ 12. $\frac{28}{48} = \frac{\blacksquare}{12}$

Write *yes* or *no* to tell whether the fractions are equivalent. If they are not, write an equivalent fraction for each fraction.

13. $\frac{6}{8}, \frac{18}{32}$ 14. $\frac{1}{5}, \frac{5}{25}$ 15. $\frac{4}{6}, \frac{24}{36}$ 16. $\frac{33}{120}, \frac{11}{10}$

17. $\frac{7}{49}, \frac{2}{7}$ 18. $\frac{10}{30}, \frac{1}{3}$ 19. $\frac{25}{115}, \frac{5}{23}$ 20. $\frac{4}{16}, \frac{2}{32}$

21. $\frac{3}{5}, \frac{2}{10}$ 22. $\frac{8}{12}, \frac{2}{3}$ 23. $\frac{24}{32}, \frac{8}{16}$ 24. $\frac{18}{27}, \frac{6}{9}$

25. $\frac{75}{100}, \frac{2}{4}$ 26. $\frac{1}{3}, \frac{3}{24}$ 27. $\frac{20}{21}, \frac{40}{42}$ 28. $\frac{7}{8}, \frac{15}{16}$

Lesson 6.3 *(pages 178–179)*

Write each pair of fractions by using the LCD.

1. $\frac{3}{7}, \frac{1}{14}$ 2. $\frac{5}{8}, \frac{2}{4}$ 3. $\frac{6}{9}, \frac{1}{3}$ 4. $\frac{6}{10}, \frac{3}{5}$

5. $\frac{7}{11}, \frac{10}{22}$ 6. $\frac{3}{5}, \frac{5}{6}$ 7. $\frac{4}{7}, \frac{1}{4}$ 8. $\frac{6}{9}, \frac{5}{6}$

9. $\frac{3}{8}, \frac{5}{6}$ 10. $\frac{12}{18}, \frac{1}{6}$ 11. $\frac{2}{3}, \frac{3}{7}$ 12. $\frac{6}{8}, \frac{2}{4}$

Lesson 6.4 *(pages 180–181)*

Use the LCD to write like fractions.

1. $\frac{1}{3}, \frac{5}{18}$

2. $\frac{4}{6}, \frac{1}{24}$

3. $\frac{5}{12}, \frac{11}{24}$

4. $\frac{1}{2}, \frac{5}{16}$

5. $\frac{3}{8}, \frac{1}{24}$

6. $\frac{7}{15}, \frac{8}{45}$

7. $\frac{3}{4}, \frac{2}{5}$

8. $\frac{11}{13}, \frac{1}{2}$

9. $\frac{2}{3}, \frac{4}{5}$

10. $\frac{6}{10}, \frac{1}{15}$

11. $\frac{3}{4}, \frac{5}{7}$

12. $\frac{7}{8}, \frac{1}{12}$

13. $\frac{1}{6}, \frac{3}{10}$

14. $\frac{5}{6}, \frac{5}{9}$

15. $\frac{3}{4}, \frac{5}{6}$

16. $\frac{2}{12}, \frac{1}{8}$

Use <, >, or = to compare the fractions.

17. $\frac{1}{3} \,\bullet\, \frac{2}{9}$

18. $\frac{4}{7} \,\bullet\, \frac{10}{21}$

19. $\frac{5}{6} \,\bullet\, \frac{3}{4}$

20. $\frac{8}{24} \,\bullet\, \frac{2}{6}$

21. $\frac{15}{24} \,\bullet\, \frac{18}{32}$

22. $\frac{5}{30} \,\bullet\, \frac{13}{78}$

23. $\frac{8}{25} \,\bullet\, \frac{16}{45}$

24. $\frac{12}{25} \,\bullet\, \frac{7}{9}$

25. $\frac{5}{6} \,\bullet\, \frac{4}{5}$

26. $\frac{4}{12} \,\bullet\, \frac{7}{12}$

27. $\frac{5}{8} \,\bullet\, \frac{11}{12}$

28. $\frac{3}{4} \,\bullet\, \frac{7}{9}$

29. $\frac{1}{9} \,\bullet\, \frac{2}{15}$

30. $\frac{2}{3} \,\bullet\, \frac{3}{4}$

31. $\frac{6}{10} \,\bullet\, \frac{8}{40}$

32. $\frac{11}{12} \,\bullet\, \frac{7}{8}$

33. $\frac{4}{8} \,\bullet\, \frac{5}{10}$

34. $\frac{5}{8} \,\bullet\, \frac{7}{10}$

35. $\frac{7}{8} \,\bullet\, \frac{6}{7}$

36. $\frac{7}{9} \,\bullet\, \frac{21}{27}$

Lesson 6.5 *(pages 182–183)*

Choose a strategy and solve.

1. Five students, A through E, just put their papers on the teacher's desk. B was not first but was before A. C put his paper on the desk between A and E. D was before A. Whose paper is at the bottom of the stack?

2. Kelly, Brenda, Diane, and Mary competed in a talent contest. Kelly competed after Diane but before Brenda. Mary competed just before Brenda. Diane competed first. In what order did the girls compete?

Lesson 6.6 *(pages 184–185)*

Tell whether the number is prime or composite.

1. 19   2. 17   3. 45   4. 9   5. 121   6. 13   7. 27

Write the factors of each number.

8. 22   9. 36   10. 8   11. 28   12. 42   13. 65   14. 100

Lesson 6.7 *(pages 186–187)*

Write the prime factorization. Use a factor tree.

1. 34
2. 26
3. 14
4. 45
5. 52

6. 81
7. 80
8. 75
9. 69
10. 105

11. 38
12. 54
13. 40
14. 49
15. 32

16. 42
17. 60
18. 22
19. 28
20. 34

Write the prime factorization in exponent form.

21. 4
22. 20
23. 63
24. 68
25. 76

26. 88
27. 108
28. 243
29. 128
30. 40

31. 30
32. 18
33. 42
34. 110
35. 400

36. 44
37. 96
38. 56
39. 90
40. 24

Lesson 6.8 *(pages 188–189)*

Write the common factors of each pair of numbers.

1. 4, 16
2. 12, 60
3. 3, 27
4. 9, 27

5. 25, 100
6. 8, 48
7. 7, 56
8. 45, 65

9. 23, 69
10. 18, 90
11. 21, 15
12. 18, 20

13. 15, 95
14. 2, 30
15. 9, 21
16. 20, 32

17. 16, 24
18. 24, 30
19. 16, 30
20. 15, 45

Write the GCF of each pair of numbers.

21. 18, 20
22. 30, 27
23. 15, 24
24. 24, 32

25. 14, 35
26. 33, 55
27. 60, 72
28. 44, 60

29. 36, 63
30. 60, 42
31. 60, 75
32. 48, 68

33. 62, 124
34. 42, 56
35. 36, 120
36. 48, 54

37. 4, 12
38. 24, 28
39. 9, 15
40. 32, 48

41. 15, 24
42. 12, 18
43. 15, 21
44. 16, 20

45. 4, 48
46. 21, 15
47. 15, 45
48. 18, 90

Lesson 6.9 (pages 192–193)

Write the GCF of the numerator and denominator.

1. $\dfrac{24}{30}$ 2. $\dfrac{14}{42}$ 3. $\dfrac{9}{63}$ 4. $\dfrac{6}{18}$ 5. $\dfrac{8}{48}$

6. $\dfrac{25}{50}$ 7. $\dfrac{18}{20}$ 8. $\dfrac{12}{72}$ 9. $\dfrac{110}{130}$ 10. $\dfrac{15}{25}$

Write the fraction in simplest form.

11. $\dfrac{20}{50}$ 12. $\dfrac{6}{18}$ 13. $\dfrac{42}{49}$ 14. $\dfrac{16}{18}$ 15. $\dfrac{21}{72}$

16. $\dfrac{25}{100}$ 17. $\dfrac{33}{36}$ 18. $\dfrac{21}{24}$ 19. $\dfrac{5}{5}$ 20. $\dfrac{40}{44}$

21. $\dfrac{48}{52}$ 22. $\dfrac{20}{25}$ 23. $\dfrac{42}{90}$ 24. $\dfrac{10}{24}$ 25. $\dfrac{18}{21}$

Lesson 6.10 (pages 194–195)

Write the fraction as a mixed number or a whole number.

1. $\dfrac{44}{9}$ 2. $\dfrac{65}{4}$ 3. $\dfrac{39}{13}$ 4. $\dfrac{68}{11}$ 5. $\dfrac{31}{4}$

6. $\dfrac{57}{11}$ 7. $\dfrac{28}{12}$ 8. $\dfrac{49}{7}$ 9. $\dfrac{145}{15}$ 10. $\dfrac{192}{8}$

Write the mixed number as a fraction.

11. $6\dfrac{1}{3}$ 12. $3\dfrac{11}{12}$ 13. $4\dfrac{7}{8}$ 14. $8\dfrac{1}{3}$ 15. $2\dfrac{13}{25}$

16. $5\dfrac{3}{8}$ 17. $6\dfrac{2}{3}$ 18. $7\dfrac{5}{9}$ 19. $12\dfrac{1}{2}$ 20. $17\dfrac{2}{3}$

Lesson 6.11 (pages 196–197)

Choose a strategy. Then solve.

1. Guy spent $\dfrac{2}{5}$ of his time reading, $\dfrac{1}{3}$ writing, $\dfrac{1}{4}$ talking and $\dfrac{3}{8}$ dreaming. On which activity did Guy spend the most time?

2. There are 48 rolls on the shelf. If there are 24 more sourdough rolls than French rolls, how many French rolls are on the shelf?

3. Camille and Pierre will work 30 hours each this month at the beach picking up trash. Camille has already worked 5 more hours than Pierre, who has worked 18 hours. How many more hours does Camille need to work?

4. Tammy had 60 marbles. She gave $\dfrac{1}{5}$ of her marbles to John. She gave $\dfrac{1}{3}$ of what she had left to Yakov and the rest to Paula. How many marbles did Paula receive?

CHAPTER 7

Lesson 7.1 (pages 206–207)

Tell whether the estimate is a little less than or a little more than the answer given. Write < or >.

1. $\frac{15}{16} + \frac{1}{4}$ ● 1

2. $6\frac{1}{2} - 3\frac{3}{4}$ ● 3

3. $1\frac{1}{3} + 2\frac{1}{6}$ ● 3

4. $8\frac{3}{8} - 2\frac{1}{3}$ ● 6

5. $5\frac{1}{9} + 6\frac{3}{7}$ ● 11

6. $4\frac{1}{6} - 3\frac{2}{3}$ ● 1

Estimate the sum or difference.

7. $\frac{1}{9} + \frac{5}{8}$

8. $\frac{5}{6} + \frac{7}{8}$

9. $\frac{8}{9} - \frac{1}{6}$

10. $\frac{5}{6} - \frac{5}{8}$

11. $2\frac{11}{12} - \frac{1}{9}$

12. $3\frac{1}{3} + 4\frac{1}{8}$

13. $5\frac{7}{9} - 4\frac{12}{13}$

14. $4\frac{3}{13} + 5\frac{2}{15}$

Lesson 7.2 (pages 208–209)

Find the sum or difference. Write your answer in simplest form.

1. $\frac{1}{7} + \frac{3}{7}$

2. $\frac{8}{13} - \frac{5}{13}$

3. $\frac{4}{10} + \frac{5}{10}$

4. $\frac{3}{7} - \frac{2}{7}$

5. $\frac{5}{9} + \frac{8}{9}$

6. $\frac{9}{11} - \frac{3}{11}$

7. $\frac{5}{6} + \frac{1}{6}$

8. $\frac{2}{3} - \frac{1}{3}$

9. $\frac{3}{4} + \frac{2}{4}$

10. $\frac{7}{8} - \frac{3}{8}$

11. $\frac{4}{5} + \frac{3}{5}$

12. $\frac{2}{15} + \frac{3}{15}$

Lesson 7.3 (pages 210–211)

Find the sum or difference. Write your answer in simplest form.

1. $\begin{array}{r} \frac{3}{8} \\ -\frac{1}{12} \\ \hline \end{array}$

2. $\begin{array}{r} \frac{2}{3} \\ +\frac{5}{12} \\ \hline \end{array}$

3. $\begin{array}{r} \frac{5}{6} \\ +\frac{8}{9} \\ \hline \end{array}$

4. $\begin{array}{r} \frac{11}{12} \\ -\frac{5}{6} \\ \hline \end{array}$

5. $\begin{array}{r} \frac{4}{5} \\ -\frac{1}{4} \\ \hline \end{array}$

6. $\begin{array}{r} \frac{2}{3} \\ +\frac{5}{7} \\ \hline \end{array}$

7. $\begin{array}{r} \frac{3}{4} \\ -\frac{2}{5} \\ \hline \end{array}$

8. $\begin{array}{r} \frac{1}{3} \\ +\frac{2}{5} \\ \hline \end{array}$

9. $\begin{array}{r} \frac{7}{10} \\ -\frac{1}{4} \\ \hline \end{array}$

10. $\begin{array}{r} \frac{7}{8} \\ +\frac{5}{6} \\ \hline \end{array}$

11. $\begin{array}{r} \frac{1}{6} \\ +\frac{1}{2} \\ \hline \end{array}$

12. $\begin{array}{r} \frac{3}{4} \\ +\frac{1}{6} \\ \hline \end{array}$

13. $\begin{array}{r} \frac{5}{6} \\ +\frac{2}{3} \\ \hline \end{array}$

14. $\begin{array}{r} \frac{3}{15} \\ +\frac{2}{5} \\ \hline \end{array}$

15. $\begin{array}{r} \frac{5}{6} \\ +\frac{3}{4} \\ \hline \end{array}$

16. $\begin{array}{r} \frac{1}{3} \\ +\frac{1}{9} \\ \hline \end{array}$

Lesson 7.4 *(pages 212–213)*

Find the sum. Write your answer in simplest form.

1. $4\frac{1}{2}$
$+ 5\frac{1}{4}$
_____

2. $3\frac{2}{5}$
$+2\frac{7}{10}$
_____

3. $2\frac{6}{7}$
$+1\frac{3}{14}$
_____

4. $8\frac{1}{3}$
$+ 1\frac{1}{3}$
_____

5. $1\frac{1}{8}$
$+ 2\frac{3}{8}$
_____

6. $3\frac{5}{6}$
$+1\frac{5}{6}$
_____

7. $4\frac{1}{5}$
$+2\frac{3}{10}$
_____

8. $9\frac{2}{3}$
$+ 8\frac{1}{5}$
_____

9. $5\frac{1}{6}$
$+ 2\frac{2}{3}$
_____

10. $2\frac{6}{7}$
$+ 3\frac{1}{3}$
_____

11. $6\frac{4}{9}$
$+ 2\frac{2}{9}$
_____

12. $8\frac{1}{6}$
$+ 2\frac{1}{2}$
_____

13. $7\frac{3}{10}$
$+ 4\frac{1}{2}$
_____

14. $4\frac{1}{3}$
$+ 5\frac{3}{5}$
_____

15. $1\frac{1}{2}$
$+ 1\frac{2}{9}$
_____

16. $10\frac{9}{10}$
$+ \quad \frac{3}{5}$
_____

17. $22\frac{4}{5}$
$+ 17\frac{5}{9}$
_____

18. $32\frac{11}{12}$
$+25\frac{5}{6}$
_____

19. $47\frac{7}{8}$
$+ 39\frac{3}{5}$
_____

20. $23\frac{10}{11}$
$+ 9\frac{1}{2}$
_____

21. $1\frac{3}{8} + 1\frac{2}{3}$

22. $5\frac{2}{5} + 6\frac{7}{10}$

23. $6\frac{2}{3} + 2\frac{3}{4}$

Lesson 7.5 *(pages 214–215)*

Draw a diagram for Exercises 1–4. Then solve.

1. Merle wants to hang a 1.5-foot poster on a 6.5-foot wall. If she centers the poster, how far will it be from each end of the wall?

2. Laurie walked $1\frac{1}{9}$ miles south, and $2\frac{4}{9}$ miles east. How many more miles does she need to walk to complete her 5-mile walk?

3. Ely has a total of 320 books. He says that $\frac{3}{16}$ of his book collection consists of novels, and $\frac{3}{8}$ of the collection are biographies. The rest are reference books. How many are reference books?

4. Eric wants to mount a 3-inch decal on a square window with 51-inch sides. If he centers the decal, how far will it be from each end of the window?

Lesson 7.6 *(pages 218–219)*

Tell whether you must rename the greater number. Write *yes* or *no*. Then rename if necessary.

1. $6 - 1\dfrac{1}{3}$

2. $4\dfrac{3}{8} - 2\dfrac{1}{8}$

3. $3\dfrac{2}{15} - 2\dfrac{4}{15}$

4. $5\dfrac{5}{6} - 3\dfrac{1}{6}$

5. $2\dfrac{1}{3} - 1\dfrac{2}{3}$

6. $6 - 1\dfrac{3}{16}$

Find the difference.

7. $6 - 4\dfrac{1}{8}$

8. $10 - 3\dfrac{1}{6}$

9. $8\dfrac{1}{5} - 4\dfrac{4}{5}$

10. $3\dfrac{1}{8} - 1\dfrac{2}{8}$

11. $3\dfrac{1}{3} - 1\dfrac{2}{3}$

12. $5\dfrac{2}{7} - 2\dfrac{5}{7}$

Lesson 7.7 *(pages 220–221)*

Find the difference. Write the answer in simplest form.

1. $\begin{array}{r} 8\frac{7}{8} \\ -2\frac{5}{8} \\ \hline \end{array}$

2. $\begin{array}{r} 8\frac{11}{12} \\ -5\frac{7}{12} \\ \hline \end{array}$

3. $\begin{array}{r} 6\frac{6}{15} \\ -5\frac{11}{15} \\ \hline \end{array}$

4. $\begin{array}{r} 2\frac{1}{8} \\ -\frac{3}{8} \\ \hline \end{array}$

5. $\begin{array}{r} 6 \\ -2\frac{3}{10} \\ \hline \end{array}$

6. $\begin{array}{r} 6\frac{2}{13} \\ -3\frac{7}{13} \\ \hline \end{array}$

7. $\begin{array}{r} 4\frac{1}{6} \\ -1\frac{5}{6} \\ \hline \end{array}$

8. $\begin{array}{r} 7\frac{12}{13} \\ -5\frac{6}{13} \\ \hline \end{array}$

9. $\begin{array}{r} 3\frac{1}{7} \\ -1\frac{5}{7} \\ \hline \end{array}$

10. $\begin{array}{r} 12 \\ -8\frac{3}{8} \\ \hline \end{array}$

Lesson 7.8 *(pages 222–223)*

Change to the LCD if necessary. Then tell whether you must rename to subtract. Write *yes* or *no*.

1. $6\dfrac{4}{5} - 2\dfrac{1}{2}$

2. $3\dfrac{1}{6} - 1\dfrac{5}{6}$

3. $2\dfrac{5}{6} - 1\dfrac{1}{3}$

4. $2\dfrac{1}{8} - 1\dfrac{5}{8}$

5. $3\dfrac{1}{7} - 1\dfrac{4}{7}$

6. $4\dfrac{3}{4} - 2\dfrac{5}{6}$

Find the difference. Write the answer in simplest form.

7. $3\dfrac{1}{5} - \dfrac{4}{5}$

8. $4\dfrac{1}{8} - 2\dfrac{7}{24}$

9. $5\dfrac{7}{8} - 2\dfrac{1}{4}$

10. $6\dfrac{1}{3} - 1\dfrac{5}{6}$

11. $6\dfrac{4}{15} - 3\dfrac{2}{5}$

12. $7\dfrac{1}{8} - 3\dfrac{15}{24}$

13. $2\dfrac{1}{2} - 1\dfrac{8}{9}$

14. $5\dfrac{2}{3} - 4\dfrac{2}{5}$

15. $9\dfrac{1}{10} - 3\dfrac{9}{20}$

Lesson 7.9 (pages 224–225)

Find the difference.

1. $8\frac{11}{12}$
$-7\frac{3}{4}$

2. $10\frac{1}{4}$
$-3\frac{1}{12}$

3. $5\frac{5}{8}$
$-1\frac{1}{3}$

4. $9\frac{3}{4}$
$-4\frac{1}{6}$

5. $8\frac{1}{6}$
$-5\frac{1}{3}$

6. $3\frac{4}{5}$
$-2\frac{9}{10}$

7. $10\frac{1}{3}$
$-6\frac{5}{6}$

8. $6\frac{3}{8}$
$-3\frac{1}{2}$

9. $5\frac{1}{4}$
$-4\frac{5}{6}$

10. $8\frac{2}{3}$
$-6\frac{7}{8}$

11. $9\frac{1}{8}$
$-7\frac{1}{3}$

12. $6\frac{7}{8}$
$-1\frac{7}{12}$

13. $5\frac{5}{6}$
$-1\frac{1}{4}$

14. $5\frac{3}{4}$
$-2\frac{1}{2}$

15. $6\frac{1}{2}$
$-2\frac{1}{16}$

16. $8\frac{6}{15}$
$-2\frac{7}{9}$

17. $22\frac{4}{5}$
$-17\frac{1}{9}$

18. $32\frac{1}{12}$
$-25\frac{5}{6}$

19. $47\frac{1}{8}$
$-39\frac{3}{5}$

20. $23\frac{2}{11}$
$-9\frac{1}{2}$

21. $4\frac{1}{5} - 2\frac{4}{5}$

22. $8\frac{1}{3} - 2\frac{1}{6}$

23. $3\frac{2}{3} - 1\frac{1}{3}$

Lesson 7.10 (pages 226–227)

Choose a strategy. Then solve.

1. Josie painted $\frac{1}{3}$ of her fence in the morning and $\frac{1}{2}$ of what was left in the afternoon. What fraction of the fence does she still need to paint to finish the job?

2. Maria spent $15.00 at the pet store. She bought dog food with $\frac{2}{5}$ of her money, a dog collar for $\frac{1}{5}$, and flea shampoo with the rest of her money. How much was the shampoo?

3. Mr. Jones spent $3\frac{1}{2}$ hours running errands. He spent $1\frac{1}{4}$ hours at the grocery store and $\frac{5}{8}$ hour at the hardware store. The rest of the time was spent driving. How long did Mr. Jones spend driving?

4. Corey left her front door and walked $1\frac{1}{3}$ miles east. Then she walked $\frac{1}{2}$ mile south, $\frac{2}{3}$ mile east, $\frac{1}{6}$ mile south and 2 miles west. How far from her front door is she?

CHAPTER 8

Lesson 8.1 *(pages 236–237)*

Draw a model for each problem. Tell whether the product in **a** is the same as the product in **b**.

1. a. $0.6 \times 0.4 = 0.24$
 b. $\dfrac{3}{5} \times \dfrac{2}{5} = \dfrac{6}{25}$

2. a. $\dfrac{5}{8} \times \dfrac{1}{2} = \dfrac{5}{16}$
 b. $0.6 \times 0.5 = 0.3$

3. a. $0.2 \times 0.4 = 0.08$
 b. $\dfrac{1}{5} \times \dfrac{2}{5} = \dfrac{2}{25}$

4. a. $\dfrac{2}{3} \times \dfrac{1}{5} = \dfrac{2}{15}$
 b. $0.65 \times 0.5 = 0.325$

Lesson 8.2 *(pages 238–239)*

Solve. Write the product in simplest form.

1. $\dfrac{7}{12} \times \dfrac{6}{7}$

2. $\dfrac{1}{4} \times \dfrac{1}{4}$

3. $\dfrac{2}{5} \times \dfrac{5}{8}$

4. $\dfrac{1}{6} \times \dfrac{2}{5}$

5. $\dfrac{8}{9} \times \dfrac{9}{10}$

6. $\dfrac{5}{7} \times \dfrac{14}{25}$

7. $\dfrac{3}{10} \times \dfrac{20}{30}$

8. $\dfrac{4}{9} \times \dfrac{3}{8}$

9. $\dfrac{1}{6} \times \dfrac{3}{4}$

10. $\dfrac{2}{9} \times \dfrac{6}{10}$

11. $\dfrac{1}{8} \times \dfrac{4}{5}$

12. $\dfrac{3}{7} \times \dfrac{14}{21}$

13. $\dfrac{1}{9} \times \dfrac{2}{3}$

14. $\dfrac{3}{5} \times \dfrac{1}{2}$

15. $\dfrac{4}{11} \times \dfrac{1}{4}$

16. $\dfrac{1}{6} \times \dfrac{7}{8}$

Lesson 8.3 *(pages 240–241)*

Simplify the factors.

1. $\dfrac{1}{5} \times \dfrac{5}{6}$

2. $\dfrac{1}{3} \times \dfrac{3}{5}$

3. $\dfrac{1}{2} \times \dfrac{8}{15}$

4. $\dfrac{6}{11} \times \dfrac{2}{3}$

5. $\dfrac{3}{7} \times \dfrac{7}{15}$

6. $\dfrac{7}{12} \times \dfrac{3}{14}$

7. $\dfrac{7}{8} \times \dfrac{24}{49}$

8. $\dfrac{2}{6} \times \dfrac{9}{18}$

9. $\dfrac{1}{2} \times \dfrac{2}{3}$

10. $\dfrac{11}{12} \times \dfrac{6}{8}$

11. $\dfrac{1}{8} \times \dfrac{4}{9}$

12. $\dfrac{3}{4} \times \dfrac{8}{9}$

13. $\dfrac{5}{7} \times \dfrac{14}{10}$

14. $\dfrac{2}{5} \times \dfrac{15}{4}$

15. $\dfrac{7}{12} \times \dfrac{6}{21}$

16. $\dfrac{7}{8} \times \dfrac{16}{6}$

Choose a method. Then find the product. Write the product in simplest form.

17. $\dfrac{3}{4} \times \dfrac{1}{2}$

18. $\dfrac{7}{8} \times \dfrac{4}{5}$

19. $\dfrac{2}{3} \times \dfrac{3}{8}$

20. $\dfrac{3}{8} \times \dfrac{4}{13}$

21. $\dfrac{4}{9} \times \dfrac{3}{5}$

22. $\dfrac{5}{6} \times \dfrac{19}{20}$

23. $\dfrac{3}{7} \times \dfrac{14}{21}$

24. $\dfrac{3}{7} \times \dfrac{5}{9}$

25. $\dfrac{14}{25} \times \dfrac{5}{7}$

26. $\dfrac{8}{9} \times \dfrac{3}{16}$

27. $\dfrac{11}{24} \times \dfrac{12}{22}$

28. $\dfrac{5}{9} \times \dfrac{3}{15}$

Lesson 8.4 *(pages 242–243)*

Use rounding to estimate the product.

1. $\dfrac{5}{6} \times \dfrac{2}{5}$ **2.** $\dfrac{1}{3} \times \dfrac{10}{11}$ **3.** $\dfrac{1}{4} \times \dfrac{5}{12}$ **4.** $\dfrac{15}{16} \times \dfrac{9}{10}$ **5.** $\dfrac{6}{11} \times \dfrac{8}{17}$

Use compatible numbers to estimate the product.

6. $\dfrac{1}{3} \times 89$ **7.** $\dfrac{1}{2} \times 101$ **8.** $\dfrac{2}{5} \times 69$ **9.** $\dfrac{5}{6} \times 131$ **10.** $\dfrac{3}{4} \times 158$

Tell whether the estimate is reasonable. Write *yes* or *no*.

11. $\dfrac{2}{5} \times 40 \approx 20$ **12.** $\dfrac{4}{9} \times 200 \approx 180$ **13.** $\dfrac{1}{4} \times 800 \approx 200$ **14.** $\dfrac{1}{8} \times 30 \approx 4$

15. $\dfrac{7}{8} \times \dfrac{2}{5} \approx 1$ **16.** $\dfrac{6}{11} \times 120 \approx 70$ **17.** $\dfrac{3}{8} \times 50 \approx 20$ **18.** $\dfrac{3}{4} \times 100 \approx 30$

Lesson 8.5 *(pages 244–245)*

Tell whether the product will be less than both factors, between both factors, or greater than both factors.

1. $\dfrac{1}{6} \times \dfrac{2}{3}$ **2.** $\dfrac{1}{8} \times 4\dfrac{1}{2}$ **3.** $\dfrac{5}{6} \times 2\dfrac{3}{4}$ **4.** $2\dfrac{1}{3} \times 2\dfrac{1}{2}$

5. $5\dfrac{5}{6} \times \dfrac{3}{5}$ **6.** $3\dfrac{7}{8} \times \dfrac{5}{6}$ **7.** $4\dfrac{1}{12} \times 1\dfrac{3}{7}$ **8.** $6\dfrac{1}{3} \times 4\dfrac{4}{7}$

Find the product.

9. $2\dfrac{1}{6} \times 3\dfrac{1}{3}$ **10.** $5\dfrac{1}{5} \times 6\dfrac{7}{8}$ **11.** $3\dfrac{3}{4} \times 2\dfrac{1}{8}$ **12.** $1\dfrac{9}{11} \times 1\dfrac{1}{10}$

13. $1\dfrac{2}{11} \times 1\dfrac{9}{13}$ **14.** $\dfrac{3}{7} \times 4\dfrac{5}{11}$ **15.** $5\dfrac{1}{2} \times 7\dfrac{1}{3}$ **16.** $\dfrac{1}{9} \times 3\dfrac{3}{5}$

17. $2\dfrac{1}{3} \times 3\dfrac{1}{5}$ **18.** $8\dfrac{1}{6} \times 6\dfrac{1}{2}$ **19.** $1\dfrac{3}{4} \times 2\dfrac{3}{5}$ **20.** $9\dfrac{1}{10} \times 6\dfrac{1}{3}$

Lesson 8.6 *(pages 246–247)*

Write an equation. Then solve.

1. This week, Karim worked $2\dfrac{1}{3}$ times more than the 15 hours he worked last week. How many hours did he work this week?

2. Natalie earned $1\dfrac{1}{8}$ times more this year than she did last year. If she earned \$16,000 last year, how much did she earn this year?

3. Rob walks $11\dfrac{2}{5}$ miles every day. How many miles does he walk in 5 days?

4. Maria sold twice as many toys as her age. She is $24\dfrac{1}{2}$ years old. How many toys did she sell?

Lesson 8.7 *(pages 250–252)*

Write the reciprocal of the divisor.

1. $4 \div \dfrac{1}{5}$ **2.** $6 \div \dfrac{2}{7}$ **3.** $8 \div \dfrac{2}{3}$ **4.** $1 \div \dfrac{1}{10}$ **5.** $\dfrac{2}{5} \div \dfrac{5}{6}$

Complete the multiplication sentence. Then find the quotient of the division sentence.

6. $\dfrac{1}{8} \div \dfrac{1}{16} = \blacksquare$ $\dfrac{1}{8} \times \dfrac{\blacksquare}{\blacksquare} = \blacksquare$

7. $\dfrac{1}{2} \div \dfrac{1}{4} = \blacksquare$ $\dfrac{1}{2} \times \dfrac{\blacksquare}{\blacksquare} = \blacksquare$

Lesson 8.8 *(pages 254–255)*

Tell whether the quotient will be greater than or less than 1.

1. $12 \div \dfrac{1}{8}$ **2.** $3 \div \dfrac{1}{10}$ **3.** $\dfrac{8}{9} \div \dfrac{1}{3}$ **4.** $\dfrac{5}{8} \div \dfrac{3}{4}$

5. $\dfrac{2}{3} \div \dfrac{5}{12}$ **6.** $\dfrac{1}{8} \div \dfrac{2}{3}$ **7.** $\dfrac{2}{7} \div \dfrac{1}{3}$ **8.** $6 \div \dfrac{11}{12}$

Find the quotient.

9. $6 \div \dfrac{1}{4}$ **10.** $8 \div \dfrac{2}{5}$ **11.** $\dfrac{3}{10} \div \dfrac{6}{7}$ **12.** $\dfrac{7}{8} \div \dfrac{3}{4}$

13. $\dfrac{11}{12} \div \dfrac{1}{6}$ **14.** $\dfrac{3}{4} \div \dfrac{7}{8}$ **15.** $\dfrac{5}{6} \div \dfrac{11}{12}$ **16.** $\dfrac{5}{9} \div \dfrac{2}{3}$

17. $9 \div \dfrac{1}{3}$ **18.** $6 \div \dfrac{1}{8}$ **19.** $\dfrac{5}{11} \div \dfrac{15}{20}$ **20.** $12 \div \dfrac{3}{4}$

21. $\dfrac{1}{2} \div 10$ **22.** $\dfrac{1}{8} \div \dfrac{7}{16}$ **23.** $\dfrac{9}{10} \div \dfrac{4}{5}$ **24.** $\dfrac{8}{9} \div \dfrac{1}{3}$

Lesson 8.9 *(pages 256–257)*

Write the multiplication sentence.

1. $3\dfrac{1}{6} \div \dfrac{1}{2}$ **2.** $4\dfrac{4}{5} \div 2\dfrac{1}{3}$ **3.** $5\dfrac{1}{3} \div \dfrac{4}{9}$ **4.** $\dfrac{1}{3} \div 3\dfrac{3}{5}$

Find the quotient.

5. $3\dfrac{1}{8} \div 2\dfrac{1}{4}$ **6.** $3\dfrac{1}{2} \div \dfrac{1}{2}$ **7.** $4\dfrac{4}{5} \div \dfrac{9}{10}$ **8.** $\dfrac{5}{8} \div 6\dfrac{1}{4}$

9. $2\dfrac{2}{9} \div 1\dfrac{2}{3}$ **10.** $9\dfrac{1}{4} \div \dfrac{1}{8}$ **11.** $\dfrac{2}{5} \div 6\dfrac{1}{4}$ **12.** $4\dfrac{1}{8} \div \dfrac{3}{7}$

13. $1\dfrac{7}{8} \div 5\dfrac{1}{2}$ **14.** $2\dfrac{2}{3} \div 5\dfrac{1}{6}$ **15.** $9\dfrac{1}{6} \div 4\dfrac{1}{3}$ **16.** $\dfrac{5}{3} \div 8\dfrac{1}{3}$

17. $3\dfrac{1}{4} \div 5\dfrac{1}{2}$ **18.** $8\dfrac{1}{6} \div \dfrac{11}{12}$ **19.** $\dfrac{1}{4} \div 1\dfrac{3}{5}$ **20.** $1\dfrac{7}{8} \div 6\dfrac{1}{3}$

21. $11\dfrac{1}{7} \div \dfrac{2}{21}$ **22.** $12\dfrac{1}{8} \div \dfrac{1}{16}$ **23.** $1\dfrac{2}{3} \div 1\dfrac{7}{15}$ **24.** $6\dfrac{1}{8} \div \dfrac{7}{10}$

Lesson 8.10 *(pages 258–259)*

Write as a decimal.

1. $\dfrac{19}{100}$ 2. $\dfrac{1}{25}$ 3. $\dfrac{2}{5}$ 4. $\dfrac{14}{20}$ 5. $\dfrac{11}{50}$ 6. $\dfrac{41}{100}$

7. $\dfrac{4}{9}$ 8. $\dfrac{1}{100}$ 9. $\dfrac{1}{20}$ 10. $\dfrac{27}{40}$ 11. $\dfrac{13}{250}$ 12. $\dfrac{7}{9}$

13. $\dfrac{4}{5}$ 14. $\dfrac{2}{3}$ 15. $\dfrac{3}{5}$ 16. $\dfrac{7}{8}$ 17. $\dfrac{2}{9}$ 18. $\dfrac{11}{12}$

Use a calculator. Find an equivalent decimal.

19. $\dfrac{15}{30}$ 20. $\dfrac{1}{9}$ 21. $\dfrac{4}{5}$ 22. $\dfrac{3}{11}$ 23. $\dfrac{27}{100}$ 24. $\dfrac{23}{50}$

25. $\dfrac{2}{3}$ 26. $\dfrac{7}{11}$ 27. $\dfrac{1}{12}$ 28. $\dfrac{1}{6}$ 29. $\dfrac{9}{40}$ 30. $\dfrac{9}{100}$

31. $\dfrac{1}{250}$ 32. $\dfrac{6}{50}$ 33. $\dfrac{8}{75}$ 34. $\dfrac{1}{50}$ 35. $\dfrac{5}{12}$ 36. $\dfrac{4}{11}$

37. $\dfrac{1}{15}$ 38. $\dfrac{5}{9}$ 39. $\dfrac{9}{11}$ 40. $\dfrac{7}{100}$ 41. $\dfrac{4}{9}$ 42. $\dfrac{9}{15}$

Write as a fraction in simplest form.

43. 0.66 44. 0.9 45. 0.08 46. 0.05 47. 0.125 48. 0.038

49. 0.15 50. 0.2 51. 0.75 52. 0.35 53. $0.3\overline{3}$ 54. 0.54

55. 0.45 56. 0.55 57. $0.08\overline{3}$ 58. 0.4 59. $0.\overline{36}$ 60. 0.875

61. $0.91\overline{6}$ 62. 0.11 63. 0.625 64. 0.16 65. 0.01 66. 0.18

Lesson 8.11 *(pages 260–261)*

Solve by using a simpler problem.

1. Anna gave away $\frac{1}{5}$ of the yellow ribbons the club had, and Tina gave away $\frac{7}{10}$ of what was left. If Tina gave away 840 ribbons, how many ribbons did the club have when it started?

2. Patrick read $\frac{1}{3}$ of his book on Saturday and $\frac{1}{5}$ on Sunday. He still has 280 pages to read. What is the total number of pages in the book?

3. Ms. Hollingsworth, the manager of a retail store, pledged to give $\frac{1}{10}$ of the store's sales for the day to the school fund-raiser for band uniforms and $\frac{1}{20}$ of the store's sales that day to a local youth organization. If Ms. Hollingsworth's store gave away $750, what were the store's sales for that day?

4. Randy is a stock clerk at a discount store. His boss gave him 140 packages of price stickers. There are 240 stickers in each package, and Randy had 30 packages left over. How many stickers did Randy use?

CHAPTER 9

Lesson 9.1 *(pages 270–272)*

Find the missing number.

1. 15 m = ▉ dm

2. 40 cm = ▉ dm

3. 40 L = ▉ mL

4. 35 g = ▉ kg

5. 4,583 mm = ▉ m

6. 35.28 kg = ▉ g

7. 12 cm = ▉ mm

8. 500 mL = ▉ L

9. 3 m = ▉ km

10. 0.385 kg = ▉ g

11. 675 g = ▉ mg

12. 1,000 m = ▉ km

Lesson 9.2 *(pages 274–275)*

Choose the most reasonable estimate. Write **a**, **b**, or **c**.

1. length of a closet   **a.** 2 mm   **b.** 2 m   **c.** 2 km

2. height of a newborn   **a.** 40 m   **b.** 40 mm   **c.** 40 cm

3. thickness of a dime   **a.** 1 dm   **b.** 1 cm   **c.** 1 mm

4. walk around the block   **a.** 300 mm   **b.** 30 dm   **c.** 0.25 km

Choose the appropriate unit. Write *cm, m,* or *km.*

5. height of a table

6. diameter of a dime

7. height of a skyscraper

8. length of a bookcase

9. length of a road

10. width of a book

11. height of a tree

12. distance between cities

13. length of a skirt

Lesson 9.3 *(pages 276–277)*

Solve by using estimation.

1. A computer technician tells Lisa that the part needed to repair her computer is $145.90 and labor is $95.00 an hour. If it takes the technician 2 hours, about how much will the repair cost?

2. The distance between Carol's house and Key West is 300 miles. If her car gets 34 miles to a gallon of gasoline, about how many gallons of gasoline will she need to make the round trip?

3. Joey's car holds 12 gallons of gasoline and gets 28 miles per gallon. About how many full tanks will he need for a 1,500 mile trip?

4. Betty makes $4.75 per hour. About how many hours does she need to work to make $250?

Lesson 9.4 *(pages 278–279)*

Change to the given unit.

1. $35\,kg = \blacksquare\,g$

2. $95\,L = \blacksquare\,mL$

3. $12{,}000\,g = \blacksquare\,kg$

4. $4\,mL = \blacksquare\,L$

5. $675\,g = \blacksquare\,kg$

6. $3{,}645\,mL = \blacksquare\,L$

7. $0.69\,L = \blacksquare\,mL$

8. $4.8\,kg = \blacksquare\,g$

9. $6.2\,L = \blacksquare\,mL$

10. $1{,}000\,g = \blacksquare\,kg$

11. $0.9\,g = \blacksquare\,kg$

12. $500\,g = \blacksquare\,kg$

13. $0.1\,L = \blacksquare\,mL$

14. $0.05\,kg = \blacksquare\,g$

15. $21\,mL = \blacksquare\,L$

Lesson 9.5 *(pages 280–281)*

Tell which measurement is more precise.

1. 6 km or 5,980 m

2. 0.2 L or 200 mL

3. 45 mm or 4 cm

4. 1,508 m or 1.5 km

5. 8.2 cm or 82.5 mm

6. 400 m or 0.4 km

7. 4 km or 4.1 km

8. 6.98 mm or 6.9 mm

9. 30 cm or 300 mm

10. 30 mg or 325 mg

11. 6 cm or 65 mm

12. 1 kg or 500 g

13. 5 km or 4,902 m

14. 30 L or 30.5 L

15. 160 mL or 0.2 L

Lesson 9.6 *(pages 282–283)*

Tell whether to estimate or use a tool to measure. If you would use a tool, tell which tool.

1. amount of fabric to make a dress

2. time it takes to get to the theater

3. length of dresser for bedroom

Describe an everyday situation to fit the requirements.

4. capacity that requires a precise measurement

5. length that can be estimated

6. measuring mass with a tool

Estimate the sum.

7. $40\,m + 9.5\,m + 1.25\,m + 3.9\,m$

8. $2.3\,g + 0.1\,g + 1.04\,g + 3.9\,g$

Find the sum or difference.

9. $40\,mg + 200.1\,mg + 3.59\,mg + 1\,mg$

10. $5\,g - 0.256\,g - 3.25\,g - 1.22\,g$

11. $200\,L - 12.23\,L - 100.6\,L - 50.156\,L$

12. $59.5\,m + 0.12\,m + 12.69\,m + 5.3\,m$

Lesson 9.7 *(pages 286–287)*

Estimate the product or the quotient.

1. $50 \text{ ft} \times 12$
2. $6{,}008 \text{ in.} \div 36$
3. $92 \text{ yd} \times 3$
4. $551 \text{ ft} \div 3$
5. $48 \text{ mi} \times 5{,}280$
6. $8 \text{ yd} \times 1{,}760$

Tell by what number to multiply or divide. Then change the units.

7. 15 feet to inches
8. 108 inches to yards
9. 27 yards to feet
10. 20 miles to feet
11. 10,560 feet to miles
12. 8 yards to inches

Change to the given units.

13. $459 \text{ in.} = \blacksquare \text{ ft} \blacksquare \text{ in.}$
14. $10{,}569 \text{ ft} = \blacksquare \text{ mi} \blacksquare \text{ yd}$
15. $5 \text{ mi} = \blacksquare \text{ yd}$
16. $395 \text{ in.} = \blacksquare \text{ ft} \blacksquare \text{ in.}$
17. $430 \text{ ft} = \blacksquare \text{ yd} \blacksquare \text{ ft}$
18. $672 \text{ in.} = \blacksquare \text{ yd} \blacksquare \text{ ft}$
19. $320 \text{ ft} = \blacksquare \text{ yd} \blacksquare \text{ ft}$
20. $216 \text{ in.} = \blacksquare \text{ yd} \blacksquare \text{ ft}$
21. $7 \text{ mi} = \blacksquare \text{ yd}$

Change to the given unit. Write any remainder in fraction form.

22. $1{,}760 \text{ ft} = \blacksquare \text{ mi}$
23. $33 \text{ in.} = \blacksquare \text{ ft}$
24. $27 \text{ in.} = \blacksquare \text{ yd}$
25. $122 \text{ in.} = \blacksquare \text{ ft}$
26. $156 \text{ in.} = \blacksquare \text{ yd}$
27. $31 \text{ ft} = \blacksquare \text{ yd}$
28. $288 \text{ in.} = \blacksquare \text{ yd}$
29. $205 \text{ ft} = \blacksquare \text{ yd}$
30. $21{,}120 \text{ ft} = \blacksquare \text{ mi}$

Lesson 9.8 *(pages 288–289)*

Change to the given unit.

1. $4 \text{ oz} = \blacksquare \text{ lb}$
2. $30 \text{ qt} = \blacksquare \text{ c}$
3. $6 \text{ lb } 8 \text{ oz} = \blacksquare \text{ oz}$
4. $5\frac{1}{8} \text{ lb} = \blacksquare \text{ oz}$
5. $3\frac{1}{4} \text{ gal} = \blacksquare \text{ pt}$
6. $42 \text{ oz} = \blacksquare \text{ c}$
7. $10\frac{1}{2} \text{ pt} = \blacksquare \text{ c}$
8. $33 \text{ qt} = \blacksquare \text{ gal}$
9. $108 \text{ oz} = \blacksquare \text{ pt}$
10. $9{,}500 \text{ lb} = \blacksquare \text{ T}$
11. $49 \text{ pt} = \blacksquare \text{ qt}$
12. $2\frac{1}{2} \text{ T} = \blacksquare \text{ lb}$
13. $5 \text{ lb } 3 \text{ oz} = \blacksquare \text{ oz}$
14. $36 \text{ c} = \blacksquare \text{ qt}$
15. $96 \text{ oz} = \blacksquare \text{ lb}$
16. $6\frac{1}{2} \text{ qt} = \blacksquare \text{ pt}$
17. $5 \text{ c} = \blacksquare \text{ fl oz}$
18. $16\frac{1}{2} \text{ pt} = \blacksquare \text{ c}$
19. $1\frac{1}{2} \text{ lb} = \blacksquare \text{ oz}$
20. $10 \text{ lb } 6 \text{ oz} = \blacksquare \text{ oz}$
21. $7 \text{ pt} = \blacksquare \text{ fl oz}$
22. $8 \text{ oz} = \blacksquare \text{ lb}$
23. $1{,}000 \text{ lb} = \blacksquare \text{ T}$
24. $1 \text{ qt} = \blacksquare \text{ gal}$

Lesson 9.9 *(pages 290–291)*

Find the sum or difference.

1. 4 ft 3 in.
    +2 ft 5 in.

2. 2 ft 8 in.
    +3 ft 1 in.

3. 6 ft 6 in.
    +5 ft 6 in.

4. 2 yd 1 ft
    +3 yd 1 ft

5. 4 yd 2 ft
    +5 yd 1 ft

6. 6 yd 2 ft
    +1 yd 2 ft

7. 7 ft 2 in.
    −4 ft 10 in.

8. 4 yd 1 ft
    −1 yd 2 ft

9. 9 ft 6 in.
    −3 ft 9 in.

Lesson 9.10 *(pages 292–293)*

Change to the given unit.

1. 50 min = ▓ sec

2. 360 min = ▓ hr

3. 15 hr = ▓ min

4. 6:30 A.M. = ▓ : ▓ hours

5. 4 days = ▓ hr

6. 7:15 P.M. = ▓ : ▓ hours

7. 264 hr = ▓ days

8. 3:25 P.M. = ▓ : ▓ hours

9. 3 hr = ▓ sec

Find the sum or difference.

10. 2 hr 15 min
    +3 hr 55 min

11. 7 min 20 sec
    −6 min 25 sec

12. 3 hr 5 min
    −1 hr 40 min

13. 1 min 30 sec
    +   90 sec

14. 2 min 59 sec
    +9 min 5 sec

15. 6 hr 18 min
    −1 hr 26 min

Lesson 9.11 *(pages 294–295)*

Use the following schedule to solve Exercises 1–4.

1. Of the flights listed, which one is the fastest?

2. Karen has a meeting this morning at 10 A.M. that will last 3 hours. It takes her 45 minutes to get to the airport from the meeting. What is the earliest flight she can take?

3. What is the difference in time between the departure of Flight 139 and Flight 494?

Airline Schedule Atlanta to Miami		
Flight #	Departs	Arrives
265 (1 stop)	11:55 A.M.	2:10 P.M.
139 (nonstop)	1:40 P.M.	3:30 P.M.
494 (nonstop)	2:05 P.M.	4:10 P.M.

4. If the meeting lasted only $2\frac{1}{2}$ hours, which flights could Karen take?

CHAPTER 10

Lesson 10.1 (pages 304–305)

Draw a picture to show the ratio.

1. The ratio of red roses to yellow roses is 8:2.

2. The ratio of 9-year-olds to 10-year-olds is 5:6.

3. The ratio of tinted glass to clear glass is 10:15.

4. The ratio of salads to soups is 11:5.

Write the ratio in two other ways.

5. 30:7

6. three to six

7. $\dfrac{8}{9}$

8. ten to twelve

9. 10:3

10. eleven to two

Lesson 10.2 (pages 306–307)

Write a ratio that describes each rate.

1. 4 for a quarter

2. 60 mi per 120 min

3. 15 for $2.00

4. 10 muffins for $2.99

5. 45 words per min

6. 10 for $1.00

Find the unit rate or unit price. Remember to express the second term.

7. $1.25 for 10

8. 12 for $60.60

9. 900 mi per 15 hr

10. 3 for $9.00

11. 405 mi for 15 gal

12. $3.95 for 5

13. $4.20 a dozen

14. 1,750 words per 35 min

15. 600 people per sq mi

Lesson 10.3 (pages 308–309)

Tell whether the ratios are equivalent. Write *yes* or *no*.

1. $\dfrac{3}{5}; \dfrac{9}{25}$

2. $\dfrac{4}{3}; \dfrac{100}{75}$

3. $1:4; 16:64$

4. $4:9; 24:54$

5. $8:5; 12:15$

6. $\dfrac{3}{2}; \dfrac{6}{3}$

7. $7:12; 21:36$

8. $\dfrac{4}{5}; \dfrac{81}{100}$

Find the term that makes the ratio equivalent.

9. $\dfrac{5}{4}; \dfrac{\blacksquare}{8}$

10. $\dfrac{1}{9}; \dfrac{\blacksquare}{63}$

11. $9:4; 36:\blacksquare$

12. 3 to 8; 60 to $\blacksquare$

13. 2 to 9; $\blacksquare$ to 72

14. $40:5; 200:\blacksquare$

15. $\dfrac{12}{15}; \dfrac{24}{\blacksquare}$

16. $\dfrac{60}{45}; \dfrac{\blacksquare}{15}$

Lesson 10.4 (pages 310–311)

Write the cross products.

1. $\dfrac{4}{6} = \dfrac{2}{3}$ **2.** $\dfrac{8}{12} = \dfrac{2}{3}$ **3.** $\dfrac{1}{2} = \dfrac{m}{16}$ **4.** $\dfrac{12}{x} = \dfrac{32}{40}$

Tell whether the ratios make a proportion. Write *yes* or *no.*

5. $\dfrac{2}{45}; \dfrac{6}{130}$ **6.** $\dfrac{6}{9}; \dfrac{9}{12}$ **7.** $\dfrac{2}{3}; \dfrac{12}{18}$ **8.** $\dfrac{8}{5}; \dfrac{40}{25}$

Lesson 10.5 (pages 312–313)

Tell whether the ratios make a proportion. Write *yes* or *no.*

1. $\dfrac{5}{7}; \dfrac{15}{21}$ **2.** $\dfrac{10}{11}; \dfrac{100}{101}$ **3.** $\dfrac{43}{100}; \dfrac{22}{50}$ **4.** $\dfrac{24}{29}; \dfrac{72}{87}$

5. $\dfrac{9}{3}; \dfrac{45}{15}$ **6.** $\dfrac{17}{12}; \dfrac{51}{36}$ **7.** $\dfrac{8}{19}; \dfrac{16}{38}$ **8.** $\dfrac{7}{16}; \dfrac{15}{30}$

Write the cross products. Then solve.

9. $\dfrac{2}{3} = \dfrac{n}{120}$ **10.** $\dfrac{4}{11} = \dfrac{28}{n}$ **11.** $\dfrac{6}{n} = \dfrac{42}{35}$ **12.** $\dfrac{4}{20} = \dfrac{16}{n}$

13. $\dfrac{7}{12} = \dfrac{x}{108}$ **14.** $\dfrac{x}{35} = \dfrac{3}{7}$ **15.** $\dfrac{x}{15} = \dfrac{10}{150}$ **16.** $\dfrac{8}{x} = \dfrac{96}{36}$

Lesson 10.6 (pages 314–315)

Use the scale drawing of the lot, the house, and the garage. Write
the proportion you can use to find the actual dimensions.

1. width of the lot

2. length of the lot

3. width of the house

4. length of the garage

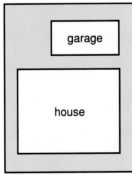

1 cm = 6 m

Lesson 10.7 (pages 316–317)

Use a centimeter ruler and the scale drawing for Lesson 10.6. Solve.

1. What is the actual width of
the garage?

2. What is the actual length of
the lot?

3. What is the actual width of
the house?

4. What is the actual width of
the lot?

Lesson 10.8 (pages 320–321)

Tell what percent is shaded.

1. 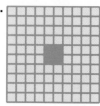 2. 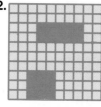 3. 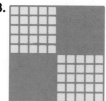 4.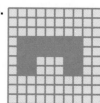

Lesson 10.9 (pages 322–323)

Write the decimal as a percent.

1. 0.28 2. 0.5 3. 0.19 4. 0.04 5. 1.28

6. 0.4 7. 0.45 8. 0.75 9. 0.8 10. 2.05

Write the percent as a decimal.

11. 10% 12. 43% 13. 12% 14. 6% 15. 35%

16. 9% 17. 85% 18. 90% 19. 79% 20. 155%

Lesson 10.10 (pages 324–325)

Write the fraction as a percent.

1. $\dfrac{13}{50}$ 2. $\dfrac{4}{25}$ 3. $\dfrac{2}{5}$ 4. $\dfrac{13}{20}$ 5. $\dfrac{9}{10}$

6. $\dfrac{7}{10}$ 7. $\dfrac{9}{20}$ 8. $\dfrac{8}{25}$ 9. $\dfrac{47}{50}$ 10. $\dfrac{1}{25}$

Write the percent as a fraction in simplest form.

11. 50% 12. 32% 13. 44% 14. 75% 15. 12%

Lesson 10.11 (pages 326–327)

Use the method of your choice to find the percent of the number.

1. 10% of 20 2. 30% of 60 3. 60% of 35 4. 50% of 96

5. 70% of 200 6. 20% of 100 7. 80% of 40 8. 40% of 70

9. 35% of 120 10. 65% of 80 11. 45% of 120 12. 55% of 900

13. 25% of 32 14. 70% of 140 15. 15% of 40 16. 75% of 60

Lesson 10.12 *(pages 328–329)*

Use mental math to find the percent of the number.

1. 25% of 400   **2.** 20% of 40   **3.** 2% of 200   **4.** 50% of $3.50

5. 10% of 65   **6.** 30% of 300   **7.** 200% of 12   **8.** 75% of 24

9. 100% of 10   **10.** 40% of 60   **11.** 150% of 20   **12.** 20% of $5.50

13. 200% of 40   **14.** 50% of $9.00   **15.** 30% of 120   **16.** 1% of 1,000

Lesson 10.13 *(pages 330–331)*

Suppose you know about what 10% of a number is. Tell how you can estimate the given percent.

1. 35%   **2.** 16%   **3.** 24%   **4.** 55%   **5.** 28%

Choose the most compatible numbers. Write **a, b,** or **c.**

6. 18% of 95
    a. 10% of 100
    b. 20% of 200
    c. 20% of 100

7. 46% of 130
    a. 40% of 150
    b. 50% of 150
    c. 50% of 100

8. 27% of 41
    a. 30% of 40
    b. 20% of 45
    c. 20% of 40

9. 39% of $45.95
    a. 40% of $50
    b. 30% of $40
    c. 30% of $50

10. 52% of 95
    a. 50% of 200
    b. 50% of 50
    c. 50% of 100

11. 78% of 2,842
    a. 70% of 2,000
    b. 80% of 2,500
    c. 80% of 3,000

Tell whether the estimate is an overestimate or underestimate.

12. 6% of 790 $\approx$ 48   **13.** 97% of 50 $\approx$ 50   **14.** 15% of 190 $\approx$ 40

Lesson 10.14 *(pages 332–333)*

Choose a strategy and solve.

1. Maureen made a scale model of her patio, using a scale of 1 in. = 4 ft. The length of the model is 11 inches. What is the actual length of Maureen's patio?

2. Leonore spent $40 on a gift for her mother. Then she bought computer paper for $27 and ribbons for $38. She had $15 left. How much money did she have to start?

3. James travels 60 mi a day to and from work. He works 5 days a week. His car gets 25 mi per gallon of gasoline. How many gallons does James use every week?

4. Rob bought a stereo on credit. His payments are $25.75 per month for 24 months. If Rob had paid cash for the stereo, he would have saved $68. What is the cash price of the stereo?

CHAPTER 11

Lesson 11.1 *(pages 342–343)*

Tell what geometric figure is suggested.

1. star in the sky   **2.** stove top   **3.** open scissors   **4.** piece of pipe

Use Figure A for Exercises 5–6.

Figure A

5. Name three points.

6. Name three line segments.

Use Figure B for Exercises 7–8.

Figure B

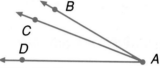

7. Name three rays.

8. Name three angles.

Lesson 11.2 *(pages 344–347)*

Tell what the blue symbol means.

1. $\overleftrightarrow{AB}$ **2.** $\angle E$ **3.** $\overrightarrow{AB}$ **4.** $\overleftrightarrow{AB} \perp \overleftrightarrow{CD}$ **5.** $\overleftrightarrow{EF} \parallel \overleftrightarrow{GH}$

6. $\overline{KL} \perp \overline{MN}$ **7.** $\overline{OP}$ **8.** $\overleftrightarrow{AB} \parallel \overleftrightarrow{CD}$ **9.** $\angle ABC$ **10.** $\overleftrightarrow{AB} \perp \overleftrightarrow{CD}$

Use Figure C for Exercises 11–14. Tell whether the lines are parallel, perpendicular, intersecting, or skew.

11. $\overleftrightarrow{AB}$ and $\overleftrightarrow{CD}$ **12.** $\overleftrightarrow{AB}$ and $\overleftrightarrow{GH}$

13. $\overleftrightarrow{AB}$ and $\overleftrightarrow{EF}$ **14.** $\overleftrightarrow{EF}$ and $\overleftrightarrow{CD}$

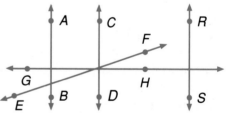

Use a compass and a straightedge.

15. Trace $\overline{CD}$. Construct $\overline{AB}$ congruent to $\overline{CD}$.

16. Trace $\overline{RS}$. Then bisect it.

Lesson 11.3 *(pages 348–349)*

Name the angles. Write *acute, right,* or *obtuse.*

1.   **2.**   **3.**

4.   **5.**   **6.**

Lesson 11.4 *(pages 350–351)*

Use a protractor to measure each pair of angles. Write <, >, or ≅.

1.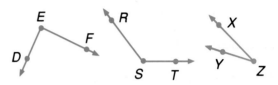

∠ABC ● ∠DEF

2. ∠ABC ● ∠DEF

3. ∠ABC ● ∠DEF

Use a compass and a straightedge.

4. Trace ∠DEF. Construct ∠ABC ≅ ∠DEF.

5. Trace ∠RST. Construct ∠KLM ≅ ∠RST.

6. Trace ∠XYZ. Construct ∠MNO ≅ ∠XYZ.

Lesson 11.5 *(pages 352–353)*

Make a circle graph.

1. Zach spends 60% of his monthly budget on rent, 25% on a car payment, 10% on food, and 5% on miscellaneous expenses. Make a circle graph showing his monthly expenses.

2. Adam spent 30% of his vacation in London, 25% in Paris, and 45% in Geneva. Make a circle graph showing how much time was spent in each city.

3. In a living room, 20% of the floor space is covered by a couch, 30% by a bookcase, and 10% by a coffee table. The remaining 40% is empty. Make a circle graph showing this.

4. Jackie's wardrobe consists of 20% dresses, 10% skirts, 45% slacks, and 25% shirts. Make a circle graph showing her wardrobe contents.

Lesson 11.6 *(pages 354–355)*

Use the drawing for Exercises 1–6. Find and name each type of triangle.

1. right

2. obtuse

3. acute

4. scalene

5. equilateral

6. isosceles

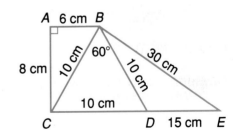

Write the measure of the third angle of the triangle.

7. 10°, 70° ■°

8. 30°, 40° ■°

9. 60°, 60° ■°

10. 90°, 20° ■°

Lesson 11.7 (pages 356–357)

Name the polygon.

1. **2.** **3.** **4.** **5.**

Lesson 11.8 (pages 360–361)

Using graph paper draw a polygon similar to the one shown and a polygon congruent to the one shown.

1. **2.** **3.** **4.**

 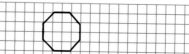

Lesson 11.9 (pages 362–363)

Trace the figure. Then draw the lines of symmetry.

1. **2.** **3.** **4.**

   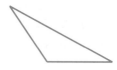

Tell whether the figure has rotational symmetry. Write *yes* or *no*.

5. **6.** **7.** **8.**

Lesson 11.10 (pages 364–365)

Tell whether the second figure is a translation, a rotation, or a reflection.

1. **2.** **3.**

Trace and label a translation, a rotation, and a reflection of the given figure.

4. **5.** **6.** **7.**

Lesson 11.11 *(pages 366–367)*

Complete the table.

	Figure	Number of Faces	Number of Edges	Number of Vertices
1.	Rectangular prism	▦	▦	▦
2.	Triangular pyramid	▦	▦	▦
3.	Rectangular pyramid	▦	▦	▦
4.	Cone	▦	▦	▦
5.	Triangular prism	▦	▦	▦

Lesson 11.12 *(pages 368–369)*

Use a geoboard and rubber bands. Begin with a 3-by-2 rectangle.
Make changes as directed. Then name the new shape.

1. Stretch both bases the same amount.

2. Shrink one base to a point.

3. Move one base to the right without stretching or shrinking.

4. Stretch both ends of one base the same amount.

5. Move the center of one side one unit away from the rectangle.

6. Move the center of each side one unit away from the rectangle.

Lesson 11.13 *(pages 370–371)*

Find a pattern and solve.

1. Mike is using red and white tiles to cover his kitchen floor. If the pattern Mike uses is R, R, W, R, R, W, what will be the color of the eighteenth tile?

2. Jane runs every day. Monday she ran 2 mi, Tuesday 3 mi, Wednesday 5 mi, and Thursday 8 mi. If the pattern continues, how many miles will she run on Saturday?

3. Mark is building a model of a tower out of blocks. He used 65 blocks in the first layer, 60 blocks in the second layer, 54 blocks in the third layer, and 47 blocks in the fourth layer. If the pattern continues, how many blocks will he use in the seventh layer?

4. Silvia saved $1 her first week at work, $2 the second week, and $4 the third week. If the pattern continues, how much will she save the sixth week?

CHAPTER 12

Lesson 12.1 *(pages 380–381)*

Find the perimeter of the polygon.

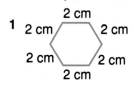
1 2 cm, 2 cm, 2 cm, 2 cm, 2 cm, 2 cm

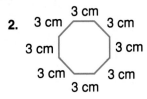
2. 3 cm, 3 cm, 3 cm, 3 cm, 3 cm, 3 cm, 3 cm

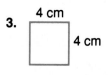
3. 4 cm, 4 cm

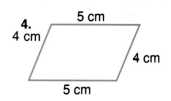
4. 5 cm, 4 cm, 4 cm, 5 cm

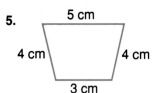
5. 5 cm, 4 cm, 4 cm, 3 cm

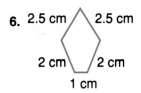
6. 2.5 cm, 2.5 cm, 2 cm, 2 cm, 1 cm

7. regular pentagon
11 cm each side

8. equilateral triangle
$12\frac{1}{2}$ in. each side

9. rectangle
$l = 8$ m, $w = 7$ m

Lesson 12.2 *(pages 382–383)*

Find the area of the rectangle.

1. 6 in., 2 in.

2. 16 yd., 10 yd.

3. 9 m, 1.5 m

4. $l = 3$ in., $w = 15$ in.

5. $l = 6$ m, $w = 5$ m

6. $l = 13$ m, $w = 12$ m

7. $l = 5$ yd, $w = 12$ yd

8. $l = 7$ cm, $w = 8$ cm

9. $l = 35$ m, $w = 14.5$ m

Lesson 12.3 *(pages 384–385)*

Find the area of the parallelogram.

1. $b = 4$ m, $h = 8$ m

2. $b = 5$ m, $h = 3$ m

3. $b = 0.5$ m, $h = 3$ m

4. $b = 3$ in., $h = 1.8$ in.

5. $b = 6$ in., $h = 8.5$ in.

6. $b = 3.8$ m, $h = 2.3$ m

7. $b = 15$ cm, $h = 3.3$ cm

8. $b = 1.2$ in., $h = 6$ in.

9. $b = 2.1$ m, $h = 32$ m

Find the area of the triangle.

10. $b = 5$ yd, $h = 6$ yd

11. $b = 3$ yd, $h = 9$ yd

12. $b = 4$ m, $h = 12$ m

13. $b = 9$ in., $h = 20$ in.

14. $b = 6.5$ m, $h = 12$ m

15. $b = 2.4$ m, $h = 6.6$ m

16. $b = 6.2$ m, $h = 2.6$ m

17. $b = 1.1$ cm, $h = 2.4$ cm

18. $b = 9.9$ m, $h = 1.2$ m

Lesson 12.4 *(pages 386–387)*

Use a formula and solve.

1. Bill is carpeting a rectangular room that has a width of 11 ft and a length of 16 ft. How many square feet of carpeting will he need?

2. Jane wants to cover her front window with solar film. Her window is 6.5 ft by 3.2 ft. How much solar film does she need?

3. Claude needs a new triangular mainsail for his sailboat. His mainsail is 20 ft high and 10 ft wide. What is the area of his mainsail?

4. Louise wants to screen her 8 patio windows. Each is 6 ft by 5 ft. How much screen does she need?

Lesson 12.5 *(pages 388–389)*

Find the area of the shaded part of the figure.

1.
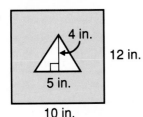

2.
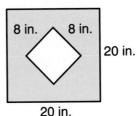

3.
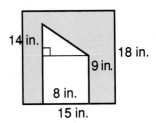

Lesson 12.6 *(pages 390–391)*

Draw the rectangle with the greatest area. Label the length of the sides.

1. $P = 40$ units   2. $P = 68$ units   3. $P = 88$ units   4. $P = 12$ units   5. $P = 96$ units

Draw a rectangle that has double the dimensions of the given rectangle. Find the perimeter of both.

6. $l = 4$ cm, $w = 8$ cm

7. $l = 2$ cm, $w = 8$ cm

8. $l = 5$ cm, $w = 9$ cm

9. $l = 13$ cm, $w = 11$ cm

10. $s = 6$ cm

11. $l = 7$ cm, $w = 9$ cm

Double the dimensions of the given rectangle. Find the area of both.

12. $l = 8$ in., $w = 6$ in.

13. $s = 5$ cm

14. $l = 9$ cm, $w = 2$ cm

15. $l = 2\frac{1}{2}$ ft, $w = 1\frac{3}{4}$ ft

16. $s = 35$ mm

17. $l = 5.2$ m, $w = 3.7$ m

Lesson 12.7 *(pages 394–395)*

Use Figure A for Exercises 1–6. Find and name the circle and its parts.

1. two diameters

2. two radii

3. two chords

4. center

5. circle

6. intersecting line segments

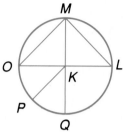

Figure A

Lesson 12.8 *(pages 396–397)*

Find the circumference. Round your answer to the nearest tenth. You may want to use a calculator.

1.
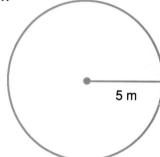
5 m

2.
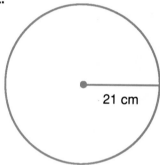
21 cm

3.
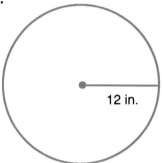
12 in.

4. diameter = 9 in.

5. diameter = 4 m

6. radius = 16 in.

7. diameter = 20 in.

8. diameter = 13 in.

9. radius = 10 in.

Lesson 12.9 *(pages 398–399)*

Find the area of the circle. Round to the nearest tenth.

1.
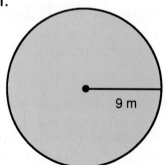
9 m

2.
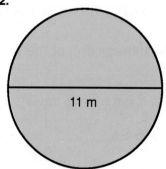
11 m

3.
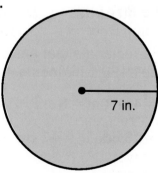
7 in.

4. $r = 4$ in.

5. $d = 6$ m

6. $r = 9$ yd

7. $r = 2.8$ in.

8. $d = 25$ in.

9. $r = 7.4$ yd

10. $d = 3.2$ m

11. $r = 0.8$ m

Lesson 12.10 *(pages 400–401)*

Find the surface area.

1.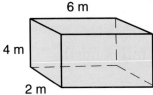
6 m
4 m
2 m

2.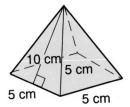
10 cm
5 cm
5 cm   5 cm

3.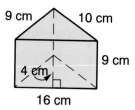
9 cm   10 cm
9 cm
4 cm
16 cm

Lesson 12.11 *(pages 402–403)*

Find the volume.

1.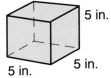
5 in.
5 in.
5 in.

2.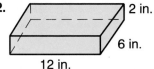
2 in.
6 in.
12 in.

3.
4 m
2 m
1 m

4. $l = 3$ cm, $w = 2$ cm, $h = 5$ cm

5. $l = 9$ m, $w = 7$ m, $h = 1$ m

6. $l = 8$ in., $w = 6$ in., $h = 10$ in.

7. $l = 12$ in., $w = 2$ in., $h = 1$ in.

Lesson 12.12 *(pages 404–405)*

Make a model and solve.

1. The dining room is a rectangle 10 ft long and 8 ft wide. A table 2 ft long and 3 ft wide will be put inside the room. How many square feet of space will be left after the table is placed in the dining room?

2. Corey wants to store a glass bowl in a cube-shaped box. The widest point of the bowl has a diameter of 12 in. The height is 9 in. What is the smallest box Corey can use?

3. Stuart made a basket in the shape of a rectangular prism 9 in. long, 6 in. wide, and 7 in. high. He wants to cover the bottom with plastic cubes that are 3 in. long on each side. Stuart has 15 cubes. Does he have enough cubes to cover the bottom of the basket?

4. The sitting room is a rectangle 8 ft wide and 9 ft long. A bookcase 6 ft long and 2 ft wide will be put inside the room. How many square feet will be left after the bookcase is placed in the sitting room?

CHAPTER 13

Lesson 13.1 *(pages 414–415)*

Describe the opposite of the situation.

1. gaining 5 pounds   **2.** 10 steps up   **3.** 3 miles north

Give an integer to represent the situation. Then describe the
opposite situation and give an integer to represent it.

4. 45 ft underground

5. stock market up 100 points

6. loss of $50

7. 4 ft up the flagpole

8. 1,500 ft above sea level

9. increase of 10 members

10. weight loss of 10 pounds

11. up 3 flights

Lesson 13.2 *(pages 416–417)*

Act out the situation to solve each problem.

1. The Igloos took possession of the
football on their own 10-yd line.
They gained 20 yd, lost 5 yd, gained
28 yd, and lost 6 yd. On what yard
line were the Igloos after those
4 plays?

2. Joyce leaves her front door and
walks 3 blocks east, 1 block south,
2 blocks west, 3 blocks south, and
one block west. How far is she from
her front door?

3. Anna leaves her front door and
walks $\frac{1}{2}$ block east, 3 blocks north,
10 blocks west, 2 blocks south,
4 blocks east, and 1 block south.
How far is she from her front door?

4. Ryan left his garage and drove
6 miles south, 2 miles east, 10 miles
south, and 2 miles west. How far
was he from his garage?

Lesson 13.3 *(pages 418–419)*

Compare. Use < or >.

1. 0 ● ⁻4   **2.** ⁻3 ● ⁺2   **3.** ⁻1 ● 0   **4.** ⁺5 ● ⁻3

5. ⁻6 ● ⁺6   **6.** ⁻4 ● ⁻5   **7.** ⁻8 ● ⁻9   **8.** ⁺1 ● ⁻2

Order the integers from least to greatest. Use <.

9. 3, ⁻1, ⁻2, ⁻4

10. ⁺6, ⁻5, ⁺4, ⁻1

11. ⁻7, ⁺5, ⁻3, ⁻4, 0

12. ⁺20, ⁺10, ⁺15, ⁻10, ⁻15

Lesson 13.4 (pages 420–423)

Use counters or a number line. Find the sum.

1. $^+4 + {}^+5$
2. $^+3 + {}^-5$
3. $^-6 + {}^-7$

4. $^-5 + {}^+10$
5. $^-1 + {}^+2$
6. $^+11 + {}^-8$

7. $^+13 + {}^-9$
8. $^-8 + {}^-11$
9. $^-15 + {}^-10$

10. $^+23 + {}^-14$
11. $^-41 + {}^+26$
12. $^-8 + {}^+11$

13. $^+9 + {}^-2$
14. $^+25 + {}^+1$
15. $^-16 + {}^-4$

16. $^+7 + {}^-14$
17. $^+11 + {}^+5$
18. $^-18 + {}^+20$

19. $^-8 + {}^-8$
20. $^-13 + {}^-15$
21. $^+7 + {}^+11$

22. $^+8 + {}^+16$
23. $^-3 + {}^+5$
24. $^-2 + {}^-7$

25. $^+12 + {}^-12$
26. $^-19 + {}^+5$
27. $^+23 + {}^+15$

Lesson 13.5 (pages 424–425)

Use counters to find the difference.

1. $^-3 - {}^+2$
2. $^-9 - {}^-8$
3. $^-4 - {}^-1$

Complete each of the following.

4. $^-3 - {}^+6 = {}^-3 + \blacksquare$
5. $^+10 - {}^-4 = {}^+10 + \blacksquare$

6. $^+5 - {}^-10 = {}^+5 + \blacksquare$
7. $^-2 - {}^+3 = {}^-2 + \blacksquare$

8. $^-7 - {}^-5 = {}^-7 + \blacksquare$
9. $^+9 - {}^+4 = {}^+9 + \blacksquare$

10. $^+6 - {}^-10 = {}^+6 + \blacksquare$
11. $^-3 - {}^-18 = {}^-3 + \blacksquare$

12. $^+8 - {}^+7 = {}^+8 + \blacksquare$
13. $^-5 - {}^+11 = {}^-5 + \blacksquare$

14. $^+2 - {}^-1 = {}^+2 + \blacksquare$
15. $^+16 - {}^-9 = {}^+16 + \blacksquare$

Rewrite each subtraction expression as an addition expression.
Solve.

16. $^+12 - {}^-8$
17. $^+7 - {}^+5$
18. $^+16 - {}^-24$

19. $^-5 - {}^-1$
20. $^+6 - {}^-20$
21. $^+11 - {}^+1$

22. $^+100 - {}^+1$
23. $^-3 - {}^+2$
24. $^+8 - {}^-7$

25. $^-4 - {}^-9$
26. $^+18 - {}^+2$
27. $^+10 - {}^-2$

Lesson 13.6 *(pages 428–429)*

Find the sum or difference.

1. $6 + 3$
2. $^-8 + ^-5$
3. $9 - ^-4$

4. $4 + ^-5$
5. $8 + 9$
6. $^-7 + ^-7$

7. $^-10 + ^-8$
8. $11 - ^-3$
9. $0 + ^-9$

10. $3 - 8$
11. $^-2 - ^-7$
12. $12 - 5$

13. $^-7 + 3$
14. $^-7 + ^-8$
15. $6 + ^-5$

16. $^-14 + 8$
17. $6 + ^-6$
18. $^-9 - 6$

19. $9 - 4$
20. $9 - ^-2$
21. $^-6 + 4$

22. $^-10 - ^-8$
23. $5 - ^-2$
24. $^-14 + ^-3$

25. $^-15 + ^-6$
26. $^-35 + ^-20$
27. $15 + ^-45$

Lesson 13.7 *(pages 430–431)*

Use the map. Tell the directions needed to get from the starting point to the given location.

1. theater

2. park

3. zoo

4. stadium

5. pool

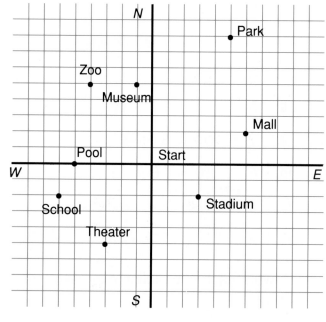

Trace the map. Locate each point on the map by following the given directions.

6. Go 6 blocks east, 2 blocks north

7. Go 3 blocks east, 2 blocks south

8. Go 5 blocks west

9. Go 1 block west, 5 blocks north

10. Go 6 blocks west, 2 blocks south

11. Go 5 blocks east, 8 blocks north

Lesson 13.8 (pages 432–435)

Write the ordered pair for each point.

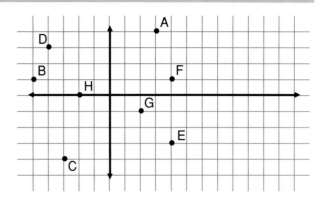

1. point A
2. point E
3. point B
4. point F
5. point C
6. point G
7. point D
8. point H

Use graph paper to make a coordinate plane. Locate the point for each ordered pair.

9. $A(4,3)$
10. $B(5,^-4)$
11. $C(4,0)$
12. $D(^-2,5)$

13. $E(^-3,^-5)$
14. $F(^-4,2)$
15. $G(^-2,^-8)$
16. $H(4,^-6)$

17. $I(0,^-5)$
18. $J(3,0)$
19. $K(0,4)$
20. $L(0,2)$

21. $M(^-4,^-2)$
22. $N(^-3,6)$
23. $P(7,7)$
24. $Q(^-6,0)$

Lesson 13.9 (pages 436–437)

Sean plans to use the health spa during his 6-week vacation to play racquetball. He can buy a pass, pay regular fees, or use a permit.

Choice 1
A 6-week pass costs $100.

Choice 2
The regular fee is $8 per game.

Choice 3
A permit costs $50 in advance. Then the cost is $4 per game.

Copy and complete the table.

	Times played per week	Cost for Six Weeks		
		Choice 1	Choice 2	Choice 3
1.	1	▨	▨	▨
2.	2	▨	▨	▨
3.	3	▨	▨	▨
4.	4	▨	▨	▨

5. What does the table show about the cost of the three choices for a player who plays racquetball two times a week or less?

6. Sean decides he would play 3 times a week. He selected Choice 2. Give one advantage of this choice over Choice 3.

CHAPTER 14

Lesson 14.1 *(pages 446–447)*

Write a word expression for the algebraic expression.

1. $4h$

2. $\dfrac{x}{5}$

3. $n + 3$

4. $y + 10$

5. $d - 8$

6. $m - 5$

7. $6b$

8. $\dfrac{12}{y}$

9. $25 - x$

10. $a + 6$

11. $7c$

12. $8 + a$

Copy and complete the table. Write an algebraic expression or an equation.

	Word Expression	Algebraic Expression or Equation
13.	b less than 2 is 15	■
14.	y divided by 5	■
15.	eighteen is three times g	■
16.	a and eight equals twelve	■
17.	c plus nine	■
18.	six more than x is ten	■
19.	b divided by 6 = 5	■

Lesson 14.2 *(pages 448–449)*

Write the number in the form $\dfrac{a}{b}$.

1. 3.5

2. 0.68

3. 0.39

4. $5\dfrac{6}{11}$

5. 25.2

6. $4\dfrac{5}{8}$

7. 0.93

8. $2\dfrac{12}{13}$

9. 58%

10. 4.7%

Tell what rational numbers you would use in the given situation.

11. to express flight numbers

12. to express sale prices

13. to express hat sizes

14. to express a business loss

15. to express a comparison between games won and games played

16. to express mass on a gram scale

Lesson 14.3 *(pages 450–451)*

Evaluate the expression $x - 17$ for each value of x.

1. $x = 9$ **2.** $x = {}^-5$ **3.** $x = 1\frac{1}{3}$ **4.** $x = 25.06$ **5.** $x = {}^-90$

Evaluate the expression $m \div 4$ for each value of m.

6. $m = 25$ **7.** $m = 12.5$ **8.** $m = \frac{1}{16}$ **9.** $m = 3\frac{1}{8}$

10. $m = 16$ **11.** $m = \frac{2}{3}$ **12.** $m = 15$ **13.** $m = 24.9$

Evaluate the expression $9b$ for each value of b.

14. $b = 27$ **15.** $b = 6\frac{1}{8}$ **16.** $b = 25.4$ **17.** $b = 90\%$

18. $b = 4.5$ **19.** $b = \frac{2}{3}$ **20.** $b = 4.02$ **21.** $b = \frac{5}{18}$

Lesson 14.4 *(pages 452–453)*

Tell the inverse of the operation in the equation.

1. $x + 2 = 90$ **2.** $y - 4 = 10$ **3.** $\frac{1}{2} + z = 7$

Use inverse operations. Solve the equation.

4. $x - 253 = 792$ **5.** $y + 29 = 148$ **6.** $x + 6\frac{1}{3} = 25\frac{1}{2}$

7. $x - \frac{7}{8} = 3$ **8.** $y + \frac{5}{12} = \frac{7}{12}$ **9.** $y - \frac{9}{10} = \frac{1}{10}$

10. $y + 3{,}400 = 6{,}876$ **11.** $x - \frac{3}{8} = 16\frac{1}{2}$ **12.** $x - 356 = 0$

13. $y + \frac{1}{9} = 4\frac{1}{3}$ **14.** $x - 46 = 46$ **15.** $y + 39\frac{1}{2} = 48\frac{1}{16}$

Lesson 14.5 *(pages 454–455)*

Write an equation. Then solve.

1. Monica wants to read a 500-page novel in 3 days. She reads 145 pages the first day and 198 pages the second day. How many pages must she read the third day to meet her goal?

2. Al is saving money to buy a bicycle that costs $295. He has already saved $179. How much more does he need to save?

3. Yves wrote 90 words fewer than Chuck in his book report. Chuck wrote 625 words. How many words did Yves write?

4. Rita has $230 more than her brother who has $190. How much money does Rita have?

Lesson 14.6 (pages 458–459)

Tell what integers to add or subtract to solve the equation.

1. $x = 2 + 3$

2. $y - 5 = 9$

3. $z - 1 = 15$

4. $c + 4 = 5$

5. $g - 13 = 1$

6. $a + 8 = 20$

Solve the equation.

7. $x = 14 + {}^-9$

8. $y + {}^-6 = {}^-20$

9. $x = {}^-2 + {}^-3$

10. $x = 21 + {}^-12$

11. $y - 16 = 49$

12. $x + {}^-35 = 215$

13. $y + {}^-3 = {}^-41$

14. $x - 16 = {}^-9$

15. $y + 3 = 15$

16. $y - {}^-7 = 26$

17. $x - 13 = 15$

18. $y + 6 = 2$

Lesson 14.7 (pages 460–461)

Tell whether $^-3$ is a solution of the inequality. Write *yes* or *no*.

1. $x < 0$

2. $x < {}^-5$

3. $x + 5 > 1$

Tell whether 5 is a solution of the inequality. Write *yes* or *no*.

4. $y + 3 > 10$

5. $y - 10 < 0$

6. $y - 1 < 0$

Draw a number line that shows the solutions of the inequality.

7. $x > 4$

8. $a < 0$

9. $b < 2\frac{1}{3}$

10. $y > 7$

11. $x < {}^-3$

12. $d > {}^-5$

13. $c > 2.5$

14. $x < 1.2$

15. $b > {}^-1.5$

Lesson 14.8 (pages 462–463)

Copy and complete the table. Then write an expression using *y* to show the value of *x*.

1.

x	2	3	4	5	6	7	8
y	4	6	8	10	■	■	■

2.

x	0	1	2	3	4	5	6	7
y	$^-2$	$^-1$	0	1	2	■	■	■

3.

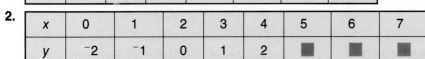

x	0	1	2	3	4	5	6	7	8
y	3	4	5	6	7	■	■	■	■

Lesson 14.9 *(pages 464–465)*

Name the ordered pairs in each table.

1.
x	12	9	6	3
y	4	3	2	1

2.
x	5	6	7	8
y	1	2	3	4

3. What expression using y can you write to show the value of x in Exercise 1?

4. What expression using y can you write to show the value of x in Exercise 2?

Use the expression to help you complete the table. Then graph the ordered pairs on a coordinate plane.

5. $x - 3$

x	3	4	5	6	7
y	0	■	■	■	■

6. $\dfrac{x}{2}$

x	10	12	14	16	18
y	5	6	■	■	■

7. $2x + 6$

x	2	3	4	5	6
y	10	12	■	■	■

8. $3x + 1$

x	2	3	4	5	6
y	7	10	■	■	■

Lesson 14.10 *(pages 466–467)*

Solve. Use logical reasoning.

1. A chess club has 25 members. Of these members, 5 have played in a state tournament, 8 have played in a city tournament, and 4 have played in both kinds of tournaments. How many members have never played in a tournament?

2. The results of a survey of 75 people show 31 collect only stamps, 26 collect only postcards, and 8 do both. How many people do not collect stamps or postcards?

3. The results of a survey of 90 people show 30 attend only football games, 20 attend only soccer games, and 8 do both. How many people do not attend football or soccer games?

4. A survey of 120 computer programmers shows that 50 write Cobol, 30 write Pascal, and 15 do both. How many programmers do not write Cobol or Pascal?

The Learning Resources can be traced, colored, and cut out.
These resources can be used as tools to help you understand
math concepts and solve problems.

Plane Geometric Shapes

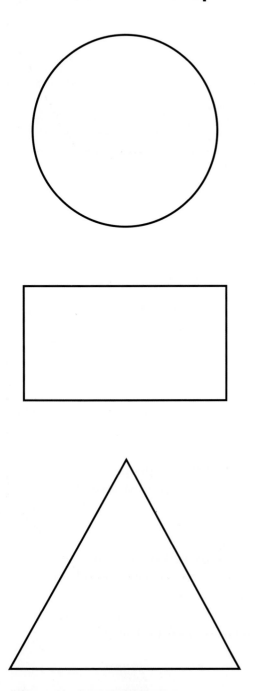

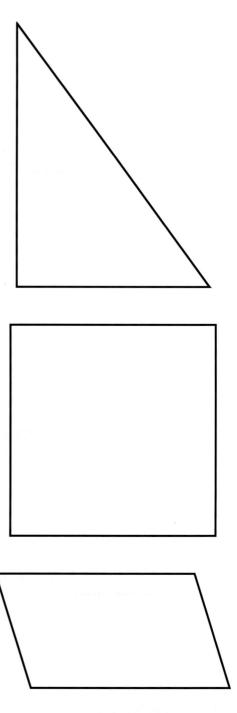

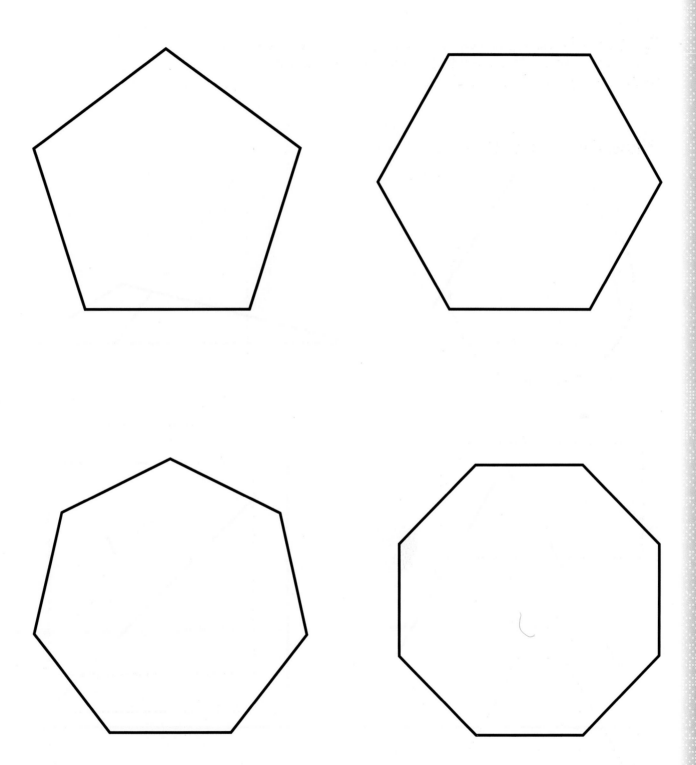

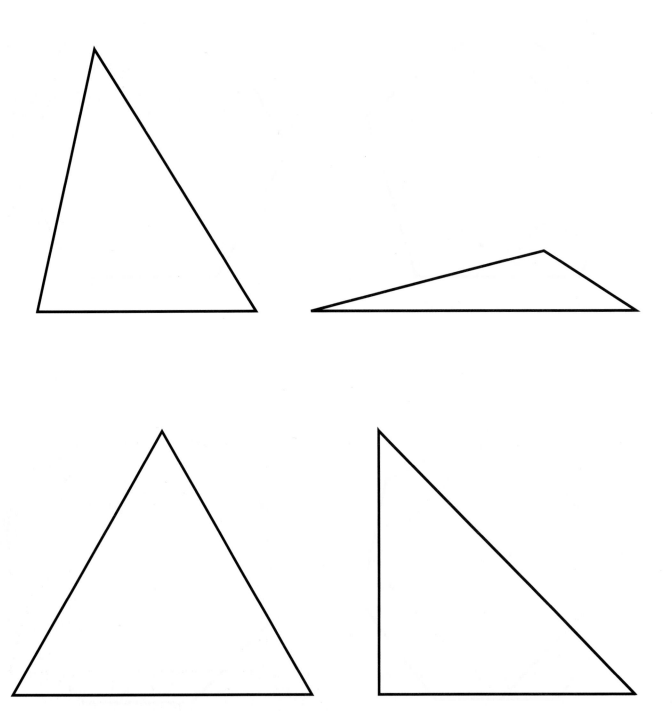

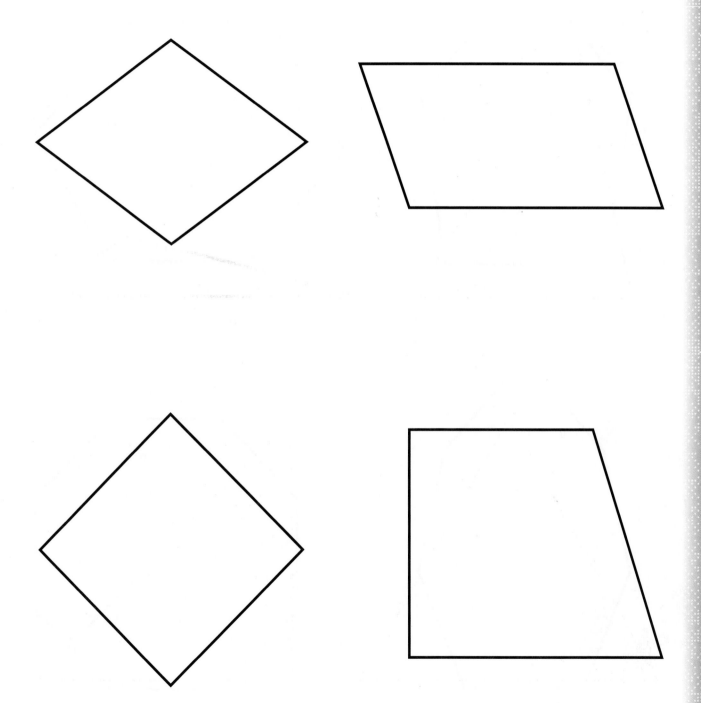

More Polygons

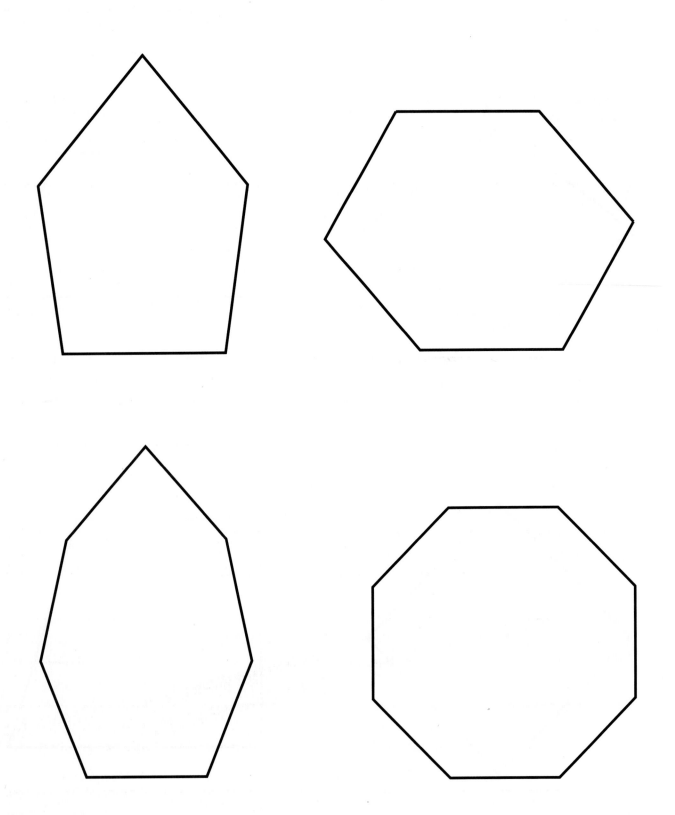

Fraction Bars

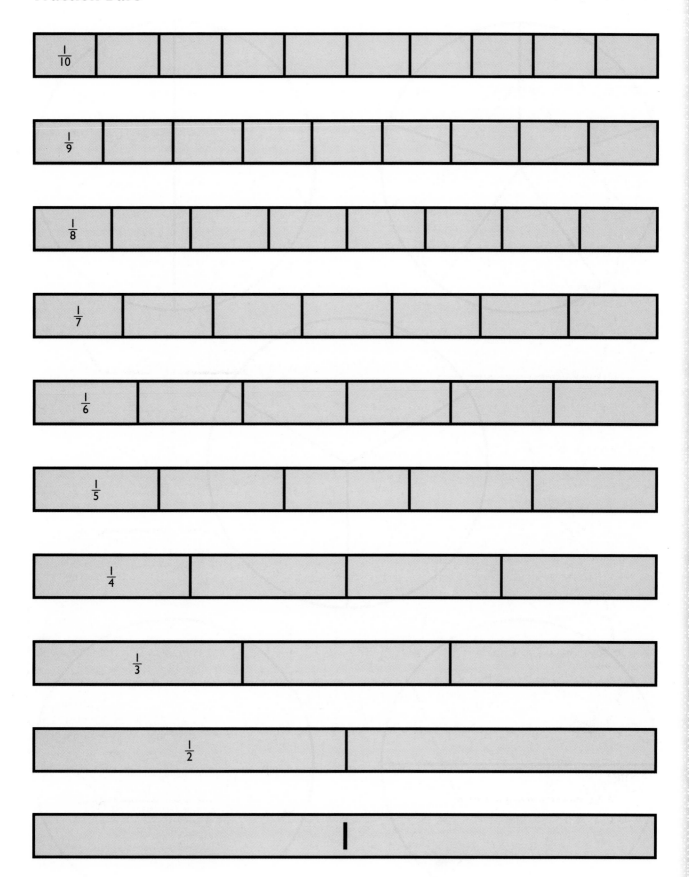

Fraction Circles

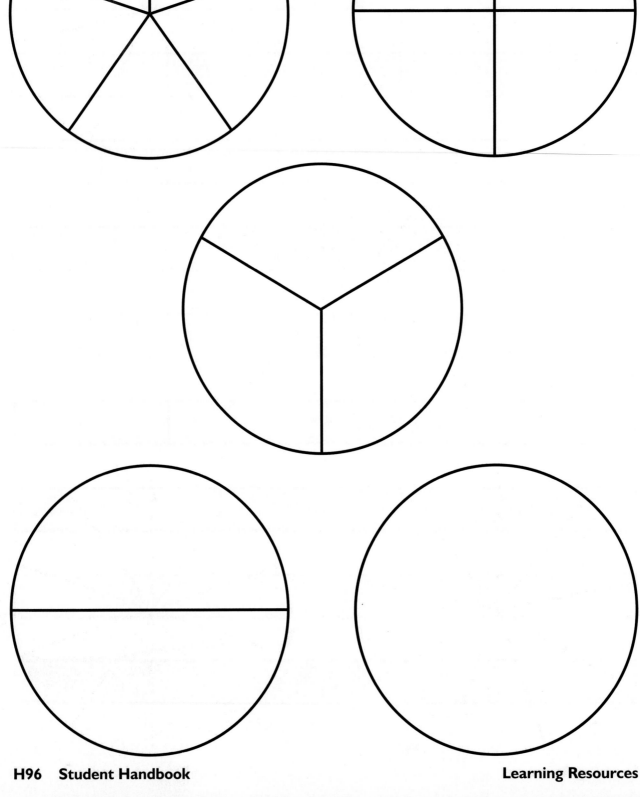

More Fraction Circles

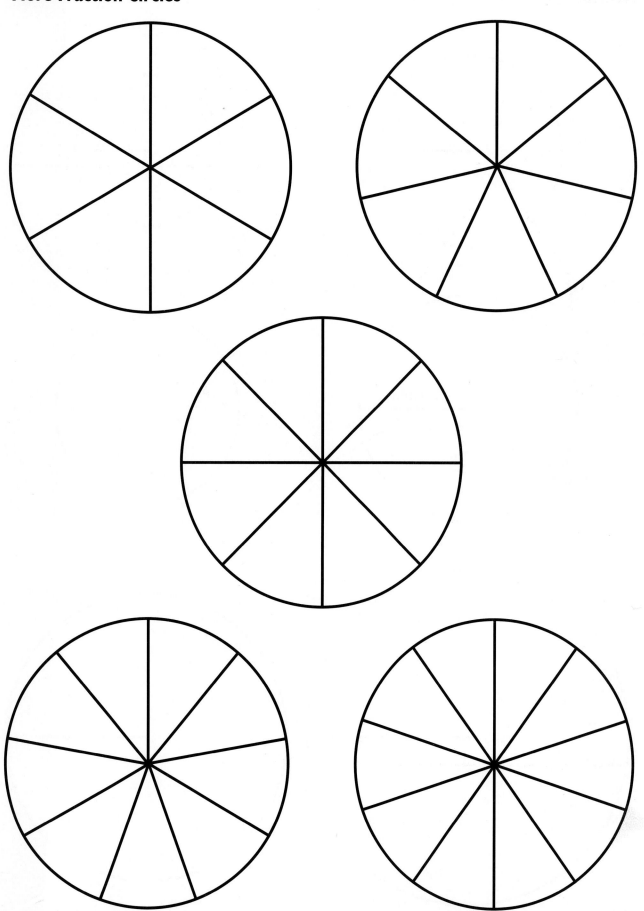

Circles

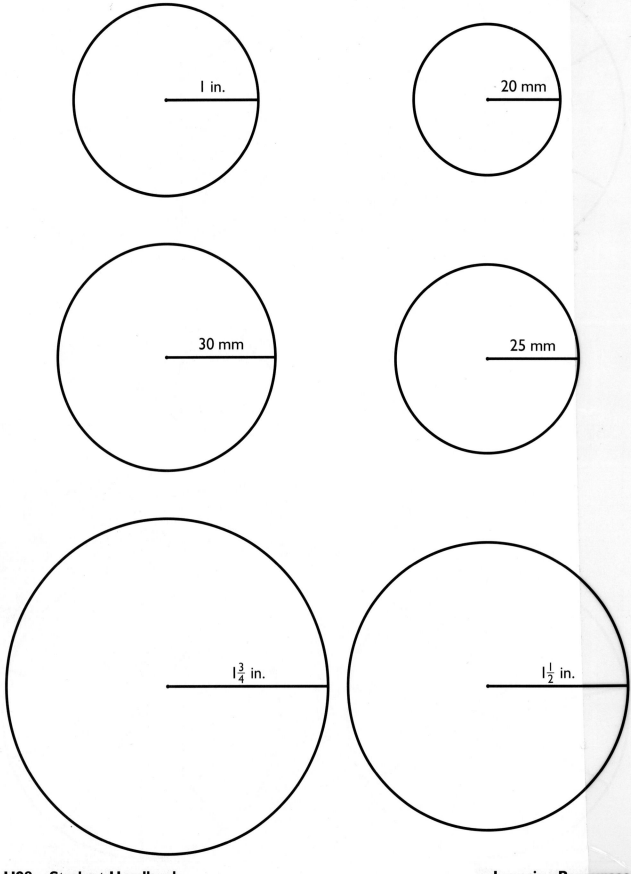

1 in.

20 mm

30 mm

25 mm

$1\frac{3}{4}$ in.

$1\frac{1}{2}$ in.

Solid Geometric Shape

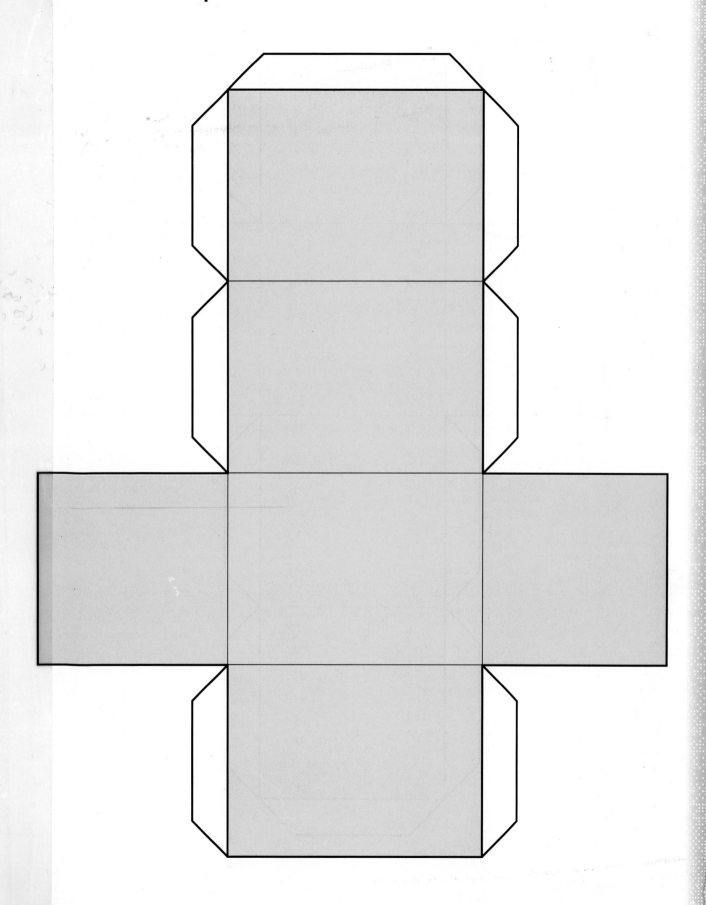

Solid Geometric Shape

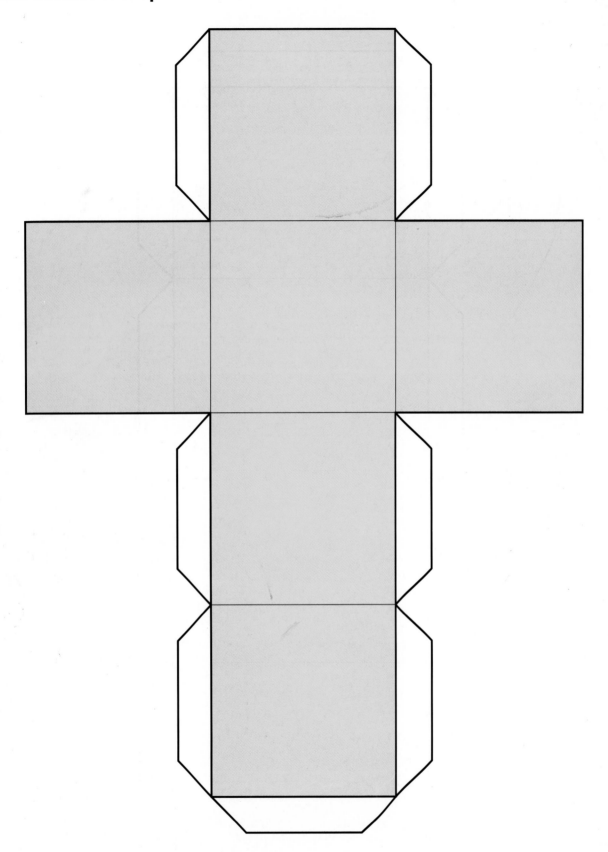

Solid Geometric Shape

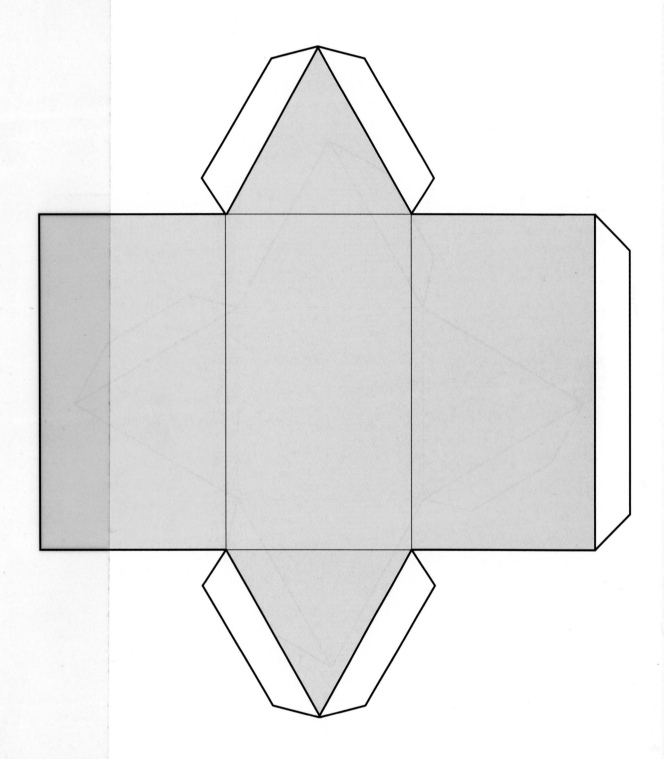

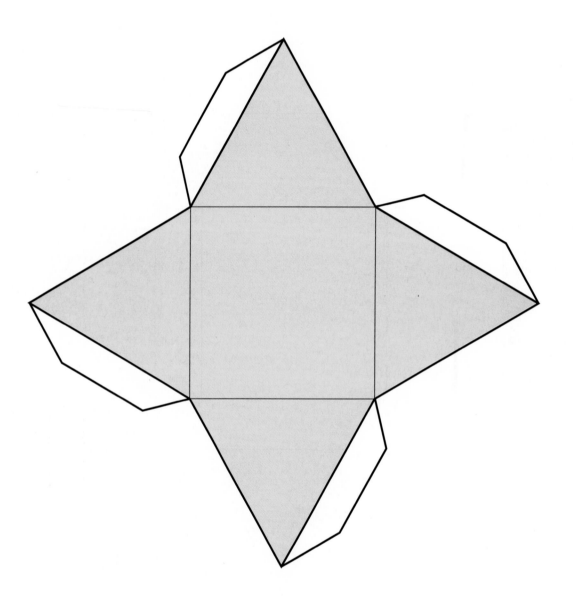

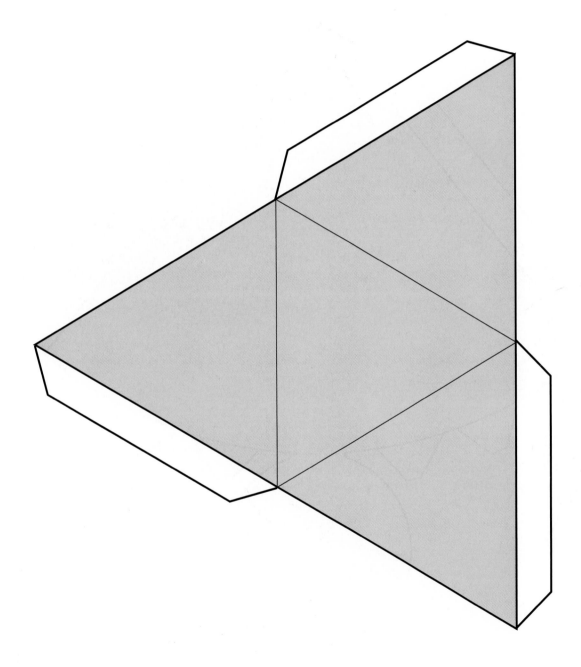

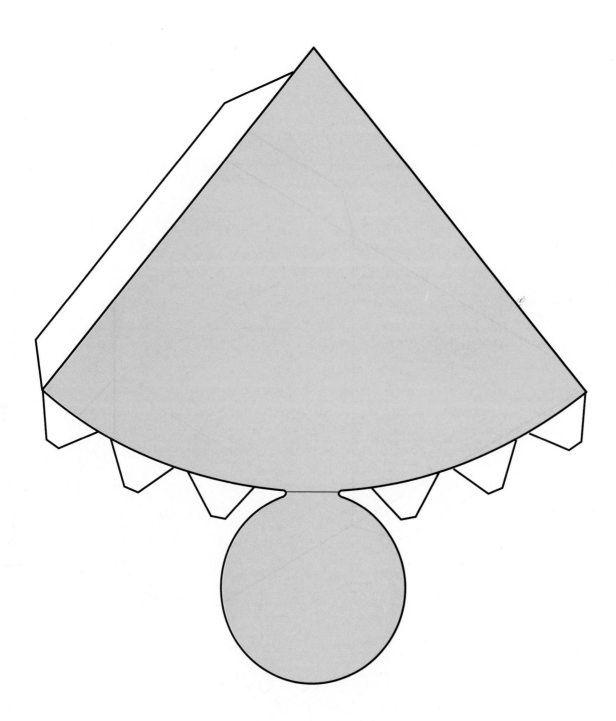

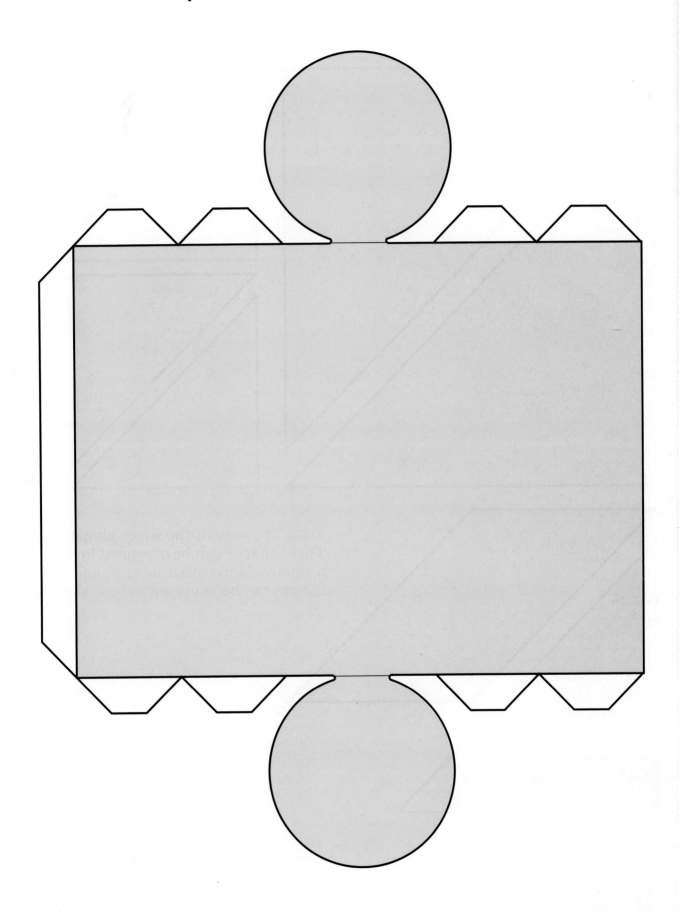

Trace and cut out the seven shapes. These shapes can be arranged to form a square. Many other designs and figures can be made with these shapes.

CREDITS

Harcourt Brace & Company Photographs

KEY: (t) top, (b) bottom, (l) left, (r) right, (c) center.

6(t) & (c), 10 & 12, Jerry White; 16, Jerry White; 18, Earl Kogler; 20(t), Rob Downey; 20(b, all), Jerry White; 21, Ron Kunzman; 22(t), Chris Lawery; 22(b), Britt Runion; 26, Jerry White; 28, Chris Lawery; 34, 40, 44 & 50, Jerry White; 56(t), (c) & (b) & 57, Chris Lawrey; 61, Jerry White; 62, Chris Lawrey; 63(c), Ron Kunzman; 66(inset), Terry Sinclair; 68, Jerry White; 75, Ron Kunzman; 78, Jerry White; 80, Richard Haynes; 86, Jerry White; 90, Britt Runion; 91(t) & (b), Ron Kunzman; 96, Chris Lawrey; 97, 104, 107 & 108, Jerry White; 114, Chris Lawery; 115, Annette Stahl; 116(t), Chris Lawrey; 116(b), Maria Paraskevas; 118 & 120, Annette Stahl; 121, Jerry White; 122, Ron Kunzman; 124(t) & (b), Chris Lawrey; 126, Annette Stahl; 127, Jerry White; 128, Ron Kunzman; 130, Maria Paraskevas; 132, Ron Kunzman; 134(inset) & 135(inset), Jerry White; 136, 138, 140 & 141, Annette Stahl; 146, Maria Paraskevas; 147, Ron Kunzman; 152, 156(b), 158, 162, 163 & 164, Jerry White; 166, Ron Kunzman; 168, Britt Runion; 173(inset), Ron Kunzman; 177, Annette Stahl; 178, Rob Downey; 179, Jerry White; 180, Greg Leary; 181, Jerry White; 182, Greg Leary; 183, 184 & 190, Jerry White; 191, Terry Sinclair; 192, 196 & 198, Jerry White; 200, Britt Runion; 201, Ron Kunzman; 202, Maria Paraskevas; 204–205(background), Earl Kogler; 204(inset), 205(inset), 207 & 216, Jerry White; 218, Annette Stahl; 222 & 224, Maria Paraskevas; 226, Annette Stahl; 228, Jerry White; 230, Britt Runion; 231(t), Mark Antman; 231(b), Ron Kunzman; 236, Jerry White; 238(t), Maria Paraskevas; 240, Jerry White; 242(t), Nancy Tobin; 242(b), 244(t) & (b), 210 & 212(t) & (b), Jerry White; 248, Ron Kunzman; 251(t) & (b), Jerry White; 254 & 256, Maria Paraskevas; 258, 259, 260(b) & 262, Jerry White; 264, Britt Runion; 268(inset), 269(inset) & 270, Jerry White; 274(all), Ron Kunzman; 275(tl), Jerry White; 275(tc), Ron Kunzman; 275(tr), 275(b), 276 & 277, Jerry White; 278(all), Ron Kunzman; 279, Jerry White; 280(t) & (b) & 281, Maria Paraskevas; 282 & 283, Jerry White; 284, Ron Kunzman; 286, Terry Sinclair; 288(l), 289, 290(b), 292 & 294, Jerry White; 296, Ron Kunzman; 298, Maria Paraskevas; 302(TV) & 303(inset) & 304, Ron Kunzman; 308 & 309, Jerry White; 311, Beverly Brosius; 314, Rob Downey; 316, Jerry White; 318, Ron Kunzman; 320, Maria Paraskevas; 322, Greg Leary; 326(t) & (b), Maria Paraskevas; 327, Beverly Brosius; 328, 329, 330(t), 331, 332 & 333(l), 333(r) & 335, Jerry White; 336, Maria Paraskevas; 337, Jerry White; 340(inset), Ron Kunzman; 343, Maria Paraskevas; 348, Rob Downey; 352(l) & (c), 354(t), 356 & 358, Jerry White; 368, Maria Paraskevas; 372, Ron Kunzman; 374, Maria Paraskevas; 378(inset) & 379(inset), Jerry White; 380, Ron Kunzman; 382, Maria Paraskevas; 384, 386 & 387, Ron Kunzman; 388, Victoria Bowen; 389, Ron Kunzman; 390(t) & (b), Maria Paraskevas; 392, Jerry White; 393, Maria Paraskevas; 394, Ron Kunzman; 396 & 398, Maria Paraskevas; 401, Ron Kunzman; 402, Jerry White; 404, Jerry White; 406, Ron Kunzman; 408 & 409, Maria Paraskevas; 412(inset), Terry Sinclair; 416(t), Ron Kunzman; 416(b) & 418(b), Jerry White; 420, Maria Paraskevas; 421 & 422, Victoria Bowen; 424 & 425, Rob Downey; 426, Ron Kunzman; 430(t), Jerry White; 430(b), Maria Paraskevas; 434, Jerry White; 438, Ron Kunzman; 440, Maria Paraskevas; 445(foreground), Ron Kunzman; 447, 448(c) & 452(t), Jerry White; 452(c), Ron Kunzman; 452(b), Beverly Brosius; 453 & 456, Jerry White; 462, Victoria Bowen; 463, 466, 468 & 470, Maria Paraskevas; 471(t), Jerry White; 471(c) & (b), Ron Kunzman; 475, Rodney Jones; 479, 492 & 492–H1, Jerry White; H1, Ron Kunzman; H4, Earl Kogler; H5, Jerry White; H8, Rob Downey; H10, Jerry White; H14, Maria Paraskevas; H16, Rob Downey; H17, Maria Paraskevas; H18, Jerry White; H22, Maria Paraskevas; H24, Rob Downey; H28(b) & H29(b), Jerry White; H30(b), Rob Downey; H31(all), Annette Stahl; M1, Maria Paraskevas; Rob Downey.

All Other Photographs

xxiv–1(background), NASA/The Picture Cube; xxiv(inset), Robert Rathe/Stock, Boston; 1(inset), NASA; 2(t), Steve Drexler/Stock Photos/The Image Bank; 2(b), Giraudon/Art Resource; 3, Spencer Jones/Bruce Coleman, Inc.; 6(b), Thomas Kitchin/Tom Stack & Assoc.; 8(t), Lawrence Schiller/The New Ingot Co.; 8(b), Susan McCartney/Photo Researchers; 13, Roy Morsch/Bruce Coleman, Inc.; 14, Comstock; 17, Brett Froomer/The Image Bank; 19, Al Messerschmidt/South Florida Images; 24, Grgg Mancuso/Stock, Boston; 25, David Jeffrey/The Image Bank; 32–33(background), David Madison; 32(inset), Francis Marion College; 33(inset), Damian Strohmeyer/Sports Illustrated; 36, Adam J. Stoltman/duomo; 38, Wayne Gretzky/Focus on Sports; 41, Al Tielemans/duomo; 42(t) & (b) & 43, Focus on Sports; 45(t), Art Resource; 45(b), Noboru Komine/Photo Researchers; 46, Robert E. Daemmrich/TSW; 48(t), Richard Dole/duomo; 48(b), Sports Illustrated; 52, David Madison; 54, Mary Kate Denny/PhotoEdit; 58, Focus on Sports; 63(t) & (b), David Madison; 64, Culver Pictures; 66–67(background), Harvey Lloyd/The Stock Market; 66–67(foreground), Blaine Harrington/The Stock Market; 67(inset), Blaine Harrington/The Stock Market; 70, Bruce Thomas/The Stock Market; 72, Greek National Tourist Organization; 76, David Stone/Berg & Assoc.; 79, Ned Gillette/The Stock Market; 82, Frank Labua/TSW; 84, Jon Riley/TSW; 94–95(background), Georger Holton/Photo Researchers; 94(inset), Tom Stack/Tom Stack & Assoc.; 98, Bob Daemmrich/Stock, Boston; 100, Ulrike Welsch/Photo Researchers; 102, Joseph A. DiChello; 103, Kenneth L. Weaver/Berg & Assoc.; 106, Bob McKeever/Tom Stack & Assoc.; 109(t) & (b), Mark Downey; 110, Victor Englebert/Photo Researchers; 112, NASA; 123, Four by Five/SUPERSTOCK; 134–135(background), Jeff Cadge/The Image Bank; 149, DW Productions/The Image Bank; 150, Marc & Evelyne Bernheim/Woodfin Camp & Assoc.; 153, Ted Spiegel/Black Star; 154, David Madison/duomo; 156(t), Focus on Sports; 165, Reuters/Bettmann; 165(inset), UN Photo 176855/M. Grant; 169, Al Francekevich/The Stock Market; 172–173(background), DPI; 172(inset), Joe Towers/The Stock Market; 174(TV), DW Productions/The Image Bank; 174(screen), DPI; 186, Jean Francois Causse/TSW; 188, J. Paul Kennedy/The Stock Market; 214, Kirk Schlea/Berg & Assoc.; 215, Mug Shots/The Stock Market; 217, Scala/Art Resource, New York; 220, Don Mason/The Stock Market; 232, Ted Mahieu/The Stock Market; 234–235(background), Henry T. Kaiser/Stock Imagery; 234(inset), John Neubauer/PhotoEdit; 235(inset), Stock Imagery; 238(b), Suzanne Brookens/The Stock Market; 247, McKinney/FPG; 249, Paul Jude/Science Photo Source/Photo Researchers; 250, Lee Fostger/FPG; 253, L. Villota/The Stock Market; 260(t), Elizabeth Zuckerman/PhotoEdit; 261, David Young Wolff/PhotoEdit; 268–269(background), Jurgen Vogt/The Image Bank; 285, Susan Lapides/Woodfin Camp & Assoc.; 288(r), Julian Baum/Bruce Coleman, Inc.; 290(t), Debbie Leavitt/Nawrocki Stock Photo; 302–303(background) & 302(screen), Paul J. Sutton/duomo; 310(t & b), Photofest; 319(t), Arvind Garg/Photo Researchers; 319(b), Daniele Pellegrini/Photo Researchers; 330(b), Michael Montgomery/Positive Image Photography; 338, Jewel Craig/Photo Researchers; 340–341(background), TSW; 341(inset), Runk/Schoenberger from Grant Heilman; 344, Breck P. Kent/Earth Scenes; 345(t) & (b) & 346, Murray Alcosser/The Image Bank; 350, Chris Rogers/The Stock Market; 352(r), Nicholas deVore III/Bruce Coleman, Inc.; 354(t), Larry Ulrich/DRK; 359, Don Mason/The Stock Market; 360(t), Tim Davis/Photo Researchers; 360(b), Renee Lynn/Photo Researchers; 362, John Gerlach/DRK; 366(t), Roberto de Gugliemo/Science Photo Library/Photo Researchers; 366(b), Antonio Rosario/The Image Bank; 370(t), Robert Frerck/TSW; 370(b), Werner Forman Archive/Art Resource; 376, Comstock; 378–379(background), Joe Azzara/The Image Bank; 397, R. Laird/FPG; 412–413(background), Ned Gillette/The Stock Market; 413(inset), Bill Wasserman/The Stock Market; 414, Carl Purcell; 418(t), Jerry Cooke/Photo Researchers; 428(t), Jim Holland/Stock, Boston; 428(b), Dave Watts/Tom Stack & Assoc.; 429, R. Laird/FPG; 431, Mugshots/TSW; 432, Luis Villota/The Stock Market; 436, G. Marche/FPG; 437, Stephen Marks/Stock Photos/The Image Bank; 444–445(background), Nikolay Zurek/FPG; 444(inset), Norman Owen Tomalin/Bruce Coleman, Inc.; 446(t), Steven Hunt/The Image Bank; 446(b) & 448(t), Comstock; 448(b), Michel Tcherevkoff/The Image Bank; 450(t), Joe Towers/The Stock Market; 450(b), David M. Doody/Tom Stack & Assoc.; 455, Pete Rosendale/TSW; 457, The Granger Collection; 459, Tom Stack/Tom Stack & Assoc.; 464, Makoto Iwafuji/the Stock Market; 467, Alvis Upitis/The Image Bank; 474, G. Contorakes/The Stock Market; 474 & 475, Ted Horowitz/The Stock Market; H2, Troy Maben/David R. Frazier Photo Library; H6, Ann Duncan/Tom Stack & Assoc.; H12, Walter Chandoha; H26(t) & (b), Comstock; H27, Jerry Tobias/Sharp Shooters; H28(t), Mary Kate Denny/PhotoEdit; H29(t), P & G Bowater/The Image Bank; H29(c), Bob Burch/Bruce Coleman, Inc.; H30(t), Mary Kate Denny/PhotoEdit; H32(t), Janeart/The Image Bank; H32(b), Bill Varie/The Image Bank.

ILLUSTRATIONS: Alex Bloch 4, 7, 9, 11, 15, 25, 27, 29, 35, 51, 53, 99, 109, 131, 189, 191, 193, 227, 241, 244, 258, 265, 266, 281, 299, 300, 306, 307, 312, 313, 323, 359, 405, 415, M9, M11; **Ellen Appleby** 122T, 364; **Shirley Bruell** 23, 139, 143, 151, 157, 163, 305; **Richard Courtney** 460; **Fred Daunno** 101, 113, 119, 159, 291; **Dennis Davidson** 460T, 465; **JAK Graphics** 14, 227, 288, 291, 305, 321, 353, 362, 364, 416, 423, 428, 437; **Larry Moore** 137, 161, 175, 221, 272, 273, 287, 295, 417, 449; **Dominick Micolupo** 342; **Sal Murdocca** 39, 47, 59, 69; **Curt Thurston** 458, 463; **Fred Winkowski** 13, 37, 49, 55, 57, 73, 83, 85, 87, 105, 111, 113, 125, 186, 195, 273, 317

Table of Measures

METRIC | CUSTOMARY

Length

METRIC	CUSTOMARY
1 kilometer (km) = 1,000 meters (m)	1 foot (ft) = 12 inches (in.)
1 decimeter (dm) = 0.1 meter	1 yard (yd) = 3 feet, or 36 inches
1 centimeter (cm) = 0.01 meter	1 mile (mi) = 1,760 yards, or 5,280 feet
1 millimeter (mm) = 0.001 meter	

Capacity

METRIC	CUSTOMARY
1 kiloliter (kL) = 1,000 liter (L)	1 cup (c) = 8 fluid ounces (fl oz)
1 milliliter (mL) = 0.001 liter	1 pint (pt) = 2 cups
	1 quart (qt) = 2 pints
	1 gallon (gal) = 4 quarts

Mass/Weight

METRIC	CUSTOMARY
1 kilogram (kg) = 1,000 grams (g)	1 pound (lb) = 16 ounces (oz)
1 milligram (mg) = 0.001 gram	1 ton (T) = 2,000 pounds

Time

1 hour (hr) = 60 minutes (min)

1 minute = 60 seconds (sec)

Formulas

$P = a + b + c$	$P = 2l + 2w$
$A = lw$	$A = bh$
$A = \frac{1}{2}bh$	$C = \pi d$, or $2\pi r$
$\pi = \pi r^2$	$V = lwh$

Symbols

Symbol	Meaning	Symbol	Meaning
$=$	is equal to	$\overleftrightarrow{AB}$	line AB
$\neq$	is not equal to	$\overline{AB}$	line segment AB
$>$	is greater than	$\angle ABC$	angle ABC
$<$	is less than	$\parallel$	is parallel to
10^2	ten squared	$\triangle ABC$	triangle ABC
10^3	ten cubed	$\perp$	is perpendicular to
10^4	ten to the fourth power	$\cong$	is congruent to
$2.\overline{6}$	repeating decimal	π	pi (about 3.14)
$P(Y)$	probability of event Y	$^\circ$	degrees
$\approx$	is approximately equal to	$^+2$	positive 2
$1:3$	ratio of 1 to 3	$^-2$	negative 2
$\overrightarrow{AB}$	ray AB	$(^-5,3)$	ordered pair $^-5,3$

Glossary

A

absolute copy   A copy of a cell or a group of cells in a spreadsheet; the computer makes an exact copy of the information *(page 481)*

acute angle   An angle whose measure is greater than 0° and less than 90° *(page 348)*

acute triangle   A triangle in which all angles are acute *(page 354)*

algebraic expression   An expression that is written using one or more variables *(pages 52, 446)*

angle   A figure formed by two rays that meet at a common endpoint called a vertex *(page 342)*
Example:

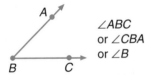

∠ABC
or ∠CBA
or ∠B

area   The number of square units needed to cover a surface *(page 382)*

Associative Property of Addition   The property which states that three or more addends can be grouped in any order without changing their sum *(page 34)*
Example: $(2 + 3) + 5 = 2 + (3 + 5)$

Associative Property of Multiplication   The property which states that three or more factors can be grouped in any order without changing their product *(page 68)*
Example: $(5 \times 2) \times 6 = 5 \times (2 \times 6)$

average   The number obtained by dividing the sum of a set of numbers by the number of addends *(page 11)*

B

bar graph   A graph that uses separate bars (rectangles) of different heights (lengths) to show and compare data *(page 140)*

base   A number used as a repeated factor *(page 20)*
Example: $8^3 = 8 \times 8 \times 8$
The base is 8. It is used as a factor three times.

base   The standard grouping of a numeration system *(page 5)*

base   A side of a polygon or a face of a solid figure by which the figure is measured or named *(pages 366, 384)*
Examples:

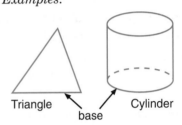

Triangle   Cylinder
base

bisect   To divide into two equal parts *(page 346)*

C

capacity   The amount a container will hold when filled *(page 278)*

category (or field)   A type of information in a data base, such as names or phone numbers *(page 489)*

cell   In a spreadsheet, a block area in which data or formulas can be entered; the cell is located by an address consisting of a letter and a number *(page 481)*

center of a circle   The point inside a circle that is the same distance from each point on the circle *(page 394)*
Example:

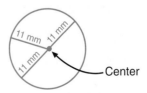

Center

chord   A line segment whose endpoints lie on a circle *(page 394)*
   Example:

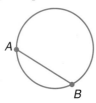

circle   The set of points in a plane that are the same distance from a given point called the center of the circle *(page 394)*

circle graph   A graph using a circle that is divided into pie-shaped sections showing percents or parts of the whole *(pages 148, 352)*

circumference   The distance around a circle *(page 396)*

clipboard   An area in a computer's memory in which the program stores information to be moved or copied from one location or document to another location or document *(page 484)*

common denominator   A number that is a multiple of the denominators of two or more fractions *(page 179)*

common factor   A number that is a factor of two or more numbers *(page 188)*

common multiple   A number that is a multiple of two or more given numbers *(page 174)*

Commutative Property of Addition   The property of addition which states that when the order of two addends is changed, the sum is the same *(page 34)*
   Example:
    $9 + 4 = 4 + 9$

Commutative Property of Multiplication   The property of multiplication which states that when the order of two factors is changed, the product is the same *(page 68)*
   Example:
    $3 \times 5 = 5 \times 3$

compatible number   A number that is close to the actual number and is easy to compute mentally *(page 98)*

compensation   Changing one addend and adjusting the other addend to keep the balance *(page 34)*
   Example: $16 + 9$
    $(16 - 1) + (9 + 1)$
    $15 + 10 = 25$

complementary angles   Two angles whose measures have a sum of 90° *(page 349)*

composite number   A whole number greater than 1 with more than two whole-number factors *(page 184)*

cone   A solid figure with a circular base and one vertex *(page 366)*
   Example:

congruent figures   Figures that have the same size and shape *(page 360)*

coordinate plane   A plane formed by a horizontal line (*x*-axis) that intersects a vertical line (*y*-axis) at a point called the origin *(page 432)*
   Example:

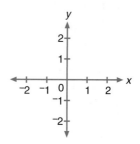

counting principle   The process of multiplying the number of choices in one set by the number of choices in another set to find the total number of outcomes *(page 158)*

cross products   Two equal products obtained by multiplying the second term of each ratio by the first term of the other ratio in a proportion *(page 311)*
   Example: $\dfrac{2}{3} = \dfrac{6}{9}$
    $2 \times 9 = 3 \times 6$
     $18 = 18$

cube   A rectangular solid figure with six congruent square faces *(page 366)*
   Example:

customary measurement system   A measurement system that measures length in inches, feet, yards, and miles; capacity in cups, pints, quarts, and gallons; weight in ounces, pounds, and tons; and temperature in degrees Fahrenheit *(pages 286, 418)*

cylinder   A solid figure with two parallel bases that are congruent circles *(page 366)*

data   A set of information *(page 136)*

data base   A computer program used to organize, sort, and find the kind of information that is normally kept in a list or on file cards *(page 488)*

decimal system   A numeration system based on grouping by tens *(page 4)*

degree   A unit for measuring angles *(page 348)*

degree Celsius (°C)   A metric unit for measuring temperature *(pages 13, 418)*

degree Fahrenheit (°F)   A customary unit for measuring temperature *(pages 13, 418)*

denominator   The number below the fraction bar in a fraction; tells the total number of equal parts or groups into which the whole or group has been divided *(page 176)*

desktop   An area in a computer's memory in which documents or files are stored *(page 484)*

diagonal   A line segment that joins the vertices of a polygon but is not a side *(page 357)*
   Example:

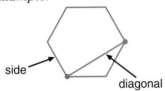

side   diagonal

diameter   A chord that passes through the center of a circle *(page 394)*

difference   The answer in a subtraction problem *(page 35)*

Distributive Property of Multiplication over Addition   The property which states that multiplying a sum by a number is the same as multiplying each addend by the number and then adding the products *(page 68)*
   Example: $4 \times (3 + 5) = 32$
   $(4 \times 3) + (4 \times 5) = 32$

dividend   The number to be divided in a division problem *(page 100)*

divisible   A number is divisible by another number if the quotient is a whole number and the remainder is zero *(page 96)*

divisor   The number by which a dividend is divided in a division problem *(page 96)*

edge   The line segment where two faces of a solid figure meet *(page 366)*

equation   A mathematical sentence that uses an equals sign to show that two quantities are equal *(page 56)*

equilateral triangle   A triangle in which all three sides are congruent *(page 354)*

equivalent fractions   Two or more fractions that name the same number *(page 176)*

equivalent ratios   Ratios that name the same comparisons *(page 308)*

estimate   An answer that is close to the exact answer and is found by rounding, by using front-end digits, or by using compatible numbers *(page 14)*

expanded form   A number written as the sum of the products of its digits and powers of 10 *(page 6)*
   Example:
   3,251
   $3,000 + 200 + 50 + 1$

exponent   A number that tells how many times a base is to be used as a factor *(page 20)*
   Example: $2^3 = 2 \times 2 \times 2 = 8$
   The exponent is 3 because 2 is multiplied by itself 3 times.

expression   A name for a number that contains at least one of the operations of addition, subtraction, multiplication, and division *(page 122)*
   Examples: $n + 5, a - b, 8 \times 4$

face   One of the polygons of a solid figure *(page 366)*

factor   A number that is multiplied by another number to find a product *(page 184)*

factor tree A diagram that shows the prime factors of a number *(page 186)*
Example:

file The electronic form of information stored together as a group on a disk or on a computer's hard drive *(page 484)*

formula In a spreadsheet, a set of instructions that tells the computer to do a calculation or to perform a task *(page 486)*

fraction A number that names part of a group or part of a whole *(page 192)*

gram A metric unit for measuring mass *(pages 270, 278)*

greater than (>) More than in size, quantity, or amount; the symbol > stands for *is greater than (page 10)*
Example: Read 7 > 5 as *seven is greater than five.*

greatest common factor (GCF) The largest number that is a factor of two or more numbers *(page 188)*
Example:
18 is the GCF of 54 and 72.

height The length of a perpendicular segment from the base to the opposite side or vertex of a polygon or solid figure *(pages 384, 403)*
Examples:

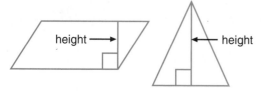

hexagon A six-sided polygon *(page 356)*

histogram A bar graph that shows the number of times data occurs within certain ranges or intervals *(page 144)*

independent events Events that have no influence on each other *(page 162)*

inequality A mathematical sentence containing < (less than) or > (greater than) to show that two expressions do not represent the same quantity *(page 460)*
Examples:
$2 \times 3 < 8; 6 + 5 > 9$

integers The set of whole numbers and their opposites *(page 414)*
Examples:
$\ldots, {}^{-}3, {}^{-}2, {}^{-}1, 0, 1, 2, 3, \ldots$

intersecting lines Lines that cross at exactly one point *(page 344)*
Example:

$\overset{\leftrightarrow}{DE}$ intersects $\overset{\leftrightarrow}{AC}$.

inverse operations Operations that undo each other; addition and subtraction are inverse operations; multiplication and division are inverse operations *(page 38)*
Examples:
$29 - 13 = 16, 16 + 13 = 29$
$15 \div 3 = 5, 5 \times 3 = 15$

isosceles triangle A triangle in which at least two sides and two angles are congruent *(page 354)*

label In a spreadsheet, text read as characters, not as a number value *(page 480)*

least common denominator (LCD) The smallest number, other than zero, that is a multiple of two or more denominators *(page 179)*

least common multiple (LCM) The smallest number, other than zero, that is a multiple of two or more given numbers *(page 174)*

less than (<) Smaller in size, quantity, or amount; the symbol < stands for *is less than (page 10)*
Example: Read 6 < 8 as *six is less than eight.*

line   A straight path that goes on forever in opposite directions *(page 342)*
    Example:

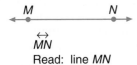

    Read: line *MN*

line graph   A graph in which line segments are used to show changes over time *(page 146)*

line of symmetry   A line that divides a figure into two congruent parts *(page 362)*

liter   A metric unit for measuring capacity *(pages 270, 278)*

LOGO   A computer language used primarily to draw graphic designs; it can also perform calculations *(page 476)*

mass   The amount of matter in an object *(page 278)*

mean   The average of a group of numbers *(page 154)*

median   The middle number or the mean of the two middle numbers of a group of numbers arranged in numerical order *(page 154)*

meter   A metric unit for measuring length *(page 270)*

metric system   A measurement system that measures length in millimeters, centimeters, meters, and kilometers; capacity in liters and milliliters; mass in grams and kilograms; and temperature in degrees Celsius *(page 270)*

mixed number   A number that is made up of a whole-number part and a fraction or a decimal part *(page 194)*

mode   The number or numbers that occur most often in a collection of data; there can be more than one mode or none at all *(page 154)*

multiple   The product of a given number and a whole number *(page 174)*

negative integer   The opposite of a positive whole number; zero is neither positive nor negative *(page 414)*

numeration system   A system of reading and writing numbers *(page 2)*

numerator   The number above the fraction bar in a fraction; tells how many of the equal parts of a whole are being considered *(page 176)*

obtuse angle   An angle whose measure is greater than 90° and less than 180° *(page 348)*

obtuse triangle   A triangle in which exactly one angle is obtuse *(page 354)*

octagon   An eight-sided polygon *(page 356)*
    Example:

opposites   Two numbers whose points on the number line are the same distance from 0, but are on opposite sides of 0 *(page 418)*

ordered pair   A pair of numbers used to locate a point on a coordinate plane *(page 431)*

order of operations   The order in which operations are done; first, do the operations within parentheses; then, multiply and divide from left to right; and last, add and subtract from left to right *(page 18)*

origin   The point on the coordinate plane where the *x*-axis and the *y*-axis intersect, (0,0) *(page 432)*

outcome   A possible result in a probability experiment *(page 160)*

overestimate   An estimate that is greater than the actual answer *(page 36)*

parallel lines   Lines in a plane that do not intersect *(page 344)*
    Example:

$\overleftrightarrow{AB} \parallel \overleftrightarrow{CD}$
Read: *AB* is parallel to *CD*.

parallelogram   A quadrilateral in which opposite sides are parallel and congruent *(page 356)*

pentagon   A five-sided polygon *(page 356)*
Example:

percent   The ratio of a number to 100; percent means per hundred *(page 320)*

perimeter   The distance around a polygon *(page 380)*

perpendicular lines   Lines that intersect to form 90°, or right, angles *(page 344)*
Example:

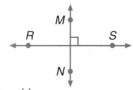

$\overleftrightarrow{RS} \perp \overleftrightarrow{MN}$
Read: *RS* is perpendicular to *MN*.

pi **(π)**   The ratio of the circumference of a circle to its diameter; π≈3.14 or $\frac{22}{7}$ *(page 397)*

pictograph   A graph that uses pictures or symbols to represent numbers *(page 140)*

place value   The value of a digit as determined by its position in a number *(page 6)*

plane   A flat surface that goes on forever in all directions *(page 342)*
Example:

Read: plane *P*

point   An exact location in space; usually represented by a dot *(page 342)*
Example:

• *P*

Read: point *P*

polygon   A closed plane figure whose sides are line segments *(page 356)*

positive integer   A whole number that is greater than 0 *(page 414)*

precision   A property of measurement that is related to the unit of measure used; the smaller the unit of measure used, the more exact the measurement is *(page 280)*

prime factorization   A number written as the product of all its prime factors *(page 186)*
Example: $24 = 2 \times 2 \times 2 \times 3$,
or $2^3 \times 3$

prime number   A whole number greater than 1 whose only factors are itself and 1 *(page 184)*

prism   A solid figure whose bases are congruent, parallel polygons and whose other faces are parallelograms *(page 366)*
Examples:

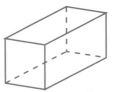

Rectangular Prism   Triangular Prism

probability (P)   The chance that an event will occur expressed as the ratio of the number of favorable outcomes to the number of possible outcomes *(page 160)*

procedure   A set of commands that directs the computer *(page 476)*

product   The answer in a multiplication problem *(page 68)*

Property of One for Multiplication   The property which states that the product of 1 and any factor is the factor *(page 68)*
Examples:
$3 \times 1 = 3; 1 \times a = a$

proportion   An equation which states that two ratios are equivalent *(page 310)*

Example: $\frac{2}{3} = \frac{4}{6}$

pyramid   A solid figure whose base is a polygon and whose other faces are triangles with a common vertex *(pages 366, 401)*
Examples:

Triangular Pyramid   Rectangular Pyramid

quadrilateral   A four-sided polygon *(page 356)*

quotient   The answer in the division operation *(page 96)*

radius   A line segment with one endpoint at the center of a circle and the other endpoint on the circle *(page 394)*
   Example:

random sample   A group chosen by chance so that each item has an equal chance of being chosen *(page 138)*

range   The difference between the greatest and least numbers in a set of numbers *(page 154)*

rate   A ratio that compares different kinds of units, such as miles per hour, beats per minute, or students per class *(page 306)*

ratio   A comparison of two numbers *(page 304)*
   Examples: 3 to 5, 3:5, $\frac{3}{5}$

rational number   Any number that can be expressed as a ratio in the form of $\frac{a}{b}$ where a and b are integers and $b \neq 0$ *(page 448)*

ray   A part of a line that has one endpoint and goes on forever in only one direction *(page 342)*
   Example:

A ———————→ B $\overrightarrow{AB}$
Read: ray *AB*

reciprocal   One of two numbers whose product is 1 *(page 252)*

rectangle   A parallelogram with four right angles *(page 356)*

recursion   The ability of a procedure to repeat a set of commands by calling itself *(page 478)*

reflection   A flip of a geometric figure across a line of symmetry to obtain a mirror image *(page 364)*
   Example:

line of
symmetry

regular polygon   A polygon in which all sides and all angles are congruent *(page 357)*

relation   A set of ordered pairs *(page 463)*

repeating decimal   A decimal in which one digit or a series of digits repeats endlessly *(page 258)*
   Example: 0.333 . . ., or $0.\overline{3}$

rhombus   A parallelogram with four congruent sides *(page 356)*

right angle   An angle whose measure is 90° *(page 348)*

right triangle   A triangle in which exactly one angle is a right angle *(page 354)*

rotation (turn)   A turn of a figure about a fixed point without reflection *(page 364)*
   Example:

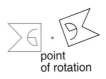

point
of rotation

rotational symmetry   A figure has rotational symmetry if it matches exactly when turned less than 360° about a point *(page 362)*

sample   A group of people or objects chosen from a larger group to provide data to make predictions about the larger group *(page 138)*

scale   The ratio of the size of the object or the distance in a drawing to the actual size of the object or the actual distance *(page 315)*

scale drawing   A reduced or enlarged drawing whose shape is the same as an actual object and whose size is determined by the scale *(page 314)*

scalene triangle   A triangle in which no sides are congruent *(page 354)*

similar figures   Figures having the same shape but not necessarily the same size *(page 360)*

simplest form   A fraction is in simplest form when the numerator and denominator have no common factor greater than 1 *(page 192)*

skew lines   Lines that are in different planes, are not parallel, and do not intersect *(page 344)*

Examples:

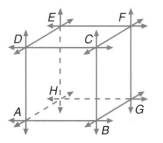

$\overleftrightarrow{AB}$ and $\overleftrightarrow{FG}$,
$\overleftrightarrow{DA}$ and $\overleftrightarrow{BG}$,
$\overleftrightarrow{EH}$ and $\overleftrightarrow{BG}$, and
$\overleftrightarrow{CB}$ and $\overleftrightarrow{AH}$
are skew lines.

solid figure A geometric figure that exists in three or more planes *(page 366)*

spreadsheet A computer program that organizes information in rows and columns and does calculations with numbers and formulas *(page 480)*

square A rectangle with four congruent sides *(page 356)*

square To square a number means to multiply it by itself *(page 22)*
   Example:
      25 is the square of 5 because $5^2 = 25$.

square root One of the two equal factors of a number *(page 22)*
   Example: 5 is the square root of 25 because $5^2 = 25$ and $\sqrt{25} = 5$.

standard form The form in which numerals are usually written, with digits 0 through 9, separated into periods by commas *(page 6)*
   Example: 634,578,910

stem-and-leaf plot A method of organizing data in order to make comparisons; the ones digits appear horizontally as leaves, and tens and greater digits appear vertically as stems *(page 156)*
   Example:

Stem	Leaves
1	3 4 4 6 7
2	1 2 2 3 3
3	0 0 2 3 4

straight angle An angle whose measure is 180° *(page 348)*

supplementary angles Two angles whose measures have a sum of 180° *(page 349)*

surface area The sum of the areas of all the faces or surfaces of a solid figure *(page 400)*

······ **T** ······

translation (slide) A movement of a geometric figure to a new position without turning or flipping it *(page 364)*

Example:

Figure   Translation

trapezoid A quadrilateral with only two parallel sides *(page 356)*

tree diagram A diagram that shows all the possible outcomes of an event *(page 158)*
   Example:

coin toss   heads   tails

triangle A three-sided polygon *(page 354)*

······ **U** ······

underestimate An estimate that is less than the actual answer *(page 36)*

unit rate A rate in which the second term is 1 *(page 306)*

unlike fractions Fractions whose denominators are not the same *(page 180)*

······ **V** ······

variable A letter used to represent one or more numbers *(page 52)*

vertex The point where two rays meet; the point of intersection of two sides of a polygon; the point of intersection of three edges of a solid figure *(page 342)*

volume The number of cubic units that can fill a container *(page 402)*

···**W**··**X**··**Y**··**Z**···

weight The measure of the force of gravity on an object *(page 289)*

x-axis The horizontal axis on the coordinate plane *(page 432)*

y-axis The vertical axis on the coordinate plane *(page 432)*

Zero Property of Addition The property which states that the sum of any number and zero is that number *(page 34)*
   Example: $3 + 0 = 3$

Zero Property of Multiplication The property which states that the product of 0 and any number is 0 *(page 68)*
   Example: $3 \times 0 = 0$

Index

Index

MATH FUN MAGAZINE

Have fun solving these brain teasers!

> As you learn
> new things this year,
> you will be able
> to solve problems
> that might have
> stumped you at first.
> So, keep trying!

These brainteasers don't stump me!

Double SCOOP DILEMMA

**Be a detective and use the given clues to solve this puzzle.
You may find it helpful to make a table of choices.**

George, Hiram, and Leeanna walk into an ice cream shop to buy double dip ice cream cones. They have a choice of five different flavors and two kinds of cones. Each friend chooses a different combination of two flavors and a cone.

Use the clues given below to determine what kind of double dip ice cream cone each friend chooses.

FEATURED FLAVORS

- **MINT CHOCOLATE CHIP**
- **BANANA NUT**
- **ROOT BEER MARBLE**
- **FUDGE MARSHMALLOW**
- **CHERRY SWIRL**

CLUES

- George does not like fruit in his ice cream.
- Hiram is allergic to nuts.
- Leeanna does not like chocolate or root beer.
- Hiram likes root beer and chooses it.
- George loves chocolate, so he chooses both chocolate flavors.
- Hiram's other choice is cherry swirl.
- The two friends who choose the same flavor choose sugar cones.
- One person chooses a plain cone.

I'VE GOT YOUR

NUMBER

Here are
some puzzles for those
with a calculating mind.
Use a calculator to help you
solve each puzzle.

1 Continue these calculations
to reveal an interesting pattern.
Show the final computation and its result.

$9 \times 9 + 7 = 88$
$98 \times 9 + 6 = 888$
$987 \times 9 + 5 = 8,888$

2 Copy the numbers and circles onto your own paper.
Insert operation signs ($+$, $-$, $\times$) to make the number sentences correct.

a. 12 ◯ 3 ◯ 4 ◯ 5 ◯ 67 ◯ 8 ◯ 9 = 100

b. 12 ◯ 3 ◯ 4 ◯ 5 ◯ 6 ◯ 7 ◯ 89 = 100

c. 123 ◯ 4 ◯ 5 ◯ 67 ◯ 89 = 100

d. 1 ◯ 2 ◯ 34 ◯ 56 ◯ 7 ◯ 8 ◯ 9 = 100

3 Follow these steps.

Step 1   Choose any four-digit number. Write it.
Step 2   Rearrange the digits to form another four-digit number.
         Write it.
Step 3   Subtract the lesser number from the greater number.
         Write the difference.
Step 4   Add the digits of the difference.
Step 5   If the sum of the digits of the difference is a two-digit number,
         rearrange the digits of the difference and repeat Steps 3 and 4
         until the sum of the digits of the difference is a one-digit number.

What do you notice about the sum of the digits?

THE RIGHT STUFF

**See if you have the right stuff
to solve these number arrangement puzzles.**

1 Copy this figure onto your own paper. Arrange the numbers 1–9 in the nine empty spaces to get a sum of 17 along each side.

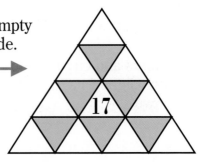

2 Copy this figure onto your own paper. Arrange the numbers 1–9 in the nine empty spaces to get a sum of 23 along each side.

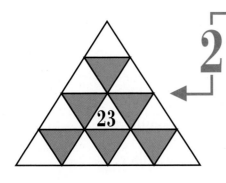

3 Copy the 3 x 3 grid onto your own paper. Fill in the three spaces with the given numbers as shown. Nine consecutive counting numbers form a path through the grid. The three given numbers are part of that path. All the numbers follow only a vertical or a horizontal path.
Complete the grid to make a path of consecutive counting numbers.

	29	30
	33	

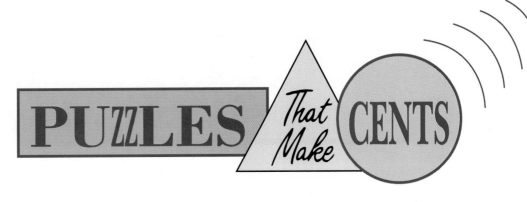

PUZZLES *That Make* CENTS

Here are four brainteasers about money. See if you can solve each one without passing the buck!

1 Mike has six American coins for a total amount of $1.15. With his coins, Mike cannot give Jill exact change for a dollar bill. He cannot give Tim exact change for a 50-cent piece. He cannot give Shawn change for a quarter, or Maria change for a dime, or Cindy change for a nickel. What are Mike's six coins?
HINT: Some of the coins may be the same kind.

2. Mary Lou has two cans of equal size. One can is full of nickels. The other can is half full of dimes. Which can has more money in it? How do you know?

3. Mr. Parks was about to begin a job that would last 30 days. His boss said, "I will give you a choice of salary plans. You can be paid $1,000 a day for the entire job, or you can start with a wage of 1 cent for the first day and have your pay double for each day afterward." Which salary plan offers Mr. Parks the most money? Explain.

4 An archaeologist found two gold coins while digging in Rome, Italy. Each coin was dated 32 B.C. The archaeologist realized the coins were fake. How did she know?

What's Next?

Sometimes you can predict what comes next
if you detect a pattern.
Try to solve each of these puzzles involving a pattern.
Look for clues to help you.

1 What letter comes next?
Once you find the pattern,
the answer is as simple
as one, two, three!

O T T F F S S ___

2 What design comes next?
Look carefully at the figures.
Take time to reflect on each one.

3 Below are all the letters of the alphabet, except *Z*.
Each letter has been placed above or below the line for a
reason. Does *Z* belong above or below the line?
Don't let this pattern throw you a curve!

A   E F H I K L M N   T V W X Y
___
B C D   G   J   O P Q R S U

4 Copy the figures
onto your own paper.
Draw the next figure
in the pattern.
Don't stumble
end-over-end looking
for the answer!

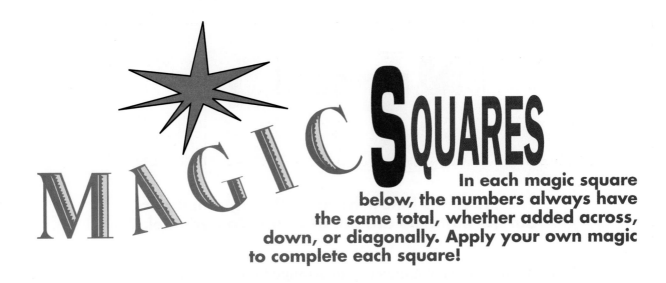

MAGIC SQUARES

In each magic square below, the numbers always have the same total, whether added across, down, or diagonally. Apply your own magic to complete each square!

1. In Square A, the sum of each row is 34. Copy Square B onto your own paper. Then fill in numbers that are 35% of each number in Square A. Do the new numbers still make a magic square? If so, what is the sum of each row?

7	6	11	10
14	9	8	3
12	15	2	5
1	4	13	16

Square A

Square B

2. Copy the square onto your paper. Write a fraction in each box so that each row, column, and diagonal adds up to 1. One fraction is given.

	$\frac{5}{15}$	

3. Magic squares work with both positive and negative numbers. Copy this square onto your paper. Fill the square with numbers so that each row, column, and diagonal adds up to ⁻24. Two numbers are given.

	⁻8	
		32

4. Magic squares also work with decimals. Copy this square onto your paper. Fill in numbers so that each row, column, and diagonal adds up to 3.3. Three numbers are given.

	1.1	
	1.3	0.8

M7

The problems below have all the right numbers, but the numbers are out of order. Can you help?

Jake cut out dozens of numbers and arranged the numbers for a class display on division. Unfortunately, the wind blew Jake's divisors and dividends off the board.

Rearrange the numbers in each box below so that they equal the quotient shown.

Example: $\boxed{8\ 8\ 3} = 4.75 \longrightarrow 8\overline{)38}$ with 4.75 above

1. $\boxed{4\ 6\ 9}$ = 24
2. $\boxed{0\ 9\ 9}$ = 10
3. $\boxed{1\ 5\ 8}$ = 3.6
4. $\boxed{2\ 4\ 8}$ = 20.5
5. $\boxed{6\ 1\ 2}$ = 0.5
6. $\boxed{2\ 9\ 8}$ = 3.625

7. $\boxed{1\ 8\ 5}$ = 16.2
8. $\boxed{7\ 1\ 0}$ = 0.7
9. $\boxed{7\ 6\ 2}$ = 33.5
10. $\boxed{3\ 0\ 4}$ = 7.5
11. $\boxed{0\ 2\ 5}$ = 0.25
12. $\boxed{1\ 1\ 1}$ = 11

Jake also cut out numbers to arrange for a class display on addition. Each problem used the digits 1 through 9. This time, the wind blew away all but one digit in each problem. Supply the missing numbers for Jake. The sum of the numbers is given. The sum of the digits in each number is given to the right.

13.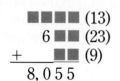

```
    ■■■■  (13)
  6 ■■    (23)
+   ■■    (9)
  8,0 5 5
```

14.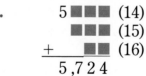

```
  5 ■■■  (14)
    ■■■  (15)
+   ■■   (16)
  5,7 2 4
```

Now just suppose...

**These problems contain true facts about animals.
Now just suppose something weird happened.
Could you find the solution?**

1 A swarm of 50,000 bees weighs 10 pounds.
Now just suppose an overweight bee decided to go on a diet.
If the bee weighed twice as much as an average bee,
what would be the weight of the overweight bee?

2 A grasshopper can jump a distance of 2 feet.
Now just suppose a grasshopper got the hiccups
and jumped 1,000 times without stopping. How many yards
would the grasshopper have jumped?

3 A camel can drink 25 gallons of water in half an hour.
If your job is to give a camel water from a quart pitcher,
how many times will you need to fill the pitcher with water
for the camel to drink for an hour?

4 All ants have 6 legs. Now just suppose you were buying
ant shoes. Naturally, each ant needs 3 pairs. The Acme Ant
Shoe Store is having a sale. You can buy 2 pairs of shoes
for $4 each and get a third pair for half price. How much
would you spend to buy shoes for one dozen ants?

5 A dog is as old at 12 years as a person is at 84.
Now just suppose your dog is having his actual
100th birthday. How old is your dog in "dog years"?

GOING AROUND IN SQUARES

**All of the puzzles below are about squares.
See if you can "square off" with each puzzle and solve it!**

1 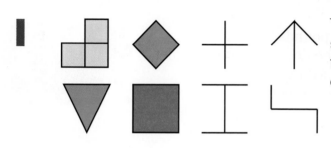 Which two of these shapes, when connected to each other, will make exactly four squares?

2 Copy this dot grid onto your own paper. How many squares can you draw within the dots? Each corner of the square must touch a dot. One square has been drawn for you.

3 **How many other squares contain exactly the same design as the square bordered by bold lines?**
HINT: the squares can be in any position.

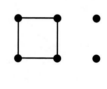

4 Carefully copy or trace the five shapes shown. Cut out the shapes. Then fit them together to make a square. It can be done!

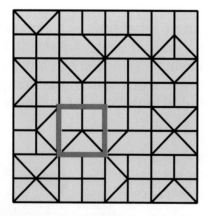

GETTING INTO SHAPE

Here are some picture puzzlers of all shapes and sizes. Study them closely before answering, and you will be in fine shape yourself!

1 How many squares and how many triangles can you find in each of these figures?

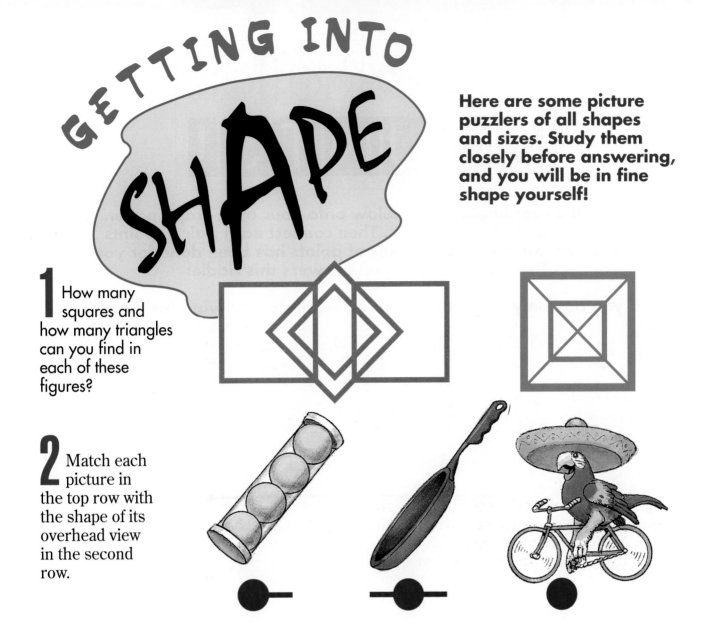

2 Match each picture in the top row with the shape of its overhead view in the second row.

3 Copy this figure onto your own paper. Divide the figure into five sections so that all five numbers (1, 2, 3, 4, and 5) are included in each section.

2	1	3	4	3
5	2	5	2	4
4	3	1	4	1
3	5	2	1	3
1	4	5	2	5

4 Copy this figure onto your own paper. How many circles of the same size as these can you add that will be touching, but not crossing, both of these circles?

Coordination COUNTS!

Copy the coordinate plane below onto your own graph paper.
Plot each pair of coordinates. Then connect each pair of points
with a straight line. The first pair of points has been done for you.
The message you spell answers this riddle:

If you buy only 10¢ worth of nails, what do you want for them?

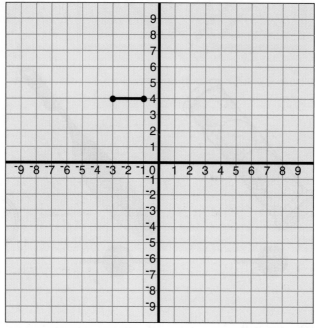

1.	(⁻3,4) (⁻1,4)	14.	(⁻3,⁻1) (⁻3,⁻4)
2.	(⁻2,1) (⁻2,4)	15.	(⁻3,⁻4) (⁻1,⁻4)
3.	(1,1) (1,4)	16.	(⁻3,⁻2) (⁻1,⁻2)
4.	(1,4) (3,4)	17.	(1,⁻1) (⁻1,⁻4)
5.	(1,3) (3,3)	18.	(1,⁻1) (2,⁻4)
6.	(1,1) (3,1)	19.	(2,⁻1) (2,⁻4)
7.	(4,1) (4,4)	20.	(3,⁻1) (5,⁻1)
8.	(4,4) (5,1)	21.	(4,⁻1) (4,⁻4)
9.	(5,1) (5,4)	22.	(8,⁻1) (6,⁻1)
10	(⁻4,⁻1) (⁻6,⁻1)	23.	(6,⁻1) (6,⁻3)
11.	(⁻6,⁻1) (⁻6,⁻4)	24.	(6,⁻3) (8,⁻3)
12.	(⁻6,⁻4) (⁻4,⁻4)	25.	(8,⁻3) (8,⁻4)
13.	(⁻1,⁻1) (⁻3,⁻1)	26.	(8,⁻4) (6,⁻4)

TOOTH PiCK REMOVAL

Arrange 24 toothpicks to form the figure below.

1 Remove 10 toothpicks so that 2 squares remain.

2 Remove 12 toothpicks so that 2 squares remain.

3 Remove 8 toothpicks so that 2 squares remain.

4 Remove 7 toothpicks so that 3 squares remain.

Catchy PUZZLERS

Here are some "catchy" problems that may seem impossible to solve. Yet each one has a logical answer. All you must do is find the "catch"!

1 During a half-inning in a softball game, 7 players came to bat, but no man crossed home plate. How was this possible?

2 A bus driver picked up 23 passengers along his bus route. Only 1 passenger got off the bus before the end of the line. At the end of the route, there were still 23 people on the bus. How was this possible?

3 Eight adults were huddled under an umbrella measuring only 2 feet in diameter. No one got wet. How was this possible?

4 Rita had 2 coins in her purse. They totaled 35¢. One of the coins was not a dime. How was this possible?

5 Jennifer was born in 1960, but by 1990 she had had only 7 birthdays. How was this possible?

M14

Letter Perfect

The puzzles on this page have mysterious letters that will surely challenge you.
See if you can find some "letter-perfect" solutions!

 1 For each statement below, figure out what the letters stand for. The subject might be weights, measures, science, sports, music, or anything else!

Example:

52 = W in a Y 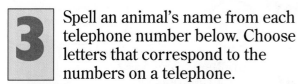 **Weeks in a Year**

a. 12 = I in a F

b. 16 = O in a P

c. 9 = P in the S S

d. 4 = Q in a D

e. 11 = P on a F T

f. 100 = C in a M

g. 2,000 = P in a T

h. 180 = D in a S A

i. 50 = S in the U S

j. 29 = D in F in a L Y

k. 8 = P in a G

2 Jay Jason is a radio disc jockey. What is unusual about his business card? Study the letters closely, but don't take all year to figure out the answer!

> J. JASON
>
> DJ FM / AM

3 Spell an animal's name from each telephone number below. Choose letters that correspond to the numbers on a telephone.

Example:

243-3824   CHEETAH

a. 447-2333

b. 365-7446

c. 678-7424

d. 536-7273

e. 467-4552

f. 885-8873

Strange But True

These word problems contain facts that may seem strange, but the facts are all true. Can you solve each problem?

1 The highest temperature recorded in the United States was 134° Fahrenheit. How many degrees Celsius was this?

2 A piece of pie eaten just once a week will add 3 pounds of body weight in a year. How many ounces of body weight are gained after each piece of pie is eaten?

3 The longest recorded flight by a pigeon was 5,400 miles in 55 days. What was the pigeon's average speed in miles per hour, assuming the bird slept 8 hours a day?

5 Suppose you spent one dollar per minute. About how many years would it take you to spend one billion dollars?

I solved every problem! Did you?

4 The average American makes 382 telephone calls in a year. How many telephone calls does a person average in a month?